Professional Conduct

Professional Conduct

Inns of Court School of Law

Institute of Law, City University, London

OXFORD

UNIVERSITY PRESS

OXFORD

UNIVERSITY PRESS

Great Clarendon Street, Oxford OX2 6DP

Oxford University Press is a department of the University of Oxford.
It furthers the University's objective of excellence in research, scholarship,
and education by publishing worldwide in

Oxford New York

Auckland Bangkok Buenos Aires Cape Town Chennai
Dar es Salaam Delhi Hong Kong Istanbul Karachi Kolkata
Kuala Lumpur Madrid   Melbourne Mexico City Mumbai Nairobi
Sao Paulo Singapore Taipei Tokyo Toronto

Oxford is a registered trade mark of Oxford University Press
in the UK and certain other countries

Published in the United States
by Oxford University Press Inc., New York

British Library Cataloguing in Publication Data

Data available

Library of Congress Cataloging in Publication Data

Data available

ISBN 0-19-927290-5

1 3 5 7 9 10 8 6 4 2

Typeset by Style Photosetting Limited, Mayfield, East Sussex
Printed in Great Britain
on acid-free paper by
Ashford Colour Press, Gosport, Hampshire

FOREWORD

These Manuals are designed primarily to support training on the Bar Vocational Course, though they are also intended to provide a useful resource for legal practitioners and for anyone undertaking training in legal skills.

The Bar Vocational Course was designed by staff at the Inns of Court School of Law, where it was introduced in 1989. This course is intended to equip students with the practical skills and the procedural and evidential knowledge that they will need to start their legal professional careers. These Manuals are written by staff at the Inns of Court School of Law who have helped to develop the course, and by a range of legal practitioners and others involved in legal skills training. The authors of the Manuals are very well aware of the practical and professional approach that is central to the Bar Vocational Course.

The range and coverage of the Manuals have grown steadily. This year, the major revisions of last year have been consolidated and updated to ensure currency and to reflect the changing demands of Bar students.

This updating and revision is a constant process and we very much value the comments of practitioners, staff and students. Legal vocational training is advancing rapidly, and it is important that all those concerned work together to achieve and maintain high standards. Please address any comments to the Bar Vocational Course Director at the Inns of Court School of Law.

With the validation of other providers for the Bar Vocational Course it is very much our intention that these Manuals will be of equal value to all students wherever they take the course, and we would very much value comments from tutors and students at other validated institutions.

The enthusiasm of the publishers and their efficiency in arranging production and publication of the Manuals is much appreciated.

The Hon. Mr Justice Elias
Former Chairman of the Advisory
Board of the Institute of Law
City University, London
August 2004

OUTLINE CONTENTS

DETAILED CONTENTS

PREFACE

'Ethics — a small county east of London?'

The main reason you will read this Manual is because as an intending barrister, your understanding and application of professional conduct and ethics will be the foundation of all you achieve at the Bar. This Manual represents the guidance you will require as a barrister to steer you through these sometimes problematic areas of practice.

Of course the focus of this Manual is on the development of your skills to effectively deal with professional conduct matters as the intending practitioner. You can never work in isolation at the Bar. You will come into contact with and represent a variety of individuals from all walks of life and the way in which you choose to carry out your dealings is under increasing public scrutiny. It is important therefore, that this Manual contains practical advice and guidance from those at the 'coal-face' of practice and from others such as the National Consumer Council, who can help your understanding of the relationship with your clients, as well as setting out the Code of Conduct (see **Appendix 1**) and other key practical texts such as the Code for Crown Prosecutors.

You are a member of a professional body whose reputation is linked to each and every one of its members. The need to maintain the highest standards is an ongoing obligation for the Bar. As an intending member you will soon recognise how helpful other members of the Bar are with regard to professional conduct matters and of the support the Bar Council itself will give you. However, you will not be able to draw upon the support of others if you are unable to identify potential areas of difficulty. To help you to develop these crucial skills you must first identify the fundamental principles set out in the Code of Conduct and question the application of the spirit of the Code based on these fundamental tenets

when no express provision can be found. This Manual will help you to develop these skills by discussing situations that frequently arise during the differing assessment areas you will undertake during the Bar Vocational Course, where the application of the Code and its spirit is paramount.

Furthermore, the guidance set out in this Manual will then encourage you to think further about your obligations towards helping to 'protect individuals and groups from the abuse of public and private power' (The Lord Chancellor's Advisory Committee on Legal Education and Conduct, 1996). This concept, know as the 'ethical challenge' should ensure that your understanding of professional conduct and ethics reaches further than a simple familiarisation with the Code of Conduct and of the complaints procedure for dealing with transgressions. Indeed, in meeting this challenge the Manual will also encourage you to think carefully about your own moral standpoint and how this could impact upon your response to the ethical dilemmas you will meet in practice. After all, as an intending practitioner, the recognition of your own subjective personal morality should then ensure that it does not interfere with your practice as a lawyer.

The approach this Manual takes towards your development of a disciplined way of working will be of great value throughout your career at the Bar. It will help to ensure that you become a respected member of the profession and in time you may be giving advice to junior members of the Bar, as to the most suitable approach to professional conduct problems.

Kate R Stead LL.B (Hons)., M.Phil (Cantab),
Barrister,
Lecturer in Law, ICSL

Introduction

Paragraph 301 of the Code of Conduct states that:

A barrister ... must not:
- (a) engage in conduct whether in pursuit of his profession or otherwise which is:
  - (i) dishonest or otherwise discreditable to a barrister;
  - (ii) prejudicial to the administration of justice; or
  - (iii) likely to diminish public confidence in the legal profession or the administration of justice or otherwise bring the legal profession into disrepute.

You are hoping to join this profession at a time of change. The courts, for example, are no longer the exclusive adversarial platforms of barristers, but are now open to solicitor advocates, in-house solicitors and the employed Bar. The Bar is therefore focusing on opportunities such as Bar Direct, the Human Rights Act and quality standards. The Bar is increasing in size and income, there is an increased number of female practitioners (28%) and an increasing representation among ethnic minority groups (7%). However, even in these changing times there is nothing more important to practice at the Bar than the way in which barristers conduct themselves, and the regard in which they are held by their peers, judges they appear before, their instructing solicitor and members of the public with whom they come into contact during their professional lives.

1.1 The Code of Conduct

Underpinning the profession is the Code of Conduct (the Code) and no matter what challenges you will face individually or as part of a profession, your comprehension and application of the Code must be thorough. Without this solid foundation the Bar's efforts in the face of change would crumble to nothing. The way you conduct yourselves in practice and towards those whom you meet in your professional lives is rightly under scrutiny. Barristers never work in isolation. Ignoring the application of the Code not only affects an individual's reputation and career at the Bar, it can have far reaching implications to those affected by such oversights and thus the behaviour of the Bar as a profession is brought into question. Consequently, the Code set out in **Appendix 1** is perhaps the most important text to comprehend and then apply throughout your career at the Bar.

1.2 The ethical challenge

It would be comforting to think that at this stage of your legal training the Code will expressly deal with all professional conduct situations. Of course during the BVC and in early practice it becomes apparent that not only does the letter of the Code need to be understood, but also the application of its spirit to many situations is crucial. **Chapter 4**, 'the letter and spirit of the Code' prompts you to think carefully about they way in which you choose to interpret the Code and it also suggests that you recognise the 'underpinning values' of the Code. This approach is vital if as a barrister you are to operate within the spirit of the Code, where there is no letter, albeit that this is so often based on an interpretation of the combination of the fundamental tenets. Indeed, the chapter also advises that you are wise to be aware of your own personal morality and that it does not cloud your objective professional judgment in dealing with the ethical difficulties you will meet in practice.

Accepting that the Code is designed to ensure ethical practice at the Bar, your analysis of professional conduct issues must also take place within the context of an important principle identified by the Lord Chancellor's Advisory Committee on Legal Education and Conduct (ACLEC). The committee in its first report on Legal Education and Training (April 1996) identified 'the ethical challenge' (para 1.21):

From the earliest stages of education and training, intending lawyers should be imbued not only with the standards and codes of professional conduct, but also more generally with the obligations of lawyers to help protect individuals and groups from the abuse of public and private power.

ACLEC recognised therefore that 'familiarisation of the professional codes of conduct and the machinery for enforcing them' (p 17) was not enough. Trainee lawyers must be made aware through effective training of their wider obligations to society.

Fair treatment of individuals is a factor which Lady Justice Hale comments upon in a speech to the Bar Council (December 2002):

... the public perception should not be of a profession fighting hard to keep things as they are, which the public will see as mainly for its own benefit rather than for the public good, but of a profession fighting hard for equal protection of the laws, and equal access to justice, most needed by the powerless rather than the powerful.

1.3 A profession under scrutiny

Popular perceptions about the Bar are often wrong. Conclusions portrayed in the media about alleged 'fat cat' lawyers overlook the £2.5 million worth of pro bono work the Bar undertakes or of the many lawyers struggling to make ends meet. Michael Scott CBE DSO, the Lay Complaints Commissioner (LCC) to the General Council of the Bar in his 5th Annual Report (2001) recognises the difficulties faced by some in practice and states:

Members of the public who think a barrister's life begins at 10 am by alighting from the Rolls and gently easing into a large lunch, should see the serious financial difficulties many face at the unglamorous end of, say, magistrates' courts and the like.

You may be puzzled as to why it is necessary to mention such problems. The answer is simple — whatever difficulties are encountered, financial or otherwise, the application of the

Code of Conduct remains paramount. Cutting corners, being rude to a difficult professional client or not being aware of a client's specific needs are not options.

Every day the way in which you choose to conduct your affairs is rightly under scrutiny by all parties you come into contact with. For example, in the context of criminal trials recent case law has highlighted defence counsels' professional duties with regard to procedural errors by the prosecution. The judiciary have clearly set out that such matters should be identified and dealt with at the earliest opportunity and not left until the last minute because criminal proceedings are not a game (*R v Gleeson* The Times, 30 October 2003 and *Hughes v DPP* [2003] EWHC 2470).

As you become fully versed in the letter of the Code and its application, it is useful to read a list recently compiled by Mark Stobbs (General Council of the Bar, Head of Professional Conduct) setting out the main reasons for complaints against barristers.

Principal Reasons for Complaints Against Barristers

Poor Services to Clients
This can cover a wide variety of circumstances but typical examples are:

- arriving late at court or for a conference without reasonable excuse;
- behaving rudely or abruptly to the client — no matter how difficult the client may be;
- failing to ensure that the client properly understands advice or the consequences of any decision or settlement;
- giving negligent advice or failing to take steps to protect the client's interest;
- double-booking and other clerks' room errors.

Misconduct
All of the above cases can amount to misconduct as well if the facts are sufficiently serious. The following types of action will also amount to misconduct:

- breach of confidence;
- expressing personal opinions in the press in matters which are continuing and in which you have been instructed;
- acting where you have an interest or where another client has an interest which is opposed to that of your client;
- bullying your client and threatening to withdraw if your client does not accept a settlement or plead guilty;
- making allegations of fraud without a proper basis for so doing no matter how hard your client may press you to do so;
- coaching or rehearsing a witness in their evidence;
- holding yourself out as a barrister when offering legal advice if you have not completed pupillage or complied with the other practising requirements;
- misleading the court or continuing in a case where your client has misled the court or failed to disclose a document that the law requires to be disclosed.

Personal Problems
Generally, the Bar Council does not seek to make judgements about individuals' personal lives, but there are times when conduct outside practice can call a person's suitability to remain a barrister into question. Particular examples include:

- being convicted of a criminal offence or being charged with a serious criminal offence — both must be reported to the Bar Council;
- being adjudicated bankrupt or made subject to an Individual Voluntary Arrangement or a Directors Disqualification Order which must, again be reported to the Bar Council;
- using the qualification to obtain an advantage that would not otherwise be given or to intimidate another person;

- failing to comply with the order of a court;
- other dishonest or disreputable behaviour which is likely to bring the Bar or the administration of justice into disrepute.

Breaches of the Practising Rules

- Failing to pay the insurance premium to the Bar Mutual Indemnity Fund or practising certificate fee;
- not complying with compulsory continuing education scheme.

Given the number of complaints stemming from the relationship between a barrister and the lay client, it is worth noting that the Professional Conduct and Complaints Committee of the Bar Council have commented in the General Council of the Bar Annual Report 2001 that:

It is clear from a number of the complaints considered by the PCC that some members of the Bar could place client care more at the forefront of their professional behaviour — by ensuring, for example, that their lay client understands the reasons for a particular outcome.

1.4   Fair treatment

The Bar is committed to equal opportunities. An integral part of good professional conduct is the attitude, which you adopt and display towards the variety of people with whom you come into contact in your professional life. These range from colleagues in chambers, opponents, the judiciary, professional clients, lay clients, witnesses and court staff, to other professionals such as police officers, doctors, probation officers and social workers. You will be dealing with people from every walk of life, every socio-economic group, with differing mental abilities, customs, religions and expectations. It is crucial that you treat people courteously and fairly and that you are scrupulous to avoid discriminating directly or indirectly against any person on grounds of race, colour, ethnic or national origin, nationality, citizenship, sex, sexual orientation, marital status, disability, religion or political persuasion (see the Code para 305.1). Such discrimination is not only a breach of the Code; it is also a breach of the Bar's Equality Code (see Miscellaneous Guidance in Section 3 of the Code in **Appendix 1**).

Your success at the Bar will depend more than anything upon the way that you treat other people. **Chapter 3**, 'working at the Bar today', sets out how you can develop your awareness of and approach to treating people fairly. As such, the chapter contains information on the sources of guidance relating to fair treatment, harassment and discrimination and sets out invaluable advice for your practice at the Bar today. **Chapter 2** which deals with 'professional relationships' is also a very useful source of guidance in ensuring that you behave towards others with the courtesy, respect and sensitivity that the Bar requires of its members. It draws upon the experience of barristers, solicitors, judges, clerks and organisations to which the lay client turns, such as the National Consumer Council and the Bar Council's professional conduct department. It also contains key practical texts such as the Code for Crown Prosecutors in an attempt to ensure that whatever your role is in proceedings you will know the sources of guidance that an intending barrister needs.

1.5   The consequences of misconduct

Barristers who choose the approach of keeping their head in the sand when faced with professional conduct issues in practice will inevitably meet problems. They will fall down the path of sleepless nights; their reputation will be soiled and because any failure to comply with the Code will constitute professional misconduct and may result in liability for disciplinary proceedings (see para 901 of the Code), they may find, at worst, that they are disbarred from practice or suspended for a period of time. Consequently, because the Code of Conduct has a 'remorseless grip' and the 'disciplinary system of the Bar is very strong' (LCC 5th Annual Report 2001) barristers who choose to ignore the early warning signs in a case do so at their peril. Disciplinary proceedings are the most obvious consequence following a transgression of the Code, not to mention the possibility of a wasted costs order. If you gain a reputation as a sharp practitioner, your life in practice will become very difficult. Your fellow practitioners will treat you suspiciously, judges will give you a hard time, solicitors will no longer brief you and you will lose the trust of your clerk. If you cannot command the respect of those you regularly come into contact with, it becomes readily apparent that you will not have a career at the Bar. Remember the Bar is a small profession and the 'grapevine' is extremely effective. Your reputation at all times must be untarnished. **Chapter 6** is a useful guide to the Bar Council's complaints procedure.

1.6   Practical advice

In his keynote speech to the Inns of Court School of law (2001, 2002) Michael Pooles QC, a member of the Bar Council's Professional Conduct and Complaints Committee, reminds all trainee lawyers that, 'If you have to ask yourself whether a matter constitutes a professional conduct difficulty, then the answer to this question is inevitably yes and the matter must then be dealt with'.

Chapter 7, 'BVC, practice and professional conduct', is designed to help further with your analysis of professional conduct and ethical difficulties. It provides you with a central source of reference of specific problem areas which can occur frequently in practice and which you will meet during your participation in the key skill areas on the BVC and may well be examined upon. It therefore focuses on professional conduct problems pertinent to the following skills: conference, advocacy, negotiation, opinion writing and drafting. The chapter refers to relevant sources of guidance to ensure that intending barristers are fully aware of why a certain approach to these issues is necessary. It includes, for example, Bar Council guidance on dealing with previous convictions and matters arising under the Proceeds of Crime Act 2002. Additionally, **Chapter 5** is a useful overview of court etiquette and takes you through many of the customs you will meet in practice.

It is hoped as you read the specific provisions of the Code and of the discussions relating to the potential areas of difficulty in practice, your skills in the following areas will develop:

- the *identification* of potential professional conduct issues;
- the *sources* of guidance on particular issues;
- the necessity of applying the *spirit* of the Code where there is no letter;
- the need to recognise obligations towards *fair treatment*; and
- how you would deal *practically* with the matter.

1.7   BVC, pupillage and professional conduct

Throughout the ICSL Bar Vocational Course you will be able to monitor the development of these skills set out above. The professional conduct course begins with an introductory Keynote speech given by a member of the Professional Conduct and Complaints Committee. This is followed by two panels of practitioners of differing call who will discuss the problems set out in **Chapter 8**. During the BVC, in both large and small groups, professional conduct teaching continues with PTX's deliberately containing areas of difficulty. In addition to this, you will also attend a number of small group sessions, which deal with a number of conference scenarios devised to increase your awareness of professional conduct and ethical difficulties and to think through how best to approach these issues. It is during these sessions that you are encouraged to use the Bar Council's web site as a source of the most current version of the Code (www.barcouncil.org.uk) and to make use of the ethical guidance contained therein. You are advised to keep a separate note of all professional conduct matters arising on the course and your approach to them, together with a note of the suggested response. As part of the professional development course you should reflect upon the way in which you are approaching these issues and keep a note of the sources of information used to help with your response. Very importantly you will be examined on professional conduct during your undertaking of the skills assessments. Hence, by keeping a note for the purposes of reflection, you will also have a central reference source setting out the likely areas you will be examined upon. This approach to professional conduct issues will also be useful in pupillage when the Bar Council expects that you will continue with the monitoring of this area of practice with the use of the pupillage checklist.

1.8   Conclusion

In conclusion, taking the right approach to professional conduct and ethical difficulties from the outset of your professional training is crucial. One word sums up all that has been set out above. That word is '*Awareness*'. Being alert to professional conduct and ethical difficulties and knowing both the Code and its application will hold you in good stead throughout your career at the Bar and you will, in time, inspire others through your professionalism, to join this respected profession. This commitment to a disciplined way of working, no matter the breadth and depth of our practices, no doubt underpins Matthias Kelly QC's comments in his role as chairman of the Bar (Inaugural Speech December 2002):

We prove our value as specialist advocates and advisers on a daily basis in courts and tribunals across the country to all clients be they ordinary citizens, trade unions, governments or major commercial organisations in difficulty. For hundreds of years the Bar has been there to advise, represent and advocate the client's cause. That's what makes us the fiercely independent profession we are today. That's why we survive and grow. Governments come and go. Clients with a need for our services are always there. The Bar is strong and determined to continue to deliver high quality services to all who need those services.

Professional relationships

Whether instructed for the prosecution or defence, claimant or defendant, applicant or respondent, as counsel you must consider a number of responsibilities beyond those to your client. Of course everything possible must be done on behalf of the client, but counsel has a number of wider duties. Miscarriages of justice can and do occur when counsel forget or ignore their duties to the court, to their professional client and the Crown Prosecution Service, and to other members of the profession. There is even a duty to the Legal Aid Services Commission. A barrister should be concerned in the administration of justice, and **not** to win at all costs.

It is not uncommon for these duties to conflict, eg, over the disclosure of some evidence or an authority harmful to your case. Frequently the question is not straightforward. It is important that from the earliest days you can at the very least recognise that there is a potential problem so that you can then take steps, eg, discussion with a senior barrister or telephoning the Professional Conduct and Complaints Committee, to ensure that the right answer is reached.

In this chapter we consider a number of ways in which the duty to one's client is, and must be, fettered, so that ultimately justice is achieved. More broadly we consider the range of professional relationships that the barrister will enter into in the course of practice and the duties and obligations that are owed in conducting each relationship successfully and to the appropriate ethical standard. In addition there is practical advice from some of those on the other side of the various relationships with counsel. A senior solicitor, a senior clerk and the National Consumer Council to whom dissatisfied lay clients can turn, all contribute practical guidance and advice which, if heeded, will provide you with a sense of how to make your professional relationships work effectively in day-to-day practice.

2.1 Relationship with the court

2.1.1 Duties and responsibilities owed to the court

Time and again, the judiciary have stressed the paramount duty of counsel to the court. In *Rondel v Worsley* [1969] 1 AC 191, 227 Lord Reid put it in this way:

Every counsel has a duty to his client fearlessly to raise every issue, advance every argument, and ask every question, however distasteful, which he thinks will help his client's case. But, as an officer of the Court concerned in the administration of justice, he has an overriding duty to the Court, to the standards of his profession, and to the public, which may and often does lead to a conflict with his client's wishes or with what the client thinks are his personal interests.

In the same case, Lord Denning MR explained the nature of the duty to the court in these terms:

[Counsel] must accept the brief and do all he honourably can on behalf of his client. I say 'all he honourably can' because his duty is not only to his client. He has a duty to the Court which is paramount. It is a mistake to suppose that he is the mouthpiece of his client to say what he wants: or his tool to do what he directs. He is none of these things. He owes allegiance to a higher cause. It is the cause of truth and justice. He must not consciously misstate the facts. He must not knowingly conceal the truth. He must not unjustly make a charge of fraud, that is, without evidence to support it. He must produce all the relevant authorities, even those that are against him. He must see that his client discloses, if ordered, the relevant documents, even those that are fatal to his case. He must disregard the most specific instructions of his client, if they conflict with his duty to the court. The code which requires a barrister to do all this is not a code of law. It is a code of honour. If he breaks it, he is offending against the rules of the profession and is subject to its discipline. But he cannot be sued in a Court of law. Such being his duty to the Court, the barrister must be able to do it fearlessly. He has time and time again to choose between his duty to his client and his duty to the Court. ([1966] 3 WLR 950, 962.)

2.1.1.1   Examples of duties and responsibilities

Your overriding duty to the court to act with independence in the interests of justice incorporates many separate responsibilities. These are set out in the Code of Conduct and include a duty:

(a) To assist the court in the administration of justice, and not to deceive or knowingly or recklessly mislead the court (para 302). Note that ss 27 and 28 of the Courts and Legal Services Act 1990 are amended by s 42 of the Access to Justice Act 1999. This imports an overriding duty on advocates to the court to act with independence in the interests of justice. This would include, eg, correcting any misleading information which is incorporated in your client's affidavit and which on your instructions, is inaccurate. In *Abraham v Justsun* [1963] 2 All ER 402, 404 Lord Denning MR explained this duty further:

[It is an] advocate's duty to take any point which he believes to be fairly arguable on behalf of his client. An advocate is not to usurp the province of the judge. He is not to determine what shall be the effect of legal argument. He is not guilty of misconduct simply because he takes a point which the tribunal holds to be bad. He only becomes guilty of misconduct if he is dishonest. That is, if he knowingly takes a bad point and thereby deceives the court.

(See also, *Memory Corporation and Another v Sidhu and Another* [2000] 1 WLR 1443.)

(b) To act with due courtesy to the court (Section 3, Miscellaneous Guidance, General Standards, para 5.5).

(c) To bring to the attention of the court all relevant decisions and legislative provisions of which you are aware, whether or not their effect is favourable to your case (para 708(c)). (See *Copeland v Smith and Another* [2000] 1 All ER 457.)

(d) To bring any procedural irregularity to the attention of the court during the trial (para 708(d)). (See *R v L (Glen Bernard)* The Times, 12 January 2001 and *Re B (Appeal: lack of reasons)* [2003] EWCA Civ 881; [2003] 2 FLR 1035.)

(e) To advise that all relevant documents be disclosed and withdraw from the case if such advice is not followed (para 608(d) and (e)).

(f) To record the proceedings. You have a duty to take a note of the judge's reasons for his decision and have it typed as soon as there is any question of an appeal (see *Letts v Letts* The Times, 8 April 1987).

(g) Not to devise facts which will assist in advancing your lay client's case or settle a groundless statement of case or other document (para 704). In *Steamship Mutual Underwriting Association Ltd v Trollope & Colls Ltd* The Times, 31 March 1986, May LJ put it in these terms:

> ... To issue a writ when there was no evidential basis upon which a statement of claim could be founded and without any intention to serve one was an abuse of the process of the court.

(h) Not to allege fraud in any statement of case or other document without clear instructions to do so and without reasonably credible material which as it stands establishes a prima facie case of fraud (para 704(c)). (See *Medcalf v Mardell (Wasted Costs Order)* [2001] Lloyd's Rep PN 146.)

(i) Not to assert a *personal* opinion of the facts or the law to the court unless invited to do so by the court (para 708(b)).

(j) Not to make statements or ask questions which are merely scandalous or intended or calculated only to vilify, insult or annoy either a witness or some other person (para 708(g)).

2.1.1.2 Wasted costs orders: civil and criminal

The barrister is also under a duty to take all reasonable and practicable steps to avoid unnecessary expense or waste of the court's time (Section 3, Miscellaneous Guidance, Written Standards for the Conduct of Professional Work, General Standards, para 5.11); this includes a duty not to waste an appellate court's time. In *Ainsbury v Millington* The Times, 13 March 1987, Lord Bridge stated that it was:

> ... the duty of counsel and solicitors in any pending appeal in publicly funded litigation whenever an event occurred which arguably disposed of the matter in contention, either to ensure that the appeal was withdrawn by consent or, in the absence of agreement, to bring the facts promptly to the attention of the appellate court and to seek directions.

Note that counsel could be made liable personally for costs thrown away (see Supreme Court Act 1981, s 51(6) and CPR, Part 48, r 48 and PD 48). Similar orders could follow under CPR, Part 44, r 44 (assessment of costs). Section 19 of the Prosecution of Offences Act 1985, gave the magistrates' courts, the Crown Court and the Court of Appeal power, where satisfied that one party to criminal proceedings has incurred costs as a result of an unnecessary or improper act or omission by, or on behalf of, another party to the proceedings, to make an order as to the payment of those costs. Section 19A, which was inserted by the Courts and Legal Services Act 1990, gives similar powers to disallow or (as the case may be) order the legal or other representative concerned to meet the whole of any wasted costs or any part of them. 'Wasted costs' means any costs incurred by a party:

- as a result of any improper, unreasonable or negligent act or omission on the part of any representative or any employee of a representative; or

- which, in the light of any such act or omission occurring after they were incurred, the court considers it is unreasonable to expect that party to pay.

There have been a number of cases in which courts, including the Court of Appeal, have made wasted costs orders against barristers. In *Re A Barrister (Wasted Costs Order No 1 of 1991)* [1992] 3 WLR 662, the Court of Appeal recommended a three-stage test:

- Had there been an improper, unreasonable or negligent act or omission?
- If so, had any costs been incurred by any party in consequence thereof?
- If so, should the court exercise its discretion to disallow, or order the representative to meet, the whole of any part of the relevant costs and, if so, what specific sum was involved?

In the Court of Appeal case of *Ridehalgh v Horsefield* [1994] 3 WLR 462 Sir Thomas Bingham MR made it clear that the judgment was applicable to criminal as well as civil courts, and made the following points.

(a) 'Improper' covered, but was not confined to, conduct which would ordinarily justify serious professional penalty. It was not limited to significant breach of the relevant code of professional conduct. It included conduct which was improper according to the consensus of professional, including judicial, opinion, whether it violated the letter of a professional code or not.

(b) 'Unreasonable' described conduct which was vexatious, ie, designed to harass the other side rather than advance the resolution of the dispute. Conduct could not be described as unreasonable simply because it led to an unsuccessful result, or because other more cautious legal representatives would have acted differently. The acid test was whether the conduct permitted of a reasonable explanation. If it did, the course adopted might be regarded as optimistic and reflecting on a practitioner's judgment, but it was not unreasonable.

(c) 'Negligent' should be understood in an untechnical way to denote failure to act with the competence reasonably expected of ordinary members of the profession. It was not a term of art and did not necessarily involve an actionable breach of the legal representative's duty to his own client.

(d) A legal representative was not acting improperly, unreasonably or negligently simply because he acted for a party who pursued a claim or defence which was plainly doomed to fail.

(e) However, a legal representative could not lend his assistance to proceedings which were an abuse of process, and was not entitled to use litigious procedures for purposes for which they were not intended, eg, by issuing proceedings for reasons unconnected with success in the action, pursuing a case which was known to be dishonest or knowingly conniving at incomplete disclosure of documents.

(f) Any judge considering making a wasted costs order must make full allowance for the fact that an advocate in court often had to make decisions quickly and under pressure.

(g) Legal professional privilege might be relevant. If so, the privilege was the client's which he alone could waive. Judges should make full allowance for the inability of respondent lawyers to tell the whole story. Where there was room for doubt, the respondent lawyers were entitled to the benefit of it. It was only when, with all allowance made, a lawyer's conduct of proceedings was quite plainly unjustifiable that it could be appropriate to make the order.

(h) When a solicitor sought the advice of counsel, he did not abdicate his own professional responsibility. He had to apply his mind to the advice received. But the more specialised the advice, the more reasonable it was likely to be for him to accept it.

(i) A threat to apply for a wasted costs order should not be used as a means of intimidation. However, if one side considered that the conduct of the other was improper, unreasonable or negligent and likely to cause a waste of costs, it was not objectionable to alert the other side to that view.

(j) In the ordinary way, such applications were best left until after the end of the trial.

(k) As to procedure, the respondent lawyer should be told very clearly what he was said to have done wrong. No formal process of discovery would be appropriate. Elaborate statements of case should in general be avoided. The court could not imagine circumstances in which the applicant could interrogate the respondent lawyer or vice versa. The legal representative must have opportunity to show cause why an order should not be made (Rules of the Supreme Court 1965, Ord 62, r 11(4)), but this did not mean that the burden was on the legal representative to exculpate himself. (Note that this was written before the introduction of the Civil Procedure Rules 1998.)

In *R v Ullah* The Times, 11 November 1999, the Court of Appeal held that it was only a significant fault by trial counsel or a solicitor that could found a challenge to a jury's verdict. The proper and convenient approach was to apply the *Wednesbury* test.

In *Re A Barrister (Wasted Costs Order No. 4 of 1992)* The Times, 15 March 1994, the Court of Appeal held that a barrister who practised at home without a clerk must not rely wholly on instructing solicitors to notify him of the dates and times of cases. He was responsible for keeping abreast of listing details and should have adopted a system which enabled him to do so.

In *Re A Barrister (Wasted Costs Order No. 4 of 1993)* The Times, 21 April 1995, the Court of Appeal held that a judge should not impose such a Draconian penalty as a wasted costs order without taking into account the daily demands of practice and the difficulties associated with time estimates.

2.1.1.3 Problems

(1) In the course of legal argument, your opponent advances a proposition of law to the court in support of their client's case, but fails to produce a particular reported decision of which you are aware and which would plainly be of assistance. Without it you are likely to win; with it you may well fail. What do you do? Does your answer depend upon for whom you are acting and whether in civil or criminal proceedings?

(2) Whilst sitting in court waiting for your case to be called, you listen to the previous case. Counsel for the claimant is seeking to persuade the judge that the maximum time that the judge can allow the defendant to vacate the claimant's premises is 14 days. The defendant is unrepresented. The judge is an assistant recorder with clearly little experience of landlord and tenant law. You are aware that the judge has a discretion to allow the defendant a maximum period of six weeks. Do you do anything?

(3) You start to cross-examine a prosecution witness about matters which you consider to be vital to your client's case. The judge, having heard argument on the matter, disallows your line of questioning. You are convinced the judge is wrong and that your client will thereby be convicted. What, if anything, can you do?

2.1.2 Specific responsibilities of prosecuting counsel

Prosecuting counsel plays a very important role within the criminal justice system to ensure that the system operates openly and fairly. You must be familiar with a number of sources of guidance. See also **2.3.2.1** which sets out the Code for Crown Prosecutors and **2.3.3** which includes the CPS instructions for prosecuting advocates.

The role and responsibilities of prosecuting counsel are fully set out in Section 3, Miscellaneous Guidance, Written Standards for the Conduct of Professional Work (Standards Applicable to Criminal Cases, para 11) including guidance to counsel on the role of the prosecution in relation to the sentencing process. Although those provisions are not repeated here, it is important to be familiar with their content. The following paragraphs merely highlight some further aspects of those responsibilities, and are not a comprehensive guide in themselves.

2.1.2.1   The relationship between prosecuting counsel and the judge

This relationship was considered in the Farquharson Committee Report in 1986. The following passage is reproduced from Archbold's *Criminal Pleading, Evidence and Practice*, paras 4–76 to 4–80, Vol 1, 1995 by kind permission of Sweet & Maxwell (an abbreviated version of this passage appears at 4–96 of the 2003 edition of *Archbold*). The committee stated:

> It is a matter of curiosity that the respective rights and duties of the Judge and Prosecution Counsel have never been clearly defined. The most likely explanation is that whenever a difference has arisen between the two as to which course to take in particular circumstances, it has usually been resolved by discussion. Such authority as there is suggests that there has been some change of view on the topic by the Court of Appeal over the last thirty years.
>
> In 1948 in the case of *Soanes* 32 Cr App R 136 Prosecution Counsel in an Indictment for murder agreed with defence Counsel to accept a plea of guilty to infanticide. The Judge, Singleton J refused to accept it on the grounds that there was nothing on the depositions which could justify such a course. As a matter of history the trial proceeded on the charge of murder and the jury convicted of infanticide. In the Court of Criminal Appeal Goddard LCJ said this:
>
>> '... it is impossible to lay down a hard and fast rule in any class of case in which a plea for a lesser offence should be accepted by counsel for the Crown — and it must always be in the discretion of the Judge whether he will allow it to be accepted — in the opinion of the Court, where nothing appears on the depositions which can be said to reduce the crime from the more serious offence charged to some lesser offence for which a verdict may be returned, the duty of Counsel for the Crown would be to present the offence charged in the Indictment ...'
>
> In 1980 in *R v Coward* 70 Cr App R 70 at 76 Lawton LJ said:
>
>> 'It is for Prosecuting Counsel to make up their own minds what pleas to accept. If the judge does not approve he can say so in open Court and then the Prosecution will have to decide what course to take.'
>
> We approach the problem by considering whether Counsel acting on behalf of the Prosecution may or should decide to offer no evidence on any particular count in an Indictment or on the Indictment itself, without the approval of the Judge. When taking such a decision it is usual for Counsel to explain his reasons for doing so to the Judge. It is open then to the Judge to express his own views and if he disapproves of the course taken by Counsel he will no doubt say so. In those circumstances, Counsel is under an obligation to reconsider the matter, both personally and with his junior, if he has one, and his Instructing Solicitor. Whilst great weight should be given to the Judge's view, if Counsel still feels that the Prosecution's decision is the correct one then he must persist in the course he originally proposed. He will have much more information about the background and weight of the case than the Judge who will only have the depositions and exhibits. Counsel is therefore in the best position to make the decision and although one would expect that Counsel would rarely have to take the course of offering no evidence in defiance of the opinion of the Judge, in the final analysis the decision must be his.
>
> There is now no doubt that where Counsel for the Prosecution wishes to proceed on a properly laid Indictment the Judge cannot prevent him doing so because he is of the opinion that the evidence is too weak for the Prosecution to succeed. See *R v Chairman of London County Sessions, ex p Downes*, 37 Cr App R 148. Nor may the Judge refuse to allow the Prosecution to proceed on an Indictment on the grounds that he disapproves of the course being taken unless it amounts to an abuse of the process of

the Court. The explanation must be that Counsel for the Prosecution has the carriage of the proceedings and it is for him to decide in a particular case whether to proceed or not to proceed.

In accepting a plea of guilty to a lesser offence or offences Counsel for the Prosecution is in reality making a decision to offer no evidence on a particular charge. It follows in our opinion that if Counsel is entitled to decide whether he should offer no evidence on the Indictment as a whole, as we think he is, then correspondingly, it must be for him to decide whether or not to proceed on a particular count in an Indictment. This is subject to three important qualifications:

(a) It is sometimes the practice when Prosecution Counsel decides to accept a plea to a lesser count for him to invite the approval of the Judge. Counsel may feel it appropriate to do so in cases where it is desirable to reassure the public at large that the course proposed is being properly taken, or when he has been unable to reach agreement with his Instructing Solicitor.

As we have already said, Counsel is not bound to invite the Judge's approval but if he does so, then he must of course abide by the Judge's decision. 'When Counsel for the Crown invites the Judge to give approval to some course which he wishes to take the seeking of that approval is no idle formality. The Judge in such circumstances is not a rubber stamp to approve a decision by Counsel without further consideration, a decision which may or may not be right.' *R v Broad* 68 Cr App R 281, *per* Roskill LJ.

(b) While the Judge will not have all the information available to Counsel he will have derived considerable knowledge of the case from the depositions and exhibits; certainly enough to enable him to decide upon the right sentence after receiving the appropriate report and hearing any mitigation. There may well be cases where the Judge so disapproves of the decision taken by Prosecution Counsel to accept a plea to a lesser offence that he cannot consistently with his duty, as he sees it, proceed to sentence on that basis. The Judge may take the view that Counsel's decision proceeds from caprice or incompetence, or simply that he entirely disagrees with the decision however carefully Counsel has arrived at it. The Judge cannot in such circumstances be expected to lend himself to a process which in his judgment amounts to an abuse or to injustice. While for the reasons already given the Judge cannot insist on Prosecution Counsel proceeding on the major charge he may decline to proceed with the case without Counsel first consulting with the Director of Public Prosecutions, on whether he should proceed in the light of the comments the Judge will have made. In an extreme case he may think it right to invite Counsel to seek the advice of the Attorney-General. In the final analysis, when these steps have been taken, the Judge has no power to prevent Counsel proceeding. Indeed any attempt by him to do so would give the impression that he was stepping into the arena and pressing the Prosecution case. However, we are of the opinion that the occasions when counsel felt it right to resist the Judge's views would be rare.

These views are in accordance with the Guidelines to Prosecution Counsel given by the Bar Committee of the Senate of the Four Inns of Court and the Bar (dated 9 May, 1984) to the following effect:

'Counsel may in his discretion invite the trial Judge to assist him in his decision (whether to offer no evidence or to accept or to refuse pleas tendered by the accused) but he is never under a duty to do so nor should he do so as a means of avoiding his personal responsibility.' 'Counsel should in any case be ready to explain his decision in open Court and to reconsider it in the light of any observations made by the trial Judge.'

This guidance has recently received the approval of the Court of Appeal and must now be taken to be the proper approach for a Judge when he is informed by Prosecuting Counsel that he does not intend to proceed. See *R v Jenkins* (1985) 83 Cr App R 152.

(c) Sometimes a decision has to be made to offer no evidence during the course of the trial; and similarly pleas of guilty may be tendered to lesser counts. While the Prosecution case is being presented the decision as to what course to take in these circumstances remains with Counsel.

After the prosecution case is completed, once the Judge has ruled that there is a case to answer or where he has not been invited to do so but the case is proceeding, then in our view the prosecution cannot be discontinued nor pleas of guilty to lesser charges be accepted without the consent of the Judge. *Ex hypothesi* there is at this stage a case to answer and it would, in our view, be an abuse of process for the Prosecution to discontinue without leave. In such a situation while the Judge may rule that the case shall proceed and be considered by the Jury it would not be the duty of Counsel to cross-examine the defence witnesses or address the Jury if he was of the view that it would not be proper to convict.

The only exception to this rule is when the Attorney-General enters a *nolle prosequi* which can be done at any stage of the proceedings.

4.   *Prosecuting counsel in the Court of Appeal*

In the event of an Appeal against conviction or a reference by the Secretary of State Prosecution Counsel's view can be no more than persuasive. Section 2 of the Criminal Appeal Act 1968 expressly provides that:

> 'The Court of Appeal should allow an Appeal ... if they think that ...'

In other words by Statute the decision is vested exclusively in the Court of Appeal.

If Prosecution Counsel has formed the view that the Appeal should succeed he should acquaint the Court with the view and explain the reasons for it. If the Court disagrees with him Counsel is entitled to adhere to his view and is not obliged to conduct the Appeal in any way which conflicts with his own judgment. At the same time it remains Counsel's duty to give assistance to the Court if requested to do so.

5.   *In summary it is our opinion that:*

(a) It is the duty of Prosecution Counsel to read the instructions delivered to him expeditiously and to advise or confer with those instructing him on all aspects of the case well before its commencement.

(b) A solicitor who has briefed Counsel to prosecute may withdraw his instructions before the commencement of the trial up to the point when it becomes impracticable to do so, if he disagrees with the advice given by Counsel or for any other proper professional reason.

(c) While he remains instructed it is for Counsel to take all necessary decisions in the presentation and general conduct of the prosecution.

(d) Where matters of policy fall to be decided after the point indicated in (b) above (including offering no evidence on the Indictment or on a particular count, or the acceptance of pleas to lesser counts) it is the duty of Counsel to consult his Instructing Solicitor/Crown Prosecutor whose views at this stage are of crucial importance.

(e) In the rare case where Counsel and his Instructing Solicitor are unable to agree on a matter of policy, it is, subject to (g) below, for Prosecution Counsel to make the necessary decisions.

(f) Where Counsel has taken a decision on a matter of policy with which his Instructing Solicitor has not agreed, then it would be appropriate for the Attorney-General to require Counsel to submit to him a written report of all the circumstances, including his reasons for disagreeing with those who instructed him.

(g) When Counsel has had the opportunity to prepare his brief and to confer with those instructing him, but at the last moment before trial unexpectedly advises that the case should not proceed or that pleas to lesser offences should be accepted, and his Instructing Solicitor does not accept such advice, Counsel should apply for an adjournment if instructed so to do.

(h) Subject to the above, it is for Prosecution Counsel to decide whether to offer no evidence on a particular count or on the Indictment as a whole and whether to accept pleas to a lesser count or counts.

(i) If Prosecution Counsel invites the Judge to approve the course he is proposing to take, then he must abide by the Judge's decision.

(j) If Prosecution Counsel does not invite the Judge's approval of his decision it is open to the Judge to express his dissent with the course proposed and to invite counsel to reconsider the matter with those instructing him, but having done so, the final decision remains with Counsel.

(k) In an extreme case where the Judge is of the opinion that the course proposed by Counsel would lead to serious injustice, he may decline to proceed with the case until Counsel has consulted with either the Director or the Attorney-General as may be appropriate.

2.1.3 Further duties

There are further duties of prosecuting counsel which are not expressly included in the Code.

2.1.3.1 To inform the defence of any known previous convictions of any prosecution witness

See *R v Collister and Warhurst* (1955) 39 Cr App R 100. It should be noted that previous convictions include any disciplinary offences/findings and criminal cautions against police witnesses.

2.1.3.2 To call or tender witnesses at trial

The current scheme is governed by the Criminal Procedure and Investigations Act 1996 (the 1996 Act). Under this Act committal proceedings are held without live witnesses. The court still decides whether there is a case to answer, with or without consideration of evidence. If with consideration of evidence, this will be written only.

By virtue of the 1996 Act, sch 2, para 1(2), a statement tendered at committal under s 5B 'may without further proof be read as evidence on the trial of the accused' provided (para 1(3)(c)) that the accused does not object. However, even if the accused does object, that objection may be overridden by the court of trial if that is in the interests of justice (Sch 2).

The exceptions to the general rule that the prosecution must call (or tender for cross-examination) all the witnesses whose evidence was used in the committal proceedings are those set out in the cases of *R v Russell-Jones* [1995] 3 All ER 230 and *R v Armstrong* [1995] 3 All ER 831:

- the defence has consented to the written statement of that witness being read to the court;
- counsel for the prosecution takes the view that the evidence of that witness is no longer credible; or
- counsel for the prosecution takes the view that the witness would so fundamentally contradict the prosecution case that it would make more sense for that person to be called as a witness for the defence.

There remains a limit to the prosecution's discretion, namely that it must be exercised in the interests of justice, so as to promote a fair trial.

2.1.3.3 To adduce all the evidence upon which you intend to rely to prove the defendant's guilt before the close of your case

This is provided that such evidence is then available.

2.1.3.4 To disclose not only all of the evidence that will be called at trial, but also information of which the defence may be unaware and which will not be part of the prosecution case

This duty is dealt with mainly in the Criminal Procedure and Investigations Act 1996. The statutory scheme is covered in the *Criminal Litigation and Sentencing Manual*.

In essence, there is a duty on the police officer investigating the offence to record and retain information and material gathered during the investigation. The prosecution must inform the defence of certain categories of that material that it does not intend to rely on at trial: 'primary disclosure by prosecutor'. The defence then has a duty to inform the prosecution of the case that it intends to present at trial. The prosecution then has a duty to present further material to the defence which might be reasonably expected to assist the accused's defence as disclosed by the defence: 'secondary disclosure by prosecutor'. After this, applications can be made to the court where there is a dispute as to whether the prosecution should disclose certain material. Where public interest immunity is involved, the 1996 Act expressly preserves the existing common law.

The prosecutor remains under a continuing duty to review questions of disclosure.

The prosecution's duty of primary disclosure applies to summary trial where the accused pleads not guilty. The defence may make voluntary disclosure. In such a case, the prosecution will be obliged to make secondary disclosure.

It should be noted that para 11.2 to Standards Applicable to Criminal Cases in Section 3, Miscellaneous Guidance, Written Standards for the Conduct of Professional Work, provides:

Prosecuting counsel should bear in mind at all times whilst he is instructed:

   ...

     (ii)   that he should use his best endeavours to ensure that all evidence or material that ought properly to be made available is either presented by the prosecution or disclosed to the defence.

2.1.3.5 To consider whether witness statements need to be edited

See *Practice Direction* [1986] 2 All ER 511 for the relevant considerations and practice on editing witness statements.

2.1.3.6 To be familiar with the *Practice Direction: Crown Court (Plea and Directions Hearings)* [1995] 1 WLR 1318

The purpose of a Pleas and Directions Hearing (PDH) is to ensure that all necessary steps have been taken in preparation for trial and to provide sufficient information for a trial date to be arranged. The *Practice Direction* stresses that 'it is expected that the advocate briefed in the case will appear in the PDH wherever practicable'. With the demands of a busy practice this will not always be possible. Pupils and junior tenants should be very conscious of the fact that it is regarded as a serious dereliction of duty for counsel to turn up at a PDH and say 'Sorry, this isn't my brief and I can't provide the information required'. If you are going to appear at a PDH in the place of counsel who will be appearing in the case, go armed with all the relevant information, and there is a lot of it to gather together! Information required includes informing the court of the issues in the case, number of witnesses and the form their evidence will take, exhibits and schedules to be admitted at trial, points of law and admissibility of evidence that will arise at trial, applications for evidence to be given via television links etc, witness availability, length of witness testimony, counsel availability.

2.1.3.7 Problems

(1)   You are instructed to prosecute a case in which the allegation is that the defendant and associates burst into the victim's flat intent on causing injury. The victim, seeing the group arrive, tried to escape by jumping off the fifth floor balcony. He fell and was seriously injured. The defendant was charged with causing grievous bodily harm with intent. After the victim has given evidence, you are shown a note by the officer in the case which the officer says was written by the victim about ten days before these events. It shows that at that time the victim was threatening suicide. You do not think that that is the reason why he jumped that day and it certainly does not accord with the evidence the victim has just given. What do you do, if anything, about the note?

(2)   In the course of a ruling given following argument by counsel for both prosecution and defence, the judge gives reasons which are based on a case cited in argument. The ruling is favourable to you, the prosecution. It is, however, clear that the judge has misunderstood the passage quoted. What do you do?

(3)   You arrive in court to prosecute a defendant. You realise that the defendant was a client of a solicitor's firm for which you worked during the holidays. You learnt details about the defendant which might well help you in prosecuting the case. The defendant does not appear to recognise you. Do you do anything?

2.1.4   Specific responsibilities of defence counsel

You are referred to the Standards Applicable to Criminal Cases, para 12 (see **Appendix 1**) and to Guidance on Preparation of Defence Case Statements in Section 3, Miscellaneous Guidance, for a full consideration of these responsibilities. It is not proposed to repeat them here. The most common ethical problems associated with defending, other than those which involve a (potential) conflict of interest, tend to arise in the following circumstances where:

- a client confesses his or her guilt. Coping in this situation is dealt with in para 13 of the Standards Applicable to Criminal Cases 'Confessions of Guilt';
- a client changes his or her instructions;
- a client insists upon you conducting the case in a manner which you consider detrimental to his or her interests, eg, by calling unhelpful witnesses; or
- you find yourself in the position of being a material witness.

These points will be considered in detail during the Professional Conduct Course classes (see **Chapter 8** for professional conduct problems).

Although the primary responsibility of defence counsel in a criminal case is to endeavour to protect the client from conviction except by a competent tribunal and upon legally admissible evidence sufficient to support a conviction for the offence charged (para 12.1 of the Standards Applicable to Criminal Cases), this does not displace the overriding duty to the Court. It is important, however, to bear in mind the duty of confidentiality owed to the lay client which must not be breached (para 702). As with prosecuting counsel, defence counsel should be familiar with the duties and obligations imposed by the *Practice Direction: Crown Court (Pleas and Directions Hearings)* [1995] 1 WLR 1318.

2.1.4.1   Problems

(1)   You represent a defendant in a trial at the Crown Court having advised and appeared (without your instructing solicitor having been present) at the magistrates' court. The defendant, having been given the new caution, did not answer any question in his or her police interview. During your client's cross-examination by the prosecution, it is suggested that the account he or she is giving has been thought up recently. You know that he or she gave that account to you on the first remand date. You were alone with him or her at the time. What should you do?

(2)   There is crucial prosecution evidence of your client's presence at the scene of the crime at a material time. Your instructions are that your client was present but merely an onlooker, not a participant in the crime. You conduct your cross-examination on that basis and do not challenge the evidence of your client's presence at the scene. When he or she gives evidence, the defendant denies his or her presence at the material time by saying that he or she had just left the scene. The judge points out the difference and demands that you clarify the situation.

(3)   Your client is pleading guilty in the magistrates' court. Your instructions are that he or she has a number of previous convictions. The police antecedents given to the court show him or her as a person of good character. How do you mitigate? Would your ap-

proach be different if the omitted previous conviction had involved the imposition of a suspended sentence of which the defendant was in breach by virtue of the instant conviction?

2.1.5   Access to the judge

2.1.5.1   *Turner* directions

The Court of Appeal has stressed the need for strict compliance with the directions given by that court in *R v Turner* [1970] 2 QB 321 on seeking guidance from the judge, in particular, upon the question of sentence (see also *Attorney-General's Reference (No. 44 of 2000)* The Times, 25 October 2000). Those directions are now set out in full:

Before leaving this case, which has brought out into the open the vexed question of so-called 'plea-bargaining', the court would like to make some observations which may be of help to judges and to counsel and, indeed, solicitors. They are these:

1. Counsel must be completely free to do what is his duty, namely to give the accused the best advice he can and if need be advice in strong terms. This will often include advice that a plea of guilty, showing an element of remorse, is a mitigating factor which may well enable the court to give a lesser sentence than would otherwise be the case. Counsel of course will emphasise that the accused must not plead guilty unless he has committed the acts constituting the offence charged.

2. The accused, having considered counsel's advice, must have a complete freedom of choice whether to plead guilty or not guilty.

3. There must be freedom of access between counsel and judge. Any discussion, however, which takes place must be between the judge and both counsel for the defence and counsel for the prosecution. If a solicitor representing the accused is in the court he should be allowed to attend the discussion if he so desires. This freedom of access is important because there may be matters calling for communication or discussion, which are of such a nature that counsel cannot in the interests of his client mention them in open court. Purely by way of example, counsel for the defence may by way of mitigation wish to tell the judge that the accused has not long to live, is suffering maybe from cancer, of which he is and should remain ignorant. Again, counsel on both sides may wish to discuss with the judge whether it would be proper, in a particular case, for the prosecution to accept a plea to a lesser offence. It is of course imperative that so far as possible justice must be administered in open court. Counsel should, therefore, only ask to see the judge when it is felt to be really necessary, and the judge must be careful only to treat such communications as private where, in fairness to the accused person, this is necessary.

4. The judge should, subject to the one exception referred to hereafter, never indicate the sentence which he is minded to impose. A statement that on a plea of guilty he would impose one sentence but that on a conviction following a plea of not guilty he would impose a severer sentence is one which should never be made. This could be taken to be undue pressure on the accused, thus depriving him of that complete freedom of choice which is essential. Such cases, however, are in the experience of the court happily rare. What on occasions does appear to happen however is that a judge will tell counsel that, having read the depositions and the antecedents, he can safely say that on a plea of guilty he will for instance, make a probation order, something which may be helpful to counsel in advising the accused. The judge in such a case is no doubt careful not to mention what he would do if the accused were convicted following a plea of not guilty. Even so, the accused may well get the impression that the judge is intimating that in that event a severer sentence, maybe a custodial sentence would result, so that again he may feel under pressure. This accordingly must also not be done.

The only exception to this rule is that it should be permissible for a judge to say, if it be the case, that whatever happens, whether the accused pleads guilty or not guilty, the sentence will or will not take a particular form, eg, a probation order or a fine, or a custodial sentence.

Finally, where any such discussion on sentence has taken place between judge and counsel, counsel for the defence should disclose this to the accused and inform him of what took place.

See also *Criminal Litigation and Sentencing Manual*.

2.1.5.2 A view for change

There is, however, a feeling among some senior members of the profession that these rules are unnecessarily restrictive and that while caution must be exercised, there are occasions when court time and costs could be saved by a more flexible and 'sensible approach'. This argument was supported by Robin Gray QC in the following paper. It is stressed that this was his personal view and not to be used as a justification for ignoring your duty to comply with the directions in *R v Turner*.

Seeing the Judge on Sentence: Should the Parameters be Extended?
For many years now, and more particularly since the case of *Turner* (1970) 54 Cr App R 352; [1970] 2 QB 321, counsel for defendants have been nervous about seeing the judge on sentence and judges themselves have been even more nervous in agreeing to a request to see them.

This seems to me to result from an unrealistic approach to the problem and an unreasonable fear of accusations of 'plea bargaining' putting unfair pressure on defendants. I believe this fear is unfounded and, if a sensible approach were adopted by the courts, a substantial shortening of trials would result and a considerable saving in cost. I doubt if it is an exaggeration to say that over 95 per cent of those charged with crime are guilty of some criminal offence, if not the precise offence with which they are charged.

It may well be for that reason that three questions are frequently asked in conference with counsel, although the client is protesting his innocence:

(1) What will I get if I'm convicted?; (2) Will I go to prison?; (3) How long will I get?

These are questions which counsel should be able to answer but can never give more than an educated guess, bearing in mind tariffs, precedents, etc.

When a person is arrested, no doubt the police officer will say 'you'd do better to put your hands up to this', the solicitor will say 'you'll get less on a plea', the barrister will say 'you appreciate that the judge is likely to feel more kindly disposed if you plead guilty', and yet the judge cannot say 'if you plead guilty, you'll get less or won't go inside', although everybody knows, and the client can and should be told, that all the authorities on sentencing enjoin the judges to give a reduction, sometimes substantial, for a plea of guilty.

So how do we answer the three questions posed above?

(1) *What will I get if I'm convicted?*
In the last resort there is only one person who knows the sentence which is about to be passed and that is the trial judge himself, and indeed an honest answer to the question is 'it may depend on who the judge is'. Judges do not vary to any great degree in their sentencing, except in rare cases, but there is no doubt that some are more lenient than others and in borderline cases some will pass non-custodial and others custodial sentences.

Accordingly, there is only one way in which one can ever positively answer the client's question and that is by asking the judge at the trial. Unfortunately, since *Turner* (above), if the judge is prepared to discuss the matter with counsel at all, there are considerable limitations on what he or she can say. A judge has to be approached by counsel through the clerk of the court and very often the answer comes back: 'the judge will not see you on sentence'.

(2) *Will I go to prison?*
This question can only be answered if the judge is satisfied as to the nature of the sentence, whatever the plea. Waller LJ made this clear in *Ryan* (1977) 67 Cr App R 177, with these words:

> ... the only permissible communication of intended sentence is that, whatever happens about the plea, the sentence will or will not take a particular form, and secondly, that the judge must not indicate what he will do on a plea of guilty and say nothing about a conviction after pleading not guilty.

Clearly, therefore, there is no problem if the judge decides that, whatever the plea, a non-custodial sentence will be imposed. He or she can say so. The difficulty arises in the borderline cases, where the judge feels that on a plea of guilty a non-custodial sentence can be imposed, but simply does not know how he or she would be minded at the end of a trial if the defendant were to plead not guilty. It would obviously be wrong for the judge ever to say 'if you plead you'll go free, but if you fight you'll go inside', as in *Bird* (1978) 67 Cr App R 203. That is putting obvious pressure on the defendant, and in any event a judge cannot know the final sentence in a case where a non-custodial sentence is a possibility until the end of the trial.

However, should it be wrong for a judge to say simply 'If you plead now, you'll go free' without any reference to what the situation would be after a fight? Waller LJ's dicta (above) clearly stated that it would be wrong. (See also *Atkinson* (1978) 67 Cr App R 201.)

However, there is a strong argument to say that the risk which the defendant chooses to take in those circumstances if he decides to plead not guilty is a no greater risk than he already appreciates he is taking, having been advised by competent counsel and solicitor that he runs a risk of a heavier sentence if he persists in fighting. Indeed the judge would not be going as far as that. He or she would simply be saying in effect: 'I can tell you that if you plead now, you won't go inside, but I'm afraid I simply can't say whether the position will remain the same by the end of the trial. It may be the same, it may not'; whereas counsel in any event, doing his duty, would already have said 'I can't tell you whether you'll go inside or not, but you certainly have a far better chance if you plead guilty'.

(3)   *How long will I get?*

Waller LJ's dicta in *Ryan* (above) also allow a judge to indicate that the sentence will be custodial in any event, but that is not of any great assistance if it is not known how long the sentence will be. It is in this area that it may be that there is a stronger case than in any other situation for arguing that the rules of practice should be altered. There are very many serious cases in which the defendant's persistence in his innocence is simply brought about by the fact that he will on conviction, or so he believes, be sentenced to a far longer sentence than in fact the judge would have in mind, and counsel cannot disabuse him.

It seems to me that there should be nothing wrong in a judge telling counsel in *any* case that the *maximum* sentence will be 'so many' years of imprisonment, plea or fight. If the judge cannot give even a maximum indication at the outset of a trial, not yet being in possession of sufficient facts, he should be entitled to give such an indication *at any stage* of the trial. I believe this would lead to a substantial increase in pleas of guilty and an enormous saving of court time.

As an example, I defended a man charged with fraud, in 1987. The defence was one of 'subjective honesty', but I was told that he would take my advice whether to plead guilty or not on his version of events. He said that, if he were to receive no more than four years' imprisonment, he would think seriously of changing his plea. The judge, whom I approached through the clerk of the court, refused to see counsel on sentence at all. I could not, therefore, even know the *maximum* sentence. The trial lasted eight weeks, the defendant was convicted, and he was sentenced to four years' imprisonment. Eight weeks of public money was wasted.

Counsel can still attempt to approach the judge, whether or not their client has indicated an intention to plead, but more often than not, as the law stands at present, it comes to nothing.

2.1.5.3   Situations where it is permissible to see the judge

Although most judges will refuse to see counsel on a matter of sentence, there are a variety of other situations in which it is permissible and indeed advisable for counsel to ask to see the judge. These include:

- if your client is thinking of pleading guilty but, for instance, wants to discuss the matter with your instructing solicitor who is not present at court that day, counsel may see the judge and ask for an overnight adjournment. To mention that the client is thinking of pleading guilty in these circumstances is sensitive information that ought not to be mentioned in open court;

- if the defendant has given information or assistance to the police he or she may not wish details to be given to the judge in open court. His or her safety or that of his or her family may be at risk;

- any matters that would be embarrassing to the defendant if mentioned in open court, for instance, if he or she is suffering from an illness that may make him or her appear drowsy or uninterested whilst in court;

- any matters that are personal to counsel and would be embarrassing to mention in open court, eg, illness, a bereavement necessitating an adjournment etc.

2.2 Relationship with the lay client

2.2.1 Duties and responsibilities owed to the lay client

First and foremost, the profession requires strict observance of the 'cab-rank' rule: see paras 601 and 602 of the Code of Conduct. You must accept any instructions or brief to represent any client, at a proper professional fee (para 604(b)), in the field(s) in which you profess to practise irrespective of the nature of the case or any belief or opinion which you may have formed as to the character, reputation, cause, conduct, guilt or innocence of that person. The cab-rank rule applies whether your client is paying privately or is publicly funded.

Note that any instructions in a publicly funded matter shall, in specified circumstances, be deemed to be at a proper professional fee (para 604(b)).

Many of the duties and responsibilities you owe to the lay client are dealt with in the Code of Conduct. Before you accept any brief or instructions, you must satisfy yourself that you are competent and have adequate time to prepare and do the particular case (para 603). If at any time in any matter you consider it would be in the best interests of any client to have different representation, you must immediately so advise the client (para 607). You have an added obligation to consider whether the best interests of the client would be served by instructing or continuing to instruct you (para 606.1). You must also consider the best interests of the client and whether it is suitable for them to instruct more than one advocate (para 606.2); and whether in the interests of the lay client or the interests of justice, to instruct a solicitor or other authorised litigator or other appropriate intermediary either together with or in place of you (para 606.3); and how several parties are represented or advised (para 606.4). If, however, the client insists that you do the case, you are bound by the 'cab-rank' rule subject to it being the sort of work you are competent to undertake. It is also obviously important to determine in any case whether a conflict of interest exists or arises which prevents you from acting/continuing to act for that client.

Your duties to the lay client include a responsibility:

(a) To promote fearlessly and by all proper and lawful means the lay client's best interests and to do so without regard to your own interests or to any consequences to yourself or to any other person (including any other professional client or other intermediary or another barrister) (para 303(a)).

(b) To owe your primary responsibility as between the lay client and any professional client or other intermediary to the lay client and not to permit the intermediary to limit your discretion as to how the interests of the lay client can best be served (para 303(b)).

(c) To preserve the confidentiality of your client's affairs (para 702).

(d) To act with reasonable competence and maintain professional independence.

(e) To keep your lay client informed of the estimate and likely impact of costs. In *Singer (formerly Sharegin) v Sharegin* [1984] FLR 114, 119, Cumming-Bruce LJ expressed the duty in this way:

> I conclude by emphasising the immense importance of the obligation upon solicitors and counsel in all these cases (financial disputes) to form accurate estimates as to costs, to inform their lay client what the impact of costs is likely to be, to inform the lay client of the probable estimate of the totality of costs on both sides so that the lay client can fully understand the enormous financial risks they may incur if they insist on sticking to what they regard as their own sensible point of view and so refuse to make or accept an offer involving much compromise on both sides.

(f) To advise your lay client, when a conflict of interest arises between your lay client and a professional client or other intermediary, that it would be in his or her interests to instruct another professional adviser or representative (para 703).

(g) To owe your primary duty to your lay client, in cases funded by the Legal Services Commission, subject only to compliance with para 304 (see para 303(c)).

(h) To advise your client (and professional client) where it becomes apparent that funding in any case by the Legal Services Commission has been wrongly obtained by false or inaccurate information, and to withdraw from the case where action is not taken by the client to remedy the situation immediately (para 608(c)).

In order to provide a practical and objective insight into the relationship between counsel and the lay client, the then chairman of the National Consumer Council, David Hatch CBE, JP, and Marlene Winfield, the then Acting Head of Policy Research and Strategy at the National Consumer Council, wrote the following essay on barristers and their lay clients.

Barristers and their Lay Clients

> We believe that the excellence of the Bar will not simply be judged by the quality of its advice and advocacy. The Bar, like other professions and businesses, needs to display a wider, more all-round excellence: value for money and good client communications are an essential part of the modern profession.
>
> *Report of the Bar Standards Review Body*, September 1994

> In future a solicitor will increasingly need to have a reason to instruct counsel rather than to do the work himself, or to refer it to his in-house advocacy department or to an agency solicitor. Moreover, he will need to have a reason which can be explained to the client.
>
> *The Work of the Young Bar*, November 1993

A changing world

When today's fledgling barristers enter pupillage and practice, they will enter a world very different from that of their predecessors. The young barrister of today will face new types of work requiring different relationships with lay clients. Examples might include: providing or participating in alternative methods of dispute resolution such as mediation, arbitration and neutral case evaluation; coaching lay clients to be their own advocates; developing expertise in areas of social welfare law in order to take direct referrals from advice agencies operating under legal aid contracts.

Even in the traditional forms of work, things are changing. There is increasing specialisation by both barristers and solicitors. In areas such as personal injury and medical negligence, the harm that 'dabblers' can do is being recognised. Anecdotal evidence suggests that in all areas of the law lay clients are less content to take a passive role than they once were. Increasingly they want to be informed and consulted, to participate in decision-making. And they are more ready to complain if they feel they are not getting a good service.

Other changes to the nature of the traditional work of barristers are coming about as a result of the new Civil Procedure Rules 1998. New procedures have been introduced for dealing with multi-party actions, medical negligence, housing cases, and more generally with cases involving sums of money under £10,000. New procedures are streamlined, less adversarial and cheaper. A large share of the savings should be made on legal fees.

At the same time, competition is hotting up. Increased rights of audience and a desperate search for new sources of work, have driven solicitors into court in increasing numbers. Even that traditional training ground for new barristers, the magistrates' court, is equally likely these days to feature showdowns between salaried prosecutors and young solicitors.

Meanwhile, the size of the Bar has increased rapidly, by nearly a quarter in recent years. This means that more people are chasing fewer briefs. And as if that were not enough, the 1993 joint working party on the young Bar discovered other worrying trends: an apparent decline in levels of fees in the early years and increasing debt arising from barristers' training.

The many changes afoot pose threats, but they also offer opportunities for young barristers. What they all have in common is that they call for new ways of working with lay clients and their lay advisers. Those most likely to succeed in the brave new streamlined world of Woolf reforms and alternatives to trial will be those least afraid to explore new types of working relationships. It might be as well to start that exploration by learning from the mistakes of the past.

Working with lay clients

To a certain extent, barristers are shielded from the criticism of lay clients by solicitors. When something goes wrong, the solicitor is usually the first port of call. However, Action for Victims of Medical Accidents, AVMA, with over 19,000 medical negligence clients having passed through its doors, has experienced the highs and the lows of barristerial performance in an area of the law where sensitivity is perhaps most needed.

AVMA staff make the following observations about client care, based on their experience of accompanying lay clients on visits to counsel:

Inexperienced lay clients need to be adequately prepared by the solicitor for conferences with counsel. Clients need to know what to expect from the barrister and what the barrister expects from them. They also need to know what they are and are not allowed to do, for example, if they can speak directly to the barrister.

Lay clients need to be given a clear idea of who is making the decisions, the solicitor or barrister, and who is ultimately responsible for the conduct of the case.

Clients should be asked at an early stage what they hope to achieve by legal action. Thereafter, they should be asked their opinions.

It is essential that at the outset the client is given a clear idea about the difficulties of the case, the likely outcome and the potential costs.

Some clients are left feeling that their concerns were not addressed. If the client's concerns are not considered relevant, the reasons should be explained to them.

When a solicitor and barrister talk in legal jargon, it often excludes the client from the discussion.

If the solicitor and barrister wish to speak without the lay client being present, the purpose should be made clear.

Both solicitors and barristers should consider the client's needs as well as their own when determining the time and place of meetings. Factors such as ease of access for people with disabilities and availability of lavatories should be considered when fixing venues. Consideration should be given to where the client will feel most comfortable and thus best able to participate: chambers can be difficult to find and daunting places. Clients might prefer to meet in the solicitor's office, particularly if they have been there before. Wherever the meeting, clients should be given good directions.

When meetings are not well-organised or structured, clients can be left feeling that the barrister was not familiar with the case.

Simple kindnesses should not be forgotten. One AVMA staff member told of a stressful five hour conference during which the clients, who had travelled a long way and started very early in the morning, were not even offered a cup of coffee.

The above comments represent a mixture of good client care, common sense and basic courtesy. Lapses would be particularly out of place in medical accident cases, an area of the law where people can be extremely vulnerable. But, arguably, going to law for any reason is potentially stressful for lay clients, who will always benefit from sensitivity on the part of the barrister.

At a time of fierce and increasing competition between barristers, and between barristers and solicitors, those barristers — young and old — offering a high standard of client care will have a competitive edge.

...

Looking to the future

The future is by no means all gloom and doom. The young Bar can look forward to new opportunities in areas such as alternative dispute resolution, new civil justice fast track procedures, social welfare law, and the burgeoning area of public policy. But if young barristers are to compete with the new generation of solicitors, increasingly trained in both client care and advocacy skills, they too must adopt a more client-centred approach. A fine line has to be walked between providing good client care and retaining the objectivity that is the Bar's hallmark. The training of young barristers needs to grapple with how the changing expectations of lay clients can best be met within the Code of Conduct of the Bar and its working practices.

David Hatch CBE JP
Chairman [to December 2000]
National Consumer Council
and
Marlene Winfield
Acting Head of Policy Research and Strategy [to October 2000]
National Consumer Council

2.2.1.1   Problems

(1)   Your client bombards you with instructions, both before and during the trial. He or she insists you put each one to the various witnesses, who are all children your client is said to have abused. Your client insists on giving evidence even though he or she has previous similar convictions. He or she is also adamant that you call a witness that you suspect will destroy his or her case. How do you conduct the trial?

(2)   Whilst discussing with your client his or her witness statement outside court, you query his or her explanation of a certain event. The client tells you that is not what really happened but 'it was what the solicitor told me to say'. The solicitor is not present but has sent an articled clerk. What, if anything, do you do?

(3)   Your client loses his claim for a residence order in respect of his children. Upon leaving court, he mumbles 'She'll be sorry, I'll make sure she doesn't live to enjoy them'. How do you react?

2.3 Relationship with the professional client and other intermediaries

2.3.1 Duties and responsibilities owed to the professional client and other intermediaries

You may now accept instructions from professional clients (see paras 401 and 1001) and from members of approved professional bodies, for example, accountants and surveyors. In the latter cases, you must comply with the BarDIRECT Rules and Recognition Regulations reproduced in Annexe F of the Code of Conduct (see para 401).

With regard to your relationship with those who instruct you, problems can arise in circumstances where they seek to limit the way in which you present the case; where they take a different view of the lay client's prospects of success; where you consider they have been remiss/negligent in their handling of the client's affairs, or where they consider you have 'let them down' by not being available to do a case or have been guilty of delay. Many of these problems are due to poor communication, lack of control of your clerk or an unjustifiable attitude that you are somehow superior to them.

It is important that you foster good relations with those who instruct you, discuss any differences of opinion, and ensure that he or she is kept fully informed of any potential difficulties or conflicting dates in your diary. Your clerk should always inform any person who seeks to instruct you on a case if there is likely to be a conflicting engagement. Watch the chambers diary yourself to ensure this is being enforced. Do not delay your paperwork. If some delay cannot be avoided due to other pressing work, telephone them and explain the position so that he or she is free to instruct other counsel.

Do not criticise your solicitor or those who instruct you in front of the lay client without first discussing your view with the solicitor or the person who instructs you. Do not criticise your solicitor or those who instruct you in court unless they agree that some fault lies with them and they accept that the court must be told to prevent the lay client suffering the consequences.

A further area in which the relationship with a solicitor, in particular, may become problematical, arises out of the growth of the number of solicitors with rights of audience in the higher courts. This can lead to a variety of difficulties — not least if you are co-defending with a solicitor whose firm is acting for your defendant too, and who may be more likely to go to him or her than you. Be tactful.

The Legal Services Committee of the Bar Council has provided guidance on the area of solicitors acting as juniors to silks, which it quaintly describe as 'mixed doubles'. The committee stressed the importance of ensuring that the right amount of advocacy expertise is properly used, and in particular:

- if a case requires both a leader and junior, it is inappropriate for a solicitor advocate to try to perform both roles;
- the junior in any case (whether he or she be a barrister or solicitor advocate) must have appropriate skills and experience for the roles he or she is to perform and must be competent and available to perform the junior work required by the leader including examination of witnesses, the preparation of skeleton arguments and chronologies, the drafting of statements of case etc as the case may require;
- if a case is suitable for a silk to conduct alone, there should be no junior. But, if a junior is genuinely necessary, it would be manifestly inappropriate for a solicitor without rights of audience to seek to dispense with a junior on the basis that he or

she will carry out the junior work, excluding advocacy, whilst also acting as a solicitor.

Guidance upon your main duties to the professional client and other intermediaries can be found in paras 603, 610, 701(e), 703, 706 and 707 of the Code. Remember that your primary duty is to the lay client (para 303(b)). Note also Annexe G which covers the Terms of Work on which Barristers Offer their Services to Solicitors and the Withdrawal of Credit Scheme 1988.

2.3.1.1   Making the relationship work

A barrister's practice will depend largely upon the way in which he or she behaves towards and works with those who instruct him or her, particularly with his or her instructing solicitors. The relationship requires counsel to understand clearly what it is that solicitors expect from them. It also requires counsel to understand what is likely to alienate a solicitor. In order to provide a practical insight into the relationship between solicitor and counsel, there follows an essay by a senior solicitor on making the relationship work. It is written from the perspective of civil work (specifically medical negligence).

A Solicitor's View on the Barrister's Relationship with the Professional Client

Preface

The author specialises in claimant medical negligence litigation funded predominantly by legal aid. At the time of writing, he was a partner at Bolt Burdon, a firm that holds a legal aid franchise, and was in charge of supervising the firm's policy on the use of 'approved sub-contractors', which includes barristers.

The starting premise for this article was the general myth that traditionally the relationship between solicitors and barristers has been an uneasy alliance. Do barristers really think that they are the intellectual superiors of solicitors, who are always having to look to counsel to sort out ill-prepared cases? Do solicitors really think that barristers are arrogant snobs who blame solicitors when well-prepared cases fall apart because they have not bothered to read the papers properly? The reality, I think, is that at the extremes both are true, but for most of the time barristers and solicitors work very well together, and lay clients benefit from the combination of skills.

Preparation for court

Competent solicitors will ensure that the case has been prepared thoroughly from the outset, and by the time of trial will normally have met with counsel and experts on two or three occasions. On each of those occasions counsel will have had very full instructions, and will have been encouraged to think forward to ensure that at the pre-trial conference there are no glaring omissions in the evidence. So, the first piece of advice is that you should always think ahead — both in practical terms and legal terms. On a number of occasions I have sat in conferences with counsel knowing that the papers have not been read properly, and with the sinking feeling that I will get poorly drafted statements of case that will need amendment, and that in the weeks before trial counsel will suddenly want information that he or she could have asked for at the first conference. This is very annoying and does little to inspire confidence in the lay client.

In the weeks leading up to a trial I expect to work fairly closely with counsel. Typically we arrange a pre-trial conference for two or three weeks before the trial, and even with the best prepared case there will always be further work to be done before the brief is delivered. I expect and welcome telephone conversations about particular aspects of the case, and I am always encouraged as the questions become more complex, as it indicates that counsel is making a proper analysis of the papers. If there are to be settlement negotiations I expect to conduct them, unless we are at court, and I would not expect counsel to speak with opposing counsel without first discussing the prospect with me. Generally I think settlement negotiations are better conducted by solicitors. It is difficult to rationalise why this is so, as it has to be acknowledged that counsel will have a better understanding of the law and evidential strengths and weaknesses of the case. I think that it is partly because the solicitor manages the case for a long time and should have a better 'feel' for the case and understanding of how the opposing legal team behave, and partly because solicitors are not constrained by the thought that they may have to present the case in court, which enables us to be tougher in negotiation.

I expect a barrister to have a thorough knowledge of matters of law and procedure. I will happily defer to counsel's views on these matters, but I expect a reasoned discussion of why a particular course of action is being taken. A competent solicitor will not be happy to spend three to four years preparing a case, only to abdicate responsibility for it when it comes to trial.

An uneasy alliance?

Most of the solicitors and barristers that I know are specialists in their fields. They are confident of their abilities, and do their respective jobs very well. For many it was not ever thus. I trained in a very general practice, where I was expected to carry out all types of contentious and non-contentious work. When working with counsel I invariably had only a very superficial understanding of the case. In some instances this did not really matter, because I was the clerk sent along to sit behind counsel at trial, and make no more contribution than to take notes. In other cases it did matter, because I was dealing with cases that were beyond my competence and experience. Mostly the barristers I worked with were very kind about this, but I would have forgiven any of them for thinking that he or she was the real lawyer, because on those occasions they undoubtedly were. I think much has changed in the training of solicitors since then and certainly in my firm we try to make sure that trainees have a proper and appropriate role to play in the preparation of cases.

When done properly, the solicitor's job is a complex and demanding one. We gather a great deal of information, narrow it down, and fashion it into a well-prepared and well-thought-out case that can then be finished off by counsel. Appropriate metaphors are elusive. Clients often ask if we are like GPs and barristers are like hospital specialists, but I think of the process more in terms of the case being a large cargo ship, perhaps an oil tanker, with the solicitor as its captain. As it approaches port a pilot comes on board to guide it through the treacherous rocks and shallows. The pilot is the barrister. Without him or her the ship will not get through the treacherous rocks and shallows, but he or she should still remember that the captain has managed to bring the vessel all the way from Africa. Which metaphor brings me rather neatly to my first anecdote which comes from the time when I was a shipping lawyer. I admit that I was not very interested in shipping law, and consequently was not a very good shipping lawyer. However, I was reasonably competent, and the barrister I was instructing, although very intelligent, was not much more experienced than me. He was a nice man, and during the conference he sympathised with me as he knew what it was like to be a solicitor 'standing at the photocopier all day'. Now I know that the mysteries of a solicitor's office can sometimes be difficult for counsel to understand, but to clear any doubt that is in your minds I can honestly say that the person who stands at a photocopier all day is a copying clerk, not a solicitor.

Returning to my main theme, I have no doubt that some solicitors still allow their cases to be 'counsel driven', but they are increasingly a thing of the past. It may interest you to know that there is a strong financial incentive for this. When my costs are taxed I can claim a higher hourly rate if I can show that as a specialist solicitor I was able to run the case with minimal use of counsel. As your career progresses, and you are able to move into a specialist area of law, you will start to get instructions from solicitors who also specialize, and when that happens the relationship can be a very good one.

So, I hope that I have now firmly established that solicitors are real lawyers, and that we have no doubts about the value of our work being equal to the value of the work performed by counsel. Now I will tell the truth, or at least the rest of the truth in so far as it applies to me, and, I suspect to quite a lot of solicitors. In a small corner of our minds we have a lingering jealousy of barristers — jealous because they spend more of their time thinking about interesting legal points, jealous because all of the drama attaches to the final days in court, rather than the three years of preparation, jealous because there are more television dramas about barristers than there are about solicitors, and jealous because barristers have more opportunity to dress up as eighteenth-century clergymen. Of course we are not jealous of the barrister's responsibility as the final presenter and advocate of the case, or jealous of the red eyes and tobacco-reeking breath that evidence the Sunday nights spent preparing for the Monday morning trial.

Ironically we still think that our job is harder. Your job may be intellectual and occasionally very stressful, but ours is continually stressful, often very frustrating, frequently intellectual, and above all never-ending. At the end of the conference or trial you give the papers back to us, but we have to carry on dealing with them, along with dozens of other cases. Too much drudgery and too little drama. Thus it was that I was very surprised to learn that barristers apparently think that they have the more difficult job. This revelation came to me only recently, when a very complicated medical negligence case settled just before trial. There was an enormous amount of paperwork, my expert witnesses were brilliant, but slightly eccentric, my client was nice, but near hysterical. My counsel was very able, but was delaying really getting to grips with the papers until the last possible moment. When the case settled, everyone concerned with it, including the defendant's lawyers, breathed a huge sigh of relief. When I spoke with counsel on the telephone, I was very surprised to find that he had anticipated that his task would be more difficult than mine. Did he not realise that all he had to do was turn up at court and present the case, whereas I had to orchestrate the whole thing, and make sure that papers and people (him included) were matched up and sent to the right place at the right time?

Behaviour towards the lay client

Most clients are scared of lawyers. It is scary for them to telephone a solicitor, and scary for them to walk into a solicitor's office for the first time. Happily most of them soon overcome that fear and build up a relationship of trust with their solicitor. However, the experience of litigation is still a stressful one, particularly when it involves professionals looking into very personal matters, as is often the case in a medical negligence claim.

Barristers are even scarier for the clients. The first meeting is usually a conference with counsel, and beforehand I reassure them that the purpose of the conference is to have a friendly, informal discussion about the case. Mostly the barristers I instruct never let me down. They are polite and do everything they can to put the clients at ease. One of the things I think about when selecting a barrister is how he or she will meet the needs of the case, and the client. If I have an exceptionally timid client I choose an exceptionally nice barrister. Occasionally I have very bullish clients who can be quite aggressive and difficult to control. In those circumstances I tend to choose a barrister who is more concerned with getting to the point than being charming. Having said that, on one notable occasion when I did that, within about 20 minutes the conference had turned into an all-out argument between the barrister and my client.

The only time when I have had cause to complain about a barrister arose out of a conference attended by my assistant. The client was a single woman in her late forties who had sustained gynaecological injuries as a result of medical negligence. The conference was with a male barrister, and was to be attended by two male medical experts. Inevitably it had to involve a detailed discussion of very intimate matters for my client, and as she was a rather shy woman, I knew she would be very apprehensive. I chose the barrister because he was recommended to me by some colleagues as being exceptionally intelligent, and very clear in his understanding of medical matters. I assumed that he would read the papers and realise that the client would have to be dealt with sensitively. He did just the opposite. First, he had a male pupil sitting in with him. Of course I have no objections to people training by observation, but it would have been courteous for him to ask my assistant, or indeed the client if she was happy to have yet another strange man discussing her very personal life. Secondly, he opened the conference not by talking about the weather, or the many general questions that had to be discussed, but by asking her if she was sexually active, and when was the last time that she had a sexual partner. Apparently the poor client tried her best to answer, but was clearly humiliated and uncomfortable.

I will never instruct that barrister again, although I should emphasise that it was an exceptional experience. Generally the barristers I use are very nice to my clients, and indeed that is one of the reasons why I use them. Perhaps I am in the fortunate position of using mostly very senior barristers who have had many years to practise their communication skills.

For any young professional starting out on his or her career, communicating with clients can be an area of weakness, and that is completely understandable. You will be working in a complicated field, uncertain about your ability to do the job, and the client may think that you look so young that you can't possibly be a properly qualified barrister. Therefore the temptation may be to prove that you are, by making everything sound so complicated that the client will think that you must be clever because he or she cannot understand a word you are saying.

Also, there is the all-embracing atmosphere of the legal profession, particularly in the Temple, where the centuries of wisdom will permeate your being, and you may find yourself acquiring the habits, dress and speech of a Chancery judge. That may make you seem and feel like a real barrister, and whilst to some extent we all have to act out our chosen role in order to placate our clients, remember that not all clients are stupid, and that solicitors in particular will not be terribly patient if very young barristers become too theatrical in presenting their professional selves.

Do you call your lay client/your solicitor by their first name, or address them formally? With lay clients you should always start by calling them Mr, Mrs or Ms. As you get to know them better you may move on to first name terms, but it is important to establish the professional relationship from the outset. It is always easy to get more friendly, but very difficult to withdraw from familiarity when, for example, you have to give unpalatable advice to an angry client. As for your instructing solicitors, I am sure that practice varies. I believe that it is probably sensible to address your instructing solicitors formally at first, particularly if they are older than you. If there is a substantial age difference you should continue to do so until invited to do otherwise. If there is not a big age difference I think you should move on to first name terms fairly soon, and in fact I find it rather odd when a barrister, particularly one of similar age to me, insists on calling me Mr Donovan. As far as I am concerned we are working in a team together, and it would concern me if I thought that my barrister would prefer to keep me at arm's distance — just like the potentially difficult lay client.

With all of this there is a substantial element of human nature, and ordinary social skills, and really the best person that you can be is yourself. (Although in saying that, I assume that you are intelligent, confident and charming. If you are not it will be necessary for you to act as much as possible, and it may even help to dye your hair grey!)

Behaviour at court

You now take centre stage. To a certain extent the case is yours, and it will sink or swim with you. However, do not forget that your lay client is the true owner, and that your solicitor has had custody of the case for much longer than you. You must involve the lay client, particularly if there is a possibility of settlement. Clients become very emotionally involved in their cases, and although many of them will be terrified on the day, and may just want you to sort it all out for them, I think it is much healthier for a client to be involved fully in the reasoning behind a settlement. That way when he or she goes home, and the fear disappears and friends and relatives start to give the client advice about the damages that they would have insisted upon, there is less scope for the client to feel cheated.

Many solicitors send a trainee clerk to court. This generally makes financial sense because a senior solicitor's costs will not be recoverable in full where counsel is instructed. Thus it is that sometimes the person sitting behind you will have only a superficial knowledge of the case. That will mean more work for you, but if that person is a trainee solicitor it presents a golden opportunity for you to make a friend and do some marketing. Solicitors, particularly junior solicitors, prefer to instruct barristers that they like.

Like barristers, solicitors have considerable egos, and it is important that you remember this if you wish to be instructed again. I recently had a very complicated case listed for a two week trial in the High Court. Half-way through, the defence began to collapse, and the judge rose to allow the three parties to negotiate a settlement. By that stage counsel for all sides had become deeply involved in the case. There was much debate about case law, and I was relying heavily upon the skills of my QC and junior counsel. However, having had conduct of the case for four years it was important that I be involved in discussions, both for the client's sense of security, and proper conduct of the case. Happily my own counsel appreciated that, but counsel for one of the defendants clearly did not. We were having one of those court corridor conversations where all of us were huddled into a close group. The defendant's barrister wanted to make a remark to one of my counsel, who was standing to one side of me. Instead of facing all three of us when speaking, he walked into the centre of the circle, stood with his back to me (the frayed tail of his wig was literally six inches away from my nose) and began discussing terms with my counsel. Possibly this was just bad manners, but such behaviour does perpetuate myths about barristers' views of the worth of solicitors, and once again, if you want to get instructions it is best to avoid doing things like that.

Delay and incompetence

Reading through the professional conduct rules of the Bar I find that paragraphs 501 [now 603] and 601 [now 701] stipulate that a barrister should not take on work if he or she does not expect to carry it out within a reasonable time, and that if he or she finds himself or herself too busy to complete work already taken on, he or she must inform the professional client.

I am sorry to say that in my experience these rules are continually flouted. With one or two exceptions, the barristers that I work with are all very pleasant and intelligent people who never let me down in conference or at court. However, time and again I have to wait and wait for written work. My reminder letters go unanswered, and my chasing telephone calls are met with promises that are made to be broken. My clients wonder why their cases stop, directions orders have to be ignored; experts do not get the draft statements of case that they really needed to read whilst the conversation from the conference was fresh in their mind, and defendants' solicitors apply to strike me out for want of prosecution. If you chose to take note of only one thing in this paper, let it be this. Solicitors are very busy people who have to juggle many things in order to keep their large case loads moving along. A slow barrister is just one more thing to worry about, and it is a bitter irony indeed when your own barrister's involvement in a case can cause more problems than the opposing solicitors.

On at least two occasions in the last year I have had good cases that have moved along very well until counsel was instructed. In each case the barristers were experienced people, chosen because of their many excellent qualities. The conferences went very well, and finished with promises that the draft statements of case would be with me within a week. The weeks and months then slipped by, and despite reminder letters, faxes and phone calls, the statements of case did not come. Eventually there were applications to strike out by the defendants. This involved me in a great deal of work, for which I will not be paid, and even threats of personal costs orders against my firm. In my clients' eyes I became incompetent, and the cases having come from important referral sources, the reputation of my firm suffered. Fortunately in each case we were able to salvage the situation, but had we not done I might also have been facing a professional negligence claim.

Quality standards applied by solicitors to barristers

My firm has a legal aid franchise ['contract' under the Community Legal Service]. This means that we have to set quality standards for our clients, and ensure they are stuck to. As the partner in charge of the 'Register of Sub-Contractors' I am responsible for monitoring the performance of the other professionals that we use on behalf of our clients, most notably counsel. When staff in the firm have good or bad experiences with counsel, they send a note to me, and I report on those notes at our weekly fee earners' meetings. This is not a matter of choice. If we want to keep the legal aid franchise we have to show that the people that we instruct will do a good job. Thus it was that I recently had to send a fax to a barrister that I like very much, to say that six months was too long to wait for a written advice, and that if it was not supplied within two weeks, I would have to ask him to return the papers and no further instructions would be sent to him. I thought about adding that under his own rules of professional conduct he should probably have returned them a long time ago in any event, but decided that he should know that.

Quality control standards such as the legal aid franchise are part of modern business culture. The solicitors that instruct you have to be increasingly accountable to their clients; we in turn are your clients and it is much better for you to say that the papers will be with us in three months, and for us to know that that is true, rather than for you to say that the papers will be with us next week, when there is no real expectation that they will arrive before next year.

This is, of course, very tough on a young barrister who is trying to build up a following. When you eventually start to get some work you will not wish to turn cases away for fear of losing your professional clients, and indeed solicitors operate in exactly the same way. We might be too busy now, but we are worried about whether we will have enough work to do next year. Nevertheless, in my firm we have made a policy decision not to take on work if we cannot progress the work that we have reasonably quickly, and I would have no difficulty with a barrister saying that he or she is too busy to take on any work at present, but will be taking cases in two months' time. That would suggest to me that he or she is reliable and sensible, and I would at least have certainty when I did instruct him or her. You should also be working towards building up a long-term relationship with your instructing solicitor, and being honest about how busy you are will not harm that. In fact in some respects being busy can enhance your reputation, and I would be happy to say to a client that I am instructing a certain barrister because although he or she is busy now, he or she will give his or her whole attention to the work when the time comes.

Fees

As most of my work is legally aided it is seldom that I have to agree fees with counsel's clerk. However, when I do, I expect to be given an hourly rate for the barrister I want to instruct. Once again, I now work in an environment where I have to give very precise costs information to my clients, and thus I need counsel's chambers to operate in a similar way. I would not instruct a barrister on behalf of a private client on the basis of an old-fashioned style of valuation of the case by counsel's clerk upon receiving the papers. I need to be able to say to my clients that they can either have barrister X for £150, or barrister Y for £160.

The barrister's clerk

Much has been written recently about how barristers' chambers are acknowledging that they are modern businesses. This is all to the good. From the outside it seems that traditionally the clerks have observed a veneer of deference and respect towards barristers, whereas in reality they have controlled much of the power and of the wealth within chambers. A junior barrister is not a young aristocrat, and his or her clerk is not his or her trusty family retainer. They are both there to do a job in what should be a modern business environment, and I think it would be better for all concerned if that was acknowledged. In modern business good manners and respect are enough. Dickensian deference, particularly if it is false, can only breed resentment and poor working relationships.

It is difficult to give advice on how you can get the best out of your clerks, but from a solicitor's point of view the following points are helpful. Encourage them to adopt a professional attitude towards marketing. Obviously this will not be your decision as a pupil, or a new tenant, but every chambers should have a brochure giving details of its barristers, their experience and specialisation. The clerks should be ready to send that out very quickly. You should also try to ensure that they know where your areas of interest lie, so that if an opportunity does come up they will be able to mention your name. Some of the barristers that I use most regularly were originally introduced to me when a clerk suggested that they take over a case where my original choice had to drop out. Make sure that your clerk is rigorous about passing on telephone messages, and prompt in delivering fee notes. If he or she is not doing so, let your instructing solicitors know that the fault does not lie with you.

Getting work

Referring once more to my firm's policy on sub-contractors, part of our quality control system is only to use counsel that come recommended by a suitable source — for example, another solicitor who has worked with the barrister. Unfortunately specialist medical negligence solicitors are not a very good source of work for newly qualified barristers. We tend to use only very experienced counsel who have also taken the trouble to attend the same medical courses as we do in order to learn about medicine. Moreover, we do not have many hearings, and if you go into medical negligence work too early you will spend too much of your time drafting statements of case, and not enough time on your feet in court, and it seems to me that the best thing that a young barrister can do is to spend as much time in court as possible, learning how to be an effective advocate.

When you do start to specialise it will be a good idea to market yourself to the solicitors who have the work that you want. You do this partly by cross-referrals between solicitors, but also by turning up at places where they tend to congregate, and getting your face known. For example, if you were to specialise in medical negligence you would be able to meet the solicitors who control most of the work by attending medical courses run by AVMA (Action for Victims of Medical Accidents, the medico-legal charity) or any of the numerous medico-legal conferences that take place. Those courses are expensive, but in addition to showing that you are committed to the work, and that you are taking steps to acquire the necessary medical knowledge, you will also have the opportunity to meet the solicitors from whom you want instructions. However, if you have only just finished your pupillage, your efforts might be wasted, because most of those specialist solicitors will be dealing only with the more complex cases, and they will not wish to send them to a newly qualified barrister. In contrast, if you wait until you can display the scars and experience of a few years experience as an advocate, and no longer look like a school leaver, specialist solicitors will be more likely to consider instructing you when you show an interest in their field.

Summary

If my contribution had been limited to a few exhortations, which it probably should have been, they would be as follows. Make sure that you know the law. Read your papers very thoroughly. Be professional but be yourself. Work with your solicitor as a team. Be well-organised. Be well-organised. Be well-organised.

Postscript

The day after I wrote this article I had a meeting with a client. I was very pleased about her case, because she was a nice woman, and I had used all my skills and experience to help her get her claim off the ground. I believed in the case when no-one else would, and I guided her through the system, and even waited a very long time for her to pay my bills. The case is now looking very strong indeed, and she will soon get a fairly large award of damages. Counsel has been involved, but only very minimally. Thus at the end of the meeting I was sitting back, modestly thinking about how lucky she was to have a solicitor who was not only a wonderful human being, but also a very shrewd and experienced lawyer. And what did she say to me? She said, 'Wasn't our counsel good and will you go on to be a barrister?' I said, 'No, I wouldn't want to be away from my photocopying'.

Terence Donovan
Litigation Solicitor
Bindman & Partners

2.3.1.2 Problems

(1)   You are asked to advise on quantum in a personal injuries case where the defendants have offered to negotiate a settlement. It is clear that the claimant's general damages will be substantial but their assessment is not straightforward. In conference you state that in your opinion the case is worth £30,000 to £35,000 on full liability. Your solicitors (who value the case more highly) ask you for an opinion in writing that the bracket is £40,000–£45,000 in order to support their negotiations and to achieve a settlement at £35,000. What should you do?

(2)   You act for the claimant in civil proceedings. Unlike your client, the defendant has the benefit of a full legal aid certificate. You arrive at court on the day fixed for the hearing to find that the defendant's solicitor has forgotten to warn any of his or her witnesses. The judge accedes to the defendant's request for an adjournment. The defendant's solicitor is in fact well known to you and briefs you on a regular basis. What application, if any, do you make for costs?

2.3.2   Relationship with the crown prosecution service

In August 1994 the Crown Prosecution Service first issued two Service Standards dealing with the delivery of instructions and pre-trial preparation. These are important, and are now reproduced with amendments:

Service Standard on Timely Delivery of Instructions to Counsel in the Crown Court

1   Introduction

   1.1 It is essential that prosecuting Counsel is instructed as early as possible after committal or date of transfer.

   1.2 Timely delivery of instructions will ensure early preparation of the case and will enable Counsel to consider CPS views on the acceptance of pleas or to seek timely formal admissions in contested cases.

   1.3 Cases in which Counsel is required to give urgent advice, to settle the indictment or to attend a fixed date hearing will naturally assume priority.

   1.4 Where Counsel is instructed to advise on evidence or to settle the indictment, a reply date should be clearly marked on the brief.

1.5 Areas should be realistic when setting reply dates and allow Counsel adequate time in which to advise or to draft the indictment.

1.6 In many cases where Counsel is instructed to settle the indictment, it will be clear that an extension beyond the 28th day will be required. Areas should be alert to this possibility and make the necessary application well before the 28th day.

2   Target dates

2.1 All Areas should set target dates for the delivery of instructions to Counsel in Crown Court cases in accordance with the following timetable:

Type of case	Date of delivery after committal, transfer or receipt of notice of appeal
Trials up to 3 days Most pleas of guilty Committals for sentence Appeals against sentence Appeals against conviction (This covers all standard fee cases)	14 days
Trials lasting 3 days or more Pleas of guilty to serious offences	21 days

2.2 The target dates should be regarded as maxima and every effort made to improve upon them.

2.3 Preparation of the case pre-committal should ensure that Counsel can be fully instructed immediately after committal or transfer.

2.4 Delivery of instructions to Counsel should not be dependent upon the receipt of formal documentation from the Crown Court. If necessary, authenticating certificates and depositions can be dispatched to Counsel separately, after delivery of the instructions.

2.5 Within the above timetable, Areas must give priority to custody cases, child abuse cases and other cases involving children or vulnerable witnesses.

Service Standard on Pre-trial Preparation by Counsel

1   Introduction

1.1 Prosecution decisions made by the CPS are governed by the Code for Crown Prosecutors issued under section 10 of the Prosecution of Offences Act 1985. All Counsel instructed by the CPS must be familiar with the principles set out in the Code and must apply them at all stages throughout the life of the case.

1.2 The duties set out in this standard apply in all cases whether or not Counsel has been specifically instructed on the matters herein.

1.3 Where two or more Counsel are instructed to prosecute in the same case, it will be sufficient for one of them to carry out some of these duties provided that, where Junior Counsel gives advice, it is done with the knowledge and approval of Leading Counsel.

1.4 Upon receipt of instructions to prosecute on behalf of the CPS, Counsel will read the papers within the time scale appropriate to the case.

1.5 Having read and considered the papers, Counsel will, where necessary, advise in writing on any matter requiring such advice, and will indicate whether a conference is required.

1.6 Whether or not formal written advice has been given, when Counsel has read the papers within the time scale appropriate to the type of case, the CPS must be given formal notification to this effect.

2   The indictment

2.1 If instructed to do so, Counsel will settle the indictment within any time limit imposed.

2.2 If the indictment is already settled, Counsel will check the indictment for both substance and form. If the indictment is defective in any way, Counsel will notify the CPS forthwith with advice on any proposed amendments.

3   *The evidence*

3.1 If, in Counsel's opinion, the evidence available does not support any count in the indictment to the standard required by the Code for Crown Prosecutors, Counsel will advise or confer on this aspect of the case, identifying the relevant evidential insufficiency.

3.2 Counsel will appreciate that there needs to be a realistic prospect of conviction against each defendant in respect of each count in the indictment. The evidential test to be applied under the Code is an objective test and means that a jury, properly directed in accordance with the law, is more likely than not to convict the defendant of the charge alleged.

3.3 If, having considered the evidence available to support the indictment, Counsel feels that further evidence is necessary, Counsel will provide written advice as to precisely what is required.

3.4 If, in Counsel's opinion, a plea of guilty to an offence other than that charged is or might be acceptable to the Crown, Counsel will confer with the CPS on the matter or will advise in writing giving reasons for the view taken.

3.5 Counsel will eliminate all unnecessary material in the case so as to ensure an efficient and fair trial and, in particular, will consider the need for certain witnesses and exhibits.

3.6 Counsel will consider both the order of witnesses to be called and the timing of their attendance and, in appropriate cases, will provide a list of witnesses in order and time of call.

4   *Disclosure*

4.1 Counsel will consider whether all witness statements, documents and other material listed on the schedules supplied by the police have been properly disclosed to the defence in accordance with the Attorney General's Guidelines and the authorities on disclosure.

5   *Preparation of documents*

5.1 Counsel will, in appropriate cases, draft a case summary for transmission to the court.

5.2 Counsel will consider the possibility of admissions and, in appropriate cases, draft such admissions for agreement by the defence.

5.3 Counsel will advise on the preparation of documents for the court and jury in good time before the hearing date.

6   *Time scales*

6.1 According to the type of case, Counsel will read the case papers and advise as necessary within the following time scale:

Type of case	Date of delivery after committal, transfer or receipt of notice of appeal
Trials up to 3 days Most pleas of guilty Committals for sentence Appeals against sentence Appeals against conviction (This covers all standard fee cases)	7 days
Trials lasting 3 days or more Pleas of guilty to serious offences	14 days
Cases of substantial complexity or gravity or those likely to last over 10 days	21 days

6.2 The target dates should be regarded as maxima and every effort made to improve upon them.

6.3 Conversely, it is acknowledged that there will always be exceptional cases in which the above target dates cannot be met. The CPS will identify these cases at the time the instructions are delivered and will consult Counsel with a view to agreeing a target date.

6.4 If Counsel is unable to meet the target date set out in the above time scale, the CPS must be notified so that a revised date can be agreed.

In addition reference should be made to Section 3, Miscellaneous Guidance of the Code of Conduct (Service standard on return briefs agreed with the CPS) and **2.1.2**.

2.3.2.1 Code for Crown Prosecutors

The Phillips Royal Commission emphasised the need for those who prosecute to follow clear and consistent criteria when deciding whether or not to bring a prosecution. Since 1986 these have been set out in the Code for Crown Prosecutors issued pursuant to s 10 of the Prosecution of Offences Act 1985. It is important for both prosecuting and defence counsel to ensure that they have an up-to-date Code, and to be familiar with it. A new edition of the Code was issued in October 2000. It will be highly relevant to the decision not just of whether or not to carry on with a case, but also the acceptability or otherwise of proposed pleas. The Code is reproduced below.

The Code for Crown Prosecutors

1   Introduction

1.1 The decision to prosecute an individual is a serious step. Fair and effective prosecution is essential to the maintenance of law and order. Even in a small case a prosecution has serious implications for all involved — victims, witnesses and defendants. The Crown Prosecution Service applies the Code for Crown Prosecutors so that it can make fair and consistent decisions about prosecutions.

1.2 The Code helps the Crown Prosecution Service to play its part in making sure that justice is done. It contains information that is important to police officers and others who work in the criminal justice system and to the general public. Police officers should take account of the Code when they are deciding whether to charge a person with an offence.

1.3 The Code is also designed to make sure that everyone knows the principles that the Crown Prosecution Service applies when carrying out its work. By applying the same principles, everyone involved in the system is helping to treat victims fairly and to prosecute fairly but effectively.

2   General Principles

2.1 Each case is unique and must be considered on its own facts and merits. However, there are general principles that apply to the way in which Crown Prosecutors must approach every case.

2.2 Crown Prosecutors must be fair, independent and objective. They must not let any personal views about ethnic or national origin, sex, religious beliefs, political views or the sexual orientation of the suspect, victim or witness influence their decisions. They must not be affected by improper or undue pressure from any source.

2.3 It is the duty of Crown Prosecutors to make sure that the right person is prosecuted for the right offence. In doing so, Crown Prosecutors must always act in the interests of justice and not solely for the purpose of obtaining a conviction.

2.4 It is the duty of Crown Prosecutors to review, advise on and prosecute cases, ensuring that the law is properly applied, that all relevant evidence is put before the court and that obligations of disclosure are complied with, in accordance with the principles set out in this Code.

2.5 The CPS is a public authority for the purposes of the Human Rights Act 1998. Crown Prosecutors must apply the principles of the European Convention on Human Rights in accordance with the Act.

3   *Review*

3.1 Proceedings are usually started by the police. Sometimes they may consult the Crown Prosecution Service before starting a prosecution. Each case that the Crown Prosecution Service receives from the police is reviewed to make sure that it meets the evidential and public interest tests set out in this Code. Crown Prosecutors may decide to continue with the original charges, to change the charges, or sometimes to stop the case.

3.2 Review is a continuing process and Crown Prosecutors must take account of any change in circumstances. Wherever possible, they talk to the police first if they are thinking about changing the charges or stopping the case. This gives the police the chance to provide more information that may affect the decision. The Crown Prosecution Service and the police work closely together to reach the right decision, but the final responsibility for the decision rests with the Crown Prosecution Service.

4   *The Code Tests*

4.1 There are two stages in the decision to prosecute. The first stage is *the evidential test*. If the case does not pass the evidential test, it must not go ahead, no matter how important or serious it may be. If the case does meet the evidential test, Crown Prosecutors must decide if a prosecution is needed in the public interest.

4.2 This second stage is *the public interest test*. The Crown Prosecution Service will only start or continue with a prosecution when the case has passed both tests. The evidential test is explained in section 5 and the public interest test is explained in section 6.

5   *The Evidential Test*

5.1 Crown Prosecutors must be satisfied that there is enough evidence to provide a 'realistic prospect of conviction' against each defendant on each charge. They must consider what the defence case may be, and how that is likely to affect the prosecution case.

5.2 A realistic prospect of conviction is an objective test. It means that a jury or bench of magistrates, properly directed in accordance with the law, is more likely than not to convict the defendant of the charge alleged. This is a separate test from the one that the criminal courts themselves must apply. A jury or magistrates' court should only convict if satisfied so that it is sure of a defendant's guilt.

5.3 When deciding whether there is enough evidence to prosecute, Crown Prosecutors must consider whether the evidence can be used and is reliable. There will be many cases in which the evidence does not give any cause for concern. But there will also be cases in which the evidence may not be as strong as it first appears. Crown Prosecutors must ask themselves the following questions:

Can the evidence be used in court?

(a)   Is it likely that the evidence will be excluded by the court? There are certain legal rules which might mean that evidence which seems relevant cannot be given at a trial. For example, is it likely that the evidence will be excluded because of the way in which it was gathered or because of the rule against using hearsay as evidence? If so, is there enough other evidence for a realistic prospect of conviction?

Is the evidence reliable?

(b)   Is there evidence which might support or detract from the reliability of a confession? Is the reliability affected by factors such as the defendant's age, intelligence or level of understanding?

(c)   What explanation has the defendant given? Is a court likely to find it credible in the light of the evidence as a whole? Does it support an innocent explanation?

(d)   If the identity of the defendant is likely to be questioned, is the evidence about this strong enough?

(e) Is the witness's background likely to weaken the prosecution case? For example, does the witness have any motive that may affect his or her attitude to the case, or a relevant previous conviction?

(f) Are there concerns over the accuracy or credibility of a witness? Are these concerns based on evidence or simply information with nothing to support it? Is there further evidence which the police should be asked to seek out which may support or detract from the account of the witness?

5.4 Crown Prosecutors should not ignore evidence because they are not sure that it can be used or is reliable. But they should look closely at it when deciding if there is a realistic prospect of conviction.

6   The Public Interest Test

6.1 In 1951, Lord Shawcross, who was Attorney-General, made the classic statement on public interest, which has been supported by Attorneys-General ever since: 'It has never been the rule in this country — I hope it never will be — that suspected criminal offences must automatically be the subject of prosecution'. (House of Commons Debates, volume 483, column 681, 29 January 1951.)

6.2 The public interest must be considered in each case where there is enough evidence to provide a realistic prospect of conviction. A prosecution will usually take place unless there are public interest factors tending against prosecution which clearly outweigh those tending in favour. Although there may be public interest factors against prosecution in a particular case, often the prosecution should go ahead and those factors should be put to the court for consideration when sentence is being passed.

6.3 Crown Prosecutors must balance factors for and against prosecution carefully and fairly. Public interest factors that can affect the decision to prosecute usually depend on the seriousness of the offence or the circumstances of the suspect. Some factors may increase the need to prosecute but others may suggest that another course of action would be better.

The following lists of some common public interest factors, both for and against prosecution, are not exhaustive. The factors that apply will depend on the facts in each case.

Some common public interest factors in favour of prosecution

6.4 The more serious the offence, the more likely it is that a prosecution will be needed in the public interest. A prosecution is likely to be needed if:

(a) a conviction is likely to result in a significant sentence;

(b) a weapon was used or violence was threatened during the commission of the offence;

(c) the offence was committed against a person serving the public (for example, a police or prison officer, or a nurse);

(d) the defendant was in a position of authority or trust;

(e) the evidence shows that the defendant was a ringleader or an organiser of the offence;

(f) there is evidence that the offence was premeditated;

(g) there is evidence that the offence was carried out by a group;

(h) the victim of the offence was vulnerable, has been put in considerable fear, or suffered personal attack, damage or disturbance;

(i) the offence was motivated by any form of discrimination against the victim's ethnic or national origin, sex, religious beliefs, political views or sexual orientation, or the suspect demonstrated hostility towards the victim based on any of those characteristics;

(j) there is a marked difference between the actual or mental ages of the defendant and the victim, or if there is any element of corruption;

(k) the defendant's previous convictions or cautions are relevant to the present offence;

(l) the defendant is alleged to have committed the offence whilst under an order of the court;

(m) there are grounds for believing that the offence is likely to be continued or repeated, for example, by a history of recurring conduct; or

(n) the offence, although not serious in itself, is widespread in the area where it was committed.

Some common public interest factors against prosecution

6.5 A prosecution is less likely to be needed if:

(a) the court is likely to impose a nominal penalty;

(b) the defendant has already been made the subject of a sentence and any further conviction would be unlikely to result in the imposition of an additional sentence or order, unless the nature of the particular offence requires a prosecution;

(c) the offence was committed as a result of a genuine mistake or misunderstanding (these factors must be balanced against the seriousness of the offence);

(d) the loss or harm can be described as minor and was the result of a single incident, particularly if it was caused by a misjudgement;

(e) there has been a long delay between the offence taking place and the date of the trial, unless:

- the offence is serious;
- the delay has been caused in part by the defendant;
- the offence has only recently come to light; or
- the complexity of the offence has meant that there has been a long investigation;

(f) a prosecution is likely to have a bad effect on the victim's physical or mental health, always bearing in mind the seriousness of the offence;

(g) the defendant is elderly or is, or was at the time of the offence, suffering from significant mental or physical ill health, unless the offence is serious or there is a real possibility that it may be repeated. The Crown Prosecution Service, where necessary, applies Home Office guidelines about how to deal with mentally disordered offenders. Crown Prosecutors must balance the desirability of diverting a defendant who is suffering from significant mental or physical ill health with the need to safeguard the general public;

(h) the defendant has put right the loss or harm that was caused (but defendants must not avoid prosecution solely because they can pay compensation); or

(i) details may be made public that could harm sources of information, international relations or national security.

6.6 Deciding on the public interest is not simply a matter of adding up the number of factors on each side. Crown Prosecutors must decide how important each factor is in the circumstances of each case and go on to make an overall assessment.

The relationship between the victim and the public interest

6.7 The Crown Prosecution Service prosecutes cases on behalf of the public at large and not just in the interests of any particular individual. However, when considering the public interest test Crown Prosecutors should always take into account the consequences for the victim of the decision whether or not to prosecute, and any views expressed by the victim or the victim's family.

6.8 It is important that a victim is told about a decision which makes a significant difference to the case in which he or she is involved. Crown Prosecutors should ensure that they follow any agreed procedures.

Youths

6.9 Crown Prosecutors must consider the interests of a youth when deciding whether it is in the public interest to prosecute. However Crown Prosecutors should not avoid prosecuting simply because of the defendant's age. The seriousness of the offence or the youth's past behaviour is very important.

6.10 Cases involving youths are usually only referred to the Crown Prosecution Service for prosecution if the youth has already received a reprimand and final warning, unless the offence is so serious that neither of these were appropriate. Reprimands and final warnings are intended to prevent re-offending and the fact that a further offence has occurred indicates that attempts to divert the youth from the court system have not been effective. So the public interest will usually require a prosecution in such cases, unless there are clear public interest factors against prosecution.

Police cautions

6.11 These are only for adults. The police make the decision to caution an offender in accordance with Home Office guidelines.

6.12 When deciding whether a case should be prosecuted in the courts, Crown Prosecutors should consider the alternatives to prosecution. This will include a police caution. Again the Home Office guidelines should be applied. Where it is felt that a caution is appropriate, Crown Prosecutors must inform the police so that they can caution the suspect. If the caution is not administered because the suspect refuses to accept it or the police do not wish to offer it, then the Crown Prosecutor may review the case again.

7   *Charges*

7.1 Crown Prosecutors should select charges which:

(a)   reflect the seriousness of the offending;
(b)   give the court adequate sentencing powers; and
(c)   enable the case to be presented in a clear and simple way.

This means that Crown Prosecutors may not always continue with the most serious charge where there is a choice. Further, Crown Prosecutors should not continue with more charges than are necessary.

7.2 Crown Prosecutors should never go ahead with more charges than are necessary just to encourage a defendant to plead guilty to a few. In the same way, they should never go ahead with a more serious charge just to encourage a defendant to plead guilty to a less serious one.

7.3 Crown Prosecutors should not change the charge simply because of the decision made by the court or the defendant about where the case will be heard.

8   *Mode of Trial*

8.1 The Crown Prosecution Service applies the current guidelines for magistrates who have to decide whether cases should be tried in the Crown Court when the offence gives the option and the defendant does not indicate a guilty plea. (See the 'National Mode of Trial Guidelines' issued by the Lord Chief Justice.) Crown Prosecutors should recommend Crown Court trial when they are satisfied that the guidelines require them to do so.

8.2 Speed must never be the only reason for asking for a case to stay in the magistrates' courts. But Crown Prosecutors should consider the effect of any likely delay if they send a case to the Crown Court, and any possible stress on victims and witnesses if the case is delayed.

9   *Accepting Guilty Pleas*

9.1 Defendants may want to plead guilty to some, but not all, of the charges. Alternatively they may want to plead guilty to a different, possibly less serious, charge because they are admitting only part of the crime. Crown Prosecutors should only accept the defendant's plea if they think the court is able to pass a sentence that matches the seriousness of the offending, particularly where there are aggravating features. Crown Prosecutors must never accept a guilty plea just because it is convenient.

9.2 Particular care must be taken when considering pleas which would enable the defendant to avoid the imposition of a mandatory minimum sentence. When pleas are offered, Crown Prosecutors must bear in mind the fact that ancillary orders can be made with some offences but not with others.

9.3 In cases where a defendant pleads guilty to the charges but on the basis of facts that are different from the prosecution case, and where this may significantly affect sentence, the court should be invited to hear evidence to determine what happened, and then sentence on that basis.

10   *Re-starting a Prosecution*

10.1 People should be able to rely on decisions taken by the Crown Prosecution Service. Normally, if the Crown Prosecution Service tells a suspect or defendant that there will not be a prosecution, or that the prosecution has been stopped, that is the end of the matter and the case will not start again. But occasionally there are special reasons why the Crown Prosecution Service will re-start the prosecution, particularly if the case is serious.

10.2 These reasons include:

(a) rare cases where a new look at the original decision shows that it was clearly wrong and should not be allowed to stand;

(b) cases which are stopped so that more evidence which is likely to become available in the fairly near future can be collected and prepared. In these cases, the Crown Prosecutor will tell the defendant that the prosecution may well start again; and

(c) cases which are stopped because of a lack of evidence but where more significant evidence is discovered later.

2.3.3 Prosecuting Counsel and the Crown Prosecution Service

In May 2000, the Crown Prosecution Service issued a document entitled 'CPS Instructions for Prosecuting Advocates'. This sets out the policy and procedure for advocates prosecuting on behalf of the CPS. The document is reproduced below.

CPS Instructions for Prosecuting Advocates
These instructions are incorporated into every prosecution brief.

Any advocate prosecuting on behalf of the Crown Prosecution Service will be expected to be familiar with the material in the booklet and to apply these instructions.

Copies will be supplied to all advocates on the list.

1 Custody Time Limits
Where defendants are remanded in custody the advocate should, at any hearing, request that the trial take place within the custody time limit. If this is not possible the advocate must apply to the court to extend the custody time limit. Whenever the court makes an order which will result in the custody time limit expiring before the start of the trial, an application must be made to extend or further extend the time limit to a date 7 days after the start of the trial. Any refusal by the court to do so, with reasons, should be endorsed on the brief.

When making an application to extend a CTL, the advocate must be in possession of sufficient information to satisfy the court that the conditions set out in the Prosecution of Offences Act 1985, s 22(3) are met. In particular the advocate should (a) provide the court with a chronology to demonstrate that the prosecution has acted with all due diligence and expedition and (b) demonstrate that there is good and sufficient cause to justify an extension — the case of *R v Manchester Crown Court, ex p McDonald* refers. If the advocate does not have sufficient information to deal with (a) and (b) above then the CPS representative at court should be contacted as soon as possible.

2 Plea and Directions Hearings
The advocate is referred to the *Practice Direction (Crown Court: Plea and Direction Hearings)* [1995] 1 WLR 1318, [1995] 4 All ER 379, which governs the completion of the Judge's Questionnaire immediately prior to the PDH by prosecution and defence advocates.

In cases involving young witnesses, the advocate must be prepared at the PDH to provide the court with all the relevant information to enable the judge to complete the supplementary pre-trial check list.

At the conclusion of the PDH, the advocate should ensure that any directions are clearly endorsed on the brief and that a copy of the signed Questionnaire is requested from the Court for any action by the Crown Prosecution Service.

3 Alternative Pleas
When pleas are offered which are not dealt with specifically in the instructions the advocate must discuss the pleas with the Crown Prosecution Service before giving any undertaking to the defence or court.

4 Disclosure/Unused Material
The following rules are set out in order that prosecuting advocate can assist the court when considering disclosure:

- primary disclosure of unused material must take place as soon as reasonably practicable after committal;
- primary disclosure is of material which in the prosecutor's opinion might undermine the prosecution case;
- following primary disclosure, the defence have 14 days to provide a defence statement or to apply for an extension to the time limit in order to do so;
- secondary disclosure is of material which might assist the defence case as revealed in the defence statement. This will take place as soon as reasonably practicable after receipt of the defence statement;
- secondary disclosure can only take place after provision and consideration of the defence statement and the advocate should firmly resist any application for the disclosure of additional material before the defence statement has been provided;
- only after secondary disclosure has taken place can the defence apply for the disclosure of additional material.

If, during the course of the trial, the advocate becomes aware of the existence of further unused material, a written endorsement should be made, detailing the nature of the material, when it was disclosed or the reasons for withholding it. The Crown Prosecution Service representative at court must be informed of decisions made.

Should the advocate disagree with any of the disclosure decisions early consultation with the reviewing prosecutor is advised.

5   *R v Edwards*

It is considered that the prosecution is under a duty to disclose to the defence details of a criminal conviction recorded against a police officer. In relation to criminal cautions, disciplinary findings of guilt and pending criminal or disciplinary matters and criminal or disciplinary matters which have not resulted in charges but where the interests of justice may require disclosure of information it is considered that the prosecution has a discretion to disclose relevant matters to the defence. The Criminal Procedure and Investigations Act 1996 has not altered these arrangements; police officers will not apply a relevance test as per the Code of Practice.

In order to comply with the duty of disclosure, the police and Home Office have agreed that police officers making witness statements will reveal to the Crown Prosecution Service details of all such matters with the following exceptions:

- Disciplinary records which have been expunged in accordance with The Police Regulations;
- Disciplinary findings resulting in a caution;
- Complaints which have not resulted in a disciplinary finding of guilt;
- Disciplinary findings in respect of charges arising out of neglect of health, improper dress or untidiness or entering licensed premises (unless the CPS has made a specific request);
- Criminal cautions that are more than 5 years old at the time of submission of the file, unless the officer has been convicted of or cautioned for a further criminal offence.

All criminal convictions whether 'spent' or otherwise will be shown. It is also the responsibility of the police to reveal details of disciplinary or other pending criminal matters during the lifetime of a case. The officer concerned should also notify the Crown Prosecution Service of any change in circumstances which makes the previous notification of a disciplinary matter/criminal conviction no longer pertinent (eg a successful appeal).

The advocate should resist any request for information that goes beyond the scope of the decision. If a judge makes an order for additional disclosure the Crown Prosecution Service representative at court should be informed immediately.

Where disciplinary information is disclosed, which at the time of trial will be expunged from the officer's record or which has been overturned by reason of a successful appeal the defence must be informed of the change of circumstances. Attempts by the defence to introduce such matters must be vigorously opposed, the argument being that as a matter of law, expunged records are not subject to disclosure under *R v Edwards*. Whenever the appropriate way forward is uncertain, the advocate is asked to seek directions from the court.

It is possible that requests by the defence for information in connection with disciplinary matters may fall within the doctrine of public interest immunity which protects police complaints investigation material from production. The advocate's attention is drawn to *R v Chief Constable of West Midlands Police, ex p Wiley* [1994] 3 WLR 433.

In respect of the 'second limb' of *R v Edwards* (that a jury can be made aware of an acquittal in a previous case by virtue of which a police officer's evidence is demonstrated to have been disbelieved), Crown Prosecution Service policy assumes that a disciplinary investigation will have taken place and that any disciplinary findings of guilt will have been revealed to the Service in accordance with the terms of the agreement reached.

Where officers are either:

(i)   suspended pending the completion of enquiries;

(ii) not charged or suspended but where the interests of justice require revelation of information;

the foregoing procedures do not apply. The defence will be advised of those officers who are suspended but whose evidence is still relied on. Where under (ii) details have been revealed to the Crown Prosecution Service, they will be disclosed only in those cases when, and to the extent that, the current law requires it.

The advocate will be familiar with the decision in *R v McCarthy* (1993) 158 JP 283 which was concerned with a situation where criminal proceedings had been instituted against an officer and as a result of those proceedings, the prosecution had decided that the officer would not be called as a witness in another case. It was held that there was a duty to disclose that other case, not simply the fact and substance of the proceedings, but also the nature of the case against that officer. In future similar circumstances, the Service will take steps to ensure that sufficient information is available to enable the defence to be provided with an outline of the nature of the case against the officer.

The advocate's attention is drawn to *R v O'Connor*, unreported, CA 29.10.96. Where serious allegations of misconduct have been made against police officers, the trial judge has discretion to allow in re-examination evidence of absence of previous convictions and disciplinary findings.

6   Witness Issues

In all cases involving a child (whether as victim or witness) the advocate is instructed to use their best endeavours to fix an early trial date and to resist any attempt to delay the listing of the case. (Schedule 6, para 7 Criminal Justice Act 1991.)

Where relevant, consideration should be given to the order of witnesses and timing of their attendance paying particular attention to victims (especially those who are vulnerable or intimidated), child witnesses and professional or expert witnesses. That order should be agreed with the defence. If agreement cannot be reached before or at the PDH, the advocate should invite the judge to make a direction that the defence confirm their witness requirements within seven days in writing.

The advocate is reminded that the Code of Conduct permits barristers appearing at court to introduce themselves to witnesses and explain court procedures. The CPS regards this personal contact as particularly important so far as victims of crime are concerned.

The advocate's attention is also drawn to the duty imposed by the Code to ensure that those facing unfamiliar court procedures are put at ease. This is particularly important in the case of nervous or vulnerable witnesses.

Guidance has been issued by the Lord Chancellor's Department that unless it is necessary for evidential purposes, defence and prosecution witnesses should not be required to disclose their addresses in open court. Exceptionally, it will be appropriate for the defence and prosecution to make application for non-disclosure, in open court, of the names of witnesses.

Where application has been made for a live television link under the provisions of s 32(1)(a) or 32(1)(b) Criminal Justice Act 1988 or for a video recording of a child's evidence to be used under s 32A(2) Criminal Justice Act 1988 and the application is opposed the advocate will be instructed to appear at the hearing and argue for leave to be granted. Should the application fail, an application for the use of screens for the witness should be considered.

Details of any applications should be noted on the PDH questionnaire.

The Crown Prosecution Service will not release video tapes without a written undertaking from the defence to comply with the undertaking contained in the Memorandum of Good Practice.

7   Fitness to be Tried

Should the question of the defendant's fitness to be tried become a live issue, the attention of the trial judge should be drawn to the provisions of s 4(2) Criminal Procedure (Insanity) Act 1964 as amended.

8   Offences in Prison

In 1992 changes to the Prison Rules ended the disciplinary role of the Board of Visitors. Internal disciplinary proceedings are now reserved to prison governors. The maximum penalty which can be imposed by the Governor is 42 additional days within a prisoner's existing sentence (not applicable to life sentence prisoners), 28 days forfeiture of privileges or stoppage of earnings, 14 days cellular confinement and other lesser sanctions.

The 1992 guidance was given to Governors by the Home Office in order to help them to identify those cases which would normally merit a police investigation and if appropriate, a prosecution rather than internal disciplinary action.

Any case which reaches court has already passed through three filters — the prison governor, the police and the Crown Prosecution Service. The public interest now requires a prosecution in a wider range of offences committed in prison than was the case before 1992.

It is important to remember when assessing where the public interest lies that:

- an offence which may otherwise be regarded as minor can assume a much greater significance when committed in an institution, because of the wider impact upon discipline;
- one public interest factor to be considered, as set out in the Code for Crown Prosecutors, is that the offence was committed against a person serving the public, unless there are public interest factors pointing away from prosecution which clearly outweigh this aggravating factor.

9   Media Reporting

In high profile cases there may be problems which arise from the reporting of cases where part of the proceedings are heard in chambers. In order to ensure accurate press reporting, the judge should be invited in appropriate cases, to:

- consider announcing the substance of any judgement made in chambers in open court and;
- give guidance about how the matter should be reported.

Consideration should be given in relevant cases to making orders under s 39 of the Children and Young Persons Act 1933. The advocate should be familiar with the Contempt of Court Act 1981.

10   Sentencing Issues

Procedures for dealing with antecedent information are set out in the *Practice Direction (Crime: Antecedents)* [1997] 1 WLR 1482, [1997] 4 All ER 350.

Advocates are under a positive duty to draw to the judge's attention any failure to give adequate and proper directions on the law, and to ensure that the judge gives all essential directions to the jury in summing up the case.

The advocate must be in a position to assist the court in relation to its sentencing powers and where there is a 'victim' statement to ensure that any relevant matters are brought to the court's attention.

The advocate will be provided with a copy of the pre-sentence report (PSR) by virtue of s 50 of the Crime (Sentences) Act 1997. Section 50(5) sets out strict parameters within which the information derived from the PSR can be used or disclosed. The information 'shall only be used or disclosed for the purposes of (a) determining whether representations as to matters contained in the report need to be made to the court or (b) making such representations to the court'. The PSR must be returned to the CPS with the brief at the conclusion of the case.

If in mitigation the defence make assertions which are unfair or run contrary to the Crown's case, the advocate should object and if the defence persist, invite the court to rule on the issue, holding a Newton Hearing if the case had been a guilty plea. Where relevant the advocate should direct the court's attention to the provisions of ss 5861 of the CPIA 1996 and notify the Crown Prosecution Service whenever an order is made.

The advocate is instructed to note any exceptional or particular circumstances found by the court for not imposing a mandatory or minimum sentence under the Crime (Sentences) Act 1997 ss 2, 3 and 4 and whether the sentence was unduly lenient.

The advocate remains instructed throughout the case and must attend any sentence hearing.

11   Racially Aggravated Offences

The Crime and Disorder Act 1998 ss 29–32 created various racially aggravated offences of assault, criminal damage, public order offences and harassment. These offences have higher maximum penalties than the corresponding basic offence. Where the aggravated offence is available, it must be charged. A court cannot take into account any racially aggravating factors at sentence, if an offence contrary to ss 29–32 was available but not charged.

Where racially aggravated common assault or criminal damage is charged, the jury cannot return alternatives of common assault or criminal damage (where the value or under £5,000) under the Criminal Law Act 1967. It will be necessary to consider including alternative counts on the indictment and to make it clear to the defence that this is not an invitation to accept a plea to the basic offences but is a means of dealing with alternatives where there is no power in law to return alternative counts unless specifically indicted.

For offences not covered by ss 29–32 (for example, s 18 OAPA 1861), racial hostility or motivation is a factor that increases the seriousness of the offence. Whenever there is evidence of racial motivation, the advocate *must* bring this to the attention of the court. The court must state in open court if it finds the offence was racially aggravated (CDA s 82). Advocates must be cautious in accepting pleas where an aggravated offence is available eg s 18 OAPA 1861 reduced to s 20 precludes sentencing for racial aggravation. An offence contrary to s 29 should be considered.

If the defendant disputes racial motivation for the offence, the advocate should ask the court to consider a Newton hearing on the basis that the difference on the facts may be material to sentence. The advocate should make a full note of the court's remarks when passing sentence.

It is especially important that the advocate has a statement setting out the effects of the crime upon the victim, when prosecuting a racially aggravated offence under ss 29–32 CDA 1998, or where racial aggravation is an issue under s 82.

R v Saunders [2000] Crim LR 314, went on to consider the approach the court should adopt in sentencing racially aggravated offences and relevant factors to be taken into account in determining the appropriate sentence.

The court expressed the view that it would often be helpful if the sentencer first considered the appropriate sentence for the offence in the absence of racial aggravation and then added a further term for the racial element so that the total sentence reflected the overall criminality.

The sentence would depend on all the circumstances of the particular case. Relevant factors would include:

- Nature of hostility, whether by language, gestures or weapons;
- The length of the hostility and whether it was isolated, repeated or persistent;
- The location of the hostility and whether public or private;
- The number of persons demonstrating hostility and the number of persons the subject of demonstration of hostility;
- The presence or absence of any other features.

A discount would be appropriate in accordance with general sentencing principles for factors such as genuine remorse, a guilty plea and good conduct.

12   Unduly Lenient Sentences

Attention is drawn to the provisions of ss 35 and 36 Criminal Justice Act 1988. If the advocate considers that the sentence imposed may be unduly lenient, a representative of the Crown Prosecution Service should be informed on the day of sentence or the next working day in view of the very stringent time limits which apply to this procedure.

13   Sex Offenders Act 1997

Where the defendant has been found to have done the act charged as listed in Sch 1 of the Sex Offenders Act 1997 the advocate is instructed to remind the court of its power to make a s 5 certification. The advocate is instructed to ensure that the evidence of the ages of the victim and defendant are before the court where age is relevant to notification.

14   Protection from Harassment Act 1997

Upon conviction of the defendant for an offence contrary to s 4(1) and (4) or in the alternative under s 4(5) of 2(1) and (2) of the Protection from Harassment Act 1997 the advocate is instructed to apply to the court for a restraining order under s 5 of the Act. Should the court decide not to make such an order the reason should be recorded on the brief.

NB: Similar power if case charged as Racially Aggravated Harassment under s 32 of Crime and Disorder Act 1998.

15   Confiscation (DTA 1994)

1. Following conviction, the advocate is instructed to apply to the Crown Court for a confiscation order against the defendant pursuant to s 2(1)(a) Drug Trafficking Act 1994 (DTA 1994). Once this application is made, the Crown Court is under a duty to consider the making of a confiscation order and fix the matter for a confiscation hearing.

2. If the defendant offers pleas to the counts on the indictment or to offences which are not drug trafficking offences or to lesser offences which are not drug trafficking offences, the acceptance of such pleas may limit the power of the Crown Court to make a confiscation order. *Accordingly, the advocate is instructed to contact the reviewing lawyer to discuss the issue of confiscation before the acceptance of pleas.*

3. If the defendant pleads guilty either in the magistrates' court (plea before venue and then committed to the Crown Court for sentence) or in the Crown Court or he is convicted after trial, the advocate is instructed to apply for an adjournment of 28 days so that the prosecution can serve the prosecutor's statement required under s 11 DTA 1994 upon the defence and the Crown Court and a confiscation hearing can be held. Service of the prosecutor's statement does not arise until after conviction since the Crown Court has no power to make a confiscation order in the absence of a conviction for a drug trafficking offence, ss 2(1) and 11(3) DTA 1994.

Postponed determinations

4. If the Crown Court is not minded to delay sentence, the Crown Court is able to sentence the defendant first and postpone consideration of the making of the confiscation determination for up to 6 months from the date of conviction, s 3 DTA 1994. If the confiscation determination is postponed then the Crown Court cannot sentence the defendant to a monetary order until after the confiscation determination is made. More than one postponement can be made in the same case, but unless there are exceptional circumstances the total postponements should not be for more than six months from the date of conviction.

5. Postponements may be made on application by the defendant or the prosecutor or by the Crown Court itself. Postponement can be made by the Crown Court if it requires further information before making the determination whether the defendant has benefited from drug trafficking, or determining the amount to be recovered in his case.

6. *The advocate is instructed to ensure that the confiscation hearing is fixed for a date within six months of the date of conviction.*

7. The advocate is referred to the cases of *Shergill* [1999] 1 All ER 485, *Cole* (unreported) [referred to *Shergill*], *France* [1999] 1 Cr App R (S) 85, *Edwards* [2000] 1 Cr App R (S) 98 and to rule 34 Crown Court Rules 1982 (SI 1982 No. 1109) [*Blackstone's* 2000 edition Appendix 1]. The advocate should note that any application to extend the time limit above must be made *before* the expiry of the six month time limit and that the matter must be dealt with in open court rather than administratively. *The advocate is instructed to ensure that any application to extend the time limit complies with these requirements.*

Confiscation hearing

Determining benefit

8. The Crown Court must determine whether the defendant has benefited from drug trafficking. A defendant benefits from drug trafficking if he has at any time received any payment or other reward in connection with drug trafficking carried on by him or another person. ***This includes any benefit received by the defendant prior to the DTA 1994 coming into force*** (3rd February 1995), s 2(3).

Amount to be recovered

9. If the defendant has benefited from drug trafficking, the Crown Court must determine the amount to be recovered. This involves the Crown Court determining:

    (1) the total value of the proceeds of the defendant's drug trafficking — this amount is the total benefit from all drug trafficking carried out by the defendant, not just from the offence of which the defendant has been convicted. This is the aggregate values of the payments and other rewards. When calculating the proceeds, the Crown Court is concerned with gross receipts, not profit, *Banks* [1997] 2 Cr App R (S) 110. The Crown Court does not reduce the amount of the proceeds to take account of expenses incurred by the defendant; and

    (2) the amount that the defendant can pay (the DTA 1994 calls this 'the amount that might be realised') — this is the total value of the defendant's realisable assets and the value of any 'gifts' (transfers made by the defendant at an undervalue to others or for no consideration). The value of legitimately acquired assets is calculated as part of the amount that might be realised. There is no requirement on the prosecution to prove that the defendant's assets were acquired from drug trafficking under the DTA 1994. In assessing the amount that the defendant can pay the Crown Court aggregates

        (i) the gross value to the defendant of his assets, less the value held in the property by others including secured creditors and

        (ii) the value of all transfers made by the defendant to others as 'gifts' (see the requirements set out in s 8(1)(a) or 8(1)(b) as to when transfers can qualify as 'gifts').

    The defendant bears the burden of showing that the amount that might be realised is less than the proceeds of drug trafficking, s 5.

'Realisable property'

10. 'Realisable property' is defined as any property held by the defendant and includes any property held by any person to whom the defendant has made a gift caught by the DTA 1994, s 6(2). Property is held by a defendant if he has any interest in the property, s 62(5)(a). Interest includes a right, s 62(3). If property falls within this definition of 'realisable property', there is **no** discretion to leave it out of account when assessing the amount that the defendant can pay since the DTA 1994 defines the amount that might be realised as the total values of **all** the defendant's realisable property, s 6(1). The value to be applied to the defendant's interest in a property is the market value, s 7(1). Where there is a third party interest in that property, it is the defendant's beneficial interest in the property which is assessed as the amount that he can pay and its value is the open market value of that interest. The only deductions permitted from the amount that the defendant can pay are priority obligations as defined in s 6(4).

11. Matrimonial home — this constitutes part of the defendant's realisable property provided that he has an interest in it. The value of the defendant's beneficial interest in the property is the open market value of the property, ie not one that is affected by the residency or other interest of a wife or other third party. This approach mirrors that adopted by the High Court in matrimonial cases. Also, it is consistent with the power of the High Court to order any person holding realisable property to give it to the receiver for the purpose of enforcing a confiscation order, s 29. The only deductions permitted from this value are priority obligations as defined in s 6(4).

12. ***The advocate is requested to ensure that the Crown Court states what property is being taken into account when assessing the amount to be recovered in respect of this defendant.***

Third parties

13. The advocate will be aware that there is no locus standi for third parties to make representations to the Crown Court during the course of the confiscation proceedings, except when they are called by the defendant. If there is a dispute as to the defendant's interest in the property (such as a claim from a third party of a beneficial interest in property), it is for the Crown Court to make a determination as to the amount by which the defendant has benefited from drug trafficking and the amount that might be realised at the time the confiscation order is made as best it can on the information available to it.

14. The High Court is the appropriate forum to determine the ownership or interests of third parties in the property. Full opportunity will be given to the third parties to make representations as to their interest in the property at the enforcement stage, either of their own volition or when a receiver is appointed to sell sufficient of the defendant's assets to pay the confiscation order.

Prosecutor's statement

15. Section 11 DTA 1994 requires the prosecutor to give the Crown Court a prosecutor's statement dealing with whether the defendant has benefited from drug trafficking together with an assessment of the defendant's proceeds from drug trafficking. The prosecutor's statement should also set out the information available to the prosecutor that led him to request the Crown Court to make the assumptions (see paragraph (19) below).

16. The Crown Court may require the defendant to indicate the extent to which he accepts any allegation in the prosecutor's statement and, if he does not accept the allegation, to provide particulars of any matter upon which he wishes to rely, s 11(5).

17. The defendant may accept the allegations in the prosecutor's statement, and for the purpose of determining whether the defendant has benefited from drug trafficking, or of determining the proceeds of drug trafficking, the Crown Court may treat his acceptance as conclusive of the matters to which it relates.

18. The Crown Court can have regard to any evidence given in the trial; the contents of the prosecutor's statement and any defence statements; any evidence given in the confiscation hearing, *Dickens* [1990] 2 WLR 1384, in making the determinations above. Additionally, the Crown Court may require the defendant to provide information, s 12.

Assumptions

19. In addition to any direct evidence heard for the purpose of making the determinations above, the Crown Court must assume that (s 4(2) DTA 1994):

    (1) all property in which the defendant has an interest was received as a payment or reward in connection with drug trafficking; and
    (2) that any property transferred to the defendant in the six years before the institution of the present proceedings was received from his or her drug trafficking;
    (3) that any expenditure of the defendant's in the six years ending with the institution of proceedings was made out of payments received from his or her drug trafficking;
    (4) any property transferred to the defendant was free of any other interest.

NOTE: The assumptions do not apply to drug trafficking offences which are drug money laundering offences (s 4(5)).

20. Once the Crown Court has made the assumptions, the onus is on the defendant to rebut them by demonstrating to the Crown Court that he has obtained the property or made the expenditure from legitimate sources. The assumptions are cumulative in their effect. In other words, the defendant has to negative all of the assumptions in respect of each property or each item of expenditure before he can submit that it is from a legitimate source.

21. The Crown Court must not make the assumptions if the assumption is shown to be incorrect in the defendant's case or if the Crown Court is satisfied that there would be a serious risk of injustice in the defendant's case if the assumption was to be made in relation to that property or expenditure, s 4(4). The defendant bears the burden of proving the serious risk of injustice and, and in discharging that burden, the defendant must show that the injustice is something

other than the intentionally harsh consequence of making a confiscation order, *Dore* [1997] 2 Cr App R (S) 152. Where the Crown Court does not make an assumption, it must state its reasons. ***The advocate is requested to note any property in respect of which the Crown Court does not make any assumptions together with the reasons given by the Crown Court.***

22. These assumptions can be made both to determine whether the defendant has benefited from drug trafficking, and if he has, to assess the value of his proceeds from drug trafficking.

Confiscation order

23. The Crown Court makes a confiscation order to the full value of the defendant's proceeds of drug trafficking. However, if the defendant satisfies the court that there are insufficient assets to meet this, the court must make an order in the amount that might be realised. Where the court orders this amount to be paid (ie an amount lower than the defendant's proceeds of drug trafficking), it must issue a certificate setting out its findings (s 5(2)). ***The advocate is instructed to ensure that the Crown Court issues such a certificate.***

24. Additionally, the Crown Court must settle a term of imprisonment in default of payment of the confiscation order. The terms to be served are the same as those applicable to fines, as set out in s 31(3A) of the Powers of Criminal Courts Act 1973 and paragraph 5–518 of *Archbold*, 2002 edition [now see s 139(4) of the Powers of Criminal Courts (Sentencing) Act 2000 and paragraph 5–396 of *Archbold*, 2002 edition]. ***The advocate is instructed to ensure that the Crown Court fixes a term of imprisonment in default.***

Standard of proof

25. The standard of proof required to determine any question arising under the confiscation determination as to whether the defendant has benefited from any offence, or the amount he has to pay, is the ***civil standard***, s 2(8).

Payment of the confiscation order

26. The Crown Court merely has the power to make a confiscation order in a sum of money. The Crown Court has no power to direct payment from a particular source nor can the Crown Court order confiscation of a particular asset. The Crown Court has no discretion to mitigate the confiscation order. For example, if the defendant has an interest in the family home, its value must be calculated. This is so even if the effect of the confiscation order may be to render the defendant and dependent relatives homeless.

27. The confiscation order is enforced either through the magistrates' court as though it were a fine (s 9) or by the CPS applying to the High Court for the appointment of a receiver.

28. There is no power within the DTA 1994 for the Crown Court to direct that third parties such as the banks or police should pay monies held by them over to the magistrates' court in satisfaction of the confiscation order. Any monies held by third parties can only be paid to the magistrates' court with the authority of the defendant, or by civil action taken by the magistrates' court (as a result of garnishee orders or distress warrants) or by the appointment of a receiver by the High Court.

Time to pay

29. The Crown Court may give the defendant time to pay the confiscation order. However, if the Crown Court gives the defendant a lengthy period in which to pay, the defendant effectively benefits from his crime as he has the benefit of any subsequent interest or capital appreciation that accrues on his assets. There is no provision for such interest or appreciation to be confiscated because the order has to be an order for a definite sum of money. Enforcement action cannot be taken by the magistrates' court until the time to pay has lapsed.

30. The Crown Court should be invited to consider making the confiscation order payable forthwith. Concern may be expressed that the defendant needs time to sell property. However, it is usually most practical and efficient for the CPS to apply for a receiver to be appointed by the High Court to sell property.

31. The sentence of imprisonment in default imposed by the Crown Court does not automatically come into force when the time to pay has lapsed. It is as a result of the magistrates' court

taking enforcement proceedings when a warrant of commitment to prison in default of payment is issued. The magistrates' court will not take enforcement proceedings until the appeal period of 28 days has elapsed.

Confiscation and sentence

32. Where a Crown Court makes a confiscation order it must take account of that before imposing any monetary order such as a fine; forfeiture order under s 27 of the Misuse of Drugs Act 1971; or deprivation order under s 143 of the Powers of Criminal Courts Act 2000. Additionally, the Crown Court must ignore the fact that a confiscation order has been made when it determines the appropriate sentence. See s 2(5).

Confiscation and forfeiture

33. The Crown Court cannot usually make a forfeiture order when it has made a confiscation order. This is because forfeiture falls to be considered after confiscation, see paragraph 33 above. The value of the asset is usually calculated when the confiscation order is considered. It therefore should not be forfeited, *R v Stuart and Bonnett* (1989) 11 Cr App R (S) 90.

34. The Crown Court may make a confiscation order and a forfeiture order only where the defendant's benefit from drug trafficking is less than the value of his realisable property. In such circumstances, the remainder of the realisable property may be liable to forfeiture provided that it satisfies the criteria under s 27 of the Misuse of Drugs Act 1971. However, this is a rare occurrence. The Crown Court can make a forfeiture order where it has decided not to make a confiscation order (for example, because it has decided that the defendant has not benefited from drug trafficking).

16   Confiscation (CJA 1988 PART VI)

Under the Criminal Justice Act 1988 Part VI, the Crown Court can make a confiscation order after conviction for a relevant offence (and any TICs), where the offender has benefited from criminal conduct. All offences before the Crown Court except drug trafficking and terrorism offences (which have their own confiscation legislation) are relevant offences. As with the Drug Trafficking Act 1994, a confiscation order under the CJA 1988 is an order to pay a sum of money. It is not an order which transfers the title to property.

Advocates will be aware that the Criminal Justice Act 1988 has been amended on a number of occasions. It is important to establish what version of the Act applies by reference to the date of offence. What follows relates to offences committed from the 1st November 1995.

The confiscation procedures are similar but not identical to those of the Drug Trafficking Act 1994 above. When *written* notice is given under the CJA 1988, the prosecution advocate should seek an adjournment for service of the prosecutor's statement under s 73. The Crown Court is then under a duty to consider making a confiscation order. The confiscation hearing must be held within six months of conviction, unless there are exceptional circumstances which justify a later hearing *and* application to extend is made within the six-month period (CJA s 72A). Advocates should ensure that these time limits are observed.

Under the DTA, the court must assume all property held by the defendant at conviction and for the previous six years was the proceeds of drug trafficking. Under the version of the CJA 1988 which applies to offences committed from 1st November 1995, assumptions about property *may* be made if various conditions are met. These are that

- the prosecution's written notice claims they should apply
- the defendant has been convicted of 2 qualifying offences in the current proceedings (or has a previous qualifying conviction in the last six years), and
- *all* these offences were committed after the 1st November, 1995 (s 72AA).

When a confiscation order is made, the prosecution advocate is instructed to ensure that the court fixes a term of imprisonment in default for non-payment.

If no confiscation order is made, the prosecuting advocate must ensure that CPS Central Confiscation Branch is notified immediately, so that any restraint or charging orders may be discharged.

17   Abuse of Process and Human Rights Act

1. The House of Lords decision in *R v DPP, ex p Kebilene and others* [1999] 3 WLR 972 is helpful if an application is made by the defence to stay proceedings on the grounds that they amount to an abuse of process by reason of an alleged breach of the European Convention on Human Rights (the Convention). It is of particular application in the period up to the implementation of the Human Rights Act 1998 (HRA) on 2 October 2000.

2. Although a terrorist case, *Kebilene* has implications for **all** cases prior to full implementation of the HRA. The House of Lords quashed the declaration of the Divisional Court that the continuing decision of the DPP to proceed with the prosecution was an unlawful act. Absent dishonesty or *mala fides* or some exceptional circumstance, the decision of the Director to consent to a prosecution is not amenable to judicial review.

3. The House also found that once the HRA is in force, arguments that domestic legislation is incompatible with the Convention should be brought during the trial or appeal process, the defendants not being entitled to an additional remedy of judicial review.

4. However, prior to the implementation of the HRA, the majority of the House believed that in 'blatant and obvious' cases it may be open to a defendant to submit that the prosecution is an abuse of process insomuch as it is so unfair and wrong that the court should not allow a prosecutor to proceed with it. **Such cases would be of an exceptional nature and it would be, therefore, only very rarely that such applications would be appropriate.**

5. There are two categories of challenges which the defence may make in applications to stay proceedings. The first category is where the defence allege that a statutory provision breaches the Convention and so may be incompatible with the Convention. The second category is where the grounds for the application are that the Convention has been breached in some other way, for example, evidence obtained in breach of Convention rights.

Incompatibility of domestic legislation

6. Where the defence suggest that a statutory provision is incompatible with the Convention, the court should be reminded that there are three remedies available to the defence:

- the defendant can persuade the court to interpret the statutory provision consistently with the Convention;
- if there is a 'blatant and obvious' breach, the defendant may be able to submit that the prosecution is an abuse of process. The strength of such an argument would depend on a number of factors including:
  - whether there is in fact a blatant and obvious breach;
  - whether it would be impossible to have a fair trial and whether the trial process can cure the alleged breach;
  - in many cases it will only be possible to establish after trial whether there has been a breach;
  - a convicted defendant will be able to raise the question of the safety of the conviction on appeal;
  - in cases of irremediable incompatibility between the statutory provision and the Convention, stays should not be allowed because of the principle of parliamentary sovereignty.
- the convicted defendant can raise Convention points on appeal heard after 2 October 2000 and may then seek from the Court of Appeal or High Court a declaration of incompatibility.

7. Where there are concerns about the vulnerability of a statutory provision, the prosecuting advocate should look at the nature of the provision and in particular whether the provision places a burden of proof on the defendant.

8. Statutory presumptions, which place an **evidential burden** on the defendant, do not breach the presumption of innocence. Such a burden requires only that the defendant must adduce sufficient evidence to establish a specific defence. For example, by cross-examining prosecution witnesses or calling evidence.

9. Statutory presumptions, which transfer the **persuasive burden** on the defendant, may violate the presumption of innocence and thus may breach the Convention. However, with the exception of a mandatory presumption of guilt, the matter may not be capable of being fully assessed until after all the evidence has been heard. Even then, if the conclusion is reached that prima facie the provision breaches the presumption of innocence, other factors may need to be considered by the court:

   • whether the burden of proof on the prosecution itself is heavy;
   • whether the burden on the defendant is something readily in the defendant's knowledge or to which the defendant readily has access;
   • the nature of the threat faced by society which the provision is designed to combat.

10. If a finding is made that a statutory presumption breaches the presumption of innocence, this does not automatically mean that it is incompatible with the Convention. In *Kebilene*, although the House of Lords expressed no concluded view as to the compatibility of s 16A Prevention of Terrorism (Temporary Provisions) Act 1989 with article 6(2), their Lordships suggested that a finding of incompatibility was not inevitable because each case has to be examined on its own merits. Furthermore, whether the burden which the accused has to discharge is unreasonable is unlikely to be known until all the evidence has been heard.

Procedural and evidential breaches

11. Other alleged breaches of the Convention, (for example, obtaining evidence in breach of a Convention right), should not provide a basis to stay proceedings. The trial process itself can deal with allegations of unfairness (*R v Khan* [1996] 3 WLR 162; *Schenk v Switzerland* (1988) 13 EHRR 242).

In conclusion

12. A court should not, therefore, normally grant a stay before the implementation of the HRA having regard to the remedies in paragraph 6 above and the following general points:

   • a stay would conflict with the decision in *Kebilene* that until 2 October 2000 the HRA does not alter the law;
   • even once the HRA is fully implemented, the Crown Court cannot declare a provision incompatible;
   • the routine grant of stays would disrupt the process of criminal trials in the lead up to 2 October 2000.

13. The advocate is asked to inform the Crown Prosecution Service if any issues involving the HRA arise during the conduct of the case. If any issues are raised, the advocate is asked to make a short note of the point, the arguments put forward and the judge's ruling.

18   Costs

The advocate is instructed to apply for costs in all cases unless it is considered to be inappropriate, in which case the Crown Prosecution Service representative at court should be informed.

In the event of an acquittal, the advocate is referred to ss 16(2), 19 and 19a Prosecution of Offences Act 1985 and reg 3 of the Costs in Criminal Cases Regulations 1986.

You may find, on occasion, that a dispute arises between you and your instructing solicitor as to whether or not to continue with a prosecution or whether to accept a proposed plea. This problem was addressed by the committee presided over by Farquharson J (May 1986) on the role of prosecuting counsel. The summary of the recommendations of the committee, set out in para 11.6 of the Written Standards for the Conduct of Professional Work in Section 3, Miscellaneous Guidance to the Code of Conduct, is adopted as part of the Code. The full text of the committee's Report is reprinted in *Archbold: Criminal Pleading, Evidence & Practice* 1995 Re-issue Volume 1 at paras 4-71–4-80. The 2002 edition of *Archbold* does not reproduce the full text of the committee's Report but does contain the committee's summary of its views. This can be found at para 4-95. It is reproduced below in so far as it deals with the relationship between prosecuting counsel and his or her instructing solicitor. You should also note that since the publication of the committee's findings, new Farquharson guidelines have been produced. They can be located at the CPS website on www.cps.gov.uk.

2.3.3.1   The relationship between prosecution counsel and his instructing solicitor/the crown prosecutor

Generally speaking, a Prosecuting Solicitor is in the same position as any other Solicitor instructing Counsel. This will be the case when instructions are received from the Crown Prosecutor, acting as Instructing Solicitor. He will not brief counsel whose competence he doubts and in whose judgment he has no faith. Moreover, he has available the ultimate sanction of the Professional Client that, if he does not like the way his work is done, he can brief other Counsel thereafter. There will remain rare occasions when an experienced Prosecuting Solicitor is not prepared to accept the advice of Counsel upon whose judgment he would normally rely. If the difference of opinion is about an unimportant aspect of the prosecution, then it will be resolved by the usual give and take which informs discussion between members of the profession. Sometimes the difference is more fundamental as, for example, where there is a conflict between Prosecution Counsel, wishing to accept a manslaughter plea in a murder case, and his Instructing Solicitor who does not. In such circumstances, it is the view of the majority of us that the Prosecuting Solicitor/Crown Prosecutor should be in the same position as other Instructing Solicitors: if he feels it is necessary, he should be entitled to take a second Opinion, either by taking in a Leader, to advise or by withdrawing the instructions from Counsel originally briefed and instructing other Counsel. There will come a point before the commencement of the trial, however, when it will cease to be practicable for him to withdraw his instructions. It is fundamental to our thinking that, from this point, Prosecution Counsel must be accepted as being in control of the case. In the vast majority of trials, Prosecution Counsel will not normally be attended by an experienced Prosecuting Solicitor/Crown Prosecutor: he is more likely to be attended by an unqualified Clerk. The only other person in Court equipped to give an opinion on a matter requiring decision is likely to be the Police Officer in the case. Whilst it is proper for Counsel to seek and consider their views, there can be no substitute for the view of Counsel himself.

We have suggested that the moment from which Prosecution Counsel's control should start is the point, before the commencement of the trial, when it becomes impracticable for his instructions to be withdrawn. This seems to us to allow for the present common experience of pleas to different or lesser counts being offered by the defence and considered by Prosecution Counsel when the parties are at Court but before the trial has begun. There has been a measure of dissension in the committee about this with one view being advanced that Prosecution Counsel's authority to consider and accept pleas should run from the time that he receives his brief to prosecute. Whilst recognising both the force and the convenience of that view, the majority of the Committee has concluded that the Prosecuting Solicitor has authority to withdraw his instruction for proper cause up to the point which we have indicated. Once the case reaches Court, so that it becomes impracticable as well as undesirable for instructions to be withdrawn (other than in the extreme circumstances of Counsel being unable to continue for physical or mental reasons), it is for Counsel to make the necessary decisions on all matters relating to the general conduct of the trial. These will include, for example: what evidence should be called; which witnesses, in the event, are to be relied upon and which are to be abandoned; what submissions are appropriate to be made to the Judge on matters of law and/or to the Judge and jury on the existence and strength of the evidence required and available to prove the count(s) in the indictment.

We recognise that there is a significant distinction between decisions on matters of 'policy' and other decisions which have to be made. We refer to the latter hereafter as 'evidential' decisions. We do not regard any of the decisions referred to in the examples just given as being 'policy' decisions. In our view, 'policy' decisions should be understood as referring only to non-evidential decisions on the acceptance of pleas of guilty to lesser counts or groups of counts or available alternatives; offering no evidence on particular counts; and the withdrawal of the prosecution as a whole.

On 'policy' matters, we consider that the proper practice is and should continue to be that Prosecution Counsel should act contrary to his instructions only in circumstances which give him no alternative. Before reaching that stage, he will have to consider his duty to those for whom he acts, his duty to the Court and his duty to do only that which he considers to be proper. If those considerations lead him to a different view from that held by those who instruct him, he will have to act accordingly. Consideration of the views of the Prosecuting Solicitor/Crown Prosecutor, important at every stage when any kind of decision has to be taken, is crucially important with regard to 'policy' decisions.

It is our experience, as well as that of the Prosecuting Solicitors' Society, that differences of view between Prosecution Counsel and those instructing him, be they on evidential or 'policy' matters, are almost always resolved by discussions between them. There is no reason to and we do not expect this to change. Nonetheless, we have had to consider what should be the position if the very remote possibility of an unresolved conflict should occur in fact and in circumstances where it will not be possible or desirable to obtain an adjournment. The exigencies of trials usually require immediate and effective decisions by somebody. In our view, there is no alternative to the practical position that Prosecution Counsel must take those decisions and do what he conscientiously believes to be right.

The ultimate authority for any prosecution is and will be the Attorney-General, under whose superintendence the Crown Prosecution Service will be administered by the Director and to whom Prosecution Counsel are and always will be answerable. It would be impracticable, generally, to refer a dispute on a 'policy' matter to one of the Law Officers during the course of a case. Not only are they unlikely to be immediately available, but it would take time for a Law Officer to familiarise himself with the details of the particular case sufficiently to make an informed decision. Therefore, if Prosecution Counsel, in discharging his duty, has found it necessary to proceed with the case on the basis of his own view as to the correct decision with which the Prosecuting Solicitor/Crown Prosecutor has not agreed, it would be appropriate for the Attorney-General, *ex post facto,* to require Counsel to submit to him a written report of all the circumstances, including his reason for disagreeing with those who instructed him. We would expect the Attorney-General so to require when the disagreement has been about a 'policy' decision. We would welcome such a practice and rule.

We emphasise that it is Prosecution Counsel's duty to read the instructions delivered to him expeditiously and to confer with those instructing him well before the commencement of the trial, so that either the evidential and 'policy' decisions (where the need for them is identifiable) can be agreed or the opportunity will be available without adjourning the trial, to withdraw instructions or to take in a leader. The purpose is to ensure the early preparation of the case and to make timely contact with the defence, either informally or in the context of a Case Conference. For this purpose to be achieved, we recognise that both Prosecuting Solicitor/Crown Prosecutor and Defence Solicitors must deliver proper instructions as early as possible and that Defence Counsel will have to give as high a priority to early preparation as we suggest that Prosecution Counsel must give. We draw attention to rule 141 of the Code of Conduct for the Bar. (See now para 701 of the Code.)

It would be unacceptable for Prosecution Counsel, who has had the opportunity to prepare his brief and to confer with those instructing him, to advise at the last moment before the trial begins that, for example, the case ought not to proceed or that pleas to lesser offences should be accepted. If such a situation should arise, the Instructing Solicitor must be consulted before his advice is put into effect, and if the Instructing Solicitor is unable to accept it, and instructs Counsel to apply for an adjournment, the application should be made. If an adjournment is granted it would provide an opportunity for the Director to be consulted before any decision is made as to the future conduct of the case.

After the introduction of the Crown Prosecution Service, there will remain a number of prosecutions which will be conducted independently of the Service: the most important will be those conducted by the Revenue, Customs and Excise and other government departments with their own legal sections. We suggest that the principles and the thinking underlying the practices which we have outlined above should apply to such prosecutions.

This Report contemplates the procedures of the Crown Court. Where in a Magistrates' Court, Counsel is not attended by a representative of the Prosecuting Solicitors different considerations will apply: Counsel should not act contrary to his instructions and should seek the authority of those instructing him before departing from them.

It is the minority view of one of our number that all policy decisions, as defined in this paragraph, should in the future be made by the Crown Prosecutors.

2.3.3.2   Problem

A jury fails to agree in a case in which you have prosecuted. Given the nature of the case and the evidence available to you, their inability to reach a verdict is wholly understandable. You take the view that on the customary retrial the prosecution is almost certain to fail. You also consider that a rehearing would cause considerable distress to the principal witness. You decide to offer no further evidence when the case is relisted. Your instructing solicitors do not agree. How do you deal with the situation?

2.4   Relationship with other members of the profession

2.4.1   Duties and responsibilities to the profession as a whole

The main obligations which you are bound to observe are set out in the Code of Conduct and include a duty:

(a) To uphold at all times the standards set out in the Code of Conduct and to comply with its provisions.

(b) Not to engage directly or indirectly in any other occupation if your association with that occupation may adversely affect the reputation of the Bar or prejudice your ability to attend properly to your practice (para 301(b)).

(c) To ensure that you are insured with Bar Mutual Indemnity Fund Limited against claims for professional negligence (paras 204; 402).

(d) To have a current Practising Certificate (para 202).

(e) To ensure your practice is efficiently and properly administered (para 403).

(f) To exercise your own personal judgment in all your professional activities (para 306).

(g) Not to permit your absolute independence, integrity and freedom from external pressures to be compromised or to compromise your professional standards in order to please your client, the court or a third party (para 307).

(h) Not to engage in any advertising or promotion in connection with your practice other than as may be permitted by the provisions of the British Codes of Advertising and Sales Promotion, and otherwise permitted under para 710.2 (paras. 710.1; 710.2).

(i) As a barrister in independent practice, must not practise from the office of or in any unincorporated association with any person other than a barrister except as permitted by para 810 (para 403).

2.4.2   Duties and responsibilities owed to other members of the profession

The most important aspect of your relationship with other members of the Bar is to ensure that you never knowingly mislead or deceive them. It is equally important to treat them with courtesy (para 701). Your other responsibilities include a duty:

(a) To inform counsel previously instructed in the same matter that you have received a brief or set of instructions in place of that other barrister (this appears to be a custom rather than a duty under the Code).

(b) To return, unread, a document belonging to another party which has come into your possession other than by the normal and proper channels (para 608(f)); para 7.2 to the General Standards in Written Standards for the Conduct of Professional Work in Section 3, Miscellaneous Guidance).

(c) To pay, upon receipt of any fees in respect of work done by another barrister, the whole of that fee forthwith to the other barrister (para 406.1).

(d) To pay any pupil except where they are in receipt of an award or remuneration which is paid on terms that it is in lieu of payment for any individual item of work, for any work done for you which, because of its value to you, warrants payment (para 805.2).

In the course of negotiating with a view to a compromise, your relationship with your opponent is of particular importance. The ethics of negotiation are discussed further in **Chapter 7**.

2.4.3 Relationship with the clerks

In the early days of practice, it is quite common for members of the Bar to shy away from ever challenging the authority of the clerks in chambers. Whilst it is important to recognise the position of the clerks and build up a good rapport, trust and working relationship with them, it is vital that you remember you are responsible for ensuring that your practice is properly and efficiently administered. If your clerk makes an error, you must take the blame. Remember that you employ the clerks, they do not employ you. On occasions it may be necessary to 'have words with' the clerks. Do so in a polite manner and on a one to one basis. Do not embarrass the clerks in front of each other or other members of chambers. If you do not succeed in obtaining the clerks' co-operation, consider speaking to your head of chambers.

The following short essay is by Martin Griffiths, Chairman of the Institute of Barristers' Clerks and a senior clerk in the Chambers of David Phillips QC, and it provides a practical insight into the relationship between barrister and clerk.

Relations between Barrister and Clerk
One of the most important people in the personal and professional life of a barrister is the barrister's clerk. The title 'clerk' does little justice to the role that the barrister's clerk plays. The popular image remains one of a slightly rough and ready 'wide boy' who exerts an inordinate amount of control and influence over his or her barristers and without whom solicitors can get nothing done. Unfortunately, this image is perpetuated by the caricatures that frequently appear in TV dramas.

The modern clerk, however, is an experienced and skilful manager at the helm of what is often a multi-million pound business. He or she does much to guide the careers of the barristers in chambers and is the link between the barristers who supply a service and the solicitors who are the customers.

The clerk's role is unusual. He or she is the agent and business manager of the barrister, the ultimate manager of the support team within chambers and the personal adviser to the barrister on all aspects of his or her professional life. Of necessity the barrister may share many problems, both professional and personal, with the clerk and a real friendship may develop between the two.

When the barrister first starts in chambers the senior clerk may appear a remote and forbidding individual. This may be particularly true in a large set of chambers where the principal point of contact between the barrister and the clerks' room is a more junior clerk. However, as manager of the clerking team, the senior clerk will always be monitoring the development and progress of the new barrister. Initially, the new barrister is dependent upon the clerk for providing him or her with work and giving him or her introductions to appropriate solicitors. In the early years the barrister will be very dependent upon this supply of work. As the barrister gains experience and establishes a reputation with solicitor clients, he or she will hopefully develop a practice of his or her own. During this period the clerk is likely to advise the barrister on how to conduct himself or herself and tell him or her what he or she should or should not do.

Whilst the new barrister should, of course, respect the experience of his or her clerk, the clerk should not be regarded as unapproachable. A relationship needs to develop between the two so that there is easy communication; the barrister must be able to feel free to seek advice and to be able to raise concerns or indeed complaints about the management of his or her practice; the clerk needs to understand the strengths, weaknesses and interests of the barrister in order to be able to direct his or her career appropriately.

Communication is probably one of the most important aspects of the smooth running of the barrister's life. Without information the clerk cannot clerk.

- Tell the clerks what you think will happen to cases that you are booked for. Is the case likely to settle, is it listed for trial and you expect it to plead, is the time estimate too short?
- Be punctual and consistent. If you usually arrive in chambers at 9.00 am but tomorrow do not expect to be in until 10.00 am, say so. It is no good if at 9.05 am the clerk needs to send somebody to court on an urgent matter and is waiting for you to walk through the door. Notify your clerk of any changes to your normal routine so that he or she can plan accordingly.
- Always ensure that you telephone chambers with a progress report from court. Ring to say that you are finished and are returning to chambers, ring at lunchtime to say that the case will finish today, or will not and will last until tomorrow lunchtime. The clerk cannot properly plan without adequate warning and up-to-date information.
- Provide prompt and accurate information regarding work done for the purposes of billing. Each chambers will have its own system of time sheets. Complete these and legal aid claim forms promptly on completing any piece of work. The sooner the bill is sent, the sooner you will get paid.

The level and collection of fees is often a subject of discussion between barrister and clerk. Some barristers have absolutely no idea of the fee that a particular case can command; some believe that the fee should be far higher than can realistically be obtained, others undervalue their services dramatically. With experience some have a good idea and can be of tremendous assistance to the clerk in assessing what a particular case is worth. It is important to tell your clerk what is involved in a particular matter for without this information he or she will be assessing or negotiating in the dark. If you have a problem with the level of fees that are being obtained for you, or with the speed with which the fees are being collected, discuss the situation with the clerk. You may have got hold of the wrong end of the stick and not understand the problem; alternatively, he or she may be unaware that a problem exists and only by discussing it can the situation be rectified. If you cannot resolve the difficulty, raise the matter with your pupil master or mistress, with whom you may still have a strong relationship even though you are well past pupillage, or raise it with the head of chambers who has a duty to ensure that the chambers are managed properly.

All chambers are different and will operate in a slightly different way. In some the members of chambers will always be addressed formally, eg, Mr Smith, Miss Jones, Mrs Brown. In others the senior clerk will be on first name terms with the barristers but will expect his or her staff to address members of chambers formally, in other sets everyone may be on first name terms. Each chambers is different and I would advise that you err on the side of caution until you establish the house style. Having said that, I doubt if any senior clerk would these days expect to be addressed by anything other than his or her first name by the barristers.

As I have said, each chambers operates in a slightly different manner and hopefully when you start your second six months, or upon your arrival as a practising barrister, the senior clerk will run through how the chambers function. A few golden rules may well be as follows:

- Stay out of the clerks' room unless you have necessary business there. It is often a crowded and certainly a busy room and you gossiping to another member of chambers, or a clerk who has other duties, is not helpful.

- Keep personal telephone calls in chambers to a minimum. Do not expect the clerks to take telephone calls for you to organise your busy social life, sort out the cricket team fixtures or arrange a holiday for a dozen people.
- Let the clerk know when you are contemplating going on holiday before making the booking. It won't be very helpful suddenly to find that the five most junior members of chambers are all on holiday at the same time.
- Ensure that bills for chambers' expenses and clerk's fees are paid promptly.
- Feed back to your clerks news and views that you pick up from other barristers and your solicitors at court.

Remember that at all times your clerk is monitoring the work that you do and your progress. He or she will have views as to your future development and hopefully will wish to discuss these with you. Do not hesitate to share your views with him or her because at the end of the day the pair of you are a partnership.

2.4.3.1 Problems

(1)   A colleague in chambers comes to your room to discuss with you a quantum in a case in which he or she is giving some preliminary advice. He or she gives you the outline of the medical report and after you have exchanged valuations of the level of general damages, leaves you with the words 'We have terrible problems on liability'. Some months later, you receive instructions to settle a defence and, having read the papers, you realise that it is the same case which you discussed with your colleague. Do you continue to deal with the papers?

(2)   You have a row with your clerks. During the following week, one of the pupils in chambers asks your advice upon a brief he or she has been given for the next day. You realise it is a case you advised upon last year, yet the clerks have informed you that you have no work for the following day. What do you do?

3

Working at the Bar today

3.1 Introduction

Britain in the 21st century is a richly diverse and multi-cultural society. Statistics from the 2000 census shows that 4.6 million people, 7.9% of the population, are from a non-white ethnic group. In certain urban areas such as London, West Midlands, Greater Manchester and West Yorkshire, the percentage figure is much higher. Surveys by local education authorities show that over 100 different home languages are spoken. This diversity is further reflected by the number of religious beliefs, changes in the nature of the family, positive changes with regard to gender roles and the rights of the disabled, children and the gay and lesbian community. However, despite many positive changes in attitude, it is a society in which discrimination still exists and in which access to justice for all remains a burning issue. Yet, it is also a society whose diversity adds to the dynamism, excitement and challenges that you face as lawyers, irrespective of the area of practice you choose to enter.

The First Report on Legal Education and Training published in April 1996, the Lord Chancellor's Advisory Committee on Legal Education and Conduct (ACLEC) stated:

From the earliest stages of legal education and training, intending lawyers should be imbued not only with the standards and codes of professional conduct, but also more generally with the obligations of lawyers to help protect individuals and groups from the abuse of public and private power.

In the spirit of this statement, the aims of this chapter are to consider how the Code of Conduct operates in the areas of discrimination, diversity and equality of opportunity and how it impacts on your responsibilities to all those you work with, whether as colleagues or clients. To simply understand the Code is not enough, if barristers working at the Bar today are to rise to the obligation 'to help protect individuals and groups from the abuse of public and private power'. To effectively represent individuals you need to have an understanding of the different views, beliefs and customs of all those that make up Britain's diverse and multi-cultural society. The second part of this chapter gives some general guidance and sources of information that will help you meet this challenge. The barrister that has this understanding will not only have risen to this challenge, but will have completed a vital step in having a vibrant and successful practice.

3.2 The Code of Conduct and discrimination

An act of direct discrimination by a barrister amounts to a breach of the Code of Conduct. Paragraph 305.1 of the Code states:

A barrister must not in relation to any other person (including a client or another barrister or a pupil or a student member of an Inn of Court) discriminate directly or indirectly or victimize because of race, colour, ethnic or national origin, nationality, citizenship, sex, sexual orientation, marital status, disability, religion or political persuasion.

The breadth of this provision means that it covers a barrister's relationship with all of those people with whom he or she comes into contact in the course of carrying out a professional practice.

3.2.1 Fair representation: the 'cab-rank' rule

Fair treatment under para 305 would include fair representation, though this concept is specifically enshrined in para 603 of the Code and is known as the 'cab-rank' rule.

A barrister in independent practice must comply with the 'cab-rank rule' and accordingly except only as otherwise provided in paragraphs 603, 604, 605 and 606, he must in any field in which he professes to practice in relation to work appropriate to his experience and seniority and irrespective of whether his client is paying privately or is publicly funded:

    (a) accept any brief to appear before a court in which he professes to practice;
    (b) accept any instructions;
    (c) act for any person on whose behalf he is instructed;
    and to do so irrespective of
        (i) the party on whose behalf he is instructed
        (ii) the nature of the case and
        (iii) any belief or opinion which he may have formed as to the character reputation cause conduct guilt or innocence of that person.

(See also paras 104, 303 of the Code and para 2.2 of the Written Standards for the Conduct of Professional Work in Section 3, Miscellaneous Guidance.)

The only permissible exceptions to the 'cab-rank' rule are set out in paras 603–610 of the Code. The rule otherwise means that a barrister must accept a brief or instructions to represent a client, no matter how repugnant the client is to the barrister on political, religious or moral grounds. Consequently, if the system is correctly and properly adhered to at all times, whatever a barrister's individual views are, effective representation of an individual is rightly ensured.

3.2.2 The Equality Code for the Bar

The Equality Code for the Bar (the Equality Code) was adopted by the Bar Council in 1995. The Equality Code is described as 'a guide to good equal opportunities practice to which all barristers in independent practice must have regard'. A comprehensive summary of the Equality Code can be found in Section 3, Miscellaneous Guidance of the Code of Conduct in **Appendix 1**.

3.2.2.1 Content

The Equality Code might be seen to have two main areas of concern. First, it covers the regulatory and legislative framework governing barristers in the field of discrimination and equal opportunities (chapter 1). In that connection, it very helpfully defines unlawful and prohibited discrimination (chapter 2) and provides guidance on harassment (chapter 3). Secondly, it covers anti-discrimination and equal opportunities obligations and policies across a range of areas of chambers activity and management (chapters 4–7).

3.2.2.2   Status of the Equality Code

It is worth distinguishing between the status of the Code and the Equality Code. Whilst it is the case that by virtue of para 403 of the Code, a barrister must have regard to the provisions of the Equality Code, not every breach of the Code will render a barrister liable to disciplinary proceedings. Paragraph 305 of the Code prohibits a barrister from any act of direct or indirect discrimination and para 901 of the Code states that a barrister's failure to comply with the provisions of the Code 'shall constitute professional misconduct'. Thus, breaches of the Equality Code may well amount to professional misconduct under para 305.1 of the Code, but will not automatically do so. Under para 305.3 acts of indirect discrimination will not amount to a breach of the Code, if they were committed without any intention of treating the claimant less favourably on any ground in that paragraph to which the complaint relates. In short, the Equality Code provides an evidential standard against which allegations of discrimination may be judged, and an invaluable guide to good practice, which it would be foolish for individual barristers or sets of chambers to ignore.

3.2.2.3   Statutory obligations

Barristers and their clerks should remember that in addition to the provisions of the Code and the Equality Code, they are subject to a number of statutory obligations. Section 26A of the Race Relations Act 1976 and s 35A of the Sex Discrimination Act 1975, both enacted by s 64 of the Courts and Legal Services Act 1990, effectively outlaw discrimination by barristers or their clerks on grounds of race or sex. The Disability Discrimination Act 1995 prohibits barristers from discriminating on grounds of disability. An individual alleging discrimination can bring proceedings against a barrister or set of chambers in a county court within six months of the alleged act of discrimination.

3.2.2.4   Discrimination and harassment

Discrimination, both direct and indirect, is defined in chapter 2 of the Equality Code. You should familiarise yourselves with the concept of direct discrimination centred around the idea of 'less favourable treatment' and indirect discrimination whereby a condition or requirement is applied equally to everyone, but some individuals or groups who are unable to comply, suffer a detriment as a result and the requirement cannot be shown to be objectively justifiable in spite of its discriminatory effect.

You should be aware that the Bar Council has recently amended the Code of Conduct to make it professional misconduct to discriminate against an application for pupillage or tenancy on the grounds of age (except where such discrimination can be shown to be reasonably justified). See para 305.2 of the Code. In view of this change, the Bar Council has produced guidance on age discrimination in pupillage and tenancy selection (see the Code, Section 3, Miscellaneous Guidance set out in **Appendix 1**). This chapter also gives information on discrimination on the grounds of sexual orientation and disability.

Harassment is dealt with in chapter 3 of the Equality Code. Harassment which would not have occurred but for the race, sex or disability of the recipient, may constitute unlawful direct discrimination. The chapter specifically highlights avenues of redress for individuals suffering harassment, but these are also relevant for any act of unlawful discrimination. These include chambers grievance procedures, complaints to the relevant student officers about a sponsor or pupil master/mistress, complaints to the PCC where the harasser is a barrister, complaints to a county court or employment tribunal alleging harassment as a form of direct discrimination and referral to the police where the act is a criminal offence. A recipient may also raise the matter informally with the Inns' Student Officers, members of Chambers and sympathetic organisations such as the Association of Women Barristers. The Bar Council's Equal Opportunity Officers offer confidential advice on all of these matters including reference to the Bar Council's Harassment Mediation Panel, where appropriate. Sources of help and advice are listed at **3.4** below.

3.3 Effective representation in a diverse society

We cannot be a beacon to the world unless the talents of all the people shine through. Not one black high court judge; not one black chief constable or permanent secretary; not one black army officer above the rank of colonel. Not one Asian either. Not a record of pride for the British establishment.

Prime Minister Tony Blair, 1997

The Bar itself is slowly changing and gradually becoming more representative of the society it serves. In October 2000 of the 8,263 barristers recorded by the Bar Council, 2,263 (24.5%) were women and 784 (8.7%) were from ethnic minority and mixed backgrounds.

As the Equality Code points out, 'Direct discrimination may frequently be subconscious, based on stereotypical assumptions about particular minority ethnic groups or about the difference in capabilities, characteristics, personalities and motivation between women and men'. From whatever background a barrister comes, at some time all will need help and advice on the customs and beliefs of the individuals that they represent. The Judicial Studies Board (JSB), the body responsible for training all those who sit in a judicial capacity, have issued specific guidance on these matters in the Equal Treatment Bench Book. Whilst this book is aimed at those sitting in a judicial capacity, you are advised that it holds equally invaluable information for those who are representing others. The full text of the Equal Treatment Bench Book is available on the JSB website at http://www.jsboard.co.uk. In addition, two easy-to-use companion booklets have been produced dealing with racial matters and general equality before the courts. These are reprinted in full below and offer a general introduction to some of the matters dealt with in more detail in the Equal Treatment Bench Book.

RACE AND THE COURTS
Foreword by the Honourable Mr Justice Keene
Chairman of the Equal Treatment Advisory Committee.

All of us who sit in a judicial capacity, whether full-time or part-time, are operating today in a society which is one of great diversity in race, culture and religion. Gone are the days when a judge or magistrate could assume that an innate sense of fairness, together with a knowledge of the law, was all that was required to carry out his or her function successfully. We need in addition an understanding of the customs of all those who appear in the civil and criminal courts in whatever capacity, and most of us need some help in obtaining that understanding. This booklet, produced by the Equal Treatment Advisory Committee on behalf of the Judicial Studies Board, has that object in mind.

It is intended as an easy-to-use companion to the revised section of the Equal Treatment Bench Book dealing with racial matters. It is no substitute for that Bench Book, which provides the detailed material and which avoids the over-simplification inevitable in a brief publication such as this. Nonetheless, used in conjunction with the Bench Book, this booklet is designed to be a practical working guide in an area where the judiciary is under greater public scrutiny than ever before. I hope that you will find it of value on these vitally important matters.

David Keene
September 1999

1. *Introduction*

> Although, like all judges, I speak only for myself, it can safely be assumed that the judiciary are implacably opposed to racism and that no one who harbours racist views is fit to be a judge.
>
> *Lord Justice Rose, Chairman, Criminal Justice Consultative Council, 14 July 1999*

Justice in a modern and diverse society must be 'colour conscious', not 'colour blind'.

This means that those who administer justice must be aware of, and responsive to, the differences among people who come to court in any capacity, while remaining fair, independent and impartial.

How can judges meet this challenge?

This short guide offers some pointers. It complements the Judicial Studies Board's *Equal Treatment Bench Book* and is intended to be used as a quick, practical reference rather than as an alternative to it.

a. *Why does this matter?*

It is fundamental to the stability of society that everyone should have confidence and trust in the institutions and agencies of justice. The judicial oath itself embodies the concept of equal treatment 'without fear or favour, affection or ill will'. However, there is evidence of a widespread lack of confidence in the justice system, particularly among the Black and Asian communities. The task of ensuring that in terms of rights, remedies and treatment, courts and tribunals are perceived as fair, presents the judiciary and those who work in the administration of justice with a major challenge.

> Crime and fear of crime became a major public preoccupation. Did this fear of crime help to demonise certain groups in the public mind? We are all familiar with the image of the uncontrollable pre-teens stealing car after car on deprived estates; we are all familiar with the portrayal of 'muggers' as being, on the whole, young black men; we are familiar with the derogatory terminology of 'rat boys', the barely concealed message of 'bogus asylum seekers'. These messages help us identify people to blame instead of making us look for solutions.
>
> *Lord Navnit Dholakia OBE*
> *Chair, National Association for the Care and Resettlement of Offenders, July 1999*

b. *What does this mean in practice?*

If people believe that justice and fair treatment are not 'on offer' for them, this may influence their attitudes and approach to the institutions of justice. They will not expect to see figures of authority from their own communities, in particular black or Asian judges. They may also expect to encounter ignorance about their own cultures and backgrounds or stereotypical assumptions, for example that they represent the 'problem' rather than possibly being a victim of it. If they have also experienced social and economic disadvantage, their sense of alienation and distrust will be more acute. Sullenness, aggression or posturing in court might be a mark of disrespect for the tribunal, but it might equally be an outward display of these fears and expectations.

> There is a striking and inescapable need to demonstrate fairness, not just by police services, but across the criminal justice system as a whole, in order to generate trust and confidence within minority ethnic communities, who undoubtedly perceive themselves to be discriminated against by 'the system'. Just as justice needs to be 'seen to be done' so fairness must be 'seen to be demonstrated' in order to generate trust.
>
> *Stephen Lawrence Inquiry Report, para 46.30*

2.   Some basic principles

What therefore can judges do to demonstrate fairness and build confidence? The basic principles can be expressed in a short list of dos and don'ts:

- Treat everyone who comes to court with dignity and respect — 'do as you would be done by.'

- Everyone has prejudices. Recognise and guard against your own.

- Be well-informed — being independent and impartial does not mean being isolated from issues which affect people from minority communities.

- Don't assume that treating everyone in the same way is the same thing as treating everyone fairly. It would not be fair to treat a wheelchair user in the same way as someone who is able to walk, for example expecting him or her to climb stairs to reach a courtroom.

- Be 'colour conscious', not 'colour blind'. Fair treatment involves taking account of difference.

- Don't make assumptions: all white people are not the same. Nor are all black, or Asian, or Chinese or Middle Eastern people.

- Don't project cultural stereotypes: for example that all young black people avoid eye contact. Most young black and Asian people are second and third generation British born citizens and may be no different from any other teenager when faced with authority figures.

- Don't perceive people from ethnic minority communities as 'the problem' — the problem may lie in the working methods and traditions of some institutions which may put some groups, such as women, people with disabilities or people from racial minorities, at an unfair disadvantage.

- If in doubt — ask. A polite and well-intentioned inquiry about how to pronounce a name or about a particular religious belief or a language requirement will not be offensive when prompted by a genuine desire to get it right.

3.   Putting it in context

The 1991 census offered respondents a choice of seven categories for describing their own ethnic group: White, Black-Caribbean, Black-African, Indian, Pakistani, Bangladeshi and Chinese as well as 'Other'.

A breakdown of the figures in the 1991 census is:

UK population	56 million
Racial minority groups	3.251m (5.8%)
of which:	
Black	1.016m (1.9%)
Asian	1.729m (3%)
Chinese/other	.529m (0.9%)

48% of the UK's minority population of all ages was born here and three quarters hold British nationality. The proportion is of course much higher among the young.

The largest single racial minority group is the Indian community at 1.5% of the general population, next is the Pakistani group (1%) and the third largest is the African Caribbean community (0.9%).

Over half of all racial minority groups live in South Eastern England. Outside the major cities in the UK, minority ethnic groups generally form less than 2% of the local population. Members of minority communities, however, suffer a disproportionate degree of social disadvantage. Some 40% of the black and Indian groups and 63% of Pakistanis and Bangladeshis live in low income or council estate areas compared with under 20% of the white population.

Six per cent of the UK population of working age is from racial minority groups. A 1993 Labour Force Survey showed unemployment rates of 15% among Indian people, 25% of African Caribbeans, 28% of Bangladeshis, 30% of Pakistanis and 37% of Africans, compared with 9.5% among the white population. In some parts of London six out of every ten young black men aged 16–24 are unemployed. Unemployment among racial minority groups does not seem to be related to educational achievement — a 1994 Labour Force Survey found that 48% of young people from minority groups were in post-16 full-time education compared with 31% of young white people.

4.   Race and justice

> Race issues go to the heart of our system of justice, which demand that all are treated as equals before the law. This is recognised not only in the standard embodiment of justice as a figure blindfolded but also in the terms of the judicial oath.
>
> It is therefore a matter of the gravest concern if members of the ethnic minorities feel they are discriminated against by the criminal justice system: more so if their fears were to be borne out in reality.
>
> *The late Lord Taylor of Gosforth, Lord Chief Justice, 1995.*

Despite a disproportionate number of black people in prison, and some public perceptions to the contrary, there is no evidence that black people commit more crime than white people.

However:

- Black people are four to five times more likely than white people to be stopped and searched by the police.
- Black people are more likely to be arrested than white people or people from other ethnic groups; cautioning is used less often for black than white or other ethnic groups.
- 7% of people on probation orders, 10% of those on community service orders and 18% of the prison population are from minority groups.
- A 1992 study of sentencing in the Crown Court found that when a range of legally relevant variables were taken into account, black defendants stood between 5% and 8% greater chance of an immediate prison sentence.

What has been found by the British Crime Surveys is that people from racial minorities are disproportionately the victims of crime.

Surveys have revealed highly negative perceptions of the criminal justice system among members of racial minorities. For example:

- Only 11% of young black people in a 1994 survey believed that 'judges give fair and equal treatment to everyone in this country' compared to 25% of young white people.
- A 1995 survey found that 78% of black respondents felt that the police would treat a white victim more seriously than a black victim.
- 18% of complaints to the Police Complaints Authority are from black people.

Statistical material and research concentrates overwhelmingly on race within the criminal justice system. Little is so far known about the effect on racial minorities of other types of proceedings. Some factors that may be relevant here are:

- In family proceedings, a need for understanding of different family patterns and structures.
- Problems arising from subjective assessments of what is a 'good parent'.
- Increase in the numbers of litigants in person, who may not understand vital procedures eg the pre-action protocols under the Civil Procedure Rules and some of whom may not have English as a first language.

Steps that can be taken by those who sit judicially to promote greater openness and equality in the justice system are:

- Making themselves aware of the impact of the system on different communities and what it means for those coming to court, whether as claimants, victims, witnesses, representatives or suspects.
- Recognising the different impact of the system of justice on different groups.
- Effectively managing court and tribunal hearings to ensure that they are free from any form of discrimination.

- In the light of the Crime and Disorder Act 1998, being alert to possible racist motivations for crimes that may have been missed by the police or CPS.
- Helping to support local victim support groups and encouraging other appropriate community-based groups to become involved in providing support.

> It is incumbent upon every institution to examine their policies and the outcome of their policies and practices to guard against disadvantaging any section of our communities.
>
> *Stephen Lawrence Inquiry Report*

5. Managing fairness

Discrimination

Discrimination can be:

- **Direct**: Where a person is treated less favourably on grounds of race, colour, religion, gender, ethnic or national origin, or disability, than others would be in similar circumstances.
- **Indirect**: Where a requirement is applied equally to all groups, but has a disproportionate effect on the members of one group because a considerably smaller number of members of that group can comply with it. This applies whether intentional or not.
- **Institutional**: Defined by the Stephen Lawrence Inquiry Report as '... *the collective failure of an organisation to provide an appropriate and professional service to people because of their colour, culture or ethnic origin. It can be seen or detected in processes, attitudes and behaviour which amount to discrimination through unwitting prejudice, ignorance, thoughtlessness, and racist stereotyping which disadvantage minority ethnic people.*' Institutional racism does not mean that all individuals in an organisation are racist, but that their structures and working methods may have an unfair outcome.

6. Communicating fairness

General points

The responsibility for ensuring equality and fairness of treatment rests on everyone involved in the administration of justice. A litigant, claimant, defendant or representative may not encounter a member of the judiciary until the final stages of his or her case, but may only think in terms of a single system — finer points about who does what are meaningless. If anyone feels hard done by at any stage, it reflects on everyone who represents that system.

Judges can communicate fairness and impartiality in a court setting in various ways. Individually they can:

- Be polite, courteous and patient at all times.
- Get names and modes of address correct.
- Make provision for oath-taking in accordance with different religions.
- Avoid making assumptions based on stereotypes or misinformation.
- Take the initiative to find out about different local cultures and religions.
- Take care not to use offensive words or terminology.
- Display an understanding of differences and difficulties with a well-timed and sensitive intervention where appropriate.

In partnership with court administrators they can:

- Encourage the availability of court documents and advance information in different local languages.
- Encourage the provision of access to interpreters.
- Encourage the provision of appropriate facilities for all court users.
- Help to promote a high standard of service to all court users.
- Support the provision of posters and leaflets in English and local minority languages.

Appropriate words — dos and don'ts

However committed a judge may be to fairness and equality, he or she may still give the opposite impression by using inappropriate, dated or offensive words. There are no right answers. Language and ideas are living and developing all the time. Some words that were once acceptable no longer are. The following can be advanced with confidence:

- **Black**: acceptable to people of African or Caribbean origin. Some Asian people are happy to be called black and some are not. 'Black and Asian' is preferable (though see below on the use of 'Asian').
- **Coloured**: an offensive term that should never be used.
- **Non-white**: implies a negative value judgement. Should not be used.
- **People of colour**: common in the USA but not so usual here.
- **Visible minorities**: acceptable, with wider scope than 'black'.
- **Racial minorities**: alternative to 'ethnic minorities'. Both are acceptable.
- **Ethnics**: a deeply offensive term that should never be used.
- **Ethnic monitoring**: acceptable when applied to systems of monitoring.
- **African Caribbean**: preferable to West Indian or Afro-Caribbean. Younger people may prefer to be called black, or black British.
- **African**: acceptable, as is naming the country from which a person or family may have originated eg Nigerian.
- **Asian**: should be used with care. People prefer to identify themselves by reference to their country eg Indian, Pakistani and Bangladeshi, region eg Bengali, Punjabi, or religion eg Muslim, Hindu or Sikh. Younger people born in Britain may call themselves British or British Asians. If the country is not known, Asian or South Asian is acceptable.
- **Paki**: not acceptable.
- **Negro/negroid**: not acceptable.
- **Oriental**: not acceptable. The proper name such as Chinese, Malaysian, Vietnamese etc should be used.
- **Mohammedan**: not acceptable. Muslim should be used.
- **Half-caste**: not acceptable. Mixed race should be used instead.
- **Immigrants**: it is inaccurate to apply this generalisation to racial minorities in the United Kingdom, many of whom are British born.

7.   Religious diversity in Britain

Christianity has not only played a major part in the evolution of society among the white population in Britain, but has also attracted a significant number of adherents within minority groups. There are a number of Asian and Chinese churches, and indeed black churches are currently the fastest growing within the Christian Communion. In the course of a working day, judges may, however, encounter people with a variety of different religious beliefs — or none. There are, in addition, many degrees of devotion within the practice of any faith.

- **African religions**
  People from African countries may be Muslims, Christians or followers of indigenous African religions with their own practices. In some cases it may be relevant to ascertain an individual's area of origin. In all cases, when in doubt, ask what is needed in terms of oath taking or other court facilities.
- **Chinese religions**
  Many religions are practised in China, including Buddhism, Christianity and Islam. Chinese religions include Confucianism and Daoism. Unless they are Christians or Muslims, most Chinese witnesses prefer to affirm.
- **Buddhism**
  There are several Buddhist traditions commonly practised in the UK. Commitment to the Three Jewels is a key element; the Buddha, the Dhamma (teachings) and the Sangha (community of monks or nuns). With a lunar calendar, festivals and special days vary from

year to year. Holy days fall on full- and half-moon days. Most Buddhists usually choose to affirm.

- **Hinduism**

  Holy books are the Vedas; main religious festivals are MahaShivaratri (February), Janmashtami (August), Vinayaka Chauth (August), Dussehra or Navaratri (October), Durga Puja (October), Diwali (November), Holi (March). Oath is taken on the Gita, (which is an extract from the Vedas).

- **Judaism**

  The holy book is the Hebrew Bible (Tenach). Festivals include Rosh Hashanah (New Year, held in September/October), Yom Kippur (holiest day of the year, held 10 days after Rosh Hashanah), Pesach (March/April), Shavout (May/June), Sukkot (autumn). Holy day is Saturday (from Friday sunset). Prayers are said three times a day.

- **Islam**

  Main festivals include Eid-ul-Fitr (held after the one-month fast of Ramadan) and Eid-ul-Adha. Friday is the holy day and many will wish to attend the mosque at midday. The holy book is the Qur'an (Koran) and prayers are said five times a day. Muslims prefer to wash before handling the Qur'an and may want to cover their heads when taking the oath. During Ramadan (which may fall at various times of the year), most, if not all, Muslims may fast and will therefore not eat or drink from dawn to dusk.

- **Rastafari**

  The holy book is the Bible. Festivals include Ethiopian Constitution Day (16 July), the birthday of Emperor Haile Selassie 1 (23 July), Marcus Garvey's birthday (17 August), Ethiopian New Year's Day (11 September), anniversary of the coronation of Haile Selassie (2 November), Ethiopian Christmas (7 January). Rastafarians may take the oath on either the Old or New Testaments, or may prefer to affirm.

- **Sikhism**

  The holy book is the Guru Granth Sahib. Main festivals include Vaisaki (13 April), Diwali (October/November), Guru Nanak's birthday (November/December), Guru Gobind Singh's birthday (December or January), Guru Arjan Dev's Martyrdom (May/June). The Sunder Gutka, an extract from the Guru Granth Sahib, has been treated as the appropriate form of a Sikh holy book to be used in courts in the UK.

8. Oath-taking. Some practical points

The Oaths Act 1978 accords statutory precedence to Christianity, but it is essential that proper respect is paid to the religious beliefs of all litigants.

The holy book of people from any community who often come to a court should be available: it is likely that most demand will be for the Gita, the Qur'an and the Sunder Gutka.

- Religious practices in relation to oath taking should be handled sensitively — not as though they are a nuisance.

- Not everyone from racial minority communities is religious: some may prefer to affirm.

- Muslim, Hindu and Sikh women may prefer to affirm if having to give evidence during menstruation or shortly after childbirth.

- Requests to wash hands, feet or other body parts before taking the oath should be treated sympathetically.

- Some witnesses may want to remove shoes or cover their heads or bow with folded hands.

- Holy books should be covered at all times when not in use in cloth or velvet bags. When uncovered, they should only be touched by the person taking the oath, not by an usher or other court staff. They should not be marked inside or out.

9. Names and naming systems

Naming systems vary between minority groups and some are complex. A few basic principles may be stated:

- It is more important to treat people with courtesy and address them properly than to try to learn all the different naming systems.

- Ask people how they would like to be addressed, how to pronounce their name and how to spell it.
- Ask for full name: first, middle and last. Do not ask for 'Christian' name or 'surname'.
- Do not record or address a male Muslim or Sikh by his religious name only; eg Mohammed or Allah, or Singh — check in case these are last names.
- Do not record or address a female Muslim or Sikh by her religious name only: eg Begum, Bibi or Kaur.

EQUALITY BEFORE THE COURTS
Foreword by Lord Justice Keene
Chairman of the JSB's Equal Treatment Advisory Committee

In September 1999, the Judicial Studies Board published a booklet entitled *Race and the Courts*, which was intended as an easy-to-use companion to the guidance on race that had just been published as part of the JSB's new Equal Treatment Bench Book. That booklet was extremely well received, particularly by lay magistrates and members of tribunals.

In order that all members of society are treated on an equal basis, Parliament has enacted a number of statutes with respect to groups such as children and those with disabilities, and the Equal Treatment Bench Book has now been extended to include coverage of these and other groups which might be at risk of unequal treatment. This second leaflet is intended to build on the success of the first by, once again, providing a summary of the key points contained in that guidance. It is no substitute for the Bench Book, which provides the detailed material that avoids the over-simplification inevitable in a brief publication such as this and is available in full on the JSB's website at www.jsboard.co.uk.

It is perhaps worth noting that, for the sake of succinctness, the terms 'judge', 'court' and 'trial' have been used throughout.

Many of the general principles included in the booklet will be familiar to you. I do hope, however, that you find this practical, working guide of some help in an area where the judiciary continues to be under increasing public scrutiny.

David Keene August 2001

1. *Equal treatment — some dos and don'ts*

Do's	Don'ts
• ascertain how parties wish to be addressed.	• underestimate the stress and worry faced by those appearing in court, particularly when the ordeal is compounded by an additional problem such as disability or having to appear without professional representation.
• make a point of obtaining, well in advance if possible, precise details of any disability or medical problem from which a person who is appearing before you suffers.	
• allow more time for special arrangements, breaks etc to accommodate special needs at the trial.	• overlook the use — unconscious or otherwise — of gender-based, racist or 'homophobic' stereotyping as an evidential shortcut.
• give particular thought to the difficulties facing disabled people who attend court — prior planning will enable their various needs to be accommodated as far as possible.	• allow advocates to attempt overrigorous cross-examination of children or other vulnerable witnesses.
• try to put yourself in their position — the stress of attending court should not be made worse unnecessarily, through a failure to anticipate foreseeable problems.	• use words that imply an evaluation of the sexes, however subtle — for instance, 'man and wife', 'girl' (unless speaking of a child), 'businessmen'.
• bear in mind the problems facing unrepresented parties.	• use terms such as 'mental handicap', 'the disabled' — use instead 'learning disability', 'people with disabilities'.

Do's	Don'ts
• admit a child's evidence, unless the child is incapable of giving intelligible testimony.	• allow anyone to be put in a position where they face hostility or ridicule.
• ensure that appropriate measures are taken to protect vulnerable witnesses, for instance children, those with mental or physical disabilities or those who are afraid or distressed.	
• be understanding of people's difficulties and needs.	

2. Disability

'It is estimated that there are at least 8.5 million people who currently meet the definition of disabled person.'

It is estimated that there are at least 8.5 million people who currently meet the definition of disabled person under the Disability Discrimination Act 1995. This provides that a 'disability' is any 'physical or mental impairment which has a substantial and long-term adverse effect on ... normal day-to-day activities'. 'Disability' may for example relate to mobility, manual dexterity, physical co-ordination, incontinence, speech, hearing or sight, memory, and ability to concentrate, learn or understand.

The Disability Discrimination Act 1995, Youth Justice and Criminal Evidence Act 1999 and Human Rights Act 1998 all impose on courts a duty to take account of disabilities. Courts must be able to accommodate the special needs of litigants, defendants and witnesses arising from disability.

Under the Disability Discrimination Act 1995 it is unlawful to discriminate against disabled persons in the provision of facilities and services. There is a duty on all service providers — including courts — to take reasonable steps to change any practice which makes it impossible or unreasonably difficult for disabled persons to make use of a service which they provide to other members of the public.

The Human Rights Act 1998 also provides support for disabled litigants, particularly in respects of the right to a fair trial. Awareness of the issues which disability may raise in the management of a trial are important in this respect, and special arrangement may have to be made with regard to:

- memory and comprehension — form of questioning, courtroom procedures;
- mobility — access requirements; sufferer may be unable to attend court;
- communication — visual aids, speech interpreters;

'The Human Rights Act 1998 also provides support for disabled litigants.'

- some forms of disability mean concentration is impaired, or the person needs to eat or drink more frequently, or take medication, or go to the lavatory at frequent intervals;
- the presence of carers or helpers may be necessary, perhaps even in the dock or witness box;
- the order in which evidence is heard — attending court can be even more stressful for disabled people than for others, so it might be helpful to arrange the hearing of evidence so that they are not kept waiting.

Some types of disability

'All court rooms should be fitted with an induction loop.'

- **Alzheimer's disease** — most sufferers of this progressive disease are elderly. It can take the form of lapses of memory and unsettling behaviour patterns. The stress of appearing in court can have a detrimental effect.
- **Autism** — a lifelong development disability which impedes the ability to communicate and to relate socially.
- **Cerebral palsy** — sufferers experience disorders of movement as well as posture and communication problems.

- **Cerebral vascular accidents ('stroke')** — symptoms can include weakness or paralysis, speech difficulties, loss of balance and incontinence.
- **Deafness** — this covers a range of hearing impairments. All court rooms should be fitted with an induction loop. The use of sign language interpreters may be necessary.
- **Diabetes** — this can be controlled by medication, but sufferers can experience symptoms ranging from irritability to slurred speech and loss of consciousness.
- **Down's syndrome** — this is associated with a low IQ and varying communication difficulties.
- **Dyslexia** — sufferers have difficulty with information processing and short-term memory.
- **Epilepsy** — sufferers have seizures or fits which may be brought on by the stress of a court appearance.

'... the presence of carers or helpers may be necessary, perhaps even in the dock or witness box.'

- **Incontinence** — this may arise in conjunction with other disabilities or in isolation, and may worsen with stress. Additional breaks in proceedings may have to be arranged.
- **Inflammatory bowel disease** — a pre-arranged signal for an urgent trip to the lavatory may be necessary.
- **Mental health problems** — these vary greatly and the judge will have to make a careful assessment of affected individuals and how to deal with them in the witness box.
- **Motor neurone disease** — a progressive degenerative disease with symptoms extending to loss of limb function and wasting of muscles.
- **Multiple sclerosis** — symptoms can include visual damage and restricted movement and sufferers are likely to fatigue rapidly.
- **Spina bifida and hydrocephalus** — the range of mobility is wide, and some sufferers have impaired brain function.
- **Thalidomide sufferers** — usually limb disabled; some have hearing impairment.
- **Visual impairment** — one of the commonest disabilities. The best method of communicating in court should be established at the outset.

'The best method of communicating in court should be established at the outset.'

The Juries Act 1974 provides that it is for the judge to determine whether or not a person should act as a juror. In the event of a person with disabilities being called for jury service, the presumption is that the person should so act unless the judge is of the opinion that the person will not, on account of their disability, be capable of acting effectively as a juror. The full-time attendance of a carer for a jury member would, however, pose difficulties because it would be an incurable irregularity for the carer to retire with the jury to the jury room.

'... it is for the judge to determine whether or not a person should act as a juror.'

3. Mental incapacity

'There is a presumption that an adult is capable until the contrary is proved.'

An adult who lacks mental capacity will not be able to make decisions that others should act upon. He or she will not be able to enter into contracts, administer his or her own affairs or conduct litigation.

There is a presumption that an adult is capable until the contrary is proved, but this may be rebutted by a specific finding of incapacity. Lawyers must be able to recognise incapacity when it exists, and to cope with the legal implications.

The legal definition of mental capacity will differ for different purposes, and the severity of the test and means of assessment may depend upon the nature and implications of the particular decision.

There is no universal test of capacity. Where doubt arises as to mental capacity, legal tests may vary according to the particular transaction or act involved.

It has been stated that the individual must be able to:

(a) understand and retain information, and

(b) weigh that information in the balance to arrive at a choice.

When making assessments, different professions apply different criteria:

- the medical profession is concerned with diagnosis and prognosis;
- care workers classify people according to their degree of independence and competence in performing certain skills;
- the lawyer is concerned with whether the individual is capable of making a reasoned and informed decision and of communicating that decision.

'Where doubt arises as to mental capacity, legal tests may vary according to the particular transaction or act involved.'

4.   Those appearing without legal representation

There are various reasons why people choose to represent themselves, rather than instructing a lawyer. For many, it is because they do not qualify for Legal Services Commission funding. Whatever their reason for not employing a lawyer, unrepresented parties are likely to be stressed and worried. There may be much at stake, and yet they may be unaware of basic legal principles and court procedures. It is to be expected that they will be experiencing feelings of fear, ignorance, frustration, bewilderment and disadvantage, especially if appearing against a represented party. Judges must try to maintain a balance between assisting the unrepresented party and protecting their represented opponent from problems arising from the unrepresented party's lack of legal knowledge.

'There may be much at stake, and yet they may be totally unaware of basic legal principles and court procedures.'

a.   Problems that may face those without legal representation

Those who appear without legal representation:

- may lack understanding of legal terminology and specialist vocabulary;
- may be ignorant of law and procedure and in some cases may have difficulty with reading and writing;
- may have no experience of advocacy;
- may lack objectivity;
- may lack the ability to cross-examine or test evidence;
- may not grasp the true issues of a case;
- may have difficulty in marshalling facts;
- may fail to understand court orders or directions, or their obligations to comply with pre-hearing directions;
- may not appreciate the importance of documentary or photographic evidence, or the duty to disclose documents;
- may misunderstand the purpose of a hearing;
- may need court papers to be translated if English is not their first language;
- are unlikely to have ready access to legal textbooks or libraries.

At the hearing, the judge should explain to an unrepresented party:

- who he or she is and how he or she should be addressed;
- who everybody else is, and their respective functions;
- that the unrepresented party should tell the judge immediately he or she does not understand something;
- the purpose of the hearing and the issue which is to be decided;
- the rule that only one person at a time may speak and that each side will have a full opportunity to present its case;
- that a party may take notes (but not tape-recordings);
- that if the unrepresented party would like a short break in the proceedings, he or she has only to ask;
- that the issue is decided on the evidence, documented and oral, before the court and nothing else.

b.   Cross-examination by the defendant

Throughout a trial, a judge must be ready to assist a claimant or defendant in the conduct of his or her case, particularly when they are examining or cross-examining witnesses and giving evidence. The judge should always ask whether they wish to call any witnesses, and should be ready to restrain any unnecessary, intimidating or humiliating cross-examination by an unrepresented defendant.

In criminal cases, for certain offences of assault, child cruelty or of a sexual nature, the Youth Justice and Criminal Evidence Act 1999 prohibits unrepresented defendants from cross-examining adult witnesses and child witnesses. The Act also gives courts the discretion to forbid such cross-examination in other types of case.

After the hearing, unrepresented parties often do not understand the outcome of the case or the reasons for it, especially if they have lost. A judge should always set out clearly the reasons for the decision.

The judge should also explain the requirement to seek permission to appeal, if appropriate, and should tell the unrepresented party to consider his or her rights of appeal, but explain that the court cannot give any advice as to the exercise of those rights.

5.   Children in court

The appearance in court of a child or young person — as victim, witness or defendant — requires particular procedures to be followed. A significant number of vulnerable witnesses are children, and there are various initiatives to protect them — it is important for the judge to be conversant with these facilities. The testimony of the child must be adduced as effectively and fairly as possible. The judge must be satisfied as to the child's competence; this issue should be dealt with as early as possible in proceedings. Under the Youth Justice and Criminal Evidence Act 1999, a lack of competence in a witness is described as an inability to understand questions or to give answers which can be understood. Any hearing to determine competence shall be in the presence of the jury and may include expert evidence. A judge should be aware of the sort of stresses and worries affecting a child in court.

'Adolescent witnesses are more likely to exhibit adverse psychological reactions to the stress of appearing in court than younger ones.'

These may include fear of the unknown, fear of retaliation or publicity, pressure to withdraw a complaint, fear of having to relate personal details before strangers, fear of having to see the defendant or of being sent to prison, or feelings of guilt connected with family breakdown. Adolescent witnesses are more likely to exhibit adverse psychological reactions to the stress of appearing in court than younger ones. At trial, it is very important for the judge to give the child directions on:

- the need to tell the truth;
- the importance of leaving nothing out when answering questions;
- the need to say so if the child does not understand a question;
- the importance of not guessing the answers to questions;
- the need to tell the judge if the child has any problem of any sort at any time during the hearing.

Judges should ensure that advocates do not attempt over-vigorous cross-examination, and that they use language which is free of jargon and which is appropriate to the age of the child. Judicial vigilance is always necessary.

a.   Special measures and children's evidence

The Criminal Justice Acts of 1988 and 1991 allowed children's evidence to be given via live TV link and later by previously recorded video. Provision for children's evidence to be given in special ways extends back to the Children and Young Persons Act 1933. The Youth Justice and Criminal Evidence Act 1999 has introduced further measures, which extend to children and young persons, as well as witnesses who are suffering from mental or physical disorders or whose evidence is likely to be impaired by reason of fear or distress:

- witnesses may be shielded by screens;
- the court can be cleared so that evidence may be given in private;

- evidence-in-chief, cross-examination and re-examination may all be carried out by video-recordings;
- evidence may be given through an intermediary, who may also explain questions and answers to and from the witness, to enable them to be understood;
- the court can make available any device to aid communication with a witness suffering from any disability.

A judge conducting a trial involving a video recording of an earlier interview should be thoroughly conversant with the Home Office Memorandum of Good Practice on Video Recorded Interviews with Child Witnesses for Criminal Proceedings, which provides guidance on how to conduct such interviews with children, including how to confine their answers to comply with the law of evidence.

The *Memorandum* is of principal relevance to criminal proceedings, although its guidance is also of use in civil and family proceedings.

The judge has absolute discretion as to whether or how to admit the evidence of children. The first question must be the potential relevance of what the child may have to say. Much will also depend on the age of the child and the nature of the case.

6. Gender

There have been many positive changes in society regarding gender roles. Law-makers and law-enforcers have in the past, however, mostly been men and a male outlook can still prevail. The disadvantages that women can suffer range from inadequate recognition of their contribution to the home or society to an underestimation of the problems women face as a result of gender bias.

> - 67 per cent of women are employed, as opposed to 78 per cent of men.
> - women's employment is more likely to be casual or part-time.
> - 60 per cent of all primary carers for another adult are women.

Despite the increasing number of women in the workforce, they remain primarily responsible for unpaid domestic duties. The economic contribution of such labour can be undervalued, resulting in disadvantageous assessments of damages and liability in civil actions, including the settlement of property claims.

In court, women can feel patronised and disbelieved as witnesses. A recent Home Office survey revealed that significant (most often disadvantageous) stereotyping exists in the manner in which women are sentenced. Sexual complainants, and those complaining of sexual harassment in discrimination cases, can suffer when there is unnecessarily over- rigorous cross-examination regarding their previous sexual history, or where the assailant is known to them.

7. Domestic violence

Research commissioned by the Northern Ireland Office shows two out of every five serious assaults on women involve a current or former partner. Violent behaviour is often a means of coercion, control and reinforcement of power over the other partner in a relationship. The difficulty always stems from the fact that until allegations are proven, they remain as such.

> - two women are killed every week by their current or former partners.
> - domestic violence accounts for 25 per cent of all violent crime.
> - one in four women experience domestic violence, which can escalate during pregnancy or when a woman attempts to leave her violent partner.

Recent guidance encourages the Crown Prosecution Service and courts to take into account the paramount need to ensure the safety of the woman and any children of the household, in particular by ensuring that their whereabouts are not revealed. When granting bail or an injunction, other factors to take into account are: any history of violence in the relationship, the seriousness of the allegations, the victim's injuries, the use of any weapon and whether the attack was planned, whether any subsequent threats have been made, and the effect on any children.

'Between a third and a half of all perpetrators of domestic violence also physically abuse children in their care.'

When appearing in court, there are analogies to be drawn with vulnerable witnesses, such as the possibility of intimidation, the need for escort to and from court, and the presence of supporters in court. Other specific measures should be considered, such as providing screens in court, allowing the giving evidence by television link and the video-recording of testimony. The consequences of leaving the perpetrator of the violence alone with the woman in any part of the building should be considered most sensitively. Domestic violence, particularly that occurring over a long period of time, can affect the ability to give coherent testimony. Much depends upon the quality of legal advice received, and whether there are innovative procedures in place, such as the use of Polaroid cameras in police stations.

An apparent inability to change or leave a violent situation should not be interpreted as an acceptance of the violence, so as to render the woman responsible for the violence, or serve to undermine a woman's credibility.

Between a third and a half of all perpetrators of domestic violence also physically abuse children in their care. The effect of domestic violence upon children might include post-traumatic anxieties such as depression, anxiety, behavioural problems, and other psychosomatic symptoms. Readers are referred to Section 5 of the Report to the Lord Chancellor on the question of parental contact in cases where there is domestic violence, which contains guidelines for good practice in such cases, and can be found at www.lcd.gov.uk/family/abflmfr.htm.

8.   Sexual orientation

There is a historical background of widespread discrimination against homosexuals. Verbal abuse and physical violence are not infrequently directed against homosexuals, and discrimination in the workplace is not uncommon. Perceptions of prejudice by the gay and lesbian community extend to their experiences in court. There is no evidence that homosexuality implies a propensity to commit crime, nor is there an established link with paedophile orientation. Judicial decision-makers need to be aware of the harm done to people, and to the reputation of the judicial system, by such stereotypical assumptions.

The Human Rights Act 1998 raises a number of issues relating to the equal treatment of homosexuals and lesbians, most particularly whether the respect for family life under Article 8 includes homosexual couples. It will certainly be argued that the employees of public authorities cannot be dismissed on the grounds of sexuality, and this is likely to have implications both for the private sector and for the Employment Tribunal.

Concerns about undermining the institution of marriage assume that to promote the rights of one category of citizen necessarily undermines those of another. That argument would seem curious if applied to the rights of women versus men, or to the rights of a racial minority versus the majority.

Families that do not strictly conform to the traditional model are an increasingly common social reality. There is no evidence that children are excessively teased because their parents are unmarried, or even because their parents are gay. Indeed, such children do equally well as those brought up by heterosexual parents in terms of emotional wellbeing, sexual responsibility, academic achievement and avoidance of crime.

It is misguided to:

- attribute feminine characteristics to gay men, or masculine characteristics to lesbians;
- make any assumptions as to the sexual orientation of transvestites or transsexuals. Where there is a question relating to a person's gender, the person should be asked what gender they consider themselves to be, and what gender they would prefer to be treated as;
- assume that AIDS and HIV positive status are necessarily indicative of homosexual activity.

3.4 Sources of useful information

3.4.1 The Bar Council: Equal opportunities

Equal opportunities at the Bar is directed by four Bar Council committees: the race relations committee set up in 1984, the sex discrimination committee set up in 1992 and the disability committee set up in 1991. Their work is co-ordinated by the equal opportunities committee on which the Chairman of the Bar sits, which was set up in 1998.

The equal opportunity officers are based at 3 Bedford Row (tel: 020 7242 0082, email: equalopps2@barcouncil.org.uk). If you wish to speak to an equal opportunities officer in confidence there is a confidential line (tel: 020 7242 0768). Their role is to provide guidance on any equal opportunities or discrimination matters to chambers wishing to improve their equal opportunity practice, to barristers with equal opportunity problems or queries, Practice Managers, clerks, pupils, BVC or law students. They work independently of all other Bar Council departments and report to the chief executive.

3.4.2 Other support groups at the Bar

South East Circuit Minorities Committee
Elpha Lecointe
Coram Chambers
Ground Floor
4 Brick Court
Temple
London EC4Y 9AD
Tel: 020 7797 7766
Fax: 020 7797 7700
Email: mail@coramchambers.co.uk

Association of Muslim Lawyers (AML)
PO Box 148
High Wycombe
Bucks HP13 5WY
Email: sofbash@aol.com
Website: www.aml.org.uk

Association of Women Barristers (AWB)
Frances Burton (Chairperson)
Ground Floor
10 Old Square
Lincoln's Inn
London   WC2A 3SU
Email: francesburton@dial.pipex.com / frances.burton@uwe.ac.uk
Tel: 07775 655088

Vicky Milner (Vice-Chairperson)
MOD Legal Team
Metropole Building
Northumberland Avenue
London WC2N 5BL
Email: LA7@mod.gsi.gov.uk
Tel: 020 7218 9423

Administration postal address:
Association of Women Barristers
c/o 3 Bedford Row
London WC1R 4DB
Email: awbeditor@aol.com
Website: www.womenbarristers.co.uk

Bar Lesbian and Gay Group (BLAGG)
Damien Lochrane
3 Pump Court
Temple
London EC4Y 7AJ
Tel: 020 7353 1315
Email: blagg_uk@yahoo.co.uk

Society of Asian Lawyers (SAL)
Ali Zaidi
c/o Edwin Coe (Solicitors)
2 Stone Buildings
Lincoln's Inn
London WC2A 3TH
Tel: 07766 600526
Email: ali.zaidi@edwincoe.com
Website: www.societyofasianlawyers.com

Society of Black Lawyers (SBL)
Umair Abiden (Administrative Officer)
Room 9, Winchester House
First Floor
11 Cranmer Road
Kennington Park
London SW9 6EJ
Tel: 020 7735 6592
Fax: 020 7820 1389
Email: national-office@sbl-hq.freeserve.co.uk

3.5 Conclusion

The obligations of lawyers to help protect individuals and groups from the abuse of public and private power, has been identified by ACLEC as the 'ethical challenge'. The guidance set out in this chapter will help you to meet that obligation. However, unless you are prepared to seek guidance, if necessary, to understand the views, beliefs and customs of all those who appear before the courts, you will risk individuals through their legal experiences, believing that justice and fair treatment are not options for them. You must therefore remember the advice set out in the JSB guidance on 'Race and the courts' that, 'the responsibility for ensuring equality and fairness of treatment rests on everyone involved in the administration of justice'. You are shortly to become part of this system, embracing this important aspect of your professional conduct is crucial if you are to gain the respect of all individuals you come into contact with at the Bar today and generate the necessary trust and confidence of all sections of the community.

4

The letter and spirit of the Code

4.1 The lawyer joke

A layperson, an accountant and a lawyer were all asked: 'What do two and two make?'
The layperson replied: 'Four, of course.'
The accountant replied: 'Four — or five.'
The lawyer replied: 'What do you want it to make?'

Lawyers are the butt of many jokes, many of which flow from a perception that lawyers are capable of acting quite unethically in pursuit of their client's interests. While this perception has, fortunately, never developed in the UK to the extent that it has in the USA, the characteristics of practice in common law jurisdictions exposes lawyers to many ethical dilemmas, and responses to these vary. This chapter (and indeed this Manual) will provide you with some answers, but in other areas it will simply provide you with a framework within which you will still have to make your own decisions. In these cases it should provide you with tools and ideas which may help you to arrive at conclusions which satisfy the ethical demands of practice.

The issues have been neatly presented by Ross Cranston:

An important policy issue is the extent to which the Code of Conduct ought to be infused by wider ethical notions. There are two aspects to this. One is encapsulated in the question: 'Can a good lawyer be a bad person?'. In other words, are the standards in the Code of Conduct untenable when laid alongside ethical thought or common morality? The second aspect is that if there is a discrepancy between the Code of Conduct and secular ethical thought, what is special about barristers that exempts them from the precepts of the latter? To put it another way, how is it that barristers can decide ethically on a course of action for a client which is different from that which they would adopt for themselves?

(Cranston, R (ed): *Legal Ethics and Professional Responsibility* (Oxford, Clarendon 1996) at p 5)

4.2 The Code of Conduct

The Bar Code of Conduct provides you with the rules and standards that should inform all aspects of your practice at the Bar. It looks, at first sight, very much like a statute and this recognition should lead you to approach it with respect, but also to consider carefully how you should use it. It is not a statute, but a Code of Conduct.

There is a risk that, if the Code is perceived as essentially like any other piece of legislation, you will approach it in the same way. Why should this be a problem? It stems from the underlying principle within UK substantive law that all actions are permitted unless they are forbidden. Thus Acts that regulate behaviour are to be construed in a restrictive manner and loopholes may properly be exploited.

For example, the Theft Act 1968, s 9 provides:

(1) A person is guilty of burglary if:
    (a) he enters any building or part of a building as a trespasser and with intent to steal anything in the building or part of a building in question, to inflict on any person in it any grievous bodily harm or to rape any woman in it, or to do unlawful damage to the building or anything in it; or
    (b) having entered any building or part of a building as a trespasser, he steals or attempts to steal anything in the building or that part of it or inflicts or attempts to inflict on any person in it any grievous bodily harm.

Your client has entered a building as a trespasser but with no particular intention, and, once inside decides to do unlawful damage to property within the building. Your advice to him should be to plead not guilty to a charge of burglary. This is because his actions fall within neither paragraph of the subsection even though his actions have produced the same result as behaviour which would lead to guilt (had he formed the intention to cause the damage before, rather than after entering the building). This conclusion may be hard for a layperson to understand but would be natural to any lawyer versed in statutory interpretation.

To adopt the same approach to following the Code may enable you to avoid successful disciplinary proceedings by the Bar Council. In other words, in so far as it acts in an analogous manner to a criminal statute, the Code may be treated in the same way. However, to approach the Code in this way could carry dangers for the reputation of the profession. Your interpretation of the Code should be informed by ethical values and where the Code permits a variety of responses your choice between them should be similarly informed.

An example of how the Code regulates your professional response arises from para 704:

704 A barrister must not devise facts which will assist in advancing the lay client's case and must not draft any statement of case, witness statement, affidavit, notice of appeal or other document containing:

...

    (c) any allegation of fraud unless he has clear instructions to make such allegation and has before him reasonably credible material which as it stands establishes a prima facie case of fraud; ...

The concept of 'reasonably credible material' inherently carries a degree of subjectivity. Suppose that you have been instructed by your lay client that the opponent has been perpetrating a fraud. It is not uncommon for hostility between the parties to lead to all sorts of allegations which are discovered later to be impossible of formal proof. That being the case it would be unwise to incorporate such an allegation into any draft on the client's assertion alone. What, however, if the client (who has behaved in a temperate manner throughout) tells you that the opposing party has admitted to committing fraud, but no other independent evidence is available? What if, in addition, the client is prepared to make a statement of truth in respect of this allegation? Would such a statement be 'reasonably credible material' given that it is in essence no more than the original assertion presented formally in a way which is admissible in court? Should you still insist on some independent evidence?

In practical terms you would doubtless advise your professional client to seek independent evidence to corroborate your lay client's oral evidence before settling a statement of case which contained an allegation of fraud. If it is not forthcoming, should you pursue the allegation? The only guidance the Code offers is that the material must be credible and establish a *prima facie* case. The assertion of an intemperate client would clearly be inadequate (it is the mischief the rule is designed to avoid). To rely on a statement of truth may be sufficient to avoid a finding of misconduct (although if there were no other evidence the client should be advised of the dangers of pressing the matter in court: a wasted costs order may loom). However, to refuse to incorporate such an allegation in those circumstances will upset your client, and is likely to upset them more if the allegations are in fact well-founded. You must not let your independence be compromised (para 307(a) and (c)) yet you should act on your client's behalf (para 303(a)).

Note that the House of Lords decision in *Medcalf v Weatherill and another* [2002] 3 WLR 172 (for details see **7.5.4.2**) while addressing this area, does not resolve this issue. If you check the specific guidance on this matter on the Bar Council website you will find:

The Professional Standards Committee (PSC) takes the view that there is no litmus test for determining whether it is proper to allege fraud. As Lord Bingham made clear: 'Council is bound to exercise an objective professional judgment whether it is in all circumstances proper to lend his name to the allegation'. That decision will depend on the individual facts of each case.

It should be noted that although paragraph 704 refers specifically to fraud, the same principle would apply to any other allegation of serious misconduct.

No doubt you should err on the side of caution and advise that further evidence should be obtained if possible, but it may not be available. Moreover, if, after settling the statement of case, it becomes clear that there is no credible evidence of fraud (for example, the opposing party may have made the admission to provoke a reaction or as an act of bravado) or if other facts come to light showing that the allegation of fraud has no prospect of success, you will no doubt recognise that the fraud allegation should no longer be pursued. It is submitted that the proper approach is not to seek a 'way around' the provisions of the Code, but to consider underlying values, so that your response is likely to assist to maintain the Bar's reputation as a thoroughly ethical profession. Fortunately, problems as awkward as this should not be a daily occurrence, and you should remember that advice will be available from your Head of Chambers or from the Bar Council. (The Professional Conduct Hotline is 020 7242 0082).

An understanding of the underpinning values will give you a basis for deciding ethical questions beyond what the Code provides. Remember that behaviour prohibited by the Code is not made acceptable by a contrary underpinning value, but an underpinning value might validate conduct upon which the Code is silent or in circumstances which generate conflict between its provisions. Ultimately, where, having thought through matters in this degree of depth, you remain uncertain as to the proper way of proceeding, you should contact the Bar Council hotline available for advice in emergencies.

4.3 Underpinning values

Here is a number of values which may be said to underpin the Code of Practice. It is not intended to be exhaustive.

- Justice.
- Respect for the law.
- Client autonomy.
- Confidentiality.
- Honesty.

4.3.1 Conflict in underpinning values

Conflict between values is inherent in legal practice. Lord Reid makes this clear in his opinion in *Rondel v Worsley* [1969] 1 AC 191, 227:

Every counsel has a duty to his client fearlessly to raise every issue, advance every argument and ask every question, however distasteful, which he thinks will help his client's case. But, as an officer of the court concerned with the administration of justice, he has an overriding duty to the court, to the standards of his profession, and to the public, which may and often does lead to a conflict with his client's wishes or what the client thinks are his personal wishes.

Consider a concrete situation. If your client in a criminal matter has provided you with information which is relevant (but adverse) to your case you will be faced with a conflict between maintaining confidentiality and not misleading the court. A perusal of the Code will throw up relevant provisions.

104   The general purpose of this Code is to provide the requirements for practice as a barrister and the rules and standards of conduct applicable to barristers which are appropriate in the interests of justice and in particular:

(a) in relation to barristers in independent practice to provide common and enforceable rules and standards which require them:

(i) to be completely independent in conduct and in professional standing as sole practitioners;

(ii) to act only as consultants instructed by solicitors and other approved persons;

(iii) to acknowledge a public obligation based on the paramount need for access to justice to act for any client in cases within their field of practice ...

301   A barrister must have regard to paragraph 104 and must not:

(a) engage in conduct whether in pursuit of his profession or otherwise which is:

(i) dishonest or otherwise discreditable to a barrister;

(ii) prejudicial to the administration of justice; or

(iii) likely to diminish public confidence in the legal profession or the administration of justice or otherwise bring the legal profession into disrepute ...

302   A barrister has an overriding duty to the Court to act with independence in the interests of justice: he must assist the Court in the administration of justice and must not deceive or knowingly or recklessly mislead the Court.

702   Whether or not the relation of counsel and client continues a barrister must preserve the confidentiality of the lay client's affairs and must not without the prior consent of the lay client or as permitted by law lend or reveal the contents of the papers in any instructions to or communicate to any third person (other than another barrister, a pupil or any other person who needs to know it for the performance of their duties) information which has been entrusted to him in confidence or use such information to the lay client's detriment or to his own or another client's advantage.

708   A barrister when conducting proceedings in Court: ...

(e) must not adduce evidence obtained otherwise than from or through the client or devise facts which will assist in advancing the lay client's case ...

These rules are helpful in identifying what is expected in relation to each of the underlying values. However, they provide little guidance as to how conflicts should be resolved. In fact, the conflict identified occurs so regularly in practice that a proper way of responding is well-established. You will not necessarily be required to withdraw unless your client wishes you to present information you now know to be incorrect. Your precise duties will depend on the nature of the information being withheld. This may range from a full confession to dishonesty in obtaining public funding or an indication of past offences of which the prosecution appears to be unaware. You will find detailed guidance as to how to respond ethically to these different situations at **7.2** below.

Note that further guidance on the preparation of witness statements is available on the Bar Council website. This is expressly described as applying to civil matters only as barristers do not draft witness statements in criminal cases. Thus you should note that striking a balance between different values might produce different results in the criminal and the civil context.

This itself throws up an important value, associated with client autonomy and justice. Our adversarial system of justice requires as close as possible an approach to equality of arms. The assumption is that representation by competent and qualified lawyers achieves that equality. In a civil matter the parties are to some extent equal (although one may be able to spend more money than the other in preparing the case). In a criminal matter, however, it is normal to find individuals (often impecunious and possibly facing loss of liberty) with all the forces and resources of a powerful state arranged against them. This goes some way to explaining:

- the cab rank rule, which requires a barrister to accept any case which is within his competence and ability to undertake (there are exceptions — see Part VI of the Code), and

- the lesser expectations to disclose adverse factual information in criminal, as opposed to civil matters (given that the task is for the prosecution to prove the case, not for the defendant to prove his innocence).

So your response to a clash of underlying values may need to differ depending on the context.

You may find yourself in a situation where you face such a clash of values or where you are challenged by a client holding different values to your own. Consider the following situations.

EXAMPLE

What if my client is impecunious and facing a wealthy opponent?

For example, you are acting *pro bono* for an unemployed client who claims to have been unfairly dismissed for fighting at work. Your professional client instructs you to contact the respondent's lawyers in order to seek a settlement. The evidence from a number of witnesses and from personnel records suggests that your client had, indeed, been fighting, had done so on many occasions, and was only dismissed after proper warnings had been given. In conference, however, your client continues to deny the allegation while offering no explanation for the evidence against him. You are confident that should the matter proceed to trial your client will lose. You are, however, aware that many cases can result in a technical finding of unfair dismissal for procedural failings, even if the compensation in such cases is likely to be minimal. Your lay client has indicated that he is willing to accept £2,000 in settlement. You recognise, moreover, that for the employer to defend the claim, should you make many demands on them for disclosure or further questions, will cost them over £2,000.

Should you contact the employer, pointing out that the hearing will be a long one and that you will be requiring considerable disclosure of documents and answers to detailed questions about personnel practices in the firm, suggesting that your client will withdraw the case if they pay £2,000 in settlement? To do so would promote the value of client autonomy and (by subverting the normal consequences of inequalities in wealth) promote a particular view of social justice.

Should you, instead, avoid putting that pressure on the employer when negotiating, recognising that it might make it less likely that the employer will settle for £2,000? To do so would promote the values of respect for the law and a particular (but different) perception of justice.

The Code does not prevent either course, provided you are acting on your client's instructions after giving proper advice. This is thus one example where your own values may have an impact on your choice of whether to use the 'we'll make this expensive for you' tactic.

What if my client is seeking to achieve, by instructing me, a goal which I regard as immoral?

For example, your clients, who are a couple seeking to have an exceptionally bright child, wish to carry out genetic checks to screen out any foetuses which appear not to be intelligent. You feel strongly that this is an abuse of the genetic research which has been done. Although the motive appears to be one which is forbidden under the relevant legislation you understand that similar checks (which are permitted) can indirectly provide information which would enable them to screen for intelligence.

Should you simply advise them that their proposed course of action would contravene the law and that they should not therefore attempt to pursue it? To do so may promote the value of (your particular view of) morality. This itself will be based on a value such as the integrity of the individual (in this case the unconceived child).

Should you, instead, indicate how they might achieve their goal without technically breaking the law? To do so would promote the value of client autonomy.

When considering the propriety of your response you must remember that your duty is to act for your client and you should not make moral judgements about your client's actions. You should also consider what your client needs to know in order to make a properly informed decision. These principles are addressed in the Code and clearly prioritise the value of client autonomy.

What if my client is seeking to achieve, by instructing me, a goal which involves a breach of the law?

For example, you are instructed by solicitors to advise a corporate client which wishes to reduce some of its production costs. The proposed savings will increase the risk of a release of toxic chemicals into a river. Such a release will constitute a breach of regulations designed to protect the environment and expose the client company to the risk of fines. However, you are aware that the local authority with responsibility for enforcing those regulations is extremely short of finance and is unable to make regular checks. A minor release is therefore unlikely to be noticed.

Should your advice be to explain the legal situation and simply point out that the proposed cost reductions place the company at risk of breach of illegal action for which they might suffer a penalty? To do so may promote the value of respect for the law.

Should your advice extend to your assessment of the very small risk of discovery? To do so may promote the value of client autonomy.

Does the principle indicated in the previous example (that you should not make moral judgements about your client's actions) apply equally here, when the proposed action involves your client committing a criminal offence? The Code indicates that you must do nothing dishonest or bring the profession into disrepute. Incitement to break the law clearly falls within that concept. You can therefore protect yourself from breach of the Code by giving clear advice not to break the law. However you may be doing that in the realistic knowledge that your client may well ignore you and break the law. Note that if this has occurred to you it is probably your own sensitivity to ethical issues that alerts you to the risk that this may have the effect of indirectly inciting a breach of the law.

You will see that none of these three examples produce a single, clearly correct answer. Regrettably, this may well arise in practice. I have my personal preferences as to the most appropriate response, but you may well take a different view. Any such difference will flow in part from the personal values that you or I espouse. For this reason we need to be aware of those values and how they impact on our responses when faced with ethical dilemmas (as we undoubtedly will be). At the same time it is important that we remember that we must not apply our personal values unrestrained. As barristers we are bound by the Code and that recognition may assist when you are faced with a conflict of potentially-applicable values. You cannot justify a departure from the clear requirements of the Code by pleading an inconsistent personal value, no matter how strongly you espouse it.

4.4 Role morality

One concept which may assist in resolving conflicts of this sort is that of role morality. A lawyer may be required to do something for a client which she could not morally justify doing for herself. That proposition may initially appear to be wrong, or at least counter-intuitive. However, it is explained to a degree by the recognition that the basis of litigation in the UK is adversarialism. The lawyer is the skilled partisan advocate of the client and is (in theory) opposed by a similarly skilled partisan advocate for the opponent. The neutral decision-maker is neither lawyer but the tribunal.

This concept only works if the lawyer is genuinely partisan and the parties are equitably resourced. A client whose lawyer adopts a neutral role will be severely disadvantaged if opposed by a client whose lawyer adopts a partisan approach. In order to shoulder this burden properly lawyers may well have to seek to achieve conclusions of which they disapprove, or carry out actions which they would not carry out on their own behalf. To justify this, many have introduced the idea of 'role morality'. This concept prioritises the value of client autonomy and is the source of the cab-rank rule (see Code, para 601). Many lawyers regard it as enabling them to do for their clients what they would not do for themselves.

It may have surprising consequences. As Boon and Levin point out:

Paradoxically, whilst lawyers are expected to act co-operatively, altruistically and ethically when dealing *with* their clients, they are expected to be unco-operative, selfish and possibly unethical in pursuing the objectives *of* their clients, assuming that this is what the client wishes. This creates considerable moral strain.

(Boon, A and Levin, J, *The Ethics and Conduct of Lawyers in England and Wales* (Oxford, Hart 1999) at 165)

That moral strain will alert you to the fact that while the concept of role morality may justify your doing for your client what you would not do for yourself, it does not give you guidance as to how far you can go. Take an example.

> It may well be that if you clearly owed a debt you would not take advantage of the limitation provisions to evade it. However, would you apply the same moral judgement if it were your client who owed the debt? Suppose, for example, your client is very short of money and had forgotten the debt, which is owed to a large corporation? Suppose, instead, your client is the large corporation and the person owed the debt is impecunious?

Your view may be identical in those two situations or you may regard their relative wealth as a key issue. That is a matter for you. However, identifying the issue should make it clear that role morality, while potentially justifying actions which you would feel uncomfortable about on your own behalf, does not resolve questions about whether a particular course of action is ethically acceptable. For that, once again, you need to follow the Code and, where necessary, consider your underlying values.

The underpinning principle here is client autonomy. The Code permits you to do whatever your client wants provided that it is not illegal, you are not dishonest and you give the court the full benefit of your knowledge of the law, whether helpful to your case or not. Equally, you must provide your client with advice that helps them to take an informed decision as to whether to pursue a case or not. It would be improper (as with the second example at **4.3.1**) to prioritise your views over those of your client. There is nothing to stop you identifying ethical considerations to your client, but the decision must remain theirs.

The adversarial nature of the UK legal system may be some justification for a barrister behaving differently in professional and personal contexts, but it also carries its own limits to professional behaviour. Because (unlike in an inquisitorial system) the court does not have the resources to explore the truth for itself, it relies on the honesty of advocates and their ability to research the law fully. This is the source of the requirements not to mislead the court and to cite authorities that go against your client's interests. This should identify two insights:

(a) A claim to role morality does not justify all behaviour. A balance between conflicting values must still be maintained. This is clear from the Marre Report (para 6.1):

> The client is frequently acting under physical, emotional or financial difficulties and may well wish to take every step he can, whether legal or extra-legal, to gain advantage over the other party. In this situation the lawyer has a special duty and responsibility to advise his client as to the legal and ethical standards which should be observed and not to participate in any deception or sharp practice.

(Lady Marre, CBE, *A Time for Change: Report of the Committee on the Future of the Legal Profession* (General Council of the Bar and Council of the Law Society, London 1998))

This is helpful guidance, but leaves much to the individual lawyer.

(b) No advocate will be able to meet the standards expected unless the requisite knowledge, understanding and skills have been mastered. The knowledge, understanding and skills that you have acquired in your undergraduate study and which you are now developing on your Bar Vocational Course are central to your effectively meeting the demands of an adversarial system. Competence itself is an ethical issue.

For further discussions of role morality, see Boon, A and Levin, J, *The Ethics and Conduct of Lawyers in England and Wales* (Oxford, Hart 1999) at 195–198 and Nicolson, D and Webb, J, *Professional Ethics: Critical Interrogations* (Oxford, OUP 1999) at 169–171.

4.5 Ethical behaviour and self-interest

It is often said that ethical behaviour is in the individual lawyer's best interest because 'the Bar is a small profession and your reputation will quickly get around'. Barely hidden behind this assertion is the suggestion that if you acquire a reputation for poor ethical standards opponents will not trust you and you will find it increasingly difficult to meet your clients' needs. This may be true. However, it is important to recognise that ethics and self-interest should not be equated.

Some help may be available from the recognition that taking a long-term view of self-interest is highly likely to be an ethically safer approach than taking a short-term view. Thus, an approach which ensures that you have a reputation for honesty is likely to enable you to represent many future clients in negotiation. It is also therefore likely to enhance your long-term income. Willingness to deceive an opponent may achieve something your current client values but will inhibit your ability to come to desirable solutions for future clients. Not only would this inhibit long-term income, it would involve a breach of the Code (para 301(a)).

One other aspect of self-interest is worth addressing here. You have an interest in your profession continuing to be perceived as in good ethical standing. If you comply with the provisions of the Code this will preserve you from the risk of disciplinary proceedings. However, where the Code provides a framework within which different courses of action are permitted you should be alert to maintain the highest possible ethical standards.

This insight helps us to identify those aspects of self-interest which will assist us to maintain high ethical standards, but relying on self-interest is altogether insufficient. It ignores most of the underpinning values which we have identified earlier and leaves the individual lawyer without ethical guidance. Thus it remains necessary to comply with the requirements of the Code and to consider its underpinning values in those situations where conflicts nevertheless arise.

4.6 The lawyer joke again

So which of the three was acting most ethically? I have no problem with the layperson's response and am sufficiently ignorant to accept that there may be justification for the accountant's response. However, to judge the lawyer I need to go back to my core values again. If I prioritise client autonomy this lawyer may be responding perfectly correctly. There are few situations in reality where one simple answer is the only one available. The lawyer here is seeking the client's instructions as to what the desired outcome is. It may be that that outcome is not legally available, in which case the lawyer should advise the client to that effect. It may be readily available, in which case the lawyer is in the fortunate position of giving the client good news. It is just as likely, however, that the answer is somewhere between the two. How far should you go to achieve the client's desired result? That is a matter of your professional responsibility. The Code of Conduct is your guide ('a barrister must not ... compromise his professional standards in order to please his client the Court or a third party' — Code, para 307(c)) which makes it clear that you should never allow your personal values to override the requirements of the Code. Within the boundaries provided by the Code, however, the final decision is yours.

Court etiquette

5.1 Introduction

Each time you appear in court you are on a public stage, in full view of the judge, the client and, usually, the public at large. How you appear and conduct yourself in front of that audience is of great importance if you are to do the job of a barrister properly. If you are discourteous, inappropriately dressed or do not behave in the way that you ought to, you risk alienating the tribunal you are seeking to persuade. Remember that as a barrister you are always appearing on behalf of someone other than yourself: unfavourable views formed about you by the tribunal because of an unprofessional manner may rebound onto your client. Some of the requirements of the etiquette that you must observe are to be found in written sources, such as the Code of Conduct, or the occasional Practice Direction (e.g, *Practice Direction (Court Dress) (No. 2)* [1995] 1 WLR 648), but others have been established through custom, tradition and commonsense.

5.2 Courtesy

It should go without saying that in every sphere of practice you ought to be courteous, and this is reinforced by the Code of Conduct, which states '[a] barrister must at all times be courteous to the Court and to all those with whom he has professional dealings' (para 5.5 of the Written Standards for the Conduct of Professional Work in Section 3, Miscellaneous Guidance). You are, of course, required by the Code of Conduct to '... promote and protect fearlessly and by all proper and lawful means the client's best interests and do so without regard to [your] own interests or to any consequences to [yourself] or to any other person ...' (para 303(a)), but this does not give you *carte blanche* to be as rude as you like to judges, witnesses or your opposing counsel. Ultimately, discourtesy by counsel in court could amount to a contempt.

5.3 Dress in court

The Code of Conduct requires that '... a barrister's personal appearance should be decorous, and his dress, when robes are worn, should be compatible with them.' (para 5.12 of the Written Standards for the Conduct of Professional Work in Section 3, Miscellaneous

Guidance). In practice, this means that you should dress conservatively. A courtroom is not the place to make an individual fashion statement: you may like wearing paisley waistcoats and bright orange socks, but save that for your own time. As a barrister you are a professional: dress like one. Dressing conservatively means, amongst other things:

(a) Men should wear a suit (the traditional black jacket and grey striped trousers is an alternative, although less common now amongst younger members of the Bar). Do not wear blazers or linen jackets in court, even in hot weather. Either single or double breasted suits are acceptable, but a waistcoat should be worn if the former is chosen. Suits and dresses should be dark in colour, ie, black, dark navy or grey, and of a traditional cut. In May 1995 the then Lord Chief Justice, Lord Taylor of Gosforth, decided that it was perfectly acceptable for women to wear trousers when appearing in court.

(b) Dresses or blouses should be long sleeved and high to the neck, even in warmer weather.

(c) Shirts or blouses should be predominantly white; collars should be white. For men (when robes are worn) a separate wing collar is the norm: avoid, as has been seen in court, a dress evening shirt.

(d) Shoes should be black; avoid wearing boots in court.

(e) Jewellery should be discreet: avoid studs and rings through places other than ears. Men should avoid wearing an ear-ring in court.

(f) When a wig is worn, wear it so that it covers your hair as far as possible; avoid fringes showing at the front, and keep long hair neatly tied back.

The Professional Conduct Committee of the Bar Council has been asked about the propriety of a barrister who customarily wears a turban to do so in place of a wig. The Committee was of the view that such matters were properly determined by the court concerned rather than the committee itself. However, it expressed the view that it is entirely reasonable for a barrister who customarily wears a turban to do so in court in place of a wig.

5.4 Robes

For counsel, being robed means wearing wig, gown, and bands. You will be robed when you appear in open court in County Courts, the Crown Court, the High Court, the Court of Appeal, and the House of Lords.

It is unnecessary to robe when you appear before a judge in private, or generally in chambers or before a magistrates' court, tribunal or arbitrators.

It is generally unnecessary to robe when you appear before a Master or district judge, whether sitting in open court or in private. If, however, the district judge is sitting in robes in open court it is desirable that you also appear robed. For this reason it is always advisable, though rather inconvenient, to take your robes to court in case the district judge before whom you are appearing on a private matter chooses to take the matter robed and in open court.

Always turn up to your chambers prepared to appear in court in robes, even if you were planning a day on papers, ie, wear a suit, have your robes with you and a collarless shirt to hand. It is not at all unusual for you to arrive at chambers to be told by your clerk that you are in open court on an urgent matter, when you thought you were going to have a paper-work day!

5.5 Customs

Much of court etiquette is derived from custom. Some of the more common customs are:

(a) Do not move or speak whilst a witness is being sworn; you should stay completely still and silent whilst this is being done, even if you are not involved in the case.

(b) Do not enter or leave court whilst a verdict is being taken, or when a defendant is being sentenced.

(c) When the judge enters the courtroom you must stand; he or she will normally bow to counsel before being seated — you should return the bow. You should also bow to the judge when leaving court, and, if you have just come in to a court when the judge is already sitting, as you sit down.

(d) Do not stare (indeed try not to look) at members of a jury when they come into court to deliver their verdict. At this stage they have made their decision: you can no longer influence them one way or the other, and there is no reason why you should make them feel uncomfortable by trying to guess their verdict.

(e) You should not show your emotions at a verdict, or a judge's ruling.

(f) By convention, briefcases are not usually carried by counsel when robed. Do not take a bag into court (other than a handbag). If you have to, for whatever reason, ensure it is concealed as far as possible. Similarly, newspapers and other miscellaneous items should be kept from the view of the tribunal you are before.

(g) There is a courtesy known as 'dressing the judge' which should be observed. A judge in robes should never be left without a member of the Bar being in court, unless the judge has indicated that he or she can leave. If your case is over, and you are the only barrister in court, do not leave unless the judge has given such an indication. In virtually every case the judge will so indicate.

(h) If your opponent rises to object, sit down. Two barristers should never be on their feet at the same time unless being addressed directly by the judge.

(i) Sometimes you will go into court where leading counsel will be appearing; by convention junior barristers sit in the row behind leading counsel, rather than the same one. Constraints of space sometimes mean that this is not always observed.

In addition to the above customs there are also a number of less common situations where there is still an element of custom and etiquette, eg, on the death of a judge, it will usually fall to the most senior member of the Bar present in the robing room that day to perform some form of valediction before the business of the court is resumed.

5.6 Modes of address

Reference should be made to the *Advocacy Manual* which contains a guide to the appropriate modes of addressing the court and the use of the correct form of address.

5.7 Problems

(1) You are instructed to represent the defendant in a High Court case at 10.30 am, at the Royal Courts of Justice. You sleep through your alarm clock and, to your horror, wake up at 10 am. The Court is an hour's journey from your home. What do you do?

(2) You are the junior pupil in chambers. At 4.30 pm on Thursday your clerk tells you that you have two cases listed at Exeter Crown Court for the following day: one at 10 am in court one, and one at 10.30 am, in court two, and that no one else in chambers is available to do either of them. At 10.35 am you are still conducting the case in court one, when you are passed a note by the usher from court two that that court has convened and that the judge is waiting for you and furious to know that you are in a different court. What do you do?

Professional misconduct: the complaints procedure

6.1 General

As part of its regulatory role, the Bar Council has a duty to investigate and, where appropriate, prosecute complaints against barristers. The procedures that it follows in doing so are laid down, or repeated, in the Code of Conduct.

(a) The Complaints Rules — Annexe J.

(b) Disciplinary Tribunal Regulations 2000 (repeated as Annexe K).

(c) Hearings before the Visitors Rules 2002 (repeated as Annexe M).

(d) Summary Procedure Rules — Annexe L.

(e) Adjudication Panel and Appeals Rules — Annexe P.

The structure of the system is outlined in the diagram at **6.15** below. There are two important figures in the procedure: the Complaints Commissioner and the Professional Conduct and Complaints Committee (PCC).

6.2 The Complaints Commissioner

The Complaints Commissioner is responsible for overseeing the investigation of complaints against barristers. The Commissioner is neither a barrister nor a solicitor and has power to dismiss complaints which are clearly unmeritorious without referring them to the PCC. In addition, the Commissioner advises the PCC about issues of inadequate professional services and compensation and plays an important role in presenting the lay client's perspective.

6.3 Professional conduct and Complaints Committee (PCC)

Under the present system, the PCC comprises around 40 members of the Bar, two lay members (chosen by rota from a panel of lay representatives appointed by the Complaints

Commissioner) and the Chairman and Vice-Chairman of the PSC who are members ex-officio.

Apart from dealing with complaints, the PCC also deals with applications and queries from members of the Bar concerning Code of Conduct matters, in so far as these concern the exercise of discretion or questions of interpretation. The Committee also considers whether to waive particular provisions of the Code in individual cases.

6.4 The nature of complaints

Under the present system about 500 complaints are received each year from a wide variety of complainants including members of the lay public, prisoners, judges, solicitors and other members of the Bar. Of these, about 60% are dismissed by the Commissioner. The remainder are considered by the PCC.

The nature of complaints can vary widely but the most common, in descending order of frequency, are probably as follows:

(a) Dissatisfied lay clients (especially prisoners) alleging:
   (i)   incompetence and/or negligence;
   (ii)   undue pressure to accept a settlement or to plead guilty;
   (iii) poor advocacy, style or tactics.

(b) Misbehaviour in court, especially rudeness to other counsel or to the judge and failure to accept the latter's rulings.

(c) Failure to pay debts. These are normally accepted as being within the Committee's jurisdiction only if use of the status of barrister or a degree of moral turpitude is involved.

(d) Maladministration of, or misbehaviour in, chambers.

(e) Reports of driving, public order or criminal convictions. The last of these almost invariably result in reference to a disciplinary tribunal, often with the most severe consequences.

6.5 Present complaints procedure

When a complaint has been received (other than one made by the Bar Council of its own motion) it is referred to the Complaints Commissioner who will give initial instructions on how the complaint should be investigated. In a relatively small number of cases it is likely that it will be obvious that the complaint as it stands shows no evidence of misconduct or of inadequate professional service. In such cases the Commissioner is able to dismiss the complaint immediately. In other cases, the matter may be suitable for conciliation or should be adjourned (for example because an appeal is pending). In the majority of cases, however, the Commissioner will seek further information and at this stage the comments of the barrister concerned with the complaint will be sought.

It is likely that the Commissioner will also approach the instructing solicitor (if there is one) for comments, together with other relevant witnesses at the same time. All comments are then sent to the complainant for further comments. Once these have been received the papers are sent to the Commissioner for further consideration.

If, having considered the papers, the Commissioner is satisfied that there is no *prima facie* evidence of professional misconduct or of inadequate professional service on the barrister's part, the complaint may be dismissed. Otherwise, it will be referred to the PCC. A member of the PCC will be asked to examine the file and prepare a report on the complaint for the PCC to consider.

The report will summarise the background, the detailed nature of the complaint and the arguments for and against, and recommending a decision. This is tabled at the first available Committee meeting which the Sponsor Member can attend when the complaint is discussed in full and a decision is reached.

The primary purpose of consideration by the PCC is to determine whether a *prima facie* case of misconduct or inadequate professional services has been disclosed. The Committee considers only documentary evidence and none of the parties attend. Having considered the evidence, the PCC may:

(a) with the concurrence of both lay representatives attending, dismiss the complaint or determine that no further action should be taken; or,

(b) adjourn the matter for further enquiries; or,

(c) require counsel to attend on the Chairman of the PCC or other person to receive advice as to his future conduct or to advise the barrister in writing as to his future conduct (this does *not* amount to a finding of professional misconduct);

(d) find a *prima facie* case of inadequate professional service, in which case the matter will be referred to an adjudication panel;

(e) find a *prima facie* case of professional misconduct (whether with or without inadequate professional service) whereupon, depending upon the seriousness of the matter and whether there is a significant dispute as to facts, the PCC may refer the matter to one of an informal hearing, a summary procedure panel or a disciplinary tribunal.

The complainant is invariably informed of the Committee's decision and, if it is dismissed, if no further action is taken or if the matter is dealt with informally, is told the outline reasons for the Committee's decision and, if appropriate, the nature of the advice given.

6.6   Adjudication Panels

Adjudication Panels exist to consider complaints where the PCC has only found that there is a *prima facie* case of inadequate professional service. This is defined as:

... such conduct towards the lay client (or in the case of an employed barrister the person to whom he has supplied the professional service in question) or performance of professional service for that client which falls significantly short of that which is to be reasonably expected of a barrister in all the circumstances.

Their procedures are governed by the Adjudication Panel and Appeals Rules. The panel may:

- dismiss the complaint;
- require the barrister to apologise to the lay client;
- require the barrister to repay or reduce the fee;
- require the barrister to pay compensation up to £5,000 to the lay client.

A finding of inadequate professional service may only be made where the person making the complaint is the lay client or their representative.

Adjudication Panels normally sit in private and reach their decisions on the papers in front of them. Both the complainant and barrister will have been invited to make further representations about the matter and, in particular, any loss that has been suffered. A barrister may attend the panel and/or be represented there if he or she wishes.

6.7 Informal hearings

Where the PCC considers that there is a *prima facie* case of misconduct but that it is relatively trivial, it may refer the matter to a panel comprising three barristers (usually chaired by a QC) sitting with a lay representative. If the panel finds either misconduct or inadequate professional services to have been established, it may advise as to future conduct or reprimand the barrister. A panel making a finding of inadequate professional service may order the same remedies as an Adjudication Panel.

6.8 Summary hearings

Summary hearings are held under the authority of Summary Procedure Rules. Panels, each consisting of a silk as chairman, a lay representative and at least one, and up to three barristers. Procedure is informal. Proceedings are based on an agreed statement of facts, although witnesses can, with the prior permission of the chairman of the panel, be heard. Hearings may be held in public or, if the barrister wishes and the chairman of the tribunal consents, in private. Both the defendant and the PCC can be represented by counsel (although the latter is unusual) and evidence, where applicable, is taken on oath.

6.9 Tribunals

Disciplinary tribunals are held under the authority of and are organised by the Council of the Inns of Court and consist of a Chairman (a High Court or Circuit judge) together with two practising members of the Bar and two lay representatives. Both oral and documentary evidence is taken. Hearings are normally held in public. Both the defendant and the

PCC (as prosecuting authority) are represented by counsel and evidence is taken, where appropriate, on oath.

6.10 Penalties

If charges of professional misconduct are found proved, a summary hearing or a tribunal may sentence a barrister to be:

(a) disbarred (disciplinary tribunals only);

(b) suspended from practice for a prescribed period, with or without conditions (for three months only in the case of a summary hearing);

(c) ordered to pay a fine to the Bar Council of up to £5,000 (£500 in the case of summary hearings);

(d) ordered to forgo or repay fees;

(e) reprimanded;

(f) permanently or temporarily excluded from undertaking publicly-funded work;

(g) advised as to his or her future conduct.

A barrister may be reprimanded or be given advice as to his or her future conduct by the tribunal or summary hearing panel itself, or by attendance on a nominated person.

Summary Hearings and Disciplinary Tribunals may also make findings of inadequate professional service and order the same remedies as an Adjudication Panel.

6.11 Appeals

Findings of professional misconduct and subsequent sentences by summary hearings and disciplinary tribunals are subject to appeal under the Hearings Before the Visitors Rules 2002. Findings of inadequate professional service may be appealed to an Appeals Panel under the Adjudication Panel and Appeal Rules. The Bar Council may appeal against a lenient sentence of a disciplinary tribunal.

6.12 Publication of findings and sentence

The proceedings of, and decisions by, the PCC, informal hearings or adjudication panels are not published unless the barrister concerned so requests. All other findings of professional misconduct are published unless the tribunal or summary hearing panel decides otherwise.

6.13 Conciliation

In some cases, where it is clear to the Commissioner that misconduct is not involved, the Commissioner may consider that it is most appropriate for the barrister to attempt some informal conciliation with the complainant. This may arise, for example, in cases where it is clear that the complainant simply has not understood what has gone on or where some minor problem has arisen over delay or confusion in clerking which is not serious enough to amount to misconduct. It is often most satisfactory if such difficulties can be resolved between the parties rather than by formal findings and an investigation. It should be stressed, however, that in suggesting this the Commissioner has not reached any formal view as to whether an issue of inadequate professional service is involved.

In these circumstances, the Commissioner will suggest that the barrister should approach the complainant to see whether it is possible to resolve the difficulties informally. It is up to the barrister to decide what response to this is appropriate. It may, for example, be reasonable to offer some sort of explanation or financial compensation or to refer the matter to a Chambers complaints procedure (if one exists). It is equally open to the barrister to make no response at all but if it is not possible to resolve the dispute, the complainant may return the matter to the Bar Council for a formal investigation.

6.14 Legal Services Ombudsman

The Legal Services Ombudsman, who is neither a barrister nor a solicitor, is appointed under the Courts and Legal Services Act 1990 to oversee the handling of complaints against members of the legal professions. If complainants are dissatisfied with the way their complaints have been dealt with, they have the right to request the Ombudsman to examine the PCC's treatment of the complaint and decide whether it was investigated fully and fairly. The Ombudsman then asks to see the PCC's file. If, after considering the matter, the Ombudsman thinks the complaint was not dealt with properly, the Ombudsman can recommend or require further action including, in certain circumstances, reconsideration of the matter by the PCC or the payment of compensation by the Bar Council and/or by the barrister(s) concerned.

Complaints have to be referred to the Legal Services Ombudsman within three months of the letter notifying the complainant of the PCC's decision. The Ombudsman has no power to investigate the substance of a complaint that has been decided by a court or by a disciplinary tribunal or where an appeal is being, or could still be, made against the PCC's decision though the Ombudsman may look at the Bar Council's handling of the matter. He or she will also not normally intervene while the PCC is still investigating the matter and will in fact only do so if there appears to have been unreasonable delay or if other strong reasons exist.

6.15 Complaints system structure

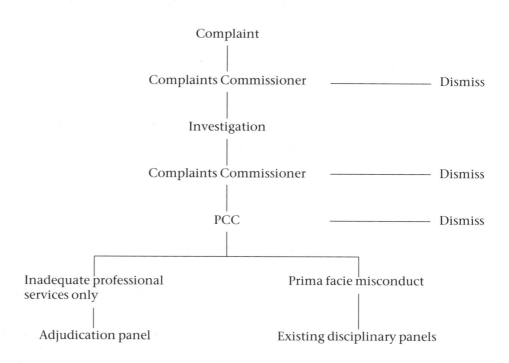

6.16 Advice to counsel who are the subject of a complaint

The number of complaints received by the Bar Council from lay clients and others has increased steadily over the last ten years and it is becoming increasingly likely that, at one stage or another, a barrister, particularly if he or she specialises in criminal or family work, will be required to respond to a complaint. Counsel will normally be informed of this in a letter from the Bar Council enclosing a copy of the material sent by the complainant to the Bar Council. That letter will indicate that counsel's comments are required within three weeks of its date.

It is worth making clear that, at this stage, the Bar Council or the Commissioner has not taken any view on the merits of the complaint. The majority of complaints are dismissed but in many cases the complainant will not have supplied sufficient information to allow the Commissioner to deal with the matter without seeking counsel's comments. The Legal Services Ombudsman oversees the working of the system and has power to refer matters back to the PCC for reconsideration. For this reason it is generally safer to seek counsel's comments where there may be any doubt about a particular complaint. Counsel should feel free to contact the Secretariat to discuss the handling of the complaint, the procedure generally or to seek advice. Clearly the Secretariat cannot advise on whether there is or is not a *prima facie* case of misconduct and cannot give a barrister advice on how to present his or her case. That said, the following questions arise frequently.

6.16.1 I am in a long case and cannot prepare my response adequately in time

The Secretariat is usually able to agree reasonable extensions for good reasons over the telephone. Generally it is most important that a barrister should at least make contact with the Secretariat even if he or she is not able to produce a full response by the deadline. Barristers should make every effort to produce their response as soon as is reasonably possible. The PCC can and does take action against barristers who are unreasonably dilatory in preparing their replies.

6.16.2 This matter took place many months ago and I have little recollection of the case

There is no reason why counsel cannot approach his or her instructing solicitors for a copy of the original instructions in the case and such other details as he or she may need in order to refresh his or her memory. It is certainly open to him or her to seek an extension of time in order to obtain such documentation.

6.16.3 May I approach solicitors and other witnesses for their views?

There is no reason why counsel should not approach instructing solicitors, judges, etc to provide statements or other information in support of counsel.

6.16.4 The client has issued/is likely to issue proceedings against me in negligence

Counsel should seek the advice of the BMIF on how to deal with the complaint. Normally consideration of such a complaint is adjourned until the matter has been considered by the civil courts. In any case if, on the advice of your insurers or for reasons of professional privilege, it is inappropriate for certain matters to be sent to the complainant which, nevertheless, it would be helpful for the Commissioner or the Committee to see, such material can be withheld from the complainant. If this is the case, counsel should make it clear which parts of the response should not be sent to the complainant.

6.16.5 What should I say in my response?

The content of the response to the complaint is very much a matter for the individual barrister to consider. There is nothing to stop him or her seeking advice from other colleagues or his or her head of chambers or a member of the Barristers' Complaints Advisory Service as to his or her reply. A good rule is to address specific allegations but not include comment or material 'just in case'. Simply refer to the further details or evidence which is available and can be supplied if required.

6.16.6 How will it affect my application for silk or judicial appointment?

A complaint which has been dismissed is not at present required to be mentioned to the Department for Constitutional Affairs (DCA) in connection with any application for silk or judicial appointment and the Bar Council will not disclose such a complaint, though the barrister may have to do so. The Bar Council will, however, disclose any finding of professional misconduct or any unresolved complaint. The exact effect of such disclosure is for the DCA to consider and will clearly depend on the circumstances of each case. It may be worth noting, however, that a finding of professional misconduct by one of the informal panels has not proved an insuperable barrier to preferment in the past.

6.16.7   Should I be represented at tribunals or panel hearings?

Barristers are almost invariably represented before disciplinary tribunals and may approach other counsel direct in order to be so represented. There is a long tradition at the Bar of very senior silks agreeing to act for no fee in such cases. It is, however, in each case, a matter for the individual concerned as to whom he or she seeks to approach and whether he or she needs to instruct solicitors on these matters. If a barrister has difficulty finding suitable counsel, then the Secretariat is usually able to assist. The individual should bear in mind that he or she will not always get his or her costs back even after a successful defence at a tribunal. Representation in front of panels and summary hearings is less common. There is, however, nothing to prevent a barrister from being represented if he or she wishes.

6.16.8   Is there any organisation that can help me?

The Bar Council recently established the Barristers' Complaints Advisory Service (BCAS) which consists of about 70 barristers of all levels of seniority and types of practice who are prepared to advise barristers on how to deal with complaints. A list of members and details of the scheme are included in the material sent to chambers when they are asked for comments on complaints. The London Common Law and Commercial Bar Association operates a similar scheme.

6.17   Legal Services Ombudsman: recommendations for compensation

As has been explained, the Ombudsman has power to consider the decisions of the Commissioner and the PCC and, on occasion, to recommend or require that the barrister concerned pay compensation direct to the lay client. The Bar Council is consulted about such recommendations but it is not its normal policy to make representations about the awards, unless those awards appear to it to be unreasonable. In dealing with the Ombudsman, barristers are recommended to contact the BMIF about any recommendations or requirements that they pay compensation.

6.18   Interim suspension and fitness to practise

The Bar Council has recently introduced rules to deal with cases where a barrister has been charged or convicted of a serious criminal offence or is medically unfit to practise. These rules essentially allow the Bar Council to suspend a barrister from practice pending a final decision on his or her future.

The provisions are contained at para 905(c) which requires a barrister to report to the Bar Council if he or she is charged with a serious criminal offence (as defined in s 116 of the Police and Criminal Evidence Act 1984) or a relevant criminal offence (which covers everything apart from fixed penalty or parking offences). Barristers who report themselves under these provisions will be considered under the Interim Suspension Rules in Annex N to the Code of Conduct. These effectively give the Bar Council power to suspend a barrister until the matter is dealt with by a disciplinary tribunal. It was thought inappropriate for members of the Bar to be able to continue practising while serious charges or convictions which might call into question their suitability to be barristers were over their heads. The rules empower the Bar Council to set early dates for hearings and to enable the barrister concerned to make appropriate representations.

The Fitness to Practice Rules are used where it comes to the attention of the Bar Council that a barrister may be unfit for medical reasons to practise. Essentially, the rules allow the Bar Council to require a barrister to attend on their appointed medical adviser for an examination. On receipt of a report from the medical adviser the panel can consider whether a barrister is unfit to practise by reason of medical incapacity (including addiction) and that a suspension is necessary for the protection of the public. The rules can be found at Annex O to the Code of Conduct.

The BVC, practice and professional conduct

7.1 General introduction

This chapter will focus on professional conduct problems pertinent to the key skills you will undertake during the Bar Vocational Course. It therefore concentrates on the following assessment areas: conference, advocacy, negotiation, opinion writing and drafting.

Undoubtedly the issues discussed will arise in practice. A sound understanding of these areas will ensure that when you are conducting a case you can identify these professional conduct points and, as a result, because you will be familiar with the fundamental tenets of the Code and of relevant statutory law (ref. the Proceeds of Crime Act 2002), the matters can be properly dealt with at the earliest opportunity, no matter in what context the problem arises.

All the contributors to this chapter are experienced lecturers, academic authors and subject co-ordinators at the ICSL and as such, are not only drawing on their own experiences of practice in these areas, but upon the types of professional conduct points which you will inevitably be examined upon as you complete your skills assessments. Consequently, it is particularly useful not only to use this chapter as a central source of reference for professional conduct difficulties, but also as you go through the BVC to take a note of your approach to the areas which have arisen in your small group discussions. You will then be in a position, as the course progresses, to check upon your development in handling these areas and how it compares to the advice set out below.

7.2 Conference skills

Conferences come in a variety of forms, most often involving the lay client, with or without the professional client in attendance. In some cases, for example, when you are prosecuting on behalf of a body such as the CPS, Serious Fraud Office or Customs and Excise, your conference may involve a number of other people. It would not be unusual, for example, to have a conference involving Crown Prosecutors, police officers and forensic scientists in a serious criminal case. At the other end of the range, you may be sent to the magistrates' court with little information and have to deal with finding your lay client and maybe even taking instructions through a wicket in a cell door or while standing in a corridor.

As stated in the *Conference Skills Manual*, these problems often arise without warning and in situations where you cannot readily seek advice. This means that you have to have a sound understanding of the principles which guide a barrister in practice, as well as the spirit of the Code. There are common duties which apply in all of these situations and they are discussed below.

7.2.1   Instructions from your lay client

With limited exceptions, the instructions that you receive from your lay client are to be treated in the strictest confidence. The Code states:

702   Whether or not the relation of counsel and client continues a barrister must preserve the confidentiality of the lay client's affairs and must not without the prior consent of the lay client or as permitted by law lend or reveal the contents of the papers in any instructions to or communicate to any third person (other than another barrister, a pupil or any other person who needs to know it for the performance of their duties) information which has been entrusted to him in confidence or use such information to the lay client's detriment or to his own or another client's advantage.

Clearly, you will expect to be able to use your client's instructions to cross-examine, draft statements of case or even draft witness statements. This will necessarily involve disclosing those instructions and the client will have given you permission to do so. A problem may, however, arise when the client makes a disclosure to you in conference, which he or she does not want to have revealed. A number of common disclosures are considered below.

7.2.2   Whether to disclose?

7.2.2.1   Disclosure to the National Criminal Intelligence Service (NCIS) under the Proceeds of Crime Act 2002 (POCA).

In practice you must be aware of how the POCA 2002 impacts on your disclosure obligations to NCIS, when as counsel you are concerned in an arrangement which you know or suspect relates to the proceed of crime. For example, in the context of agreeing a settlement in an ancillary relief matter, your client reveals that a proportion of her husband's assets stem from business earnings which have not been declared to the Inland Revenue. What should you do next?

In summary, you will need to consider whether:

1. The property concerned amounts to 'criminal property' under the Act and

2. If it does — you must know the procedure under the Act, which must be followed, taking into account whether the good practice set out by Butler Sloss P in *P v P* [2003] EWHC Fam 2260 should also be adhered to.

Consequently, you must not only be familiar with the Act itself, but of the relevant sources of guidance to aid your understanding of its practical implications. The Bar Council's amended guidance is set out in full below. Whilst it may not expressly address all the difficulties involved in dealing with such matters, it is a very useful general guide and it clearly takes into account the good practice advice mentioned above. Given that at present there is very little case law guidance on the practical interpretations of the statutory wording, you must be prepared regularly to check recent case law on this area together with the Bar Council's and NCIS's website for any updates (for the web site addresses see the guidance below). The important point to remember is that all this groundwork is necessary so that you do not carry out the 'prohibited act' and therefore avoid criminal liability under the Act! Please refer to the Conference manual for additional guidance.

AMENDED GUIDANCE ON THE PROCEEDS OF CRIME ACT

Note to the Bar — Proceeds of Crime Act

In the case of *P v P* [2003] EWHC Fam 2260, in the context of an application for ancillary financial relief in a matrimonial case the President of the Family Division dealt with the following issues:

(i) whether and in what circumstances it is permitted to act in relation to an arrangement and

(ii) whether and in what circumstances a legal adviser, having made an authorised disclosure, is permitted to tell others of the fact that s/he has done so.

The case is important. It can be accessed from this link: www.bailii.org.uk

In the light of the decision we have amended the guidance on the Proceeds of Crime Act and this appears below. The amendments are underlined for ease of reference.

The National Criminal Intelligence Service (NCIS) has revised its guidance to legal advisers in the light of *P v P* (see the NCIS website www.ncis.co.uk). In particular NCIS now states that where a solicitor has already made disclosure and obtained consent there is no need for a barrister instructed subsequently to do so (where there is no change of circumstances).

The Law Society is updating its Proceeds of Crime Act guidance in the light of *P v P*. It will appear in due course on the Law Society website at www.lawsociety.org.uk.

THE PROCEEDS OF CRIME ACT 2002

Guidance to Barristers — December 2003

1. This guidance is no substitute for reading the Act and being familiar with it. Contravention of the Act is a criminal offence.

2. Part 7 of the Act is most likely to affect members of the Bar. Set out below are those sections likely to require the closest scrutiny.

3. By section 328(1) a person commits an offence if he enters into or becomes concerned in an arrangement which he knows or suspects facilitates (by whatever means) the acquisition, retention, use or control of criminal property by or on behalf of another person.

4. By section 340(3) property is criminal property if:

5. (a) it constitutes a person's benefit from criminal conduct or it represents such benefit (in whole or part and whether directly or indirectly), and

6. (b) the alleged offender knows or suspects that it constitutes or represents such a benefit.

7. For example, property that represents the benefit of the non-payment of tax constitutes criminal property for the purposes of the Act.

8. Where a barrister advises a client in respect (say) of how to enforce his rights in respect of certain property is the barrister 'concerned in an arrangement which ... facilitates the acquisition etc of criminal property' (assuming that the property is criminal within the meaning of the Act)? He probably is. Where the barrister knows or suspects that as a result of following his advice his client may (eg) acquire criminal property the barrister will be said to be concerned in such an arrangement. (See *P v P* [2003] EWHC Fam 2260, where the point was not contested.)

9. Where the parties to litigation agree a settlement where the subject matter of the litigation is (at least in part) criminal property within the meaning of the Act, this too will be said to be an arrangement within the meaning of the Act (see *P v P*).

10. The examples are not exhaustive. You are advised to consider your position in the light of the facts of each case. Remember that under section 328(1) suspicion (that the arrangement facilitates by whatever means the acquisition etc of criminal property) is enough.

Disclosure

11. Section 328(2) provides defences. Most pertinent is section 328(2)(a) ... a person does not commit such an offence if:

   (a) he makes an authorised disclosure under section 338 and (if the disclosure is made before he does the act mentioned in subsection (1)) he has the appropriate consent.

12. By section 335 (so far as is relevant at this stage) the disclosure is to and the appropriate consent is from a constable (in fact the National Criminal Intelligence Service, NCIS).

13. Where a member of the Bar is instructed to advise/appear in court in circumstances where he will become involved in an arrangement as described in section 328 he must consider whether he should make a disclosure to NCIS before acting/continuing to act. He should ask his solicitor whether the solicitor has already made a disclosure and has consent (a solicitor, in answering such a question would not be committing the offence of tipping off because his disclosure to the barrister is not likely to prejudice any investigation — see subsection 333(1)(b) and below).

14. Where the barrister considers that, in order to continue to act without committing a criminal offence, he should make disclosure (and the solicitor has not already done so), subject to his assessment of the impact of sections 333 and 342 as to which see below, he should inform his client that in order to continue to act without committing a criminal offence the barrister must make a disclosure to NCIS and seek NCIS consent before continuing to act. He should also inform his client that in order for the client to proceed without committing a criminal offence the client should seek NCIS consent. Thereafter events will take one of three courses:–

   (i) The client objects to this course of action in which case he will no doubt withdraw instructions. If he does so there is no difficulty and there is no need for the barrister to make a disclosure.

   (ii) If the client objects to the report and does not withdraw instructions the barrister should withdraw from the case to avoid committing the offence. There is no duty upon the barrister to make a disclosure in those circumstances.

   (iii) If the client agrees to the proposed course of action the barrister makes disclosure to NCIS and seeks consent. The barrister should consider (and advise his client in this regard) whether he should make the disclosure jointly with his client. If the client makes a report, he also has the protection of the defence. In practical terms it may well be the case that the disclosure is made jointly by barrister, solicitor and client.

15. A disclosure report must be made in writing. The report may be downloaded from www.ncis.co.uk. Consent may be express or deemed. NCIS has 7 working days (the notice period) within which to notify the person making the disclosure of its consent/refusal, starting with the first working day after the person makes disclosure. If no notice is received from NCIS during the notice period a person is deemed to have appropriate consent. If a notice of refusal is served on the person making the disclosure there is then a moratorium period (31 days starting with the day on which the person receives notice of refusal). At the expiry of that period the person is deemed to have consent.

16.   Where the solicitor has already made a disclosure to NCIS the barrister's position is different. NCIS have confirmed that there is no need in those circumstances for the barrister to make a disclosure and seek consent before continuing to act. Since the barrister knows that disclosure has been made both sections 333 and 342 will come into play (see below).

Tipping Off

17.   By subsection 333(1) A person commits an offence if—

(a) he knows or suspects that a disclosure falling within section 337 or 338 has been made and

(b) he makes a disclosure which is likely to prejudice any investigation which might be conducted following the disclosure referred to in paragraph (a).

18.   There is a defence (section 333(2)(c)) if a person is a professional legal adviser and the disclosure falls within subsection (3) — ie 'it is a disclosure to ... a client ... in connection with the giving by the adviser of legal advice to the client (see also (b) — to any person in connection with legal proceedings or contemplated legal proceedings).'

19.   In short the barrister is entitled to tell his client of the disclosure if he does so in connection with the giving of legal advice.

20.   BUT NB section 333(4) 'But a disclosure does not fall within the subsection (3) if it is made with the intention of furthering a criminal purpose'. It is plain from the decision in *P v P* that the intention must be that of the legal adviser, not the client.

21.   Where, eg, a barrister has made a disclosure in respect of another party in the proceedings (or knows or suspects that such disclosure has been made) the barrister must ensure he does not tip off that party (subject to the defence of LPP contained in section 333(3)(b) (see paragraphs 18–20 above). 'Unless the requisite improper intention is there, the solicitor should be free to communicate such information to his/her client or opponent as is necessary and appropriate in connection with the giving of legal advice or acting in connection with actual or contemplated legal proceedings' (para 65 *P v P*)

Prejudicing Investigations — Part 8 of the Act

22.   By section 342 if a person knows or suspects that a confiscation investigation, a civil recovery investigation or a money laundering investigation is being or is about to be conducted he commits an offence if he makes a disclosure which is likely to prejudice the investigation.

23.   There is a defence where the disclosure is made by a professional legal adviser in connection with the giving of legal advice to the client etc (see section 342(3)(c) and s 342(4)) but see also section 342(5) — where the disclosure is made with the intention of furthering a criminal purpose. Again, the decision in *P v P* makes clear that the intention is that of the legal adviser, not the client. See also paragraphs 18–20 above.

24.   Where a barrister knows or suspects that an investigation is taking place or is about to begin he should be very careful as to what, if anything, he tells his client.

Good Practice once a disclosure has been made

25.   Butler Sloss P suggested that good practice (rather than statutory obligation) should permit the authorities time to do their job without frustration (paragraph 67 of the judgment). There would be no harm in a short delay between reporting by a legal adviser and the disclosing of the fact of the report. She tied the proposed timetable to the consent/moratorium timetable.

26. She suggested (paragraph 67 of the judgment) that in most cases a delay of, at most 7 working days from the making of the report by the solicitor to NCIS, would not cause difficulty to the solicitor in respect of his duty to his client.

27. Butler Sloss P went on to say that where appropriate consent was refused and a 31 day moratorium was imposed, best practice would suggest that the legal adviser and NCIS should agree on the degree of information to be disclosed during the moratorium period without harming the investigation. In the absence of agreement, or in urgent circumstances, the guidance of the court may be sought.

28. Barristers should consider in each case whether the good practice set out by Butler Sloss P may be followed.

29. NB if, for whatever reason the barrister is not able to tell his client that a disclosure has been made (eg where the solicitor has already made a disclosure and to inform the client would be tipping off), it is difficult to see how he may continue to act for him. The barrister must withdraw without giving the reason. An amendment to the Code of Conduct may be required as a result of this legislation.

Regulated Sector

30. Section 330 creates an offence of failing to disclose where the person who should make the disclosure is in the regulated sector. Barristers do not come within the current definition of the regulated sector under schedule 9 of the Act. But the Treasury has reserved to itself the power to amend schedule 9. At present it mirrors the current regulations. It is expected that schedule 9 will be amended to mirror the 2003 regulations. In short, sections of the Bar will come within the regulated sector and be caught by (amongst other provisions) section 330. This will lead to further changes in the guidance set out above.

The Regulations

31. The Money Laundering Regulations of 2003 were laid before parliament on 28th November 2003. They will come into force on 1st March 2004. Barristers involved in financial transactions as defined within the regulations will be caught by the regulations with requirements for money laundering procedures. Further guidance will be given in this regard.

16 December 2003

7.2.2.2 Confessions

Every barrister has been asked by someone 'how can you represent someone when you know that they are guilty?' The answer that you may have given is that you are not the judge or a juror and if your client says that he or she is not guilty then those are the instructions you follow in presenting his or her case. So far so good. But what happens if the client actually tells you that he or she did commit the offence?

Using a criminal case as an example and assuming that the client's instructions to date have been that he or she wants to plead not guilty, what do you do when the client appears to admit to you in conference that he or she did commit the offence? In the first place do not panic. Recognise that there is a potential problem and continue your questioning to explore exactly what the client is saying — he or she is not a lawyer and may not appreciate what defences are available. If your questioning reveals that, without doubt, the client has told you that he or she does not have a defence, then you will need to advise on this clearly and advise him or her that the best course of action would be to plead guilty and make the most of the mitigation.

If the client tells you that, nonetheless, he or she wishes to continue to plead not guilty, you will need to consider your duty to the court. The Code expresses it as follows:

302 A barrister has an overriding duty to the Court to act with independence in the interests of justice: he must assist the Court in the administration of justice and must not deceive or knowingly or recklessly mislead the Court.

You may not make representations to the court that you know to be untrue — this would involve you in misleading the court. You will need to explain this to the client. He or she may well be concerned that this 'overriding' duty means that you will have to reveal his or her guilt to the court. You may well be concerned that your duty to the court appears to clash with your duty of confidentiality to your client.

The correct approach is that, first, you cannot reveal the client's instructions without his or her permission. However, you equally cannot put forward any positive case that he or she is not guilty as this would be knowingly misleading the court. You may, however, still test the prosecution evidence in cross-examination. This means that you can explore with a witness how reliable his or her evidence is, but you cannot put any positive case to him or her on behalf of your client. For example, if the issue were identification you might well question a witness about the conditions in which the identification was made, but if your instructions are that the identification was correct then you cannot put to the witness that he or she was mistaken in that identification. Practically, it makes it extremely difficult to run a successful case or to make any clear closing speech. You will have to explain all of this to the client and also remind him or her of the potential advantages of pleading guilty in terms of sentencing, reiterating your advice to plead guilty. If the client chooses to ignore that advice, as he or she is entitled to do, you may be wise to have the client endorse your brief to say that you have advised him or her of the consequences of his or her choice.

7.2.2.3 Information damaging to your client's case

Your lay client may reveal information in conference, which would be damaging to his or her case. For example, if the client discloses that he or she has previous convictions which the CPS do not seem to know about and wants to keep those secret at trial. In such a situation, you will advise the client that you have a duty of confidentiality and that, without his or her express permission, you cannot disclose the previous convictions to the court. However, you will also remind yourself that you have a duty not to mislead the court. While you do not have to volunteer information damaging to your client's case, if the judge were to ask you, for instance, whether your client wanted a good character direction in the summing up then you would be in an uncomfortable position.

In your conference, you will have to advise your client that this may happen and will need to ask whether he or she will allow you to disclose the previous convictions. If he or she says no, then when you are in court you will simply have to tell the judge that you are unable to answer any such direct question. The judge and prosecutor will easily work out why that is and the prosecutor will probably take the opportunity to have the client's record re-checked by police. You will certainly not get a good character direction. The effect, therefore, is the same as if you had revealed the previous convictions — but without the credit to your client of 'coming clean'. You should advise of this in your conference and may suggest that he or she would gain credit for being so honest.

The Bar Council has offered guidance to barristers on that they can and cannot say in such situations. The full text is available on the Bar Council website (www.barcouncil.org.uk), but some key points are extracted below:

In circumstances where counsel is aware of previous convictions, regardless of the nature of the case or potential sentence, counsel should give the defendant clear advice as to all the options. He should:

- Inform the defendant that the information as to the previous conviction will remain confidential unless the client specifically waives privilege;
- Inform the defendant that whilst the information remains confidential, he will be restricted in what he can say in mitigation;
- Advise the defendant that nothing can be said as to the defendant's record which expressly or impliedly adopts the position as outlined by the prosecution and in particular, that nothing can be said as to:

  (a)   the absence of convictions of the type or gravity of the undisclosed conviction;
  (b)   a period of time as being free from convictions if the undisclosed conviction occurred during that period;
  (c)   the absence of a particular sentence or disposal in the defendant's antecedents if such sentence or disposal was in fact imposed in respect of the undisclosed conviction; or
  (d)   an apparently good character of the defendant.

- Specifically advise the defendant as to the nature of the sentencing exercise if the court became aware of the undisclosed conviction, whether by virtue of the defendant's voluntary disclosure or by some other means.
- Advise the defendant as to the possibility of the prosecution subsequently discovering the undisclosed conviction;
- Advise of the real possibility that failure of counsel to refer to the defendant's antecedents would not go unnoticed by experienced prosecution counsel or judge. This could lead to an adjournment, to the matter being relisted for alteration of the sentence, or to a reference by the Attorney-General under section 36 of the Criminal Justice Act 1998.

The defendant should be told that the choice as to what course to adopt is his, but that if he decides to reveal the qualifying conviction, he would be entitled to expect significant credit from the court.
...

The Bar Council's guidance notes also make clear that this would not be an appropriate situation for counsel to withdraw.

7.2.2.4   Prosecutors

The Criminal Procedure and Investigations Act 1996 creates a positive duty for prosecutors to disclose information which undermines the Crown's case or which is helpful to the defendant's. Section 9 of the 1996 Act makes this a continuing duty to review information. This is a far heavier burden than that on defence counsel. The Code for Crown Prosecutors makes this clear:

2.4   It is the duty of Crown Prosecutors to review, advise on and prosecute cases, ensuring that the law is properly applied, that all relevant evidence is put before the court and that obligations of disclosure are complied with, in accordance with the principles set out in this Code.

This duty to disclose damaging information illustrates the different approach that defending and prosecuting counsel are obliged to take. The Code for Crown Prosecutors states clearly that the Prosecutor should not be primarily motivated by winning the case.

2.3   It is the duty of Crown Prosecutors to make sure that the right person is prosecuted for the right offence. In doing so, Crown Prosecutors must always act in the interests of justice and not solely for the purpose of obtaining a conviction.

If some piece of information (a disciplinary finding against a police officer, for example) were to come to light during a conference, your advice would have to be that it must be disclosed — even though it might expose your witness to cross-examination.

7.2.2.5   Civil cases

In civil matters, counsel is bound by the same duty of confidentiality to the lay client and the duty not to mislead the court. However, in fast track and multi-track cases, the parties are obliged to disclose any documents within their control which relate to the proceedings. This means that if counsel were told in conference about a relevant document which had not been disclosed, he or she would have to advise the client to disclose it to the other party. If the client refused, then counsel would have to advise that he or she could not continue to act for the client unless that disclosure were made. The Code of Conduct deals with this situation as follows:

608   A barrister must cease to act and if he is a barrister in independent practice must return any instructions: ...

> (e) if having become aware during the course of a case of the existence of a document which should have been but has not been disclosed on discovery the client fails forthwith to disclose it.

Before withdrawing from the case, counsel is obliged to consider whether he or she is prejudicing the client by the timing of that withdrawal. He or she is also obliged to explain why it is necessary to withdraw from the case. The Code says:

610   A barrister must not:

> (a) cease to act or return instructions without having first explained to the client his reasons for doing so;
>
> ...
>
> (d) except as provided in paragraph 608 return any instructions or withdraw from a case in such a way or in such circumstances that the client may be unable to find other legal assistance in time to prevent prejudice being suffered by the client.

However, the wording of para 610 clearly suggests that the client's failure to make proper disclosure will be an overriding consideration — even if the revelation occurs during a trial. For guidance on disclosure of illegally obtained evidence refer to the Bar Council's web site, 'Guidance on Illegally Obtained Evidence in Civil and Family Proceedings'.

7.2.2.6   Public funding

It may well be that your lay client has the benefit of public funding through the Legal Services Commission (LSC). This adds another dimension to your duties in conference as the Code says that a barrister has a duty to the LSC in the following terms:

303   A barrister:

> ...
>
> (c) when supplying legal services funded by the Legal Services Commission as part of the Community Legal Service or the Criminal Defence Service owes his primary duty to the lay client subject only to compliance with paragraph 304.

304   A barrister who supplies legal services funded by the Legal Services Commission as part of the Community Legal Service or the Criminal Defence Service must in connection with the supply of such services comply with any duty imposed on him by or under the Access to Justice Act 1999 or any regulations or code in effect under that Act and in particular with the duties set out in Annex E.

Annex E deals with counsel's obligations when drafting opinions on the suitability of cases for public funding by the LSC. At para 20, this states that:

> Counsel acting under a funding certificate is under a duty to bring to the attention of the Commission any matter which might affect the client's entitlement to funding, or the terms of his or her certificate, at whatever stage of the proceedings that might occur.

In criminal matters, there is a similar duty to report abuse of the system. The relevant regulations under the Access to Justice Act 1999 are contained within the Criminal Defence Service (General) (No 2) Regulations 2001 (SI 2001/1437). This provides:

24.   Notwithstanding the relationship between or rights of a representative and client or any privilege arising out of such relationship, where the representative for an applicant or assisted person knows or suspects that that person:

    (a) has intentionally failed to comply with any provision of regulations made under the Act concerning the information to be furnished by him; or

    (b) in furnishing such information has knowingly made a false statement or false representation the representative shall immediately report the circumstances to the Commission.

If your publicly-funded lay client revealed facts in conference which would affect this entitlement, you would have to advise him or her to pass the correct information to the LSC immediately. If the client refuses to do this, then you will have to explain that you cannot continue to act:

608 A barrister must cease to act and if he is a barrister in independent practice must return any instructions: ...

    (c) if in any case funded by the Legal Services Commission as part of the Community Legal Service or Criminal Defence Service it has become apparent to him that such funding has been wrongly obtained by false or inaccurate information and action to remedy the situation is not immediately taken by the client;

    (d) if the client refuses to authorise him to make some disclosure to the Court which his duty to the Court requires him to make ...

If you are forced to withdraw, para 610(a) of the Code obliges you to explain to your lay client why you are doing so, and, as far as possible, not to leave your client in a position where he or she will suffer prejudice (para 610(d)). However, as noted above, the wording of the Code makes clear that counsel cannot in any circumstances continue to act when he or she believes that one of the conditions within para 608 of the Code applies.

7.2.2.7   Sensitive information

The client may reveal information in conference that he or she wishes to be kept confidential, but which you believe would assist either at trial or in mitigation. For example, he or she may be able to assist the police by revealing the names of others involved in the same offence. This would assist the mitigation considerably. The duty of confidentiality to the client means that without his or her express permission you cannot reveal that information — even if you believe that it is in his or her interests to do so. You should advise clearly on how you believe that revealing the relevant information would assist him or her. However, if your client is clear that he or she will not reveal it, remember that it is your client's case and not yours. Only your client can say what is in his or her 'best interests', once he or she has been given the full picture by you.

In these circumstances, you may wish to invite the client to endorse your brief to say that you have advised him or her about the consequences of not revealing the relevant information and that he or she has nonetheless decided not to do so. This should protect you from any complaint that he or she might make about your advice if, for example, your client receives a more serious sentence than he or she was expecting.

7.2.3 The professional client

As a general rule you would expect your solicitor (or the firm's representative) to attend a conference between you and a lay client. He or she will take notes, record action points and, depending on how involved he or she is with the case, participate in talking to the lay client and clarifying points. The solicitor also acts as a witness to what is discussed. There may be times when you do not have this luxury — for example, in your early cases where you may meet the client for the first time at court and conduct your conference then and there. Solicitors, mindful of costs, may also not attend some court hearings simply to keep costs down for their clients. This raises a number of professional conduct issues:

706 A barrister in independent practice who is instructed by a professional client should not conduct a case in Court in the absence of his professional client or a representative of his professional client unless the Court rules that it is appropriate or he is satisfied that the interests of the lay client and the interests of justice will not be prejudiced.

The Code does not make it mandatory that the professional client attends with you at court — indeed he or she will rarely attend at the magistrates' court. You will have to decide whether your lay client risks being prejudiced by this absence. Take a careful note of your instructions from your client and be prepared to explain to him or her, and, if necessary, the judge, why the solicitor is not there. The client may be unhappy that the solicitor (perhaps someone who deals with him or her regularly, or the only lawyer he or she believes is dealing with the case) is not there at court. It may also help to build your lay client's confidence if you can demonstrate your knowledge of the case and your skill in conference and as an advocate.

7.2.4 Witnesses

It is not prohibited for a barrister to meet and speak to witnesses. Extreme caution is, however, needed to avoid any suggestion of coaching witnesses. The Code says:

705 A barrister must not:
  (a) rehearse practise or coach a witness in relation to his evidence; ...

You must, of course, exercise care not to coach your lay client or suggest how the evidence should be given at any time. This caution extends to all witnesses of fact in a case. Remember also that interviewing witnesses includes not only sitting down in an interview room, but also chatting in the corridor or over a cup of coffee about the case. You need to be conscious of what you say about the case at all times.

You may have a conference which involves an expert witness or someone giving character evidence on your client's behalf. The same rules apply — that you are not to seek to influence the way that the witness gives his or her evidence (save by your expertise in questioning in court). This does not prevent you from asking experts questions about matters within their expertise, or their view on the evidence given by other experts, only your suggesting the answers that they should give.

If a witness of fact attends court in a criminal matter and wants to give evidence on behalf of the defendant then you will want to know what he or she will say. If you have no proof from the witness and if you have a professional client in attendance then you will be able to leave it to him or her to take a proof from the witness. If you are alone then this leaves you in a more difficult position. The Code states that:

401 A barrister in independent practice whether or not he is acting for a fee: ...

> (b) must not in the course of his practice: ...
>> (iv)   except as permitted by paragraph 707, take any proof of evidence in any criminal case ...

If the only other option is to seek an adjournment of the case, then the best course of action may be to take the proof yourself. This Code says that this may be permissible if necessary:

> **707**   A barrister in independent practice who attends Court in order to conduct a case in circumstances where no professional client or representative of a professional client is present may if necessary interview witnesses and take proofs of evidence.

This situation is most likely to arise in the magistrates' court, where you may well be representing your client without your professional client in attendance. As the professional client will almost always be in attendance at the Crown Court, it will seldom be necessary to take a proof or interview witnesses in such matters.

You will have to take care not to lead the witness or coach him or her in any way. If the witness asks you what he or she should say then your advice must be to tell the truth. You would be very unwise to offer any more information than that. If you take a note of what the witness says to you, you may wish to have the witness sign it as an accurate record of what he or she told you.

At court you will never speak to or contact a witness while he or she is giving evidence, save by asking questions in examination-in-chief or cross-examination. The Code expressly prohibits such contact:

> **705**   A barrister must not: ...
>> (c)   except with the consent of the representative for the opposing side or of the Court, communicate directly or indirectly about a case with any witness, whether or not the witness is his lay client, once that witness has begun to give evidence until the evidence of that witness has been concluded.

This prohibition extends even to your client — for example, if the case is adjourned overnight while your client is still giving evidence you will not speak to him or her until the next day, after he or she has finished his or her evidence. If this situation is likely to arise, then you will need to explain this to your client before he or she goes into the witness box. If you are seen to be speaking to him or her (even if you are not discussing the evidence) it will appear that you are coaching your client and you can expect opposing counsel to protest to the judge in the strongest terms.

7.2.5   Fair treatment

It should hopefully come as no surprise that the Code of Conduct forbids you to discriminate in the following terms:

> **305.1**   A barrister must not in relation to any other person (including a client or another barrister or a pupil or a student member of an Inn of Court) discriminate directly or indirectly or victimise because of race, colour, ethnic or national origin, nationality, citizenship, sex, sexual orientation, marital status, disability, religion or political persuasion.

The Code has also been amended to forbid discrimination on the grounds of age.

What this means in terms of conference skills is that you must be sensitive to the differing needs of your lay client. The range of issues this may cover is necessarily wide. For example, you may be unfamiliar with the naming system of your client's culture, or you may find that your client has never learned to read — you may even find his or her lifestyle or personal views unattractive. Of course, whether or not you like your client or the way that your client lives his or her life — or any other of your personal prejudices — must not affect your dedication to conducting his or her case as effectively as possible. Equally, if you are unsure how to pronounce your client's name or how to address him or her, use your common sense and show your client the courtesy of asking.

Fair treatment goes beyond these obvious points. If your client could not read, for example, it would be up to you to do all you could to enable him or her to take a full part in proceedings. In consultation with your client, you would seek to find ways of overcoming that problem. Ignoring the problem would amount to discrimination.

Most importantly, your duty not to discriminate requires you to be aware of what discrimination is and the wide variety of circumstances where you might be found to be discriminating inappropriately. The examples above are merely the tip of the iceberg. It is recognising that there is a problem which is vital to dealing with a situation correctly. Once you know that there is a problem, you will then have to use your common sense and your sense of what is right, within the spirit of the Code, to deal with it depending on the individual circumstances. Remember, if you are in doubt, you can always consult another member of chambers or, in emergencies, the Bar Council's adviser on professional conduct problems.

7.2.6   What the lay client is entitled to expect from you

Finally, remember that your duty to the lay client includes giving full and accurate advice to him or her on all matters. This involves you in applying the spirit of the Code, as well as good business sense. Your function is to give information to your client on options and consequences, as well as your opinion on which line of action he or she should pursue and why. It is never your function to make choices for your client or to force him or her to do what you want.

Thinking back, for example, to the client who has information on others involved in his or her offending. Your duty to your client is to advise him or her on what might be done with that information, the consequences of what he or she decides to do and also your opinion on the best course of action to pursue. You will give your client the information that he or she needs to make a fully informed decision. Your opinion on the best course of action may be to reveal this information to the judge so that your client can receive maximum credit when being sentenced. You will explain to your client why you think that this best serves his or her interests, but make clear that the final decision is his or hers to make. If you have done your job in fully informing your client about the potential choices then he or she is ideally placed to make a decision. If the client decides not to follow your advice and you feel that this is a mistake, you may wish to have your client endorse your brief stating that he or she understands the consequences of the choice and that he or she still wishes to proceed in this way. As long as your client's choice does not involve your having to act unethically, then you will have to run the case as he or she instructs. It is, after all, your client's case.

Many trainee barristers seem to believe that the lay client's function is simply to listen respectfully to counsel's wise pronouncements, rather than play an active part in the conference. This is not correct. You are providing a service for which you are being paid and the lay client is entitled to expect professionalism and courtesy at all times rather than irritation or condescension. Remember that the most important person in any conference is your lay client.

7.3 Advocacy skills

The role of an advocate in court is very demanding and you will soon find yourself in challenging and highly stressful situations. Throughout, however, your conduct must meet the rightly demanding standards of the profession. If you do so you will avoid adverse criticism and know that you have acted to the best of your abilities in the interest of your client. For a recent example of unprofessional behaviour see *Boodram v State of Trinidad and Tobago* [2002] 1 Cr App R 12. In that case defence counsel conducting a trial for murder had failed to realise that it was in fact a retrial. This was described as 'the worst case of the failure of counsel to carry out his duties in a criminal case that their lordships have come across' (para 40).

This section will help you to identify the main duties of the advocate; it is not exhaustive and should be read in the context of the general guidance offered in the rest of this Manual. Many of the rules of professional conduct that are relevant to courtroom advocacy are longstanding, however, the precise wording of the rules and duties do change from time to time to adapt to the changing circumstances of modern life. It is therefore vital that you are up-to-date with any amendments to the rules. A full and up-to-date version of the Code is available on the Bar Council web site www.barcouncil.org.uk.

In the context of advocacy, the main areas of the Code for BVC students to concentrate on are:

(a) Part III which contains the Fundamental Principles, including the duty not to act dishonestly or bring the profession into disrepute and the particular duties to the court and to act in the best interests of the client. It also includes the duties to the Legal Services Commission and not to discriminate on grounds of race, sex and so forth and the duties which safeguard a barrister's independence.

(b) Part VII which sets out the duties of barristers when conducting work including the general duties to act courteously and promptly, the duty of confidentiality, duties where there is a conflict between clients, duties when drafting documents and appearing in court, the rules concerning contact with witnesses, media comment and advertising.

One of the main concerns for practising barristers is striking the balance between the overriding duty to the court and promoting the client's case:

(a) A barrister has an overriding duty to the court to act with independence in the interests of justice: he must assist the court in the administration of justice and must not deceive or knowingly or recklessly mislead the court. (Code para 302)

(b) A barrister must promote and protect fearlessly and by all proper and lawful means the lay client's best interests and do so without regard to his own interests or to any consequences to himself or to any other person (including any professional client or other intermediary or another barrister). (Code para 303(a))

See *R v McFadden* (1976) 62 Cr App R 187, where James LJ at page 190 offered the following stark observation on the competing considerations of duty to the court and the status of the Bar Council's guidance.

The Bar Council issues statements from time to time to give guidance to the profession in matters of etiquette and procedure. A barrister who conforms to the Council's rulings knows that he cannot be committing an offence against professional discipline. But such statements, although they have strong persuasive force, do not bind courts. If therefore a judge requires a barrister to do, or refrain from doing, something in the course of a case, the barrister may protest and may cite any relevant ruling of the Bar Council, but since the judge is the final authority in his own court, if counsel's protest is unavailing, he must either withdraw or comply with the ruling or look for redress in a higher court.

In this section we will discuss some of the duties that should help inform your decision about how to act in the face of such significant competing interests. Before doing so you will be advised to know where else you can find guidance on your duties and conduct in court.

7.3.1 Guidance on duties and conduct in court

7.3.1.1 The Crown Prosecutors' Code

The Crown Prosecution Service (CPS) is a public service for England and Wales headed by the Director of Public Prosecutions (DPP) and is answerable to Parliament through the Attorney-General. While the police are responsible for investigating crime, the CPS are the public prosecutors; however, they co-operate closely with the police whilst remaining independent of them.

The DPP is empowered under s 10 of the Prosecution of Offences Act 1985, to give guidance on the general principles to be applied when making decisions about prosecutions and this is the main function of the Code for Crown Prosecutors. For the purposes of this Code, 'Crown Prosecutor' includes members of staff in the Crown Prosecution Service who are designated by the DPP under s 7A of the Act and are exercising powers under that section. The code sets out the basic principles Crown Prosecutors should follow when they make case decisions. The Code helps the Crown Prosecution Service to play its part in making sure that justice is done. It contains information that is important to police officers and others who work in the criminal justice system and to the general public. The Code is also designed to make sure that everyone knows the principles that the Crown Prosecution Service applies when carrying out its work. By applying the same principles, everyone involved in the system is helping to treat victims fairly and to prosecute fairly but effectively.

The Code is a public document. It is set out in full in **Chapter 2** and is available on the CPS web site: www.cps.gov.uk. Translations into other languages are available, as are audio and braille copies.

7.3.1.2 Guidance for prosecuting counsel

In the mid-19th century Crompton J said that prosecuting counsel 'are to regard themselves as ministers of justice, and not to struggle for a conviction' (*R v Puddick* (1865) 4 F & F 497). Nearly a century and a half later the Court of Appeal repeated the concept of ministers of justice in *R v Gonez* [1999] All ER (D) 674. The role of the prosecuting counsel was also the focus of the Farquharson Committee in 1986. It concluded that such counsel have wide duties to the court and the public at large. Prosecuting counsel, it said, are under a duty to present cases for the prosecution fairly to the jury and that they have a greater independence of those instructing them than that enjoyed by other counsel. Prosecuting counsel should not strive unfairly to obtain convictions; they must not press a case beyond the limits that the evidence permits. The Written Standards for the Conduct of Professional Work, appended to the Bar's Code of Conduct at para 11.6 remind prosecuting counsel at all times to have regard to the Farquharson Committee report. Further and more detailed discussion of the conclusions of the committee can be found in *Blackstone's Criminal Practice*, 2004, para D13.5. Additionally, the Farquharson guidelines have recently been produced and although the principles established by the Farquharson Committee will continue to apply, this new guidance can be found attached to the Code in the miscellaneous guidance section or on the CPS website.

Paragraph 11 of the Written Standards of the Bar's Code of Conduct sets out the responsibilities of prosecuting counsel in detail. These standards and principles apply as appropriate to all practising barristers, whether in independent practice or employed and whether appearing as counsel in any given case or exercising any other professional capacity in connection with it (para 11A). Paragraph 11.1 encapsulates the spirit of Mr Justice Crompton's statement:

Prosecuting counsel should not attempt to obtain a conviction by all means at his command. He should not regard himself as appearing for any party. He should lay before the Court fairly and impartially the whole of the facts which comprise the case for the prosecution and should assist the Court on all matters of law applicable to the case.

For example, a prosecutor should take special care not to prejudice the defendant's trial by engendering inappropriate amounts of sympathy for the alleged victim of an assault.

7.3.1.3   Equal Treatment Benchbook

When working as an advocate in court you will have your ability to deal with people regularly tested. One of the keys to being effective in court is to know and understand the people you deal with and address. The trial process rests on the presumption that everyone in court has an ability to follow and understand oral communication and nowhere is this presumption more significant than in the oral testimony of the witnesses. The advocates and the judge will all have highly developed skills in questioning witnesses, analysing their evidence, and communicating their arguments to the jury. If at any point the witnesses or jury fail to comprehend the questions, answers or arguments (ie the oral communications) the trial system begins to fail justice. The Judicial Studies Board's Equal Treatment Benchbook (ETB) has identified what it labels 'cross-cultural misunderstanding' as one way in which oral communication can fail the justice system. Guidance is offered on all aspects of interpersonal communication in a multi-cultural and multi-faith society. Not only is helpful guidance offered on technical matters such as oaths and affirmations but also on interpreting how people answer questions and display respect in court. In addition there are sections on disability, gender and sexuality. The full text of the ETB is available on the web site: www.jsboard.co.uk.

7.3.2   Advocacy and professional conduct

7.3.2.1   General

In the context of civil practice it has been said that a barrister has complete authority over the conduct of litigation and all that is incidental to it, but not over matters which are collateral to the case: *Swinfen v Lord Chelmsford* (1860) 5 Hurl & N 890. Lord Esher MR stated (at 143) in *Matthews v Munster* (1888) LR 20 QBD 141:

... When the client has requested counsel to act as his advocate ... he thereby represents to the other side that counsel is to act for him in the usual course, and he must be bound by that representation so long as it continues ... The request does not mean that counsel is to act in any other character than that of advocate or to do any other act than such as an advocate usually does. The duty of counsel is to advise his client out of court and to act for him in court, and until his authority is withdrawn he has, with regard to all matters that properly relate to the conduct of the case, unlimited power to do that which is best for his client.

Under the Civil Procedure Rules 1998, r 1.3 the parties are required to help the court to further the overriding objective, that is to enable the court to deal with cases justly. The Access to Justice Act 1999, s 42 has inserted a new provision into the Courts and Legal Services Act 1990, s 27 (rights of audience), that any person exercising a right of audience before any court has a duty to the court to act with independence in the interests of justice and that duty shall override any other obligation with which it is inconsistent (other than an obligation under the criminal law). Should you receive instructions that are in conflict with these requirements you may find yourself to be professionally embarrassed and need to withdraw from the case.

As a barrister you have a duty to the court to ensure that it is informed of all relevant decisions and legislative provisions of which you are aware whether they are favourable or unfavourable to the contention which you are arguing (Code para 708(c)). Similarly any procedural irregularity must be brought to the court's attention during the hearing — you must resist the temptation to reserve the matter for an appeal (Code para 708(d)). These provisions are reiterated in the Written Standards at para 5.10(c).

7.3.3 Submissions

It is well known that counsel should not give evidence personally in court. However, inadvertent attempts to do so do occur. You should avoid statements that personalise your submissions, so avoid 'I think', 'I feel' and 'I believe'. If you remember that your role in court is to speak on behalf of your client and the judge will only accept your submissions you should be able to avoid this pitfall.

Similarly when appearing in a case you should maintain a professional detachment. Do not attempt to impose your own personality onto the application. So, avoid expressions of personal opinion, do not thank judges for administering justice in your client's favour and likewise, resist the temptation to express disappointment when they do not! (In any event the hearing may not be the end of the matter — are there meritorious grounds of appeal?) You should also avoid visible or audible reactions to your opponent's case as it is presented in court — wait until you have an opportunity to reply. And if the judge's questions are inconvenient or unhelpful to your case maintain a poker face and attempt to turn your answer to your client's advantage.

The following provisions of the Code are of direct relevance to submissions and applications, but most of them equally apply to trial advocacy. Remember that these duties apply to both oral advocacy and written advocacy (for example skeleton arguments).

(a) Preservation of *confidentiality* of lay client's affairs (para 702).

Clients sometimes give their lawyers information on the understanding that it will not be communicated to others — including the court. Occasionally this information would be of assistance to their case. In such circumstances you must get the lay client's express permission to disclose the fact. It is often wise to have the client endorse your brief to confirm his or her permission — this is particularly advisable if the professional client is not present. If the court or an opponent attempts to draw you on a point that your client has identified as confidential you must still respect your client's wishes. Neither the court nor an opponent is in a position to require you to make a disclosure, though of course both are at liberty to draw their own conclusions. In civil proceedings the court can use its wide powers to stay proceedings until the information is disclosed. This may be a wholly consistent manoeuvre by the judge in order to meet the overriding objective of the rules of enabling the court to deal with cases justly, see CPR, r 1.1.

(b) Counsel must not deceive or knowingly or recklessly *mislead* the Court (para 302). Fortunately few barristers would countenance the former, but the latter can occur often through poor preparation and sheer carelessness. Note that recklessness will leave you on the wrong side of the line — hence the importance of finding adequate time for thorough preparation, marking your brief in such a way that you can find relevant facts readily and giving yourself adequate time to answer questions. If your brief or the pre-hearing client conference is unable to supply the answer do not speculate as to what it might be. The court will be sympathetic that you are not in possession of all the facts in a case (so long as you are not personally at fault) especially at the interim stage.

(c) A barrister must not adduce *evidence* obtained otherwise than from or through the client or devise facts which will assist the lay client's case (para 708(e)).

(d) A barrister must not devise facts which will assist in advancing his lay client's case (Written Standards para 5.8).

This follows on from what has just been said about avoiding speculation and filling in gaps. It also reminds us that a barrister cannot (in the ordinary run of events) give evidence in open court. (For the extraordinary circumstances when it is appropriate for counsel to give evidence see the Court of Appeal's guidance to the Bar Council and Law Society in *R v Jaquith* [1989] Crim LR 563.) Whilst you should do everything in your legitimate powers to promote the cause of your client there are limits and this is one of the most significant.

7.3.3.1   Full and frank disclosure

In civil applications that are without notice there is a duty to give full and frank disclosure. This means that adverse facts and potential arguments that the other side either does intend to raise or may raise should be brought to the attention of the judge. The Civil Procedure Rules require parties to address in their evidence 'all material facts of which the court should be made aware' (PD 25, para 3.3). However, it is not sufficient to assume that the judge is aware of an adverse fact simply because it is in the witness statement or your skeleton argument. You have a duty to draw the court's attention to such facts orally. This is a continuing duty, so if something material subsequently comes to light before the return date the court must be informed of it. Failure to disclose will usually result in an order being set aside as of right and would additionally be a breach of the Code of Conduct, in particular the duty not mislead the court (para 302).

7.3.4   Trial advocacy

Before conducting — indeed before planning — a trial you need to be aware of the limits placed on contact with witnesses within the Code. Basically witness coaching is not permitted in England and Wales (see para 705(a)). In most cases the solicitor is the main conduit for instructions and can relay important messages to the lay client. These and other points that are relevant to client conferences are dealt with in **7.2** above and discussed at length in the *Conference Skills Manual* (**Chapter 9**).

The special guidance for prosecuting counsel has been discussed, that for defence counsel is given in the Written Standards at para 12. The essence of this guidance is found at para 12.1:

When defending a client on a criminal charge, a barrister must endeavour to protect his client from conviction except by a competent tribunal and upon legally admissible evidence sufficient to support a conviction for the offence charged.

The rest of para 12 and the following paragraph on confessions of guilt should be read carefully before preparing the case, making any contact with the prosecutor, offering advice to clients in conference and attending court to represent them.

Attendance of counsel at court is considered in para 16 of the Written Standards. These should be read with care, as some of the guidance is complex. However one point is clear:

Defence counsel should ensure that the defendant is never left unrepresented at any stage of his trial. (Written Standards para 16.2.1)

7.3.4.1 Formulating a theory of the case and witness handling

One of the most important aspects of trial preparation is the theory of the case — a reasoned explanation of your side's case that will form the basis of your closing speech. Your sources are the uncontested evidence in the case and your client's version of the matters that are in issue. Naturally there are professional conduct considerations attached to the formulation of case theories. First and foremost of these is the duty to limit your theory to the facts in the case (according to your client's instructions and those facts that are not in issue) and any reasonable inferences that can be drawn from those facts. There are special limits for prosecutors, as has been set out previously under para 11.1 of the Written Standards.

On the other hand a defence barrister:

Must not suggest that a victim, witness or other person is guilty of crime, fraud or misconduct or make any defamatory aspersion on the conduct of any other person or attribute to another person the crime or conduct of which his lay client is accused unless such allegations go to a matter in issue (including the credibility of the witness) which is material to his lay client's case and which appear to him to be supported by reasonable grounds. (Code of Conduct para 708(j) and Written Standards para 5.10(h))

When appearing for either the defence or prosecution you:

must not make statements or ask questions which are merely scandalous or intended or calculated only to vilify insult or annoy either a witness or some other person; (Code of Conduct para 708(g) and Written Standards para 5.10(e))

must if possible avoid the naming in open Court of third parties whose character would thereby be impugned; (Code of Conduct para 708(h) and Written Standards para 5.10(f))

With these very significant caveats your theory of the case will lead you to formulating a short explanation of why the events took place and why your client's version of the events is the preferable one. Not only will this form the basis of your closing address but it will also suggest themes that will run through your examination of your own witnesses and cross-examination of those of your opponent. Thus checking that your theory does not offend any of the rules of professional conduct is an essential stage in its formulation.

You will have to exercise personal judgement upon the substance and purpose of questions asked and statements made, since you are personally responsible for the conduct and presentation of your case. See Code of Conduct para 708(a) and Written Standards para 5.10(a). This is in keeping with para 306 of the Code of Conduct:

A barrister is individually and personally responsible for his own conduct and for his professional work: he must exercise his own personal judgement in all his professional activities.

7.3.4.2 Cross-examination

After the other side has brought out evidence from its witness in chief examination, or in civil trials has tendered the witness statement as evidence, you are given the opportunity to question that witness to advance your client's case. You can achieve this in ways that are positive or negative:

Positively:

- seek or emphasise agreement between your client's case and what this witness has just said or can say;
- elicit additional information from the witness that did not come out in examination-in-chief.

Negatively:

- undermine the evidence of this witness;
- undermine this witness.

The rule against unnecessary unpleasant statements and insults that applied to formulating a theory of the case and examination-in-chief is perhaps even more pertinent to cross-examination, so it is worth repeating it. Code of Conduct para 708(g) and Written Standards para 5.10(e) states:

A barrister when conducting proceedings at Court: ...
must not make statements or ask questions which are merely scandalous or intended or calculated only to vilify insult or annoy either a witness or some other person.

Tempting as it may be to get carried away during a particularly successful cross-examination it will in all likelihood damage rather than advance your client's case. Judicial reprimands in open court not only embarrass counsel they can also potentially jeopardise the lay clients' case.

7.3.4.3   Putting your case

A crucial feature of cross-examination is the obligation to put your case. You must put your client's version of a particular event to a witness who is in a position to dispute that version. You may not want to do so, because the witness will disagree with your version of events, but you must. Indeed, if the denial or disagreement is unconvincing this will have an impact in the jury: they may not believe the witness. Even if you strongly suspect that the witness will deny your case convincingly, you must still put the relevant questions to that witness. You cannot merely leave the point and deal with it in your closing speech — the Code prevents you from following this route. Code of Conduct para 708(i) and Written Standards para 5.10(g) states:

A barrister when conducting proceedings at Court: ...
must not by assertion in a speech impugn a witness whom he has had an opportunity to cross-examine unless in cross-examination he has given the witness an opportunity to answer the allegation.

So, if you fail to put your case to the witness:

(a) You are acting incompetently at best, unethically at worst.

(b) You run a danger that you will not be allowed to deal with that point in your closing speech.

(c) When your client goes into the box and gives his or her evidence, and adduces evidence that the jury has not heard put to the other side's witnesses, it may conclude that the defendant has recently invented it.

If through your own fault you have failed to put the client's case; you will have to explain to the judge that it is your fault and not your client's. Witnesses may need to be recalled, the trial delayed and all parties inconvenienced. The consequences therefore are likely to be embarrassing in the extreme.

7.3.4.4 Conclusion of the trial and sentencing

At the conclusion of the judge's summing up the prosecuting counsel is under a duty to draw to the judge's attention any apparent omissions or errors of fact or law (Written Standards para 11.7). If you are acting as defence counsel you would not appear to be under such a duty (except in the case of provocation in a murder trial: *R v Cox* [1995] 2 Cr App R 513). However, if you were not to assist the court at this stage you could jeopardise any subsequent appeal raised by your client.

In relation to sentence, prosecuting counsel should not attempt by advocacy to influence the court with regard to sentence. Indeed if a defendant is unrepresented it is proper for prosecuting counsel to inform the court of any mitigating circumstances about which he or she is instructed (Written Standards para 11.8(a)). The prosecutor also should assist the court with sentencing guidelines and statutory provisions and other technical matters relevant to compensation, forfeiture and restitution (Written Standards para 11.8(b)–(d)). Further the prosecutor should draw the attention of the defence to any assertion of material fact made in mitigation which the prosecutor believes to be untrue. If the defence persists with the assertion prosecuting counsel should invite the court to have the matter determined in a Newton hearing (Written Standards para 11.8(e)).

There are also duties for defence counsel in the sentencing process. If a barrister acting for the defence is instructed to submit in mitigation anything which casts aspersions on the conduct or character of a victim or witness in the case, you must notify the prosecution in advance so as to give prosecuting counsel sufficient opportunity to consider the requirement for a Newton hearing (Written Standards para 12.2(k)).

It is sometimes appropriate for counsel — both for the prosecution and the defence — to see the judge prior to sentencing. Specific guidance is offered on this in *Practice Direction (Criminal: Consolidated)* [2002] 3 All ER 904, para 45.3–5. It is essential that you understand the limits on such contact and what you can expect judges to indicate about the sentence and perhaps more importantly what they will not indicate.

7.3.4.5 Appeals

When deciding whether to appeal the outcome of a case and especially when settling ground of appeal you must remember the guidance offered in the Code of Conduct. This includes the dogmatic statement that counsel should not settle grounds of appeal unless they consider that such grounds are properly arguable (para 704(b) and Written Standards para 17.3). Further if at any stage you are of the view that the appeal should be abandoned, you should at once set out your reasons in writing and send them to your professional client (Written Standards para 17.6). Naturally you should not devise facts which will assist in advancing the lay client's case and a barrister must not draft grounds of appeal or any other document containing:

(a) any statement of fact or contention which is not supported by the lay client or by their instructions;

(b) any contention which he does not consider to be properly arguable;

(c) any allegation of fraud unless he has clear instructions to make such allegation and has before him reasonably credible material which as it stands establishes a prima facie case of fraud; ...

provided that nothing in this paragraph shall prevent a barrister drafting a document containing specific factual statements or contentions included by the barrister subject to

confirmation of their accuracy by the lay client or witness.
(Code of Conduct para 704)

7.4 Negotiation

Professional conduct is as important in negotiation as in any other aspect of a barrister's work. The Code of Conduct applies equally to your conduct as a negotiator as it does to your conduct as an advocate. Of particular relevance to negotiation are those paragraphs which are applicable to all practising barristers (paras 301–307) and those under Part VII relating to the conduct of work by practising barristers. Note in particular the duty in para 701(a) to be courteous, in para 702 the duty of confidentiality, in para 703 the duties in respect of conflicts between lay client and intermediaries, and para 704 the duty not to mislead which although headed 'drafting documents' is of more general application. You should also have regard to the Written Standards for the Conduct of Professional Work of the Code of Conduct, under the Conduct of Work at paras 5.5 and 5.11.

As with other aspects of your work as a barrister, the Code can only give general guidance on ethical rules when negotiating, it cannot deal specifically with every situation that may arise. Although negotiations are conducted privately with only those involved knowing what happened, it is as important to act as ethically as when you are acting in the public eye (eg as an advocate in court). Your reputation is based on how you conduct yourself in practice whether in public or private. The Bar is a small profession!

This section highlights the more common professional conduct issues that arise where a barrister is instructed to negotiate a settlement on behalf of his or her client. It focuses on the general duties when negotiating a settlement in a civil case, as negotiating in a criminal case (or plea bargaining) has very specific rules which are beyond the scope of this Manual. When instructed to negotiate a settlement, a barrister needs to be aware of his or her duties to a variety of people: the professional client, the lay client, the opposing lawyer (whether barrister or solicitor) and the court (when negotiating a settlement within the litigation process). The section is divided into four parts, each one dealing with one of these four relevant relationships.

7.4.1 The professional client

Both the solicitor and counsel may become involved in seeking to negotiate a settlement in a case. The division of roles should be kept clear. You might be asked to advise the solicitor on possible terms of settlement, in which case the solicitor will proceed with any negotiation. Alternatively, you might be instructed to try to settle a case, in which case you must keep the solicitor informed.

(a) Keep your professional client informed of developments. If such a client is present, listen to his or her views on the merit of any proposal that has been made.

(b) Be courteous and even-tempered in your dealings with your professional client. Do not argue in front of the lay client. If there is a difference of opinion between you, discuss it out of the lay client's hearing.

(c) Do not, however, keep your professional client happy at the expense of your lay client's interests. For example, do not advise your client to reject a fair offer of compromise merely because your solicitor insists that his firm, rather than the one proposed, handles the conduct of the sale of the property in dispute. The Code states:

303(b)   A barrister owes his primary duty as between the lay client and any professional client or other intermediary to the lay client and must not permit the intermediary to limit his discretion as to how the interests of the lay client can best be served ...

703   If a barrister in independent practice forms the view that there is a conflict of interest between his lay client and a professional client or other intermediary (for example because he considers that the intermediary may have been negligent) he must consider whether it would be in the lay client's interest to instruct another professional adviser or representative and, if he considers that it would be, the barrister must so advise and take such steps as he considers necessary to ensure that his advice is communicated to the lay client (if necessary by sending a copy of his advice in writing directly to the lay client as well as to the intermediary).

7.4.2   The lay client

A lawyer is negotiating for the client. The lawyer is the expert, the professional adviser and representative acting on behalf of the client. However, it is the client's case. The professional conduct issues which arise as a result are as follows.

7.4.2.1   Act only on instructions and within your client's instructions

As a lawyer, you act as your client's agent in a negotiation and general agency rules apply. You have actual authority to act only within the client's instructions and should never settle outside this actual authority. However, from the other party's point of view, you are acting for the client and have the apparent or ostensible authority to settle a case after proceedings have been issued. The extent of this apparent authority can of course be cut down by giving the other side notice of any limit on it. If you act outside your actual authority but bind the client because the agreement comes within your apparent authority you will be in breach of duty to your client and liable to him or her.

You must therefore only negotiate when your client instructs you to do so, and you can only negotiate within the authority given to you by your client. You must ensure that you really do understand the client's objectives, interests and needs and pursue these in the negotiation and that you have your client's clear authority to either propose or accept an offer of compromise.

Your brief will normally contain a lot of information which makes it clear what the client will or will not accept, ie, sets the parameters of your actual authority in negotiating a settlement. However, there may well be matters of detail on which it is not clear exactly what the client wants. Making it apparent to the other side that any negotiation is subject to the authorisation or approval of the client, leaves you open to agree detail on condition that the client does approve (ie, giving notice of the limited authority). By setting this parameter, it leaves you free to try to tie up the detail in the best way possible without binding the client.

7.4.2.2   Ensure that the client's claim is legitimate

Although it is the lay client's case, you have a duty not to knowingly allow yourself to be used as a tool to obtain settlement in respect of a groundless or fraudulent claim. If your client's case is without any foundation, you should not act for him or her. The Code sets out:

704   A barrister must not devise facts which will assist in advancing the lay client's case and must not draft any statement of case, witness statement, affidavit, notice of appeal or other document containing:

(a) any statement of fact or contention which is not supported by the lay client or by his instructions;

(b) any contention which he does not consider to be properly arguable;

(c) any allegation of fraud unless he has clear instructions to make such allegation and has before him reasonably credible material which as it stands establishes a prima facie case of fraud;

(d) in the case of a witness statement or affidavit any statement of fact other than the evidence which in substance according to his instructions the barrister reasonably believes the witness would give if the evidence contained in the witness statement or affidavit were being given in oral examination;

provided that nothing in this paragraph shall prevent a barrister drafting a document containing specific factual statements or contentions included by the barrister subject to confirmation of their accuracy by the lay client or witness.

7.4.2.3 Ensure your client's interests are protected

As counsel, it is also your duty to ensure your client's interests are adequately protected by the machinery of the compromise. For example, a judgment debt is likely to affect your client's prospects of obtaining future credit, whereas an agreement to pay the debt contained in a Tomlin order will not. For further guidance on enforcement of orders see the *Civil Litigation Manual*.

7.4.2.4 Advise the client clearly and fully on their case

You also have a duty, as counsel, to ensure that when the client decides whether or not to accept an offer or agree to settle, the decision is a fully informed one. You must advise the client both of your view of the case and of what, in your judgement, is the best course of action. Ensure that the client understands how the strengths and weaknesses of the case or any procedural or evidential matters affect the chances of achieving the objectives that he or she is seeking. Ensure that he or she is aware of the risks involved in making, accepting or rejecting an offer of compromise, for example, the incidence of costs, and that he or she understands the nature and effect of any agreement and/or any undertaking he or she is proposing to give to the court. The terms of the settlement must be fully explained as must the effect, in particular that settlement will mean the end of the matter and there will normally be no possibility of reopening it or seeking more.

Failing to advise the client properly or just accepting a decision where the client clearly does not understand his or her legal position or consequences of the decision is a breach of duty to the client.

7.4.2.5 It is the client's decision, not yours

Decisions about substantive matters, eg, whether or not to negotiate, what issues are open to negotiation and whether or not an offer should be accepted, must be made by the client. It is the client's case and you must ensure that any decision about whether to settle or not is that of the client and not yours. Whether the settlement is acceptable must be measured against the client's objectives, needs and interests. Having advised fully (see above), you must then accept the client's decision and abide by it. If the client is not prepared to accept a settlement, that is his or her prerogative. The only exception to this may arise if the client is funded by the Community Legal Service. The solicitor will be under a duty to report to the Regional Director of the Community Legal Service that the client has declined to accept an offer to settle (Funding Code Procedures, Section 12 Reporting Obligations, C43.2.vi.a Duties of the Solicitor). In such a case advice may have been required from a barrister on the merits of the case prior to funding being granted. You may have given that advice which included an assessment of quantum. If the settlement offer is within that which you advised, then you too may fall under the duty of any Legal Representative in the Funding Code Procedures (C44 i) to ensure that the Regional Director is informed, if it appears to you that the client has required the case to be conducted unreasonably, or so as to incur an unjustifiable expense to the Fund or has unreasonably required that the case be continued.

7.4.2.6   Conditional fee agreements

Barristers are increasingly entering conditional fee agreements whereby no fee is charged if the client loses the case but the barrister receives a 'success' fee if the client wins. These agreements raise novel practical problems and have significant potential pitfalls for the Bar. In particular, it is recognised that a conditional fee agreement could impact on the barrister/client relationship in respect of settling a case.

Guidance is given by the General Council of the Bar in its 'Conditional Fee Guidance' set out under Rules and Guidance on the Bar Council website (www.barcouncil.org). Part I deals specifically with Ethical Guidance. The paragraphs of particular relevance to negotiation are:

Conditional Fee Guidance

6.   Form of agreement
The barrister should ensure that no term increases or tends to increase inappropriate pressure on the lay client to reach a settlement.

9.   Impartiality/conflict of interest
Having accepted instructions to act under a CFA, a barrister shall thereafter give impartial advice to the lay client at all times and take all reasonable steps to identify and declare to the lay client and to the instructing solicitor any actual or apparent conflict of interest between the barrister and the lay client.

10.   Advice and interests of lay client
During the currency of a CFA, the barrister should use his/her best endeavours to ensure that:

    (a)   any advice given by the barrister in relation to the case is communicated and fully explained to the lay client;

    (b)   any offer of settlement is communicated to the lay client forthwith;

    (c)   the consequences of particular clauses in the solicitor/lay client agreement and the solicitor/barrister agreement are explained to the client as and when they become relevant, particularly after an offer of settlement has been made.

This last obligation applies in particular to the financial consequences which may arise from the making of an offer to settle the case including consideration of (1) any increase in the offer of settlement; (2) 'conventional' costs consequences; and (3) the success fees which are or may become payable.

11.   Advising on settlement
When advising on a settlement of the action the barrister should at all times have in mind his/her obligation under paragraph 303(a) of the Code to 'promote and protect fearlessly and by all proper and lawful means the lay client's best interests and do so without regard to his own interests or to any consequences to himself or to any other person (including any professional client or other intermediary or another barrister)'. The barrister's duty must be, when advising the client on a settlement or on a payment in or Part 36 offer, to advise as to the best course of action from the lay client's point of view only.

12.   Disagreement over settlement
Difficulties may arise when the lawyers disagree about the wisdom of continuing the case or accepting an offer, whether that disagreement is:

    (a) between them on the one part and the lay client on the other; or

    (b) between solicitor and counsel; or

    (c) between leading and junior counsel.

In such event careful consideration must be given to the lay client's interests. Every effort should be made to avoid unfairly putting the lay client in the position where having begun proceedings s/he is left without representation. However, where, for example, counsel has been misled about the true nature of the evidence or the lay client is refusing to accept firm advice as to the future conduct of the case, the terms of the CFA may permit counsel to withdraw. Before taking this serious step the barrister will have to check carefully whether s/he is entitled to withdraw.

13.   Withdrawal from the case

The barrister may withdraw from the case in any of the circumstances set out in the CFA agreement, but only if satisfied that s/he is permitted to withdraw pursuant to Part VI of the Code. In the event that the CFA agreement does not contain a term that the barrister may withdraw from the case in particular circumstances, but the Code requires the barrister to withdraw in those circumstances, the Code takes priority over the agreement.

If you are acting under a CFA agreement you will need to ensure that your advice to your client satisfies these requirements, in particular that you advise the client on the best course of action for him or her regardless of your own position on any success fee. In addition, you must ensure that your advice on the offer of settlement and the consequences of the CFA agreement is clear to the client, in particular advising on the usual costs consequences of settlement and any success fee payable. You should also make clear the consequences of not accepting the settlement and ensure that the client is clear on the net gain of such action (the likely better sum/outcome, the prospects of getting it and the further costs consequences of continuing including any likely success fee).

7.4.2.7   Client confidentiality

Your duty not to divulge information entrusted to you in confidence by your client without his or her consent continues after the case, even if it has been dealt with by way of a negotiated compromise. If you are acting under a conditional fee agreement, the guidance of the Bar Council in para 14 is that the fact that the action is funded by means of a CFA, and the terms of a CFA, should not be disclosed to the other parties to the action without the express written permission of the lay client, or save in so far as such disclosure is required by the court, the CPR, statute, rule, order, or Practice Direction.

7.4.3   The opponent

Negotiating with the other side raises the most difficult issues of professional conduct. These can be roughly divided between those matters which raise issues of confidentiality and/or privilege and those which raise issue of tactics and general behaviour in the negotiation.

7.4.3.1   Confidentiality/privilege

The first general principle is that you should avoid discussing a case without instructions. Remember you are acting for the client and must act on instructions whether express or implicit.

'Without prejudice'

Negotiations with a view to settlement should be conducted 'without prejudice' whether by letter, fax, phone or face-to-face meeting. This basically means that the contents of the negotiation cannot be revealed to the court to assist it to determine the case. While any negotiation with a view to compromise is impliedly without prejudice, the position is also frequently expressly stated, eg, by putting the words 'without prejudice' on a letter. Negotiations between counsel with a view to a compromise are impliedly made 'without prejudice'. Such discussions are in effect privileged and must not be repeated in court or in open correspondence. In the event of a failure to reach a satisfactory compromise, warn your client not to repeat in court what has been said during the negotiation. More detailed guidance on the evidential position of 'without prejudice' communications is contained in the *Evidence Manual*.

There are two exceptions to the rule that what was discussed in a negotiation is privileged and cannot be repeated. The first is where an admission of fact, which should properly have been openly disclosed, is made in the course of negotiations. For example, 'My client now admits he gave your client a gift of £500 although the balance of his claim for £2,000 was a loan.' The umbrella of 'without prejudice' does not protect such an admission. You may therefore use the admission if it is in your lay client's best interests to do so, though you should inform your opponent of your intention to do this. On the other hand, 'My client is prepared to waive £500 of his claim provided your client pays him the balance of £1,500 within 28 days' is not an admission. It is a concession made 'without prejudice' in the context of an offer of compromise.

The second is where agreement is reached. The phrase 'without prejudice' was discussed in *Guiness Peat Properties v Fitzroy Robinson Partnership* [1987] 2 All ER 716, where it was held to mean 'without prejudice to the position of the writer if the terms he proposes are not accepted'. If a 'without prejudice' offer is accepted it is a formal agreement to settle the claim, is immediately binding, and can be revealed. If the offer is not accepted it is ignored, and nothing said in a letter making the offer can be used as evidence (*Rush v Tompkins Ltd v GLC* [1988] 3 WLR 939).

Discussions between counsel about a possible settlement or how to assist the case to run smoothly frequently take place without either client being present. Both counsel may therefore be more informal than if the clients are present, using language and saying things which might not be said if the clients are present. However, you must always remember that your first duty is to your client; that you are negotiating on their behalf. Your duty of confidentiality means that you should not reveal anything to the other side that might be damaging to your client or their case. As a general rule, you should not disclose anything that your client would not wish the other side to know. If something is revealed to you by your opponent which it is in your client's interest to know or which may affect the way in which you conduct the case, you must disclose this to the client. You should also tell your opponent that you will inform your client.

Do not be persuaded to reveal matters which you feel you should not or not inform your client of things you feel you should by your opponent saying or implying that 'counsel to counsel' discussions exempt you from your duty to your client. There is no such thing within the Code of Conduct or professional ethics as 'counsel to counsel confidentiality'!

7.4.3.2 Behaviour/tactics in the negotiation

As counsel, you have a duty to conduct negotiations in a fair, honest, courteous and trustworthy manner. You should never compromise your professional integrity. This does not mean that you should adopt an apologetic approach to negotiating. The importance of fair play should not detract from your duty to promote the interests of the lay client fearlessly. Frustration may tempt you on occasions to forget this: *don't let it*. A reputation for underhandedness or sharp practice will be retained long after the event. The old maxim 'you can fool some of the people all of the time' has little application at the Bar. The grapevine is far too effective! You need to be conscious that, even if the behaviour comes within the ethical boundaries (which are often difficult to determine), the tactics you use will invariably affect the reputation you build. If, for example, you use aggressive tactics you will get a reputation for being confrontational which may be difficult to get rid of.

Misleading your opponent

Some tactics are clearly dishonest and unethical, eg, deliberately misleading your opponent by pretending to have evidence you do not have. They are against the Bar's Code of Conduct and, even if they do not amount to an offence, eg, fraud, using them can result in being debarred. You must never deliberately deceive or mislead your opponent in order to achieve a more favourable offer of compromise (see para 301 of the Code of Conduct).

It is, however, acceptable to use 'bluff', allowing an opponent to form an impression without positively misleading him. However, managing or manipulating information may become sufficiently 'tricky' or misleading to amount to professional misconduct. A barrister's job is to promote the client's case as an advocate. You can quite properly pitch the case at its highest when trying to reach a settlement, even though you may not necessarily succeed in proving the whole case in court. There is not always a clear line between doing the best for your client and misleading or unfair tactics. But you must not pretend that you do know a fact or have particular instructions if this is simply not true. You must also not knowingly conceal something which ought properly to have been disclosed, for example a document, in the hope of securing a more favourable settlement.

Failing to act courteously

While it is absolutely acceptable to be assertive in your manner, aggressive behaviour may become sufficiently insulting or rude to amount to a breach of your professional duty to act courteously. Avoid bickering with your opponent; it does not do your client any good. Nor is it wise to lose your objectivity by taking on the persona of your client in the course of negotiations. For example, 'Your client is totally dishonest, he has already stolen £2,000 from us'. This merely serves to antagonise.

Use of threats

'Threat' is defined as 'a conditional commitment by a negotiator to act in a way that appears detrimental to the other party unless the other party complies with a request', in Donald G. Gifford's book *Legal Negotiation: Theory and Applications* ((1989) (St Paul: Min-West Publishing Co), p 143). Not all threats are unethical. Many negotiation tactics, although not phrased as threats, implicitly involve them, eg, 'the final offer' is basically a threat to end the negotiation if the offer is not accepted.

Difficulties arise in considering actions which a client might take if he or she does not get the desired result from the opponent. Clearly, it would be dishonest and unprofessional to suggest that your client intended to do something he or she did not intend. In addition, your client may be considering action that is not legitimate because it is illegal or impractical, in which case you should be advising your client in strong terms not to take it.

Even where the client has threatened to take particular legitimate action if their demands are not met, eg that they will 'go to the press unless the opponent does X', whatever the facts, counsel must tread a fine line between following the client's instructions and avoiding the aggressive use of threats to secure a favourable outcome. It is unprofessional and unethical to make threats that are tantamount to blackmail. On the other hand it is quite legitimate to point out potential consequences. The dividing line between a legitimate statement and an unethical threat is not clear. This is a difficult area and there is no clear guidance in the Code of Conduct. It frequently comes down to a question of the manner in which the information is imparted to one's opponent.

When in doubt, err on the side of caution, ie do *not* threaten 'My client will go to the press unless your client does XYZ', as this is really simply a threat. However, you may inform the opponent in appropriate language that your client is indicating an intention to go to the newspapers, eg 'I think it is only fair to tell you that my client is so upset by this/ feels so strongly about this that she's talking of going to the newspapers'. Although the difference between these two approaches is subtle, it is nevertheless there. The second example is merely a statement of the client's possible intention and *not* linked to any demand in respect of her case.

Going back on your word

Do not go back on your word, or subsequently pretend you did not say something, in order to cover your own mistake or indiscretion. Such behaviour is unacceptable. If you have made an error, admit it.

Acting without authority

Do not make an offer or commit your client to an agreement without instructions or authority to do so. Make it clear to your opponent when your proposal is subject to your lay client's agreement. For example, 'If my client were prepared to do XYZ, would your client do ABC?'

Litigants in person

The above considerations apply whether or not your opponent is a lawyer or a litigant in person. However, where your opponent is a litigant in person you have the additional consideration of ensuring that you do not abuse your professional status and knowledge. This can produce other difficult issues, such as how much and the way in which you explain the law as you understand it, eg to what extent you include in your explanation any points of law which go against you.

7.4.4 The court

The fact that you are seeking to negotiate a settlement may deceive you into thinking of the case as being subject only to your decisions. Never forget the ultimate role of the court and the need for its approval where you are seeking a consent order. The judge may suggest some amendments to your draft order.

If negotiations are taking place at court, keep the court informed of the possibility of a compromise. It may be sufficient to relay this information to the court via the court clerk or usher. At times, it may be necessary to explain this to the judge or tribunal. Provide the court with a realistic estimate of the further time you need to discuss any proposals. Inform the court immediately upon reaching agreement. The Code states:

701 A barrister:

(a) must in all his professional activities be courteous and act promptly conscientiously diligently and with reasonable competence and take all reasonable and practicable steps to avoid unnecessary expense or waste of the Court's time and to ensure that professional engagements are fulfilled ...

Paragraph 5.11 of the Written Standards states:

A barrister must take all reasonable and practicable steps to avoid unnecessary expense or waste of the Court's time. He should, when asked, inform the Court of the probable length of his case; and he should also inform the court of any developments which affect information already provided.

If you have time, draw up draft minutes of the agreed terms or order.

When you go into court, either hand up the draft, or, in the absence of a written draft, inform the court of the terms which have been agreed between the parties 'subject to Your Honour/Your Lordship's approval'. It may be necessary even where you have a draft order, to take the judge through its terms. Invite the judge to make the order in the terms proposed.

If agreement is reached between the parties away from the court, for example, in correspondence, remind your professional client to inform the court as soon as possible.

7.4.5 Conclusion

This section has highlighted the various professional conduct issues which arise when a barrister is instructed to negotiate a settlement on behalf of his or her client in a civil case. Acting ethically and professionally in your dealings with your lay and professional client and your opponent in a negotiation is every bit as important as it is when you act as an advocate in court. The way you behave in these circumstances is as open to action by the Bar Council and will have as much, if not more, impact on your reputation.

7.5 Opinion writing and drafting

In written work, you must display the same high standards of integrity and honesty that apply in all other aspects of your practice. The Code of Conduct has a lot to say about the conduct of written work. This section is designed to give you some guidance on matters that arise frequently in opinion writing and drafting in civil and criminal cases.

7.5.1 General provisions relevant to written work

When undertaking any written work on behalf of a client you should have a comprehensive knowledge of:

- the Code of Conduct ('the Code');
- the Written Standards for the Conduct of Professional Work ('the Written Standards');
- Guidance on Preparation of Defence Case Statements;
- Guidance on Preparation of Witness Statements;
- the Funding Code.

The Written Standards in particular provide a guide to the way in which you should carry out your work. They must be read in conjunction with the Code and are to be taken into account in determining whether a disciplinary offence has been committed.

In undertaking any written work, advisory or drafting, or indeed any oral advisory work, you must always bear in mind the fundamental principles of the Code. In particular you:

(a) must not engage in conduct whether in pursuit of your profession or otherwise which is:

(i) dishonest or otherwise discreditable;

(ii) prejudicial to the administration of justice; or

(iii) likely to diminish public confidence in the legal profession or the administration of justice or otherwise bring the legal profession into disrepute (Code para 301);

(b) have an overriding duty to the court to act with independence in the interests of justice; you must assist the court in the administration of justice and not deceive or knowingly or recklessly mislead the court (Code para 302);

(c) must promote and fearlessly protect the lay client's best interests by all lawful and proper means and without regard to any consequences to yourself or your professional client (Code para 303);

(d) are individually and personally responsible for your conduct and for your professional work; you must exercise personal judgment in all your professional activities (Code para 306);

(e) must not allow your independence integrity or freedom from external pressures to be compromised, or do anything which would lead to an inference that they have been compromised (para 307).

Although these fundamental principles lie at the heart of all written work which you may be asked to undertake on behalf of a lay client, the Code and Written Standards and the Guidance issued by the Bar Council under the Code offer specific guidance in relation to certain types of work which you may be instructed to carry out.

7.5.2 Your duty on receipt of papers

When you obtain instructions to advise or draft a document, you must read them as soon as possible, to ensure that you are competent to deal with the matter, and have adequate time to carry out the task given the pressures of your other work (see para 701(b) and (c) of the Code and para 3.1 of the Written Standards). You must not delay in carrying out this task. You should aim to do this within a few days, or immediately if the instructions are urgent, because if the case is beyond your competence, or you cannot fulfil the task within the required time or a reasonable time, then the professional client must be informed and the instructions passed on to another barrister. Of course, you cannot return instructions without first explaining to your client the reason for doing so, and you obviously cannot pass the papers on to another barrister without the consent of your client (Code para 610).

If you do accept the instructions, then you must ensure that you do the work within the time requested or agreed, or within a reasonable time. If there is a time limit laid down by the Civil Procedure Rules within which the work should be done (for example, filing a Defence, serving Witness Statements, filing a Notice of Appeal) then you must ensure the work is done and returned to your instructing solicitor in good time to enable him or her to comply with the time limit. A failure to comply with time limits laid down by the Civil Procedure Rules may result in your lay client's case being struck out, so drafting work must usually be given priority over advisory work.

Solicitors are frequently heard to complain that a failure to carry out written work within the requested or agreed time, or within a reasonable time, is a very common failing of the Bar. In practice, it sometimes happens that cases run on longer than intended, or urgent and serious matters arise, so that agreed time limits cannot be met or the work requested cannot be undertaken within a reasonable time. If this does happen, it is important to telephone your instructing solicitor immediately. The lay client may be able and prepared to wait, but if he or she is not, then you must return the instructions to the professional client or to another barrister acceptable to your professional and lay client (para 701(e) of the Code and para 5.6 of the Written Standards).

It follows that you must actively manage your practice and keep a close eye on the volume of work that you have. Be realistic and honest about (a) the length of time it will take you to complete each item of work and (b) the work that you are competent to do, having regard to your knowledge and expertise. Do not feel obliged to accept instructions in a complex case involving copyright and passing off if your primary area of expertise is family work and you do not know the first thing about copyright or passing off. Indeed, if you know, or ought to know, that you are not competent to handle the instructions, it would be a clear breach of the Code to accept them.

7.5.3   Opinion writing

7.5.3.1   General principles

Any advice that you give should be 'practical, appropriate to the needs and circumstances of the particular client, and clearly and comprehensively expressed' (para 5.7 of the Written Standards). This is obvious. However, in the remainder of this section, some guidance will be given about your professional obligations when specific types of advice are sought.

7.5.3.2   Advice for the benefit of the Legal Aid Board/Legal Services Commission

If you undertake publicly-funded work you have additional professional responsibilities that you must always follow when it comes to providing written advice about the case. In publicly-funded cases, you will almost always be asked to provide a written opinion before proceedings are issued, and also quite often after service of witness statements, to determine whether it is appropriate for the matter to go to trial. In relation to opinions provided under Legal Aid Certificates granted before April 2000, the Opinion must comply with the *Legal Aid Guidelines* (to be found in the Legal Aid Handbook or on the Bar Council's website). In respect of Legal Services Certificates provided under the Funding Code, the advice must comply with Annex E of the Code of Conduct *'Guidelines on Opinions under the Funding Code'*. Both sets of guidelines are in fairly similar terms and give guidance to barristers on what an Advice or Opinion must contain as to the merits of funding or continuing to fund a case.

Generally, Opinions must be prepared in accordance with *The Funding Code* (see www.legalservices.gov.uk). When you are instructed to advise in writing, you must decide whether a conference is necessary, for example to assess the credibility or reliability of a lay client's evidence.

When you write the Opinion, you must ensure that it states (a) the level of service under which the Opinion is given (or applied for) and (b) the case category into which the proceedings fall. In addition, every Opinion on the merits should comply with the following matters in so far as they are relevant to the issues raised in the particular case:

(a) Where factual issues are involved, set out the factual disputes in sufficient detail to enable the Commission to assess their relative strengths and express a clear opinion on whether the applicant's evidence would be accepted by the court, and give reasons for that opinion.

(b) Where there are issues or disputes of law, these must also be summarised in sufficient detail to enable the Commission to come to a view without having to have recourse to materials outside the Opinion. Express a clear view on whether the applicant's case on the law would be accepted by the court, and give reasons for that opinion.

(c) Draw attention to any lack of evidence, which might have a bearing on the applicant's case or any other factor which might affect the outcome of the case.

(d) State the prospects of success, and in particular specify whether they are:

    (i)   very good (greater than 80%);

    (ii) good (60%–80%);

    (iii) moderate (50%–60%);

    (iv) borderline (which means that the prospects of success are not poor, but because there are difficult disputes of fact, law or expert evidence, it is not possible to say that the prospects of success are better than 50%). In this case, the fact, law or expert evidence, which leads you to put the case in this category must be identified;

    (v) poor (less than 50% so the claim is likely to fail);

    (vi) unclear (the case cannot be put into any of the above categories because further investigation is needed; in which case, you must also indicate what further investigation is needed).

(e) Cost benefit: the Opinion must set out the benefit to the client, and put a figure on the likely level of damages the client would receive if successful at trial, allowing for any reduction for contributory negligence or otherwise. Likely damages should also be discounted if there is any doubt as to whether the opponent will be able to pay the money award.

(f) Where the application is for investigative help to be granted or continued, the Opinion should indicate what investigations need to be conducted. It should also show that there are reasonable grounds for believing that when the investigative work has been carried out, the claim will be strong enough, in terms of prospects of success and cost benefit, to justify a grant of full representation.

(g) If the case has a wider public benefit, you should set out the nature of the benefit and the parties affected by it.

(h) Finally you should suggest or formulate any appropriate limitation or condition on the certificate, if it is appropriate to do so, in order to safeguard the Fund.

7.5.3.3 What advice do you give if you become aware that your lay client has improperly obtained public funding?

Sometimes your lay client may provide you with information which suggests that public funding has been wrongly obtained by false or misleading information. If this is the case, you cannot simply turn a blind eye to the matter. You should explore the matter, tactfully, with your lay client and/or instructing solicitor. If it becomes apparent that funding has been improperly obtained, your duty, as counsel, is clearly spelt out by paras 303 and 304 and Annex E paras 20 and 22 of the Code of Conduct (see **7.2.2.5** above). In addition to these provisions, Rule C44 of the *Funding Code Procedures* also provides that counsel must inform the Regional Director if, *inter alia*, it appears that the lay client may have given inaccurate, misleading or incomplete information, or new information or a change of circumstances has come to light which may affect the terms or continuation of the Certificate.

Your obligations under the Code of Conduct are therefore clear. You must inform the Commission of any matter which may affect your lay client's entitlement to funding or the terms or continuation of a Certificate. You should discuss the matter with your lay client, explain the nature of the duty imposed on you, and urge him or her personally to make the disclosure required (although personal disclosure by the lay client does not appear to negate the duty imposed on counsel). Note that para 22 of Annex E provides that where you are under a duty to draw matters to the attention of the Commission, you can do so by drawing the matter to the attention of your instructing solicitor, and asking him or her to pass it on to the Commission, or you can contact the Commission directly if that is appropriate in the circumstances of the case. In addition to the reporting obligations set out above, you must cease to act if the lay client refuses to take action to remedy the situation. In these circumstances, you are effectively put in the position of having to make the disclosure to the Commission against your lay client's wishes, and this would obviously make any continuing professional relationship with him or her extremely difficult.

7.5.3.4   Advice on disclosure

In civil cases, it is your duty to advise your client that all relevant documents must be disclosed, even if they are fatal to his or her case (see para 608 of the Code and **7.2.2.4** above). If the lay client fails to follow your advice, you must withdraw from the case.

Applications made 'without notice' impose an even stricter obligation of disclosure on the lay client. In applications of this type, which will usually involve obtaining an urgent injunction or a freezing or search order, you must ensure that full and frank disclosure is made to the court. The duty of disclosure is really that of your lay client, but it is policed by the lawyers. If you fail to ensure that your lay client complies with it, or fail to draw the attention of the court to matters which should be disclosed, then you may be misleading the court, or engaging in conduct which is prejudicial to the administration of justice. You would therefore be in breach of your duties under paras 301 and 302 of the Code. Any failure to make full and frank disclosure may also result in the order being discharged. An order for costs may also be made against your lay client (or perhaps a wasted costs order may be made against you or your instructing solicitors).

Therefore, in advising a client who wishes to obtain urgent 'without notice' interim relief, such an as injunction, a freezing order, or a search order, it is imperative that your lay client understands the nature of the duty of full and frank disclosure. If necessary you must ask questions of the client to ensure that this duty is complied with. If you are asked to draft any document, such as a witness statement, you must also ensure that all relevant matters are fully and properly disclosed in it.

7.5.3.5   Advice following receipt of further information

It is not uncommon for counsel to be asked to advise at an early stage of an action. Subsequently, you may be sent instructions to settle statements of case, or witness statements or advise on a different aspect of the matter. Sometimes the fresh instructions will contain material that will alter the advice which you gave previously.

If you find yourself in this position, you should reassess any previous advice following receipt of further information if you are instructed to do so. Even if you are not instructed to reconsider your previous advice, you should at least warn your instructing solicitor that your previous views have to be reconsidered as a result of the change of circumstances. A failure to do so may lead to a wasted costs order against you: *C v C (Wasted Costs Order)* [1994] 2 FLR 34.

7.5.3.6   Opinions under conditional fee agreements

If you are instructed to act under a conditional fee agreement ('CFA') then you may face a number of ethical problems, not least when you are instructed to carry out written work. The Bar Council CFA Panel has drawn up a lengthy document to offer guidance to those undertaking CFA work. The *Conditional Fee Guidance* does not form part of the Code of Conduct, but you are strongly advised to follow the guidance to ensure compliance with the Code.

If you are acting under a CFA, then during the currency of the CFA agreement, you should use your best endeavours to ensure that:

(a) Any advice you give is communicated and fully explained to the lay client.

(b) Any offer of settlement is communicated to the lay client immediately.

(c) The consequences of particular clauses in the solicitor/lay client agreement and the solicitor/barrister agreement are explained to the lay client as and when they become relevant, particularly after an offer of settlement has been made. This last obligation in particular would require you to give advice on the usual costs consequences of settlement and the success fee that may become payable.

(d) In advising on settlement you must bear in mind only the interests of the lay client (and not your own interests, such as the 'success fee' that may become payable on settlement under the CFA). In order to avoid any allegation by lay clients that they were pressured into an unfavourable settlement, you should give advice in writing, which includes the following matters:

   (i)   the sum offered in settlement;

   (ii) the success fee payable to lawyers on the settlement, assuming it is not recoverable from the other side;

   (iii) whether the settlement is, in your opinion, a good one;

   (iv) an assessment of the prospects of getting more money if the case proceeds, and if so, the likely sum that may be recovered, and an assessment of the prospects of getting less or nothing at all;

   (v)   where you advise that the sum offered in settlement is not adequate, then you must also advise on the likely sum that will be expended in costs, the likely success fee payable in the event that the client succeeds in recovering more at the end of the day, and the net gain to the client taking these matters into account.

(e) The same considerations apply when considering and advising on whether to make a Part 36 offer and on the amount of the offer.

7.5.3.7 Advice in criminal cases

The Code of Conduct and the Written Standards apply equally to criminal cases. However there are a number of other specific duties which you must also bear in mind by virtue of the Written Standards.

In particular, para 11.4(c) of the Written Standards provides that prosecuting counsel should:

(i)   decide whether any additional evidence is required, and if it is, advise in writing, setting out precisely what additional evidence is required with a view to serving it on the defence as soon as possible;

(ii) consider whether all the witness statements in the possession of the prosecution have been properly served on the defendant;

(iii) eliminate all unnecessary material so as to ensure an efficient and fair trial, and also consider the need for particular witnesses and exhibits;

(iv) draft appropriate admissions and serve them on the defence;

(v)   in all Class 1 and Class 2 cases and in other cases of complexity, draft a case summary for transmission to the court.

Defence counsel must consider whether:

(i) any enquiries or further enquiries are necessary, and if so, should advise in writing as soon as possible;

(ii) details of an alibi are required and if so, draft an appropriate notice;

(iii) it is appropriate to call expert evidence for the defence, and advise solicitors to comply with the rules of the Crown Court in relation to notifying the prosecution of the contents of the evidence to be given;

(iv) any admissions can be made with a view to saving time and expense at trial, with the aim of admitting as much evidence as can be admitted in accordance with his or her duty to client;

(v) he or she wishes to examine any exhibits, and if so, should ensure that appropriate arrangements are made to examine them as promptly as possible.

7.5.3.8   Advice on appeal

Frequently barristers are asked to advise on appeal. In criminal cases, defence counsel must always consider whether there are any grounds of appeal against conviction or sentence.

Paragraph 17 of the Written Standards draws counsel's attention to the Guide to Proceedings in the Court of Appeal Criminal Division. In particular, defence counsel is encouraged to follow the procedures set out in paras 1.2 and 1.4 of the Guide. In addition para 17.2 of the Written Standards provides that:

(i) If his client pleads guilty or is convicted, a defence barrister should see his client after sentence in the presence of his professional client or representative. If he is satisfied that there are no reasonable grounds of appeal he should advise orally and confirm this in writing using the form set out in Appendix 1 to the Guide. No further advice is necessary unless a full written advice is required by the lay client, or it is necessary on the particular facts of the case.

(ii) If he is satisfied that there are reasonable grounds for appeal or he needs more time to consider the position then he should give oral advice in these terms, and certify in writing using the form in Appendix 1 of the Guide. Counsel would then provide written advice to the professional client as soon as possible and in any event within 14 days.

Quite often clients may want you to settle appeal documents even if you advise that the appeal is completely hopeless. In these circumstances, you must take care not to settle any grounds of appeal that you do not consider to be properly arguable (para 704 of the Code of Conduct and para 5.11 of the Written Standards). In criminal cases, para 17.3 of the Written Standards states:

Counsel should not settle grounds of appeal unless he considers that such grounds are properly arguable, and in that event, he should provide a reasoned written opinion in support of such grounds.

7.5.3.9   Solicitor asks you to give advice which does not reflect your true opinion

You must not permit your absolute independence, integrity and freedom from external pressures to be compromised or compromise your professional standards in order to please your client, the court or a third party (Code para 307). You therefore must not alter your opinion to suit the needs of any professional client or lay client, and nor should you provide advice, for any purpose, which does not reflect your true opinion.

7.5.3.10   What advice do you give if you consider your solicitor to be negligent

In practice, you may sometimes consider that your lay client may have a claim against your instructing solicitors. For example, the client's case may have been struck out because your instructing solicitors failed to serve witness statements on time. In a property dispute, you may conclude that your client has no legal title to a particular piece of land due to the negligence of your instructing solicitors who acted for the lay client during the purchase of the land. Your instructing solicitor may send you a lot of work, and you know that he or she will not want the lay client to become aware that the firm may have caused the lay client's predicament. What do you do in these circumstances?

Guidance can be obtained from paras 303 and 703 of the Code of Conduct and para 3.3 of the Written Standards. Your duty under these provisions can be broken down into the following parts:

(a) You must promote and protect fearlessly and by all proper and lawful means the lay client's best interests.

(b) You must do so without regard to your own interests or to any consequences to yourself or to any other person, including your instructing solicitors. The fact that you may receive no further instructions from the solicitors must not be allowed to influence your advice. Nor should you permit your instructing solicitor, in any way, to limit your discretion or influence your opinion on how the interests of the lay client would best be served.

(c) As between your lay client and your instructing solicitor, your primary duty is owed to the lay client.

(d) You should always be alert to the possibility of a conflict of interest between the lay client and the professional client, and any such conflict must be resolved in favour of the lay client.

(e) If you form the view that there is a conflict of interest between your lay client and your instructing solicitor (for example, because it appears that the latter may have been negligent) then you must consider whether it would be in the lay client's best interests to instruct another professional adviser or representative. If you consider that it would, you must advise in those terms. You must also take such steps as you consider necessary to ensure that your advice is communicated to the lay client, if necessary by sending a copy of your advice in writing directly to him or her, as well as to the professional client (see para 703 of the Code).

(f) In advising, bear in mind that it may not always be sensible for a lay client to instruct another firm of solicitors to act on his or her behalf immediately, even if it does appear that your instructing solicitors have been negligent. An example of when it might be proper for your instructing solicitors to continue to act for the time being, is where an appeal is pending against an order striking out the claim for failure to follow a procedural step in the action. However even in these circumstances, it may be appropriate to ask the solicitors or the Solicitors Indemnity Fund to fund the appeal. It is equally clear that a firm of solicitors should not continue to act if there is any doubt over whether the litigation should be continued, or if the lay client would clearly be best advised to pursue a remedy against his or her solicitors rather than a third party. The facts of each case must be carefully considered.

(g) Finally, as a matter of common courtesy, always telephone your instructing solicitor and give him or her advance warning of the nature of the advice that it is your professional duty to give to the lay client. This may do much to preserve the relationship between you and your instructing solicitor for the future.

7.5.4   Drafting

7.5.4.1   General principles

Paragraph 704 of the Code offers general advice on drafting any statement of case, witness statement, affidavit, notice of appeal or other document.

704   A barrister must not devise facts which will assist in advancing the lay client's case and must not draft any statement of case, witness statement, affidavit, notice of appeal or other document containing

> (a) any statement or fact or contention which is not supported by the lay client or by his instructions;
>
> (b) any contention which he does not consider to be properly arguable.

You must not settle any statement of case or any document which contains abusive or scandalous allegations or any allegation which is intended to insult, vilify or annoy the other party or any other person (para 708(g)).

These general rules must be borne in mind every time you are asked to draft any document. In relation to para 704(b) of the Code, it is impossible to lay down any detailed rules about whether or not something is 'properly arguable'. However, it is clear that a contention will not be 'properly arguable' if it gives rise to no claim or defence at law, or, if properly analysed, there is absolutely no evidence to support it. You must therefore have a firm grasp of the relevant substantive law when drafting any legal document. Furthermore, you must ensure that any contention you put in a document can be properly argued on the facts of the particular case.

7.5.4.2   Pleading fraud

Sometimes a lay client will make allegations of fraudulent or dishonest conduct against the opposing party. Both the lay client and the professional client may ask you to include these allegations in any statement of case that you are instructed to draft. However, you are under a very strict duty not to draft any statement of case, witness statement, affidavit, notice of appeal or other document containing any allegation of fraud unless you have 'clear instructions' to make such an allegation and you have before you 'reasonably credible material which as it stands establishes a *prima facie* case of fraud' (Code para 704(c)). Although this paragraph only refers to fraud, any other dishonourable or dishonest conduct should not be alleged without similar material.

The House of Lords (agreeing with the dissenting judgment of Wilson J in the Court of Appeal) have considered this provision in *Medcalf v Weatherill & Another* [2002] 3 WLR 172. In this case, a wasted costs order was sought by the opposing party from leading and junior counsel ('the barristers') acting for the other party. They had settled a notice of appeal and a skeleton argument containing allegations of fraud, which the court found were not justified by the evidence. The barristers defended the application on the ground that they had not been able to persuade their lay clients to waive privilege, and that being so, it was impossible for the court to know on what material they had acted, and so the application ought to be dismissed.

In the Court of Appeal, Peter Gibson LJ and Schiemann LJJ (Wilson J dissenting), took the view that para 704(c) required a barrister to have reasonably credible material establishing a *prima facie* case of fraud before they could draft an allegation of fraud. That material had to be evidence that could be put before the court to make good the allegation. If there is material before counsel which could not be used in court, the existence of the material could not justify pleading fraud.

Wilson J carefully considered the meaning of the phrase 'reasonably credible material which as it stands establishes a *prima facie* case of fraud'. In his view, the word 'material' in what is now para 704(c) of the Code was wider than evidence in its proper form, and the phrase 'as it stands' means 'at face value'. He took the view (para 80) that, 'To construe the word "establishes" as something that can be achieved only by evidence admissible in court is, in this context, arguably to read too much into it'. In the absence of any evidence as to what the barristers did have before them when pleading the allegations of fraud in the notice of appeal and skeleton argument, he did not feel that he could come to a positive conclusion that the Code of Conduct had been breached.

In the House of Lords, Lord Bingham, agreeing with Wilson J, had this to say:

Paragraph 606(c) [now 704(c)] lays down an important and salutary principle. The parties to contested actions are often at daggers drawn, and the litigious process serves to exacerbate the hostility between them. Such clients are only too ready to make allegations of the most damaging kind against each other. While counsel should never lend his name to such allegations unless instructed to do so, the receipt of instructions is not of itself enough. Counsel is bound to exercise an objective professional judgment whether it is in all the circumstances proper to lend his name to the allegation. As the rule recognises, counsel could not properly judge it proper to make such an allegation unless he had material before him which he judged to be reasonably credible and which appeared to justify the allegation. At the hearing stage, counsel cannot properly make or persist in an allegation which is unsupported by inadmissible evidence, since if there is not admissible evidence to support the allegation the court cannot be invited to find that it has been proved, and if the court cannot be invited to find that the allegation has been proved the allegation should not be made or should be withdrawn. I would however agree with Wilson J that at the preparatory stage the requirement is not that counsel should necessarily have evidence before him in admissible form but that he should have material of such a character that would lead responsible counsel to conclude that serious allegations could properly be based upon it. I could not think, for example, that it would be professionally improper for counsel to plead allegations, however serious, based on the documented conclusions of a DTI inspector or a public inquiry, even though counsel had no access to the documents referred to and the findings in question were inadmissible hearsay. On this point I would accept the judgment of Wilson J.

It is clear from this that:

(a) Allegations of fraud cannot and should not be made simply because the lay client instructs you to make them.

(b) Allegations of fraud should never be made in the absence of 'clear instructions'. You should insist on written instructions from the lay client before you draft any allegation of fraud.

(c) You must scrutinise the papers carefully and decide whether there is enough material to justify pleading an allegation of fraud. The material must be credible and, as it stands, establish a *prima facie* case of fraud.

(d) If the material relied upon includes or consists of the evidence of a witness, it would be prudent to ensure that a signed statement is obtained from the witness before such an allegation is made.

(e) If an allegation of fraud is drafted but it later becomes clear, at any stage of the proceedings, that it cannot be substantiated (for example, because a witness has retracted his or her statement) then you should inform the opposing side immediately that the allegation of fraud is not being pursued.

7.5.4.3   Drafting orders for interim relief

Quite often counsel is instructed to make an application and draft an order for interim relief such as an injunction, search order, or freezing order. If you are instructed to make such an application, you should ensure that you personally undertake the task of drafting the order, and do so as quickly as possible. A copy of the order must be lodged with the court before the oral hearing starts, except in exceptional circumstances.

Mummery LJ had this to say in *Memory Corporation plc v Sidhu (No 2)* [2000] 1 WLR 1443 at 1459(H)–1460(E) about counsel's duty in relation to such hearings:

It is the particular duty of the advocate to see that the correct legal procedures and forms are used; that a written skeleton argument and a properly drafted order are prepared by him personally and lodged with the court before the oral hearing; and that at the hearing, the court's attention is drawn by him to unusual features of the evidence adduced, to the applicable law and to the formalities and procedure to be observed.

It is unsatisfactory for an advocate to hand to the court for the first time during the course of an urgent hearing a long and complex draft order that requires close reading and careful scrutiny by the Court. If the advocate is unable to produce a draft order for the judge to read before the oral hearing starts then the application should not be made, save in the most exceptional circumstances, until the order has been drafted and lodged.

I emphasise the special responsibility of the advocate for the preparation of draft orders for the use of the court. There may be a convenient precedent to hand on the word processor of the instructing solicitor or in their files or in counsel's chambers, but it is the duty of the advocate actually presenting the case on the oral hearing of the application to settle the draft order personally so as to ensure that he is thoroughly familiar with the detail of it and so in the best possible position to respond to the court's concerns and to assist the court on the final form of the order.

If the order differs in any respect from the standard form of order used in such applications, it is also important to draw this to the attention of the court. Failure to do so may render you in breach of your duty not to mislead the court.

7.5.4.4   Witness statements

In relation to witnesses, you may be asked to see a lay client or a witness in conference with a view to discussing their evidence. You may be asked to do this to assess the credibility of the witness or advise on the strength of the case generally, or to take a proof of evidence which can then be used as the basis of a witness statement. You may also be asked to draft a witness statement on behalf of the lay client or some other witness of fact. In civil cases, counsel is increasingly asked to draft and prepare witness statements because the witness statement will usually stand as that witness's evidence-in-chief at the trial of the action. In this section, guidance will be given in relation to:

- the contact which you may have with a witness in both civil and criminal cases;
- the rules you must adhere to when drafting witness statements.

Contact with witnesses

There is no longer any rule which prevents a barrister from having contact with any witness other than the lay client. Under the Code of Conduct (para 705) it is clear what you must not do. You must not:

- rehearse, practise or coach a witness in relation to his evidence;
- encourage a witness to give evidence which is untruthful or which is not the whole truth.

See **7.2** above for further discussion on this point.

In relation to witnesses other than the lay client, you should exercise your discretion and consider very carefully whether and to what extent contact is appropriate for the purpose of interviewing witnesses or discussing with them the substance of their evidence bearing in mind that:

(a) it is not your function, but rather that of your instructing solicitor, to investigate the case and collect the evidence;

(b) even if you do not intend or wish to do so, as a figure in authority, you may subconsciously influence lay witnesses, and discussion of the evidence may unwittingly contaminate the witness's evidence;

(c) you should be alert to the risks that any discussion of the substance of the case with a witness may lead to suspicions of coaching, and thus tend to diminish the value of the witness's evidence in the eyes of the court. It may also place you in a position of professional embarrassment if you yourself became a witness in the case (see para 6.2 of the Written Standards).

In the case of a completely independent witness, you may think it prudent not to discuss the evidence with the witness at all, bearing in mind the matters set out above. If, however, after careful consideration of all matters, you decide to proceed, you should take the following steps to minimise the risk of suspicions of coaching. You should ensure that:

• before any discussion about the evidence takes place, you have been provided with a proof of the witness's evidence;

• any such discussion takes place in the presence of your instructing solicitor or a representative;

• the discussion of one witness's evidence does not take place in the presence of another witness of fact;

• care is taken not to disclose the factual evidence of another witness if it would be inappropriate to do so.

A failure to follow these steps will tend to encourage the rehearsal or coaching of a witness and increase the risk of fabrication or contamination of evidence.

You should also be alert to the distinction between settling a witness statement and the taking of a witness statement. Where you are asked to take a witness statement, as opposed to settling a witness statement from a proof of evidence of the witness which has been taken by your professional client, then it is not appropriate, except in exceptional circumstances, for you to act as counsel in the case because it risks undermining your independence as an advocate (see para 6.2.6 of the Written Standards). It should also be noted that the cab rank rule does not require a barrister to undertake the task of taking a witness statement, as opposed to settling a witness statement. Exceptional circumstances when it may be appropriate for you to take a proof of evidence and continue to act as counsel in the case would be:

• the witness is a minor;

• you have no choice, other than to take a proof, for example, in circumstances where a witness turns up at trial and there is no professional client in attendance;

• you are a junior member in a team and will not be examining the witness.

The 'Guidance on Preparation of Witness Statements' para 9(v) makes it clear that the following distinction should be borne in mind:

(a) Questioning a witness closely in order to:

(i)   enable him or her to present his or her evidence fully and accurately (this must be permissible to ensure that any witness statement that you settle is complete in content); or

(ii)   test the reliability of his or her evidence (which may be necessary to form an informed view of the merits of the case and/or the credibility of the witness)

and

(b)   Questioning a witness closely with a view to encouraging him or her to alter, massage or obscure his or her real recollection (which is clearly not permissible).

There is no objection to testing a witness's recollection robustly to ascertain the quality of the evidence or discussing the issues that may arise in cross-examination. What is objectionable is conducting a mock cross-examination of the witness or lay client or rehearsing with the witness particular lines of questioning that you propose to follow or which your opponent is likely to follow.

The rules relating to the settling or taking of witness statements in criminal cases are much more strict than in civil cases. Paragraph 6.3.1 of the Written Standards states that:

As a general principle, with the exception of the lay client, character and expert witnesses, it is wholly inappropriate for a barrister in such a case to interview any potential witness. Interviewing involves discussing with any such witness the substance of his evidence or the evidence of other such witnesses.

Drafting witness statements in a civil case

When asked to draft witness statements in a civil case, you must bear in mind the fact that the statement is likely to stand as the witness's evidence-in-chief. One of the first questions that will be asked of the witness at trial is whether he or she confirms the truth and accuracy of the statement. It is therefore critical that the statement you draft reflects that witness's evidence.

There is often some misunderstanding of the role that counsel can play in drafting a witness statement. Counsel's duty in drafting a witness statement is to:

- understand the evidence that a witness can give;
- help the witness present his or her story *in his or her own words* in a well structured, organised, coherent and persuasive way;
- ensure the witness tells his or her whole story (in other words that the statement is complete in content);
- above all, ensure that the statement reflects the witness's evidence. Paragraph 6(iv) of the Guidance on Preparation of Witness Statements states that:

Save for formal matters and uncontroversial facts, [the witness statement] should be expressed, if practicable in the witness's own words. This is especially important when the statement is dealing with the critical factual issues in the case — eg the accident or the disputed conversation. Thus the statement should reflect the witness's own description of events. It should not be drafted or edited so as to massage or obscure the witness's real evidence.

It is *not* counsel's function to:

- put a gloss on the evidence;
- draft a statement that contains words that the witness would not use, particularly in relation to the central factual issues;
- vet the accuracy of the witness's evidence (see para 5 of Guidance on Preparation of Witness Statements);
- exclude material from the statement where the omission renders untrue or misleading anything that remains in the statement.

Paragraphs 704(a) and (b) of the Code of Conduct apply equally to witness statements as they do to any other document that you may be asked to draft. Therefore, the witness statement must not contain any statement of fact which is not supported by instructions. You should not draft any statement or fact other than the evidence which in substance, according to your instructions, you reasonably believe the witness would give if the evidence contained in the witness statement or affidavit were being given in oral examination (para 704(d) of the Code). However, you can draft a document containing facts or matters which are subject to confirmation of accuracy by the lay client or witness.

Settling defence case statements in criminal cases

It is becoming increasingly common for counsel to be asked to settle defence case statements. The Bar Council has now prepared a document entitled 'Guidance on preparation of Defence Case Statements' to assist counsel undertaking this task. You should not settle the defence case statement until you have seen all relevant documents, particularly all prosecution documents and statements, and obtained full instructions from the lay client from a properly signed proof and also preferably during a conference. In particular, you must ensure that the lay client understands the importance of the defence case statement and the potential adverse effects of an inaccurate or inadequate statement.

Once the statement is drafted, you should ensure that you get proper informed approval for the draft from the lay client. This is particularly important in case the lay client challenges or disowns the statement during the trial. You ought therefore to insist on getting *written* acknowledgment from the lay client that:

- he or she understands the importance and accuracy of the defence case statement; and

- he or she has had the opportunity of considering the contents of the statement carefully and approves it.

If you entrust your solicitor with the task of obtaining this acknowledgement, then you should also prepare a short written advice to enclose with the defence case statement on the importance of obtaining the acknowledgment before the defence case statement is served. The defendant should be asked to sign the statement before it is served.

Due to the absolute necessity for the statement to be accurate, para 6 of the Guidance on Preparation of Defence Case Statements states that counsel ought not to accept any instructions to draft or settle a defence case statement unless he or she has been given adequate time and opportunity to gain proper familiarity with the case and comply with the requirements set out above.

7.5.4.5   Drafting indictments in criminal cases

Prosecution counsel is frequently asked to draft the indictment. If you do obtain instructions to undertake drafting of this type, you must do so promptly and within due time. You should also bear in mind 'the desirability of not overloading an indictment with either too many defendants or too many counts, in order to present the prosecution case as simply and as concisely as possible' (para 11.4 of the Written Standards). See also the Code for Crown Prosecutors, paragraphs 7.1–7.3. Furthermore, even if you are not instructed to settle the indictment, you should ask to see a copy of it and should check it.

7.5.5   Can you refuse to advise and/or draft a document?

You are bound by the cab rank rule (Code para 602). You must therefore accept any instructions at a proper professional fee in the fields in which you profess to practice, irrespective of the party on whose behalf you are instructed, the nature of the case or any belief or opinion that you may have formed as to the character, reputation, cause, conduct or guilt or innocence of that party. This applies whether the case is privately or publicly funded.

There are a number of circumstances in which you can refuse to act when instructed. These are set out in paras 603, 604 and 701 of the Code of Conduct. You may refuse to act if:

(a) you are required to do anything other than during the course of your ordinary working year;

(b) you do not have adequate time to deal with the papers (Code paras 603 and 701);

(c) there is a conflict of interest which would prevent you acting (such as having acted for the other side);

(d) the fee is not a proper professional fee having regard to the complexity and length and difficulty of the case, your expertise and seniority and the expenses you will incur. Note that a publicly-funded matter is deemed to be at a proper professional fee;

(e) if the work is to be done under a conditional fee agreement;

(f) if instructions are received from a solicitor or firm who has had credit facilities withdrawn by the Bar Council on the basis that the firm has been persistently late or has failed to pay counsel's fees. You must then refuse to do any work for the solicitor or firm unless payment of an agreed fee is enclosed with the papers, or you agree in advance to accept no payment for the work (Annex G1, The Terms of Work on which Barristers Offer Their Services to Solicitors and the Withdrawal of Credit Scheme 1988).

Otherwise, you must accept and carry out your instructions to the best of your ability, bearing in mind your duty under the Code and the Written Standards and the other Guidance issued by the Bar Council which has been discussed above.

7.6 Conclusion

This chapter has made it clear that professional conduct and ethical difficulties can arise throughout a case, in a variety of contexts. It has guided you through the problem areas pertinent to the key skills with a discussion of the relevant principles and other sources of guidance you will need as an intending barrister. Furthermore, several situations have been identified which are not expressly covered by the Code, but in applying its spirit with a recognition of the Code's underlying values (see **Chapter 4**), the suggested approaches should now be more easily understood.

Your alertness to these issues will ensure that they are handled appropriately paying due regard if necessary to not only the Code and the application of its spirit, but also to the 'ethical challenge' obligations discussed in **Chapter 1**. Hence, you will continue to develop the skills set out in **Chapter 1**:

- the *identification* of potential professional conduct issues;
- the *sources* of guidance on particular issues;
- the necessity of applying the *spirit* of the Code where there is no letter;
- the need to recognise obligations towards *fair treatment*; and
- how you would deal *practically* with the matter.

Of course, in practice there will be difficult situations in which you find yourself and no matter how disciplined your approach is to handling professional conduct matters, you will struggle to know the best course of action. The point is that you are already half way to dealing with the matter because you have recognised at the earliest opportunity that an issue has arisen. In such a situation do not be afraid to take guidance from fellow barristers or to phone the Bar Council. Remember the need to maintain the highest standards is an ongoing obligation for all members of the Bar — the practical advice and guidance set out in this section and throughout the Manual will only take you so far. You will know if you are cutting corners or deliberately ignoring professional conduct matters. However, it is hoped that you have already decided that the extra time and effort put to solving these areas of practice are the only way to ensure the solid foundation of a continuing and successful practice at the Bar.

Professional conduct problems

Question 1

Objectives

(a) To consider the meaning and importance of the 'Cab-rank' rule in all aspects of a practising barrister's work.

(b) To consider the meaning of 'professional embarrassment'.

A solicitor seeks to instruct you to act for notoriously bad landlords in an action for possession of premises occupied by a highly regarded charitable organisation. The case is likely to draw adverse publicity. You hold yourself out to act in landlord and tenant cases, you have no connection with either party or with the premises, you have no conflicting professional commitment and the fee offered is a proper fee for you and for the case. Your clerk tells you that he wishes you to refuse the instructions because:

(a) it is chambers' policy not to act for landlords; and

(b) he fears that your normal professional clients will be reluctant to instruct you in future cases as their clients (tenants, consumers, etc) would refuse to have as counsel one who had acted for these particular claimants.

What do you do?

Question 2

Objectives

(a) To illustrate the possibility of different interpretations of the Bar Code.

(b) To consider the relationship between the 'Cab-rank' rule and the practising barrister's duty not to discriminate nor to victimise on prohibited grounds.

You act for a father whose former wife is now cohabiting with a black boyfriend. Your client instructs you to resist her application for contact with the parties' son on thinly veiled racist grounds. Can you refuse to put forward instructions even if wrapped up as seeking to avoid 'exposing his son to a cultural environment totally alien to him ...'.

Question 3

Objectives

(a) To emphasise the continuing duty of confidentiality.

(b) To illustrate its relationship with the cause(s) of professional embarrassment.

You have successfully appeared for the claimants in an action where the unsuccessful defendants now wish to seek a Part 20 indemnity or contribution from a third party who was not a party to the original action. The defendants' solicitors were impressed with your performance and want you to be able to use your knowledge of the case against the third party. Do you accept the instructions?

Question 4

Objectives

To introduce the general rules governing the receipt of instructions.

A solicitor, who regularly instructs you and your chambers, telephones you and instructs you to attend at a particular police station where a lay client is about to be interviewed and to advise the client as necessary. The solicitor undertakes to pay you a proper fee. If the matter leads to a charge or charges being preferred, the brief is likely to come into chambers for someone of your experience.

> *(a) Can you act?*
>
> *(b) Would it make any difference if the brief would certainly be beyond your competence?*

Question 5

Objective

To show the importance of the Written Standards for the Conduct of Professional Work.

You are prosecuting a plea of guilty where the defendant is unrepresented. It is a type of case in which the Court of Criminal Appeal has given sentencing guidelines. The judge does not appear to be familiar with criminal work. You are aware from discussion with the officer in the case of a number of facts favourable to the defendant which he does not bring out when mitigating on his own behalf. What are your duties?

Question 6

Objectives

> (a) To underline that, under paras. 306 and 403 of the Bar Code, the barrister is responsible for the organisation of his or her own work.
>
> (b) To underline that, under para 701(a) of the Bar Code, advocates must in all their activities be courteous and act promptly, conscientiously, diligently and with reasonable competence and take all reasonable and practicable steps to avoid unnecessary expense or waste of the court's time and to ensure that professional engagements are fulfilled. Under para 610(d) of the Bar Code, if a case is to be returned it must be returned in good and sufficient time for the client and the court to be properly serviced when it is called on.

You have received and accepted instructions to appear in case 'A' (a civil case fixed to be heard on 20 April). You have done a lot of preparatory work upon it and have seen the professional and lay clients in conference on a number of occasions. You have also accepted instructions to defend in a serious criminal case (case 'B') expected to be tried in the week beginning 1 April and to last for five days, but which may well go on longer. Before you have conferred with the client in case 'B' you learn that it will not be heard until the week beginning 15 April. Both solicitors assert priority and both clients are anxious to have your services. Which case do you do? Why?

Question 7

Objective

To illustrate some of the 'fundamental principles' applicable to all barristers.

You have represented your client successfully in court. After the hearing, the client stuffs a £20 note in your pocket and tells you to enjoy a drink on him.

 (a) Do you keep the money?

 (b) Would it make any difference if your client instead sent you a bottle of whiskey?

Question 8

Objective

To consider scenarios where your client's instructions may render you professionally embarrassed, and the action you must take as a consequence.

 (a) The defendant in a rape case instructs you that intercourse took place between him and the victim with her consent. At trial he tells you that he did not have intercourse with her and gives you names of alibi witnesses.

 (b) Your client is mentally disturbed. His instructions differ each time you speak to him.

What should you do in these circumstances?

Question 9

Objective

To explore the relationship between the duty of disclosure and the grounds on which a practising barrister must cease to act and withdraw from a case.

You act for the claimant in civil proceedings. In the course of his evidence-in-chief, he produces several documents from his pocket which he alleges support his claim. You have never seen them before nor have they been disclosed to the defence. What do you do?

Question 10

Objective

To explore counsels' duties where conflicts of interest exist between their professional and lay clients.

You receive a set of instructions to advise and settle civil proceedings for a claimant from X and Co, a firm of solicitors who have instructed you on a number of occasions and are among your best clients. It is apparent that they have been negligent in handling the claimant's affairs. It appears to you that the claimant's chances have not been badly affected and he is likely to succeed in the litigation, but he has at least been prejudiced in the sense that, if the relevant matter 'surfaces' in the litigation, the defendants will be able to make use of it to reduce the damages or to obtain a better settlement than would otherwise have been open to them. (For example, there has been a failure to secure evidence relevant to proving the amount of the claimant's loss and damage.) What, if anything, should you do?

Question 11

Objectives

 (a) To highlight the practising barrister's overriding duty to the Court.

 (b) To highlight the concomitant duties to the lay client.

You are defending a trial at the Crown Court. In the course of giving his evidence the defendant makes an allegation which, although it is in your instructions, you had not put to the victim. It is apparent that it should have been, and the victim has gone on holiday and cannot be recalled. The judge is furious. What do you do?

Question 12

Objectives

    (a) To introduce the rules regarding media comment.

    (b) To introduce the rules regarding advertising.

You are appearing for a well-known businessman in his local magistrates' court on a charge of drink driving. After a preliminary hearing, you are approached by a reporter from the local newspaper who asks you for information about the client and the case. What should you do?

Question 13

Objective

To illustrate the relationship between a practising barrister's duty of confidentiality to the lay client and the overriding duty to the Court.

You are asked to advise, in conference, upon the acceptability of an offer of £3,000 in settlement of your client's claim for damages in a personal injury case. The medical report, which has been disclosed to the defence, is now ten months old. In the course of the conference, your client informs you that the doctor's prognosis was unduly pessimistic as his condition has improved since the report was prepared. In the circumstances, the offer is generous and more than your client is likely to receive from the court.

    (a) What advice do you give?

    (b) Would it make any difference if the client's information was contained in a more recent, but undisclosed medical report?

Question 14

Objective

To illustrate the relationship between the overriding duty to the Court and the rules under the Civil Procedure Rules 1998 regarding witnesses at trial.

You are instructed to represent the defendant in proceedings for damages for breach of contract. Upon your arrival at court, your instructing solicitor informs you that one of your witnesses has just telephoned his office to say that she is ill and cannot attend court to give evidence. Her testimony is vital to the defendant's case. You have no option but to seek an adjournment. At that moment, your opponent approaches you and asks if he can have a word with you. He indicates that he has witness difficulties and invites you to agree to an adjournment of the hearing for two weeks. In so doing:

    (a) Do you inform your opponent and the court of your own witness difficulties?

    (b) If not, do you make an application for the claimant to pay defendant's costs thrown away by the adjournment?

APPENDICES

APPENDIX 1
CODE OF CONDUCT OF THE BAR
OF ENGLAND AND WALES

CODE OF CONDUCT

OF

THE BAR OF ENGLAND AND WALES

AND

GUIDANCE ISSUED BY THE BAR COUNCIL

7th Edition

Adopted by the Bar Council on 25 March 2000

Effective from 31st July 2000

The General Council of the Bar of England and Wales
3 Bedford Row
London WC1R 4DB

THE CODE OF CONDUCT OF THE BAR OF ENGLAND AND WALES

7th EDITION

Arrangement of sections

The Bar's Code of Conduct sets out the duties which all barristers must obey. It is divided into the following sections.

Part I — the Preliminary Section which sets out details about the **commencement** of the Code, the rules governing **amendments**, the Code's **general purpose**, to whom it applies and Bar Council's powers to waive its provisions.

Part II — the Bar's Practising Requirements which sets out the rules governing the circumstances in which individuals may **practise as a barrister**, exercise **rights of audience** and **supply legal services to the public**, including the requirement to be **insured** and the prohibition on practise in **partnership**.

Part III — contains the Fundamental Principles, including the duty to not to act dishonestly or bring the profession into disrepute and the particular duties to the **Court** and to act in the best interests of the **client**. It also includes the duties to the **Legal Services Commission** and not to **discriminate** on ground of race, sex etc. and the duties which safeguard a barrister's **independence**.

Part IV — concerns barristers in independent practice only and provides that they can only **accept instructions** from solicitors or other professional clients and sets out the work barristers may not undertake. It provides further rules governing **insurance** and the duties of barristers and heads of chamber to **administer their practice** efficiently. Finally, it provides rules about **fees**.

Part V — provides the rules for **Employed Barristers** and particularly sets out the people to whom they may offer legal services.

Part VI — deals with the occasions on which barristers are required to **accept instructions** (the 'Cab-Rank rule') and when they are required to refuse or **withdraw** from a case (including **conflicts of interest**) and when they may choose to refuse or withdraw from a case.

Part VII — sets out the duties of barristers when conducting work including the general duties to act courteously and promptly, the duty of **confidentiality**, duties where there is a **conflict** between clients, duties when **drafting documents** and **appearing in court**, the rules concerning **contact with witnesses, media comment** and **advertising**.

Part VIII — sets out miscellaneous provisions concerning **pupillage**, working at a **Legal Advice Centre**, **dual qualification** and relationships with **foreign lawyers**.

Part IX — sets out duties to inform the Bar Council in the event of **criminal convictions**, **bankruptcy** etc. and the duties concerning the **complaints procedure**.

Part X — contains the **Definitions** of terms used in the Code.

Part XI — contains **Transitional Arrangements** affecting people who were barristers before this edition came into force.

The Code also contains various [provisions] which set out the rules for particular situations:

A   The International Practice Rules

B   The Registered European Lawyers Rules

C   The Continuing Professional Development Regulations

D   The Practising Certificate Regulations

E   Guidelines on Opinions under the Funding Code

F   The BarDIRECT Rules and Recognition Regulations

G   The Terms of Work on which Barristers Offer their Services to Solicitors and the Withdrawal of Credit Scheme 1988

H   The Foreign Lawyers (Chambers) Rules

I   The Employed Lawyers (Conduct of Litigation) Rules

J   The Complaints Rules

K   The Disciplinary Tribunals Regulations

L   The Summary Procedure Rules

M   The Hearings before the Visitors Rules

N   The Interim Suspension Rules

O   The Fitness to Practice Rules

P   The Adjudication Panel and Appeals Rules

Q   The Code of Conduct for Lawyers in the European Community

R   Pupillage Funding and Advertising Requirements

The Consolidated Regulations

The **Consolidated Regulations of the Four Inns of Court** set out the rules about entry to the Bar and Pupillage.

They are divided as follows:

Part I — concerning admission to an Inn

Part II — setting the rules concerning Training to be a Barrister

Part III — concerning Call to the Bar

Part IV — Admission of European and Overseas Lawyers

Part V — Pupillage and Entry into Practice

Part VI — Miscellaneous provisions including those covering admission of teachers of law, re-admission of disbarred barristers and waiver powers.

SECTION 1 CODE OF CONDUCT OF THE BAR OF ENGLAND AND WALES

Table of Contents

PART I — PRELIMINARY

101   This Code (which save as provided in paragraphs 1101 and 107 replaces all earlier Codes) was adopted by the Bar Council on 25 March 2000 with amendments approved on 10 June 2000 and came into force on 31 July 2000 (save for paragraphs 202(c) and 504 which will come into force on a date to be appointed by the Bar Council).

102   This Code includes the Annexes.

103   Amendments and additions to this Code may be made by Resolution of the Bar Council which shall be operative upon such date as the Resolution shall appoint or if no such date is appointed on the later of:

(a) the date of the Resolution; and

(b) the date when approval of the amendment or addition, if required, is given under Schedule 4 of the Act.

Amendments and additions will be published from time to time in such manner as the Bar Council may determine.

General purpose of the Code

104   The general purpose of this Code is to provide the requirements for practice as a barrister and the rules and standards of conduct applicable to barristers which are appropriate in the interests of justice and in particular:

(a) in relation to barristers in independent practice to provide common and enforceable rules and standards which require them:

(i)   to be completely independent in conduct and in professional standing as sole practitioners;

(ii)   to act only as consultants instructed by solicitors and other approved persons;

(iii) to acknowledge a public obligation based on the paramount need for access to justice to act for any client in cases within their field of practice;

(b) to make appropriate provision for employed barristers taking into account the fact that such barristers are employed to provide legal services to or on behalf of their employer.

Application of the Code

105   A barrister must comply with this Code which (save as otherwise provided) applies to all barristers whenever called to the Bar.

106   Subject to the International Practice Rules (reproduced in Annex A) this Code applies to International work and whether a barrister is practising in England and Wales or elsewhere.

107   A registered European lawyer must comply with this Code in the manner provided for by the Registered European Lawyers Rules (reproduced in Annex B).

Waiver of the Code

108   The Bar Council shall have the power to waive the duty imposed on a barrister to comply with the provisions of this Code in such circumstances and to such extent as the Bar Council may think fit and either conditionally or unconditionally.

PART II — PRACTISING REQUIREMENTS

[Amended 5 February 2001]

General

201   For the purposes of this Code:

(a) a barrister practises as a barrister if he supplies legal services and in connection with the supply of such services:

(i)   he holds himself out or allows himself to be held out as a barrister; or

(ii) he exercises a right which he has by reason of being a barrister;

(b) any reference to the supply of legal services includes an offer to supply such services.

202   Subject to the provisions of this Code a barrister may practise as a barrister provided that:

(a) he has complied with any applicable training requirements imposed by the Consolidated Regulations which were in force at the date of his Call to the Bar;

(b) he has complied with any applicable requirements of the Continuing Professional Development Regulations (reproduced in Annex C);

(c) he has a current practising certificate issued by the Bar Council in accordance with the Practising Certificate Regulations (reproduced in Annex D);

(d) he has provided in writing to the Bar Council details of the current address(es) with telephone number(s) of the chambers or office from which he supplies legal services and (if he is an employed barrister) the name address telephone number and nature of the business of his employer;

...

(f) a barrister who practises as a barrister in independent practice or as an employed barrister may not also supply legal services for reward other than in the course of his practice except as permitted by paragraph 806.

Rights of audience

203.1   A barrister may exercise any right of audience which he has by reason of being a barrister provided that:

(a) he is entitled to practise as a barrister in accordance with paragraph 202; and

(b) if he is of less than three years' standing his principal place of practice is a chambers or office which is also the principal place of practice of a qualified person who is able to provide guidance to the barrister.

203.2   For the purpose of paragraph 203.1(b) a barrister shall be treated as being of a particular number of years' standing if he:

(a) has been entitled to practise and has practised as a barrister (other than as a pupil who has not completed pupillage in accordance with the Consolidated Regulations) or as a member of another authorised body;

(b) has made such practice his primary occupation; and

(c) has been entitled to exercise a right of audience before every Court in relation to all proceedings

for a period (which need not be continuous and need not have been as a member of the same authorised body) of at least that number of years.

203.3   A person shall be a qualified person for the purpose of paragraph 203.1(b) if he:

(a) has been entitled to practise and has practised as a barrister (other than as a pupil who has not completed pupillage in accordance with the Consolidated Regulations) or as a member of another authorised body for a period (which need not have been as a member of the same authorised body) of at least six years in the previous eight years;

(b) for the previous two years

(i)   has made such practice his primary occupation, and

(ii)   has been entitled to exercise a right of audience before every Court in relation to all proceedings;

(c) is not acting as a qualified person in relation to more than two other people; and

(d) has not been designated by the Bar Council as unsuitable to be a qualified person.

203.4   This paragraph 203 is subject to the transitional provisions at paragraphs 1102 to 1105.

Supply of legal services to the public

204   A practising barrister may supply legal services to the public provided that:

(a) he complies with the requirements of paragraph 203.1; and

(b) he is covered (and in the case of an employed barrister his employer is covered) by insurance against claims for professional negligence arising out of the supply of his services in such amount and upon such terms as are currently required by the Bar Council.

205   A practising barrister must not supply legal services to the public through or on behalf of any other person (including a partnership company or other corporate body) except as permitted by paragraph 502.

PART III — FUNDAMENTAL PRINCIPLES

Applicable to all barristers

301   A barrister must have regard to paragraph 104 and must not:

(a) engage in conduct whether in pursuit of his profession or otherwise which is:

(i)   dishonest or otherwise discreditable to a barrister;

(ii)   prejudicial to the administration of justice; or

(iii)   likely to diminish public confidence in the legal profession or the administration of justice or otherwise bring the legal profession into disrepute;

(b) engage directly or indirectly in any occupation if his association with that occupation may adversely affect the reputation of the Bar or in the case of a practising barrister prejudice his ability to attend properly to his practice.

Applicable to practising barristers

[Amended 10 July 2002]

302   A barrister has an overriding duty to the Court to act with independence in the interests of justice: he must assist the Court in the administration of justice and must not deceive or knowingly or recklessly mislead the Court.

303   A barrister:

(a) must promote and protect fearlessly and by all proper and lawful means the lay client's best interests and do so without regard to his own interests or to any consequences to himself or to any other person (including any professional client or other intermediary or another barrister);

(b) owes his primary duty as between the lay client and any professional client or other intermediary to the lay client and must not permit the intermediary to limit his discretion as to how the interests of the lay client can best be served;

(c) when supplying legal services funded by the Legal Services Commission as part of the Community Legal Service or the Criminal Defence Service owes his primary duty to the lay client subject only to compliance with paragraph 304.

304   A barrister who supplies legal services funded by the Legal Services Commission as part of the Community Legal Service or the Criminal Defence Service must in connection with the supply of such services comply with any duty imposed on him by or under the Access to Justice Act 1999 or any regulations or code in effect under that Act and in particular with the duties set out in Annex E.

305.1   A barrister must not in relation to any other person (including a client or another barrister or a pupil or a student member of an Inn of Court) discriminate directly or indirectly or victimise because of race, colour, ethnic or national origin, nationality, citizenship, sex, sexual orientation, marital status, disability, religion or political persuasion.

305.2   A barrister must not in relation to any offer of a pupillage or tenancy discriminate directly or indirectly against a person on grounds of age, save where such discrimination can be shown to be objectively and reasonably justifiable.

305.3   In respect of indirect discrimination, there is no breach of paragraph 305.1 and 305.2 if the barrister against whom the complaint is brought proves that the act of indirect discrimination was committed without any intention of treating the claimant unfavourably on any ground in that paragraph to which the complaint relates.

306   A barrister is individually and personally responsible for his own conduct and for his professional work: he must exercise his own personal judgment in all his professional activities.

307   A barrister must not:

(a) permit his absolute independence integrity and freedom from external pressures to be compromised;

(b) do anything (for example accept a present) in such circumstances as may lead to any inference that his independence may be compromised;

(c) compromise his professional standards in order to please his client the Court or a third party;

(d) give a commission or present or lend any money for any professional purpose to or (save as a remuneration in accordance with the provisions of this Code) accept any money by way of loan or otherwise from any client or any person entitled to instruct him as an intermediary;

(e) make any payment (other than a payment for advertising or publicity permitted by this Code or in the case of a barrister in independent practice remuneration paid to any clerk or other employee or staff of his chambers) to any person for the purpose of procuring professional instructions;

(f) receive or handle client money securities or other assets other than by receiving payment of remuneration or (in the case of an employed barrister) where the money or other asset belongs to his employer.

PART IV — BARRISTERS IN INDEPENDENT PRACTICE

[Amended 17 November 2001]

Instructions

401   A barrister in independent practice whether or not he is acting for a fee:

    (a) may supply legal services only if he is instructed by a professional client or by a Bar-DIRECT client or is appointed by the Court;

    (b) must not in the course of his practice:

        (i)   undertake the management administration or general conduct of a lay client's affairs;

        (ii)   conduct litigation or inter-partes work (for example the conduct of correspondence with an opposite party);

        (iii) investigate or collect evidence for use in any Court;

        (iv)   except as permitted by paragraph 707, take any proof of evidence in any criminal case;

        (v)   attend at a police station without the presence of a solicitor to advise a suspect or interviewee as to the handling and conduct of police interviews;

        (vi)   act as a supervisor for the purposes of section 84(2) of the Immigration and Asylum Act 1999.

    (c) must not enter into a contract for the supply of legal services by him with any person other than a professional client or BarDIRECT client;

    (d) must if he is instructed by a BarDIRECT client comply with the BarDIRECT Rules (reproduced in Annex F).

Insurance

402.1   Every barrister in independent practice (other than a pupil who is covered under his pupil-master's insurance) must be entered as a member with BMIF.

402.2   Every barrister entered as a member with BMIF shall:

    (a) pay immediately when due the appropriate insurance premium required by BMIF for the purpose of insurance against claims for professional negligence for such amount and upon such terms as may be approved by the Bar Council from time to time;

    (b) supply immediately upon being requested to do so such information as BMIF may from time to time require pursuant to its Rules.

Administration and conduct of independent practice

[Amended 24 March 2001, 1 February 2002 and 18 May 2002]

403.1   A barrister in independent practice must not practise from the office of or in any unincorporated association (including any arrangement which involves sharing the administration of his practice) with any person other than a barrister in independent practice or any of the following:

    (a) a registered European lawyer;

    (b) subject to compliance with the Foreign Lawyers (Chambers) Rules (reproduced in Annex H) and with the consent of the Bar Council a foreign lawyer;

(c) a non-practising barrister or retired judge who is practising as an arbitrator or mediator.

403.2   A barrister in independent practice:

(a) must take all reasonable steps to ensure that:

   (i)   his practice is efficiently and properly administered having regard to the nature of his practice;

   (ii)   proper records are kept;

   (iii)   he complies with the Terms of Work on which Barristers Offer their Services to Solicitors and the Withdrawal of Credit Scheme 1988 as amended and in force from time to time (reproduced in Annex G1) and with any Withdrawal of Credit Direction issued by the Chairman of the Bar pursuant thereto.

(b) must have ready access to library facilities which are adequate having regard to the nature of his practice;

(c) must have regard to any relevant guidance issued by the Bar Council including guidance as to:

   (i)   the administration of chambers;

   (ii)   pupillage and further training; and

   (iii)   good equal opportunities practice in chambers in the form of the Equality Code for the Bar;

(d) (i)   must deal with all complaints made to him promptly, courteously and in a manner which addresses the issues raised; and

   (ii)   must have and comply with an appropriate written complaints procedure and make copies of the procedure available to a client on request.

Heads of chambers

[Amended 26 February 2002]

404.1   The obligations in this paragraph apply to the following members of chambers:

(a) any barrister who is head of chambers;

(b) any barrister who is responsible in whole or in part for the administration of chambers;

(c) if there is no one within (a) and (b) above, all the members of the chambers.

404.2   Any person referred to in paragraph 404.1 must take all reasonable steps to ensure that:

(a) his chambers are administered competently and efficiently and are properly staffed;

(b) the affairs of his chambers are conducted in a manner which is fair and equitable for all barristers and pupils;

(c) proper arrangements are made in his chambers for dealing with pupils and pupillage and, in particular,

   (i)   that all pupillage vacancies are advertised in the manner prescribed by the Bar Council;

   (ii)   that such arrangements are made for the funding of pupils by chambers as the Bar Council may by resolution from time to time require;

(iii) that in making arrangements for pupillage, regard is had to the pupillage guidelines issued from time to time by the Bar Council and to the Equality Code for the Bar;

(d) all barristers practising from his chambers whether they are members of the chambers or not are entered as members with BMIF and have effected insurance in accordance with paragraph 402 (other than any pupil who is covered under his pupil-master's insurance);

(e) all barristers practising from his chambers comply with paragraph 403(b)(iii);

(f) all employees and staff in his chambers (i) are competent to carry out their duties, (ii) carry out their duties in a correct and efficient manner, (iii) are made clearly aware of such provisions of this Code as may affect or be relevant to the performance of their duties and (iv) all complaints against them are dealt with in the manner set out in paragraph 403(e) above;

(g) all registered European lawyers and all foreign lawyers in his chambers comply with this Code to the extent required by the Registered European Lawyers Rules (reproduced in Annex B) and the Foreign Lawyers (Chambers) Rules (reproduced in Annex H);

(h) fee notes in respect of all work undertaken by all members of chambers and pupils and (unless expressly agreed with the individual) former members and pupils of chambers are sent expeditiously to clients and in the event of non-payment within a reasonable time, pursued efficiently;

(i) every barrister practising from his chambers has a current practising certificate in accordance with paragraph 202(c) of the Code of Conduct and the Practising Certificate Regulations (reproduced in Annex D).

404.3   In carrying out the obligations referred to in paragraph 404.2 any person referred to in paragraph 404.1 must have regard to any relevant guidance issued by the Bar Council including guidance as to:

(a) the administration of chambers;

(b) pupillage and further training; and

(c) good equal opportunities practice in chambers in the form of the Equality Code for the Bar.

Fees and remuneration

405   Subject to paragraph 307 a barrister in independent practice may charge for any work undertaken by him (whether or not it involves an appearance in Court) on any basis or by any method he thinks fit provided that such basis or method:

(a) is permitted by law;

(b) does not involve the payment of a wage or salary.

406.1   A barrister in independent practice who receives fees in respect of work done by another barrister must himself and without delegating the responsibility to anyone else pay forthwith the whole of the fee in respect of that work to that other barrister.

406.2   Subject to paragraph 805 a barrister in independent practice who arranges for another barrister to undertake work for him (other than a pupil or a person who has asked to do the work in order to increase his own skill or experience) must himself and without delegating the responsibility to anyone else:

(a) pay proper financial remuneration for the work done;

(b) make payment within a reasonable time and in any event within three months after the work has been done unless otherwise agreed in advance with the other barrister.

PART V — EMPLOYED BARRISTERS

[Amended 23 July 2002]

501   An employed barrister whilst acting in the course of his employment may supply legal services to his employer and to any of the following persons:

(a) any employee, director or company secretary of the employer in a matter arising out of or relating to that person's employment;

(b) where the employer is a public authority (including the Crown or a Government department or agency or a local authority):

   (i)   another public authority on behalf of which the employer has made arrangements under statute or otherwise to supply any legal services or to perform any of that other public authority's functions as agent or otherwise;

   (ii)   in the case of a barrister employed by or in a Government department or agency, any Minister or Officer of the Crown;

(c) where the barrister is or is performing the functions of a justices' clerk, the justices whom he serves;

(d) where the barrister is employed by a trade association, any individual member of the association.

502   An employed barrister may supply legal services only to the persons referred to in paragraph 501 and must not supply legal services to any other person save that whilst acting in the course of his employment:

(a) a barrister employed by a solicitor or other authorised litigator or by an incorporated solicitors' practice may supply legal services to any client of his employer;

(b) a barrister employed by the Legal Services Commission may supply legal services to members of the public;

(c) a barrister employed by or at a Legal Advice Centre may supply legal services to clients of the Legal Advice Centre;

(d) any employed barrister may supply legal services to members of the public free of charge (to any person).

503   A barrister employed to supply legal services under a contract for services may be treated as an employed barrister for the purpose of this Code provided that the contract is:

(a) in writing;

(b) (subject to any provision for earlier termination on notice) for a determinate period; and

(c) the only contract under which the barrister is supplying legal services during that period (unless the Bar Council grants a specific waiver of this requirement).

504   An employed barrister shall have a right to conduct litigation in relation to every Court and all proceedings before any Court and may exercise that right provided that he complies with the Employed Barristers (Conduct of Litigation) Rules (reproduced in Annex I).

PART VI — ACCEPTANCE AND RETURN OF INSTRUCTIONS

[Amended 30 April and 17 November 2001]

Acceptance of instructions and the 'Cab-rank rule'

601   A barrister who supplies advocacy services must not withhold those services:

(a) on the ground that the nature of the case is objectionable to him or to any section of the public;

(b) on the ground that the conduct opinions or beliefs of the prospective client are unacceptable to him or to any section of the public;

(c) on any ground relating to the source of any financial support which may properly be given to the prospective client for the proceedings in question (for example, on the ground that such support will be available as part of the Community Legal Service or Criminal Defence Service).

602   A barrister in independent practice must comply with the 'Cab-rank rule' and accordingly except only as otherwise provided in paragraphs 603 604 605 and 606 he must in any field in which he professes to practise in relation to work appropriate to his experience and seniority and irrespective of whether his client is paying privately or is publicly funded:

(a) accept any brief to appear before a Court in which he professes to practise;

(b) accept any instructions;

(c) act for any person on whose behalf he is instructed;

and do so irrespective of (i) the party on whose behalf he is instructed (ii) the nature of the case and (iii) any belief or opinion which he may have formed as to the character reputation cause conduct guilt or innocence of that person.

603   A barrister must not accept any instructions if to do so would cause him to be professionally embarrassed and for this purpose a barrister will be professionally embarrassed:

(a) if he lacks sufficient experience or competence to handle the matter;

(b) if having regard to his other professional commitments he will be unable to do or will not have adequate time and opportunity to prepare that which he is required to do;

(c) if the instructions seek to limit the ordinary authority or discretion of a barrister in the conduct of proceedings in Court or to require a barrister to act otherwise than in conformity with law or with the provisions of this Code;

(d) if the matter is one in which he has reason to believe that he is likely to be a witness or in which whether by reason of any connection with the client or with the Court or a member of it or otherwise it will be difficult for him to maintain professional independence or the administration of justice might be or appear to be prejudiced;

(e) if there is or appears to be a conflict or risk of conflict either between the interests of the barrister and some other person or between the interests of any one or more clients (unless all relevant persons consent to the barrister accepting the instructions);

(f) if there is a risk that information confidential to another client or former client might be communicated to or used for the benefit of anyone other than that client or former client without their consent;

(g) if he is a barrister in independent practice where the instructions are delivered by a solicitor or firm of solicitors in respect of whom a Withdrawal of Credit Direction has been issued by the Chairman of the Bar pursuant to the Terms of Work on which Barristers Offer their Services to Solicitors and the Withdrawal of Credit Scheme 1988 as amended and in force from time to time (reproduced in Annex G1) unless his fees are to be paid directly by the Legal Services Commission or the instructions are accompanied by payment of an agreed fee or the barrister agrees in advance to accept no fee for such work or has obtained the consent of the Chairman of the Bar.

604   Subject to paragraph 601 a barrister in independent practice is not obliged to accept instructions:

(a) requiring him to do anything other than during the course of his ordinary working year;

(b) other than at a fee which is proper having regard to:

(i)   the complexity length and difficulty of the case;

(ii)   his ability experience and seniority; and

(iii) the expenses which he will incur;

and any instructions in a matter funded by the Legal Services Commission as part of the Community Legal Service or the Criminal Defence Service for which the amount or rate of the barrister's remuneration is prescribed by regulation or subject to assessment shall for this purpose unless the Bar Council or the Bar in general meeting otherwise determines (either in a particular case or in any class or classes of case or generally) be deemed to be at a proper professional fee;[1]

(c) to do any work under a conditional fee agreement;

(d) save in a matter funded by the Legal Services Commission as part of the Community Legal Service or the Criminal Defence Service:

(i)   unless and until his fees are agreed;

(ii)   if having required his fees to be paid before he accepts the instructions those fees are not paid;

(e) in a BarDIRECT matter or in a matter where the lay client is also the professional client;

(f) to do any work under the Contractual Terms on which Barristers offer their Services to Solicitors 2001 as amended and in force from time to time (reproduced in Appendix G2) or on any other contractual terms.

605   A Queen's Counsel in independent practice is not obliged to accept instructions:

(a) to settle alone any document of a kind generally settled only by or in conjunction with a junior;

(b) to act without a junior if he considers that the interests of the lay client require that a junior should also be instructed.

606.1 A barrister (whether he is instructed on his own or with another advocate) must in the case of all instructions consider whether consistently with the proper and efficient administration of justice and having regard to:

(a) the circumstances (including in particular the gravity complexity and likely cost) of the case;

---

1 [On 30 April 2001 the Bar Council decided that, with effect from 1 May 2001, all cases subject to family graduated fees are no longer deemed to be at a proper professional fee for the purposes of paragraph 604(b).]

(b) the nature of his practice;

(c) his ability experience and seniority; and

(d) his relationship with the client;

the best interests of the client would be served by instructing or continuing to instruct him in that matter.

606.2   Where a barrister is instructed in any matter with another advocate or advocates the barrister must in particular consider whether it would be in the best interests of the client to instruct only one advocate or fewer advocates.

606.3   A barrister who in any matter is instructed either directly by the lay client or by an intermediary who is not a solicitor or other authorised litigator should consider whether it would be in the interests of the lay client or the interests of justice to instruct a solicitor or other authorised litigator or other appropriate intermediary either together with or in place of the barrister.

606.4   In cases involving several parties, a barrister must on receipt of instructions and further in the event of any change of circumstances consider whether, having regard to all the circumstances including any actual or potential conflict of interest, any client ought to be separately represented or advised or whether it would be in the best interests of any client to be jointly represented or advised with another party.

607   If at any time in any matter a barrister considers that it would be in the best interests of any client to have different representation, he must immediately so advise the client.

Withdrawal from a case and return of instructions

608   A barrister must cease to act and if he is a barrister in independent practice must return any instructions:

(a) if continuing to act would cause him to be professionally embarrassed within the meaning of paragraph 603 provided that if he would be professionally embarrassed only because it appears to him that he is likely to be a witness on a material question of fact he may retire or withdraw only if he can do so without jeopardising the client's interests;

(b) if having accepted instructions on behalf of more than one client there is or appears to be:

(i)   a conflict or risk of conflict between the interests of any one or more of such clients; or

(ii)   risk of a breach of confidence;

and the clients do not all consent to him continuing to act;

(c) if in any case funded by the Legal Services Commission as part of the Community Legal Service or Criminal Defence Service it has become apparent to him that such funding has been wrongly obtained by false or inaccurate information and action to remedy the situation is not immediately taken by the client;

(d) if the client refuses to authorise him to make some disclosure to the Court which his duty to the Court requires him to make;

(e) if having become aware during the course of a case of the existence of a document which should have been but has not been disclosed on discovery the client fails forthwith to disclose it;

(f) if having come into possession of a document belonging to another party by some means other than the normal and proper channels and having read it before he realises that it ought to have been returned unread to the person entitled to possession of it he would thereby be embarrassed in the discharge of his duties by his knowledge of the contents of the document provided that he may retire or withdraw only if he can do so without jeopardising the client's interests.

609   Subject to paragraph 610 a barrister may withdraw from a case where he is satisfied that:

(a) his instructions have been withdrawn;

(b) his professional conduct is being impugned;

(c) advice which he has given in accordance with paragraph 607 or 703 has not been heeded; or

(d) there is some other substantial reason for so doing.

610   A barrister must not:

(a) cease to act or return instructions without having first explained to the client his reasons for doing so;

(b) return instructions to another barrister without the consent of the client;

(c) return a brief which he has accepted and for which a fixed date has been obtained or (except with the consent of the lay client and where appropriate the Court) break any other engagement to supply legal services in the course of his practice so as to enable him to attend or fulfil an engagement (including a social or non-professional engagement) of any other kind;

(d) except as provided in paragraph 608 return any instructions or withdraw from a case in such a way or in such circumstances that the client may be unable to find other legal assistance in time to prevent prejudice being suffered by the client.

PART VII — CONDUCT OF WORK BY PRACTISING BARRISTERS

[Amended 19 May and 25 July 2001]

General

701   A barrister:

(a) must in all his professional activities be courteous and act promptly conscientiously diligently and with reasonable competence and take all reasonable and practicable steps to avoid unnecessary expense or waste of the Court's time and to ensure that professional engagements are fulfilled;

(b) must not undertake any task which:

(i)   he knows or ought to know he is not competent to handle;

(ii) he does not have adequate time and opportunity to prepare for or perform; or

(iii) he cannot discharge within the time requested or otherwise within a reasonable time having regard to the pressure of other work;

(c) must read all instructions delivered to him expeditiously;

(d) must have regard to any relevant Written Standards for the conduct of Professional Work issued by the Bar Council;

(e) must inform his client forthwith and subject to paragraph 610 return the instructions to the client or to another barrister acceptable to the client:

(i)   if it becomes apparent to him that he will not be able to do the work within the time requested or within a reasonable time after receipt of instructions;

(ii)   if there is an appreciable risk that he may not be able to undertake a brief or fulfil any other professional engagement which he has accepted.

(f)   must ensure that adequate records supporting the fees charged or claimed in a case are kept at least until the last of the following: his fees have been paid, any taxation or determination or assessment of costs in the case has been completed, or the time for lodging an appeal against assessment or the determination of that appeal, has expired, and must provide his professional or BarDIRECT client (or where the lay client is subsequently acting in person) the lay client) with such records or details of the work done as may reasonably be required.

Confidentiality

702   Whether or not the relation of counsel and client continues a barrister must preserve the confidentiality of the lay client's affairs and must not without the prior consent of the lay client or as permitted by law lend or reveal the contents of the papers in any instructions to or communicate to any third person (other than another barrister, a pupil or any other person who needs to know it for the performance of their duties) information which has been entrusted to him in confidence or use such information to the lay client's detriment or to his own or another client's advantage.

Conflicts between lay clients and intermediaries

703   If a barrister in independent practice forms the view that there is a conflict of interest between his lay client and a professional client or other intermediary (for example because he considers that the intermediary may have been negligent) he must consider whether it would be in the lay client's interest to instruct another professional adviser or representative and, if he considers that it would be, the barrister must so advise and take such steps as he considers necessary to ensure that his advice is communicated to the lay client (if necessary by sending a copy, of his advice in writing directly to the lay client as well as to the intermediary).

Drafting documents

704   A barrister must not devise facts which will assist in advancing the lay client's case and must not draft any statement of case, witness statement, affidavit, notice of appeal or other document containing:

(a)   any statement of fact or contention which is not supported by the lay client or by his instructions;

(b)   any contention which he does not consider to be properly arguable;

(c)   any allegation of fraud unless he has clear instructions to make such allegation and has before him reasonably credible material which as it stands establishes a prima facie case of fraud;

(d)   in the case of a witness statement or affidavit any statement of fact other than the evidence which in substance according to his instructions the barrister reasonably believes the witness would give if the evidence contained in the witness statement or affidavit were being given in oral examination;

provided that nothing in this paragraph shall prevent a barrister drafting a document containing specific factual statements or contentions included by the barrister subject to confirmation of their accuracy by the lay client or witness.

Contact with witnesses

705   A barrister must not:

(a) rehearse practise or coach a witness in relation to his evidence;

(b) encourage a witness to give evidence which is untruthful or which is not the whole truth;

(c) except with the consent of the representative for the opposing side or of the Court, communicate directly or indirectly about a case with any witness, whether or not the witness is his lay client, once that witness has begun to give evidence until the evidence of that witness has been concluded.

Attendance of professional client

706   A barrister in independent practice who is instructed by a professional client should not conduct a case in Court in the absence of his professional client or a representative of his professional client unless the Court rules that it is appropriate or he is satisfied that the interests of the lay client and the interests of justice will not be prejudiced.

707   A barrister in independent practice who attends Court in order to conduct a case in circumstances where no professional client or representative of a professional client is present may if necessary interview witnesses and take proofs of evidence.

Conduct in Court

708   A barrister when conducting proceedings in Court:

(a) is personally responsible for the conduct and presentation of his case and must exercise personal judgement upon the substance and purpose of statements made and questions asked;

(b) must not unless invited to do so by the Court or when appearing before a tribunal where it is his duty to do so assert a personal opinion of the facts or the law;

(c) must ensure that the Court is informed of all relevant decisions and legislative provisions of which he is aware whether the effect is favourable or unfavourable towards the contention for which he argues;

(d) must bring any procedural irregularity to the attention of the Court during the hearing and not reserve such matter to be raised on appeal;

(e) must not adduce evidence obtained otherwise than from or through the client or devise facts which will assist in advancing the lay client's case;

(f) must not make a submission which he does not consider to be properly arguable;

(g) must not make statements or ask questions which are merely scandalous or intended or calculated only to vilify insult or annoy either a witness or some other person;

(h) must if possible avoid the naming in open Court of third parties whose character would thereby be impugned;

(i) must not by assertion in a speech impugn a witness whom he has had an opportunity to cross-examine unless in cross-examination he has given the witness an opportunity to answer the allegation;

(j) must not suggest that a victim, witness or other person is guilty of crime, fraud or misconduct or make any defamatory aspersion on the conduct of any other person or attribute to another person the crime or conduct of which his lay client is accused unless such allegations go to a matter in issue (including the credibility of the witness) which is material to the lay client's case and appear to him to be supported by reasonable grounds.

Media comment

709.1   A barrister must not in relation to any anticipated or current proceedings in which he is briefed or expects to appear or has appeared as an advocate express a personal opinion to the press or other media or in any other public statement upon the facts or issues arising in the proceedings.

709.2   Paragraph 709.1 shall not prevent the expression of such an opinion on an issue in an educational or academic context.

Advertising and publicity

[Amended 23 March 2002]

710.1   Subject to paragraph 710.2 a barrister may engage in any advertising or promotion in connection with his practice which conforms to the British Codes of Advertising and Sales Promotion and such advertising or promotion may include:

(a) photographs or other illustrations of the barrister;

(b) statements of rates and methods of charging;

(c) statements about the nature and extent of the barrister's services;

(d) information about any case in which the barrister has appeared (including the name of any client for whom the barrister acted) where such information has already become publicly available or, where it has not already become publicly available, with the express prior written consent of the lay client.

710.2   Advertising or promotion must not:

(a) be inaccurate or likely to mislead;

(b) be likely to diminish public confidence in the legal profession or the administration of justice or otherwise bring the legal profession into disrepute;

(c) make direct comparisons in terms of quality with or criticisms of other identifiable persons (whether they be barristers or members of any other profession);

(d) include statements about the barrister's success rate;

(e) indicate or imply any willingness to accept instructions or any intention to restrict the persons from whom instructions may be accepted otherwise than in accordance with this Code;

(f) be so frequent or obtrusive as to cause annoyance to those to whom it is directed.

PART VIII — MISCELLANEOUS

[Amended 24 March 2001]

Pupils

801   A barrister who is a pupil must:

(a) comply with Part V of the Consolidated Regulations;

(b) apply himself full time to his pupillage save that a pupil may with the permission of his pupil master or head of chambers take part time work which does not in their opinion materially interfere with his pupillage;

(c) preserve the confidentiality of every client's affairs and accordingly paragraph 702 applies to him in the same way as it does to his pupil-master and to every person whom he accompanies to Court or whose papers he sees.

802   A barrister who is a pupil may supply legal services as a barrister and exercise a right of audience which he has by reason of being a barrister provided that:

(a) he has completed or been exempted from the non-practising six months of pupillage; and

(b) he has the permission of his pupil-master or head of chambers;

provided that such a barrister may during the non-practising six months of pupillage with the permission of his pupil-master or head of chambers accept a noting brief.

803.1   So long as he is a pupil a barrister in independent practice may not become or hold himself out as a member of chambers or permit his name to appear anywhere as such a member.

803.2   A barrister who is a pupil of an employed barrister or who pursuant to Regulation 46 of the Consolidated Regulations spends any period of external training with an employed barrister or with a solicitor shall be treated for the purpose of the Code as if he were during that period employed by the employed barrister's employer or by the solicitor's firm as the case may be.

Pupil-masters

804   A barrister who is a pupil-master must:

(a) comply with Part V of the Consolidated Regulations;

(b) take all reasonable steps to provide his pupil with adequate tuition supervision and experience;

(c) have regard to the pupillage guidelines issued from time to time by the Bar Council and to the Equality Code for the Bar.

805   Except where a pupil is in receipt of an award or remuneration which is paid on terms that it is in lieu of payment for any individual item of work, a barrister must pay any pupil (or in the case of an employed barrister ensure that a pupil is paid) for any work done for him which because of its value to him warrants payment.

Legal Advice Centres

806   A barrister in independent practice may supply legal services at a Legal Advice Centre on a voluntary or part time basis and, if he does so, shall in connection with the supply of those services be treated for the purpose of this Code as if he were employed by the Legal Advice Centre.

807   A barrister who is employed by a Legal Advice Centre:

(a) must not in any circumstances receive either directly or indirectly any fee or reward for the supply of any legal services to any client of the Legal Advice Centre other than a salary paid by the Legal Advice Centre;

(b) must ensure that any fees in respect of legal services supplied by him to any client of the Legal Advice Centre accrue and are paid to the Legal Advice Centre;

(c) must not have any financial interest in the Legal Advice Centre.

Dual qualification

808.1   A barrister who is a member of another authorised body and currently entitled to practise as such shall not practise as a barrister.

808.2   A barrister who becomes entitled to practise as a member of another authorised body shall forthwith inform the Bar Council and the Inn(s) of Court of which he is a member in writing of that fact.

808.3   A barrister who:

(a) has had his name struck off the roll of solicitors or been excluded from membership of an authorised body; or

(b) has at any time been found guilty of any professional misconduct or is the subject of any continuing disciplinary proceedings in relation to his professional conduct as a member of an authorised body; or

(c) has at any time been refused a practising certificate as a solicitor or had his practising certificate suspended or made subject to a condition

shall not practise as a barrister until the PCC has considered his case and, if it decides to refer the case to a Disciplinary Tribunal, until the case is finally determined.

Foreign lawyers

[Amended 18 May 2002]

809   A barrister called to the Bar under Part IV of the Consolidated Regulations (temporary membership of the Bar) may not practise as a barrister other than to conduct the case or cases specified in the certificate referred to in Regulation 39.

PART IX — COMPLIANCE

[Amended 14 July 2001]

901   Any failure by a barrister to comply with this Code shall constitute professional misconduct.

902   If the declaration made by a barrister on Call to the Bar is found to have been false in any material respect or if the barrister is found to have engaged before Call in conduct which is dishonest or otherwise discreditable to a barrister and which was not, before Call, fairly disclosed in writing to the Benchers of the Inn calling him or if any undertaking given by a barrister on Call to the Bar is breached in any material respect that shall constitute professional misconduct.

903   A barrister is subject to:

(a) the Complaints Rules (reproduced in Annex J);

(b) the Disciplinary Tribunals Regulations (reproduced in Annex K);

(c) the Summary Procedure Rules (reproduced in Annex L);

(d) the Hearings before the Visitors Rules (reproduced in Annex M);

(e) the Interim Suspension Rules (reproduced at Annex N);

(f) the Fitness to Practise Rules (reproduced at Annex O);

(g) the Adjudication Panel and Appeals Rules (reproduced at Annex P) which are concerned with inadequate professional service.

904 Pursuant to the Rules referred to in paragraph 903 a barrister may be directed to provide redress to a lay client for inadequate professional service whether or not such inadequate professional service also constitutes professional misconduct.

905 A barrister must:

(a) if he is practising, or the Bar Council has reason to believe may be practising, as a barrister:

(i) respond promptly to any requirement from the Bar Council for comments on or documents relating to the arrangements made for administering his practice and chambers or office whether or not any complaint has been received or raised arising out of those arrangements;

(ii) permit the Bar Council or any agent appointed by it to inspect forthwith and on request and at any time which is reasonable having regard to the circumstances and the urgency of the matter any premises from which he practises or is believed to practise as a barrister, the arrangements made for administering his practice and chambers or office, and any records relating to such practice and to the administration of his chambers or office.

(b) report promptly to the Bar Council if:

(i) he is charged with a serious criminal offence;

(ii) he is convicted of any relevant criminal offence; or

(iii) he is convicted of a disciplinary offence by another professional body;

(c) report promptly to the Bar Council if;

(i) bankruptcy proceedings are initiated in respect of or against him;

(ii) directors disqualification proceedings are initiated against him;

(iii) a bankruptcy order or directors disqualification order is made against him; or

(iv) if he enters into a individual voluntary arrangement with his creditors;

(d) where a complaint about a barrister has been made to or by the Bar Council, or where the Bar Council has reasonable grounds for believing that a breach of this Code may have occurred or is about to occur, or where circumstance referred to in sub-paragraph (b) or (c) above has been reported to the Bar Council, respond promptly to any request from the Bar Council for comments or information on the matter whether it relates to him or to another barrister;

(e) respond promptly to any letter of notification sent to him or attend before any tribunal panel body or person when so required pursuant to the rules referred to in paragraph 903;

(f) comply in due time with any sentence or suspension imposed or direction made or undertaking accepted by a tribunal panel body or person pursuant to the rules referred to in paragraph 903.

provided for the avoidance of doubt that nothing in this paragraph shall require a barrister to disclose or produce any document or information protected by law or in circumstances to which paragraph 702 applies.

PART X — DEFINITIONS

[Amended 24 March 2001 and 23 July 2002]

1001 In this Code except where otherwise indicated:

'the Act' means the Courts and Legal Services Act 1990 and where the context permits includes any orders or regulations made pursuant to powers conferred thereby;

'the Act of 1985' means the Administration of Justice Act 1985;

'advocacy services' means advocacy services as defined in Section 119 of the Act;

'authorised body' means any body other than the Bar Council authorised under the Act to grant rights of audience or rights to conduct litigation;

'authorised litigator' means an authorised litigator as defined in Section 119 of the Act;

'bankruptcy order' includes a bankruptcy order made pursuant to the Insolvency Act 1986 and any similar order made in any jurisdiction in the world;

'Bar' means the Bar of England and Wales;

'Bar Council' means The General Council of the Bar as constituted from time to time or a Committee thereof;

'BarDIRECT client' means a person or organisation approved as such by the Bar Council in accordance with the BarDIRECT Recognition Regulations (reproduced in Annex F);

'barrister' means an individual who has been called to the Bar by one of the Inns of Court and who has not ceased to be a member of the Bar; and in Parts III (other than paragraph 301), VI, VII and VIII of this Code means a practising barrister;

'barrister in independent practice' means a practising barrister other than an employed barrister acting in the course of his employment;

'BMIF' means Bar Mutual Indemnity Fund Limited;

'brief' means instructions to a barrister to appear as an advocate before a Court;

'Call' means Call to the Bar in accordance with the Consolidated Regulations;

'chambers' means a place at or from which one or more barristers in independent practice carry on their practices and also refers where the context so requires to all the barristers (excluding pupils) who for the time being carry on their practices at or from that place;

'client' means lay client or intermediary;

'complaint' means an allegation by any person or by the Bar Council of its own motion of professional misconduct or of inadequate professional service and includes a legal aid complaint;

'conditional fee agreement' means a conditional fee agreement as defined in Section 58 of the Act;

'Consolidated Regulations' means the Consolidated Regulations of the Inns of Court;

'Court' includes any court or tribunal or any other person or body whether sitting in public or in private before whom a barrister appears or may appear as an advocate;

'Disciplinary Tribunal' means a disciplinary tribunal constituted under the Disciplinary Tribunals Regulations (reproduced in Annex K);

'employed barrister' means a practising barrister who is employed either under a contract of employment or by virtue of an office under the Crown or in the institutions of the

European Communities and who supplies legal services as a barrister in the course of his employment;

'employer' means a person by whom an employed barrister is employed as such and any holding subsidiary or associated company corporate body or firm of that person;

'English law' includes international law and the law of the European Communities;

'European lawyer' means a person who is a national of a Member State and who is authorised in any Member State to pursue professional activities under any of the professional titles appearing in article 2(2) of the European Communities (Lawyer's Practice) Order 1999, but who is not any of the following:

(a) a solicitor or barrister of England and Wales or Northern Ireland; or

(b) a solicitor or advocate under the law of Scotland.

'foreign lawyer' means a person (other than a registered European lawyer) who is authorised by a competent professional body to practise in a system of law other than English law;

'home professional body' means the body in a Member State which authorises a European lawyer to pursue professional activities under any of the professional titles appearing in article 2(2) of the European Communities (Lawyer's Practice) Order 1999 and, if he is authorised in more than one Member States, it shall mean any such body;

'home professional title' means, in relation to a European lawyer, the professional title or any of the professional titles specified in relation to his home State in article 2(2) of the European Communities (Lawyer's Practice) Order 1999 under which he is authorised in his home State to pursue professional activities;

'home State' means the Member State in which a European lawyer acquired the authorisation to pursue professional activities under his home professional title and, if he is authorised in more than one Member State, it shall mean any such Member State;

'inadequate professional service' means such conduct towards a lay client or performance of professional services for that client which falls significantly short of that which is to be reasonably expected of a barrister in all the circumstances;

'incorporated solicitors' practice' means a body recognised under section 9 of the Act of 1985;

'instructions' means instructions or directions in whatever form (including a brief) given to a practising barrister to supply legal services whether in a contentious or in a non-contentious matter and 'instructed' shall have a corresponding meaning;

'intermediary' means any person by whom a barrister in independent practice is instructed on behalf of a lay client and includes a professional client who is not also the lay client;

'International work' shall have the meaning set out in the International Practice Rules (reproduced in Annex A);

'lay client' means the person on whose behalf a practising barrister (or where appropriate in the case of an employed barrister his employer) is instructed;

'lay representative' means a lay person appointed by the Bar Council to serve on Disciplinary Tribunals;

'legal aid complaint' shall mean a complaint so described in section 40 of the Act of 1985 as amended by the Access to Justice Act 1999;

'Legal Advice Centre' means a centre operated by a charitable or similar non-commercial organisation at which legal services are habitually provided to members of the public without charge (or for a nominal charge) to the client and:

(a) which employs or has the services of one or more solicitors pursuant to paragraph 7(a) of the Employed Solicitors' Code 1990 or for whom the Law Society has granted a waiver, or

(b) which has been and remains designated by the Bar Council as suitable for the employment or attendance of barristers subject to such conditions as may be imposed by the Bar Council in relation to insurance or any other matter whatsoever;

'legal services' includes legal advice representation and drafting or settling any statement of case witness statement affidavit or other legal document but does not include:

(a) sitting as a judge or arbitrator or acting as a mediator;

(b) lecturing in or teaching law or writing or editing law books articles or reports;

(c) examining newspapers, periodicals, books, scripts and other publications or libel, breach of copyright, contempt of court and the like;

(d) communicating to or in the press or other media;

(e) exercising the powers of a commissioner for oaths;

(f) giving advice on legal matters free to a friend or relative or acting as unpaid or honorary legal adviser to any charitable benevolent or philanthropic institution;

(g) in relation to a barrister who is a non-executive director of a company or a trustee or governor of a charitable benevolent or philanthropic institution or a trustee of any private trust, giving to the other directors trustees or governors the benefit of his learning and experience on matters of general legal principle applicable to the affairs of the company institution or trust;

'Legal Services Commission' means a body established by or under Section 1 or Section 2 of the Access to Justice Act 1999 and includes any body established and maintained by such a body;

'litigation services' means litigation services as defined in section 119 of the Act;

'Member State' means a state which is a member of the European Communities;

'non-practising barrister' means a barrister who is not a practising barrister;

'the PCC' means the Professional Conduct and Complaints Committee of the Bar Council;

'practising barrister' means a barrister who is practising as such within the meaning of paragraph 201;

'professional client' means a solicitor or other professional person by whom a barrister in independent practice is instructed that is to say:

(a) a solicitor, authorised litigator, Parliamentary agent, patent agent, trade mark agent, Notary or a European lawyer registered with the Law Society of England and Wales;

(b) a licensed conveyancer in a matter in which the licensed conveyancer is providing conveyancing services;

(c) an employed barrister or registered European lawyer;

(d) any practising barrister or registered European lawyer acting on his own behalf;

(e) a foreign lawyer in a matter which does not involve the barrister supplying advocacy services;

(f) the representative of any body (such as a Legal Advice Centre or Pro Bono or Free Representation Unit) which arranges for the supply of legal services to the public without a fee, and which has been and remains designated by the Bar Council (subject to such conditions as may be imposed by the Bar Council in relation to insurance or any other matter whatsoever) as suitable for the instruction of barristers, and which instructs a barrister to supply legal services without a fee;

'professional misconduct' shall bear the meaning given in paragraphs 901 and 902;

'the PSC' means the Professional Standards Committee of the Bar Council;

'the public' includes any lay client of a practising barrister (or in the case of an employed barrister of the barrister's employer) other than any of the persons referred to in paragraph 501;

'registered European lawyer' means a European lawyer registered as such by the Bar Council and by an Inn pursuant to a direction of the JRC under Regulation 30 of the Consolidated Regulations;

'relevant criminal offence' means any criminal offence committed in any part of the world except:

(a) an offence committed in the United Kingdom which is a fixed penalty offence for the purposes of the Road Traffic Offenders Act 1988 or any statutory modification or replacement thereof for the time being in force;

(b) an offence committed in the United Kingdom or abroad which is dealt with by a procedure substantially similar to that applicable to such a fixed penalty offence; and

(c) an offence whose main ingredient is the unlawful parking of a motor vehicle;

'right of audience' means a right of audience as defined in Section 119 of the Act;

'right to conduct litigation' means a right to conduct litigation as defined in Section 119 of the Act;

'serious criminal offence' means an offence involving dishonesty or deception or a serious arrestable offence (as defined by section 116 of the Police and Criminal Evidence Act 1984);

'solicitor' means a solicitor of the Supreme Court of England and Wales;

'Summary Procedure Panel' means a panel constituted under the Summary Procedure Rules (reproduced in Annex L);

'trade association' means a body of persons (whether incorporated or not) which is formed for the purpose of furthering the trade interests of its members or of persons represented by its members, and does not include any association formed primarily for the purpose of securing legal assistance for its members;

any reference to the masculine shall be deemed to include the feminine and any reference to the singular shall include the plural.

PART XI — TRANSITIONAL PROVISIONS

1101   In respect of anything done or omitted to be done or otherwise arising before 31 July 2000:

(a) this Code shall not apply;

(b) the Code of Conduct in force at the relevant time shall notwithstanding paragraph 101 apply as if this Code had not been adopted by the Bar Council.

1102   Any barrister called to the Bar before 1 January 2002 but who has not completed or been exempted from 12 months' pupillage in accordance with the Consolidated Regulations in force at the relevant time may practise as a barrister notwithstanding paragraph 202(a) of this Code provided that such a barrister shall not be entitled to exercise a right of audience under paragraph 203.1 unless he:

(a) has notified the Bar Council in writing of his wish to do so; and

(b) either (i) has complied with any conditions as to further training which the Bar Council may require or (ii) has been informed by the Bar Council that he is not required to comply with any such conditions.

1103   Any barrister who on 31 July 2000 was entitled to exercise any right of audience which he had by reason of being a barrister shall notwithstanding paragraph 203 of this Code remain entitled to exercise that right of audience.

1104   Any barrister who during any period before 31 July 2000 was entitled to exercise a right of audience as an employed barrister may for the purpose of paragraph 203.2(c) of this Code count that period as if he had been entitled during that period to exercise a right of audience before every Court in relation to all proceedings provided that he:

(a) has notified the Bar Council in writing of his wish to do so; and

(b) either (i) has complied with any conditions (including any conditions as to further training) which the Bar Council may require or (ii) has been informed by the Bar Council that he is not required to comply with any such conditions.

1105   Any person who was entitled on 31 July 2000 or becomes entitled before 31 July 2002 to exercise a right of audience before every Court in relation to all proceedings shall be a qualified person without having satisfied paragraph 203.3(b)(ii) of this Code if he:

(a) has satisfied the other requirements of paragraph 203.3;

(b) has notified the Bar Council in writing of his wish to act as a qualified person; and

(c) has been designated by the Bar Council as suitable so to act.

1106   Any barrister who before 31 July 2000 had delivered to the Bar Council the notification and information referred to in paragraph 212(b)(ii) of the Sixth Edition of the Code of Conduct or was exempted by waiver from that requirement shall until 31 July 2005 remain entitled to supply legal services to the public on condition that he complies with those requirements of paragraph 212(b)–(e) of the Sixth Edition of the Code of Conduct which on 31 July 2000 applied to him and provided that he shall not thereby be entitled to exercise any right of audience which he has by reason of being a barrister.

SECTION 2

Table of Annexes

ANNEXE A

THE INTERNATIONAL PRACTICE RULES

[Amended 14 July 2001 and 28 November 2002]

1. 'International work' means practice as a barrister:

    (a) where the work (i) relates to matters or proceedings essentially arising taking place or contemplated outside England and Wales and (ii) is to be substantially performed outside England and Wales; or

    (b) where the lay client carries on business or usually resides outside England and Wales provided that:

        (i)   the instructions emanate for outside England and Wales; and

        (ii) the work does not involve the barrister in providing advocacy services.

2. In connection with any International work, a barrister must comply with any applicable rule of conduct prescribed by the law or by any nation or local Bar of (a) the place where the work is or is to be performed (b) the place where any proceedings or matters to which the work relates are taking place or contemplated, unless such rule is inconsistent with any requirement of Part III of this Code ('Fundamental Principles').

3. Paragraphs 401(a) and (c) and 602 of the Code shall not apply to International work.

4. In relation to International work substantially performed outside England and Wales:

    (a) a practising barrister may enter into any association (including partnership) with any lawyer other than a member of another authorised body for the purpose of sharing any office, services or fees;

    (b) paragraphs 401(b) and 402.1 of the Code shall not apply;

    (c) paragraph 405 of the Code shall apply on the basis that the applicable law is that of the place where the work is performed;

    (d) a practising barrister employed by a foreign lawyer or foreign legal practice may supply legal services to any client of his employer; and

    (e) paragraphs 202(b) and 204 of the Code shall not apply to a barrister who is practising as a foreign lawyer and who does not:

        (i)   give advice on English law; or

        (ii) supply legal services in connection with any proceedings or contemplated proceedings in England and Wales (other than as an expert witness on foreign law).

5. A practising barrister who supplies legal services as a barrister (other than to his employer) outside England and Wales must be covered (and in the case of an employed barrister his employer must be covered) by insurance against claims for professional negligence arising out of the supply of his services in an amount not less than the minimum level of insurance cover required by law or by the rules of the Bar in the place where the services are supplied or, if there is no such minimum, the current minimum sum insured for barristers practising in England and Wales.

6. A barrister who solicits work in any jurisdiction outside England and Wales must not do so in a manner which would be prohibited if the barrister were a member of the local Bar.

ANNEXE B

THE REGISTERED EUROPEAN LAWYERS RULES

1. The Bar Council shall maintain a register of European lawyers.

2. The Bar Council shall:

    (1) enter a European lawyer on the register pursuant to a direction of the Joint Regulations Committee under Regulation 30 of the Consolidated Regulations;

    (2) remove a European lawyer from the register:
      (i) pursuant to a sentence of a Disciplinary Tribunal; or
      (ii) if the registered European lawyer ceases to be a European lawyer;

    (3) suspend a European lawyer from the register:
      (i) pursuant to a sentence of either a Disciplinary Tribunal or a Summary Procedure Panel; or
      (ii) if the European lawyer's authorisation in his home state to pursue professional activities under his home professional title is suspended; and

    (4) notify the European lawyer's home professional body:
      (i) of his entry on or removal or suspension from the register; and
      (ii) of any criminal conviction or bankruptcy order of which it becomes aware against a registered European lawyer.

3. A registered European lawyer must not hold himself out to be a barrister.

4. A registered European lawyer must in connection with all professional work undertaken in England and Wales:

    (1) use his home professional title as determined by the Joint Regulations Committee pursuant to the Consolidated Regulations;

    (2) indicate the name of his home professional body or the Court before which he is entitled to practise in that Member State; and

    (3) indicate that he is registered with the Bar Council as a European lawyer.

5. A registered European lawyer may supply legal services, including the exercise of rights of audience, under these Rules provided that:

    (1) he has paid to the Bar Council the subscription currently prescribed by the Bar Council;

    (2) in the case of a registered European lawyer who supplies legal services to the public, unless exempted by the Joint Regulations Committee he is covered by insurance against claims for professional negligence arising out of the supply of his services in England and Wales in such amount and upon such terms as are currently required by the Bar Council, and has delivered to the Bar Council a copy of the current insurance policy or the current certificate of insurance issued by the insurer;

    (3) where the professional activities in question may (but for the European Communities (Lawyer's Practice) Order 1999) be lawfully provided only by a solicitor or barrister, he must act in conjunction with a solicitor or barrister who is entitled to practise before the Court, tribunal or public authority concerned and who could lawfully provide those professional activities.

6. A registered European lawyer in connection with all professional work undertaken in England and Wales must comply with all of the provisions of the Code (except paragraphs 201 to 204, 401, 402 and 801 to 804) as if he were a barrister in independent practice or an employed barrister as the case may be and as if references in the Code to barristers included reference to registered European lawyers.

7. A registered European lawyer must inform the Bar Council of:

   (1) any investigation into his conduct by his home professional body;

   (2) any findings of professional misconduct made by his professional body; and

   (3) the withdrawal or suspension of his authorisation in his home state to pursue professional activities under his home professional title.

ANNEXE C

THE CONTINUING PROFESSIONAL DEVELOPMENT REGULATIONS

[Amended 25 July 2001]

Application

1. These Rules apply;

    (a) to all barristers who have commenced practice on or after 1 October 1997;

    (b) from 1 October 2002, to all barristers who were called to the Bar in or after 1990;

    (c) from 1 October 2003, to all barristers who were called to the Bar between 1980 and 1989; and

    (d) from 1 October 2004, to all barristers who were called to the Bar before 1980.

The Mandatory Continuing Professional Development Requirements

2. For the purpose of these Regulations the 'mandatory requirements' are those set out in paragraphs 3 to 5 below.

3. Any barrister to whom these Regulations apply and who as at 1 October 2001 had commenced but not completed the period of three years referred to in the Continuing Education Scheme Rules at Annex Q to the Sixth Edition of the Code of Conduct must complete a minimum of 42 hours of continuing professional development during that period.

4. Any barrister to whom these Regulations apply who commences practice on or after 1 October 2001 must during the first three calendar years (running from 1 January) in which the barrister holds a practising certificate complete a minimum of 42 hours of continuing professional development.

5. Any barrister to whom these Regulations apply who has completed or is not subject to either of the requirements referred to in paragraphs 3 and 4 above and who holds a practising certificate must comply with the following requirement:

    (a) If the practising certificate has been issued or renewed for a period of twelve months, the barrister must complete a minimum of 12 hours of continuing professional development during that period; and

    (b) If the practising certificate has been issued or renewed for a period of between six and twelve months, the barrister must

    (c) complete a minimum of 6 hours of continuing professional development during that period.

6. The Bar Council may, by resolution, specify the nature, content and format of courses and other activities which may be undertaken by barristers (or any category of barristers) in order to satisfy the mandatory requirements.

7. The Bar Council may, by resolution and following consultation with the Inns, Circuits and other providers as appropriate, increase the minimum number of hours of continuing professional development which must be completed in order to satisfy any of the mandatory requirements.

Waivers

8. The Bar Council shall have the power in relation to any barrister to waive any or all of the mandatory requirements in whole or in part or to extend the time within which the barrister must complete any of the mandatory requirements.

9. Any application by a barrister to the Bar Council for a waiver of any of the mandatory requirements or to extend the time within which to complete any of the mandatory requirements must be made in writing, setting out all mitigating circumstances relied on and supported by all relevant documentary evidence.

ANNEXE D

THE PRACTISING CERTIFICATE REGULATIONS

The Authority to Issue Practising Certificates

1. The Access to Justice Act 1999 (s. 46) included provision for the Bar Council to make rules prohibiting barristers from practising unless authorised by a certificate issued by the Bar Council (a 'practising certificate'). The rules may include provision for the payment of different fees by different descriptions of barristers, but the Council may not set fees with a view to raising a total amount in excess of that applied by the Council for the purposes of the regulation, education and training of barristers, and those wishing to become barristers and for any other purpose approved by the Lord Chancellor under subsection (3)(a) of s. 46 of the Access to Justice Act 1999.

2. No provision included in the rules shall have effect unless approved by the Lord Chancellor.

3. Section 46 of the Access to Justice Act 1999, as amended by Order by statutory instrument with effect from 31 January 2001, is at Appendix 1 to these rules.

Application

4. These rules shall apply to all barristers and registered European lawyers holding themselves out as offering legal services as barristers to the public or to their employer. They shall not apply to non-practising barristers.

The Calculation of Income from Practising Certificates

5. The income to be raised by the Bar Council from Practising Certificate Fees shall not exceed the forecast expenditure for the year ahead starting 1 January each year to be applied to the activities and purposes set out below, less any subventions for those purposes received from the Inns of Court.

6. The activities, including education and training, to which practising certificate fees shall be applied shall be as follows:

    (a) The formulation and implementation of rules and regulations;

    (b) The development and dissemination to the profession of guidance, recommendations and other standards (whether binding or advisory) contributing to the control, government and direction of the profession and the way in which it practises: those activities shall include the definition, review and supervision of the standards of professional conduct and work expected of members of the profession;

    (c) Participation in the legislative process in relation to proposals relevant to the organisation or conduct of the profession;

    (d) Law reform work: that is, participation in the legislative process in relation to proposals falling outside paragraph 5(c);

    (e) Support for the administration of provision of legal services to the public *pro bono*;

    (f) the furtherance of human rights;

    (g) the development of international relations.

7. The maximum sum to be raised from Practising Certificate Fees shall include, as agreed by the Lord Chancellor, the annual forecast full cost of work in the following areas:

    (a) Activities which are entirely regulatory:

    (i)   Professional Standards

    (ii) Professional Conduct and Complaints

    (iii) Equal Opportunities

    (iv) Records

  (b) Education and Training

  (c) Activities qualifying under the Statutory Instrument laid under s. 46 subsection (3)(a) of the Access to Justice Act 1999:

    (i)   Human Rights and Pro Bono administration

    (ii) Law Reform

8.   The maximum sum to be raised from Practising Certificate Fees shall include, as agreed by the Lord Chancellor, the proportion as shown of the annual forecast full cost of work in the following areas qualifying as regulatory activity or for purposes agreed under the Statutory Instrument laid under s. 46 sub-section (3)(a) of the Access to Justice Act 1999:

(a) Legal Services	80%
(b) International Relations	90%
(c) Policy	75%
(d) Remuneration	80%
(e) Public Affairs	30%
(f) Employed Bar	70%
(g) Young Bar	60%
(h) Information Technology	60%

9.   For the purpose of calculating the maximum sum to be raised from Practising Certificate Fees, Administration costs shall be added in proportion to the cost of activities set out in paragraphs 8 and 9, to include the following:

Chairman's Office
Executive Office
Council and General Management Committee work
Finance
Library/Registry
Print and Distribution
Reception and Meeting Rooms
Publications
Website
Contingency funds up to 3% of total expenditure
Provision for capital expenditure not covered by depreciation

The Issue of Practising Certificates

10. The Bar Council shall issue Full Practising Certificates at entry into independent practice in accordance with the rules set out in the Consolidated Regulations of the four Inns of Court and on entry to employment as a barrister. On the introduction of Practising Certificate Fees, the Bar Council shall issue a Practising Certificate to all barristers and registered European lawyers offering a legal service as a barrister to the public or to their employer, on receipt of the Practising Certificate Fee. The Bar Council shall give four weeks' notice of the date by which payment of the Practising Certificate Fee is due.

11.   A Practising Certificate shall be valid for one year. A barrister must inform the Bar Council of any change of category or status relating to his practice, whereupon the Bar Council shall if appropriate issue a Practising Certificate, amended as necessary, reflecting such change and subject to confirmation of payment of the appropriate Practising Certificate Fee.

12.   A Practising Certificate shall cease to be valid if a barrister is disbarred or (and for such period as he is) suspended from practice as a barrister. A Practising Certificate may be amended to reflect any qualification imposed on the barrister by the Bar Council or as a result of disciplinary proceedings.

13.   Unless disbarred or suspended, and subject to any other qualification which the Bar Council or disciplinary proceedings may impose, a barrister may qualify for a Practising Certificate for a barrister of his description provided that:

   (a) he has complied with any applicable training requirements imposed by the Consolidated Regulations which were in force at the date of Call to the Bar;

   (b) he has complied with any applicable requirements of the Continuing Professional Development Regulations;

   (c) he has provided in writing to the Bar Council details of the current address(es) with telephone number(s) of the chambers or office from which he supplies legal services and (if he is an employed barrister) the name, address, telephone number and nature of the business of his employer;

   (d) unless exempted by the Bar Council, he has paid to the Bar Council the Practising Certificate Fee currently prescribed by the Bar Council for barristers of his/her description;

   (e) with effect from such date as the Bar Council may determine, he has paid the appropriate insurance premium so as to be insured with the Bar Mutual Indemnity Fund against claims for professional negligence, as required by the Code of Conduct.

The Renewal of Practising Certificates

14.   The Practising Certificate Fee for barristers in independent practice and registered European lawyers shall be due by 1st January each year. The Practising Certificate Fee for employed barristers shall be due by 6th April each year. The Bar Council shall provide four weeks' notice of the date by which payment of the Practising Certificate Fee is due and shall confirm in writing the validity of the Practising Certificate following payment of the Practising Certificate Fee. The Practising Certificate Fee following Call to the Bar shall become due on 1st January or 6th of April of the year following the year of Call, as appropriate to each category of barrister.

Practising Certificate Fees

15.   The Bar Council shall set different fees for different descriptions of barrister, so that the projected income from these fees shall not exceed the total amount calculated under paragraphs 8 to 10 of these rules. On application of individual barristers, the Bar Council may reduce the Practising Certificate Fee in recognition of certified periods of continuous absence from practice exceeding three months. The Bar Council may reduce the Practising Certificate Fee payable by those whose certified gross fee income or salary for the previous year is less than such annual amount as the Council may decide from time to time.

16. Notification to practising barristers of the Practising Certificate Fee shall include a statement of any separate voluntary subscription to the Bar Council, other than for a Practising Certificate.

Non-Payment of the Practising Certificate Fee

17. Any practising barrister who has not paid the Practising Certificate Fee by the due date shall receive from the Bar Council notification that if the Fee is not paid within one month, their name will be passed to the Professional Conduct and Complaints Committee for that Committee to investigate and consider whether there has been a breach of paragraph 202 of the Code of Conduct.

Appendix to ANNEX D

ACCESS TO JUSTICE ACT
s. 46 Bar Practising Certificates

(1) If the General Council of the Bar makes rules prohibiting barristers from practising as specified in the rules unless authorised by a certificate issued by the Council (a 'practising certificate'), the rules may include provisions requiring the payment of fees to the Council by applicants for practising certificates.

(2) Rules made by virtue of subsection (1)—

    (a) may provide for the payment of different fees by different descriptions of applicants, but

    (b) may not set fees with a view to raising a total amount in excess of that applied by the Council for the purposes of:

        (i) the regulation, education and training of barristers and those wishing to become barristers;

        (ii) the participation by the Council in law reform and the legislative process;

        (iii) the provision by barristers and those wishing to become barristers of free legal services to the public;

        (iv) the promotion of the protection by law of human rights and fundamental freedoms; and

        (v) the promotion of relations between the Council and bodies representing the members of legal professions in jurisdictions other than England and Wales.

(3) The Lord Chancellor may by order made by statutory instrument—

    (a) amend subsection (2)(b) by adding to the purposes referred to in it such other purposes as the Lord Chancellor considers appropriate, or

    (b) vary or revoke an order under paragraph (a).

(4) No order shall be made under subsection (3) unless—

    (a) the Lord Chancellor has consulted the Council, and

    (b) a draft of the order has been laid before, and approved by a resolution of, each House of Parliament.

(5) No provision included in rules by virtue of subsection (1), and no other provision of rules made by the Council about practising certificates, shall have effect unless approved by the Lord Chancellor.

(6)   The Council shall provide the Lord Chancellor with such information as he may reasonably require for deciding whether to approve any provision of rules made by the Council about practising certificates.

ANNEXE E

GUIDELINES ON OPINIONS UNDER THE FUNDING CODE

Status of these Guidelines

1. These Guidelines are prepared by the Legal Services Commission. They are intended as statements of good practice to be followed when opinions are prepared on the merits of applications or certificates issued under the Funding Code. As statements of good practice these Guidelines should not be too rigidly applied. An opinion will, however, be rejected if it does not contain the information necessary for the Commission to make its decision under the Code.

2. These Guidelines have been agreed by the Bar Council for incorporation in the Code of Conduct of the Bar of England and Wales.

Scope

3. These Guidelines apply to legal opinions sent to the Legal Services Commission for the purpose of decisions made in individual cases under the Funding Code. The Guidelines are most relevant to decisions made under certificates or contracts covering Legal Representation or Support Funding, but also may be relevant to other levels of service.

   The Guidelines apply to counsel and to solicitors with higher rights of audience who are instructed to give an independent opinion on the merits of a case. The term 'counsel' in the Guidelines therefore includes a solicitor with higher rights of audience.

4. The Guidelines do not apply directly to solicitors giving a report to the regional office in a case which they are conducting or proposing to conduct. Such a report may be shorter and more informal than an opinion on the merits, but these Guidelines should still be borne in mind by solicitors when such reports are prepared.

Preliminary Considerations

5. All opinions must be prepared in accordance with the Funding Code and having regard to the Funding Code guidance prepared by the Commission. This guidance is set out in the Commission's Manual, and on the Commission's website at www.legalservices.gov.uk. Every person preparing an opinion must have access to and consult the guidance as necessary.

6. When counsel is instructed to provide an opinion in writing, counsel should first consider whether it is necessary to have a conference, for example to enable counsel to assess the reliability of the client's evidence in a case where that evidence is likely to be contested. Where counsel considers that a conference is necessary and would be cost effective, the costs of such a conference may be covered by the certificate provided it is within any overall cost limitation on the certificate and is justified as reasonable on assessment at the end of the case. In the case of a high cost case contract, any conference must be justified within the agreed case plan for the action.

Contents of Opinions
Issues to be Covered

7. The primary purpose of an opinion is to provide the Commission with the information and legal opinion necessary to apply all relevant Funding Code criteria, rather than to provide a personal opinion on what the funding decision should be.

8. Each opinion should state at the outset:

(a) the level of service under which the opinion is given and if appropriate, the level of service being applied for;

(b) the case category into which the proceedings fall, giving reasons if there is likely to be an issue as to which case category is appropriate.

9. In every opinion counsel should identify any potentially excluded work in the case, i.e. aspects of the case which may fall within the excluded categories in paragraph 1 of Schedule 2 of the Access to Justice Act 1999. Where excluded work arises counsel should specify any of the Lord Chancellor's directions which may bring the case back into scope.

10. It is not necessary for an opinion to discuss separately every criterion relevant to the decision. For example, it is not usually necessary for counsel to refer to the standard criteria in section 4 of the Code unless, in the particular circumstances of the case, one or more of these criteria is likely to be material to the Commission's decision. Unless otherwise instructed an opinion should always cover the following:

(a) Prospects of success (except for special Children Act proceedings or other proceedings which do not have a prospect of success criterion). The opinion should specify what constitutes a successful outcome for the client, having regard to guidance, and must specify with reasons the prospects in one of the six categories provided for in the Code. Where prospects are 'borderline', the issues of fact, law or expert evidence which give rise to that assessment must be identified. Where prospects of success are 'unclear' the necessary work to clarify prospects of success must be identified.

(b) Cost benefit (save for those cases which do not have a cost benefit criterion). The opinion must identify the benefit to the client from the proceedings and, for quantifiable claims, provide a figure for 'likely damages' as defined in the Code. See paragraph 14 below as to estimates of 'likely costs'.

(c) Where the application is for Investigative Help to be granted or continued, the opinion must deal with matters relevant to criteria 5.6.2 (the need for investigation) and 5.6.4 (prospects after investigation). The opinion should explain why there are reasonable grounds for believing that when the investigative work has been carried out the claim will be strong enough, in terms of prospects of success and cost benefit, to satisfy the relevant criteria for full representation.

(d) Where the issue is whether funding should be withdrawn on the merits, the opinion should cover matters relevant to applying criteria 14.2 to 14.4, taking into account the interests of the client, the interests of the Community Legal Service Fund and relevant guidance.

11. An opinion on merits should:

(a) where factual issues are involved (a) set out in sufficient detail, (although not necessarily at great length), the rival factual versions to enable the Commission to assess their relative strengths, and (b) express a clear opinion as to the likelihood of the applicant's version being accepted by a court and why;

(b) where legal issues or difficulties of law are involved (a) summarise those issues or difficulties in sufficient detail to enable the Commission to come to a view about them without looking outside the opinion, and (b) express a clear view as to the likelihood of the applicant's case on the law being accepted by a court and why;

(c) draw attention to (a) any lack or incompleteness of material which might bear on the reliability or otherwise of the applicant's version, and (b) any other factor which could — whether now or in the future — materially affect the assessment of the outcome of the case.

12.   Where appropriate an opinion should suggest or formulate for the Commission any limitation or condition, whether as to the scope of work that should be covered, or as to costs, which ought to be imposed on the grant of funding in order to safeguard the Fund. In complex cases, including cases proceeding on the multi-track, the opinion should, specify any future point in the proceedings at which it is likely to be sensible to re-assess the merits.

Information From Other Sources

13.   There will often be information relevant to a merits decision which is not readily available to counsel. Where such information is not included in counsel's instructions, the opinion should specify the information which should be provided by the instructing solicitors, usually in the form of a covering letter to accompany counsel's opinion.

14.   The following issues should usually be dealt with by instructing solicitors:

(a) estimates of likely costs. This includes estimates of whether costs incurred to date, likely future costs to disposal, or future costs to trial. Assessments of likely costs may be relevant not just to any cost benefit criteria, but also to other criteria such as the thresholds for support funding, or the affordability of a high cost case. Such estimates will sometimes best be made in the light of counsel's opinion as to prospects of success and the future conduct of the case. Alternatively instructing solicitors may provide relevant estimates of costs to counsel with counsel's instructions so that such figures may be incorporated in the body of the opinion;

(b) assessments of whether a case is suitable for a Conditional Fee Agreement and whether affordable insurance is available, in cases which are being considered under the General Funding Code.

Specific Issues

15.   Where it is suggested that a case has a significant wider public interest counsel's opinion should:

(a) identify the nature of the benefits which the case might bring to persons other than the client;

(b) identify the group or section of the public who might benefit from the case, if possible giving at least a rough estimate of likely numbers;

(c) where people may benefit indirectly from a test case, explain the individual issues which other clients would need to establish in order to succeed with their claims;

(d) where the public interest of the case derives from establishing an important point of law, set out that legal issue clearly and explain the likelihood of the court resolving the issue one way or another for the benefit of other cases.

16.   Where it is suggested that a judicial review or claim against a public authority raises significant human rights issues, the opinion should identify the specific articles of the Convention which may have been breached by the public body and the importance of those issues to the client and the general public.

17.   Where it is suggested that a case has overwhelming importance to the client as this is defined in the Code, the nature of the importance to the client must be identified in the opinion having regard to the Commission's guidance on this issue.

18.   In cases involving more than two parties, counsel should consider carefully whether separate representation for each client is justified (criterion 5.4.5). This is particularly important in many family cases and in appeals where the points at issue in the appeal may not require separate representation from every party to the proceedings at first instance. Counsel should consider whether the arguments on which his or her client relies will be put forward on behalf of another party whose interests in the proceedings are substantially the same. Counsel should report to the Commission with proposals for minimising representation by solicitors and counsel.

19.   In high cost cases in which the Commission will be considering whether the action is affordable in the light of available resources (criterion 6.4) counsel's opinion should address those aspects of the case which, in accordance with the Commission's guidance, are relevant to the affordability decision. It will not be possible or appropriate for counsel to consider the question of the resources available to the Commission, or the reasonableness of funding the individual case as against other cases, as these are matters solely for the Commission.

Continuing Duties to the Fund

20.   A barrister is under a specific duty to comply with the provisions of the Access to Justice Act 1999 and any regulations or code in effect under that Act (paragraph 304 of the Bar Code of Conduct). Since these duties are directed at ensuring that public funding is granted and continued only in justifiable cases, it follows that counsel acting under a funding certificate is under a duty to bring to the attention of the Commission any matter which might affect the client's entitlement to funding, or the terms of his or her certificate, at whatever stage of the proceedings that might occur.

21.   Counsel and any other legal representative acting under a certificate or contract are also subject to the specific obligations set out in Rule C44 of the Code Procedures. This includes a general obligation to inform the Regional Director of new information or a change of circumstances which has come to light which may affect the terms or continuation of a certificate.

22.   Where counsel is under an obligation to draw matters to the attention of the Commission, he or she may do so by drawing matters to the attention of his or her instructing solicitors and asking that they be passed on to the Commission, or counsel may contact the Commission directly if that is appropriate in the particular circumstances of the case.

ANNEXE F

THE BarDIRECT RULES

[Amended 14 July 2001]

1.   Subject to these rules and to compliance with the Code of Conduct (and in particular to paragraphs 401 and 403) a barrister in independent practice may accept instructions from a BarDIRECT client in circumstances authorised in relation to that client by the BarDIRECT Recognition Regulations (reproduced in Annex C1) whether that client is acting for himself or another.

2.   These rules apply to every matter in which a barrister in independent practice is instructed by a BarDIRECT client save that paragraphs 4(b) 6 7 and 9 of these rules do not apply to any matter in which a BarDIRECT Client is deemed to be a BarDIRECT Client by reason only of paragraph 7 or paragraph 8 of the BarDIRECT Recognition Regulations.

3. Not used.

4. A barrister is only entitled to accept instructions from a BarDIRECT client if at the time of giving instructions the BarDIRECT client

    (a) is identified; and

    (b) sends the barrister a copy of the Licence issued by the BarDIRECT Committee.

5. A barrister must not accept any instructions from a BarDIRECT client

    (a) unless the barrister and his Chambers are able to provide the services required of them by that BarDIRECT client;

    (b) if the barrister considers it in the interests of the lay client or the interests of justice that a solicitor or other authorised litigator or some other appropriate intermediary (as the case may be) be instructed either together with or in place of the barrister.

6. A barrister who accepts instructions from a BarDIRECT client otherwise than on the terms of the BarDIRECT Terms of Work as approved from time to time by the BarDIRECT Committee

    (a) must first agree in writing the terms upon which he has agreed to do the work and the basis upon which he is to be paid;

    (b) must keep a copy of the agreement in writing with the BarDIRECT client setting out the terms upon which he has agreed to do the work and the basis upon which he is to be paid.

7. A barrister who accepts instructions from a BarDIRECT client

    (a) must promptly send the BarDIRECT client
        (i)   a statement in writing that the instructions have been accepted (as the case may be) (1) on the standard terms previously agreed in writing with that Bar-DIRECT Client or (2) on the terms of the BarDIRECT Terms of Work (and thereafter if requested a copy of the BarDIRECT Terms of Work); or
        (ii) if he has accepted instructions otherwise than on such standard terms or on the terms of the BarDIRECT Terms of Work, a copy of the agreement in writing with the BarDIRECT client setting out the terms upon which he has agreed to do the work and the basis upon which he is to be paid;

    (b) unless he has accepted instructions on the terms of the BarDIRECT Terms of Work or on terms which incorporate the following particulars must at the same time advise the BarDIRECT client in writing of:
        (i)   the effect of paragraph 401 of the Code of Conduct as it relevantly applies in the circumstances;
        (ii) the fact that the barrister cannot be expected to perform the functions of a solicitor or other authorised litigator and in particular to fulfil limitation obligations disclosure obligations and other obligations arising out of or related to the conduct of litigation;
        (iii) the fact that circumstances may require the client to retain a solicitor or other authorised litigator at short notice and possibly during the case.

8. If at any stage a barrister who is instructed by a BarDIRECT client considers it in the interests of the lay client or the interests of justice that a solicitor or other authorised litigator or some other appropriate intermediary (as the case may be) be instructed either together with or in place of the barrister:

(a) the barrister must forthwith advise the BarDIRECT client in writing to instruct a so-licitor or other authorised litigator or other appropriate intermediary (as the case may be); and

(b) unless a solicitor or other authorised litigator or other appropriate intermediary (as the case may be) is instructed as soon as reasonably practicable thereafter the barris-ter must cease to act and must return any instructions.

9. If at any stage a barrister who is instructed by a BarDIRECT client considers that there are substantial grounds for believing that the BarDIRECT client has in some significant re-spect failed to comply either with the terms of the Licence granted by the BarDIRECT Committee or (where applicable) with the terms of the BarDIRECT Terms of Work the bar-rister must forthwith report the facts to the BarDIRECT Committee.

10. A barrister who accepts instructions from a BarDIRECT client must keep a case record (whether on card or computer) which sets out:

(a) the date of receipt of the instructions, the name of the BarDIRECT client, the name of the case, and any requirements of the BarDIRECT client as to time limits;

(b) the date on which the instructions were accepted;

(c) the dates of subsequent instructions, of the despatch of advices and other written work, of conferences and of telephone conversations;

(d) when agreed, the fee.

11. A barrister who accepts instructions from a BarDIRECT client must either himself retain or take reasonable steps to ensure that the BarDIRECT Client will retain for six years after the date of the last item of work done:

(a) copies of instructions (including supplemental instructions);

(b) copies of all advices given and documents drafted or approved;

(c) a list of all documents enclosed with any instructions;

(d) notes of all conferences and of all advice given on the telephone.

BarDIRECT

THE BarDIRECT RECOGNITION REGULATIONS

1. Authorised BarDIRECT clients are those persons and organisations and/or their members and/or their or their members' employees (as the case may be) who have from time to time been approved as such by the BarDIRECT Committee.

2. Any person or organisation wishing to be approved as an authorised BarDIRECT client shall apply in writing to the BarDIRECT Committee by completing an application form in such form and supplying such other information as the BarDIRECT Committee may from time to time or in any particular case require.

3. In approving any person or organisation as an authorised BarDIRECT client the Bar-DIRECT Committee may grant such approval in each case as the BarDIRECT Committee may think appropriate:

(a) (i)   on a provisional basis or (ii) on a full basis;

(b) (i)   for a fixed period or (ii) for a fixed period subject to extension or (iii) indefi-nitely;

(c) (i) to the person or organisation and/or (ii) to some or all of the members of the organisation and/or (iii) to some or all of the employees of the person or organisation or its members;

(d) in relation to matters concerning (i) the person or organisation and/or its members (as the case may be) and/or (ii) his or its or its members' employees and/or (iii) his or its or its members' clients or customers;

(e) subject to such limitations or conditions as the BarDIRECT Committee may think appropriate relating to:

   (i) the matters in relation to which the authorised BarDIRECT client may instruct a barrister and/or

   (ii) the courts or tribunals before which a barrister so instructed may exercise a right of audience and/or

   (iii) such other matters (including the means by which the authorised BarDIRECT client shall instruct a barrister) as seem relevant in the circumstances.

4. The BarDIRECT Committee shall issue to every person or organisation approved as an authorised BarDIRECT client a Licence in such form as the BarDIRECT Committee may from time to time or in the particular case think appropriate. Such Licence (which may be a provisional Licence or a full Licence):

   (a) shall specify (i) the name of the person or organisation who has been approved as an authorised BarDIRECT client (ii) the period (if any) for which the Licence has been granted or (as the case may be) that the Licence has been granted indefinitely and (iii) the limitations or conditions (if any) subject to which the Licence has been granted;

   (b) may if the BarDIRECT Committee think appropriate provide that unless otherwise first agreed in writing with an individual barrister or chambers all instructions accepted by any barrister from the authorised BarDIRECT client will be deemed to be given and accepted on the terms of the BarDIRECT Terms of Work as approved from time to time by the BarDIRECT Committee;

   (c) may if the BarDIRECT Committee think appropriate provide that a copy of the Licence shall be sent with every set of instructions to any barrister instructed by the authorised BarDIRECT client;

   (d) shall remain at all times the property of the General Council of The Bar to whom (or to whose duly appointed officer) it shall be surrendered on demand.

5. The BarDIRECT Committee may from time to time:

   (a) approve additional persons or organisations as authorised BarDIRECT clients;

   (b) withdraw approval (either wholly or in part) from any person or organisation as an authorised BarDIRECT client;

   (c) increase reduce or otherwise alter the period for which a person or organisation is approved as an authorised BarDIRECT client;

   (d) alter or revoke the limitations or conditions (if any) attached to any approval of a person or organisation as an authorised BarDIRECT client or impose new or additional limitations or conditions;

   (e) cancel and demand the surrender of any Licence issued under paragraph 4 of these regulations.

6.   In exercising their functions under paragraphs 1 2 3 4 and 5 of these regulations the Bar-DIRECT Committee shall comply with the statutory objectives referred to in section 17(1) of the Courts and Legal Services Act 1990 and section 1(2) of the Access to Justice Act 1999 may consult with such persons organisations or bodies as they think appropriate and shall to such extent as they may think appropriate in the particular case have regard to the following matters:

   (a) the fact that barristers in independent practice operate as a referral profession of specialist consultants;

   (b) the extent to which the person or organisation or its members (as the case may be) are likely to have a significant requirement to retain the services of a barrister for their own benefit or for the benefit of their employers employees members clients or customers (as the case may be);

   (c) the extent to which whether as a result of professional or other relevant training or by reason of practice and experience the person or organisation or its employees or members (as the case may be) are or may reasonably be expected to be
      (i)   providers of skilled and specialist services
      (ii) competent in some identifiable area of expertise or experience
      (iii) familiar with any relevant area of law
      (iv) possessed of the necessary skills to obtain and prepare information and to organise papers and information sufficiently to enable the barrister to fulfill his duties in a non-contentious matter to the client and in a contentious matter both to the client and to the court
      (v)   possessed of the necessary skills to take charge and have the general conduct of the matters in respect of which they wish to retain the services of a barrister;

   (d) the extent to which the affairs and conduct of the person or organisation or its members (as the case may be) are subject to some appropriate professional disciplinary regulatory or other organisational rules;

   (e) the extent to which the person or organisation or its members (as the case may be)
      (i)   are insured against claims for negligence in relation to their handling of matters in respect of which they wish to retain the services of a barrister
      (ii) have made and continue to comply with satisfactory arrangements for holding in separate accounts and maintaining as trust monies any monies received from third parties
      (iii) have made and continue to comply with satisfactory arrangements for ensuring that barristers' fees are promptly paid;

   (f) such other facts and matters (if any) as seem to them to be relevant in the circumstances.

7.   Notwithstanding paragraphs 2 3 and 4 of these regulations any member of any of the bodies referred to in the First Schedule to these regulations shall be deemed to be an authorised BarDIRECT client (including in relation to matters concerning that member's clients or customers) but

   (a) only in a matter of a kind which falls generally within the professional expertise of the members of the relevant body; and

   (b) not for the purpose of briefing counsel to appear in or exercise any right of audience before the Judicial Committee of the House of Lords the Privy Council the Supreme Court the Crown Court a County Court or the Employment Appeals Tribunal.

8. Notwithstanding paragraphs 2 3 and 4 of these regulations any of the following shall be deemed to be an authorised BarDIRECT client:

  (a) an arbitrator (including for these purposes an adjudicator under the Housing Grants Construction and Regeneration Act 1996) but only when instructing counsel for the purpose of advising on any point of law practice or procedure arising in or connected with an arbitration in which he has been or may be appointed;

  (b) any person who has been appointed to one of the offices of Ombudsman referred to in the Second Schedule to these regulations but only when instructing counsel for the purpose of advising on any point of law practice or procedure arising in the course of the performance of his duties.

9. Nothing in paragraphs 7 and 8 of these regulations shall prevent

  (a) any person to whom paragraph 7 or paragraph 8 applies making an application in accordance with paragraph 2 of these regulations (in which event paragraphs 3 4 5 and 6 of these regulations shall apply to such application and to any Licence issued pursuant to such application);

  (b) the BarDIRECT Committee exercising in relation to any person to whom paragraph 7 or paragraph 8 applies the powers conferred by paragraphs 5(b) 5(c) and 5(d) of these regulations (in which event paragraph 6 of these regulations shall apply).

THE FIRST SCHEDULE

Part I — Accountants and taxation advisers

(1) The Association of Authorised Public Accountants
(2) Association of Taxation Technicians
(3) The Chartered Association of Certified Accountants
(4) The Chartered Institute of Management Accountants
(5) Institute of Chartered Accountants
(6) The Institute of Chartered Accountants in Ireland
(7) Institute of Chartered Accountants in Scotland
(8) The Chartered Institute of Taxation
(9) The Institute of Financial Accountants

Part II — Insolvency practitioners

(1) Insolvency Practitioners Association

Part III — Architects surveyors and town planners

(1) The Architects Registration Council of the UK
(2) The Architects and Surveyors Institute
(3) Association of Consultant Architects
(4) The Royal Institute of British Architects
(5) The Royal Institution of Chartered Surveyors
(6) The Royal Town Planning Institute

Part IV — Engineers

(1) The Institution of Chemical Engineers
(2) The Institution of Civil Engineering Surveyors
(3) The Institution of Civil Engineers
(4) The Institution of Electrical Engineers

(5)   Institution of Mechanical Engineers

(6)   The Institution of Structural Engineers

Part V — Valuers

(1)   The Incorporated Society of Valuers & Auctioneers

Part VI — Actuaries

(1)   The Faculty of Actuaries

(2)   Institute of Actuaries

Part VII — Chartered secretaries and administrators

(1)   The Institute of Chartered Secretaries and Administrators

Part VIII — Insurers

(1)   The Association of Average Adjusters

(2)   The Chartered Institute of Loss Adjusters

(3)   The Chartered Insurance Institute

THE SECOND SCHEDULE

(1)   Parliamentary Commissioner for Administration

(2)   Commissioner for Local Administration (England)

(3)   Commissioner for Local Administration (Wales)

(4)   Health Service Commissioner

(5)   Banking Ombudsman

(6)   Building Society Ombudsman

(7)   Insurance Ombudsman Bureau

(8)   The Personal Investment Authority Ombudsman Bureau Ltd

(9)   The Legal Services Ombudsman

CONTRACTS WITH SOLICITORS

To: All Heads of Chambers
         All Clerks and Practice Managers

From: Geoffrey Vos QC, Chairman of the Fees Collection Committee

This memorandum and its attachments is important. Please circulate it to all members of your chambers

Introduction

1.   On 24th March 2001, the Bar Council approved the following (copies of which are attached hereto):—

      (1)   Amendments to the 'Terms of Work on which barristers offer their services to solicitors and the Withdrawal of Credit Scheme 1988' ('Terms of Work'), to be appended to the Code of Conduct at Annexe G1.

      (2)   The 'Contractual Terms of Work on which barristers offer their services to solicitors 2001' ('Contractual Terms') to be appended to the Code of Conduct at Annexe G2.

      (3)   Certain minor consequential changes to paragraphs 403, 603 and 604 of the Code of Conduct.

2.   The object of the changes is to allow barristers to act on the instructions of solicitors pursuant to contractual terms, should both parties wish to do so.

3.   The Code of Conduct has been altered so as to provide that the Cab-Rank rule does not apply to contractual work. In other words, a barrister is not required to accept work on the Contractual Terms or on any other contractual basis (see paragraph 604(f) of the Code of Conduct).

4.   The new Contractual Terms themselves are not mandatory. Barristers may enter into contracts with solicitors for the provision of services on other terms should they so wish. The new Contractual Terms are, however, recommended.

5.   If no agreement is made between a barrister and solicitor, the Terms of Work (as amended) will continue to apply (see paragraph 27 of the Terms of Work).

6.   Both the Terms of Work and the Contractual Terms now provide for the payment of interest on barristers' fees from one month after the dispatch of letter 'A' (as appended to each of the Terms of Work and the Contractual Terms) until payment at 2% above Bank of England Base Rate.

7.   **Clerks and practice managers should note that:—**

      (1)   **the recommended terms of letter A have changed, and**

      (2)   **para. 28 of the revised Terms of Work provide that the new terms only apply to briefs and instructions accepted on or after 24th March 2001 (the date on which the new terms were adopted). As a result, interest is only payable on fees in respect of such work.**

How can barristers contract with solicitors?

8.   A barrister wishing to accept a brief or instructions on the Contractual Terms must agree in writing to that effect (see paragraph 1 of the Contractual Terms).

9.   The terms of sections 5(2), (3) and (4) of the Arbitration Act 1996 are applied so as to define how an agreement in writing can be made (see paragraph 15(v) of the Contractual Terms).

10.   In short:
(1)   An agreement can be made in writing whether or not it is signed by the parties.
(2)   An agreement can be made by exchange of written communications (in any form).
(3)   An agreement will be an agreement in writing if it is evidenced in writing, for example if it is recorded in writing by one of the parties or by a third party (e.g. a clerk) with the authority of the parties to the agreement.

11.   In practice, if a clerk or practice manager agrees orally with a solicitor that the Contractual Terms shall apply (with the authority of the barrister concerned), and if he then confirms that oral agreement in writing to the Solicitor, the provisions will be satisfied. It would, however, be better practice to ask the solicitor to confirm that the Contractual Terms apply by a response in writing.

What kind of work is covered by the Contractual Terms?

12.   The Contractual Terms apply to all kinds of privately funded work, except work undertaken on a conditional fee basis (see paragraph 1(4) of the Contractual Terms).

13.   The Contractual Terms do not apply to any publicly funded work (see paragraph 1(3) of the Contractual Terms).

What is the effect of using the Contractual Terms?

14.   The Contractual Terms have the following significant effects:—
(1)   The complaints system operated under the Terms of Work can still be used under the Contractual Terms. Accordingly, solicitors will still be subject to directions (better known as 'black-listing') if they fail to pay fees, which are contractually due, and complaints are made.
(2)   The Joint Tribunal system will also still be applicable to resolve any dispute as to the payment of Contractual Fees. The decision of a Joint Tribunal will be final binding and conclusive (see paragraph 12(3)(a) of the Contractual Terms).
(3)   If a dispute arises from the solicitor challenging the barrister's fees, and the solicitor fails to agree to a Joint Tribunal, it will be open to a barrister to sue for his fees. It is hoped that this will be a course of last resort.

15.   A term has been included (see paragraph 12(4) of the Contractual Terms), which is intended to prevent a solicitor from refusing to pay a barrister's fees or setting off any cross-claim against the barrister (for example arising from a contention that the barrister's work was unsatisfactory or negligent), unless the solicitor has challenged the fees in due time and has agreed to submit the dispute to a Joint Tribunal. This term will help to protect a barrister against non-payment pending resolution of a negligence claim.

How do the new interest provisions work?

16.   Under the revised Terms of Work (see paragraphs 12(5) and 13(2) of the Terms of Work) and under the Contractual Terms (see paragraphs 9(3) and 11(5) of the Contractual Terms), privately paid fees will carry simple interest at the rate of 2% above Bank of England base rate from one month after the date of letter 'A'.

17.   This date has been chosen to assist administration. Letter A marks the beginning of the process of the enforcement of payment of fees. The new draft letter A (under both the Terms of Work and the Contractual Fees) warns solicitors that interest will be charged if payment is not made within one month. Letter A may be sent one month after the first fee note. So, in practice, interest will be payable from not less than 2 months after the delivery of the fee note, if the administration is efficiently undertaken.

Geoffrey Vos QC
Chairman, Fees Collection Committee

26 March 2001

ANNEXE G1

THE TERMS OF WORK ON WHICH BARRISTERS OFFER THEIR SERVICES TO SOLICITORS AND THE WITHDRAWAL OF CREDIT SCHEME 1988

(As authorised by the General Council of the Bar on 16 July 1988 and amended by authority of the General Council of the Bar on 10 November 1990, 17 July 1999, and 24 March 2001)

[*Amended 17 November 2001*]

WHEREAS:

(1) These Terms have been authorised by the General Council of the Bar and are intended to apply (save as hereinafter provided) in any case where a barrister is instructed by a solicitor;

(2) Any solicitor who sends a brief or instructions to a barrister will be deemed to instruct that barrister on these Terms unless and to the extent that the barrister and the solicitor have agreed in writing in relation to the particular matter or generally (a) that the Contractual Terms on which Barristers Offer their Services to Solicitors 2000 shall apply, or (b) to exclude or vary these Terms;

AND WHEREAS:

(3) By the established custom of the profession a barrister looks for payment of his fees to the solicitor who instructs him and not to his lay client;

(4) Except in publicly funded cases a solicitor is personally liable as a matter of professional conduct for the payment of a barrister's proper fees whether or not he has been placed in funds by his lay client;

(5) Where instructions have been given in the name of a firm all partners at that date incur personal liability and remain liable for the payment of counsel's fees incurred on behalf of the firm by a deceased bankrupt or otherwise defaulting former partner of the firm; and

(6) The liability of a sole practitioner and of partners for the liabilities of their co-partners is a continuing one and is not cancelled or superseded by any transfer of the practice or dissolution of the partnership;

WITH EFFECT from 24 March 2001 the following will take effect:

General

1. A solicitor may in his capacity as a director partner member employee consultant associate or other agent of a company firm or other body brief or instruct a barrister.

2. In any case where a barrister accepts a brief or instructions from a solicitor in his capacity as a director partner member employee consultant associate or agent of a company firm or other body:

    (1) the solicitor warrants that he is authorised by his company firm or other body to instruct the barrister;

    (2) the obligations of the solicitor under these Terms (including in particular his responsibility for the payment of the barrister's fees) shall be the joint and several obligations of him and that company firm or other body.

Instructions

3. A barrister has the duty or the right in certain circumstances set out in the Bar Code of Conduct to refuse to accept a brief or instructions and these Terms will apply only where the barrister has accepted the brief or instructions.

4. Notwithstanding that a brief or instructions have been delivered to a barrister the barrister shall not be deemed to have accepted that brief or those instructions until he has had a reasonable opportunity:

    (1) to peruse them;

    (2) in the case of a brief to agree a fee with the solicitor.

5. A barrister accepts a brief or instructions upon the understanding:

    (1) that he must and will comply with the Bar Code of Conduct;

    (2) that he will deal with instructions as soon as he reasonably can in the ordinary course of his work;

    (3) that he may return the brief or instructions in accordance with the Bar Code of Conduct, and that, if he does so, he will incur no liability to the solicitor under these terms as a result of so doing.

6. (1) Where for any reason time is of the essence the solicitor must at the time when he delivers the brief or instructions but separately from the brief or instructions themselves inform the barrister of that fact and of the particular reason for urgency in order that the barrister may decide whether in those circumstances he can accept the brief or instructions. In addition the brief or instructions must be clearly marked 'Urgent'.

    (2) In the case of publicly funded work, the solicitor must at the time when he delivers the brief or instructions (or if any relevant certificate is not then available to him as soon as reasonably practicable thereafter) supply the barrister with copies of any relevant public funding certificates.

Copies of Briefs and Instructions and Records of Advice

7. A barrister shall be entitled for the purposes of his records (but not otherwise) to retain his brief or instructions or any papers delivered therewith or (if the solicitor requires the return of such brief or instructions and papers) to take and retain a copy of such brief or instructions and papers and of any written advice PROVIDED that nothing shall entitle a barrister to exercise any lien over any brief instructions or papers.

Fees

8. Save in the case of public funding work or in the case of a Notified Solicitor a barrister and solicitor may (subject to any rules regarding contingent fees) make such agreement or arrangement between them as to the time or times whether at the time of delivery of the brief or instructions or subsequently thereto or otherwise at which the barrister's fees shall be paid as they may think fit and the barrister's fees shall be paid by the solicitor accordingly PROVIDED that every such agreement or arrangement shall be recorded in writing.

9. Save in the case of public funding work or in the case of work the fees for which are to be paid out of a fund but cannot be so paid without an order of the court a barrister may and in the case of fees payable by a Notified Solicitor a barrister (unless and except as otherwise

previously authorised in writing by the Chairman) must require his fees to be agreed and paid before he accepts the brief or instructions to which the fees relate.

10.   (1) Fees and/or charging rates shall be (i) as agreed between the barrister and the solicitor before the barrister commences work under the brief or instructions; or, in default of such agreement, (ii) a reasonable professional rate for the barrister instructed.

(2) The barrister shall submit an itemised fee note not later than three months after the work to which the fee note relates has been done or at the conclusion of the matter in which the barrister is briefed or instructed whichever is the sooner.

(3) The barrister shall as soon as reasonably practicable comply with a request by the solicitor for a fee note.

(4) Every fee note shall include the solicitor's reference and (where appropriate) the barrister's case reference number, the barrister's relevant account number for the purpose of receiving payment in publicly funded cases and (if known to the barrister) any relevant public funding certificate number and date of issue.

(5) If any fees remain outstanding at the conclusion of a case the solicitor shall as soon as reasonably practicable inform the barrister that the case has concluded.

11.   In the case of publicly funded work:

(1) The solicitor and barrister shall respectively take such steps as may be open to each of them to take under the applicable Regulations for the time being in force for the purpose of obtaining payment of the barrister's fees as soon as reasonably practicable;

(2) The solicitor shall as soon as reasonably practicable comply with a request by the barrister for information by (i) notifying the barrister of the date of issue and number and supplying the barrister with copies of any relevant public funding certificates (ii) notifying the barrister of the date of any order for assessment of costs under the relevant certificate or other event giving rise to a right to such assessment (iii) informing the barrister of the steps taken by him pursuant to paragraph 11(1) hereof;

(3) The barrister unless such information and an explanation for non-payment satisfactory to him is thereupon received from the solicitor shall then report the facts to the Chairman.

12.   In the case of work the fees for which are to be paid out of a fund but cannot be so paid without an order of the court:

(1) The solicitor shall use his best endeavours to obtain such order or orders as may be requisite to enable payment of the fees to be made as soon as reasonably practicable;

(2) The solicitor shall as soon as reasonably practicable comply with a request by the barrister for information by informing the barrister of the steps taken by him pursuant to paragraph 12(1) hereof;

(3) The barrister unless such information and an explanation for non-payment satisfactory to him is thereupon received from the solicitor shall then report the facts to the Chairman;

(4) Subject to paragraph 12(5) below, the barrister's fees shall be payable one month after the making of the order of the court required for the payment of such fees out of the fund;

(5) In the event of any breach by the solicitor of his obligations under paragraph 12(1) and/or 12(2) above, the fees will be payable forthwith and the amount outstanding from time to time will carry simple interest at the stipulated rate from one month after the date of the letter referred to in paragraph 15(1) hereof until payment.

13.   (1) Subject to any such agreement or arrangement as is referred to in paragraph 8 hereof the barrister's fees if and to the extent that such fees have not been previously paid shall unless challenged by the solicitor as hereinafter provided be paid by the solicitor within one month after the fee note relating thereto has been sent to the solicitor whether or not the solicitor has been placed in funds by his client and whether or not the case is still continuing.

(2) In the event that the barrister's fees are not paid in full in accordance with sub-paragraph (1) above, the fees outstanding from time to time will carry simple interest at the stipulated rate from one month after the date of the letter referred to in paragraph 15(1) hereof until payment if that letter includes a statement to that effect.

14.   (1) Any challenge by a solicitor to a barrister's fee (whether giving rise to an issue of competence or a dispute on quantum or otherwise) must be made by the solicitor in writing within three months after the first fee note relating to that fee has been sent to him or within one month after such letter relating to that fee as is referred to in paragraph 15(1) hereof has been sent to him whichever is the later.

(2) No challenge to a barrister's fees will be accepted either by the barrister or in the case of a complaint by the barrister to the Bar Council of failure to pay those fees by the Bar Council unless:

(a)   the challenge was made in accordance with paragraph 14(1) hereof; and

(b)   the solicitor has within 14 days of being requested to do so either by the barrister or by the Bar Council agreed in writing (i) to submit the issue or dispute giving rise to the challenge to the decision of a Tribunal (ii) to abide by and forthwith give effect to the decision of the Tribunal.

(3) If a dispute is referred to a Tribunal in accordance with paragraph 14(2) above:

(a)   The Tribunal shall act as experts and not as arbitrators and its decision shall be conclusive, final and binding for all purposes upon the solicitor and the barrister.

(b)   No payment need be made in respect of the fees (unless the Tribunal orders an interim payment) until the Tribunal has made its decision and communicated it to the parties.

(c)   If the Tribunal determines that any sum is payable in respect of the fees, paragraph 13(2) above shall apply to that sum as if it had become payable when it would have become payable if no challenge had been made, and the Tribunal shall also determine the amount payable in respect of interest thereon under that paragraph.

(4) Unless the solicitor has challenged the barrister's fees and agreed to submit the issue or dispute in accordance with paragraphs 14(1) and (2), the fees will be payable in full, without any set-off whatsoever, in the amount set out in the relevant fee note and at the time specified in paragraph 13(1) above.

15.   Save as aforesaid and subject to any such agreement or arrangement as is referred to in paragraph 8 hereof the barrister if and to the extent that his fees have not been previously paid:

(1) may at any time after the expiration of one month after the first fee note relating thereto has been sent send a reminder substantially in the form of the letter annexed hereto and marked 'A' or some reasonable adaptation thereof; and

(2) unless an explanation for non-payment satisfactory to the barrister has been received shall at the expiration of three months after the first fee note relating thereto has been sent send a further reminder substantially in the form of the letter annexed hereto and marked 'B' or some reasonable adaptation thereof; and

(3) unless an explanation for non-payment satisfactory to the barrister is thereupon received shall then report the facts to the Chairman.

Withdrawal of Credit

16.   In any case where a barrister has made a report to the Chairman in accordance with paragraphs 11(3) 12(3) or 15(3) hereof or under the equivalent terms of any contract and in any other case in which he is satisfied that it is appropriate to do so, the Chairman may write a letter in the form of one of the letters annexed hereto and marked 'C' or some reasonable adaptation thereof.

17.   (1) This paragraph applies where the following conditions are satisfied namely where:

(a)   such a letter as is referred to in paragraph 16 hereof has been sent and no explanation for non-payment satisfactory to the Chairman has been received; and

(b)   either (i) any fees referred to in such letter which are in the opinion of the Chairman properly payable remain unpaid or (ii) in the event that all such fees have been paid not more than twelve months have elapsed since payment; and

(c)   circumstances have arisen in which the Chairman would otherwise have occasion to send to any person liable for the fees or to any connected person a further letter such as is referred to in paragraph 16 hereof.

(2) In any case in which paragraph 17(1) hereof applies the Chairman shall write to such person or persons (as the case may be) to the effect that unless written representations received by him within 14 days after the date of such letter or within such extended period as he may allow justify an exceptional departure from the following course he will and unless persuaded by such representations not to do so the Chairman whether or not any fees remain unpaid shall:

(a)   issue a direction that no barrister may without the written consent of the Chairman (which consent may be sought urgently in exceptional cases) knowingly accept instructions from any person or firm named in such direction or from any person who or firm which is or has at any time since the direction was issued been a connected person unless his fees are to be paid directly by the Legal Services Commission or such instructions are accompanied by payment of an agreed fee for such work or unless he agrees in advance to accept no fee for such work; and

(b)   cause the names of the persons or firms named in such direction to be included in a list of persons and firms named in such directions to be circulated by prepaid first-class post to all such persons and firms to all the Clerks and Heads of Chambers in England and Wales to the Master of the Rolls and to the President of the Law Society notifying them of such direction.

18.   Notwithstanding anything to the contrary herein if in any case the Chairman is satisfied that it is appropriate to issue a direction such as is referred to in paragraph 17(2)(a) hereof in respect of any person or firm named in such direction and to circulate a list such as is

referred to in paragraph 17(2)(b) hereof including the names of the persons or firms named in such direction he may after giving such persons and firms due notice of why he considers it appropriate to take such course and after considering any written representations and after consultation with the Law Society issue a direction in respect of and cause the list to include the names of such persons and firms as may be appropriate.

18A. Upon issuing a direction pursuant to either paragraph 17(2)(a) or paragraph 18 hereof, the Chairman shall report the facts to the OSS and shall request the OSS to commence proceedings before the Solicitors' Disciplinary Tribunal against the persons, the firms, or the partners in the firms named in such direction.

19. The list referred to in paragraphs 17 and 18 hereof shall be circulated monthly unless there have been in the meantime no additions to or deletions from the list.

20. Any Notified Solicitor and any barrister may at any time after the expiration of six months after the name of any person or firm was first included in such a list seek the revocation of any relevant direction and the amendment of the list and the Chairman after considering any written representations and after consultation with the Law Society shall be empowered (but shall not be obliged) to accede to such application upon such terms as he considers appropriate.

Definitions and consequential provisions

21. For the purpose hereof:

(1) 'Bar Code of Conduct' shall mean the Code of Conduct of the Bar of England and Wales for the time being in force;

(2) 'brief' 'instructions' and 'lay client' shall have the meanings assigned to them respectively in the Bar Code of Conduct;

(3) 'solicitor' shall where the context admits include any solicitor liable for the fees;

(4) 'person liable for the fees' shall mean any solicitor liable for the fees and any person company firm or other body responsible by virtue of paragraph 2(2) hereof for the payment of the fees;

(5) section 5(2), (3) and (4) of the Arbitration Act 1996 apply to the interpretation of all references in these Terms to parties having agreed, or made an agreement, in writing;

(6) 'connected person' shall mean any person who from time to time is either

(a) a partner employee consultant or associate of any firm of which any person liable for the fees or any Notified Solicitor is a partner employee consultant or associate;

(b) the employer of any person liable for the fees or of any Notified Solicitor;

(c) an employee of any person liable for the fees or of any Notified Solicitor;

(d) a firm of which any person liable for the fees or any Notified Solicitor is a partner employee consultant or associate;

(7) 'Notified Solicitor' shall mean any person or firm whose name is for the time being included in the list referred to in paragraphs 17 and 18 hereof and any person who or firm which is or has at any time since the direction was issued been a connected person;

(8) 'Tribunal' shall mean a Tribunal consisting of a barrister nominated by the Chairman and a solicitor nominated by the President of the Law Society;

(9) 'the Chairman' shall mean the Chairman of the Bar Council and shall include any person including in particular the Vice Chairman of the Bar and the Chairman of the Remuneration and Terms of Work Committee and the Chairman of the Fees Collection Committee to whom the Chairman may have delegated either the whole or any part of his responsibilities hereunder;

(10) 'the OSS' shall mean the Office for the Supervision of Solicitors;

(11) 'publicly funded work' shall mean cases funded by the Legal Services Commission, the Community Legal Service or the Criminal Defence Service;

(12) where the context admits, references to fees include any interest accrued in respect of them under paragraph 13(2) hereof;

(13) the 'stipulated rate' shall mean 2% above the Bank of England base rate from time to time;

(14) any letter written by the Chairman to any person pursuant to or which would otherwise have been effective for the purposes of either the Withdrawal of Credit Scheme which came into effect on 2 March 1987 or the Withdrawal of Credit Scheme 1988 as originally enacted or in force from time to time shall in relation to such person be deemed to be such a letter as is referred to in paragraph 16 hereof.

22.   (1) Subject to sub-paragraph (2) below, any fee note and any such letter as is referred to in paragraphs 15(1) 15(2) 16 17(2) or 18 hereof may be sent and shall be treated as having been properly and sufficiently sent to each and every person liable for the fees and to each and every connected person (as the case may be) if posted by pre-paid first-class post or sent through any Document Exchange or by facsimile transmission addressed to:

(a) any person liable for the fees; or

(b) if any person liable for the fees is either a partner of or consultant to or associate of or employed by another or others to the person liable for the fees or to his employer or to his senior partner (as the case may be); or

(c) if any such person practises (whether on his own or in partnership with others or otherwise) under a name other than his own to the firm under whose name he practises;

and addressed to any place at which such person or his employer or any partner of his carries on practice.

(2) Where a firm or a sole proprietor is liable for the fees, if any letter under paragraphs 15(2), 16, 17(2) or 18 hereof is addressed to some person other than the senior partner of the firm or the sole proprietor, a copy must also be sent to the senior partner or sole proprietor at the same time.

23.   Any such letter as is referred to in paragraphs 17(2) or 18 hereof shall:

(1) identify any earlier matters of complaint;

(2) state the Chairman's proposed course of action; and

(3) enclose a copy of this document provided that any accidental omission or failure to enclose such a copy may be remedied by the sending of a separate copy as soon as the Chairman is made aware of such omission or failure.

24.   Any such direction as is referred to in paragraphs 17 or 18 hereof may contain or be amended so as to add or include any or all of the names and addresses:

(1) of any person liable for the fees;

(2) of any connected person; and

(3) if any such person practises (whether on his own or in partnership with others or otherwise) under a name other than his own of the firm under whose name he practises.

Status of these Terms

25. Neither the General Council of the Bar in authorising these Terms nor a barrister in offering his services to a solicitor on these Terms has any intention to create legal relations or to enter into any contract or other obligation binding in law.

26. Neither the sending by a solicitor of a brief or instructions to a barrister nor the acceptance by a barrister of a brief or instructions nor anything done in connection therewith nor the arrangements relating thereto (whether mentioned in these Terms or in the Bar Code of Conduct or to be implied) nor these Terms or any agreement or transaction entered into or payment made by or under them shall be attended by or give rise to any contractual relationship rights duties or consequences whatsoever or be legally enforceable by or against or be the subject of litigation with either the barrister or the General Council of the Bar.

Exclusion or variation

27. A solicitor who sends a brief or instructions to a barrister will be deemed to instruct that barrister on these Terms unless and to the extent that the barrister and the solicitor have agreed in writing in relation to the particular matter or generally (a) that the Contractual Terms on which Barristers Offer their Services to Solicitors 2000 shall apply, or (b) to exclude or vary these Terms.

Transitional

28. Unless otherwise agreed in writing:

(1) any amendment to these Terms has effect only with regard to briefs and instructions accepted on or after the date the amendment is expressed to take effect; and

(2) as regards briefs and instructions accepted before that date, these Terms continue to have effect in the form in which they stood before the amendment.

LETTER 'A'

(To be sent 1 month after fee note)

Privately funded cases

Dear Sir,

Re: _____

I refer to the fee note of [name of barrister] in respect of the above case which was sent to you on the [date].

My records indicate that this is a privately funded case in which your relationship with [Name of Barrister] is governed by the Terms of Work on which Barristers offer their Services to Solicitors and the Withdrawal of Credit Scheme 1988 (as amended; 'the Terms'). Under paragraph 13(1) of the Terms, the fees were due and payable within 1 month of the fee note.

I would be grateful if you could make arrangements for these fees to be paid or let me know when payment may be expected.

[Please note that under paragraph 13(2) of the Terms, any such fees remaining outstanding one month after the date of this letter will carry interest at 2% above the Bank of England base rate from time to time from one month after the date of this letter until payment.]*

Yours faithfully,

Clerk to [name of barrister]

* Words substantially in the form of those shown in square brackets must be included if (but only if) it is wished to charge interest on the fees which are the subject of this letter A.

Publicly funded cases

Dear Sir,   [Relevant Public Funding Certificate Number]

[Date of issue]

Re: _____

I refer to the fee note of [name of barrister] in respect of the above case which was sent to you on [date].

My records indicate that this is a publicly funded case and I would be grateful if you could let me know when payment may be expected.

Yours faithfully,

Clerk to [name of barrister]

LETTER 'B'

(To be sent 3 months after fee note)

Privately funded cases

Dear Sir,

Re:

I have referred to [name of barrister] the letter I wrote to you concerning the fees in this matter. To date payment has not been made and no explanation for the non-payment has been forthcoming.

As you know Counsel is required as a matter of professional conduct to report to the Chairman of the General Council of the Bar the fact that these fees have been outstanding for more than three months without satisfactory explanation. Unless, therefore, I hear from you within the next 14 days I regret that Counsel will have no alternative other than to make such a report.

I sincerely trust that this will not be necessary and look forward to hearing from you in early course.

Yours faithfully,

Clerk to [name of barrister]

Publicly funded cases

Dear Sir,   [Relevant Public Funding Certificate Number]

[Date of issue]

Re:

I have referred to [name of barrister] the letter I wrote to you concerning the fees in this matter. To date payment has not been received.

My records indicate that this is a publicly funded case. I must therefore ask you to notify me of:

   (a) the date of issue and number of the relevant public funding certificate(s);

   (b) the date of any order for assessment of costs under the relevant certificate or other event giving rise to a right to such assessment; and

   (c) the steps you have taken under the relevant Regulations for the purpose of obtaining payment of [name of barrister]'s fees.

Would you also supply me with copies of the relevant Public Funding Certificate(s).

As you know Counsel is required as a matter of professional conduct to report the matter to the Chairman of the General Council of the Bar unless he receives in response to this letter the information requested above and a satisfactory explanation for the fact that he has not yet been paid. Unless, therefore, I hear from you within the next 14 days I regret that Counsel will have no alternative other than to make such a report.

I sincerely trust that this will not be necessary and look forward to hearing from you in early course.

Yours faithfully,

Clerk to [name of barrister]

LETTER 'C'

First Chairman's Letter: Private

PRIVATE AND CONFIDENTIAL

RECORDED DELIVERY

The Senior Partner

Dear Sir,

I refer to Counsel's fees particulars of which are set out in the Schedule to this letter. Copies of the relevant fee notes are attached. Letters have been written regarding payment of these fees. Payment has not been received. As a result the matter has been referred to the General Council of the Bar in accordance with Counsel's professional obligations.

I would remind you of your professional obligation to pay Counsel's fees in non publicly funded matters irrespective of whether you have been placed in funds by your client.

Unless you challenged Counsel's fees in writing within 3 months after the first fee note was sent to you, or you are able to provide a satisfactory explanation for non-payment, I would ask you to pay Counsel within 14 days of the date of this letter. In addition, please provide an explanation for the delay in payment, again within 14 days of the date of this letter.

I am also enclosing for your attention a copy of the Terms of Work on which Barristers offer their services to Solicitors and the Withdrawal of Credit Scheme 1988 (as amended). You will appreciate from reading the text of the Scheme that its effect is such that, unless there is a satisfactory explanation for non-payment or you challenged the fees in time, and the Chairman has occasion to write again in respect of other outstanding fees within the period referred to in paragraph 17(1)(b) of the Scheme, then the consequences spelt out in paragraph 17(2) of the Scheme will, save in the most exceptional circumstances, follow. In other words, credit will be withdrawn. Furthermore, the Chairman will report the facts to the Office for the Supervision of Solicitors with a request that it should commence proceedings against you before the Solicitors Disciplinary Tribunal.

If, therefore, you consider that a satisfactory explanation for non-payment exists, it is in your interests to provide it *now*.

I hope that it will not prove necessary to implement the Scheme in your case and that Counsel's fees will be paid promptly when due. I am, however, concerned that you should be fully informed in advance of the problems which would arise should you fail to pay Counsel's fees on time.

Yours faithfully,

[Name]
CHAIRMAN OF THE BAR

encls:

THE SCHEDULE

Name and address of Counsel   Fees in the matter of

[Here list name(s) and address(es) of Counsel and name(s) of case(s)]

First Chairman's Letter: Publicly funded

PRIVATE AND CONFIDENTIAL

RECORDED DELIVERY

The Senior Partner

Dear Sir,

I refer to Counsel's fees, particulars of which are set out in the Schedule to this letter. Copies of the relevant fee notes are attached. Letters have been written regarding payment of these fees. Payment has not been received. As a result, the matter has been referred to the General Council of the Bar in accordance with Counsel's professional obligations.

Since this complaint relates to a publicly funded matter, I would be grateful if you would supply the following information within 14 days of the date of this letter:—

(a) notify me of the date of issue and number and supply me with copies of any relevant publicly funded certificates;

(b) notify me of the date of any order for assessment of costs under the relevant certificate or other event giving rise to a right to such assessment; and

(c) inform me of what steps you have taken under the relevant Regulations for the purpose of obtaining payment of Counsel's fees.

I am also enclosing for your attention a copy of the Terms of Work on which Barristers offer their services to Solicitors and the Withdrawal of Credit Scheme 1988 (as amended). You will appreciate from reading the text of the Scheme that its effect is such that if (1) no satisfactory explanation for non-payment of the fees referred to in the Schedule to this letter has been provided and (2) the Chairman has occasion to write again in respect of other outstanding fees within the period referred to in paragraph 17(1)(b) of the Scheme, then the consequences spelt out in paragraph 17(2) of the Scheme will, save in the most exceptional circumstances, follow. In other words, credit will be withdrawn. Furthermore, the Chairman will report the facts to the Office for the Supervision of Solicitors with a request that it should commence proceedings against you before the Solicitors Disciplinary Tribunal.

If, therefore, you consider that a satisfactory explanation for non-payment exists, it is in your interests to provide it *now*.

I hope that it will not prove to be necessary to implement the Scheme in your case, and that Counsel's fees will be paid promptly when due. I am, however, concerned that you should be fully informed in advance of the problems which would arise should you fail to pay Counsel's fees on time.

Yours faithfully,

[Name]
CHAIRMAN OF THE BAR

encls:

THE SCHEDULE

Name and address of Counsel   Fees in the matter of

[Here list name(s) and address(es) of Counsel and name(s) of case(s)]

First Chairman's Letter: Private and Publicly funded

PRIVATE AND CONFIDENTIAL

RECORDED DELIVERY

The Senior Partner

Dear Sir,

I refer to Counsel's fees, particulars of which are set out in the Schedule to this letter. Copies of the relevant fee notes are attached. Letters have been written regarding payment of these fees. Payment has not been received. As a result, the matter has been referred to the General Council of the Bar in accordance with Counsel's professional obligations.

I would remind you of your professional obligation to pay Counsel's fees in privately funded matters irrespective of whether you have been placed in funds by your client.

Unless you challenged Counsel's fees in writing within 3 months after the first fee note was sent to you, or you are able to provide a satisfactory explanation for non-payment, I would ask you to pay Counsel within 14 days of the date of this letter. In addition, please provide an explanation for the delay in payment, again within 14 days of the date of this letter.

Insofar as this complaint relates to a publicly funded matter, I would be grateful if you would supply the following information within 14 days of the date of this letter:—

(a) notify me of the date of issue and number and supply me with copies of any relevant publicly funded certificates;

(b) notify me of the date of any order for assessment of costs under the relevant certificate or other event giving rise to a right to such assessment; and

(c) inform me of what steps you have taken under the relevant Regulations for the purpose of obtaining payment of Counsel's fees.

I am also enclosing for your attention a copy of the Terms of Work on which Barristers offer their services to Solicitors and the Withdrawal of Credit Scheme 1988 (as amended). You will appreciate from reading the text of the Scheme that its effect is such that, unless there is a satisfactory explanation for non-payment or you challenged the fees in time, and the Chairman has occasion to write again in respect of other outstanding fees within the period referred to in paragraph 17(1)(b) of the Scheme, then the consequences spelt out in paragraph 17(2) of the Scheme will, save in the most exceptional circumstances, follow. In other words, credit will be withdrawn. Furthermore, the Chairman will report the facts to the Office for the Supervision of Solicitors with a request that it should commence proceedings against you before the Solicitors Disciplinary Tribunal.

If, therefore, you consider that a satisfactory explanation for non-payment exists, it is in your interests to provide it now.

I hope that it will not prove to be necessary to implement the Scheme in your case, and that Counsel's fees will be paid promptly when due. I am, however, concerned that you should be fully informed in advance of the problems which would arise should you fail to pay Counsel's fees on time.

Yours faithfully,

[Name]
CHAIRMAN OF THE BAR

encls:

THE SCHEDULE

Name and address of Counsel   Fees in the matter of

[Here list name(s) and address(es) of Counsel and name(s) of case(s)]

ANNEXE G2

THE CONTRACTUAL TERMS OF WORK ON WHICH BARRISTERS
OFFER THEIR SERVICES TO SOLICITORS 2001

(As Authorised by The General Council of the Bar on 24 March 2001)

[*Amended 17 November 2001*]

WHEREAS:

(1) These terms have been authorised by the General Council of the Bar;

(2) These terms are intended to apply in any case where a barrister is instructed by a solicitor, and both the barrister and the solicitor have agreed in writing that the barrister's retainer shall be contractually binding;

(3) Any such agreement shall operate in accordance with paragraph 27 of the Terms of Work to exclude paragraphs 1–15 and 25–26 thereof as regards the instructions to which it relates;

AND WHEREAS:

(4) By the established custom of the profession a barrister looks for payment of his fees to the solicitor who instructs him and not to his lay client;

(5) Except in cases funded by the Legal Services Commission, Community Legal Service or Criminal Defence Service a solicitor is personally liable as a matter of professional conduct for the payment of a barrister's proper fees whether or not he has been placed in funds by his lay client;

(6) Where instructions have been given in the name of a firm all partners at that date incur personal liability and remain liable for the payment of counsel's fees incurred on behalf of the firm by a deceased bankrupt or otherwise defaulting former partner of the firm; and

(7) The liability of a sole practitioner and of partners for the liabilities of their co-partners is a continuing one and is not cancelled or superseded by any transfer of the practice or dissolution of the partnership;

Application of these terms

1. These terms apply in any case where a barrister is instructed by a solicitor and where both the barrister and the solicitor have agreed in writing that the barrister's retainer shall be contractually binding subject to the following:—

    (1) these terms apply to any particular contract only insofar as they have not been expressly varied or excluded by written agreement between the barrister and the solicitor;

    (2) these terms will apply to briefs and instructions only where they have been accepted by the barrister;

    (3) these terms do not apply to publicly funded work; and

    (4) these terms do not apply to any work undertaken by a barrister on a conditional fee basis.

General

2. The solicitor may in his capacity as a director partner member employee consultant associate or other agent of a company firm or other body brief or instruct the barrister.

3. In any case where the barrister accepts a brief or instructions from the solicitor in his capacity as a director partner member employee consultant associate or agent of a company firm or other body:

    (1) the solicitor warrants that he is authorised by his company firm or other body to instruct the barrister;

    (2) the obligations of the solicitor under these terms (including in particular his responsibility for the payment of the barrister's fees) shall be the joint and several obligations of him and that company firm or other body.

Instructions

4. The barrister has the duty or the right in certain circumstances set out in the Bar Code of Conduct to refuse to accept a brief or instructions and these terms will apply only where the barrister has accepted the brief or instructions.

5. Notwithstanding that a brief or instructions have been delivered to the barrister he shall not be deemed to have accepted that brief or those instructions until he has had a reasonable opportunity:

    (1) to peruse them;

    (2) in the case of a brief, to agree a fee with the solicitor.

6. The barrister accepts a brief or instructions upon the understanding:

    (1) that he must and will comply with the Bar Code of Conduct;

    (2) that he will deal with instructions as soon as he reasonably can in the ordinary course of his work;

    (3) that he may return the brief or instructions in accordance with the Bar Code of Conduct, and that, if he does so, he will incur no liability to the solicitor under these terms as a result of so doing.

7. Where for any reason time is of the essence the solicitor must at the time when he delivers the brief or instructions but separately from the brief or instructions themselves inform the barrister of that fact and of the particular reason for urgency in order that the barrister may decide whether in those circumstances he can accept the brief or instructions. In addition the brief or instructions must be clearly marked 'Urgent'.

Copies of briefs and instructions and records of advice

8. The barrister shall be entitled for the purposes of his records (but not otherwise) to retain his brief or instructions or any papers delivered therewith or (if the solicitor requires the return of such brief or instructions and papers) to take and retain a copy of such brief or instructions and papers and of any written advice PROVIDED that nothing shall entitle the barrister to exercise any lien over any brief instructions or papers.

Fees and interest

9. Subject to the Bar Code of Conduct, the following provisions shall apply:

    (1) Fees and/or charging rates shall be (a) as agreed between the barrister and the solicitor before the barrister commences work under the brief or instructions; or, in default of such agreement, (b) a reasonable professional rate for the barrister instructed.

(2) Subject to paragraphs 11 and 12 below, the solicitor shall pay the barrister's fees in respect of work to which these terms apply within one month after receipt by the solicitor of the barrister's fee note in respect of such fees.

(3) In the event that the barrister's fees are not paid in full in accordance with sub-paragraph (2) above, the fees outstanding from time to time will carry simple interest at the stipulated rate from one month after the date of the letter referred to in paragraph 13(1) hereof until payment.

10. (1) The barrister shall submit an itemised fee note not later than three months after the work to which the fee note relates has been done or at the conclusion of the matter in which the barrister is briefed or instructed whichever is the sooner.

(2) The barrister shall as soon as reasonably practicable comply with a request by the solicitor for a fee note.

(3) Every fee note shall include the solicitor's reference and (where appropriate) the barrister's case reference number.

(4) If any fees remain outstanding at the conclusion of a case the solicitor shall as soon as reasonably practicable inform the barrister that the case has concluded.

11. In the case of work the fees for which are to be paid out of a fund but cannot be so paid without an order of the court:

(1) The solicitor shall use his best endeavours to obtain such order or orders as may be requisite to enable payment of the fees to be made as soon as reasonably practicable;

(2) The solicitor shall as soon as reasonably practicable comply with a request by the barrister for information by informing the barrister of the steps taken by him pursuant to paragraph 11(1) hereof;

(3) The barrister unless such information and an explanation for non-payment satisfactory to him is thereupon received from the solicitor shall then report the facts to the Chairman.

(4) Subject to paragraph 11(5) below, the barrister's fees shall be payable one month after the making of the order of the court required for the payment of such fees out of the fund.

(5) In the event of any breach by the solicitor of his obligations under paragraph 11(1) and/or (2) above, the fees will be payable forthwith and the amount outstanding from time to time will carry simple interest at the stipulated rate from one month after the date of the letter referred to in paragraph 13(1) hereof until payment if that letter includes a statement to that effect.

12. (1) Any challenge by the solicitor to the barrister's fee (whether giving rise to an issue of competence or a dispute on quantum or otherwise) must be made by the solicitor in writing within three months after the first fee note relating to that fee has been sent to him or within one month after such letter relating to that fee as is referred to in paragraph 13(1) hereof has been sent to him whichever is the later.

(2) No challenge to a barrister's fees will be accepted either by the barrister or in the case of a complaint by the barrister to the Bar Council of failure to pay those fees by the Bar Council unless:

(a) the challenge was made in accordance with paragraph 12(1) hereof; and

(b) the solicitor has within 14 days of being requested to do so either by the barrister or by the Bar Council agreed in *writing* (i) to submit the issue or dispute giving rise to the challenge to the decision of a Tribunal (ii) to abide by and forthwith give effect to the decision of the Tribunal.

(3) If a dispute is referred to a Tribunal in accordance with paragraph 12(2) above:

    (a)   The Tribunal shall act as experts and not as arbitrators and its decision shall be conclusive, final and binding for all purposes upon the solicitor and the barrister.

    (b)   No payment need be made in respect of the fees (unless the Tribunal orders an interim payment) until the Tribunal has made its decision and communicated it to the parties.

    (c)   If the Tribunal determines that any sum is payable in respect of the fees, paragraph 9(3) above shall apply to that sum as if it had become payable when it would have been payable if no challenge had been made, and the Tribunal shall also determine the amount payable in respect of interest thereon under that paragraph.

(4) Unless the solicitor has challenged the barrister's fees and agreed to submit the issue or dispute in accordance with paragraphs 12(1) and (2);

    (a)   the fees will be payable in full, without any deductions or set-off whatsoever, in the amount set out in the relevant fee note and at the time specified in paragraph 9(2) above

    (b)   for the avoidance of doubt, it shall not be open to the solicitor to withhold or delay such payment or any part thereof on the grounds that a claim or complaint has been made or maybe made against the barrister arising out of the brief or instruction to which the fees relate or any other ground.

13.   Save as aforesaid and if and to the extent that his fees have not been previously paid, and without prejudice to any other remedy open to him in order to recover them, the barrister:

(1) may at any time after the expiration of one month after the first fee note relating thereto has been sent send a reminder substantially in the form of the letter annexed hereto and marked 'A' or some reasonable adaptation thereof; and

(2) unless an explanation for non-payment satisfactory to the barrister has been received, shall at the expiration of three months after the first fee note relating thereto has been sent send a further reminder substantially in the form of the letter annexed hereto and marked 'B' or some reasonable adaptation thereof; and

(3) unless an explanation for non-payment satisfactory to the barrister is thereupon received shall then report the facts to the Chairman.

Withdrawal of credit

14.   (1) In any case where a barrister has made a report to the Chairman in accordance with paragraphs 11(3) or 13(3) hereof, paragraphs 16 to 24 (inclusive) of the Terms of Work shall, so far as applicable, apply to the relationship created between the barrister and the solicitor under these terms.

    (2) Paragraph 22 of the Terms of Work shall also apply to any fee note or letter referred to in paragraphs 9, 10 and 13 above as it does to those referred to in paragraphs 15–18 of the Terms of Work.

Definitions and consequential provisions

15.   For the purpose hereof:

    (i)   'Bar Code of Conduct' shall mean the Code of Conduct of the Bar of England and Wales for the time being in force;

(ii)   'brief' 'instructions' and 'lay client' shall have the meanings assigned to them respectively in the Bar Code of Conduct;

(iii)   'solicitor' shall where the context admits include any solicitor liable for the fees;

(iv)   'person liable for the fees' shall mean any solicitor liable for the fees and any person company firm or other body responsible by virtue of paragraph 3(2) hereof for the payment of the fees;

(v)   Section 5(2), (3) and (4) of the Arbitration Act 1996 apply to the interpretation of all references in these Terms to parties having agreed, or made an agreement, in writing;

(vi)   'Terms of Work' shall mean the Terms of Work on which Barristers offer their Services to Solicitors and the Withdrawal of Credit Scheme 1988 (as amended and in force from time to time);

(vii)   'Tribunal' shall mean a Tribunal consisting of a barrister nominated by the Chairman and a solicitor nominated by the President of the Law Society;

(viii)   'the Chairman' shall mean the Chairman of the General Council of the Bar (also referred to as the 'Bar Council') and shall include any person including in particular the Vice Chairman of the General Council of the Bar and the Chairman of the Remuneration and Terms of Work Committee and the Chairman of the Fees Collection Committee to whom the Chairman may have delegated either the whole or any part of his responsibilities hereunder;

(ix)   'publicly funded work' shall mean cases funded and paid directly to the barrister by the Legal Services Commission, as part of the Community Legal Service or the Criminal Defence Service.

(x)   Where the context admits, references to fees include any interest accrued in respect of them under paragraph 9(3) hereof.

(xi)   The 'stipulated rate' shall mean 2% above the Bank of England base rate from time to time.

The General Council of the Bar

16.   Neither the sending by the solicitor of a brief or instructions to the barrister nor the acceptance by the barrister of a brief or instructions nor anything done in connection therewith nor the arrangements relating thereto (whether mentioned in these Terms or in the Bar Code of Conduct or to be implied) nor these Terms or any agreement or transaction entered into or payment made by or under them shall be attended by or give rise to any contractual relationship rights duties or consequences whatsoever (except between the solicitor and barrister) or be legally enforceable by or against or be the subject of litigation with the General Council of the Bar.

LETTER 'A'

(To be sent 1 month after fee note)

Dear Sir

Re:

I refer to the Fee Note of [*Name of Barrister*] in respect of the above case which was sent to you on the [*Date*].

My records indicate that this is a privately funded case in which your relationship with [Name of Barrister] is governed by the Contractual Terms on which Barristers Offer their

Services to Solicitors 2000 (the 'Contractual Terms'). Under paragraph 9(2) of those terms, the fees were due and payable within 30 days of the Fee Note.

[Please note that under paragraph 9(3) of the Contractual Terms, any such fees remaining outstanding within one month after the date of this letter will carry interest at 2% above the Bank of England base rate from time to time from 1 month after the date of this letter until payment.]*

I would be grateful if you could now make arrangements for these fees to be paid.

Yours faithfully

Clerk to [*Name of Barrister*]

* Words substantially in the form of those shown in square brackets must be included if (but only if) it is wished to charge interest on the fees which are the subject of this letter A.

LETTER 'B'

(To be sent 3 months after fee note)

Dear Sir

Re:

I have referred to [*Name of Barrister*] the letter I wrote to you concerning the fees in this matter. To date payment has not been made and no explanation for the non-payment has been forthcoming.

As you know Counsel is required as a matter of professional conduct to report to the Chairman of the General Council of the Bar the fact that these fees have been outstanding for more than three months without satisfactory explanation. Unless, therefore, I hear from you within the next 14 days I regret that Counsel will have no alternative other than to make such a report.

I sincerely trust that this will not be necessary and look forward to hearing from you in early course.

Yours faithfully

Clerk to [Name of Barrister]

ANNEXE H

THE FOREIGN LAWYERS (CHAMBERS) RULES

1. Before permitting a foreign lawyer to practise from chambers the head of chambers or if there is no head of chambers every member of chambers must:

    (a) obtain the written undertaking of the foreign lawyer to comply with the Code as if he were a barrister in independent practice except in so far as any requirement of the Code conflicts with the rules of his own profession;

    (b) ensure that the foreign lawyer is covered by insurance against claims for professional negligence in such amount and upon such terms as are currently required by the Bar Council;

    (c) provide the Bar Council in writing with the name and details of the foreign lawyer and with a copy of the undertaking referred to in (a) above and a copy of the current insurance policy or certificate of insurance covering the foreign lawyer; and

    (d) obtain the consent in writing of the Bar Council to the foreign lawyer so practising.

2. Thereafter for so long as the foreign lawyer is permitted to practise from chambers the head of chambers or if there is no head of chambers every member of chambers must:

    (a) satisfy himself that the foreign lawyer complies with and continues to comply with the undertaking referred to in paragraph 1(a) above;

    (b) ensure that the foreign lawyer remains covered by insurance in accordance with paragraph 1(b) above and that the Bar Council has a copy of the current insurance policy or certificate of insurance covering the foreign lawyer; and

    (c) inform the Bar Council of any failure by the foreign lawyer to comply with the undertaking referred to in paragraph 1(a) above which may be known to him.

3. No barrister shall permit a foreign lawyer to practise or continue to practise from chambers of which the barrister is a member if the consent of the Bar Council to the foreign lawyer so practising has not been given or is at any time withdrawn.

4. A European lawyer registered with the Law Society of England and Wales may not practise from or be a member of chambers.

ANNEXE I

THE EMPLOYED BARRISTERS (CONDUCT OF LITIGATION) RULES

1. An employed barrister may exercise any right that he has to conduct litigation provided that:

   (a) he is entitled to practise as a barrister in accordance with paragraph 202 of the Code;

   (b) he has spent a period of at least twelve weeks working under the supervision of a qualified person or has been exempted from this requirement by the Bar Council on the grounds of his relevant experience;

   (c) if he is of less than one year's standing (or three years' standing in the case of a barrister who is supplying litigation services to any person other than a person referred to in paragraph 501 of the Code) his principal place of practice is an office which is also the principal place of practice of a qualified person who is able to provide guidance to the barrister; and

   (d) if he is of less than three years' standing, he completes at least six hours of continuing professional development on an approved litigation course during any year in which he is required to undertake continuing professional development by the Continuing Professional Development Regulations (reproduced in Annex C).

2. For the purpose of paragraph 1(c) above an employed barrister shall be treated as being of a particular number of years' standing if he:

   (a) has been entitled to practise and has practised as a barrister (other than as a pupil who has not completed pupillage in accordance with the Consolidated Regulations) or as a member of another authorised body;

   (b) has made such practice his primary occupation; and

   (c) has been entitled to exercise a right to conduct litigation in relation to every Court and all proceedings

   for a period (which need not be continuous and need not have been as a member of the same authorised body) of at least that number of years.

3. A person shall be a qualified person for the purpose of paragraph 1(c) above if he:

   (a) has been entitled to practise and has practised as a barrister (other than as a pupil who has not completed pupillage in accordance with the Consolidated Regulations) or as a member of another authorised body for a period (which need not have been as a member of the same authorised body) of at least six years in the previous eight years;

   (b) for the previous two years

       (i) has made such practice his primary occupation, and

       (ii) has been entitled to exercise a right to conduct litigation in relation to every Court and all proceedings;

   (c) is not acting as a qualified person in relation to more than two other people; and

   (d) has not been designated by the Bar Council as unsuitable to be a qualified person.

4. If an employed barrister in the conduct of litigation gives an undertaking, any breach of that undertaking shall constitute professional misconduct.

ANNEXE J

THE COMPLAINTS RULES

[Amended 25 July 2001, 9 April 2002 and 20 July 2002]

Introduction

1. These Rules prescribe the manner in which all complaints about the conduct of or services provided by barristers shall be processed.

2. The membership of the Professional Conduct and Complaints Committee ('the Committee') shall be as prescribed by the Standing Orders of the Bar Council as amended from time to time.

3. Anything required by these Rules to be done or any discretion required to be exercised by, and any notice required to be given to, the Complaints Commissioner ('the Commissioner') or the Secretary of the Committee ('the Secretary'), may be done or exercised by, or given to, any person authorised by the Complaints Commissioner to act in his stead or by the Chief Executive of the Bar Council to act instead of the Secretary of the Committee (either prospectively or retrospectively and either generally or for a particular purpose).

Procedure for dealing with complaints

4. The Secretary shall take such steps as are reasonably practicable to inform the complainant of the progress and result of his complaint.

5. Any complaint other than a complaint raised by the Bar Council of its own motion shall be referred to and considered by the Commissioner before any further step is taken in accordance with these rules. The Commissioner's powers in relation to a complaint so considered by him shall be those set out in paragraph 8 *et seq.* below.

6. (a) If a complaint is not dismissed by the Commissioner following consideration as aforesaid, or is a complaint raised by the Bar Council, it shall be investigated by the Secretary of the Committee in the manner set out in paragraph 16 *et seq.* below.

    (b) Following such investigation, the Secretary shall refer the complaint back to the Commissioner together with the results of such investigation and the Commissioner shall reconsider the complaint and the results and shall exercise the powers given to him by paragraph 21 *et seq.* below in respect of the complaint.

7. If the Commissioner does not dismiss the complaint following reconsideration under paragraph 6(b) above, he shall refer the complaint to the Committee for consideration with his observations on it, if any. The Committee's powers in relation to such a complaint shall be those set out in paragraph 26 *et seq.* below.

Commissioner's powers under paragraph 5

8. The powers of the Commissioner shall be to consider complaints made by outside persons and to determine whether in his view such a complaint discloses a *prima facie* case of professional misconduct or inadequate professional service and is apt for consideration by the Committee. In the exercise of that power he shall observe the following provisions.

9. If it appears to him that the complaint relates to a matter within the domestic jurisdiction of an Inn or a Circuit, he may refer the complaint without further consideration to the Treasurer of the Inn or the Leader of the Circuit concerned and notify the complainant of his decision.

10.   (a) If it appears to the Commissioner that the complaint arises out of a barrister's actions in a part-time or temporary judicial or quasi-judicial capacity, he shall act as follows:

　　(i)   If it appears to him that the complaint would otherwise fall to be dismissed under these provisions, he shall so dismiss it.

　　(ii) If it appears to him that the complaint would otherwise not fall to be dismissed, the Commissioner shall refer the complaint without further consideration to the person responsible for the appointment of the barrister to the judicial or quasi-judicial office concerned (whether the Lord Chancellor, a Minister of the Crown or other person as appropriate), requesting him to notify the Commissioner when the complaint has been dealt with and of any action taken, and the Commissioner shall notify the complainant of his decision so to refer it. Where the Commissioner considers it inappropriate to refer the complaint to a person other than the Lord Chancellor or a Minister of the Crown or where that other person refuses to deal with a complaint, he shall consider the complaint and, subject to (iv) below, direct it to be proceeded with in accordance with paragraph 16 *et seq.* below.

　　(iii) If the Lord Chancellor, Minister of the Crown, or other person responsible for the appointment, having dealt with a complaint, believes that it may be appropriate for further consideration by the Bar Council, he may, subject to (iv) below, refer the matter to the Commissioner who may reconsider the complaint and may, if he sees fit, direct it to be proceeded with in accordance with paragraph 16 *et seq.* below.

　　(iv) No such reference to the Commissioner as is mentioned in (iii) above by the Lord Chancellor, Minister of the Crown, or other person responsible for the appointment shall be acted upon by the Commissioner, nor shall the Commissioner exercise the powers under the last sentence of paragraph (ii) above in respect of any part of the complaint relating to anything said or done by the barrister in the exercise of his judicial functions or affecting the independence of the barrister in his judicial or quasi-judicial capacity.

　　(b) If it appears to the Commissioner that the complaint relates to the conduct of or professional services provided by a barrister who, since the events giving rise to the complaint took place, has been appointed to and continues to hold full-time judicial office and has ceased practice, the Commissioner shall not consider the complaint further and shall inform the complainant that his complaint should be directed to the Lord Chancellor.

11.   If he has not disposed of any complaint under paragraph 9 or 10 above, he shall consider whether:

　　(a) the complaint fails to disclose a *prima facie* case of professional misconduct or inadequate professional service;

　　(b) the complaint has been made more than six months after the act or omission complained of and the complaint is not of sufficient seriousness nor are there any exceptional circumstances which justify further consideration of the complaint despite the lapse of time since the matters complained of;

　　(c) the complaint is trivial;

　　(d) the complaint obviously lacks validity; or

　　(e) for any other reason the complaint ought to be dismissed summarily.

In order to decide this question, he may seek information or assistance, orally or in writing, as he thinks fit, from the complainant, any potential witness, any member of the Committee, the Secretary or the Equal Opportunities Officers of the Bar Council.

12. If he considers that it should be dismissed on any of the grounds set out in paragraph 11 above, he shall so dismiss it, and shall notify the complainant of his decision and of his reasons for it.

13. If in considering whether a complaint should be dismissed summarily the Commissioner decides that the complaint does not disclose any evidence of professional misconduct, and it appears to him that the complaint might be capable of resolution by agreement, he may invite the complainant and the barrister concerned to attempt to conciliate their differences.

14. The Commissioner may at any time adjourn consideration of a complaint for such period as he thinks fit, whether while the complainant and the barrister attempt conciliation, during the currency of related legal proceedings or for any other reason.

15. The Commissioner may reopen or reconsider a complaint which has been disposed of under paragraphs 9 10 or 12 above:

   (a) following a recommendation of the Legal Services Ombudsman that he do so, or

   (b) where new evidence becomes available to him which leads him to conclude that he should do so, or

   (c) for some other good reason.

Following such reconsideration he may take such further or different action as he thinks fit, as if the former decision had not been made.

Investigation of complaints by the Secretary

16. The investigation of complaints shall be carried out by the Secretary under the direction of the Commissioner or the Committee in such manner as they or either of them think fit. In directing the carrying out of such investigation, the Committee and the Commissioner shall have regard to the following provisions.

17. The complaint shall be sent to the barrister concerned together with a letter requiring him to comment in writing on the complaint and to make any written representations he sees fit as to his conduct or the services he has provided to the complainant. That letter shall be sent to the address notified by the barrister pursuant to paragraphs 202(d) of the Code of Conduct.

   If no response is received within 28 days of the date of posting of such letter, the Secretary may proceed as if the barrister's response had been to deny the allegations made in the complaint in their entirety.

18. The complaint should normally also be sent to any solicitor or solicitor's agent named on the form of complaint as having instructed the barrister, and if the Commissioner directs to any other person whose name and address is provided by the complainant as a person able to assist the Committee together with a letter seeking their comments upon the complaint.

19. Any comments received by the Secretary from the barrister concerned in answer to the complaint should normally be sent to the complainant, under cover of a letter seeking his response to the barrister's comments, but the Commissioner may at his discretion direct

that this step be omitted if, for example, issues of privilege or confidentiality make it inappropriate.

20. The Secretary may enter into further correspondence with any of the parties whose comments have been sought, or any other party who the Secretary, the Commissioner or the Committee think capable of affording further assistance.

Commissioners powers under paragraph 6(b)

21. When a complaint is referred to the Commissioner following investigation, as set out in paragraph 6(b) above, the Commissioner shall consider whether, on the information now available to him, it discloses a *prima facie* case of professional misconduct or inadequate professional service.

22. In order to decide this question, he may direct any further investigations to be made that he sees fit, and may seek further information or assistance from any other person whom he considers may be capable of affording it.

23. The Commissioner may at any time adjourn consideration of a complaint for such period as he thinks fit, whether during the currency of related legal proceedings or for any other reason.

24. If the Commissioner decides that a *prima facie* case of professional misconduct or inadequate professional service is not shown, he shall dismiss the complaint, and shall notify the complainant and the barrister complained against of his decision and of his reasons for it.

25. The Commissioner may reopen or reconsider a complaint which has been disposed of under paragraph 24 above:

    (a) following a recommendation of the Legal Services Ombudsman that he do so, or

    (b) where new evidence becomes available to him which leads him to conclude that he should do so, or

    (c) for some other good reason.

Following such reconsideration he may take such further or different action as he thinks fit, as if the former decision had not been made.

Powers and functions of the Committee

26. The powers of the Committee shall be as follows:

    (a) to determine whether any complaint discloses a *prima facie* case of professional misconduct, and if so to deal with it in accordance with these Rules.

    (b) to determine whether the complaint discloses a *prima facie* case of inadequate professional service by the barrister concerned and if so to deal with it in accordance with these Rules.

    (c) to prefer charges of professional misconduct before Disciplinary Tribunals (as provided by the Disciplinary Tribunals Regulations at Annex K to the Code of Conduct), to refer to such tribunals any legal aid complaint relating to the conduct of a barrister and to be responsible for prosecuting any such charges or legal aid complaints before such Tribunals.

    (d) to prefer and deal summarily with charges of professional misconduct in accordance with the Summary Procedure Rules forming Annex L to the Code of Conduct.

(e) to take such other actions in relation to complaints as are permitted by these Rules.

(f) to make recommendations on matters of professional conduct to the Professional Standards Committee, as the Committee may think appropriate.

(g) to make rulings on matters of professional conduct when the Committee considers it appropriate to do so.

(h) to exercise the power of the Bar Council under paragraph 109 of the Code of Conduct to grant waivers of the provisions of that Code either generally or in particular cases.

(i) to exercise the power of the Bar Council to designate Legal Advice Centres for the purposes of Annex H of the Code of Conduct.

27. The Committee shall consider complaints and the results of investigations thereof referred to it by the Commissioner pursuant to paragraph 7 above, together with the Commissioner's comments thereon, in such manner as it shall see fit.

28. Upon considering any complaint and subject to the provisions of paragraph 28A below, the Committee may:

(a) dismiss the complaint provided that each of the Lay Members present at the meeting consents to such dismissal, whereupon the Secretary shall notify the complainant and the barrister complained against of the dismissal and the reasons for it.

(b) determine that no further action shall be taken on the complaint.

(c) at any time postpone consideration of the complaint, whether to permit further investigation of the complaint to be made, or during the currency of related legal proceedings or for any other reason it sees fit,

(d) if the complaint does not disclose a *prima facie* case of professional misconduct but the barrister's conduct is nevertheless such as to give cause for concern, draw it to his attention in writing. The Committee may in those circumstances advise him as to his future conduct either in writing or by directing him to attend on the Chairman of the Committee or some other person nominated by the Committee to receive such advice, and may thereafter exercise the powers given to it by paragraph (e) below, or dismiss the complaint. If the Committee considers that the circumstances of the complaint are relevant to the barrister's position as a pupilmaster, it may notify the barrister's Inn of its concern in such manner as it sees fit.

If the complaint is dismissed the Secretary shall notify the complainant of the dismissal and the reasons for it.

(e) if a *prima facie* case of inadequate professional service is disclosed and the following conditions are satisfied:

(i) the complainant is the barrister's lay client or his duly authorised representative or in the case of an employed barrister the person to whom he has supplied the professional service in question, and

(ii) if a prima facie case of professional misconduct is also disclosed by the complaint, the matter is in the opinion of the Committee not serious enough to warrant treatment under sub-paragraphs (g) or (h) below,

the Committee may direct that the complaint be referred to an Adjudication Panel to be dealt with in accordance with the Adjudication Panel Rules (Annex P to the Code of Conduct).

(f) if a *prima facie* case of professional misconduct (whether with or without inadequate professional service) is disclosed but in the opinion of the Committee the matter is not serious enough to warrant treatment under sub-paragraphs (g) or (h) below, direct that the complaint be dealt with by informal attendance by the barrister to explain his conduct following the procedure set out in paragraphs 39 *et seq.* below

(g) if a *prima facie* case of professional misconduct (whether with or without inadequate professional service) is disclosed but in the opinion of the Committee there are no disputes of fact which cannot fairly be resolved by a summary procedure, provided it is satisfied that the powers of a summary procedure are adequate to deal with the gravity of the issues, deal with the matter summarily in accordance with the Summary Procedure Rules (Annex L to the Code of Conduct)

(h) if a *prima facie* case of professional misconduct (whether with or without inadequate professional service) is disclosed in circumstances where in the opinion of the Committee paragraph (g) above does not apply, direct that the complaint should form the subject-matter of a charge before a Disciplinary Tribunal.

28A.   If the Committee considers that the Complaint discloses a *prima facie* case of inadequate professional service or of professional misconduct against a registered European lawyer, the secretary shall

(i)   inform the professional body of which the registered European lawyer is a Member in his home Member State;

(ii)   offer that professional body the opportunity to make representations to the Adjudication Panel, Informal Hearing, Summary Procedure or Disciplinary Tribunal to which the Complaint has been referred; and

(iii)   notwithstanding paragraph 47 of these rules, inform that professional body of findings made by any panel under these rules or under Annexes K, L, M or N of this Code.

28B.   If the subject matter of the complaint involves a conviction for an offence of dishonesty or deception or some other serious arrestable offence (as defined by section 116 of the Police and Criminal Evidence Act 1984) the Committee shall direct that the complaint should form the subject-matter of a charge before a Disciplinary Tribunal.

29.   The Committee may reopen or reconsider a complaint which has been disposed of (except where it has been disposed of following a hearing before a Disciplinary Tribunal or the Visitors):

(a) following a recommendation of the Legal Services Ombudsman that they do so, or

(b) where new evidence becomes available to the Committee which leads them to conclude that they should do so, or

(c) for some other good reason.

30.   Following such reopening or reconsideration, the Committee may take any further or different action it thinks fit, as if the former decision had not been made, provided that if a direction under paragraph 28(h) or 28B above has been given, and charges have been forwarded to the Clerk and served on the Defendant, the Committee's actions shall be confined to instructing counsel for the Committee to

(a) offer no evidence on a charge, or

(b) apply to the Directions Judge for the making of additions to or amendments of a charge.

30A. The Bar Council shall respect the confidentiality of complaints. The Bar Council shall not disclose the fact that a complaint has been made or details of the complaint or its disposal save in the following circumstances:

(a) for the purpose of investigating the complaint;

(b) for the purpose of keeping the complainant and the barrister informed of the progress of the complaint;

(c) where the complainant and the barrister consent;

(d) where the publication of a finding is required by the provisions of the Disciplinary Tribunals Regulations 2000 or the Summary Procedure Rules or paragraphs 46 and 47A of these rules;

(e) in response to a request from the Lord Chancellor or officials of his Department in respect of an application by a barrister for silk or judicial appointment or a request from some other body or a Certificate of Good Standing in respect of a barrister, in which case

(i) if any complaint has been made against the barrister concerned which has not been dismissed by the Commissioner, disposed of by the Committee under paragraph 28(a), (d) or (e) of these rules or by any other panel to which it may have been referred by the Committee, the Bar Council shall simply indicate that a complaint has been received which has not been dismissed; and

(ii) if a finding of professional misconduct has been recorded against the barrister concerned, the Bar Council shall disclose the finding and the penalty;

(f) for any other good reason.

Disciplinary charges

31. If the Committee directs under paragraph 28(h) or 28A above that a complaint shall form the subject matter of a charge before a Disciplinary Tribunal, the following paragraphs shall have effect.

31A. If the Committee considers that

(a) the facts of the complaint are unlikely to be disputed (for example because it involves a criminal conviction),

(b) witnesses are unlikely to be called for the hearing, or

(c) the case needs to be resolved urgently,

the Committee may direct that the prosecution of the charges be expedited.

32. The Committee shall nominate one of its members ('the PCC Representative') to be responsible for the conduct of the proceedings on its behalf. If for any reason he is unable to act at any time, the Chairman of the Committee may nominate another member to act in his place. Where no further investigation is required, the PCC representative shall settle the charge having regard to the provisions of paragraph 34 below.

33. Save in cases where the charges have been settled by the PCC Representative, the Secretary or investigations officer shall arrange for the appointment of counsel to settle the charge and to present the case before the Tribunal, and may arrange for the appointment of a solicitor or such other person as may be necessary to assist counsel and prepare the case.

34.   Save in cases where the charges have been settled by the PCC Representative, counsel shall settle such charges as he considers appropriate founded upon the facts or evidence from which the complaint arose and any further or other matters which have been revealed by investigations directed by either counsel, the PCC Representative or the Committee. Such charges may be of professional misconduct and, where appropriate, of inadequate professional service, save that no charges of inadequate professional service shall be settled unless:

    (i)   the complainant is the barrister's lay client or his duly authorised representative or in the case of an employed barrister the person to whom he has supplied the professional service in question, and

    (ii)   the subject-matter of the complaint is something in respect of which the barrister would not be entitled to immunity from suit as an advocate in civil law.

35.   It shall be the responsibility of the investigations officer at the Bar Council, subject to the supervision of the PCC Representative and/or the Committee:

    (a) to forward the charge to the Clerk to the Tribunal, as required by Regulation 5 of the Disciplinary Tribunal Regulations, together with the other documents specified therein, and

    (b) to make any necessary administrative arrangements for the summoning of witnesses, the production of documents, and generally for the proper presentation of the case on behalf of the PCC Representative before the Tribunal.

36.   Enquiries shall be made of the Under- or Sub-Treasurer of the barrister's Inn and of the Bar Council concerning any previous findings of misconduct against him, so that this information may be available to be placed before the Tribunal if any charge against him is found to have been proved.

37.   If a barrister is a member of more than one Inn, references in these Rules to his Inn shall mean the Inn by which he was called, unless he is a Bencher in which case his Inn shall mean the Inn of which he is a Bencher.

38.   The Committee may, with the approval of the Finance and the Professional Standards Committees, authorise the Secretary or investigations officer in an appropriate case to arrange that Counsel, or any other person appointed pursuant to paragraph 33 above, be paid reasonable remuneration for work done on the Committee's behalf. The cost of such remuneration shall be borne by the Bar Council.

Informal Hearings

39.   Where the Committee decides under paragraph 28(f) above that a complaint should be dealt with informally it shall direct that the barrister attend upon a panel consisting of not less than two nor more than three barrister members of the Committee and one lay member, who may be the Commissioner. When the Committee directs such attendance it shall specify:

    (a) what, in summary form, are the matters upon which the Committee has found a *prima facie* case of misconduct to be disclosed and on which the barrister's explanation of his conduct is required, and

    (b) whether, on the information available to them, the Committee also regard a *prima facie* case of inadequate professional service as having been disclosed, and if so what, in summary form, are the matters arising in that regard which the barrister will also be asked to explain.

39A. The Secretary shall notify both the barrister and the complainant of the matters specified in paragraph 39. As soon as practicable thereafter he shall send them a bundle of the papers to be considered by the panel and shall invite them within 14 days (which period may be extended with the permission of the Chairman of the PCC or the Complaints Commissioner) to comment in writing on any of those matters or to send other document to which they wish the panel to have regard.

40. The Secretary shall make such further enquiries as he sees fit, or as are directed by the Commissioner or the Committee to assist the deliberation of the panel, such as whether the complainant claims to have suffered financial loss as a result of the conduct complained of, and if so the exact nature and amount of that claimed loss and the evidence available to support the claim, and from the barrister the nature of the work he carried out for the complainant out of which the complaint arose, the fee rendered for such work, and whether or not such fee has been paid.

41. Subject to the direction of the Chairman of the panel:

(a) the Secretary shall keep the complainant informed of the progress of the complaint and of any further documents and other information to be considered by the panel;

(b) the Secretary shall, so far as practicable, require the barrister and afford the complainant an opportunity to comment in advance of the hearing on any such information or documents.

42. The barrister shall attend on the panel at the day and time arranged, and shall provide to the panel orally such information as he wishes to put before them in connection with his conduct in relation to the matters specified, and shall answer so far as he is able such further questions as the panel may put to him which may relate to any aspects of the conduct complained of. The panel shall consider whether to adjourn the hearing in order to enable the complainant to comment on any information provided by the barrister at the hearing which had not previously been disclosed by him.

43. Following such hearing, the panel may reach the following decisions and shall provide reasons for reaching the decision

(a) It may conclude that the barrister's explanation of his professional conduct has been satisfactory, whereupon it shall dismiss the complaint.

(b) It may conclude that no further action shall be taken on the complaint.

(c) It may conclude that the barrister's explanation of his professional conduct has not been satisfactory, whereupon it may either orally or in writing

(i) give him advice as to his future conduct, or

(ii) reprimand him.

(d) Regardless of the conclusion reached in relation to the barrister's professional conduct, the panel may conclude that a barrister has provided inadequate professional service in respect of the subject-matter of the complaint, provided the following conditions are satisfied:

(i) the complainant is the barrister's lay client or his duly authorised representative or in the case of an employed barrister the person to whom he has supplied the professional service in question, and

(ii) the subject-matter of the complaint is not something in respect of which the barrister would be entitled to immunity from suit as an advocate in civil law.

(e) Whatever conclusion it may reach, the panel may refer any issue of policy which arises to the relevant Committee of the Bar Council.

(f) The panel may refer a matter back to the Committee for reconsideration if it considers that its powers are not sufficient to deal with the gravity of the complaint revealed at the hearing or that other issues are raised which require further consideration by the Committee.

44. If the panel is not unanimous on any issue, the finding made shall be that of the majority of them. If the panel is equally divided, the burden of proof being on the complainant the finding made shall be that most favourable to the barrister.

45. If a finding of inadequate professional service is made under paragraph 43(d), the panel shall consider what remedy should be granted to the complainant in respect of such inadequate service. The panel may:

(a) determine that it is not appropriate to take any action in respect of the complaint,

(b) adjourn consideration of the remedy to permit investigation or further investigation of the consequences of the inadequate professional service for the complainant and reconvene the panel when the results of such investigations are known,

(c) direct the barrister to make a formal apology to the complainant for the conduct complained of,

(d) direct the barrister to repay or remit all or part of any fee rendered in respect of the inadequate service,

(e) direct the barrister to pay compensation to the complainant in such sum as the panel shall direct not exceeding £5,000,

(f) direct the barrister to complete continuing professional development of such nature and duration as the Tribunal shall direct and to provide satisfactory proof of compliance with this requirement to the Committee.

In determining whether any sum is to be paid under paragraph (e) hereof, or in fixing the amount of such sum, the panel shall in particular have regard to any loss suffered by the applicant as a result of the inadequate professional service, the availability to the complainant of other forms of redress, to the gravity of the conduct complained of, and to the fee claimed by the barrister for the inadequate service.

46. An appeal shall lie at the instance of the barrister from any decision of a panel that a barrister has provided inadequate professional service, and against any decision as to the remedy to be granted to the complainant for such service in the same manner as an appeal lies from a decision of an Adjudication Panel in respect of the same matters.

46A. The Secretary shall notify both the complainant and the barrister of the decision and, if the complaint is dismissed, of the reasons for it.

47. If the panel considers that the circumstances of the complaint are relevant to the barrister's position as a pupilmaster, it may notify the barrister's Inn of its concerns in such manner as it sees fit.

Definitions

48. In these Rules unless the context otherwise requires

(a) Any term defined in the Code of Conduct shall carry the same meaning as it does in the Code of Conduct.

(b) Any reference to a person includes any natural person, legal person and/or firm. Any reference to the masculine gender includes the feminine and the neuter, and any reference to the singular includes the plural, and in each case *vice versa*.

Commencement and Transitional Provisions

49. If a complaint has been raised in the Bar Council's complaints records before 15th May 2000, these Rules shall not apply but the Complaints Rules in force immediately before that date shall apply to that complaint, save that where the PCC has referred a complaint to an informal hearing after 15th May 2000, these rules shall apply. In relation to complaints raised after the Commencement Date, the procedure set out in these Rules shall apply, save that no finding of inadequate professional service may be made against a barrister in respect of any conduct of his which took place before 13th July 1996.

ANNEXE K

THE DISCIPLINARY TRIBUNALS REGULATIONS

[Amended 4 February, 9 April 2002 and 26 July 2002]

Arrangement of Regulations

1.   Definitions

In these regulations:

(a) 'The relevant procedure' shall mean the procedure adopted by the PCC from time to time for preferring such charges.

(b) Any reference to the Inns' Council or to the members thereof shall be a reference to the Inns' Council or the members thereof other than the Officers and the Chairman of the Council of Legal Education.

(c) Other expressions shall have the meanings respectively assigned to them by Paragraph 1 of the Introduction to the Constitutions of the General Council of the Bar, the Council of the Inns of Court and the Council of Legal Education, or by Part X of the Code of Conduct.

2.   Composition of Disciplinary Tribunals

(1)   A Disciplinary Tribunal shall consist of the following five persons nominated by the President:

(a) a Judge (who may be a retired Circuit Judge or retired judge of the High Court provided that he

(i)   continues to be permitted to sit as an Additional Judge

(ii)   has done so in the last 12 months

(iii)   has, within the last 12 months and following consultation with the Chairman of the Bar, being appointed to a panel of such judges by the President)

(b) two Lay Representatives

(c) two practising Barristers of not less than five years standing and not more than 70 years of age.

Provided that:

(i)   if the Barrister charged is an Employed or Non-Practising Barrister, at least one of the barristers nominated should normally be Employed or Non-Practising;

(ii)   no Barrister or Lay Representative shall be nominated to serve on a Tribunal which is to consider a charge arising in respect of any matter considered at any meeting of the PCC which he attended;

(iii)   in the case of a registered European lawyer, one of the members of the Tribunal shall be a registered European lawyer rather than a barrister.

(2)   The President shall select another member of the relevant class to fill any vacancy in the Disciplinary Tribunal membership that has arisen prior to the substantive hearing of the charge.

(3)   At any time before the commencement of the substantive hearing of the charge, the President may cancel any or all of the nominations made pursuant to this regulation, and make such alternative nominations as in the exercise of his discretion he deems to be expedient.

(4)   The proceedings of a Disciplinary Tribunal shall be valid notwithstanding that after the convening order has been issued one or more of the members other than the Chairman or one of the Lay Representatives becomes unable to continue to act or disqualified from continuing to act, so long as the number of members present throughout the substantive hearing of the charge is not reduced below three and continues to include the Chairman and a Lay Representative.

(5)   A member of a Disciplinary Tribunal who has been absent for any time during a sitting shall take no further part in the proceedings.

3.   Sittings of Disciplinary Tribunals

The President shall appoint Disciplinary Tribunals to sit at such times as are necessary for the prompt and expeditious determination of charges preferred against barristers in accordance with the provisions of these Regulations.

4.   Clerks

The President shall appoint a person or persons to act as Clerk or Clerks to the Disciplinary Tribunals to perform the functions specified in these Regulations and such other functions as the President or the Chairman of any Tribunal may direct. No person who has been engaged in the investigation of a complaint against a barrister in accordance with the relevant procedure or otherwise shall act as Clerk in relation to disciplinary proceedings arising out of that complaint.

5.   Service of Charges

(1)   Following the formulation of the charge or charges by counsel appointed by the PCC Representative in accordance with the relevant procedure, the PCC Representative shall cause a copy thereof to be served on the barrister concerned ('the defendant'), together with a copy of these Regulations and details of any Directions sought not later than 10 weeks (or 5 weeks if the PCC has directed that the prosecution of the charges be expedited) after the date on which the complaint was referred to a Disciplinary Tribunal by the PCC.

(2)   The PCC Representative shall at the same time cause copies of the charge or charges to be supplied to the President.

6.   Representation of complainant's interests

(a) the PCC representative shall keep the complainant informed of the progress of the complaint and of any further documents and other information to be considered by the panel and shall, so far as practicable, afford the complainant an opportunity to comment in advance of the hearing on any such information of documents.

(b) It shall be the responsibility of the PCC Representative and counsel appointed by the PCC Representative to represent the interests of the complainant in relation to any charge of inadequate professional service.

7.   Convening Orders

(1)   After receipt of the copy charge or charges supplied pursuant to Regulation 5, and in any case not less than 14 days before the substantive hearing, the President shall issue an Order ('the Convening Order') specifying

(a) the date of the sitting of the Disciplinary Tribunal at which it is proposed the charge or charges should be heard

(b) the identities of those persons who it is proposed should constitute the Disciplinary Tribunal to hear his case

(c) the identity of the Clerk.

(2)   The President shall arrange for the service of the Convening Order on the defendant, and for copies thereof to be supplied to the nominated members of the Disciplinary Tribunal and the Clerk. In the order the defendant's attention will be drawn to:

(a) his right to represent himself or be represented by counsel, with or without instructing a solicitor, as he shall think fit

(b) his right to inspect and be given copies of documents referred to in the List served pursuant to Regulation 7 below

(c) his right (without prejudice to his right to appear and take part in the proceedings) to deliver a written answer to the charge or charges if he thinks fit.

(3)   The defendant shall have the right upon receipt of the Convening Order to give notice to the President objecting to any one or more of the proposed members of the Disciplinary Tribunal. Such notice shall specify the ground of objection.

(4)   Upon receipt of such objection, the President shall, if satisfied that it is properly made (but subject to Paragraph (5) of this Regulation) exercise the power conferred on

him by Paragraph (3) of Regulation 2 to nominate a substitute Member or Members of the Tribunal, and notify the defendant accordingly. Upon receipt of such notification, the defendant shall have *mutatis mutandis* in relation to such substitute Member or Members the like right of objection as is conferred by Paragraph (3) of this Regulation.

(5)   No objection to any Member of the Tribunal shall be valid on the ground that he has or may have had knowledge of a previous charge of professional misconduct or breach of proper professional standards or a charge consisting of a legal aid complaint against the defendant or any finding on any such charge, or of any sentence imposed on the defendant in connection therewith.

(6)   The Convening Order shall contain words drawing the attention of the defendant to the rights conferred by Paragraphs (2)–(5) of this Regulation.

8.   Documents to be Served

(1)   A barrister who is to be charged before a Disciplinary Tribunal shall, as soon as practicable, be supplied with:

    (a) a copy of the statement of the evidence of each witness intended to be called in support of the charge or charges

    (b) a list of the documents intended to be relied on by the PCC Representative.

(1A)   If the documents referred to in paragraph (1) of this Regulation are not supplied to the barrister at least 10 days before the date of the Preliminary Hearing then the PCC representative shall provide to the barrister and the Directions Judge at least 10 days before the date of the Preliminary Hearing:

    (a) details of the statements of evidence that are still being sought and

    (b) a statement of when it is believed that it will be practicable to supply those statements to the barrister.

(2)   Nothing in this Regulation shall preclude the reception by a Disciplinary Tribunal of the evidence of a witness a copy of whose statement has not been served on the defendant (within the time specified aforesaid, or at all), or of a document not included in the List of Documents, provided the Tribunal is of opinion that the defendant is not materially prejudiced thereby, or on such terms as are necessary to ensure that no such prejudice arises.

9.   Preliminary Hearings; Directions Judge; Powers of Chairman etc.

(1)   The President shall designate a judge or judges ('the Directions Judge(s)') to exercise the powers and functions specified in this Regulation.

(2)   The Directions Judge shall (subject to Paragraph (7) of this Regulation) hold a Preliminary Hearing for the purpose of giving directions and of taking such other steps as he considers suitable for the clarification of the issues before the tribunal and generally for the just and expeditious handling of the proceedings.

(2A)   The Preliminary Hearing shall be held not less than 10 days and not more than 4 weeks (or 3 weeks if the PCC has directed that prosecution of charges be expedited) after service of the charge or charges on the barrister. For the purpose of calculating these periods, no account shall be taken of any period outside the law terms.

(3)   The directions to be given and steps taken by the Directions Judge may concern, but shall not be limited to, the following matters:

    (a) whether the hearing should not be held in public

    (b) applications for separate hearings

    (c) applications to sever charges

(d) applications to strike out charges

(e) attendance of witnesses

(f) a requirement that the parties provide each other with the names of all witnesses to be called at the hearing within a specified time limit

(g) admission of documents, including any documents intended to be relied upon by the PCC Representative in relation to charges of inadequate professional service

(h) admission of facts, in accordance with the procedure set out at Paragraph (4) of this Regulation

(i) the estimated duration of the substantive hearing

(j) such other matters as he deems expedient for the efficient conduct of the hearing

(k) consideration of any application under Regulation 21(12)(ii)

(l) a requirement that such action as appears to him to be necessary for a fair hearing of the matter be undertaken within such period as he may decide

(m) where he is satisfied that the matter is ready for hearing by a Tribunal setting a date for the Tribunal hearing.

(3A)   The defendant may plead guilty to any charge or charges at the Directions Hearing, in which case the Tribunal shall find the defendant guilty of that charge at the Tribunal Hearing.

(4)(a) The Directions Judge may, if he thinks fit, request the defendant or his representative to state (either forthwith or in writing within such time as may be specified) whether any and if so which of such of the facts relied on in support of the charges as may be specified is disputed, and/or the grounds on which such fact is disputed.

(b) The Clerk shall cause a record to be made of the making of such a request as aforesaid, and of the defendant's response thereto, and the same shall be drawn to the attention of the Disciplinary Tribunal at the conclusion of the substantive hearing, if relevant, on the question of costs.

(5)   The powers and functions specified in this Regulation may be exercised by a Judge nominated by the President other than the Directions Judge, including the Judge designated in the Convening Order as Chairman of the Tribunal appointed to hear and determine the charge or charges against the defendant.

(6)   The Clerk shall take a note of the proceedings at a Preliminary Hearing and shall cause a record to be drawn up and served on the parties setting out the directions given or admissions made at the Preliminary Hearing, including, without prejudice to the generality of the directions given, a record of any directions which relate to any of the matters specifically set out under Paragraph (3) of this Regulation.

(7)   A defendant aggrieved by a direction given or other step taken pursuant to this Regulation may, provided that he acts promptly following the service on him of the record of any directions, give notice to the Clerk of his intention to apply for a review of such direction or step; such review will be conducted by the Chairman of the Tribunal sitting with a Lay Representative, who shall, on such application being made, give such directions or take such other steps as they see fit.

(8)   The PCC Representative and the defendant or his representative may, in advance of the date fixed for the Preliminary Hearing, agree upon the directions to be made and/or steps to be taken thereat, or that no such directions or steps are required and shall notify the Clerk in writing of such agreement; following such notification the Directions Judge

may, if he thinks fit, make directions in the terms agreed and/or direct that no Preliminary Hearing is required.

(9)   For the avoidance of doubt the Directions Judge, or the Chairman of the Disciplinary Tribunal designated in the Convening Order (or failing the Directions Judge or the Chairman, any other Judge nominated by the President) may

(a) upon the application of either party at any time extend or abridge any time limit governing the disciplinary procedures on such terms as he thinks just

(b) upon the application of either party, or of his own motion, hold further preliminary hearings for the purpose of giving any further directions or taking any other steps which he considers necessary for the proper conduct of the proceedings

(c) adjourn the preliminary hearing from time to time and for such periods of time as he considers appropriate and set such time limits as he may decide for action to be taken during such adjournments

(d) consider applications for adjournment of the Tribunal Hearing prior to that Hearing and grant such adjournments as they consider appropriate.

10.   Provision of Documents

There shall be provided to each member of the Disciplinary Tribunal prior to the commencement of the substantive hearing copies of the following documents:

(a) the Order of the President constituting the Tribunal

(b) the Charges and any particulars thereof

(c) any documents proposed to be relied on by the PCC Representative or by the defendant, unless a direction has been made at the Preliminary Hearing or otherwise, that copies of such documents be withheld

(d) any written answer to the charges submitted by or on behalf of the defendant

(e) such other documents (which may include copies of witness statements) as at the Preliminary Hearing or otherwise have been directed to be or the PCC Representative and the defendant or his representative have agreed, should be laid before the Tribunal prior to the start of the hearing

(f) the record of directions given at each preliminary hearing which has been drawn up and served on the parties pursuant to Regulation 9(6).

11.   Procedure At The Hearing

The Proceedings of a Disciplinary Tribunal shall be governed by the rules of natural justice, subject to which the tribunal may

(a) admit any evidence, whether oral or written, whether direct or hearsay, and whether or not the same would be admissible in a court of law

(b) give such directions with regard to the conduct of and procedure at the hearing, and with regard to the admission of evidence thereat, as it considers appropriate for securing that the defendant has a proper opportunity of answering the charge or otherwise as shall be just

(c) exclude any hearsay evidence if it is not satisfied that reasonable steps have been taken to obtain direct evidence of the facts sought to be proved by the hearsay evidence.

The tribunal shall apply the criminal standard of proof when adjudicating upon charges of professional misconduct, and the civil standard of proof when adjudicating upon charges of inadequate professional service, if any.

12.   Hearing in Private

The hearing before a Disciplinary Tribunal shall be in public unless at a Preliminary Hearing or otherwise it has been directed that it shall not be held in public, and this direction has not been over-ruled by the Tribunal.

13.   Decision of a Court or Tribunal

(1)   In proceedings before a Disciplinary Tribunal which involve the decision of a court or tribunal, the following rules of evidence shall apply provided that it is proved in each case that the decision relates to the defendant:

   (a) the fact that the defendant has been convicted of a criminal offence may be proved by producing a certified copy of the certificate of conviction relating to the offence; proof of a conviction in this matter shall constitute prima facie evidence that the defendant was guilty of the offence the subject thereof.

   (b) the finding and sentence of any tribunal in or outside England and Wales exercising a professional disciplinary jurisdiction may be proved by producing a certified copy of the finding and sentence.

   (c) the judgment of any civil court may be proved by producing a certified copy of the judgment.

(2)   In any case set out in Paragraph (1) of this Regulation, the findings of fact by the court or tribunal upon which the conviction, finding, sentence or judgment is based shall be admissible as *prima facie* proof of those facts.

14.   Absence of Defendant

(1)   If a Disciplinary Tribunal is satisfied that the relevant procedure has been complied with and the defendant has been duly served (in accordance with Regulation 29 of these Regulations) with the documents required by Regulations 5, 7 and 8 and the defendant has not attended at the time and place appointed for the hearing, the tribunal may nevertheless proceed to hear and determine the charge or charges, subject to compliance with Paragraph (12)(i) of Regulation 21 in the event of any charge being found proved.

(2)   If a Disciplinary Tribunal is satisfied that it has not been practicable to comply with the relevant procedure, the Tribunal shall hear and determine the charge or charges in the absence of the defendant subject to compliance with Paragraph (12)(ii) of Regulation 21 in the event of any charge being found proved.

15.   Recording of Proceedings

The Clerk shall arrange for a record of the proceedings before a Disciplinary Tribunal to be made by the employment of a shorthand writer or the use of a recording machine.

16.   Amendment of Charges

A Disciplinary Tribunal may at any time before or during the hearing direct that the charge or charges shall be amended provided always:

   (a) that the Tribunal is satisfied that the defendant will not by reason of such an amendment suffer any substantial prejudice in the conduct of his defence,

(b) that the Tribunal shall, if so requested by the defendant, adjourn for such time as is reasonably necessary to enable him to meet the charge or charges as so amended,

(c) that the Tribunal shall make such Order as to the costs of or occasioned by the amendment, or of any consequential adjournment of the proceedings, as it considers appropriate.

17. Adjournment

(1)   Subject to the provisions of the following Paragraph, the Disciplinary Tribunal shall sit from day to day until it has arrived at a finding and if any charge has been found proved until sentence is pronounced.

(2)   Notwithstanding the provisions of Paragraph (1) of this Regulation, a Disciplinary Tribunal may, if the Tribunal decides an adjournment is necessary for any reason, adjourn the hearing for such period as it may decide. In particular, if a finding of inadequate professional service is made and the Tribunal considers that an award of compensation to the complainant may be appropriate, it may adjourn to enable further investigation of that question to take place, if it does not already have the necessary material before it.

18. The Finding

At the conclusion of the hearing, the finding of the Disciplinary Tribunal on each charge, together with its reasons, shall be set down in writing and signed by the chairman and all members of the Tribunal. If the members of the Tribunal are not unanimous as to the finding on any charge, the finding to be recorded on that charge shall be that of the majority. If the members of the Tribunal are equally divided as to the finding on any charge, then, the burden of proof being on the PCC Representative, the finding to be recorded on that charge shall be that which is the most favourable to the defendant. The chairman of the Tribunal shall then announce the Tribunal's finding on the charge or charges.

19. The Sentence

(1)   If the Disciplinary Tribunal shall have found the charge or any of the charges proved, evidence may be given of any previous finding of professional misconduct or of breach of proper professional standards or of inadequate professional service or any finding on a charge consisting of a legal aid complaint against the defendant. After hearing any representations by or on behalf of the defendant the Tribunal shall set down in writing its decision as to the sentence. If the members of the Tribunal are not unanimous as to the sentence, the sentence to be recorded shall be that decided by the majority. If the members of the Tribunal are equally divided as to the sentence, the sentence to be recorded shall be that which is the most favourable to the defendant. The chairman of the Tribunal shall then announce the Tribunal's decision as to sentence.

(2)(a) A barrister against whom a charge of professional misconduct has been found proved may be sentenced by the Disciplinary Tribunal to be:

    (i)   disbarred (or in the case of a registered European lawyer, removed from the register of European lawyers);

    (ii)   suspended (or in the case of a registered European lawyer suspended from the register of European lawyers) for a prescribed period (either unconditionally or subject to conditions);

    (iii) ordered to pay a fine of up to £5,000 to the Bar Council;

    (iv) ordered to repay or forego fees;

(v)   ordered to complete continuing professional development of such nature and duration as the Tribunal shall direct and to provide satisfactory proof of compliance with this order to the PCC;

(vi)   reprimanded by the Treasurer of his Inn;

(vii) reprimanded by the Tribunal; or

(viii) given advice by the Tribunal as to his future conduct; or

(ix)   ordered by the Tribunal to attend on a nominated person to be reprimanded; or

(x)   ordered by the Tribunal to attend on a nominated person to be given advice as to his future conduct.

(b) A barrister against whom a charge of inadequate professional service has been found proved may be

(i)   directed to make a formal apology to the complainant for the conduct in relation to which the finding was made;

(ii)   directed to repay or remit all or part of any fee rendered in respect of the inadequate service;

(iii) directed to pay compensation to the complainant in such sum as the Tribunal shall direct not exceeding £5,000; or

(iv)   directed to complete continuing professional development of such nature and duration as the Tribunal shall direct and to provide satisfactory proof of compliance with this requirement to the PCC;

In determining whether any sum is to be paid under paragraph (iii) hereof, or in fixing the amount of such sum, the Tribunal shall in particular have regard to any loss suffered by the applicant as a result of the inadequate professional service, the availability to the complainant of other forms of redress, to the gravity of the conduct complained of and to the fee claimed by the barrister for the inadequate service.

(c) In any case where a charge of professional misconduct or inadequate professional service has been found proved, the Tribunal may decide that no action should be taken against the defendant.

(3)   Sections 41 and 42 of the Administration of Justice Act 1985 (as substituted by Section 33 of the Legal Aid Act 1988 and amended by Schedule 4 to the Access to Justice Act 1999) confer certain powers (relating to the reduction or cancellation of fees otherwise payable by the Legal Services Commission in connection with services provided as part of the Community Legal Service or Criminal Defence Service and to exclusion from providing representation funded by the Legal Services Commission as part of the Community Legal Service or Criminal Defence Service) on a Disciplinary Tribunal in the cases to which those Sections apply. Accordingly:

(a) Any Disciplinary Tribunal which hears a charge consisting of a legal aid complaint relating to the conduct of a barrister may if it thinks fit (and whether or not it sentences the barrister in accordance with paragraph (2) of this Regulation in respect of any conduct arising out of the same legal aid complaint) order that any such fees as are referred to in Section 41(2) of the Act of 1985 shall be reduced or cancelled.

(b) Where a Disciplinary Tribunal hears a charge of professional misconduct against a barrister it may (in addition to or instead of sentencing that barrister in accordance with Paragraph (2) of this Regulation) order that he shall be excluded from providing representation funded by the Legal Services Commission as part of the Community Legal Service or Criminal Defence Service either temporarily or for a specified period if it determines that there is good reason for the exclusion arising out of (i) his conduct in connection with any such services as are mentioned in Section 40(1) of the Act of 1985; or (ii) his professional conduct generally.

(4)   Whether or not a Disciplinary Tribunal shall have found any charge proved, if the Disciplinary Tribunal considers that the circumstances of the complaint are relevant to the barrister in his capacity as a pupilmaster, it may notify the barrister's Inn of its concerns in such manner as it sees fit.

20.   Sentence of Suspension

(1)   Any sentence of suspension may apply to the whole of a barrister's practice or to such part only as the Disciplinary Tribunal may determine.

(2)   The conditions to which a sentence of suspension may be made subject include a requirement that the barrister shall undergo such further pupillage or training or attain such standard of competence as the Tribunal may determine.

21.   Wording of the Sentence

The sentence determined by a Disciplinary Tribunal if a charge of professional misconduct has been found proved shall be recorded as follows:

(1)   Disbarment
' That ... . . be disbarred and expelled from the Honourable Society of ... . .'

(2)   Suspension
' That ... . . be suspended from practice as a barrister and from enjoyment of all rights and privileges as a member of the Honourable Society of ... . . and be prohibited from holding himself out as being a barrister without disclosing his suspension for (stating the length of the prescribed period)'. (Note: If the Tribunal decides that the sentence of suspension shall apply to part only of the barrister's practice or shall be subject to conditions, such part or such conditions (as the case may be) shall be specified in the wording of the sentence.)

(3)   Payment of Fine
' That ... . . pay a fine of £ ... . . to the Bar Council.'

(4)   Repayment or Foregoing of Fees
' That ... . . shall repay all fees (fees amounting to £ ... . .) received by him (shall forego all fees (fees amounting to £ ... . .) due to be paid to him) in connection with ... . .'

(5)   Continuing Professional Development
' That ... . . shall by [date] complete a minimum of ... hours of continuing professional development (in addition to the mandatory requirements set out in the Continuing Professional Development Regulations at Annex C to the Code of Conduct) [in the subject of ...] and provide satisfactory proof of compliance with this order to the Professional Conduct and Complaints Committee of the Bar Council.'

(6)   Reprimand
' That ... . . be reprimanded by the Treasurer of the Honourable Society of ... . .', or 'That ... . . is hereby ordered to attend ... . . to be reprimanded'.

(7)   Advice as to Future Conduct
' That ... . . has been advised by the Tribunal as to his future conduct in regard to ... . .' or ' That ... . . is hereby ordered to attend on ... . . to be given advice as to his future conduct in regard to ... . .'.

(8)   <u>Order for Reduction of Legal Aid Fees</u>

' That the fees otherwise payable to ... . . by the Legal Services Commission in connection with his services provided by him as part of the Community Legal Service or Criminal Defence Service or otherwise in relation to the items or matters specified in the first column of the Schedule hereto be reduced to the sum or sums specified in the second column of that Schedule'.

The record of the sentence shall then contain a Schedule setting out the matters referred to above.

(9)   <u>Order for Cancellation of Legal Aid Fees</u>

' That the fees otherwise payable to ... . . by the Legal Services Commission in connection with services provided by him as part of the Community Legal Service or Criminal Defence Service in relation to the items or matters specified in the Schedule hereto be cancelled'.

The record of the sentence shall then contain a Schedule identifying the items or matters referred to above.

(10)   <u>Exclusion from Legal Aid Work</u>

' That ... . . be excluded from providing representation funded by the Legal Services Commission as part of the Community Legal Service or Criminal Defence Service (as explained in Section 42(4)(b) of the Administration of Justice Act 1985 as substituted by Section 33 of the Legal Aid Act 1988 and amended by Schedule 4 to the Access to Justice Act 1999 (until ... . .) (for a period of ... . . beginning on ... . .)'.

(11)   <u>Membership of More than One Inn</u>

If the barrister is a member of more than one Inn, each Inn of which he is a member shall be mentioned in the sentence.

(12)   <u>Absence of the Barrister Charged</u>

If the barrister charged has not been present throughout the proceedings, the sentence shall include one of the following two statements:

   (i)   If the relevant procedure under Regulation 14(1) has been complied with, that the finding and sentence were made in the absence of the barrister in accordance with Regulation 14(1).

   (ii)   If the procedure under Regulation 14(2) has been complied with, that the finding and the sentence were made in the absence of the barrister and that he has the right to apply to the Directions Judge for an order that there should be a new hearing before a fresh Disciplinary Tribunal.

(13)   <u>Removal from the Register of European Lawyers</u>

' That ... be removed from the register of European lawyers maintained by the Bar Council.'

(14)   <u>Suspension from the Register of European Lawyers</u>

' That ... be suspended from the register of European lawyers maintained by the Bar Council and be prohibited from holding himself out as registered with the Bar Council or an Inn of Court without disclosing his suspension for (state length of prescribed period).' (Note: If the Tribunal decides that the sentence of suspension shall apply to part only of the registered European lawyer's practice or shall be subject to conditions, such part or such conditions (as the case may be) shall be specified in the wording of the sentence).

22.   Report of Finding and Sentence

(1)   As soon as practicable after the conclusion of the proceedings of a Disciplinary Tribunal, the chairman of the Tribunal shall prepare a report in writing of the finding on the

charges of professional misconduct and the reasons for that finding and, where applicable, the sentence. At the discretion of the chairman of the Tribunal, the report may also refer to matters which, in the light of the evidence given to the Tribunal, appear to require investigation or comment. He shall send copies of the report to the following:

(2)   In all cases

    (i)   The Lord Chancellor

    (ii)   The Lord Chief Justice

    (iii) The Attorney General

    (iv) The President

    (v)   The Chairman of the Bar Council

    (vi) The Chairman of the Professional Conduct and Complaints Committee

    (vii) The barrister charged

    (viii) The Treasurer of the barrister's Inn of Call

    (ix) The Treasurer of any other Inn of which the barrister is a member.

(3)   In cases where one or more charges of professional misconduct have been found proved and any such charge constitutes or arises out of a legal aid complaint, and/or the sentence includes an order under Regulation 20(8), (9) or (10), the Legal Services Commission.

23.   Appeal to the Visitors

(1)   In cases where one or more charges of professional misconduct have been proved, an appeal may be lodged with the Visitors in accordance with the Hearings Before the Visitors Rules:

    (a) against conviction by the defendant; and/or

    (b) against sentence, by the defendant or (with the Consent of the Chairman of the Bar or the Chairman of the PCC) the Bar Council.

(2)   In cases where no professional misconduct has been proved, but one or more charges of inadequate professional service have been proved, an appeal shall lie at the instance of the barrister from any such finding, and against any decision as to the remedy to be granted to the complainant for such service in the same manner as an appeal lies from a decision of an Adjudication Panel in respect of the same matters.

(3)   Where a defendant lodges an appeal against a sentence of disbarment, he may at the same time lodge with the Visitors an appeal against any requirement imposed pursuant to Regulation 27.

24.   Appeal: Sum Payable

Where an appeal is lodged with the Visitors by the Defendant, the Notice of Appeal must be accompanied by the sum of £250 payable to the General Council of the Bar to defray expenses, such sum to be refunded in the discretion of the Visitors in the event of an appeal which is successful wholly or in part.

25.   Action by the Barrister's Inn

(1)   On receipt of the report prepared in accordance with Regulation 22, the Treasurer of the barrister's Inn of Call shall not less than 21 days after the conclusion of the Tribunal's proceedings pronounce the sentence decided on by the Tribunal, and take such further action as may be required to carry the sentence into effect. The Treasurer shall inform the

persons specified in Paragraph (2) of Regulation 22 of the date on which the sentence is to take effect.

(2)   Similar action shall be taken by the Treasurer of any other Inn of which the barrister is a member in conjunction with the Treasurer of the barrister's Inn of Call.

(3)   In any case in which the barrister has given notice of appeal to the visitors against the finding and/or sentence of the Tribunal on the charges of professional misconduct, the action set out in paragraphs (1) and (2) of this Regulation shall be deferred until the appeal has been heard by the Visitors or otherwise disposed of without a hearing.

25A.   Action by the Bar Council

(1)   In the case of a registered European lawyer, on receipt of the report prepared in accordance with Regulation 22, the Bar Council shall not less than 21 days after the conclusion of the Tribunal's proceedings pronounce the sentence decided on by the Tribunal and take such further action as may be required to carry the sentence into effect. The Bar Council shall inform the persons specified in paragraph (2) of Regulation 22 of the date on which the sentence is to take effect.

(2)   In any case in which a registered European lawyer has given notice of appeal to the Visitors against the finding and/or sentence of the Tribunal on the charges of professional misconduct, the actions set out in paragraph (1) of this Regulation shall be deferred until the appeal has been heard by the Visitors or otherwise disposed of without a hearing.

(3)   The Bar Council shall take all such steps as may be necessary or expedient in order to give effect to any requirement made by the Tribunal pursuant to Regulation 27 below.

26.   Publication of Finding and Sentence

(1)   The following procedures are to be observed in regard to publication of the finding and sentence of a Disciplinary Tribunal:

(i)   When the Tribunal has found one or more charges of professional misconduct have been proved the President shall publish the charges found proved and the sentence as soon as he has been informed by the Treasurer(s) of the barrister's Inn(s) of the date from which the sentence is to take effect.

(ii)   When the Tribunal has found that one or more charges of inadequate professional service have been proved, the President shall not publish the charges found proved and the finding unless the barrister charged so requests.

(iii)   When the Tribunal has found that any charge whether of professional misconduct or of inadequate professional service has not been proved the President shall not publish that charge and the finding unless the barrister charged so requests.

(2)   When publishing any finding, sentence or decision in accordance with sub-paragraph (1) of this Regulation, the President shall communicate the same in writing to:—

(i)   the Lord Chancellor;

(ii)   the Lord Chief Justice;

(iii)   the Attorney General;

(iv)   the Director of Public Prosecutions;

(v)   the Treasurer of each Inn for screening in the Hall, Benchers' Room and Treasurer's Office of the Inn;

(vi)   the Leaders of the six circuits;

(vii)   the barrister concerned;

(viii) such one or more press agencies or other publications as the President may decide;

(ix) in the case of a registered European lawyer, his home professional body.

(3) Nothing in this Regulation shall prevent the Bar Council publishing the finding and sentence of the Tribunal in such manner and in such a time as it sees fit unless:

(a) the hearing was held in private; and

(b) the Chairman of the Tribunal directs that publication shall be delayed until the President has published the finding under sub-paragraph (1) of this Regulation.

27. Suspension Pending Appeal

(1) This regulation applies in relation to any barrister who has been sentenced to be disbarred or to be suspended for a period of more than one year.

(2) Where this regulation applies the Tribunal shall seek representations from the defendant and the PCC Representative as to whether it would be inappropriate to take action under paragraphs (3) or (4) below;

(3) Having heard any representations under paragraph (2) above, the Tribunal shall:

(a) unless in the particular circumstances of the case it appears to the Tribunal to be inappropriate to do so, require the Bar Council to suspend immediately the practising certificate of the barrister in question; or

(b) where that barrister does not currently hold a practising certificate, require the Bar Council not to issue any practising certificate to him.

(4) If pursuant to paragraph (3)(a) above the Tribunal concludes that it would be inappropriate to require immediate suspension it may nonetheless require the Bar Council to suspend the practising certificate of the barrister in question from such date as the Tribunal may specify.

(5) Where this regulation applies but the barrister in question is permitted to continue to practise for any period the Tribunal may require the Bar Council to impose such terms in respect of the barrister's practice as the Tribunal deems necessary for the protection of the public.

(6) If a barrister in relation to whom a requirement has been made pursuant to paragraphs (3) to (5) considers that, due to a change in the circumstances, it would be appropriate for that requirement to be varied, he may apply to the President in writing for a variation to be made.

(7) On receiving an application made pursuant to paragraph (6) above the President shall refer it to the Chairman and one of the lay representatives of the Tribunal which originally imposed the requirement.

(8) Any application made pursuant to paragraph (6) above shall be sent by the applicant, on the day that it is made, to the PCC and the PCC may make such representations as they think fit on that application to those to whom the application has been referred by the President.

(9) The persons to whom an application made pursuant to paragraph (6) above is referred may vary or confirm the requirement in relation to which the application has been made.

28. Costs

(1) A Disciplinary Tribunal shall have power to make such Orders for costs, whether against or in favour of a defendant, as it shall think fit.

(2)   Upon making such an Order a Disciplinary Tribunal shall either itself determine the amount of such costs or appoint a suitably qualified person to do so on its behalf.

(3)   Any costs ordered to be paid by or to a defendant shall be paid to or by the Bar Council.

(4)   Subject as aforesaid, all costs and expenses incurred by a Disciplinary Tribunal or by the PCC in connection with or preparatory to the hearing before the Tribunal shall be borne by the Bar Council.

29.   Service of Documents

Any documents required to be served on a barrister arising out of or in connection with disciplinary proceedings shall be deemed to have been validly served:

(1)   If sent by registered post, or recorded delivery post, or receipted hand delivery to:

(a) the address notified by such barrister pursuant to Paragraph 202(d) of the Code of Conduct of the Bar of England and Wales (or any provisions amending or replacing the same); or

(b) an address to which the barrister may request in writing that such documents be sent; or

(c) in the absence of any such request, to his last known address;

and such service shall be deemed to have been made on the fifth working day after the date of posting or on the next working day after receipted hand delivery;

(2)   If actually served;

(3)   If served in any way which may be directed by the Directions Judge or the Chairman of the Disciplinary Tribunal.

For the purpose of this regulation 'receipted hand delivery' means by a delivery by hand which is acknowledged by a receipt signed by the barrister or his clerk.

30.   Miscellaneous Provisions

(1)   Any duty or function or step which, pursuant to the provisions of these regulations, is to be discharged or carried out by the President may, if he is unable to act due to absence or any other reason, be discharged or carried out by any other member of the Inns Council, the Treasurer of any Inn or by any other person nominated in writing by the President for any specific purpose.

(2)   When the Treasurer of an Inn is a Royal Bencher, references in these Regulations to such Treasurer shall be read as references to his deputy.

31.   Exclusion from Providing Representation Funded by the Legal Services Commission — Application for Termination

(1)   A barrister who has been excluded from legal aid work under Section 42 of the Act of 1985 may apply for an order terminating his exclusion from providing representation funded by the Legal Services Commission as part of the Community Legal Service or Criminal Defence Service in accordance with this Regulation.

(2)   Any such application shall be in writing and shall be addressed to the President.

(3)   On considering any such application the President may dismiss the application or may determine that the barrister's exclusion from providing representation funded by the Legal Services Commission as part of the Community Legal Service or Criminal Defence Service be terminated forthwith or on a specified future date.

(4)   The President shall give notification of his decision in writing to the same persons as received copies of the report of the Disciplinary Tribunal which ordered that the barrister be excluded from providing such representation legal aid work.

(5)   Upon the receipt of any such report the Treasurer of the applicant's Inn of Call and of any other Inn of which he is a member shall take action equivalent to that which it took in respect of the report of the Disciplinary Tribunal which sentenced the barrister to be excluded from providing representation funded by the Legal Services Commission as part of the Community Legal Service or Criminal Defence Service.

(6)   The procedures to be observed in regard to the publication of the decision of the President on any such application as is referred to in this Regulation shall be those which were applicable to the publication of the finding and sentence whereby the applicant was excluded from providing representation funded by the Legal Services Commission as part of the Community Legal Service or Criminal Defence Service.

(7)   The President shall have power to make such order for costs as he thinks fit and Regulation 28 shall apply with all necessary modifications.

32.   Citation, Commencement, Revocations and Transitional Provisions

(1)   These Regulations may be cited as 'The Disciplinary Tribunals Regulations 2000' and shall come into operation on 15th May 2000 save that no finding of inadequate professional service may be made against a barrister in respect of any conduct of his which took place before 13th July 1996.

(2)   Subject to Paragraph (3) below, the Disciplinary Tribunals Regulations of the Council of the Inns of Court and any other rules or regulations relating to Disciplinary Tribunals made prior to the commencement of these Regulations shall cease to have effect on 14th May 2000.

(3)   In relation to any case in which a barrister was served with the charge or charges before 15th May 2000 these Regulations shall not apply and the matter shall continue to be dealt with pursuant to the Disciplinary Tribunals Regulations 1996, save that Regulation 23 shall apply to any decision made by a Disciplinary Tribunal on or after 15th May 2000.

ANNEXE L

THE SUMMARY PROCEDURE RULES

[*Amended 25 July 2001 and 9 April 2002*]

1.   Definitions

In these Rules:

   (a) 'The Act of 1985' shall mean the Administration of Justice Act 1985 as amended by the Legal Aid Act 1988 and the Access to Justice Act 1999.

   (b) 'Disciplinary Tribunal Regulations' shall mean those Regulations as amended from time to time in Annex K to the Code of Conduct of the Bar of England and Wales.

   (c) 'The defendant' shall mean the barrister against whom complaint has been made.

   (d) 'Sponsor member' shall mean the member of the PCC to whom the file was originally or subsequently assigned and who reported to the PCC on the complaint.

   (e) 'Summary case' shall mean a complaint referred by the PCC for summary determination under these Rules.

   (f) 'Summary hearing' shall mean the hearing of a summary case by a panel appointed under these Rules.

2.   Composition of Summary Hearing Panels

A panel shall consist of not more than five, and not less than three people nominated by the Chairman of the PCC which number shall include at least:

   (a) One Queen's Counsel as chairman of the panel

   (b) One Junior over five years call

   (c) One lay representative

   Provided that:

   (i) No barrister shall be nominated to serve on a panel who has acted as sponsor member in relation to the summary case to be dealt with.

   (ii) The proceedings of a summary hearing shall be valid notwithstanding that one or more of the members other than the chairman or lay representative becomes unable to continue to act or disqualified from continuing to act, so long as the number of members present throughout the substantive hearing of the charge(s) is not reduced below three and continues to include the chairman and the lay representative.

3.   Timetable

   (a) As soon as possible after referral of a case to summary procedure, the Secretary of the PCC shall write to the defendant notifying him of the PCC's decision and enclosing a copy of the Summary Procedure Rules.

   (b) The defendant shall receive as soon as possible thereafter, the documents to be served upon him together with a letter laying down a fixed time and date (normally 5 pm on a working day within 60 calendar days or less from the date of the letter) for the hearing to take place. One alternative shall be given.

   (c) The defendant shall be invited to accept one or other of the dates proposed or to provide a written representation to the Chairman of the PCC, objecting to both dates with reasons and providing two further alternative dates. The Chairman of the PCC shall consider this representation and either confirm one of the original dates or re-fix the hearing. His decision shall be final.

(d) Once fixed, a hearing date shall be vacated only in exceptional circumstances and with the agreement of the Chairman of the PCC.

4. Documents to be Served

On referral of a complaint to summary procedure, the PCC shall prepare and serve the following documents on the defendant and the complainant who shall be invited within 14 days (which period may be extended with the permission of the Chairman of the PCC or the Complaints Commissioner) to comment in writing on any of those matters or to send other document to which they wish the panel to have regard:

(a) Notification of the PCC's decision to refer the matter to summary procedure.

(b) Statement of the charges made against the barrister which may include charges of inadequate professional service provided that:

(i)   the complainant is the barrister's lay client or his duly authorised representative or in the case of an employed barrister the person to whom he has supplied the professional service in question, and

(ii) the subject-matter of the complaint is something in respect of which the barrister would not be entitled to immunity from suit as an advocate in civil law.

(c) Statement of facts upon which the charge(s) is or are founded and upon which the PCC proposes to rely.

(d) Copies of any documents which will be available to the summary hearing and which have not previously been served on the defendant. Any document shall be deemed to have been validly served in the circumstances laid down in Paragraph 29 of Disciplinary Tribunal Regulations 2000.

5. Acceptance of the Statement of Facts and of Summary Procedure

(a) In the letter of notification:

(i)   The defendant shall be required to state in writing whether or not he admits the charge(s) and, if he does not, whether or not he challenges any of the facts detailed in the statement of facts.

(ii) If he admits the charge(s) or if he does not challenge any of the facts detailed in the statement of facts, he shall also be asked to say whether he is prepared to agree that the charge(s) should be dealt with by summary procedure.

(iii) If:

(1) the only charges(s) allege(s) breach of paragraph 402 of the Code of Conduct of the Bar of England and Wales;

(2) the PCC has so directed when referring the case to summary procedure: and

(3) the defendant admits the charge(s) and agrees that the charges(s) should be dealt with by summary procedure.

he shall also be asked to say whether he wishes to attend the summary hearing.

(b) If the defendant admits the charge(s) or does not challenge any significant facts and, in either case, if he agrees that his case should be dealt with by summary procedure, the case shall proceed to a summary hearing, failing which it shall proceed to a Disciplinary Tribunal.

(c) Failure of the defendant to respond to these questions within 30 days of the date of the Secretary's letter shall be construed as refusal to admit the charge(s), to agree the statement of facts and to accept summary procedure.

6. Submission of Further Documents

(a) If, following service of and agreement to the statement of facts and of documents relevant to summary procedure, the defendant seeks to submit further proofs of evidence, representations or other material for consideration at the summary hearing, he must do so not later than 21 days before the date fixed for the hearing.

(b) If either before or at the summary hearing, it becomes apparent that the material submitted amounts to a denial of any significant fact in the statement of facts, the Chairman of the PCC or the panel shall refer the matter to a Disciplinary Tribunal.

7. Procedure

(a) Procedure at summary hearings shall be informal, the details being at the discretion of the chairman of the panel.

(aa) Subject to the direction of the Chairman of the panel, the Bar Council shall keep the complainant informed of the progress of the complaint and of any further documents and other information to be considered by the panel; and shall so far as practicable, require the barrister and afford the complainant an opportunity to comment in advance of the hearing on any such information or documents.

(b) Subject to sub-paragraph (e), the defendant shall be entitled to be represented by counsel of his choice, by a solicitor or by any other representative he may wish. The PCC should be represented by counsel (normally the sponsor member) only in particularly complex cases and subject to the prior agreement of the chairman of the panel in each case.

(bb) A summary hearing shall take place in public unless:
(i)   the panel considers that there are special reasons why the hearing ought to be held in private; and
(ii)   the defendant consents to the hearing taking place in private.

(c) No witnesses may be called at a summary hearing without the prior consent of the chairman of the panel and without the submission of a proof of evidence.

(d) Subject to sub-paragraph (e), the attendance of the defendant shall be required. Should he nevertheless fail to attend, the summary hearing may proceed in his absence, subject to the panel being satisfied that this course is appropriate, that all relevant procedures requiring the defendant's attendance have been complied with and that no acceptable explanation for the defendant's absence has been provided. Should the panel not be so satisfied, they shall have the power to adjourn the matter, to a specific date or sine die, or to refer the matter back to the PCC, as they may think fit.

(e) If the defendant has stated in response to a request under paragraph 5(a)(iii) of these Rules that he does not wish to attend the hearing, then:
(i)   the defendant shall not be required to attend and if he does not attend, shall not be entitled to be represented at the hearing: but
(ii)   the panel shall require the defendant to attend an adjourned hearing (and sub-paragraphs (b) and (d) shall apply to the adjourned hearing) if the panel consider that a sentence of suspension may be appropriate.

(f) A record of each summary hearing shall be taken electronically and the tape re-tained under the arrangements of the Secretary of the PCC for two years, until the expiry of the period allowed for notification of intention to appeal or until the con-clusion of any appeal, whichever period is longest.

8. Finding

At the conclusion of a summary hearing, the finding on each charge shall be set down in writing and signed by the chairman of the panel together with the reasons for that find-ing. If the members of the panel are not unanimous as to the finding on any charge, the finding to be recorded on that charge shall be of the majority. If the members of the panel are equally divided as to the finding on any charge, then, the burden of proof being on the complainant, the finding to be recorded on that charge shall be that which is most favour-able to the defendant. The chairman of the panel shall then announce the panel's deci-sions as to finding.

9. Sentence

(a) If the panel shall have found any charge proved, the Secretary of the PCC shall lay before the panel details of any previous finding of professional misconduct, or of breach of proper professional standards or of inadequate professional service or any finding of guilt on a charge consisting of a legal aid complaint against the defend-ant. After hearing any representations or considering any written submissions by or on behalf of the defendant, the panel's decision as to sentence shall be set down in writing and signed by the chairman. If the members of the panel are not unanimous as to the sentence, the sentence to be recorded shall be of the majority. If the mem-bers of the panel are equally divided as to the sentence, the sentence to be recorded shall be that which is most favourable to the defendant. The chairman of the panel shall then announce the panel's decision as to sentence.

(b) A barrister against whom a charge of professional misconduct has been found proved may be sentenced by the summary hearing to be:

(i) Suspended from practice for up to three months, either unconditionally or subject to conditions;

(ii) Ordered to pay a fine of up to £500 to the Bar Council;

(iii) Ordered to forego or repay all or part of his fees;

(iv) Ordered to complete continuing professional development of such nature and duration as the Tribunal shall direct and to provide satisfactory proof of com-pliance with this order to the PCC;

(v) Reprimanded;

(vi) Advised as to his future conduct.

(c) A barrister against whom a charge of inadequate professional service has been found proved may be

(i) directed to make a formal apology to the complainant for the conduct in rela-tion to which the finding was made;

(ii) directed to repay or remit all or part of any fee rendered in respect of the inade-quate service; or

(iii) directed to pay compensation to the complainant in such sum as the Tribunal shall direct not exceeding £2,000; or

(iv) directed to complete continuing professional development of such nature and duration as the Tribunal shall direct and to provide satisfactory proof of compliance with this requirement to the PCC.

In determining whether any sum is to be paid under paragraph (iii) hereof, or in fixing the amount of such sum, the summary hearing shall have regard in particular to any loss suffered by the applicant as a result of the inadequate professional service the availability to the complainant of other forms of redress, to the gravity of the conduct complained of and to the fee claimed by the barrister for the inadequate service.

(d) In any case where a charge of professional misconduct or inadequate professional service has been found proved, the summary hearing may decide that no action should be taken against the barrister.

(e) Under the powers conferred by Sections 41 and 42 of the Act of 1985, any summary hearing which hears a charge consisting of a legal aid complaint relating to the conduct of a barrister may if it thinks fit (and whether or not it sentences the barrister in accordance with paragraph 9(b) or (c) of these Rules in respect of any conduct arising out of the same legal aid complaint) order that any such fees as are referred to in Sections 41(2) of the Act of 1985 shall be reduced or cancelled.

(f) Where a summary hearing deals with a charge of professional misconduct against a barrister it may (in addition to or instead of sentencing that barrister in accordance with paragraph 9(b) of these Rules), if it determines that there is good reason for the exclusion arising out of:

(i)   His conduct in connection with any such services as are maintained in Section 40(c) of the Act of 1985, or:

(ii) His professional conduct generally:

order that he shall be excluded from providing representation funded by the Legal Services Commission as part of the Community Legal Service or Criminal Defence Service for a period of up to six months.

(g) The sentence determined by a summary hearing if a charge of professional misconduct has been proved shall be recorded as follows:

(i)   Suspension

' That ... . be suspended from practice as a barrister and from enjoyment of all rights and privileges as a member of the Honourable Society of ... and be prohibited from holding himself out as being a barrister without disclosing his suspension for (stating the length of the prescribed period)'.

(Note: If the panel decides that the sentence of suspension shall apply to part only of the barrister's practice or shall be subject to conditions, such part or such conditions (as the case may be) shall be specified in the wording of the sentence.)

(ii) Payment of Fine

' That ... pay a fine of £ ... to the Bar Council.'

(iii) Repayment or Foregoing of Fees

' That ... shall repay all fees (fees amounting to £ ...) received by him (shall forego all fees (fees amounting to £ ...) due to be paid to him) in connection with ...'

(iv) Continuing Professional Development

' That ...... shall by (date] complete a minimum of ... hours of continuing professional development (in addition to the mandatory requirements set out in the Continuing Professional Development Regulations at Annex C to the Code of Conduct) [in the subject of ...] and provide satisfactory proof of compliance with this order to the Professional Conduct and Complaints Committee of the Bar Council.'

(v)   Reprimand

' That ... is hereby reprimanded' or ' That ... is hereby ordered to attend on ... to be reprimanded'.

(vi)   Advice as to Future Conduct

' That ... has been advised by the panel as to his future conduct in regard to ...' or ' That ... is hereby ordered to attend on ... to be given advice as to his future conduct in regard to ... '.

(vii)   Order for Reduction of Fees Payable by the Legal Services Commission

' That the fees otherwise payable by the Legal Services Commission in connection with Services provided by him as part of the Community Legal Service or Criminal Defence Service to ... in relation to the items or matters specified in the first column of the Schedule hereto be reduced to the sum or sums specified in the second column of that Schedule.'

The record of the sentence shall then contain a Schedule setting out the matters referred to above.

(viii)   Order for Cancellation of Fees Payable by the Legal Services Commission

'That the fees otherwise payable by the Legal Services Commission in connection with Services provided by him as part of the Community Legal Service or Criminal Defence Service to ... in relation to the items or matters specified in the Schedule hereto be cancelled'.

The record of the sentence shall then contain a Schedule identifying the items or matters referred to above.

(ix)   Exclusion from Providing Representation Funded by the Legal Services Commission

'That ... be excluded from providing representation funded by the Legal Services Commission as part of the Community Legal Service or Criminal Defence Service (as explained in Section 42(4)(b) of the Administration of Justice Act 1985 as substituted by Section 33 of the Legal Aid Act 1988 and amended by Schedule 4 to the Access to Justice Act 1999 (until ...) (for a period of ... beginning on ...)'.

(x)   Absence of the Defendant

If the defendant has not been present throughout the proceedings, the sentence shall include the statement that the finding and sentence were made in the absence of the barrister in accordance with paragraph 7(d) of these Rules.

(xi)   Suspension from the Register of European Lawyers

'That ... be suspended from the register of European lawyers maintained by the Bar Council and be prohibited from holding himself out as registered with the Bar Council or an Inn of Court without disclosing his suspension for (state length of prescribed period).' (Note: If the Tribunal decides that the sentence of suspension shall apply to part only of the registered European lawyer's practice or shall be subject to conditions, such part or such conditions (as the case may be) shall be specified in the wording of the sentence.)

(h) Sentences under paragraphs 9(b)(i), (ii) and (iii), 9(d) and 9(e) shall not be put into effect until expiry of the period allowed for service of Notice of Appeal under Hearings before the Visitors Rules or until the conclusion of any appeal, whichever period is the longer.

(i) Sentences under paragraphs 9(b)(iv), (v) and (vi) may be put into effect at and by the summary hearing or by directing the defendant to attend on a person or persons to be nominated by the panel, as the panel may think fit. Any sentence of suspension may apply to the whole of the defendant's practice or to such part only as may be determined. The conditions to which a sentence of suspension may be made subject include a requirement that the barrister shall undergo such further pupillage or training or attain such standard of competence as the panel may determine.

(j) Whether or not the panel shall have found any charge proved, if it considers that the circumstances of the complaint are relevant to the barrister's capacity as a pupil-master, it may notify the barrister's Inn of its concerns in such manner as it sees fit.

(k) Whether or not the panel shall have found any charge proved, it may refer any matter of policy which arises to the relevant Committee of the Bar Council.

10. Costs

A summary hearing shall have no power to award costs.

11. Report of Finding and Sentence

(a) As soon as practicable after the conclusion of a summary hearing, the Secretary of the PCC shall confirm the finding and sentence to the defendant in writing.

(b) In cases where one or more charges of professional misconduct have been found proved and on expiry of the period allowed for service of Notice of Appeal under Hearings Before the Visitors Rules or on the conclusion of any appeal, whichever period is the longer, the Secretary of the PCC shall communicate the finding and sentence (as varied on appeal) and, where the latter includes orders under paragraphs 9(b)(i), (ii), (iii), 9(c) or 9(d), the date on which these were carried into effect, in writing to the following:

(i) The Lord Chancellor

(ii) The Lord Chief Justice

(iii) The Attorney General

(iv) The President of the Council of the Inns of Court

(v) The Chairman of the Bar Council

(vi) The Chairman of the PCC

(vii) The defendant

(viii) The Treasurers of the defendant's Inn of Call and of any other Inns of which he is a member.

Provided that the Lord Chancellor, the Lord Chief Justice, the Attorney General and the President shall be informed only when a charge constituting or arising out of a legal aid complaint has been found proved or the sentence includes an order of suspension for any period.

12. Appeals

(1) In cases where one or more charges of professional misconduct have been proved, an Appeal may be lodged with the Visitors against finding and/or sentence (including any

finding of inadequate professional service) in accordance with the Hearings Before the Visitors Rules in force. Notice of appeal must be accompanied by the sum of £250 payable to the Bar Council to defray expenses, a sum to be refunded in the discretion of the Visitors in the event of an appeal which is successful wholly or in part.

(2)   In cases where no professional misconduct has been proved, but one or more charges of inadequate professional service have been proved, an appeal shall lie at the instance of the barrister from any such finding, and against any decision as to the remedy to be granted to the complainant for such service in the same manner as an appeal lies from a decision of an Adjudication Panel in respect of the same matters.

13.   Action by the Defendant's Inn

In a case where the sentence, where applicable as confirmed on appeal, includes an order under paragraph 9(b)(i) and on expiry of the period allowed for service of Notice of Appeal under Hearings before the Visitors Rules or on the conclusion of any appeal, whichever period is the longer, the Secretary of the PCC shall invite the Treasurers of the defendant's Inn of Call and of any other Inns of which he is a member to pronounce the sentence of suspension as at paragraph 9(g)(i) and to take such further action as may be required to carry it into effect. As seems to them fit, the Treasurer(s) will then pronounce the sentence and inform the Secretary of the PCC of the date on which it is to take effect.

14.   Publication of Finding and Sentence

(a) The finding and sentence of a summary hearing on any charge or charges of professional misconduct shall be published.

(b) When publishing any finding and sentence in accordance with sub-paragraph (a) above, the Secretary of the PCC shall communicate the same in writing to those listed in paragraph 11(b) of these Rules, together with the following:

(i)   The Director of Public Prosecutions.

(ii)   The Treasurers of all four Inns for screening.

(iii) The Leaders of the six circuits.

(iv)   One or more press agencies or other publications, as the Chairman of the PCC may direct.

(v)   In the case of a registered European lawyer, his home professional body.

(c) When the summary hearing has found that one or more charges of inadequate professional service have been proved, the charge and finding shall not be published unless the barrister charged so requests.

(d) When the Tribunal has found that any charge whether of professional misconduct or of inadequate professional service has not been proved the President shall not publish that charge and the finding unless the barrister charged so requests.

Commencement and Transitional Provisions

15.   (a) In relation to any summary hearing arising out of a complaint which had been referred to be Summary Procedure by the Professional Conduct Committee before 15th May 2000, these Rules shall not apply but the Summary Procedure Rules in force immediately before that date shall apply to that summary hearing save that paragraphs 5(a)(iii) and 7(e) of those rules shall apply only to cases referred to summary procedure on or after 17 July 1999.

(b) No finding of inadequate professional service may be made against a barrister in respect of any conduct of his which took place before 13th July 1996.

ANNEXE M

THE HEARINGS BEFORE THE VISITORS RULES 2002

[Amended 4 February 2002]

We, the Judges of Her Majesty's High Court of Justice, in the exercise of our powers as Visitors to the Inns of Court, hereby make the following rules for the purpose of appeals to the Visitors from Disciplinary Tribunals of the Council of the Inns of Court and certain other appeals to the Visitors:

Citation and Commencement

1. These rules may be cited as the Hearings before the Visitors Rules 2002 and shall come into effect on 4 February 2002.

Interpretation

2. (1) The Interpretation Act 1978 shall apply in relation to the interpretation of these Rules as it applies for the interpretation of an Act of Parliament.

    (2) In these Rules, unless the context otherwise requires

    'answer' means the answer served pursuant to rule 11;

    'appellant' means an appellant from an order of a tribunal;

    'appellant student' means a student disciplined by or expelled from an Inn of Court, or a person refused admission to an Inn of Court as a student, who is appealing to the Visitors;

    'appellant legal practitioner' means a legal practitioner wishing to appeal to the Visitors from a decision, on review, by the JRC under Part IV of the Consolidated Regulations of the Inns of Court;

    'JRC' means the Joint Consolidated Regulations and Transfer Committee of the Inns' Council and the Bar Council;

    'Bar Council' means The General Council of the Bar;

    'defendant' means the barrister against whom an order of a tribunal was made;

    'Directions Judge' means a Judge nominated pursuant to rule 5;

    'directions function' means any of the functions and powers conferred on a Directions Judge by rule 5;

    'the Inns' Council' means the Council of the Inns of Court;

    'lay representative' means one of the lay persons appointed by the Bar Council to serve on Disciplinary Tribunals;

    'petition' means the petition of appeal served pursuant to rule 7;

    'the tribunal' means a Disciplinary Tribunal of the Council of the Inns of Court and includes a panel appointed to hear a summary case under the Summary Procedure Rules to be found at Annex L to the Code of Conduct of the Bar of England and Wales; and

    'the Visitors' means the panel nominated to hear the appeal pursuant to rule 10 or, in the case of an appeal within rule 10(4) or (5), the single judge nominated to hear the appeal.

Service of Documents

3. (1) Where pursuant to these Rules any document is to be served on any of the persons specified in the first column of the table in the Schedule to these Rules, that document shall be served on that person by sending it to the person specified and the address specified in the second column of that table against the person to be served.

(2) Such documents shall be served

(a) by recorded delivery post,

(b) by hand delivery, if a written confirmation of receipt is obtained, or

(c) by facsimile transmission, if a return facsimile confirming receipt is obtained.

Notice of Appeal

4. (1) Written notice of intention to appeal against the finding or sentence of the tribunal must be served by the appellant on the persons specified in paragraph (2) below within the period of 21 days beginning with the date on which the order of the tribunal was made or within such further time as may be allowed by the Lord Chief Justice or the Directions Judge.

(2) The persons to be served are

(a) the Lord Chief Justice;

(b) the Chairman of the Bar Council (unless the Bar Council is the appellant);

(c) the President of the Inns' Council;

(d) the Treasurer of the Inn of which the appellant or defendant (as the case may be) is a member; and

(e) if the Bar Council is the appellant, the defendant.

(3) The notice of intention to appeal shall specify the Inn of which the appellant or defendant (as the case may be) is a member.

(4) When serving a notice of intention to appeal, an appellant other than the Bar Council shall also give notice of an address at which service is to be made on the appellant.

Directions Judge

5. (1) Upon service on him of a notice of appeal under rule 4 above (whether or not served in time) the Lord Chief Justice shall nominate a single judge of the High Court or the Court of Appeal ('the Directions Judge') who is not a Bencher of the appellant's or defendant's (as the case may be) Inn to exercise the powers and functions conferred by this rule.

(2) The Directions Judge may hold a hearing in order to determine how (if at all) he should exercise the directions functions.

(3) The Directions Judge shall consider the course of any appeal in relation to which he is appointed and may at any time give such directions and take such steps as appear to him to be necessary or desirable for the purpose of securing the just, expeditious and economical disposal of the appeal.

(4) The directions that may be given and the steps that may be taken by the Directions Judge may relate to (but shall not be limited to) the following matters

(a) the anticipated duration of the hearing;

(b) the variation of any timetable specified in these Rules;

(c) further procedural steps that should be taken before the hearing;

(d) the failure by either party to comply with any timetable specified in these Rules or directed by him; and

(e) the adjournment of the hearing.

(5)   The Directions Judge may, on application made by the appellant (which must be served on the Bar Council at the time of making the application) and after giving the Bar Council the opportunity to respond to the application, vary or set aside an order made against the appellant under regulation 27(2) or (3) of the Disciplinary Tribunal Rules on such terms and subject to such conditions (if any) as he considers appropriate.

(6)   If, at any time, the Directions Judge concludes that a party has failed to comply with any obligation imposed by, or timetable specified in, these Rules or directed by him in exercise of his directions functions (as the case may be), he may also

(a) make a final order for compliance by the party in default;

(b) direct that that party may not serve a petition or answer;

(c) dismiss or strike out the petition or answer of that party;

(d) order that any further step that appears to him to be necessary or desirable in order to provide for a fair and expeditious hearing of the matter be undertaken within a specified period;

(e) direct an expedited hearing where the party in default has been prohibited from serving an answer or the answer has been struck out.

(7)   If, on an application made by the appellant, the Directions Judge concludes that payment of the sum required by the Disciplinary Tribunal Rules or by the Summary Procedure Rules to defray the expenses of the appeal would cause undue hardship to the appellant, the Directions Judge shall direct that such sum shall not be payable and that the petition of appeal may be served notwithstanding rule 7(5) below, and may grant any extension of time necessary for serving the petition of appeal.

No appeal from Directions Judge

6.   There shall be no appeal against an order of the Directions Judge.

Service of Petition

7.   (1)   A written petition of appeal containing the information required by rule 8 below must be served by the appellant on the persons specified in paragraph (2) below within the period of 42 days beginning with the date on which the order of the tribunal was made or within such further time as may be allowed by the Lord Chief Justice or the Directions Judge.

(2)   The persons to be served are

(a) the Lord Chief Justice;

(b) the Chairman of the Bar Council (unless the Bar Council is the appellant);

(c) the President of the Inns' Council;

(d) the Treasurer of the Inn of which the appellant or defendant (as the case may be) is a member; and

(e) if the Bar Council is the appellant, the defendant.

(3)   If an application for an extension of the period of 42 days specified in paragraph (1) above is made to the Lord Chief Justice or the Directions Judge before the expiry of that period, the Lord Chief Justice or the Directions Judge may, if he sees fit, extend the period within which the petition must be served.

(4)   Where no petition is served within the period specified in paragraph (1) above or (where that period has been extended pursuant to paragraph (3)) the extended period, no further action may be taken in relation to the appeal unless the Lord Chief Justice directs otherwise.

(5)   A petition of appeal may not be served, subject to any direction of the Directions Judge to the contrary under rule 5(7) above, unless any sum payable under the Disciplinary Tribunals Regulations or under the Summary Procedure Rules to defray the expenses of the appeal has been paid to the Bar Council.

Petition of Appeal

8.   (1)   The petition shall state whether the appeal is against the findings or sentence of the tribunal, or both.

(2)   The petition shall contain the following particulars

(a) the charges;

(b) a summary of the facts on which the charges were based;

(c) the findings of the tribunal;

(d) the sentence;

(e) any finding against which the appellant appeals (if any);

(f) the grounds for appeal, including for each matter appealed against the specific evidence on which the appellant will place reliance;

(g) the relief sought.

(h) if the hearing is estimated to last longer than one day, an estimate of the time required for the hearing.

(3)   In the case of an appeal against sentence the petition may also refer to

(a) any factors which it is contended make the sentence unduly severe (or lenient) in relation to the appellant's (or the defendant's) record; and

(b) to sentences in other similar cases.

Service of other documents

9.   (1)   Subject to paragraph (2) below, the appellant shall, at the same time as serving the petition, serve on the Lord Chief Justice the number of copies specified in paragraph (4) below of the transcript of the proceedings before the tribunal whose decision is being appealed or, where the tribunal in question was a panel appointed to hear a summary matter, the statement of findings and sentence of the tribunal.

(2)   If any transcript to be served pursuant to paragraph (1) above is not available when the petition is served, the copies of that transcript shall be served on the Lord Chief Justice as soon as practicable thereafter.

(3)   Not less than 14 days before the date set for the hearing of an appeal

(a) a copy of every document intended to be produced at the hearing by any party shall be served by that party on every other party; and

(b) the number of copies of any such document specified in paragraph (4) below shall be served on the Lord Chief Justice.

(4)   The number of copies required to be served on the Lord Chief Justice is

(a) if the appeal is of a type falling within rule 10(2) below, five copies; and

(b) in any other case, three copies.

Appointment of panel to hear appeal

10. (1)   When a petition is served upon him (whether or not served in time), the Lord Chief Justice shall, nominate the persons who are to hear the appeal.

(2)   An appeal against an order for disbarment or a decision of a tribunal presided over by a Judge of the High Court shall be heard by a panel comprised of

(a) three judges of the High Court or the Court of Appeal (one of whom may be a retired judge of the High Court or Court of Appeal, provided that he has not attained the age of 75 on the date set for the hearing of the appeal);

(b) a Queen's Counsel; and

(c) a lay representative.

(3)   Subject to paragraph (4) below, an appeal that is not of a type mentioned in paragraph (2) and is an appeal against a decision of a Disciplinary Tribunal shall be heard by panel comprised of

(a) a Judge of the High Court or the Court of Appeal;

(b) a barrister; and

(c) a lay representative.

(4)   An appeal that is not of a type mentioned in paragraph (2) and that is an appeal against a decision of a Disciplinary Tribunal may be heard by a Judge of the High Court or of the Court of Appeal sitting alone, if the Lord Chief Justice or the Directions Judge directs that the appeal relates solely to a point of law and is appropriate to be heard by a judge sitting alone.

(5)   Any other appeal shall be heard by a Judge of the High Court or the Court of Appeal.

(6)   No judge or barrister member of the panel shall be a Bencher of the appellant's or defendant's (as the case may be) Inn.

Answer

11. (1)   The Bar Council or, if the Bar Council is the appellant, the defendant may (or, if so directed by the Directions Judge, shall) serve on the Lord Chief Justice an answer to the petition within the period of 28 days starting with the date on which the petition is served or such further time as may be allowed by the Directions Judge.

(2)   Where an answer is served pursuant to paragraph (1) the person serving it shall also serve forthwith a copy of that answer on the appellant.

(3)   The answer shall follow the form of the petition and shall state which points in the petition are accepted and which are rejected.

(4)   The Bar Council may, in any answer it serves, refer to any factors which it is contended make the sentence unduly lenient in relation to the appellant's record or to sentences in other cases.

(5)   If, in the view of the person serving an answer, the hearing is likely to last longer than one day, the answer shall include an estimation of the time required for the hearing and the reasons for that estimation.

Date of Hearing

12. (1)   Unless it has been indicated either in the petition or answer that the time required for the hearing is likely to exceed one day, the time allocated for the hearing of an appeal shall be one day.

(2)   The appeal shall be listed by the clerk to the Visitors for a hearing on the first available date after the expiry of a period of four weeks beginning with the date of service on the Lord Chief Justice of the answer (or, where no answer is served, beginning with the last date for service of the answer under rule 11 above).

(3)   A notice of the hearing of the appeal shall be served on the Bar Council and on the appellant or defendant (as the case may be) at least 14 days before the date fixed for hearing of the appeal.

Procedure at hearing

13.   (1)   Subject to the following paragraphs of this Rule, the Visitors may give any directions with regard to the conduct of, and procedure at, a hearing of an appeal they consider appropriate.

(2)   The Visitors may give such directions before or during the hearing.

(3)   The hearing shall be held in public unless either party has made an application that the hearing shall not be in public and the public interest does not require that it shall be held in public.

(4)   A hearing may proceed in the absence of an appellant (or defendant), but not in the absence of a representative of the Bar Council.

(5)   No witness may be called at the hearing without the consent of the Visitors.

(6)   Evidence that was not before the tribunal whose decision is being appealed may be given at the hearing only in exceptional circumstances and with the consent of the Visitors.

(7)   An appellant or defendant (as the case may be) may only challenge before the Visitors a decision of a court of law on which the tribunal's decision was based in exceptional circumstances and with the consent of the Visitors.

(8)   The proceedings of the Visitors shall continue to be valid notwithstanding that one or more of the members of the panel becomes unable to continue or is or becomes disqualified from continuing to act, if the remaining members of the panel include a judge (other than a retired judge) and a lay representative.

(9)   A full shorthand record shall be made of the hearing.

(10)   A transcription of the shorthand record shall be provided upon request to either party to the hearing but at his own expense.

Findings of the Visitors

14.   (1)   The findings of the Visitors shall be pronounced in a single decision.

(2)   The findings may be pronounced in public or in private but should normally be pronounced in public unless a party to the hearing requests otherwise and the public interest does not require that the findings be pronounced in public.

(3)   The Visitors may

(a) allow an appeal in whole or in part;

(b) confirm or vary an order of the tribunal whose decision is being appealed;

(c) order a re-hearing on such terms as they may deem appropriate in the circumstances.

(4)   The Visitors shall give reasons for their decision.

(5)   The Visitors may order, in the event of an appeal which is successful wholly or in part, a refund to the appellant of any sum paid to the General Council of the Bar in accordance with the Disciplinary Tribunal Regulations of the Inns' Council.

Barrister's Exclusion from providing representation funded by the Legal Services Commission as part of the Community Legal Service or Criminal Defence Service

15.   (1)   These Rules shall apply in relation to an appeal against an order of the tribunal that a barrister's exclusion from providing representation funded by the Legal Services Commission as part of the Community Legal Service or Criminal Defence Service pursuant to section 42(3) of the Administration of Justice Act 1985 (as substituted by Section 33 of the Legal Aid Act 1988 and amended by section 24, Schedule 4, paragraphs 32 and 35 of the Access to Justice Act 1999) is not to be terminated, subject to the following modifications set out in the following paragraphs of this rule.

(2)   The petition shall contain the following particulars

(a) the date of the order of the tribunal that excluded the appellant from providing representation funded by the Legal Services Commission as part of the Community Legal Service or Criminal Defence Service;

(b) the charges in respect of which that order was made;

(c) a summary of the facts on which those charges were based;

(d) the findings of the tribunal;

(e) the findings against which the appeal is brought; and

(f) the grounds for appeal.

(3)   An order of the tribunal to terminate a barrister's exclusion from providing representation funded by the Legal Services Commission as part of the Community Legal Service or Criminal Defence Service only from a date that is subsequent to that order shall, for the purposes of any appeal, be treated as an order that the barrister's exclusion from such work is not to be terminated.

Appeals by an appellant student against a decision of an Inn

16.   (1)   These Rules shall apply in relation to an appeal by an appellant student against a decision of an Inn subject to the modifications set out in the following paragraphs of this rule.

(2)   In rules 4 and 7 references to the order, finding or sentence of the tribunal shall be construed as references to the decision of the Inn.

(3)   Any documents required by rules 4 or 7 to be served shall, in place of the persons specified in those rules, be served on

(a) the Lord Chief Justice;

(b) the Chairman of the Bar Council;

(c) the President of the Inns' Council;

(d) and the Treasurer of the Inn of which the appellant student is a member or the Treasurer of the Inn that has refused to admit the appellant student.

(4)   There shall be substituted for rule 8

'8. The petition shall contain the following particulars:

(a)   the decision of the Inn against which the appeal is brought;

(b)   a summary of the facts giving rise to the decision of the Inn;

(c)   the grounds for appeal; and

(d) the relief sought.'

(5) Paragraphs (1) and (2) of rule 9 shall not apply.

(6) The appellant student shall serve on the Lord Chief Justice, with the petition, copies of all relevant documents including any complaint in respect of the appellant and the decision of the Inn.

(7) In paragraph (3) of rule 9, for the persons specified as the persons to be served there shall be substituted the persons specified in paragraph (3) of this rule.

(8) In paragraph (1) of rule 11 and paragraph (4) of rule 13 references to the Bar Council shall be construed as references to the Inn in question.

(9) There shall be substituted for paragraph (4) of rule 11

'(4) The Inn may, in any answer it serves, refer to any factors that it took into account when making its decision, including the appellant student's record and the Inn's practice in similar cases.'

(10) Paragraphs (3) and (5) of rule 14 shall not apply.

(11) The panel appointed to hear the appeal may

(a) allow an appeal in whole or in part;

(b) confirm or vary the decision of the Inn; or

(c) order the Inn to reconsider its decision on such terms as the Visitors may determine to be appropriate in the circumstances.

(12) Rules 15 and 18 shall not apply.

Appeals not permitted under these Rules

17. (1) No appeal shall lie under these Rules from a decision of an educational institution (other than an Inn) or any officer or committee of such an institution in respect of any matter relating to a course recognised by the Bar Council as satisfying

(a) the requirements of the Academic Stage of Training for the Bar (including Common Professional Examination requirements),

(b) the Vocational Stage of Training for the Bar, or

(c) the Stage of Continuing Education and Training at the Bar, or any examination or assessment in connection with any such course.

(2) An appeal from a decision of a type mentioned in paragraph (1) above shall be made through the appropriate appeal procedures of the institution concerned.

Appeals by an appellant legal practitioner

18. (1) In an appeal by an appellant legal practitioner, these Rules shall apply subject to the modifications set out in the following paragraphs of this rule.

(2) In rules 4 and 7 any reference to the order, finding or sentence of the tribunal shall be construed as a reference to the decision, on review, of the JRC.

(3) Any documents required by rules 4 and 7 to be served shall, in place of the persons specified in those rules, be served on

(a) the JRC;

(b) the Lord Chief Justice;

(c) the Chairman of the Bar Council; and

(d) the President of the Inns' Council.

(4) There shall be substituted for rule 8

'8. The petition shall contain the following particulars

    (a)   the decision, on review, of the JRC against which the appeal is being made;

    (b)   a summary of the facts giving rise to that decision;

    (c)   the grounds for appeal; and

    (d)   the relief sought.'

(6)   Paragraphs (1) and (2) of rule 9 shall not apply but the appellant legal practitioner shall serve on the Lord Chief Justice with the petition copies of any relevant documents, which shall include the decision of the JRC against which the appeal is brought.

(7)   In paragraph (3) of rule 9, for the persons specified as the persons to be served there shall be substituted the persons specified in paragraph (1) of this rule.

(8)   In paragraph (1) of rule 11 and paragraph (4) of rule 13 the references to the Bar Council shall be construed as references to the JRC.

(9)   There shall be substituted for paragraph (4) of rule 11

    '(4)   The JRC may, in any answer it serves, refer to any factors that it took into account when making its decision, including the appellant legal practitioner's record and the JRC's practice in similar cases.'

(10)   Paragraphs (3) and (5) of rule 14 shall not apply.

(11)   The panel appointed to hear the appeal may

    (a) allow an appeal in whole or in part;

    (b) confirm or vary the decision of the JRC; or

    (c) order the JRC to reconsider its decision on such terms as the panel appointed to hear the appeal may determine to be appropriate in the circumstances.

(12)   Rules 15 and 16 shall not apply.

Costs

19.   (1)   The Visitors may make such order for costs of the appeal as they consider appropriate.

(2)   Any order for costs made may include an order for payment of the cost of any transcript required for the purposes of the appeal.

Transition

20.   (1)   Subject to paragraph (2) below, where any appeal has been commenced before 4th February 2002 but has not been completed by that date, these Rules shall apply to that appeal from that date but any steps that have been taken in relation to that appeal pursuant to any provision of the Hearings Before the Visitors Rules 2000 shall be regarded as having been taken pursuant to the equivalent provision of these Rules.

(2)   In relation to appeals brought by students registered at the Inns of Court School of Law before 1 September 1997, the procedure provided by Rule 13 of the Hearings before the Visitors Rules 1991 shall continue to apply in place of that provided by these Rules.

Revocation

22.   The Hearings before the Visitors Rules 2000 are hereby revoked.

On behalf of the Judges of Her Majesty's
High Court of Justice

Lord Chancellor
Lord Chief Justice
President
Vice-Chancellor

SCHEDULE   Rule 3(1)

ADDRESSEE AND PLACE FOR SERVICE OF DOCUMENTS

Person to be served	Addressee and place of service
The Lord Chief Justice.	Addressed to the Clerk to the Visitors at the Royal Courts of Justice, Strand, London WC2A 2LL.
The President of the inns' Council.	Addressed to the Secretary to the Council of the Inns of Court at Treasury Office, Inner Temple, London EC4Y 7HL.
The Chairman of the Bar Council.	Addressed to the Chief Executive of the General Council of the Bar at 3 Bedford Row, London, WC1R 4DB.
The JRC.	Addressed to the Chief Executive of the General Council of the Bar at 3 Bedford Row, London, WC1R 4DB.
The Treasurer of an Inn.	Addressed to the Sub-Treasurer or Under-Treasurer (as the case may be) of that Inn at the treasury office of that Inn.
An appellant, appellant student or appellant legal practitioner.	Addressed to him at the address specified by him pursuant to rule 6(3).
A defendant.	Addressed to him at— (a) the address notified by him pursuant to Paragraphs 304(a)(i) or 402(a) of the Code of Conduct of the Bar of England and Wales (or any provisions amending or replacing those paragraphs); (b) if he has specified in writing an address to which documents may be sent, that address; or (c) where no address has been notified pursuant to the provisions mentioned in paragraph (a) above or specified as mentioned in paragraph (b) above, to his last known address.

ANNEXE N

INTERIM SUSPENSION RULES

Introduction

1. These Rules are supplemental to:

   (a) the Complaints Rules;

   (b) the Disciplinary Tribunals Regulations; and

   (c) the Summary Procedure Rules;

   as approved from time to time and annexed to the Code of Conduct of the Bar of England and Wales.

Definitions

2. In these Rules:

   (a) 'the Commissioner' means the Complaints Commissioner;

   (b) 'Suspension Panel' means a Suspension Panel as provided for in rule 3 of these Rules;

   (c) 'Appeal Panel' means an Appeal Panel as provided for in rule 4 of these Rules;

   (d) 'Lay Representative' means a lay person appointed by the Bar Council to serve on Disciplinary Tribunals;

   (e) 'the Defendant' means the barrister who is the subject of a referral to a Suspension Panel pursuant to the procedure prescribed by these Rules.

Composition of Panels

3. A Suspension Panel shall consist of five members nominated by the Chairman of the PCC being:

   (a) the Chairman of the PCC or, if unable to attend, a Vice-Chairman of the PCC, who shall be Chairman of the Panel;

   (b) three other barristers of at least ten years Call one of whom shall be a Queen's Counsel and who are current members of the PCC or the PSC;

   (c) a Lay Representative

   Provided that:

   (1) no barrister (save for the Chairman or a Vice Chairman of the PCC) or Lay Representative shall be nominated to serve on a Panel which is to consider any matter which has been considered at any meeting of the PCC which he attended; and

   (2) the proceedings of a Suspension Panel shall be valid notwithstanding that one or more of the members other than the Chairman or Lay Representative becomes unable to continue to act or disqualified from continuing to act, so long as the number of members present throughout the substantive hearing is not reduced below three and continues to include the Chairman and the Lay Representative.

4. An Appeal Panel shall consist of:

   (a) The Chairman of the Bar or, if unable to attend, the Vice-Chairman, who shall be Chairman of the Panel;

(b) a representative nominated by the Treasurer of the Defendant's Inn;

(c) a Lay Representative

Provided that no individual shall sit on both the Suspension Panel and the Appeal Panel considering the same matter.

Referral to a Suspension Panel

5. Upon the Bar Council receiving notification from a barrister that he has been convicted of or charged with a Serious Criminal Offence, the Commissioner and/or the PCC shall consider whether to refer the matter to a Suspension Panel.

6. Either the Commissioner or the PCC may refer a matter to a Suspension Panel if:

(a) the matter has been referred to the Commissioner or the PCC under rule 5 above; or

(b) a complaint has been referred to the Commissioner or the PCC during the investigation of which it is disclosed that a barrister has been convicted of or charged with a Serious Criminal Offence; or

(c) in any other circumstances it is disclosed to the Commissioner or the PCC that a barrister has been convicted of or charged with a Serious Criminal Offence.

No matter shall be referred to a Suspension Panel unless the Commissioner or the PCC considers that the conviction(s) or criminal charge(s) (if such charge(s) were subsequently to lead to conviction(s)) would warrant a charge of professional misconduct and referral to a Disciplinary Tribunal.

7. As soon as practicable after the decision has been made to refer a matter to a Suspension Panel, the Secretary of the PCC shall write to the Defendant notifying him of the decision, together with a copy of these Rules, giving brief details of the conviction(s) or criminal charge(s) that have caused the referral to the Panel. The letter of notification:

(a) shall lay down a fixed time and date (normally not less than fourteen and not more than twenty-one days from the date of the letter) for the hearing to take place. One alternative shall be given;

(b) shall invite the Defendant to accept one or other of the dates proposed or to provide a written representation to the Chairman of the PCC, objecting to both dates with reasons and providing two further alternative dates not more than twenty-one days from the date of the letter of notification. Any such representation must be received by the Chairman of the PCC not more than fourteen days from the date of the letter of notification. The Chairman of the PCC shall consider any such representation and either confirm one of the original dates or re-fix the hearing. If no such representation is received within fourteen days of the date of the letter of notification the hearing shall take place at the time and date first fixed pursuant to rule 7(a) above. The Chairman's decision, which shall be notified in writing to the Defendant by the Secretary of the PCC, shall be final. Once fixed, a hearing date shall be vacated only in exceptional circumstances and with the agreement of the Chairman of the PCC;

(c) shall inform the Defendant that he may by letter to the Chairman of the PCC undertake immediately to be suspended from practice pending the disposal of any charges of professional misconduct by a Disciplinary Tribunal based on the conviction(s) or criminal charge(s) that have caused the referral to the Panel;

(d) shall inform the Defendant that he is entitled to make representations in writing or orally, by himself or by another member of the Bar on his behalf:

(1)   where a conviction or convictions have caused the referral to the Panel, as to whether a period of interim suspension should be imposed; or

(2)   where a criminal charge or charges have caused the referral to the Panel, as to whether and if so in what terms any notification should be given to professional clients and lay clients and the conditions subject to which the Defendant should be permitted to continue to practice;

pending the disposal of any charges of professional misconduct by a Disciplinary Tribunal;

(e) shall inform the Defendant that he is entitled to request an expedited hearing of any charges of professional misconduct by a Disciplinary Tribunal.

8.   If a Defendant sends a letter in accordance with rule 7(c) above which is satisfactory to the Chairman of the PCC the Chairman shall accept the undertaking contained in the letter in lieu of imposing a period of interim suspension and so inform the Defendant in writing, whereupon the Defendant shall immediately be suspended from practice until after the disposal by a Disciplinary Tribunal of any charges of professional misconduct based on the conviction(s) or criminal charges(s) that have caused.

Powers of Suspension Panels

9.   If, prior to the date fixed for a hearing under rules 7(a) or (b) above, a Defendant shall not have produced a letter in accordance with rule 7(c) above satisfactory to the Chairman of the PCC, a Suspension Panel nominated in accordance with rule 3 above shall, at the time and place notified to the Defendant in accordance with rules 7(a) or (b) above, consider:

(a) where a conviction or convictions have caused the referral to the Panel, whether a period of interim suspension should be imposed on the Defendant;

(b) where a criminal charge or charges have caused the referral to the Panel, whether the Defendant should be directed to notify his professional clients and lay clients of the criminal offence(s) with which he has been charged before undertaking any work or (as the case may be) further work for any such client.

10. At any hearing of a Suspension Panel the proceedings shall be governed by the rules of natural justice, subject to which:

(a) the procedure shall be informal, the details being at the discretion of the Chairman of the Panel;

(b) the Defendant shall be entitled to make representations in writing or orally, by himself or by another member of the Bar or a solicitor on his behalf, as to;

(1)   where a conviction or convictions have caused the referral to the Panel, why a period of interim suspension should not be imposed; or

(2)   where a criminal charge or charges have caused the referral to the Panel, why the Panel should not direct that the Defendant should notify his professional clients and lay clients of the criminal offence(s) with which he has been charged before undertaking any work or (as the case may be) further work for any such client;

pending the disposal of any charges of professional misconduct by a Disciplinary Tribunal;

(c) no witnesses may be called without the prior consent of the Chairman of the Panel and without the submission of a proof of evidence;

(d) the attendance of the Defendant shall be required. Should he nevertheless fail to attend, the hearing may proceed in his absence, subject to the Panel being satisfied that this course is appropriate, that all relevant procedures requiring the Defendant's attendance have been complied with and that no acceptable explanation for the Defendant's absence has been provided. Should the Panel not be so satisfied, it shall have the power to adjourn the hearing;

(e) the hearing shall not be in public unless so requested by the Defendant and a record shall be taken electronically. The tape of the hearing shall be retained under the arrangements of the Secretary of the PCC for two years or until any charges of professional misconduct against the Defendant based on the convictions or criminal charges which caused the referral to the Panel have been finally disposed of by a Disciplinary Tribunal and any appeal procedure has been exhausted whichever period is the longer;

(f) if it decides an adjournment is necessary for any reason, the Panel may adjourn the hearing for such period and to such time and place, and upon such terms, as it may think fit.

11.   If the members of a Suspension Panel are not unanimous as to any decision the decision made shall be that of the majority of them. If the members of the Panel are equally divided the decision shall be that which is the most favourable to the Defendant.

12.   Where a conviction or convictions have caused the referral to a Suspension Panel, at the conclusion of the hearing the Panel:

(a) may decide not to impose any period of interim suspension;

(b) may impose a period of interim suspension (either unconditionally or subject to conditions) of up to six months pending the hearing before a Disciplinary Tribunal, provided that no period of interim suspension should be imposed unless the Panel considers that it is likely that a Disciplinary Tribunal would impose a sentence of disbarment or suspension for more than twelve months for a charge or charges of professional misconduct based on the conviction or convictions that have caused the referral to the Panel and it considers that it is in the public interest that the Defendant should be suspended pending the hearing before a Disciplinary Tribunal.

(c) in lieu of imposing a period of suspension may accept from the Defendant an undertaking in writing in terms satisfactory to the Panel (and subject to such conditions and for such period as the Panel may agree) immediately to be suspended from practice pending the disposal of any charges of professional misconduct by a Disciplinary Tribunal based on the conviction or convictions that have caused the referral to the Panel;

(d) shall set down in writing signed by the Chairman of the Panel the decision of the Panel and the terms of any period of interim suspension imposed under rule 12(b) above or undertaking accepted under rule 12(c) above. The imposition of any period of suspension shall be recorded as follows:

' That ... be suspended from practice as a barrister and from enjoyment of all rights and privileges as a member of the Honourable Society of ... and be prohibited from holding himself out as being a barrister without disclosing his interim suspension for a period expiring on the ... day of ... or such earlier date as a Disciplinary Tribunal shall have disposed of any charges based on the conviction or convictions that have caused the interim suspension or such Disciplinary Tribunal may otherwise direct.' (Note: If the Panel decides that the suspension should apply to part only of the Defendant's practice or shall be subject to conditions, such part or such conditions (as the case may be) shall be recorded.)

(e) shall, if a period of interim suspension is imposed under rule 12(b) above or a written undertaking is accepted under rule 12(c) above:

(1) fix a time and date within the period of suspension imposed, alternatively inform the Defendant that such a time and date will be fixed by the Secretary of the PCC and notified to the Defendant not less than fourteen days prior to such date, when, unless a Disciplinary Tribunal shall in the meantime have disposed of any charges of professional misconduct based on the conviction or convictions that have caused the referral to the Panel, a Panel shall be convened for the purpose of reviewing the matter;

(2) inform the Defendant of his right to request a Panel to review the matter prior to the date fixed in (1) above as provided in rule 14 below;

(3) inform the Defendant of his right of appeal as provided in rule 16 below;

(4) inform the Defendant that he is entitled to request an expedited hearing of any charges of professional misconduct by a Disciplinary Tribunal and, if so requested, the Chairman of the Panel may so direct;

(f) may, if it has not already been referred to a Disciplinary Tribunal, refer the matter to a disciplinary Tribunal.

13. Where a criminal charge or charges have caused the referral to a Suspension Panel, at the conclusion of the hearing the Panel:

(a) may decide to make no direction as to the conduct of the Defendant's practice;

(b) may decide to direct the Defendant to notify his professional clients and lay clients of the criminal offence(s) with which he has been charged, in which case the Panel shall set out the terms of the written notification to be given (for such period as the Panel may think fit) to such clients and may include such comments as the Defendant may wish to make and the Panel may approve concerning the criminal charge(s). In addition to directing the notification of professional clients and lay clients, the Panel may direct that the conduct of Defendant's practice shall be subject to such conditions as the Panel may think fit;

(c) in lieu of making any direction under rule 13(b) above the Panel may accept one or more undertakings in writing in such terms and upon such conditions as the Panel may think fit as to the form of written notification to be given to any professional client or lay client and as to the conduct of the Defendant's practice;

(d) shall set down in writing signed by the Chairman of the Panel the terms of any direction or undertaking accepted under rules 13(b) or (c) above together with a copy or copies of the letter or letters approved as the form of notification to professional clients and lay clients;

(e) shall, if any direction is given or undertaking accepted under rules 12(a) or (b) above limited to any specified period:

(1) fix a time and date within that period, alternatively inform the Defendant that such a time and date will be fixed by the Secretary of the PCC and notified to the Defendant not less than fourteen days prior to the expiration of such period when, unless a Disciplinary Tribunal shall in the meantime have disposed of any charges of professional misconduct based on the criminal charge or

charges that have caused the referral to the Panel, a Panel shall be convened for the purpose of reviewing the matter;

(2) inform the Defendant of his right to request a Panel to review the matter prior to the date fixed in (1) above as provided in rule 14 below;

(3) inform the Defendant of his right of appeal as provided in rule 16 below;

(4) inform the Defendant that he is entitled to request an expedited hearing of any charges of professional misconduct by a Disciplinary Tribunal and, if so requested, the Chairman of the Panel may so direct;

(f) may, if not already referred to a Disciplinary Tribunal, refer the matter to a Disciplinary Tribunal.

14. In the event of a significant change in circumstances or other good reason the Defendant may at any time while suspended pursuant to a decision of a Suspension Panel or an undertaking under rules 12(b) or (c) above or subject to a direction or undertaking under rules 12(b) or (c) make a request in writing to the Chairman of the PCC for a Panel to be convened to review the matter. The letter must set out the details of any alleged change in circumstances or good reason. On receipt of such a letter the Chairman may in his discretion convene a Panel or refuse the request. In either case the Secretary of the PCC shall notify the Defendant in writing of the Chairman's decision. The Chairman shall not be obliged to give reasons and his decision shall be final. If the Chairman decides to convene a Panel the procedure to be followed for fixing the time and date of the hearing shall be as set out in rules 7(a) and (b) above.

15. Unless in the meantime the hearing before a Disciplinary Tribunal of any charges based on the conviction(s) or criminal charge(s) which had caused the referral to a Suspension Panel has commenced, a hearing by a Suspension Panel convened pursuant to rules 12(e)(1), 13(e)(1) or 14 above shall take place at the time and date fixed. Such hearing shall be a rehearing of the matter by the Panel which may reconsider the matter as if there had been no previous hearing. The provisions of rules 10, 11, 12 and 13 above shall apply at the first and any subsequent reconsideration of the matter save that in imposing any further period of interim suspension the Panel shall have regard to the length of any period of suspension already served by the Defendant. If the hearing before a Disciplinary Tribunal of any charges based on the conviction(s) or criminal charge(s) which had caused the referral to a Suspension Panel has commenced before the date fixed for a rehearing by a Suspension Panel, such date shall be vacated and any interim suspension or the terms of any direction made or undertaking accepted by a Suspension Panel shall continue until such charges have been disposed of by the Disciplinary Tribunal.

16. A Defendant may by letter served on the Secretary of the PCC not more than fourteen days after the date of the relevant decision of a Suspension Panel give notice of his wish to appeal against the decision.

17. Unless a Disciplinary Tribunal shall otherwise direct, any period of interim suspension shall cease or the Defendant shall cease to be bound by the terms of any direction made or undertaking accepted by a Suspension Panel or an Appeal Panel immediately upon:

(a) all charges of professional misconduct based on the conviction(s) or criminal charge(s) which had caused the referral to a Suspension Panel being disposed of by a Disciplinary Tribunal;

(b) any appeal by the Defendant against the conviction or all the conviction(s) which had caused the referral to a Suspension Panel being successful;

(c) the acquittal of the Defendant of the criminal charge or all the criminal charges which had caused the referral to a Suspension Panel;

(d) the criminal charge or all the criminal charges which had caused the referral to a Suspension Panel being withdrawn.

Appeals

18. As soon as practicable after receipt of a letter in accordance with rule 16 above the Secretary of the PCC shall convene an Appeal Panel and write to the Defendant notifying him of a fixed time and date (normally not less than fourteen and not more than twenty-one days from the date of receipt of the letter) for the hearing to take place. The Defendant may make a written representation, addressed to the Chairman of the proposed Appeal Panel, objecting to the date with reasons and providing two further alternative dates. Any such representation must be received by the Chairman of the Appeal Panel not more than fourteen days from the date of the letter of notification. The Chairman shall consider any such representation and either confirm the original date or re-fix the hearing. If no such representation is received within ten days of the date of the letter of notification the hearing shall take place at the time and date originally notified to the Defendant. The Chairman's decision, which shall be notified in writing to the Defendant by the Secretary of the PCC, shall be final. Once fixed, a hearing date shall be vacated only in exceptional circumstances and with the agreement of the Chairman of the Appeal Panel.

19. The proceedings before an Appeal Panel shall be by way of a rehearing and the provisions of rule 10 above shall apply as if for references therein to the Suspension Panel and the Chairman of the Suspension Panel there were substituted references respectively to the Appeal Panel and the Chairman of the Appeal Panel.

20. Where the appeal concerns a period of interim suspension, at the conclusion of the hearing the Appeal Panel:

(a) may remove the period of interim suspension and/or any conditions attached thereto;

(b) may confirm the period of interim suspension (subject to any conditions), impose further or alternative conditions, or substitute such shorter period (either unconditionally or subject to conditions) as may be thought fit;

(c) in lieu of confirming or imposing a period of interim suspension, may accept from the Defendant in terms satisfactory to the Chairman of the Panel an undertaking in writing to continue to be suspended from practice (subject to such conditions and for such period as the Panel may agree) pending the disposal of any charges of professional misconduct by a Disciplinary Tribunal based on the conviction or convictions that have caused the referral to the Panel;

(d) shall set down in writing signed by the Chairman of the Panel the decision of the Panel and the terms of any interim suspension confirmed or imposed under rule 20(b) above or undertaking accepted under rule 20(c) above. If the members of the Panel are not unanimous as to the decision the decision made shall be that of the majority of them. Any period of suspension which is confirmed or imposed shall be recorded as set out in rule 12(d) above;

(e) shall, if a period of interim suspension is confirmed, imposed or the subject of a written undertaking under rule 20(c) above:

(1) confirm or fix a time and date within the period of the interim suspension, alternatively inform the Defendant that such a time and date will be confirmed

or fixed by the Secretary of the PCC and notified to the Defendant not less than fourteen days prior to such date, when, unless a Disciplinary Tribunal shall in the meantime have disposed of any charges of professional misconduct based on the conviction or convictions that caused the referral to the Suspension Panel, a Suspension Panel shall be convened for the purpose of reviewing the matter;

(2) inform the Defendant of his right to request a Suspension Panel to review the matter prior to the date confirmed or fixed under (1) above as provided in rule 14 above;

(3) inform the Defendant that he is entitled to request an expedited hearing of any charges of professional misconduct by a Disciplinary Tribunal and, if so requested, the Chairman of the Panel may so direct;

(f) may, if it has not already been referred to a Disciplinary Tribunal, refer the matter to a Disciplinary Tribunal.

21. Where the appeal concerns a direction made or undertaking accepted under rules 13(b) or (c) above, at the conclusion of the hearing the Appeal Panel:

(a) may confirm, remove or modify any direction previously given by the Suspension Panel, subject to such conditions as to the Defendant's practice as the Panel may think fit;

(b) in lieu of any direction under rule 21(a) above the Panel may accept one or more written undertakings in such terms and upon such conditions as the Panel may think fit as to the form of written notification to be given to any professional client or lay client and as to the conduct of the Defendant's practice;

(c) shall set down in writing signed by the Chairman of the Panel the decision of the Panel and the terms of any direction made or undertaking accepted under rules 21(a) or (b) above together with a copy or copies of the letter or letters approved as the form of notification to professional clients and lay clients;

(d) shall, if any direction is confirmed or modified or undertaking accepted under rule 21(b) above limited to any specified period:

(1) confirm or fix a time and date within that period, alternatively inform the Defendant that such a time and date will be fixed by the Secretary of the PCC and notified to the Defendant not less than fourteen days prior to the expiration of such period when, unless a Disciplinary Tribunal shall in the meantime have disposed of any charges of professional misconduct based on the criminal charge or charges that caused the referral to the Suspension Panel, a Suspension Panel shall be convened for the purpose of reviewing the matter;

(2) inform the Defendant of his right to request a Suspension Panel to review the matter prior to the date fixed in (1) above as provided in rule 14 above;

(3) inform the Defendant that he is entitled to request an expedited hearing of any charges of professional misconduct by a Disciplinary Tribunal and, if so requested, the Chairman of the Panel may so direct;

(e) may, if it has not already been referred to a Disciplinary Tribunal, refer the matter to a Disciplinary Tribunal.

22. A pending appeal to an Appeal Panel shall not operate as a stay of any period of interim suspension or the terms of any direction or undertaking which is the subject of the appeal.

23. There shall be no right of appeal from the decision of an Appeal Panel.

Costs

24.   A Suspension Panel and an Appeal Panel shall have no power to award costs.

Report and Publication of Decisions

25.   As soon as practicable after the conclusion of a Suspension Panel hearing or an Appeal Panel hearing, the Secretary of the PCC shall confirm the decision to the Defendant in writing.

26.   In any case where a period of interim suspension is imposed or an undertaking from a Defendant is accepted as a consequence of which he is suspended from practice (either unconditionally or subject to conditions) the Secretary of the PCC shall communicate brief details thereof in writing to the following:

(a) the Lord Chancellor;

(b) the Lord Chief Justice;

(c) the Attorney General;

(d) the Director of Public Prosecutions;

(e) the President of the Council of the Inns of Court;

(f) the Chairman of the Bar Council;

(g) the Leaders of the six circuits;

(h) the Chairman of the PCC;

(i) the Defendant;

(j) the Defendant's head of chambers;

(k) the Treasurers of the Defendant's Inn of Call and of any other Inns of which he is a member;

(l) such one or more press agencies or other publications, as the Chairman of the PCC may direct.

Save in cases where interim suspension is followed by a sentence of disbarment or suspension from practice imposed by a Disciplinary Tribunal, if a Defendant ceases for whatever reason to be suspended from practice the Secretary of the PCC shall communicate brief details of the circumstances in which the Defendant has ceased to be suspended from practice to all the persons and agencies to which brief details of the interim suspension had previously been communicated pursuant to this rule.

27.   In any case where a direction is made requiring notification of a criminal charge or charges to professional clients and lay clients or any undertaking is accepted under rules 13(c) and 21(b) above the Secretary of the PCC shall communicate brief details thereof in writing to the following:

(a) the Lord Chancellor;

(b) the Lord Chief Justice;

(c) the Attorney General;

(d) the Director of Public Prosecutions;

(e) the President of the Council of the Inns of Court;

(f) the Chairman of the Bar Council;

(g) the Leaders of the six circuits;

(h) the Chairman of the PCC;

(i) the Defendant;

(j) the Defendant's head of chambers.

Service of documents

28. Regulation 29 of the Disciplinary Tribunals Regulations shall apply for the purposes of the service of any documents in connection with the procedures which are the subject of these Rules save that for the reference in Regulation 29(3) to the 'Directions Judge or the Chairman of the Disciplinary Tribunal' there shall be substituted the 'Chairman of the PCC'.

Transitional Provisions

29. These Rules shall not be applied in respect of any conviction or charge prior to 1 February 2000.

ANNEXE O

FITNESS TO PRACTISE RULES

[Amended 14 July 2001]

Introduction

1. These Rules are supplemental to:

    (a) the Complaints Rules;

    (b) the Disciplinary Tribunals Regulations;

    (c) the Summary Procedure Rules; and

    (d) the Interim Suspension Rules;

    as approved from time to time and annexed to the Code of Conduct of the Bar of England and Wales.

2. These Rules prescribe the manner in which any question concerning whether a barrister is unfit to practise, as defined in these Rules, shall be processed.

Definitions

3. In these Rules:

    (a) 'the Commissioner' means the Complaints Commissioner;

    (b) 'Medical Panel' means a Medical Panel as provided for in rule 4 of these Rules;

    (c) 'Review Panel' means a Review Panel as provided for in rule 5 of these Rules;

    (d) 'the Defendant' means the barrister whose case is referred to a Medical Panel pursuant to the procedure prescribed by these Rules;

    (e) 'Medical Expert' means a medical expert appointed by the Bar Council for the purpose of serving on Medical and Review Panels;

    (f) 'Appointed Medical Advisor' means a medical expert appointed by the Bar Council for the purpose of performing medical (including psychiatric) examinations on barristers and advising Medical and Review panels;

    (g) 'Unfit to practise' when used to describe a barrister means that he is incapacitated by reason of ill health and:

    (1) the barrister is suffering from serious incapacity due to his physical or mental condition (including any addiction); and

    (2) as a result the barrister's fitness to practise is seriously impaired; and

    (3) his suspension or the imposition of conditions is necessary for the protection of the public.

Composition of Panels

4. A Medical Panel shall consist of five members nominated by the Chairman of the PCC being:

    (a) a Chairman and two other barristers of at least ten years Call of whom the Chairman and at least one other shall be Queen's Counsel;

    (b) a Medical Expert;

    (c) a Lay Representative.

    Provided that:

(1) no barrister or Lay Representative shall be nominated to serve on a Panel which is to consider any case which may have been considered at any meeting of the PCC which he attended; and

(2) the proceedings of a Medical Panel shall be valid notwithstanding that one or more of the members other than the Chairman or Medical Expert or Lay Representative becomes unable to continue to act or disqualified from continuing to act, so long as the number of members present throughout the substantive hearing is not reduced below three and continues to include the Chairman and the Medical Expert and Lay Representative.

5. A Review Panel shall consist of:

(a) a Chairman and one other barrister nominated by the Chairman of the Bar;

(b) a representative nominated by the Treasurer of the Defendant's Inn;

(c) a Medical Expert;

(d) a Lay Representative

Provided that no individual shall sit on both the Medical Panel and the Review Panel considering the same case.

Referral to a Medical Panel

6. Where information in writing or a complaint in writing is received by the Bar Council about any barrister which raises a question whether the barrister is unfit to practise, the Commissioner shall consider whether to refer the case to a Medical Panel.

7. The Commissioner shall refer a case to a Medical Panel if:

(a) having been referred to him under rule 6 above the Commissioner considers a barrister may be unfit to practise; or

(b) a complaint of professional misconduct or inadequate professional service has been referred to the Commissioner or the PCC during the investigation of which it appears that a barrister may be unfit to practise; or

(c) in any other circumstances it appears to the Commissioner, the PCC or any other Disciplinary Panel or Tribunal that a barrister may be unfit to practise; or

(d) a barrister requests the Commissioner in writing to refer his case to a Medical Panel.

8. As soon as practicable after the decision has been made to refer a case to a Medical Panel, the Secretary of the PCC shall write to the Defendant notifying him of the decision, together with a copy of these Rules. The letter of notification shall:

(a) contain a summary of the reasons why the case has been referred to a Medical Panel;

(b) lay down a fixed time and date (normally not less than fourteen and not more than twenty-one days from the date of the letter) for a preliminary hearing of the Panel to take place. One alternative shall be given;

(c) invite the Defendant to accept one or other of the dates proposed or to provide a written representation to the Chairman of the PCC, objecting to both dates with reasons and providing two further alternative dates not more than twenty-one days from the date of the letter of notification. Any such representation must be received by the Chairman of the PCC not more than fourteen days from the date of the letter of notification. The Chairman of the PCC shall consider any such representation and either confirm one of the original dates or re-fix the hearing. If no such representation is received within fourteen days of the date of the letter of notification the hearing shall take place at the time and date first fixed pursuant to rule 8(b) above. The Chairman's decision, which shall be notified in writing to the Defendant by the Secretary of the PCC, shall be final. Once fixed, a hearing date shall be vacated only in exceptional circumstances and with the agreement of the Chairman of the PCC;

(d) inform the Defendant that he is entitled to make representations in writing or orally, by himself or by another member of the Bar on his behalf, and that he may produce medical evidence, provided (but subject to the discretion of the Chairman of the Panel to consider any form of evidence placed before it) that a proof of such evidence shall have been submitted prior to the hearing;

(e) inform the Defendant that he may be invited to attend within a period of time upon an Appointed Medical Advisor nominated by the Panel to carry out an examination of the Defendant, and requested to authorise disclosure of his medical records;

(f) inform the Defendant of his right to appeal as provided in rule 18 below.

Procedure and Powers of Medical Panels

9. At any hearing of a Medical Panel the proceedings shall be governed by the rules of natural justice, subject to which:

(a) the procedure shall be informal, the details being at the discretion of the Chairman of the Panel;

(b) the Defendant shall be entitled to make representations in writing or orally, by himself or by another member of the Bar or a solicitor on his behalf, and may produce medical evidence, provided (but subject to the discretion of the Chairman of the Panel to consider any form of evidence placed before it) that a proof of such evidence shall have been submitted prior to the hearing;

(c) the attendance of the Defendant shall be required. Should he nevertheless fail to attend, the hearing may proceed in his absence, subject to the Panel being satisfied that this course is appropriate, that all relevant procedures requiring the Defendant's attendance have been complied with and that no acceptable explanation for the Defendant's absence has been provided. Should the Panel not be so satisfied, it shall have the power to adjourn the hearing;

(d) the hearing shall not be in public unless so requested by the Defendant and a record shall be taken electronically. The tape of the hearing shall be retained under the arrangements of the Secretary of the PCC for two years or until any charges of professional misconduct against the Defendant arising out of the case have been finally disposed of through the Bar Council's procedure for complaints and any appeal procedure has been exhausted whichever period is the longer;

(e) if it decides an adjournment is necessary for any reason, the Panel may adjourn the hearing for such period and to such time and place, and upon such terms, as it may think fit.

10. If the members of a Medical Panel are not unanimous as to any decision the decision made shall be that of the majority of them. If the members of the Panel are equally divided the decision shall be that which is the most favourable to the Defendant.

11. At the conclusion of a preliminary hearing of a Medical Panel, the Panel:

(a) may give directions for a full hearing of the Panel, including:

(1) a direction within a specified period of time an Appointed Medical Advisor nominated by the Panel shall carry out an examination of the Defendant; and

(2) a request to the Defendant to authorise disclosure of his medical records to such Appointed Medical Advisor;

(b) shall warn the Defendant that if he refuses any request made under rule 11(a) above any Panel hearing his case shall be entitled to draw such adverse inferences as it may think fit from such refusal;

(c) may direct that the barrister be suspended from practice (either unconditionally or subject to conditions) for a specified period which should not save in exceptional circumstances exceed 3 months pending the full hearing of the Panel, provided that no such period of interim suspension should be imposed unless the Panel is satisfied that it is necessary to protect the public.

(d) in lieu of imposing a period of suspension under (c) above may accept from the Defendant an undertaking in writing in terms satisfactory to the Panel (and subject to such conditions and for such a period as the Panel may agree) immediately to be suspended from practice pending the conclusion of the full hearing;

(e) may accept from the Defendant an undertaking or undertakings in writing in terms satisfactory to the Panel (and subject to such conditions and for such a period as the Panel may agree) as to the conduct of the Defendant's practice pending the conclusion of the full hearing;

(f) shall set down in writing signed by the Chairman of the Panel the decision of the Panel including the terms of any directions given under rule 11(a) above and the period and terms of any interim suspension imposed under rule 11(c) above or undertaking accepted under rule 11(d) or (e) above.

(g) shall, if a period of interim suspension is imposed under rule 11(c) above or a written undertaking is accepted under rule 11(d) above:

(1) fix a time and date within the period of suspension imposed or to which the undertaking relates, alternatively inform the Defendant that such a time and date will be fixed by the Secretary of the PCC and notified to the Defendant not less than fourteen days prior to such date, when, unless a Medical Panel has concluded proceedings, a Panel shall be convened for the purpose of reviewing the matter;

(2) inform the Defendant of his right to request a Panel to review the matter prior to the date fixed in (1) above as provided in rule 15 below;

(3) inform the Defendant of his right of appeal as provided in rule 18 below;

(4) inform the Defendant that he is entitled to request an expedited full hearing of the Medical Panel and, if so requested, the Chairman of the Panel may so direct.

12. If a Medical Panel shall decide to give directions under rule 11(a) above, as soon as practicable after the report of any examination requested has been carried out (or refused) and a summary of the case against the Defendant has been prepared on behalf of the Panel, the Secretary of the PCC shall notify the Defendant. The letter of notification shall:

(a) contain:

(1) the summary of the case against the Defendant;

(2) a copy of any report produced by the Appointed Medical Advisor nominated to carry out an examination of the Defendant;

(b) lay down a fixed time and date (normally not less than fourteen and not more than twenty-one days from the date of the letter) for a full hearing of the Panel to take place. One alternative shall be given;

(c) invite the Defendant to accept one or other of the dates proposed or to provide a written representation to the Chairman of the PCC, objecting to both dates with reasons and providing two further alternative dates not more than twenty-one days from the date of the letter of notification. Any such representation must be received by the Chairman of the PCC not more than fourteen days from the date of the letter of notification. The Chairman of the PCC shall consider this representation and either confirm one of the original dates or re-fix the hearing. If no such representation is received within fourteen days of the date of the letter of notification the hearing shall take place at the time and date first fixed pursuant to rule 12(b) above. The Chairman's decision, which shall be notified in writing to the Defendant by the Secretary of the PCC, shall be final. Once fixed, a hearing date shall be vacated only in exceptional circumstances and with the agreement of the Chairman of the PCC;

(d) inform the Defendant of his right to appeal as provided in rule 18 below.

13.   At any full hearing of a Medical Panel the provisions of rule 9 above shall apply but in addition the Defendant himself or by another member of the Bar shall be entitled to cross-examine any Appointed Medical Advisor whose report is in evidence before the Panel.

14.   At the conclusion of a full hearing of a Medical Panel, the Panel:

(a) may decide to take no action;

(b) if satisfied that the Defendant is or may become unfit to practise shall have power to impose one or more of the penalties or conditions set out in rules 14(c), (d) and (e) below;

(c) may impose a period of interim suspension (either unconditionally or subject to conditions) of up to six months, but shall inform the Defendant that such period of interim suspension shall be continued without any further decision of a Panel unless determined at a review of his case as provided in rule 15 below;

(d) may impose an indefinite period of suspension;

(e) may make the Defendant's right to continue to practise, or to resume practice after any period of suspension, subject to such conditions as the Panel may think fit, including, without prejudice to the generality of the foregoing:

(1)   a requirement that the Defendant should attend one or more Appointed Medical Advisors for regular examination whose report(s) should be made available to the Chairman of the PCC and any Medical Panel or Review Panel when considering the case;

(2)   a requirement that the Defendant should attend one or more clinics or hospitals as the Panel may decide for the purposes of treatment in respect of any physical or mental condition which the Panel may think is or may become a cause of the Defendant's Unfitness to practise;

(f) in lieu of imposing any penalty or condition under rule 14(b) above the Panel may accept from the Defendant one or more undertakings in writing satisfactory to the Panel referring to such period of suspension and any conditions which the Panel would have imposed or made under rules 14(c), (d) and (e) above;

(g) shall inform the Defendant of his right to request a Panel to review his case as provided in rule 15 below;

(h) shall inform the Defendant of his right of appeal as provided in rule 18 below;

(i) shall inform the Defendant that to attempt to practise during a period of suspension or, if the Defendant's right to continue to practise is subject to one or more conditions, not to comply with any such condition, would be serious professional misconduct likely to result in a charge of professional misconduct and a hearing before a Disciplinary Tribunal;

(j) shall set down in writing signed by the Chairman of the Panel the decision of the Panel and the terms of any suspension imposed, conditions made, or undertakings accepted.

15. At any time, after a period of suspension imposed or undertaken under rules 14(d) or (f) above has expired, or in the event of a significant change in circumstances or other good reason, the Defendant may make a request in writing to the Chairman of the PCC for a Panel to be convened to review his case. Where a significant change in circumstances or good reason is relied upon the letter must set out the details of any such alleged change in circumstances or good reason. On receipt of such a letter the Chairman may in his discretion convene a Panel or refuse the request. In either case the Chairman shall inform the Defendant in writing of his decision but shall not be obliged to give reasons. The Chairman's decision shall be final.

16. At any time during which a Defendant is subject to a period of suspension or is practising subject to conditions made pursuant to these Rules the Chairman of the PCC may in his discretion convene a Panel to review that Defendant's case.

17. When a case is referred for review to a Medical Panel under rules 15 or 16 above:

(a) there shall be a rehearing of the case by the Panel and the provisions of rules 9, 10 and 13 above shall apply save that copies of the report of any expert or any proof of evidence referred to at any previous hearing of a Medical Panel in respect of the same case may be referred to;

(b) unless agreed in writing between the Chairman of the Panel and the Defendant that any of the provisions contained in rules 8, 11 and 12 shall not apply, there shall be a preliminary as well as a full hearing of the Panel and the provisions contained in rules 8, 11, 12 and 14 above shall apply thereto.

18. A Defendant may by letter served on the Secretary of the PCC not more than fourteen days after the date of the relevant decision of a Medical Panel give notice of his wish to appeal against the decision.

Appeals

19. As soon as practicable after receipt of a letter in accordance with rule 18 above the Secretary of the PCC shall convene a Review Panel and write to the Defendant notifying him of a fixed time and date (normally not less than fourteen and not more than twenty-one days from the date of receipt of the letter) for the hearing to take place. The Defendant may make a written representation, addressed to the Chairman of the proposed Review Panel, objecting to the date with reasons and providing two further alternative dates. Any such representation must be received by the Chairman of the Review Panel not more than fourteen days from the date of the letter of notification. The Chairman shall consider any such representation and either confirm the original date or re-fix the hearing. If no such representation is received within fourteen days of the date of the letter of notification the hearing shall take place at the time and place originally notified to the Defendant. The

Chairman's decision, which shall be notified in writing to the Defendant by the Secretary of the PCC, shall be final. Once fixed, a hearing date shall be vacated only in exceptional circumstances and with the agreement of the Chairman of the Review Panel.

20. The proceedings before a Review Panel shall be by way of a rehearing and the provisions of rules 9 and 13 above shall apply as if for references therein to the Medical Panel and the Chairman of the Medical Panel for the purposes of a full hearing of a Medical Panel there were substituted references respectively to the Review Panel and the Chairman of the Review Panel, save that copies of the report of any expert or any proof of evidence referred to at any hearing of a Medical Panel in respect of the same case may be referred to.

21. At the conclusion of the hearing, the Review Panel:

   (a) may allow the appeal and decide to take no action;

   (b) confirm the decision that is the subject of the appeal;

   (c) may exercise any of the powers of a Medical Panel as set out in rules 14(c), (d), (e), and (f) above;

   (d) shall inform the Defendant of his right to request a Medical Panel to review his case as provided in rule 15 above;

   (e) shall inform the Defendant that to attempt to practise during a period of suspension or, if the Defendant's right to continue to practise is subject to one or more conditions, not to comply with any such condition, would be serious professional misconduct likely to result in a charge of professional misconduct and a hearing before a Disciplinary Tribunal;

   (f) shall set down in writing signed by the Chairman of the Panel the decision of the Panel and the terms of any suspension imposed, conditions made, or undertakings accepted. If the members of the Panel are not unanimous as to the decision the decision shall be that of the majority of them.

22. A pending appeal to a Review Panel shall not operate as a stay of any period of suspension or any conditions or the terms of any undertaking which is the subject of the appeal.

23. There shall be no right of appeal from the decision of a Review Panel.

Costs

24. A Medical Panel and a Review Panel shall have no power to award costs.

Confidentiality of medical reports

25. A Defendant's medical records and any report prepared for or submitted to a Medical Panel or a Review Panel shall not be used for any other purpose than is provided for in these Rules and shall not be disclosed to any other person or body without the consent in writing of the Defendant.

Report and Publication of Decisions

26. As soon as practicable after the conclusion of a Medical Panel hearing or a Review Panel hearing, the Secretary of the PCC shall confirm the decision to the Defendant in writing.

27. Unless the decision of a Medical Panel full hearing or a Review Panel hearing is to take no action and the Defendant is permitted to continue to practise without being subject to any conditions, the Secretary of the PCC shall communicate brief details thereof in writing to the following:

(a) the Lord Chancellor;

(b) the Lord Chief Justice;

(c) the Attorney General;

(d) the Director of Public Prosecutions;

(e) the President of the Council of the Inns of Court;

(f) the Chairman of the Bar Council;

(g) the Leaders of the six circuits;

(h) the Chairman of the PCC;

(i) the Defendant;

(j) the Defendant's head of chambers;

(k) the Treasurers of the Defendant's Inn of Call and of any other Inns of which he is a member.

Service of documents

28. Regulation 29 of the Disciplinary Tribunals Regulations shall apply for the purposes of the service of any documents in connection with the procedures which are the subject of these Rules save that for the reference in Regulation 29(3) to the 'Directions Judge or the Chairman of the Disciplinary Tribunal' there shall be substituted the 'Chairman of the PCC'.

ANNEXE P

ADJUDICATION PANEL AND APPEALS RULES

[Amended 20 July 2002]

Introduction

1. Adjudication Panels ('Panels') shall be appointed by the Professional Conduct and Complaints Committee ('the Committee') to determine complaints considered by the Committee not to raise a *prima facie* case of professional misconduct, but to raise a *prima facie* case that the barrister concerned has provided inadequate professional service to the complainant.

2. Panels shall consist of the Complaints Commissioner ('the Commissioner') as chairman, one lay member of the Committee and two barrister members of the Committee, at least one of whom shall be a Queen's Counsel.

3. Anything required by these Rules to be done or any discretion required to be exercised by, and any notice required to be given to, the Complaints Commissioner ('the Commissioner') or the Secretary of the Committee ('the Secretary'), may be done or exercised by, or given to, any person authorised by the Complaints Commissioner to act in his stead or by the Chief Executive of the Bar Council to act instead of the Secretary of the Committee (either prospectively or retrospectively and either generally or for a particular purpose).

Powers of Panels

4. The powers of a Panel shall be:

    (a) to consider any complaint referred to it pursuant to paragraph 28(e) of the Complaints Rules and to direct such investigations as they see fit in respect thereof

    (b) to dismiss any complaint without making a finding as to the existence or otherwise of inadequate professional service if they conclude that due to lapse of time, disputes of fact which cannot fairly be resolved by the Panel, or for any other reason it cannot fairly be determined

    (c) to determine whether the barrister concerned has provided inadequate professional service in respect of the matter complained of

    (d) to determine what remedy should be granted to the complainant in respect of such inadequate service.

Investigation and Procedure

5. When a complaint is referred to a Panel as set out in paragraph 4(a) above the Commissioner shall consider what, if any, further investigation is required to be made in order for the panel to deal fairly with the matters falling to it for decision, and the Secretary shall make such investigations as the Commissioner or the Panel direct to assist the deliberations of the panel, such as whether the complainant claims to have suffered financial loss as a result of the conduct complained of, and if so the exact nature and amount of that claimed loss and the evidence available to support the claim, and from the barrister the nature of the work he carried out for the complainant out of which the complaint arose, the fee rendered for such work, and whether or not such fee has been paid.

6. The Secretary shall, whether or not there are to be additional investigations under paragraph 5 above, notify both the barrister and the complainant of the matters that the PCC has directed the panel to consider. As soon as practicable thereafter, he shall prepare a

bundle of papers to be considered by the panel and shall copy those to the barrister and the complainant and shall invite their written comments within 14 days (which period may be extended with the permission of the Commissioner).

7. At the expiration of the time limit specified in paragraph 6 or on completion of any enquiries made under paragraph 5, the Secretary shall copy any further papers that are to be considered by the panel to the barrister and the complainant and shall set a date for the panel to meet. Both the barrister and the complainant shall be informed of the date of the hearing and the complainant shall be invited to make any further comments in writing which must arrive not less than seven days before the date of the hearing. Such comments shall be copied to the barrister and the panel.

8. The Panel may consider complaints and the results of any investigations in whatever manner they think fit, and may adjourn consideration of any complaint at any time, and for any reason and, in particular to enable the complainant to comment on any information provided by the barrister at the hearing which had not previously been disclosed by him.

9. Following such consideration, the Panel may decide:

   (a) that for any reason the complaint cannot fairly be determined by them, whereupon it shall dismiss the complaint and shall give notice in writing of its decision and the reasons for it to the barrister and the complainant

   (b) that the complainant has not established on the balance of probabilities that the barrister concerned has provided inadequate professional service to the complainant, whereupon it shall dismiss the complaint and shall give notice in writing of its decision and the reasons for it to the barrister and the complainant

   (c) that the complainant has so established, whereupon it shall consider what remedy should be granted to the complainant in respect of the service which it has found to have been inadequate.

10. Following a finding under paragraph 9(c) above, the Panel may:

    (a) determine that it is not appropriate to take any action in respect of the inadequate service,

    (b) direct the barrister to make a formal apology to the complainant for the inadequate service provided,

    (c) direct the barrister to repay or remit all or part of any fee rendered in respect of the inadequate service,

    (d) direct the barrister to pay compensation to the complainant in such sum as the panel shall direct not exceeding £5,000.

In determining whether any sum is to be paid under paragraph (d) hereof, or in fixing the amount of such sum, the panel shall in particular have regard to any loss suffered by the complainant as a result of the inadequate professional service, the availability to the complainant of other forms of redress, to the gravity of the conduct complained of, and to the fee claimed by the barrister for the inadequate service.

11. Following any such finding as is mentioned in paragraph 9(c) hereof, the Panel shall give notice in writing to the barrister and to the complainant of the respects in which they have found the barrister to have provided inadequate professional service, and the

reasons for such finding, and of the remedy to be granted to the complainant under paragraph 10 above.

12. If the panel is not unanimous on any issue, the finding made shall be that of the majority of them. If the panel is equally divided, the burden of proof being on the complainant, the finding shall be that most favourable to the barrister.

13. Not used.

14. Following such reopening or reconsideration, the panel may take any further or different action it thinks fit, as if the former decision had not been made.

15. Whether or not the panel shall have determined that the barrister has provided an inadequate professional service, it may refer any matter of policy which arises to the relevant Committee of the Bar Council.

16. No finding of an Adjudication Panel shall be publishable except:

   (a) by the Commissioner in any annual or other report on his work, in which case the identities of the parties shall so far as possible be concealed, unless the barrister concerned seeks that any finding be published. In that case the manner and extent of publication shall be at the discretion of the Commissioner; or

   (b) if the Adjudication Panel considers that the circumstances of the complaint are relevant to the barrister's capacity as a pupilmaster, it may notify the barrister's Inn of its concern in such manner as it sees fit.

Appeals

17. An appeal shall lie at the instance of a barrister against a finding that he has provided inadequate professional service, and against any decision as to the remedy to be granted to the complainant in respect of such inadequate service.

18. Any such appeal shall be heard and determined by a panel ('the Appeal Panel') consisting of not less than three or more than five past or present members of the Committee (or of the Professional Conduct Committee established under the rules in effect immediately before the coming into effect of these Rules) of whom at least one shall be a Queen's Counsel and shall chair the panel, at least one shall be a junior of more than five years' call and at least one shall be a lay representative. None of the members of the Appeal panel shall have been members of the tribunal which made any finding appealed against.

19. An appeal shall be made by the barrister sending to the Secretary within 28 days of the date of letter notifying him of the decision appealed against a notice stating the findings to be appealed against, the decision the barrister contends for, and the grounds of such appeal, accompanied by the sum of £100 payable to the Bar Council to defray expenses.

20. Service of notice of an appeal by a barrister shall operate as a stay of any order made in favour of the complainant.

21. On receipt of such a notice, the Secretary shall notify the Commissioner of the intended appeal, and shall afford him an opportunity to respond to the grounds of appeal stated in the notice. For the purpose of so responding the Commissioner may seek information or assistance from such persons and in such manner as he sees fit.

22. On such an appeal,

(a) the procedure shall be informal, the details being at the discretion of the chairman of the Appeal Panel including whether or not there should be an oral hearing in relation to the appeal

(b) the barrister, the complainant and the Commissioner may attend or be represented

(c) the Appeal Panel may make such order as they think fit in relation to the complaint, including any order which the tribunal appealed from had the power to make, save that they may not make any order in relation to the costs of the appeal

(d) the Appeal Panel shall not allow the appeal unless they are satisfied that the tribunal appealed from reached a wrong decision on any question of law, made a finding of fact which was against the weight of the evidence or exercised any discretion granted to it on a wrong basis

(e) if the Appeal Panel allows an appeal, in whole or in part, it may in its discretion direct the refund to the barrister of the sum deposited under paragraph 16 above

(f) whether or not the appeal is allowed, the Appeal Panel may refer any issue of policy which arises to the relevant Committee of the Bar Council.

Definitions

23.   In these Rules unless the context otherwise requires

(a) Any term defined in the Code of Conduct shall carry the same meaning as it does in the Code of Conduct.

(b) 'The Complaints Rules' shall mean the rules prescribing the manner in which complaints are to be considered set out in Annex J to the Code of Conduct, and any term defined in the Complaints Rules shall carry the same meaning as it does in those Rules.

(c) Any reference to a person includes any natural person, legal person and/or firm. Any reference to the masculine gender includes the feminine and the neuter, and any reference to the singular includes the plural, and in each case *vice versa*.

Commencement and Transitional Arrangements

24.   In relation to any adjudication panel or appeal arising out of a complaint which had been referred to a panel before 15th May 2000, these Rules shall not apply but the Adjudication Panel and Appeals Rules in force immediately before that date shall apply to that panel or appeal.

ANNEXE Q

THE CODE OF CONDUCT FOR LAWYERS IN THE EUROPEAN COMMUNITY

1   PREAMBLE

1.1   The Function of the Lawyer in Society

In a society founded on respect for the rule of law the lawyer fulfils a special role. His duties do not begin and end with the faithful performance of what he is instructed to do so far as the law permits. A lawyer must serve the interests of justice as well as those whose rights and liberties he is trusted to assert and defend and it is his duty not only to plead his client's cause but to be his adviser.

A lawyer's function therefore lays on him a variety of legal and moral obligations (sometimes appearing to be in conflict with each other) towards:

the client;

the courts and other authorities before whom the lawyer pleads his client's cause or acts on his behalf;

the legal profession in general and each fellow member of it in particular; and

the public for whom the existence of a free and independent profession, bound together by respect for rules made by the profession itself, is an essential means of safeguarding human rights in face of the power of the state and other interests in society.

1.2   The Nature of Rules of Professional Conduct

1.2.1   Rules of professional conduct are designed through their willing acceptance by those to whom they apply to ensure the proper performance by the lawyer of a function which is recognised as essential in all civilised societies. The failure of the lawyer to observe these rules must in the last resort result in a disciplinary sanction.

1.2.2   The particular rules of each Bar or Law Society arise from its own traditions. They are adapted to the organisation and sphere of activity of the profession in the Member State concerned and to its judicial and administrative procedures and to its national legislation. It is neither possible nor desirable that they should be taken out of their context nor that an attempt should be made to give general application to rules which are inherently incapable of such application.

The particular rules of each Bar and Law Society nevertheless are based on the same values and in most cases demonstrate a common foundation.

1.3   The Purpose of the Code

1.3.1   The continued integration of the European Union and European Economic Area and the increasing frequency of the cross-border activities of lawyers within the European Economic Area have made necessary in the public interest the statement of common rules which apply to all lawyers from the Community whatever Bar or Law Society they belong to in relation to their cross-border practice. A particular purpose of the statement of those rules is to mitigate the difficulties which result from the application of 'double deontology' as set out in Article 4 of the E.C. Directive 77/249 of 22nd March 1977.

1.3.2   The organisations representing the legal profession through the CCBE propose that the rules codified in the following articles:

— be recognised at the present time as the expression of a consensus of all the Bars and Law Societies of the European Union and European Economic Area;

— be adopted as enforceable rules as soon as possible in accordance with national or EEA procedures in relation to the cross-border activities of the lawyer in the European Union and European Economic Area;

— be taken into account in all revisions of national rules of deontology or professional practice with a view to their progressive harmonisation.

They further express the wish that the national rules of deontology or professional practice be interpreted and applied whenever possible in a way consistent with the rules in this Code.

After the rules in this Code have been adopted as enforceable rules in relation to his cross-border activities the lawyer will remain bound to observe the rules of the Bar or Law Society to which he belongs to the extent that they are consistent with the rules in this Code.

1.4   Field of Application Ratione Personae

The following rules shall apply to lawyers of the European Union and European Economic Area as they are defined by the Directive 77/249 of 22nd March 1977.

1.5   Field of Application Ratione Materiae

Without prejudice to the pursuit of a progressive harmonisation of rules of deontology or professional practice which apply only internally within a Member State, the following rules shall apply to the cross-border activities of the lawyer within the European Union and European Economic Area. Cross-border activities shall mean:-

(a) all professional contacts with lawyers of Member States other than his own; and

(b) the professional activities of the lawyer in a Member State other than his own, whether or not the lawyer is physically present in that Member State.

1.6   Definitions

In these rules:

'Home Member State' means the Member State of the Bar or Law Society to which the lawyer belongs.

'Host Member State' means any other Member State where the lawyer carries on cross-border activities.

'Competent authority' means the professional organisation(s) or authority(ies) of the Member State concerned responsible for the laying down of rules of professional conduct and the administration of discipline of lawyers.

2   GENERAL PRINCIPLES

2.1   Independence

2.1.1   The many duties to which a lawyer is subject require his absolute independence, free from all other influence, especially such as may arise from his personal interests or external pressure. Such independence is as necessary to trust in the process of justice as the impartiality of the judge. A lawyer must therefore avoid any impairment of his independence and be careful not to compromise his professional standards in order to please his client, the court or third parties.

2.1.2   This independence is necessary in non-contentious matters as well as in litigation. Advice given by a lawyer to his client has no value if it is given only to ingratiate himself, to serve his personal interests or in response to outside pressure.

2.2   Trust and Personal Integrity

Relationships of trust can only exist if a lawyer's personal honour, honesty and integrity are beyond doubt. For the lawyer these traditional virtues are professional obligations.

2.3   Confidentiality

2.3.1   It is of the essence of a lawyer's function that he should be told by his client things which the client would not tell to others, and that he should be the recipient of other information on a basis of confidence. Without the certainty of confidentiality there cannot be trust. Confidentiality is therefore a primary and fundamental right and duty of the lawyer.

The lawyer's obligation of confidentiality serves the interest of the administration of justice as well as the interest of the client. It is therefore entitled to special protection by the State.

2.3.2   A lawyer shall respect the confidentiality of all information that becomes known to him in the course of his professional activity.

2.3.3   The obligation of confidentiality is not limited in time.

2.3.4   A lawyer shall require his associates and staff and anyone engaged by him in the course of providing professional services to observe the same obligation of confidentiality.

2.4   Respect for the Rules of Other Bars and Law Societies

Under the laws of the European Union and the European Economic Area a lawyer from another Member State may be bound to comply with the rules of the Bar or Law Society of the host Member State. Lawyers have a duty to inform themselves as to the rules which will affect them in the performance of any particular activity.

Members of organisations of CCBE are obliged to deposit their Code of Conduct at the Secretariat of CCBE so that any lawyer can get hold of the copy of the current Code from the Secretariat.

2.5   Incompatible Occupations

2.5.1   In order to perform his functions with due independence and in a manner which is consistent with his duty to participate in the administration of justice a lawyer is excluded from some occupations.

2.5.2   A lawyer who acts in the representation or the defence of a client in legal proceedings or before any public authorities in a host Member State shall there observe the rules regarding incompatible occupations as they are applied to lawyers of the host Member State.

2.5.3   A lawyer established in a host Member State in which he wishes to participate directly in commercial or other activities not connected with the practice of the law shall respect the rules regarding forbidden or incompatible occupations as they are applied to lawyers of that Member State.

2.6   Personal Publicity

2.6.1   A lawyer should not advertise or seek personal publicity where this is not permitted.

In other cases a lawyer should only advertise or seek personal publicity to the extent and in the manner permitted by the rules to which he is subject.

2.6.2 Advertising and personal publicity shall be regarded as taking place where it is permitted, if the lawyer concerned shows that it was placed for the purpose of reaching clients or potential clients located where such advertising or personal publicity is permitted and its communication elsewhere is incidental.

2.7 The Client's Interests

Subject to due observance of all rules of law and professional conduct, a lawyer must always act in the best interests of his client and must put those interests before his own interests or those of fellow members of the legal profession.

2.8 Limitation of Lawyer's Liability towards his client

To the extent permitted by the law of the Home member State and the Host member State, the lawyer may limit his liabilities towards his client in accordance with rules of the Code of Conduct to which he is subject.

3 RELATIONS WITH CLIENTS

3.1 Acceptance and Termination of Instructions

3.1.1 A lawyer shall not handle a case for a party except on his instructions. He may, however, act in a case in which he has been instructed by another lawyer who himself acts for the party or where the case has been assigned to him by a competent body.

The lawyer should make reasonable efforts to ascertain the identity, competence and authority of the person or body who instructs him when the specific circumstances show that the identity, competence and authority are uncertain.

3.1.2 A lawyer shall advise and represent his client promptly conscientiously and diligently. He shall undertake personal responsibility for the discharge of the instructions given to him. He shall keep his client informed as to the progress of the matter entrusted to him.

3.1.3 A lawyer shall not handle a matter which he knows or ought to know he is not competent to handle, without co-operating with a lawyer who is competent to handle it.

A lawyer shall not accept instructions unless he can discharge those instructions promptly having regard to the pressure of other work.

3.1.4 A lawyer shall not be entitled to exercise his right to withdraw from a case in such a way or in such circumstances that the client may be unable to find other legal assistance in time to prevent prejudice being suffered by the client.

3.2 Conflict of Interest

3.2.1 A lawyer may not advise, represent or act on behalf of two or more clients in the same matter if there is a conflict, or a significant risk of a conflict, between the interests of those clients.

3.2.2 A lawyer must cease to act for both clients when a conflict of interests arises between those clients and also whenever there is a risk of a breach of confidence or where his independence may be impaired.

3.2.3 A lawyer must also refrain from acting for a new client if there is a risk of a breach of confidences entrusted to the lawyer by a former client or if the knowledge which the lawyer possesses of the affairs of the former client would give an undue advantage to the new client.

3.2.4   Where lawyers are practising in association, paragraphs 3.2.1 to 3.2.3 above shall apply to the association and all its members.

3.3   Pactum de Quota Litis

3.3.1   A lawyer shall not be entitled to make a pactum de quota litis.

3.3.2   By 'pactum de quota litis' is meant an agreement between a lawyer and his client entered into prior to the final conclusion of a matter to which the client is a party, by virtue of which the client undertakes to pay the lawyer a share of the result regardless of whether this is represented by a sum of money or by any other benefit achieved by the client upon the conclusion of the matter.

3.3.3   The pactum de quota litis does not include an agreement that fees be charged in proportion to the value of a matter handled by the lawyer if this is in accordance with an officially approved fee scale or under the control of the competent authority having jurisdiction over the lawyer.

3.4   Regulation of Fees

3.4.1   A fee charged by a lawyer shall be fully disclosed to his client and shall be fair and reasonable.

3.4.2   Subject to any proper agreement to the contrary between a lawyer and his client fees charged by a lawyer shall be subject to regulation in accordance with the rules applied to members of the Bar or Law Society to which he belongs. If he belongs to more than one Bar or Law Society the rules applied shall be those with the closest connection to the contract between the lawyer and his client.

3.5   Payment on Account

If a lawyer requires a payment on account of his fees and/or disbursements such payment should not exceed a reasonable estimate of the fees and probable disbursements involved.

Failing such payment, a lawyer may withdraw from the case or refuse to handle it, but subject always to paragraph 3.1.4 above.

3.6   Fee Sharing with Non-Lawyers

3.6.1   Subject as after-mentioned a lawyer may not share his fees with a person who is not a lawyer except where an association between the lawyer and the other person is permitted by the laws of the Member State to which the lawyer belongs.

3.6.2   The provisions of 6.1 above shall not preclude a lawyer from paying a fee, commission or other compensation to a deceased lawyer's heirs or to a retired lawyer in respect of taking over the deceased or retired lawyer's practice.

3.7   Cost Effective Resolution and Availability of Legal Aid

3.7.1   The lawyer should at all times strive to achieve the most cost effective resolution of the client's dispute and should advise the client at appropriate stages as to the desirability of attempting a settlement and/or a reference to alternative dispute resolution.

3.7.2   A lawyer shall inform his client of the availability of legal aid where applicable.

3.8   Clients' Funds

3.8.1   When lawyers at any time in the course of their practice come into possession of funds on behalf of their clients or third parties (hereinafter called 'clients' funds') it shall be obligatory:

3.8.1.1   That clients' funds shall always be held in an account in a bank or similar institution subject to supervision of Public Authority and that all clients' funds received by a lawyer should be paid into such an account unless the client explicitly or by implication agrees that the funds should be dealt with otherwise.

3.8.1.2   That any account in which the clients' funds are held in the name of the lawyer should indicate in the title or designation that the funds are held on behalf of the client or clients of the lawyer.

3.8.1.3   That any account or accounts in which clients' funds are held in the name of the lawyer should at all times contain a sum which is not less than the total of the clients' funds held by the lawyer.

3.8.1.4   That all funds shall be paid to clients immediately or upon such conditions as the client may authorise.

3.8.1.5   That payments made from clients' funds on behalf of a client to any other person including

(a) payments made to or for one client from funds held for another client and

(b) payment of the lawyer's fees,

be prohibited except to the extent that they are permitted by law or have the express or implied authority of the client for whom the payment is being made.

3.8.1.6   That the lawyer shall maintain full and accurate records, available to each client on request, showing all his dealings with his clients' funds and distinguishing clients' funds from other funds held by him.

3.8.1.7   That the competent authorities in all Member States should have powers to allow them to examine and investigate on a confidential basis the financial records of lawyers' clients' funds to ascertain whether or not the rules which they make are being complied with and to impose sanctions upon lawyers who fail to comply with those rules.

3.8.2   Subject as after-mentioned, and without prejudice to the rules set out in 3.8.1 above, a lawyer who holds clients' funds in the course of carrying on practice in any Member State must comply with the rules relating to holding and accounting for clients' funds which are applied by the competent authorities of the Home Member State.

3.8.3   A lawyer who carries on practice or provides services in a Host Member State may with the agreement of the competent authorities of the Home and Host Member States concerned comply with the requirements of the Host Member State to the exclusion of the requirements of the Home Member State. In that event he shall take reasonable steps to inform his clients that he complies with the requirements in force in the Host Member State.

3.9   Professional Indemnity Insurance

3.9.1   Lawyers shall be insured at all times against claims based on professional negligence to an extent which is reasonable having regard to the nature and extent of the risks which each lawyer may incur in his practice.

3.9.2   When a lawyer provides services or carries out practice in a Host Member State, the following shall apply.

3.9.2.1   The lawyer must comply with any Rules relating to his obligation to insure against his professional liability as a lawyer which are in force in his Home Member State.

3.9.2.2   A lawyer who is obliged so to insure in his home Member State and who provides services or carries out practice in any Host Member State shall use his best endeavours to obtain insurance cover on the basis required in his home Member State extended to services which he provides or practice which he carries out in a Host Member State.

3.9.2.3   A lawyer who fails to obtain the extended insurance cover referred to in paragraph 3.9.2.2 above or who is not obliged so to insure in his home Member State and who provides services or carries out practice in a Host Member State shall in so far as possible obtain insurance cover against his professional liability as a lawyer whilst acting for clients in that Host Member State on at least an equivalent basis to that required of lawyers in the Host Member State.

3.9.2.4   To the extent that a lawyer is unable to obtain the insurance cover required by the foregoing rules, he shall inform such of his clients as might be affected.

3.9.2.5   A lawyer who carries out practice or provides services in a Host Member State may with the agreement of the competent authorities of the Home and Host Member States concerned comply with such insurance requirements as are in force in the Host Member State to the exclusion of the insurance requirements of the Home Member State. In this event he shall take reasonable steps to inform his clients that he is insured according to the requirements in force in the Host Member State.

4   RELATIONS WITH THE COURTS

4.1   Applicable Rules of Conduct in Court

A lawyer who appears, or takes part in a case, before a court or tribunal in a Member State must comply with the rules of conduct applied before that court or tribunal.

4.2   Fair Conduct of Proceedings

A lawyer must always have due regard for the fair conduct of proceedings. He must not, for example, make contact with the judge without first informing the lawyer acting for the opposing party or submit exhibits, notes or documents to the judge without communicating them in good time to the lawyer on the other side unless such steps are permitted under the relevant rules of procedure. To the extent not prohibited by law a lawyer must not divulge or submit to the court any proposals for settlement of the case made by the other party or its lawyers without the express consent by the other party's lawyer.

4.3   Demeanour in Court

A lawyer shall while maintaining due respect and courtesy towards the court defend the interest of his client honourably and fearlessly without regard to his own interests or to any consequences to himself or to any other person.

4.4   False or Misleading Information

A lawyer shall never knowingly give false or misleading information to the court.

4.5   Extension to Arbitrators Etc.

The rules governing a lawyer's relations with the courts apply also to his relations with arbitrators and any other persons exercising judicial or quasi-judicial functions, even on an occasional basis.

5   RELATIONS BETWEEN LAWYERS

5.1   Corporate Spirit of the Profession

5.1.1   The corporate spirit of the profession requires a relationship of trust and co-operation between lawyers for the benefit of their clients and in order to avoid unnecessary litigation and other behaviour harmful to the reputation of the profession. It can, however, never justify setting the interests of the profession against those of the client.

5.1.2   A lawyer should recognise all other lawyers of Member States as professional colleagues and act fairly and courteously towards them.

5.2   Co-operation among Lawyers of Different Member States

5.2.1   It is the duty of a lawyer who is approached by a colleague from another Member State not to accept instructions in a matter which he is not competent to undertake. He should in such case be prepared to help his colleague to obtain the information necessary to enable him to instruct a lawyer who is capable of providing the service asked for.

5.2.2   Where a lawyer of a Member State co-operates with a lawyer from another Member State, both have a general duty to take into account the differences which may exist between their respective legal systems and the professional organisations competences and obligations of lawyers in the Member States concerned.

5.3   Correspondence Between Lawyers

5.3.1   If a lawyer sending a communication to a lawyer in another Member State wishes it to remain confidential or without prejudice he should clearly express this intention when communicating the document.

5.3.2   If the recipient of the communication is unable to ensure its status as confidential or without prejudice he should return it to the sender without revealing the contents to others.

5.4   Referral Fees

5.4.1   A lawyer may not demand or accept from another lawyer or any other person a fee, commission or any other compensation for referring or recommending the lawyer to a client.

5.4.2   A lawyer may not pay anyone a fee, commission or any other compensation as a consideration for referring a client to himself.

5.5   Communication with Opposing Parties

A lawyer shall not communicate about a particular case or matter directly with any person whom he knows to be represented or advised in the case or matter by another lawyer, without the consent of that other lawyer (and shall keep the other lawyer informed of any such communications).

5.6   Change of Lawyer

5.6.1   A lawyer who is instructed to represent a client in substitution for another lawyer in relation to a particular matter should inform that other lawyer and, subject to 5.6.2 below, should not begin to act until he has ascertained that arrangements have been made for the settlement of the other lawyer's fees and disbursements. This duty does not, however, make the new lawyer personally responsible for the former lawyer's fees and disbursements.

5.6.2   If urgent steps have to be taken in the interests of the client before the conditions in 5.6.1 above can be complied with, the lawyer may take such steps provided he informs the other lawyer immediately.

5.7   Responsibility for Fees

In professional relations between members of Bars of different Member States, where a lawyer does not confine himself to recommending another lawyer or introducing him to the client but himself entrusts a correspondent with a particular matter or seeks his advice, he is personally bound, even if the client is insolvent, to pay the fees, costs and outlays which are due to the foreign correspondent. The lawyers concerned may, however, at the outset of the relationship between them make special arrangements on this matter. Further, the instructing lawyer may at any time limit his personal responsibility to the amount of the fees, costs and outlays incurred before intimation to the foreign lawyer of his disclaimer of responsibility for the future.

5.8   Training Young Lawyers

In order to improve trust and co-operation amongst lawyers of different Member States for the clients' benefit there is a need to encourage a better knowledge of the laws and procedures in different Member States. Therefore when considering the need for the profession to give good training to young lawyers, lawyers should take into account the need to give training to young lawyers from other Member States.

5.9   Disputes Amongst Lawyers in Different Member States

5.9.1   If a lawyer considers that a colleague in another Member State has acted in breach of a rule of professional conduct he shall draw the matter to the attention of his colleague.

5.9.2   If any personal dispute of a professional nature arises amongst lawyers in different Member States they should if possible first try to settle it in a friendly way.

5.9.3   A lawyer shall not commence any form of proceedings against a colleague in another Member State on matters referred to in 5.9.1 or 5.9.2 above without first informing the Bars or Law Societies to which they both belong for the purpose of allowing both Bars or Law Societies concerned an opportunity to assist in reaching a settlement.

ANNEXE R

THE PUPILLAGE FUNDING AND ADVERTISING REQUIREMENTS 2003

Funding

1. The members of a set of chambers must pay to each non-practising chambers pupil by the end of each month of the non-practising six months of his pupillage no less than:

    (a) £833.33; plus

    (b) such further sum as may be necessary to reimburse expenses reasonably incurred by the pupil on:

    (i)   travel for the purposes of his pupillage during that month; and

    (ii)   attendance during that month at courses which he is required to attend as part of his pupillage.

2. The members of a set of chambers must pay to each practising chambers pupil by the end of each month of the practising six months of his pupillage no less than:

    (a) £833.33; plus

    (b) such further sum as may be necessary to reimburse expenses reasonably incurred by the pupil on:

    (i)   travel for the purposes of his pupillage during that month; and

    (ii)   attendance during that month at courses which he is required to attend as part of his pupillage; less

    (c) such amount, if any, as the pupil may receive during that month from his practice as a barrister; and less

    (d) such amounts, if any, as the pupil may have received during the preceding months of his practising pupillage from his practice as a barrister, save to the extent that the amount paid to the pupil in respect of any such month was less than the total of the sums provided for in sub-paragraphs (a) and (b) above.

3. The members of a set of chambers may not seek or accept repayment from a chambers pupil of any of the sums required to be paid under paragraphs 1 and 2 above, whether before or after he ceases to be a chambers pupil, save in the case of misconduct on his part.

Advertising

4. All vacancies for pupillages must be advertised on a website designated by the Bar Council and the following information must be provided:

    (a) The name and address of chambers.

    (b) The number of tenants.

    (c) A brief statement of the work undertaken by chambers e.g. 'predominately criminal'.

    (d) The number of pupillage vacancies.

    (e) The level of award.

    (f) The procedure for application.

    (g) The minimum educational or other qualification required.

    (h) The date of closure for the receipt of applications.

    (i) The date by which the decisions on the filling of vacancies will be made.

Application

5.   The requirements set out in paragraphs 1 to 4 above:

(a) apply in the case of pupillages commencing on or after 1st January 2003;

(b) do not apply in the case of pupils who qualified for call to the Bar pursuant to regulations 35 (solicitors), 36 (other qualified lawyers) or 55 (teachers of the law of England and Wales of experience and distinction) of the Consolidated Regulations;

(c) do not apply in the case of pupils who are undertaking a period of pupillage in a set of chambers as part of a pupillage training programme offered by another organisation that is authorised by the Bar Council to take pupils;

(d) do not apply in the case of pupils who have completed both the non-practising and the practising six months of pupillage;

(e) save as provided in paragraph 3 above, do not apply in respect of any period after a pupil ceases, for whatever reason, to be a chambers pupil; and

(f) may be waived in part or in whole by the Pupillage Funding Committee.

6.   For the purposes of these requirements:

(a) 'chambers pupil' means, in respect of any set of chambers, a pupil undertaking the non-practising or practising six months of pupillage with a pupil-master or pupil-masters who is or are a member or members of that set of chambers;

(b) 'non-practising chambers pupil' means a chambers pupil undertaking the non-practising six months of pupillage;

(c) 'practising chambers pupil' means a chambers pupil undertaking the practising six months of pupillage;

(d) 'month' means calendar month commencing on the same day of the month as that on which the pupil commenced the non-practising or practising six months pupillage, as the case may be;

(e) any payment made to a pupil by a barrister pursuant to paragraph 805 of the Code of Conduct shall constitute an amount received by the pupil from his practice as a barrister; and

(f) the following travel by a pupil shall not constitute travel for the purposes of his pupillage:

(i)   travel between his home and chambers; and

(ii) travel for the purposes of his practice as a barrister.

INDEX

[Amended July 2000]

SECTION 3

Miscellaneous Guidance

This section contains miscellaneous guidance, advice and inform issued by the Bar Council. It does not form part of the Code of Con

INDEX

Pupillage Guidelines
Written Standards for the Conduct of Professional Work
Summary of the Equality Code for the Bar
Guidance on Age Discrimination
Guidance on Preparation of Witness Statements
Guidance on Preparation of Defence Case Statements
Service Standard on Returned Briefs agreed with the CPS
BarDIRECT Terms of Engagement
Approved List of Direct Professional Access Bodies
Joint Tribunal Standing Orders for Fee Disputes with Solicitors
Guidance on Counsel's Fee Notes
Guidance on Holding Out as a Barrister

PUPILLAGE GUIDELINES

PART I — ADMINISTRATION

A   Applications for Pupillage

1. **General**

   (a) All chambers and other training organisations authorised by the Bar Council to take pupils must have selection procedures for pupils in which applicants are recruited through fair and open competition and on the basis of merit.

   (b) All pupils must be recruited in accordance with the Equality Code or an employer's equal opportunities policy and other guidance issued by the Bar Council.

2. **Advertisement of Vacancies**

   (a) All vacancies for pupillage in chambers must be advertised in accordance with the Pupillage Funding & Advertising Requirements.

   (b) All vacancies for pupillage in organisations other than chambers are expected to be advertised in accordance with the Pupillage Funding & Advertising Requirements.

3. **Selection Procedures**

   (a) Chambers and other organisations authorised by the Bar Council to take pupils must establish and follow selection procedures that ensure that pupils are selected through fair and open competition and on the basis of merit.

   (b) In particular it is recommended that:

       (i)   selection criteria must be relevant and applied consistently to all applicants;

       (ii) short listing and other selection decisions must be undertaken by at least two people;

       (iii) applicants who are selected for interview must be sent a copy of the chambers' pupillage policy document prior to attending for interview;

       (iv) all selectors should be familiar with the contents of the Equality Code.

   (c) Records of all applicants and documentation relating to selection decisions should be kept for a period of at least one year. They should indicate the manner in which applications are disposed of and, where known, the ethnic origin and sex of each applicant.

4. **Registration**

   (a) All chambers and other organisations authorised by the Bar Council to take pupils should ensure that each pupil has registered his pupillage with the Bar Council in accordance with Regulation 42 and Schedule 14, part 1 of the Consolidated Regulations before the pupillage commences.

   (b) All pupils must be assigned a named pupil supervisor before the pupillage is registered with the Bar Council.

   (c) Each organisation must ensure that a pupil supervisor to whom a pupil is assigned is entitled to act as a pupil supervisor under CR47.1, that is that he is entered on the register of approved Pupil Supervisors kept by the Bar Council, that his practice is and has been for the previous two years his primary occupation and that his principal place of practice is a chambers or office which is also the principal place of practice of at least one other barrister or member of another authorised body who is of at least three years standing.

(d) Each organisation must ensure that no more than one pupil is assigned to a pupil supervisor at a time, unless the pupil supervisor has obtained the prior approval of the Joint Regulations Committee.

B   Funding of Pupillage

1.   All pupillages in chambers must be funded in accordance with the Pupillage Funding & Advertising Requirements.

C   Documentation and Records

1.   **Pupillage Policy Document**

(a) Every set of chambers or other organisation authorised by the Bar Council to take pupils must prepare a document or documents setting out its policies in relation to:

- the number and type of pupillages on offer
- recruitment of pupils
- the roles and duties of pupils
- the roles and duties of pupil supervisors
- the general pattern of pupillage (e.g. whether it is served with one pupil supervisor etc)
- the check list(s) used during pupillage
- arrangements for funding, including payment of expenses
- procedures for providing pupils with an objective assessment of their progress at regular intervals throughout pupillage
- complaints and grievances by pupils and pupil supervisors

(b) Every set of chambers which takes pupils should also include in its pupillage policy document its policies in relation to:

- chambers policy on payment of devilling and work completed for other members of chambers
- chambers policy on the payment of clerks fees and rent during the practising period of pupillage
- the method for fairly distributing briefs and other work amongst working pupils
- policy and procedure for the recruitment of tenants and when prospective tenants will be notified of tenancy decisions

(c) All pupils should be given a copy of the pupillage policy document when they are shortlisted for interview and reminded of it at the start of the pupillage.

2.   **Check lists**

(a) All chambers or organisations authorised by the Bar Council to take pupils must ensure that all pupils use a check list in a form either generally or specially approved by the Education & Training Department of the Bar Council.

(b) Completed check lists must be signed and dated by the pupil supervisor.

3.   **Monitoring of Pupillage**

(a) All chambers and organisations authorised by the Bar Council to take pupils must comply with the Bar Council's monitoring of pupillage scheme.

(b) Chambers and other organisations taking pupils are required to submit a pupillage return every year and to submit a copy of the pupillage policy document or documents and completed check lists when requested to do so by the Bar Council or a review panel.

PART II — CONDUCT OF PUPILLAGE

1. **Training**

    (a) Chambers and other organisations authorised by the Bar Council to take pupils should ensure that each pupil has a copy of the Pupillage File, Good Practice in Pupillage guide and the appropriate checklist by no later than the end of the first week of pupillage.

    (b) A pupil may only exercise a right of audience as a barrister in his practising six months of pupillage provided that he has completed or been exempted from the non-practising six months of pupillage and has been given permission from his pupil supervisor or head of chambers/training principal.

    (c) Pupil supervisors must ensure that the pupil has the opportunity to do all such work and gain all such experience as is appropriate for a person commencing practice in the type of work done by the pupil supervisor and in any event so as to enable the pupil to complete the check list, in particular

    (i) To ensure that the pupil has an understanding and appreciation of the operation in practice of rules of conduct and etiquette at the Bar

    (ii) To ensure that the pupil has gained sufficient practical experience of advocacy to be able to competently prepare and present a case

    (iii) To ensure that the pupil has gained sufficient practical experience of conferences and negotiation to be able to conduct the same competently

    (iv) To ensure that the pupil has gained sufficient practical experience in the undertaking of legal research and the preparation of drafts and opinions to be able to undertake the same competently

    (d) The pupil supervisor must ensure that the pupil is provided with, and retains, the appropriate check list, and completes it conscientiously and accurately. The pupil supervisor must sign and date the check list and should ensure that it is retained by chambers for a minimum of three years.

    (e) The pupil supervisor must give the pupil time off to attend the compulsory advocacy training and Advice to Counsel courses and should ensure that he or she has completed the courses satisfactorily.

2. **Distribution of Work in Chambers**

    (a) The distribution of briefs among practising pupils should be carried out in a manner fair to all pupils.

    (b) Sets of chambers in which advocacy work by practising pupils is a regular occurrence should establish a system for the purpose of regulating the distribution of briefs or instructions among pupils. The system should be made known to pupils at the commencement of pupillage. Heads of chambers should ensure that the distribution of work to working pupils is reviewed regularly. The distribution to pupils of unnamed work arriving in chambers and of work returned between members of chambers should be monitored.

3. **Certification**

    (a) Provided that the period of pupillage has been satisfactorily completed, the pupil must provide a pupil with a certificate in accordance with Consolidated Regulation 52.

    (b) If a pupil supervisor is not satisfied that the pupil has satisfactorily completed pupillage and he will not sign the certificate, he must notify the pupil of his or her options i.e. a certificate may be accepted from the pupil supervisor's Head of Chambers, the person designated by the Head of Chambers as the person in charge of pupillage, or another person acceptable to the Masters of the Bench and the Bar Council. If a pupil remains unable to obtain a relevant certificate the pupil may appeal to (a) the Masters of the Bench of the relevant Inn and then (b) the Joint Regulations Committee (Consolidated Regulation 52).

    (c) Pupil supervisors should familiarise themselves with the Equality Code for the Bar, the Pupillage File and the guide to Good Practice in Pupillage.

    (d) If the pupil supervisor leaves chambers he or she should where possible make arrangements for the pupil.

4. **Monitoring**

    (a) Chambers and other organisations authorised by the Bar Council to take pupils must have complaints and grievance procedures.

    (b) Chambers must have a policy in the event of chambers dissolving in relation to current pupils and students who have been made offers of pupillage.

    (c) All pupillage training organisations should put systems in place to ensure that checklists are adequately completed, signed off and retained until they are requested by the Bar Council.

    (d) At the end of each period of pupillage, a pupil supervisor's certificate of satisfactory completion of pupillage must be signed and submitted to the Bar Council.

    (e) At the end of each year, the head of chambers or training principal must submit to the Bar Council an annual return in the form prescribed by the Bar Council.

    (f) The pupillage policy document, annual pupillage return and completed checklists must be made available to the Bar Council on request, for the purposes of monitoring of pupillage.

    (g) Any pupil taken on as a tenant or employed barrister at the end of pupillage must have been issued with a full qualification certificate by the Bar Council.

WRITTEN STANDARDS FOR THE CONDUCT OF PROFESSIONAL WORK

GENERAL STANDARDS

1   Introduction

1.1   These Standards are intended as a guide to the way in which a barrister should carry out his work. They consist in part of matters which are dealt with expressly in the Code of Conduct and in part of statements of good practice. They must therefore be read in conjunction with the Code of Conduct, and are to be taken into account in determining whether or not a barrister has committed a disciplinary offence. They apply to employed barristers as well as to barristers in independent practice, except where this would be inappropriate. In addition to these General Standards, there are Standards which apply specifically to the conduct of criminal cases.

2   General

2.1   The work which is within the ordinary scope of a barrister's practice consists of advocacy, drafting pleadings and other legal documents and advising on questions of law. A barrister acts only on the instructions of a professional client, and does not carry out any work by way of the management, administration or general conduct of a lay client's affairs, nor the management, administration or general conduct of litigation nor the receipt or handling of clients' money.

2.2   It is a fundamental principle which applies to all work undertaken by a barrister that a barrister is under a duty to act for any client (whether legally aided or not) in cases within his field of practice. The rules which embody this principle and the exceptions to it are set out in paragraphs 303, 601, 602, 603, 604 and 605 of the Code of Conduct.

3   Acceptance of Work

3.1   As soon as practicable after receipt of any brief or instructions a barrister should satisfy himself that there is no reason why he ought to decline to accept it.

3.2   A barrister is not considered to have accepted a brief or instructions unless he has had an opportunity to consider it and has expressly accepted it.

3.3   A barrister should always be alert to the possibility of a conflict of interests. If the conflict is between the interests of his lay client and his professional client, the conflict must be resolved in favour of the lay client. Where there is a conflict between the lay client and the Legal Aid Fund, the conflict must be resolved in favour of the lay client, subject only to compliance with the provisions of the Legal Aid Regulations.

3.4   If after a barrister has accepted a brief or instructions on behalf of more than one lay client, there is or appears to be a conflict or a significant risk of a conflict between the interests of any one or more of such clients, he must not continue to act for any client unless all such clients give their consent to his so acting.

3.5   Even if there is no conflict of interest, when a barrister has accepted a brief or instructions for any party in any proceedings, he should not accept a brief or instructions in respect of an appeal or further stage of the proceedings for any other party without obtaining the prior consent of the original client.

3.6   A barrister must not accept any brief or instructions if the matter is one in which he has reason to believe that he is likely to be a witness. If, however, having accepted a brief or instructions, it later appears that he is likely to be a witness in the case on a material question of fact, he may retire or withdraw only if he can do so without jeopardising his client's interests.

3.7   A barrister should not appear as a barrister:

(a) in any matter in which he is a party or has a significant pecuniary interest;

(b) either for or against any local authority, firm or organisation of which he is a member or in which he has directly or indirectly a significant pecuniary interest;

(c) either for or against any company of which he is a director, secretary or officer or in which he has directly or indirectly a significant pecuniary interest.

3.8   Apart from cases in which there is a conflict of interests, a barrister must not accept any brief or instructions if to do so would cause him to be otherwise professionally embarrassed: paragraph 603 of the Code of Conduct sets out the general principles applicable to such situations.

4   Withdrawal from a Case and Return of Brief or Instructions

4.1   When a barrister has accepted a brief for the defence of a person charged with a serious criminal offence, he should so far as reasonably practicable ensure that the risk of a conflicting professional engagement does not arise.

4.2   The circumstances in which a barrister must withdraw from a case or return his brief or instructions are set out in paragraph 608 of the Code of Conduct; the circumstances in which he is permitted to do so are set out in paragraph 609 the circumstances in which he must not do so are set out in paragraph 610.

5   Conduct of Work

5.1   A barrister must at all times promote and protect fearlessly and by all proper and lawful means his lay client's best interests.

5.2   A barrister must assist the Court in the administration of justice and, as part of this obligation and the obligation to use only proper and lawful means to promote and protect the interests of his client, must not deceive or knowingly or recklessly mislead the Court.

5.3   A barrister is at all times individually and personally responsible for his own conduct and for his professional work both in Court and out of Court.

5.4   A barrister must in all his professional activities act promptly, conscientiously, diligently and with reasonable competence and must take all reasonable and practicable steps to ensure that professional engagements are fulfilled. He must not undertake any task which:

(a) he knows or ought to know he is not competent to handle;

(b) he does not have adequate time and opportunity to prepare for or perform; or

(c) he cannot discharge within a reasonable time having regard to the pressure of other work.

5.5   A barrister must at all times be courteous to the Court and to all those with whom he has professional dealings.

5.6   In relation to instructions to advise or draft documents, a barrister should ensure that the advice or document is provided within such time as has been agreed with the professional client, or otherwise within a reasonable time after receipt of the relevant instructions. If it becomes apparent to the barrister that he will not be able to do the work within that time, he must inform his professional client forthwith.

5.7   Generally, a barrister should ensure that advice which he gives is practical, appropriate to the needs and circumstances of the particular client, and clearly and comprehensibly expressed.

5.8   A barrister must exercise his own personal judgment upon the substance and purpose of any advice he gives or any document he drafts. He must not devise facts which will assist in advancing his lay client's case and must not draft any originating process, pleading, affidavit, witness statement or notice of appeal containing:

    (a)   any statement of fact or contention (as the case may be) which is not supported by his lay client or by his brief or instructions;

    (b)   any contention which he does not consider to be properly arguable;

    (c)   any allegation of fraud unless he has clear instructions to make such an allegation and has before him reasonably credible material which as it stands establishes a prima facia case of fraud; or

    (d)   in the case of an affidavit or witness statement, any statement of fact other than the evidence which in substance according to his instructions, the barrister reasonably believes the witness would give if the evidence contained in the affidavit or witness statement were being given viva voce.

5.9   A barrister should be available on reasonable notice for a conference prior to the day of hearing of any case in which he is briefed; and if no such conference takes place then the barrister should be available for a conference on the day of the hearing. The venue of a conference is a matter for agreement between the barrister and his professional clients.

5.10   A barrister when conducting proceedings at Court:

    (a)   is personally responsible for the conduct and presentation of his case and must exercise personal judgment upon the substance and purpose of statements made and questions asked;

    (b)   must not, unless asked to so by the Court or when appearing before a tribunal where it his duty to do so, assert a personal opinion of the facts or the law;

    (c)   must ensure that the Court is informed of all relevant decisions and legislative provisions of which he is aware, whether the effect is favourable or unfavourable towards the contention for which he argues, and must bring any procedural irregularity to the attention of the Court during the hearing and not reserve such matter to be raised on appeal;

    (d)   must not adduce evidence obtained otherwise than from or through his professional client or devise facts which will assist in advancing his lay client's case;

    (e)   must not make statements or ask questions which are merely scandalous or intended or calculated only to vilify, insult or annoy either a witness or some other person;

    (f)   must if possible avoid the naming in open Court of third parties whose character would thereby be impugned;

    (g)   must not by assertion in a speech impugn a witness whom he has had an opportunity to cross-examine unless in cross-examination he has given the witness an opportunity to answer the allegation;

    (h)   must not suggest that a victim, witness or other person is guilty of crime, fraud or misconduct or make any defamatory aspersion on the conduct of any other person or attribute to another person the crime or conduct of which his lay client is accused unless such allegations go to a matter in issue (including the credibility of the witness) which is material to his lay client's case, and which appear to him to be supported by reasonable grounds.

5.11   A barrister must take all reasonable and practicable steps to avoid unnecessary expense or waste of the Court's time. He should, when asked, inform the Court of the probable length of his case; and he should also inform the Court of any developments which affect information already provided.

5.12   In Court a barrister's personal appearance should be decorous, and his dress, when robes are worn, should be compatible with them.

6.1   Witnesses

6.1.1   The rules which define and regulate the barrister's functions in relation to the preparation of evidence and contact with witnesses are set out in paragraphs 704, 705, 706, 707 and 708 of the Code of Conduct.

6.1.2   There is no longer any rule which prevents a barrister from having contact with any witness.

6.1.3   In particular, there is no longer any rule in any case (including contested cases in the Crown Court) which prevents a barrister from having contact with a witness whom he may expect to call and examine in chief, with a view to introducing himself to the witness, explaining the court's procedure (and in particular the procedure for giving evidence), and answering any questions on procedure which the witness may have.

6.1.4   It is a responsibility of a barrister, especially when the witness is nervous, vulnerable or apparently the victim of criminal or similar conduct, to ensure that those facing unfamiliar court procedures are put as much at ease as possible.

6.1.5   Unless otherwise directed by the Court or with the consent of the representative for the opposing side or of the Court, a barrister should not communicate directly or indirectly about the case with any witness, whether or not the witness is his lay client, once that witness has begun to give evidence until it has been concluded.

6.2   Discussing the Evidence with Witnesses

6.2.1   Different considerations apply in relation to contact with witnesses for the purpose of interviewing them or discussing with them (either individually or together) the substance of their evidence or the evidence of other witnesses.

6.2.2   Although there is no longer any rule which prevents a barrister from having contact with witnesses for such purposes a barrister should exercise his discretion and consider very carefully whether and to what extent such contact is appropriate, bearing in mind in particular that it is not the barrister's function (but that of his professional client) to investigate and collect evidence.

6.2.3   The guiding principle must be the obligation of counsel to promote and protect his lay client's best interests so far as that is consistent with the law and with counsel's overriding duty to the court (Code of Conduct paragraphs 302, 303).

6.2.4   A barrister should be alert to the risks that any discussion of the substance of a case with a witness may lead to suspicions of coaching, and thus tend to diminish the value of the witness's evidence in the eyes of the court, or may place the barrister in a position of professional embarrassment, for example if he thereby becomes himself a witness in the case. These dangers are most likely to occur if such discussion takes place:

(a) before the barrister has been supplied with a proof of the witness's evidence; or

(b) in the absence of the barrister's professional client or his representative.

A barrister should also be alert to the fact that, even in the absence of any wish or intention to do so, authority figures do subconsciously influence lay witnesses. Discussion of the substance of the case may unwittingly contaminate the witness's evidence.

6.2.5   There is particular danger where such discussions:

(a) take place in the presence of more than one witness of fact; or

(b) involve the disclosure to one witness of fact of the factual evidence of another witness.

These practices have been strongly deprecated by the courts as tending inevitably to encourage the rehearsal or coaching of witnesses and to increase the risk of fabrication or contamination of evidence: *R* v *Arif* (1993) May 26; *Smith New Court Securities Ltd* v *Scrimgeour Vickers (Asset Management) Ltd* [1992] BCLC 1104, [1994] 1 WLR 1271.

That is not to suggest that it is always inappropriate to disclose one witness' evidence to another. If the witness is one to be called by the other party, it is almost inevitable that a witness' attention must be drawn to discrepancies between the two statements. Discretion is, however, required, especially where the evidence of independent witnesses is involved.

6.2.6   Whilst there is no rule that any longer prevents a barrister from taking a witness statement in civil cases (for cases in the Crown Court see below), there is a distinction between the settling of a witness statement and taking a witness statement. Save in exceptional circumstances, it is not appropriate for a barrister who has taken witness statements, as opposed to settling witness statements prepared by others, to act as counsel in that case because it risks undermining the independence of the barrister as an advocate. The Cabrank Rule does not require a barrister to agree to undertake the task of taking witness statements.

6.2.7   There is no rule which prevents a barrister from exchanging common courtesies with the other side's witnesses. However, a barrister should not discuss the substance of the case or any evidence with the other side's witnesses except in rare and exceptional circumstances and then only with the prior knowledge of his opponent.

6.3   Criminal Cases in the Crown Court

6.3.1   Contested criminal cases in the Crown Court present peculiar difficulties and may expose both barristers and witnesses to special pressures. As a general principle, therefore, with the exception of the lay client, character and expert witnesses, it is wholly inappropriate for a barrister in such a case to interview any potential witness. Interviewing includes discussing with any such witness the substance of his evidence or the evidence of other such witnesses.

6.3.2   As a general principle, prosecuting counsel should not confer with an investigator witness unless he has also discharged some supervisory responsibility in the investigation and should not confer with investigators or receive factual instructions directly from them on matters about which there is or may be a dispute.

6.3.3   There may be extraordinary circumstances in which a departure from the general principles set out in paragraphs 6.3.1 and 6.3.2 is unavoidable. An example of such circumstances is afforded by the decision in *Fergus* (1994) 98 Cr App R 313.

6.3.4   Where any barrister has interviewed any potential witness or any such witness has been interviewed by another barrister, that fact shall be disclosed to all other parties in the case before the witness is called. A written record must also be made of the substance of the interview and the reason for it.

7   Documents

7.1   A barrister should not obtain or seek to obtain a document, or knowledge of the contents of a document, belonging to another party other than by means of the normal and proper channels for obtaining such documents or such knowledge.

7.2   If a barrister comes into possession of a document belonging to another party by some means other than the normal and proper channels (for example, if the document has come into his possession in consequence of a mistake or inadvertence by another person or if the document appears to belong to another party, or to be a copy of such a document, and to be privileged from discovery or otherwise to be one which ought not to be in the possession of his professional or lay client) he should:

(a)   where appropriate make enquiries of his professional client in order to ascertain the circumstances in which the document was obtained by his professional or lay client; and

(b)   unless satisfied that the document has been properly obtained in the ordinary course of events at once return the document unread to the person entitled to possession of it.

7.3.1   If having come into possession of such a document the barrister reads it before he realises that he ought not to, and would be embarrassed in the discharge of his duties by his knowledge of the contents of the document, then provided he can do so without prejudice to his lay client he must return his brief or instructions and explain to his professional client why he has done so.

7.3.2   If, however, to return his brief or instructions would prejudice his lay client (for example, by reason of the proximity of the trial) he should not return his brief or instructions and should, unless the Court otherwise orders, make such use of the document as will be in his client's interests. He should inform his opponent of his knowledge of the document and of the circumstances, so far as known to him, in which the document was obtained and of his intention to use it. In the event of objection to the use of such document it is for the Court to determine what use, if any, may be made of it.

7.4   If during the course of a case a barrister becomes aware of the existence of a document which should have been but has not been disclosed on discovery he should advise his professional client to disclose it forthwith; and if it is not then disclosed, he must withdraw from the case.

8   Administration of Practice

8.1   A barrister must ensure that his practice is properly and efficiently administered in accordance with the provisions of paragraph 304 of the Code of Conduct.

8.2   A barrister should ensure that he is able to provide his professional client with full and proper details of and appropriate justification for fees which have been incurred, and a proper assessment of any work to be done, so that both the lay client and the professional client are able to determine the level of any financial commitment which has been incurred or may be incurred.

9   Not used.

STANDARDS APPLICABLE TO CRIMINAL CASES

10   Introduction

10.1   These standards are to be read together with the General Standards and the Code of Conduct. They are intended as a guide to those matters which specifically relate to practice in the criminal Courts. They are not an alternative to the General Standards, which apply to all work carried out by a barrister. Particular reference is made to those paragraphs in the General Standards relating to the general conduct of a case (5.8), conduct in Court (5.10), discussion with witnesses (6.1, 6.2) and the use of documents belonging to other parties (7.1, 7.2, 7.3), which are not repeated in these standards.

11   Responsibilities of Prosecuting Counsel

11A   The Standards and principles contained in this paragraph apply as appropriate to all practising barristers, whether in independent practice or employed and whether appearing as counsel in any given case or exercising any other professional capacity in connection with it.

11.1   Prosecuting counsel should not attempt to obtain a conviction by all means at his command. He should not regard himself as appearing for a party. He should lay before the Court fairly and impartially the whole of the facts which comprise the case for the prosecution and should assist the Court on all matters of law applicable to the case.

11.2   Prosecuting counsel should bear in mind at all times whilst he is instructed:

(i)   that he is responsible for the presentation and general conduct of the case;

(ii)   that he should use his best endeavours to ensure that all evidence or material that ought properly to be made available is either presented by the prosecution or disclosed to the defence.

11.3   Prosecuting counsel should, when instructions are delivered to him, read them expeditiously and, where instructed to do so, advise or confer on all aspects of the case well before its commencement.

11.4   In relation to cases tried in the Crown Court, prosecuting counsel:

(a)   should ensure, if he is instructed to settle an indictment, that he does so promptly and within due time, and should bear in mind the desirability of not overloading an indictment with either too many defendants or too many counts, in order to present the prosecution case as simply and as concisely as possible;

(b)   should ask, if the indictment is being settled by some other person, to see a copy of the indictment and should then check it;

(c)   should decide whether any additional evidence is required and, if it is, should advise in writing and set out precisely what additional evidence is required with a view to serving it on the defence as soon as possible;

(d)   should consider whether all witness statements in the possession of the prosecution have been properly served on the defendant in accordance with the Attorney-General's Guidelines;

(e) should eliminate all unnecessary material in the case so as to ensure an efficient and fair trial, and in particular should consider the need for particular witnesses and exhibits and draft appropriate admissions for service on the defence;

(f) should in all Class 1 and Class 2 cases and in other cases of complexity draft a case summary for transmission to the Court.

11.5   Paragraphs 6 to 6.3.4 of the Written Standards for the Conduct of Professional Work refer.

11.6   Prosecuting counsel should at all times have regard to the report of Mr Justice Farquharson's Committee on the role of Prosecuting Counsel which is set out in *Archbold*. In particular, he should have regard to the following recommendations of the Farquharson Committee:

(a) Where counsel has taken a decision on a matter of policy with which his professional client has not agreed, it would be appropriate or him to submit to the Attorney-General a written report of all the circumstances, including his reasons for disagreeing with those who instructed him;

(b) When counsel has had an opportunity to prepare his brief and to confer with those instructing him, but at the last moment before trial unexpectedly advises that the case should not proceed or that pleas to lesser offences should be accepted, and his professional client does not accept such advice, counsel should apply for an adjournment if instructed to do so;

(c) Subject to the above, it is for prosecuting counsel to decide whether to offer no evidence on a particular count or on the indictment as a whole and whether to accept pleas to a lesser count or counts.

11.7   It is the duty of prosecuting counsel to assist the Court at the conclusion of the summing-up by drawing attention to any apparent errors or omissions of fact or law.

11.8   In relation to sentence, prosecuting counsel:

(a) should not attempt by advocacy to influence the Court with regard to sentence: if, however, a defendant is unrepresented it is proper to inform the Court of any mitigating circumstances about which counsel is instructed;

(b) should be in a position to assist the Court if requested as to any statutory provisions relevant to the offence or the offender and as to any relevant guidelines as to sentence laid down by the Court of Appeal;

(c) should bring any such matters as are referred to in (b) above to the attention of the Court if in the opinion of prosecuting counsel the Court has erred;

(d) should bring to the attention of the Court any appropriate compensation, forfeiture and restitution matters which may arise on conviction, for example pursuant to sections 35–42 of the Powers of Criminal Courts Act 1973 and the Drug Trafficking Offences Act 1986;

(e) should draw the attention of the defence to any assertion of material fact made in mitigation which the prosecution believes to be untrue: if the defence persist in that assertion, prosecuting counsel should invite the Court to consider requiring the issue to be determined by the calling of evidence in accordance with the decision of the Court of Appeal in *R v Newton* (1983) 77 Cr App R 13.

12   Responsibilities of Defence Counsel

12.1 When defending a client on a criminal charge, a barrister must endeavour to protect his client from conviction except by a competent tribunal and upon legally admissible evidence sufficient to support a conviction for the offence charged.

12.2 A barrister acting for the defence:

(a) should satisfy himself, if he is briefed to represent more than one defendant, that no conflict of interest is likely to arise;

(b) should arrange a conference and if necessary a series of conferences with his professional and lay clients;

(c) should consider whether any enquiries or further enquiries are necessary and, if so, should advise in writing as soon as possible;

(d) should consider whether any witnesses for the defence are required and, if so, which;

(e) should consider whether a Notice of Alibi is required and, if so, should draft an appropriate notice;

(f) should consider whether it would be appropriate to call expert evidence for the defence and, if so, have regard to the rules of the Crown Court in relation to notifying the prosecution of the contents of the evidence to be given;

(g) should ensure that he has sufficient instructions for the purpose of deciding which prosecution witnesses should be cross-examined, and should then ensure that no other witnesses remain fully bound at the request of the defendant and request his professional client to inform the Crown Prosecution Service of those who can be conditionally bound;

(h) should consider whether any admissions can be made with a view to saving time and expense at trial, with the aim of admitting as much evidence as can properly be admitted in accordance with the barrister's duty to his client;

(i) should consider what admissions can properly be requested from the prosecution;

(j) should decide what exhibits, if any, which have not been or cannot be copied he wishes to examine, and should ensure that appropriate arrangements are made to examine them as promptly as possible so that there is no undue delay in the trial.

(k) should as to anything which he is instructed to submit in mitigation which casts aspersions on the conduct or character of a victim or witness in the case, notify the prosecution in advance so as to give prosecuting Counsel sufficient opportunity to consider his position under paragraph 11.8(e).

12.3 A barrister acting for a defendant should advise his lay client generally about his plea. In doing so he may, if necessary, express his advice in strong terms. He must, however, make it clear that the client has complete freedom of choice and that the responsibility for the plea is the client's.

12.4 A barrister acting for a defendant should advise his client as to whether or not to give evidence in his own defence but the decision must be taken by the client himself.

12.5.1 Where a defendant tells his counsel that he did not commit the offence with which he is charged but nevertheless insists on pleading guilty to it for reasons of his own, counsel should:

(a) advise the defendant that, if he is not guilty, he should plead not guilty but that the decision is one for the defendant; counsel must continue to represent him but only after he has advised what the consequences will be and that what can be submitted in mitigation can only be on the basis that the client is guilty.

(b) explore with the defendant why he wishes to plead guilty to a charge which he says he did not commit and whether any steps could be taken which would enable him to enter a plea of not guilty in accordance with his profession of innocence.

12.5.2   If the client maintains his wish to plead guilty, he should be further advised:

(a) what the consequences will be, in particular in gaining or adding to a criminal record and that it is unlikely that a conviction based on such a plea would be overturned on appeal;

(b) that what can be submitted on his behalf in mitigation can only be on the basis that he is guilty and will otherwise be strictly limited so that, for instance, counsel will not be able to assert that the defendant has shown remorse through his guilty plea.

12.5.3   If, following all of the above advice, the defendant persists in his decision to plead guilty

(a) counsel may continue to represent him if he is satisfied that it is proper to do so;

(b) before a plea of guilty is entered counsel or a representative of his professional client who is present should record in writing the reasons for the plea;

(c) the defendant should be invited to endorse a declaration that he has given unequivocal instructions of his own free will that he intends to plead guilty even though he maintains that he did not commit the offence(s) and that he understands the advice given by counsel and in particular the restrictions placed on counsel in mitigating and the consequences to himself; the defendant should also be advised that he is under no obligation to sign; and

(d) if no such declaration is signed, counsel should make a contemporaneous note of his advice.

13   Confessions of Guilt

13.1   In considering the duty of counsel retained to defend a person charged with an offence who confesses to his counsel that he did commit the offence charged, it is essential to bear the following points clearly in mind:

(a) that every punishable crime is a breach of common or statute law committed by a person of sound mind and understanding;

(b) that the issue in a criminal trial is always whether the defendant is guilty of the offence charged, never whether he is innocent;

(c) that the burden of proof rests on the prosecution.

13.2   It follows that the mere fact that a person charged with a crime has confessed to his counsel that he did commit the offence charged is no bar to that barrister appearing or continuing to appear in his defence, nor indeed does such a confession release the barrister from his imperative duty to do all that he honourably can for his client.

13.3   Such a confession, however, imposes very strict limitations on the conduct of the defence, a barrister must not assert as true that which he knows to be false. He must not connive at, much less attempt to substantiate, a fraud.

13.4   While, therefore, it would be right to take any objections to the competency of the Court, to the form of the indictment, to the admissibility of any evidence or to the evidence admitted, it would be wrong to suggest that some other person had committed the offence charged, or to call any evidence which the barrister must know to be false having regard to the confession, such, for instance, as evidence in support of an alibi. In other words, a barrister must not (whether by calling the defendant or otherwise) set up an affirmative case inconsistent with the confession made to him.

13.5   A more difficult question is within what limits may counsel attack the evidence for the prosecution either by cross-examination or in his speech to the tribunal charged with the decision of the facts. No clearer rule can be laid down than this, that he is entitled to test the evidence given by each individual witness and to argue that the evidence taken as a whole is insufficient to amount to proof that the defendant is guilty of the offence charged. Further than this he ought not to go.

13.6   The foregoing is based on the assumption that the defendant has made a clear confession that he did commit the offence charged, and does not profess to deal with the very difficult questions which may present themselves to a barrister when a series of inconsistent statements are made to him by the defendant before or during the proceedings; nor does it deal with the questions which may arise where statements are made by the defendant which point almost irresistibly to the conclusion that the defendant is guilty but do not amount to a clear confession. Statements of this kind may inhibit the defence, but questions arising on them can only be answered after careful consideration of the actual circumstances of the particular case.

14   General

14.1   Both prosecuting and defence counsel:

    (a) should ensure that the listing officer receives in good time their best estimate of the likely length of the trial (including whether or not there is to be a plea of guilty) and should ensure that the listing officer is given early notice of any change of such estimate or possible adjournment;

    (b) should take all reasonable and practicable steps to ensure that the case is properly prepared and ready for trial by the time that it is first listed;

    (c) should ensure that arrangements have been made in adequate time for witnesses to attend Court as and when required and should plan, so far as possible, for sufficient witnesses to be available to occupy the full Court day;

    (d) should, if a witness (for example a doctor) can only attend Court at a certain time during the trial without great inconvenience to himself, try to arrange for that witness to be accommodated by raising the matter with the trial Judge and with his opponent;

    (e) should take all necessary steps to comply with the Practice Direction (Crime: Tape Recording of Police Interviews) [1989] 1 WLR 631.

14.2   If properly remunerated (paragraph 502 of the Code), the barrister originally briefed in a case should attend all plea and directions hearings. If this is not possible, he must take all reasonable steps to ensure that the barrister who does appear is conversant with the case and is prepared to make informed decisions affecting the trial.

15   Video Recordings

15.1   When a barrister instructed and acting for the prosecution or the defence of an accused has in his possession a copy of a video recording of a child witness which has been identified as having been prepared to be admitted in evidence at a criminal trial in accordance with Section 54 of the Criminal Justice Act 1991, he must have regard to the following duties and obligations:

(a) Upon receipt of the recording, a written record of the date and time and from whom the recording was received must be made and a receipt must be given.

(b) The recording and its contents must be used only for the proper preparation of the prosecution or defence case or of an appeal against conviction and/or sentence, as the case may be, and the barrister must not make or permit any disclosure of the recording or its contents to any person except when, in his opinion, it is in the interests of his proper preparation of that case.

(c) The barrister must not make or permit any other person to make a copy of the recording, nor release the recording to the accused, and must ensure that:

    (i) when not in transit or in use, the recording is always kept in a locked or secure place, and:

    (ii) when in transit, the recording is kept safe and secure at all times and is not left unattended, especially in vehicles or otherwise.

(d) Proper preparation of the case may involve viewing the recording in the presence of the accused. If this is the case, viewing should be done:

    (i) if the accused is in custody, only in the prison or other custodial institution where he is being held, in the presence of the barrister and/or his instructing solicitor.

    (ii) if the accused is on bail, at the solicitor's office or in counsel's chambers or elsewhere in the presence of the barrister and/or his instructing solicitor.

(e) The recording must be returned to the solicitor as soon as practicable after the conclusion of the barrister's role in the case. A written record of the date and time despatched and to whom the recording was delivered for despatch must be made.

16   Attendance of Counsel at Court

16.1   Prosecuting counsel should be present throughout the trial, including the summing-up and the return of the jury. He may not absent himself without leave of the Court; but, if two or more barristers appear for the prosecution, the attendance of one is sufficient.

16.2.1   Defence counsel should ensure that the defendant is never left unrepresented at any stage of his trial.

16.2.2   Where a defendant is represented by one barrister, that barrister should normally be present throughout the trial and should only absent himself in exceptional circumstances which he could not reasonably be expected to foresee and provided that:

(a) he has obtained the consent of the professional client (or his representative) and the lay client; and

(b) a competent deputy takes his place.

16.2.3   Where a defendant is represented by two barristers, neither may absent himself except for good reason and then only when the consent of the professional client (or his representative) and of the lay client has been obtained, or when the case is legally aided and the barrister thinks it necessary to do so in order to avoid unnecessary public expense.

16.2.4   These rules are subject to modification in respect of lengthy trials involving numerous defendants. In such trials, where after the conclusion of the opening speech by the prosecution defending counsel is satisfied that during a specific part of the trial there is no serious possibility that events will occur which will relate to his client, he may with the consent of the professional client (or his representative) and of the lay client absent himself for that part of the trial. He should also inform the judge. In this event it is his duty:

(a) to arrange for other defending counsel to guard the interests of his client;

(b) to keep himself informed throughout of the progress of the trial and in particular of any development which could affect his client; and

(c) not to accept any other commitment which would render it impracticable for him to make himself available at reasonable notice if the interests of his client so require.

16.3.1   If during the course of a criminal trial and prior to final sentence the defendant voluntarily absconds and the barrister's professional client, in accordance with the ruling of the Law Society, withdraws from the case, then the barrister too should withdraw. If the trial judge requests the barrister to remain to assist the Court, the barrister has an absolute discretion whether to do so or not. If he does remain, he should act on the basis that his instructions are withdrawn and he will not be entitled to use any material contained in his brief save for such part as has already been established in evidence before the Court. He should request the trial judge to instruct the jury that this is the basis on which he is prepared to assist the Court.

16.3.2   If for any reason the barrister's professional client does not withdraw from the case, the barrister retains an absolute discretion whether to continue to act. If he does continue, he should conduct the case as if his client were still present in Court but had decided not to give evidence and on the basis of any instruction he has received. He will be free to use any material contained in his brief and may cross-examine witnesses called for the prosecution and call witnesses for the defence.

17   Appeals

17.1.1   Attention is drawn to the Guide to Proceedings in the Court of Appeal Criminal Division ('the Guide') which is set out in full its original form at (1983) 77 Cr App R 138 and is summarised in a version amended in April 1990 Volume 1 of *Archbold* at 7–173 to 7–184.

17.1.2   In particular when advising after a client pleads guilty or is convicted, defence counsel is encouraged to follow the procedures set out at paragraphs 1.2 and 1.4 of the Guide.

17.2   If his client pleads guilty or is convicted, defence counsel should see his client after he has been sentenced in the presence of his professional client or his representative. He should then proceed as follows:

(a) if he is satisfied that there are no reasonable grounds of appeal he should so advise orally and certify in writing. Counsel is encouraged to certify using the form set out in Appendix 1 to the Guide. No further advice is necessary unless it is reasonable for a written advice to be given because the client reasonably requires it or because it is necessary e.g. in the light of the circumstances of the conviction, any particular difficulties at trial, the length and nature of the sentence passed, the effect thereof on the defendant or the lack of impact which oral advice given immediately after the trial may have on the particular defendant's mind.

(b) if he is satisfied that there are more reasonable grounds of appeal or if his view is a provisional one or if he requires more time to consider the prospects of a successful appeal he should so advise orally and certify in writing. Counsel is encouraged to certify using the form set out in Appendix 1 to the Guide. Counsel should then furnish written advice to the professional client as soon as he can and in any event within 14 days.

17.3   Counsel should not settle grounds of appeal unless he considers that such grounds are properly arguable, and in that event he should provide a reasoned written opinion in support of such grounds.

17.4   In certain cases counsel may not be able to perfect grounds of appeal without a transcript or other further information. In this event the grounds of appeal should be accompanied by a note to the Registrar setting out the matters on which assistance is required. Once such transcript or other information is available, counsel should ensure that the grounds of appeal are perfected by the inclusion of all necessary references.

17.5   Grounds of Appeal must be settled with sufficient particularity to enable the Registrar and subsequently the Court to identify clearly the matters relied upon.

17.6   If at any stage counsel is of the view that the appeal should be abandoned, he should at once set out his reasons in writing and send them to his professional client.

SUMMARY OF THE EQUALITY CODE FOR THE BAR

Explanatory Note:

Mandatory requirements in the Equality Code are those which are direct requirements of legislation or the Code of Conduct of the Bar. These are indicated by use of underlined bold in the summary. The remaining bold text indicates those recommendations which are considered essential in order that chambers/barristers avoid direct, indirect and unintentional discrimination and monitor their performance. 'Should' in the text indicates best advice on the steps chambers should take to avoid discriminating either unlawfully or contrary to the Code of Conduct of the Bar. The remaining advice is recommendations for the development of good equal opportunity practice by chambers. The Equality Code for the Bar includes explanation of the legislation and case law and refers to findings of relevant research conducted for the Bar.

CHAPTER 1 — Regulatory and Legislative Framework

1. **<u>Para. 305.1 of the Code of Conduct of the Bar of England and Wales prohibits a practising barrister from discriminating directly or indirectly against or victimising anyone on the grounds of their race, colour, ethnic or national origin, nationality, citizenship, sex, sexual orientation, marital status, disability, religion or political persuasion</u>**. A barrister who is able to prove, on the balance of probabilities, that indirect discrimination was unintentional, will not be found guilty of professional misconduct.

2. **<u>Under Para. 403 of the Code of Conduct barristers in independent practice must have regard to the Equality Code for the Bar.</u>**

3. **<u>The Sex Discrimination Act 1975 and the Race Relations Act 1976, as amended by section 64 of the Courts of Legal Services Act 1990, place a duty on barristers (and barristers' clerks) not to discriminate on the grounds of race or sex</u>**. Individuals may bring complaints that they have suffered discrimination to a county court within six months of the alleged act of discrimination.

4. The Disability (Discrimination) Bill is currently before Parliament and information will be provided to chambers when it becomes law.

CHAPTER 2 — Unlawful and Prohibited Discrimination

1. Unlawful direct discrimination consists of treating a person on grounds of race, colour, ethnic or national origin, nationality or citizenship, sex or marital status less favourably than others are or would be treated in the same or similar circumstances. Less favourable treatment is regarded as being on grounds of sex, race, etc. if but for that person's race or sex he or she would not have been subjected to the less favourable treatment.

2. Indirect discrimination occurs where:

   (a) a requirement or condition is applied equally to everyone but a considerably smaller proportion of one sex or racial group than of the other persons to whom it applies can comply with it;

   (b) the particular individual cannot comply with the requirement;

   (c) it results in a detriment to them; and

   (d) the requirement cannot be shown to be objectively justifiable in spite of its discriminatory effect.

3. **It is unlawful to victimise persons by treating them less favourably because they have brought proceedings under the Race Relations or Sex Discrimination Act, have given evidence or information relating to proceedings or have alleged that discrimination has occurred. Such treatment will also breach Para. 305 of the Code of Conduct.**

4. **It is unlawful for a person to instruct, induce or attempt to induce another person to discriminate on grounds of race, colour, ethnic or national origin, nationality, citizenship, sex or marital status. Equally, it is unlawful to act on such instructions or inducement.**

5. **Employers or principals are vicariously liable for any unlawfully discriminatory act of their employees or agents in the course of their work, unless they can demonstrate that they have taken all reasonable steps to prevent such acts.** This is relevant to barristers responsibility for their clerks and other staff in chambers.

6. Positive action is the term used for lawful measures taken under the provisions of the Race Relations or Sex Discrimination Acts where one sex or particular racial or ethnic group is under-represented in particular areas of work, or to meet the special needs of particular ethnic groups.

7. The above guidance on unlawful direct or indirect discrimination applies mutatis mutandis to discrimination on other grounds prohibited under Para. 204 of the Code of Conduct (including disability and sexual orientation).

8. Sexual orientation — a Bar Lesbian and Gay Group was formed in 1994 and is represented on the Bar Council's Sex Discrimination Committee. Chambers should adopt an equal opportunity policy making it clear that chambers will not discriminate on the grounds of sexual orientation and will offer equal opportunity to potential and actual members of chambers, whatever their sexual orientation. They should also ensure that all members, staff and applicants of chambers are aware of this policy.

9. Discrimination on the grounds of disability — the Bar Council has a Disability Panel whose members will advise on disability issues. Chambers are advised to ensure, as far as is reasonably possible, that the working environment is both safe and accessible. At interviews with people who have disabilities questions should focus on the interviewee's ability, experience and job-related qualifications. Interview panels should not make assumptions about candidates' ability to perform certain tasks but, where relevant, candidates should be asked to state how they would perform certain tasks.

CHAPTER 3 — Guidance on Harassment

1. **Harassment which would not have occurred but for the race or sex of the recipient may constitute unlawful direct discrimination. Both formal and informal grievance procedures should be available and be operated sensitively by chambers.** Harassment is unwelcome conduct which is offensive to the recipient, whatever the motive or intention of the perpetrator.

2. The European Commission's Code of Practice on sexual harassment, which may be taken into account by courts and tribunals in deciding what amounts to sexual harassment, defines it as 'unwanted contact of a sexual nature or other conduct based on sex affecting the dignity of women and men at work'. It also notes that 'harassment on grounds of sexual orientation undermines the dignity at work of those affected and it is impossible to regard such harassment as appropriate workplace behaviour.'

3. Avenues of redress for individuals suffering harassment include chambers grievance procedures, complaint to the relevant Students' Officer about a sponsor or pupil master/mistress, complaints to the PCC where the harasser is a barrister, complaint to a county court or [employment] tribunal alleging harassment as a form of direct discrimination, referral to the police when an act of harassment is a criminal offence. A recipient may also raise the matter informally with Inns Students Officers, the Bar's equal opportunities officers, CLE welfare staff, members of chambers, and sympathetic organisations such as the Association of Women Barristers.

4. The Bar Council's procedures on sexual harassment include a separate confidential telephone line to the equal opportunities officer, encouragement to chambers to adopt formal and informal procedures for handling complaints of harassment, a panel of mediators to advise the complainant and, with his or her permission, to seek to mediate between the complainant and the alleged harasser, and 'safe haven' chambers who, on the recommendation of the Chairman of the Bar or the Secretary of the PCC or the equal opportunities officers, will provide pupillage or an opportunity to squat to pupils or junior tenants who are unable to remain in their chambers as a result of harassment. A streamlined PCC procedure for handling complaints of harassment including measures to protect the anonymity of complainants, is under consideration.

CHAPTER 4 — Fair Selection of Pupils and Tenants

1. **Chambers must have selection procedures for pupils and tenants in which all applications are considered on an equal and non-discriminatory footing.** Here good practice may be evidence of what is lawful.

2. **The Code of Conduct requires sets of chambers to ensure that proper arrangements are made in chambers for dealing with pupils and pupillage. The guidelines to the Code of Conduct Annex A require that each set of chambers should have a document which sets out its policies in relation to the selection of pupils. There should also be a written policy for the selection of tenants.**

3. **No pupils should be accepted in chambers who have not come through the chambers selection procedure.**

4. **Before any consideration of applications for pupillage or for tenancy takes place, a decision should be made about the number and type of vacancies to be filled.**

5. **No decision about an applicant's suitability at any stage of the process should be taken by an individual member of chambers.** Selection decisions should be taken by a committee which should include as diverse a group of members of chambers as possible. All selectors should be familiar with the content of The Equality Code and with chambers procedures and selection criteria.

6. **The timetable for processing applications should be well publicised and chambers should adhere to it.** Chambers are recommended to join the Bar Council's pupillage admissions and clearing house scheme (PACH).

7. **All applicants should be assessed in competition with each other against objective and explicit selection criteria which relate to the demands of the work. The criteria should identify the knowledge, skills and other abilities required of a barrister doing such work. They should not be changed during the selection process.** Criteria should be checked for potentially discriminatory assumptions about the mobility, lifestyle, social background, financial resources, race or sex of applicants.

8. Many people come to the Bar later in life, having pursued a different career, or for other reasons. Traditionally, seniority in chambers has reflected age. There is a perception that young junior tenants may fear competition from older pupils and junior tenants. They may also fear that older pupils and junior tenants might be reluctant to conform to chambers' expectations of junior members. These assumptions should not feature in selection decisions concerning the skills and experience of mature applicants for pupillage and tenancy. Such skills and experience should be assessed according to the agreed selection criteria.

9. Chambers should publicise all vacancies including administrative vacancies as widely as possible, unless a tenancy vacancy is only to be filled from current or former pupils. Pupillage vacancies should be advertised in the Bar Council's Chambers Pupillage and Awards Handbook. Advertisements should contain clear and accurate information about the areas of work undertaken by chambers, the selection procedures and timetables to be followed, guidance on the selection criteria to be applied and information about any awards or financial arrangements made for pupils.

10. It is recommended that chambers use an application form in preference to a CV. The questions on the application form should invite applicants to demonstrate how their knowledge, skills and abilities meet the selection criteria. Where application forms are used it is recommended that CVs are not accepted. Chambers should not request photographs of applicants.

11. **Chambers should either include separate forms for monitoring ethnic origin and the sex of applicants, or include a monitoring question on their application form.** Monitoring data should not be passed on to shortlisters or members of selection panels until the selection process has been completed.

12. Chambers should acknowledge all applications in writing and notify applicants of any decision taken upon their applications as soon as reasonably practicable.

13. **In shortlisting for interview, members of the selection committee should assess each candidate's application against the selection criteria and make their judgments independently on the basis of the information provided in the application form.** An agreed rating scale should be used and assessments should be recorded using an agreed format.

14. **Interviews should be structured to ensure that similar areas related to the selection criteria are covered in questions to all candidates in order to ensure comparability between interviews. The interview schedule and the guidelines for scoring and decision-making should be discussed and agreed between the committee members before the round of interviews begins.**

15. Questions to all applicants should cover similar areas, should give applicants similar opportunities to demonstrate the skills required by chambers and should be closely related to the selection criteria. Interview questions should be formulated so as to ensure that they elicit relevant and reliable information for the assessment of applicants with diverse backgrounds and abilities.

Interviewers should take care to ensure that any differences between applicants in the quality of their answers are not merely a reflection of differences in the way questions are asked. Key questions should be planned in advance and written down, be clear and unambiguous and reviewed for potential bias and hence unlawful discrimination. Any follow up questions should be relevant to the selection criteria. Interviewers should avoid questions about personal relationships and family composition which are irrelevant to the applicants' professional performance.

Interviewers should avoid asking any question which carries the implication that disabled applicants have not thought through the practical consequences of their particular disability and of the ways in which this is likely to affect their working and social lives.

16. Case studies or test exercises can be used in selection procedures and provide applicants with the opportunity to demonstrate their ability in an area of work in chambers. Questions used in case studies, should be related to the type of work which the barrister in that set of chambers will be expected to do. Applicants should be advised in advance that this will form part of the interview.

17. **When references are requested the referee should be asked to supply information that relates strictly to the selection criteria.** There is considerable variation in the quality of the references that candidates can obtain, particularly in the case of students, and it is recommended that references should be used only in the final check on the selected candidates and should not be introduced into the selection process.

18. **The terms of the offer should be set out in writing to pupils and tenants; they must not be directly or indirectly discriminatory; nor should they differ without good cause between one pupil or tenant and another.** Chambers should only take the final decision on pupillages or tenancies after the round of interviews has been completed.

19. **All documentation relating to selection decisions should be retained for 12 months.** Chambers should respond positively to requests for feedback from candidates.

20. **Where chambers have vacancies for experienced tenants, these should be advertised as widely as possible and notices should indicate the area of practice and number of years' call sought. Selection should be made in accordance with the principles set out above.** There are two situations which may be dealt with outside the recommended selection procedures. These are:

    (i) the approach by a set of chambers to a particular barrister or barristers whom the chambers want to recruit because of their skills or area of practice and

    (ii) the approach by a particular barrister or barristers to a set of chambers who are not looking to recruit but who may be prepared to make an offer because of the barrister(s) skills or area of practice.

    Chambers should take care that such recruitment can be justified both in terms of the needs of chambers and the skills of the barrister(s) being recruited. Chambers should check where barristers recruited in this way are invariably of the same sex or racial group that discrimination is not occurring.

21. **When selecting tenants from pupils, chambers should take care to avoid subjective judgments in the assessment of the performance of pupils. An explicit framework for the assessment of pupils' work should be agreed by the selection committee. The decision about the offer of a tenancy to a former pupil should be made by more than one member of chambers. The pupil master/mistress and at least one other member of chambers with whom the pupil has worked should independently assess the pupil against the pre-determined criteria and record their assessments in writing before they are discussed. Chambers should record all opinions on the suitability of a pupil. The right of an unexplained veto should not be granted to any member of chambers.**

22.   Chambers should recognise the value of mini-pupillages both to potential applicants and to chambers themselves and should try to ensure fairness in the grant of mini-pupillages each year.

CHAPTER 5 — Equality of Opportunity in Chambers

1.   Every set of chambers should be in a position to state its commitment to equality of opportunity by reference to the Equality Code. Reference should be made to the statement in all material sent out to prospective applicants for mini-pupillages, pupillages, tenancy or employment in chambers.

2.   **In accordance with Annex A of the Bar's Code of Conduct, Chambers should specify in writing the role and duties of pupils in chambers, the role and duties of pupil masters/mistresses, the pattern of pupillage, the method for fairly distributing briefs and other work amongst working pupils, the checklists which apply, procedures for providing pupils with an objective assessment of their progress at regular intervals during pupillage, policy and procedures for the recruitment of tenants, policy and procedures in relation to pupils not taken on as tenants (including third-six months' pupillages and squatting) and chambers complaints and grievance procedures.**

3.   Barristers should be encouraged by their heads of chambers to discuss their career development individually with the clerk. They should tell the clerk their views of their past allocation of work in relation to the development of their practices. Heads of chambers should provide the opportunity for consultation on practice development and **should ensure that clerks know and observe the advice in this Code.**

4.   **Heads of chambers are required by the Code of Conduct's Pupillage Guidelines to ensure that the distribution of work to all members of chambers, working pupils and squatters is carried out in a manner that is fair to all and without discrimination.** All pupils in chambers are entitled to experience the range of training that a pupillage in that set of chambers offers.

5.   Heads of chambers should ensure that the distribution of work to working pupils is reviewed every two months and to junior tenants at least every six months.

6.   **The distribution of unnamed work received by chambers and the re-distribution of work between members of chambers to pupils and junior tenants should be systematically monitored.**

7.   **Heads of chambers should make clear to chambers' clerks that they must not accede to discriminatory instructions from professional clients, whether solicitors or other instructing agents. Counsel may be selected only on the basis of the skills and experience required for a particular case.**

8.   **If a solicitor or instructing agent refuses to withdraw a discriminatory instruction the Code of Conduct (Annex A) requires that it should be reported at once to the head of chambers who must report it forthwith to the relevant Bar Council committee chairman.** It should be noted that solicitors are bound by their practice rule and their statutory obligations not to practise discrimination.

9.   The Bar Council's maternity leave guidelines recommend that a woman tenant's seat in chambers should remain open for up to one year while she takes maternity leave. Chambers should offer a period of 3 months maternity leave free of rent and chambers' expenses.

10. **Heads of chambers should ensure that there is open and objective recruitment for all chambers' staff vacancies. Recruitment and selection procedures for clerks and other staff employed by chambers should follow the approach set out in chapter 4 for the selection of pupils and tenants.** Chambers should have a written staff grievance policy and a maternity leave and pay policy for female staff.

CHAPTER 6 — Monitoring

The purpose of monitoring is to check on the effectiveness of equal opportunities policies and procedures.

1. **Chambers should monitor all selection decisions and the distribution of work to junior tenants and pupils by race and sex. Selection monitoring data should be analysed after each major recruitment exercise or at least annually. A senior member of chambers should have specific responsibility for monitoring procedures.**

2. **Chambers should collect monitoring data by race and sex from a question on the application form or a separate monitoring form.** Categories consistent with the census ethnic classifications are recommended. These are: white, Black–African, Black–Caribbean, Black–other (please specify), Indian, Pakistani, Bangladeshi, Chinese, and other (please specify).

3. **The following stages of the selection process should be monitored: applications received, candidates shortlisted, candidates successful at interviews, terms and amounts of pupillage awards offered.**

4. Where under-representation of a particular group is identified in the applicant monitoring data, chambers should consider the use of the positive action provisions of the Race Relations and Sex Discrimination Acts to increase the rate of applications from under-represented groups.

5. Where equality targets are used they should be based on the existing situation in chambers and need to take into account available information on the representation of particular groups in the relevant populations (such as students seeking pupillage). Quotas should not be used and are unlawful.

6. **Where work for second six months' pupils or junior tenants is allocated by the clerk, or on the clerk's suggestion, this allocation should be systematically monitored.** The ACE fees program, if available to chambers, can assist in this. Reasons for any differences in the quantity or type of work done or fees earned, or in the potential of the work or career development, between men, women, or different minority ethnic groups within chambers should be investigated and corrective action taken if necessary. The same principles apply to the allocation of work to pupils and barristers in chambers who are known to have a disability or who are openly gay, lesbian or bisexual.

7. Chambers which are measuring the effectiveness of their equal opportunities policy may wish to monitor the number of disabled applicants for pupillage, tenancy or employment. Questions about registration will not be appropriate as the majority of disabled people do not register.

8. The collection of data on sexual orientation is impractical because many lesbians, gay men and bisexuals conceal their sexual orientation.

9. Chambers should check at regular intervals that the advice in this Code has been observed by staff and members of chambers.

CHAPTER 7 — Complaints

1. **Chambers should have written grievance procedures as part of general chambers management which should include procedures for handling complaints of discrimination and harassment. They should be brought to the attention of every new pupil, tenant and chambers' employee.**

2. **There should be procedures to deal with complaints that concern selection of pupils, tenants and staff from external and internal applicants (including pupils not offered tenancies), conduct of pupillage, distribution of work in chambers, pressure or instructions to discriminate, the distribution of work, and harassment or other discrimination originating within or outside chambers.**

3. Chambers should nominate one or two senior members of chambers to act as informal advisors to potential complainants and to assist in the informal resolution of grievances.

4. **When a complaint is made confidentiality should be maintained throughout any investigatory process as far as possible and appropriate in the circumstances. Names of complainants should not be released (save to those conducting the investigation and to the person complained against) without their consent.**

5. The written procedure should indicate the allocation of responsibility or investigating complaints to at least two members of chambers, names of chambers' informal advisors, an undertaking that complainants will not be victimised nor will suffer detriment because of a complaint made in good faith, an undertaking regarding confidentiality, a requirement for the complaint to be made in writing, a time limit within which a written response should be delivered, the range of remedial actions where complaints are substantiated, identification of the relevant Bar Council committees to which the complaints may be addressed and an indication of opportunities for supportive counselling provided by the associations and groups of women lawyers, members of minority ethnic groups, disabled people and lesbians or gay men. Confidential assistance may also be sought from the equal opportunities officers.

6. Complainants of unlawful racial or sex discrimination should be informed of their legal right to apply within six months of the incident to the county court (or within three months to an [employment] tribunal for chambers' employees) and their right to consult the Commission for Racial Equality or the Equal Opportunities Commission.

7. **Where actual or potential discrimination has been identified, remedial action should be taken by chambers.**

8. A report on all complaints and findings should be made to the head of chambers. Chambers should maintain confidential records of all complaints and records of meetings. These should be reviewed annually to ensure that procedures are working effectively.

AMENDMENT TO PARA 305 OF THE CODE OF CONDUCT

GUIDANCE ON INTERPRETATION

The Lord Chancellor has approved an amendment to the Code of Conduct which makes it professional misconduct to discriminate against an applicant for pupillage or tenancy on the ground of age *except* where such discrimination can be shown to be reasonably justifiable. The revised Para. 305 has been circulated in the usual manner for Code of Conduct amendments but is attached here as *Appendix 1* to the guidelines.

The amendment prohibits discrimination on grounds of age except in the limited circumstances when it may be objectively justified. It does not demand any form of positive discrimination in favour of older applicants nor any reduction of the usual appropriate criteria in assessing their applications. Good practice guidelines for chambers are attached at *Appendix 2* for information.

This guidance document has been circulated to all sets of chambers and will be incorporated into the revised version of the *Equality Code for the Bar*.

Background to the Amendment

For some years the Bar Council has been aware of problems being experienced by mature students in obtaining pupillage. This has been one of the major focuses of comment on the Bar Council website's General Forum.

The analyses of the PACH and OLPAS statistics produced annually since 1998 for the Bar Council by Dr Twigg of Portsmouth University have shown that each year younger applicants have more success than older applicants. The latest analysis of the 1998–2001 statistics (ie four years of data) shows that, using the technique of logistic regression to assess the influence of age while controlling for other variables such as ethnicity, gender, degree class and university attended the effect of age is significant for all age groups with a general decrease in the chances of being offered a pupillage occurring with an increase in age apart from the oldest age group (see tables at *Appendix 3*).

This issue was first discussed by the Bar Council in February 2001 when it was agreed to undertake a consultation exercise with chambers, Circuits and Specialist Bar Associations.

The amendment has been drafted to take account of the responses, in particular the view that the Bar Council's age prohibition should be in the same terms as the EC Directive 2000/78/EC which establishes a framework for equal treatment in employment and provides for differences of treatment on grounds of age where such differences of treatment are 'objectively and reasonably justified by a legitimate aim ... and if the means of achieving that aim are appropriate and necessary'.

The new provision in Para. 305 applies to all pupillage and tenancy recruitment taking place after 10th July 2002. The new requirements should be drawn to the attention of members of chambers with responsibility for recruitment and selection (note this does not apply to staff recruitment).

For further guidance please contact the Equal Opportunities Officers at the Bar Council.

APPENDIX 1

Para. 305.1

'A barrister must not in relation to any other person (including a client or another barrister or a pupil or a student member of an Inn of Court) discriminate directly or indirectly or victimise because of race, colour, ethnic or national origin, nationality, citizenship, sex, sexual orientation, marital status, disability, religion or political persuasion.'

Para. 305.2

A barrister must not in relation to any offer of a pupillage or tenancy discriminate directly or indirectly against a person on grounds of age, save where such discrimination can be shown to be objectively and reasonably justifiable.

Para. 305.3

In respect of indirect discrimination, there is no breach of paragraphs 305.1 and 305.2 if the barrister against whom the complaint is brought proves that the act of indirect discrimination was committed without any intention of treating the claimant unfavourably on any ground in that paragraph to which the complaint relates.'

APPENDIX 2

AGE DISCRIMINATION IN PUPILLAGE AND TENANCY SELECTION

GUIDANCE FOR CHAMBERS

The Bar Council has agreed that '*A barrister must not in relation to any offer of a pupillage or tenancy discriminate against a person on grounds of age, save where such discrimination can be shown to be objectively and reasonably justifiable.*'

Chambers should have regard to this guidance under Para. 403(d) of the Code.

The amendment prohibits discrimination on the ground of age only. It does not demand any form of positive discrimination in favour of older applicants nor any reduction of the selection criteria chosen for the assessment of applications. It relates only to the selection of pupils and tenants and therefore has no application in other areas such as retirement or staff recruitment.

The *Equality Code for the Bar* sets out in detail recommendations for fair selection. These apply equally to the avoidance of age discrimination. Selection criteria should not explicitly or implicitly refer to age but should focus on the skills, abilities and potential of applicants when shortlisting. Where experience is required this should be stated by reference to years in practice rather than age or years of call.

In particular:

- chambers may still set criteria with regard to levels and types of experience;
- chambers may still consider the record and suitability of an individual who has, for example, pursued a number of careers without success and assess that individual's suitability for a career at the Bar in the light of that career history;
- chambers may still take account of good health (subject to the Disability legislation) as a factor against an applicant;
- chambers should not screen applications by age nor set upper or lower age limits for pupillage and tenancy recruitment (except in the limited circumstances set out below);
- chambers recruitment criteria should take account of the increased career mobility of barristers and others wishing to join the profession.

Objective Justification for Age Discrimination

The EC Directive 2000/78/EC establishes a framework for equal treatment in employment and occupation. The rule change in the Code of Conduct has been drafted to take account of the Directive's provisions.

Article 6 of the Directive provides for differences of treatment on grounds of age. In interpreting para. 1 of Article 6 'differences of treatment ...' which are objectively and reasonably justified' still prohibit the application of a blanket exclusion of all candidates by reference to any age cut off point. A decision to refuse a candidate on grounds of age can be justified only where the individual circumstances including the professional experience of a particular candidate and the likely length of his or her professional life (a difficult prediction for the Bar) have been fully considered and the chambers has nevertheless concluded for legitimate business reasons that the application should be refused on the grounds of age.

In particular:

- blanket exclusion of candidates by reference to any upper or lower age limit or age range would not be justifiable;

- each candidate must be considered individually in relation to the business needs of chambers;

- chambers are entitled to recover their investment in recruiting and training new pupils and tenants. A period of 5–10 years before retirement would be regarded as reasonable and in the absence of any specific retirement age a notional retirement age of 65 could be assumed. *But* it would still be necessary to consider each applicant individually to assess the likely period of practice before retirement or the extent to which an applicant's previous experience may contribute towards value to chambers or earnings potential over a shorter period, given that some members of chambers take up full-time judicial appointments at an increasingly early stage in their careers and that many barristers in independent practice leave within the first 10 years, it is impossible to make accurate assumptions about how long any individual will stay in chambers;

- some sets of chambers have indicated that they recruit only pupils or tenants with a reasonable chance of applying for Silk or a Judicial Appointment. This is unlikely to be regarded as reasonable because the age/experience bands for appointments are very wide. Even where candidates in the upper age range have no reasonable prospect of advancement nevertheless they may well make a valuable contribution to chambers as successful juniors;

- where a set of chambers, for whatever reason, finds it has an imbalance in the age range of members of chambers it may be justifiable to discriminate in pupillage or tenancy selection in order to secure a balance of ages;

- it is improbable that chambers would be able to justify imposing an upper/lower age limit on the grounds that its clients preferred younger/older barristers;

- assumptions about the reluctance of older applicants to undertake the more mundane tasks of pupillage or accept pupillage supervisors who are younger than them would not amount to justifiable reasons for rejection on the grounds of age.

APPENDIX 3

Extracts from: the Twigg analysis of the latest PACH data

Table 4: Pupillage versus age by gender 1998–2001

		Age Category					
	Pupillage	20–24	25–29	30–34	35–39	40–44	45+
Men	No	1243	933	461	321	154	156
		73%	82%	84%	91%	95%	92%
	Yes	468	203	88	31	8	14
		27%	18%	16%	9%	5%	8%
Women	No	1479	661	280	242	150	114
		78%	78%	82%	91%	91%	96%
	Yes	429	186	61	24	15	5
		23%	22%	18%	9%	9%	4%

Table 7: The percentage chance of being offered a pupillage by age group, university and degree classification for white males without a CPE/Diploma, 1998–2001

Those figures in parentheses represent estimates for women in the sub-groups where there may be an effect for a particular age-gender interaction.

Age of applicant	University	Degree Classification		
		First	2:1	2:2
20–24	Oxbridge	87	64	37
	Old Civic	58	27	11
	New Civic	52	22	9
	Ex-Poly	32	12	4
25–34	Oxbridge	82	55	30
		(87)	(65)	(39)
	Old Civic	50	21	8
		(60)	(29)	(12)
	New Civic	43	17	17
		(53)	(24)	(9)
	Ex Poly	26	9	3
		(34)	(12)	(4)
35–39	Oxbridge	69	37	17
	Old Civic	32	11	4
	New Civic	27	9	3
	Ex-Poly	14	4	1
40–44	Oxbridge	56	26	10
		(76)	(47)	(23)
	Old Civic	22	7	2
		(41)	(16)	(6)
	New Civic	17	5	2
		(35)	(13)	(5)
	Ex-Poly	9	3	1
		(20)	(6)	(2)
45+	Oxbridge	68	38	17
	Old Civic	33	12	4
	New Civic	27	9	3
	Ex-Poly	14	4	2

GUIDANCE ON PREPARATION OF WITNESS STATEMENTS

PREPARING WITNESS STATEMENTS FOR USE IN CIVIL PROCEEDINGS

DEALINGS WITH WITNESSES

GUIDANCE FOR MEMBERS OF THE BAR

[*Amended 3 February 2001*]

Introduction

1. The purpose of this paper, which has the approval of the Professional Standards Committee of the General Council of the Bar, is to offer guidance to members of the Bar instructed to prepare or settle a witness statement and as to dealings with witnesses. Guidance already exists for practice in some Courts, notably Appendix 4 to the Chancery Guide, Part H1 of the Commercial Court Guide and CPR Part 32 and PD 32, paragraphs 17 to 25 to which attention is drawn. The intention is that this paper should be consistent with that guidance.

2. This guidance is not applicable to criminal proceedings. Attention is drawn to the Guidance Note 'Written Standards for the Conduct of Professional Work' in Section 3 of the Code of Conduct.

Witness statements

3. The cardinal principle that needs to be kept in mind when drafting or settling a witness statement is that, when the maker enters the witness box, he or she will swear or affirm that the evidence to be given will be the truth, the *whole truth* and nothing but the truth. In most civil trials almost the first question in chief (and not infrequently the last) will be to ask the witness to confirm, to the best of his belief, the accuracy of the witness statement. It is therefore critical that the statement is one that accurately reflects, to the best of Counsel's ability, the witness's evidence.

4. Witnesses often misunderstand the function of those drafting and settling witness statements. The function of Counsel is to understand the relevant evidence that a witness can give and to assist the witness to express that evidence in writing. It is important it is made clear to the witness (by reminder to the professional client or the witness, if seen by Counsel) that the statement once approved is *the witness's* statement. Ultimately it is the witness's responsibility to ensure that the evidence he gives is truthful. It is good practice to remind witnesses expressly of this from time to time, especially where Counsel is assisting the witness to formulate in his own words a particular aspect of the evidence or putting forward a particular piece of drafting for the witness's consideration (which is expressly permitted by the proviso to Rule 704 of the Code of Conduct).

5. It is not Counsel's duty to vet the accuracy of a witness's evidence.[1] We all may doubt the veracity of our clients and witnesses occasionally. Counsel is, of course, entitled and it may often be appropriate to draw to the witness's attention other evidence which appears to conflict with what the witness is saying and is entitled to indicate that a Court may find a particular piece of evidence difficult to accept. But if the witness maintains the evidence, it should be recorded in the witness statement. If it is decided to call the witness, it will be for the Court to judge the correctness of the witness's evidence.

---

1   If para. 6 of Appendix 4 of the Chancery Guide suggests otherwise, the PSC respectfully disagrees. The position would, of course, be different if to Counsel's knowledge the witness statement contained untruths: see *ZYX Music GmbH v King* [1995] 3 All ER 1.

6.   It follows that the statement:

(i)   Must accurately reflect the witness's evidence. Rule 704 of the Code of Conduct states:

'A barrister must not devise facts which will assist in advancing the lay client's case and must not draft any ... witness statement [or] affidavit ... containing:

...

(d)   in the case of a witness statement or affidavit any statement of fact other than the evidence which in substance according to his instructions the barrister reasonably believes the witness would give if the evidence contained in the witness statement or affidavit were being given in oral examination;[2]

provided that nothing in this paragraph shall prevent a barrister drafting a document containing specific factual statements or contentions included by the barrister subject to confirmation of their accuracy by the lay client or witness.'

(ii)   Must not contain any statement which Counsel knows the witness does not believe to be true. Nor should the witness be placed under any pressure to provide other than a truthful account of his evidence.

(iii)   Must contain all the evidence which a witness could reasonably be expected to give in answer to those questions which would be asked of him in examination-in-chief. The witness statement should not be drafted or edited so that it no longer fairly reflects the answers which the witness would be expected to give in response to oral examination-in-chief in accordance with the witness's oath or affirmation. Although it is not the function of a witness statement to answer such questions as might be put in cross-examination, great care should be exercised when excluding any material which is thought to be unhelpful to the party calling the witness and no material should be excluded which might render the statement anything other than the truth, the whole truth and nothing but the truth. While it is permissible to confine the scope of examination-in-chief to part only of the evidence which a witness could give, that is always subject to Counsel's overriding duty to assist the Court in the administration of justice and not to deceive or knowingly or recklessly to mislead the Court (Rule 302 of the Code of Conduct). Consequently, it would be improper to exclude material whose omission would render untrue or misleading anything which remains in the statement. It would also be improper to include fact A while excluding fact B, if evidence-in-chief containing fact A but excluding fact B could not have been given consistently with the witness's promise to tell the truth, the whole truth and nothing but the truth. Whether it is wise and in the client's interest in any given case to exclude unfavourable material which can properly be excluded is a matter of judgment.

(iv)   Save for formal matters and uncontroversial facts, should be expressed if practicable in the witness's own words. This is especially important when the statement is dealing with the critical factual issues in the case — e.g. the accident or the disputed conversation. Thus the statement should reflect the witness's own description of events. It should not be drafted or edited so as to massage or obscure the witness' real evidence.

---

2   CPR Part 32.4(1).

(v)   Must be confined to admissible evidence that the witness can give, including permissible hearsay.[3] Inadmissible hearsay, comment and argument should be excluded.

(vi)   Should be succinct and exclude irrelevant material. Unnecessary elaboration is to be avoided. It is not the function of witness statements to serve as a commentary on the documents in the trial bundles. Nor are they intended to serve as another form of written argument.

7. Sometimes it becomes apparent, after a witness statement has been served, that the witness's recollection has altered. This may happen if the witness sees or hears how another witness puts the facts in a witness statement served by another party. Where Counsel learns that the witness has materially changed his evidence—

(i)   He should consider with, and if necessary advise, his professional or BarDirect client whether, in the circumstances, a correction to the original statement needs to be made in order to avoid another party being unfairly misled.

(ii)   Where a correction to the original statement is appropriate, this should be done by recording the changed evidence in an additional witness statement and serving it on the other parties (and if appropriate filing it at court). If this is impracticable, e.g. because it occurs very shortly before the hearing, the other parties should be informed of the change immediately and the statement should be corrected at an early stage in court.

(iii) The underlying principle is that it is improper for a litigant to mislead the court or another party to the litigation.[4]

(iv)   If a lay or BarDirect client refuses to accept Counsel's advice that disclosure of a correction should be made, Counsel's duty is to withdraw from further acting for the client.

Formalities

8. A witness statement:

(i)   Should be expressed in the first person;

(ii)   Should state the full name of the witness and the witness's place of residence or, if the statement is made in a professional, business or other occupational capacity, the address at which he works, the position he holds and the name of the firm or employer;

(iii) Should state the witness's occupation or if he has none his description;

(iv)   Should state if the witness is a party to the proceedings or is an employee of such a party;

(v)   Should usually be in chronological sequence divided into consecutively numbered paragraphs each of which should, so far as possible, be confined to a distinct portion of the evidence;

(vi)   Must indicate which of the statements in it are made from the witness's own knowledge and which are matters of information and belief, indicating the source for any matters of information and belief;

---

3 32PD, para. 18.2 requires the witness to indicate which of the statements are matters of information and belief and the source for any such matters.

4 On the duty to make disclosure of material changes of evidence and new documents, see generally *Vernon v Bosley (No. 2)* [1999] QB 18

(vii) Must include a statement by the witness that he believes that the facts stated in it are true;

(viii) Must be signed by the witness or, if the witness cannot read or sign it, must contain a certificate made by an authorised person as to the witness's approval of the statement as being accurate;[5]

(ix) Must have any alterations initialled by the witness or by the authorised person;

(x) Should give in the margin the reference to any document or documents mentioned;

(xi) Must be dated.

There are further formal requirements in 32PD, paras 17–19, relating to intitulement, exhibits, pagination, production and presentation, to which attention is directed.

Dealings with Witnesses

Counsel seeing witnesses.[6]

9. The old rules preventing Counsel from seeing a witness, other than the client, have been progressively relaxed over recent years. The current position in civil proceedings can be summarised as follows:

(i) There is no longer any rule which prevents a barrister from having contact with any witness. Indeed, in taking witness statements and generally, it is the responsibility of a barrister, especially when the witness is nervous, vulnerable or apparently the victim of criminal or similar conduct, to ensure that those facing unfamiliar court procedures are put as much at ease as possible.

(ii) Although there is no longer any rule which prevents a barrister from having contact with witnesses, a barrister should exercise his discretion and consider very carefully whether and to what extent such contact is appropriate, bearing in mind in particular that it is not the barrister's function (but that of his professional client) to investigate and collect evidence.

(iii) The guiding principle must be the obligation of Counsel to promote and protect his lay client's best interests so far as that is consistent with the law and with Counsel's overriding duty to the Court (Code of Conduct paragraphs 302, 303). Often it will be in the client's best interests that Counsel should meet witnesses whose evidence will be of critical importance in the case, so as to be able to form a view as to the credibility of their evidence and to advise the lay client properly;

(iv) A barrister should be alert to the risks that any discussion of the substance of a case with a witness may lead to suspicions of coaching, and thus tend to diminish the value of the witness's evidence in the eyes of the court, or may place a barrister in a position of professional embarrassment, for example, if he thereby becomes himself a witness in the case. These dangers are most likely to occur if such discussion takes place:

(a) before the barrister has been supplied with a proof of the witness's evidence; or

(b) in the absence of the barrister's professional client or his representative.

---

5 See 32PD, para. 21.

6 This is largely taken from guidance Note 'Written Standards for the Conduct of Professional Work' in Section 3 of the Code of Conduct approved by the Lord Chancellor's Advisory Committee on Legal Education and Conduct and the designated judges.

(v) Rule 705 of the Code of Conduct provides that a barrister must not rehearse practise or coach a witness in relation to his evidence. This does not prevent Counsel giving general advice to a witness about giving evidence e.g. speak up, speak slowly, answer the question, keep answers as short as possible, ask if a question is not understood, say if you cannot remember and do not guess or speculate. Nor is there any objection to testing a witness's recollection robustly to ascertain the quality of his evidence or to discussing the issues that may arise in cross-examination. By contrast, mock cross-examinations or rehearsals of particular lines of questioning that Counsel proposes to follow are not permitted. What should be borne in mind is that there is a distinction, when interviewing a witness, between questioning him closely in order to enable him to present his evidence fully and accurately or in order to test the reliability of his evidence (which is permissible) and questioning him with a view to encouraging the witness to alter, massage or obscure his real recollection (which is not). The distinction was neatly drawn by Judge Francis Finch in *In Re Eldridge*[7] in 1880, where he said:

> While a discreet and prudent attorney may very properly ascertain from witnesses in advance of the trial what they in fact do know and the extent and limitations of their memory, as guide for his own examinations, he has no right legal or moral, to go further. His duty is to extract the facts from the witness, not to pour them into him; to learn what the witness does know, not to teach him what he ought to know.'

At the risk of stating the obvious, this is a difficult area calling for the exercise of careful judgment.

(vi) A barrister should also be alert to the fact that, even in the absence of any wish or intention to do so, authority figures do subconsciously influence lay witnesses. Discussion of the substance of the case may unwittingly contaminate the witness's evidence.

(vii) There is particular danger where such discussions:

(a) take place in the presence of more than one witness of fact; or

(b) involve the disclosure to one witness of fact of the factual evidence of another witness.

These practices have been strongly deprecated by the courts as tending inevitably to encourage the rehearsal or coaching of witnesses and to increase the risk of fabrication or contamination of evidence: *R v Arif* (1993) May 26; *Smith New Court Securities Ltd v Scrimgeour Vickers (Asset Management) Ltd* [1994] 1 WLR 1271.

(viii) That is not to suggest that it is always inappropriate to disclose one witness's evidence to another. If conflicting witness statements have been obtained from different witnesses or served by the other side, it may be appropriate or necessary for a witness to be further questioned about, or have his attention drawn to, discrepancies between statements. Discretion is, however, required, especially where the evidence of independent witnesses is involved.

(ix) Whilst there is no rule that any longer prevents a barrister from taking a witness statement in civil cases, there is a distinction between the settling of a witness statement and taking a witness statement. Save in exceptional circumstances, it is not appropriate for a barrister who has taken witness statements, as opposed to

---

7   New York Court of Appeals; 37 NY 161, 171.

settling witness statements prepared by others, to act as Counsel in that case because it risks undermining the independence of the barrister as an advocate. Exceptional circumstances would include:

(a) The witness is a minor one;

(b) Counsel has no choice but to take the proof and this is the only practical course in the interests of justice — this would apply, for instance, where a witness appears unexpectedly at Court and there is no one else competent to take the statement;

(c) Counsel is a junior member of a team of Counsel and will not be examining the witness.

The Cab Rank rule does not require a barrister to agree to undertake the task of taking witness statements.

(x) A barrister should be prepared to exchange common courtesies with the other side's witnesses. However, a barrister should only discuss the substance of the case or any evidence with the other side's witnesses in rare and exceptional circumstances and then only with the prior knowledge of his opponent.

16 January, 2001

GUIDANCE ON PREPARATION OF DEFENCE CASE STATEMENTS

THE PREPARATION OF DEFENCE CASE STATEMENTS PURSUANT TO THE
CRIMINAL PROCEDURE AND INVESTIGATIONS ACT 1996

GUIDANCE ON THE DUTIES OF COUNSEL

(As approved by the PCCC on 24 September 1997)

1. It is becoming increasingly common for solicitors to instruct counsel to draft or settle Defence Case Statements, required under section 5 of the Criminal Procedure and Investigations Act 1996. Often these instructions are given to counsel with no or little previous involvement in the case shortly before the expiry of the time limit.

2. The relevant legislation is set out at §12–56 *et seq.* of the 2002 edition of *Archbold*. In summary, however:

    (i) The time limit for compliance is short — 14 days from service of prosecution material or a statement that there is none. The permitted grounds for an extension of time are limited;[1]

    (ii) The contents of the Defence Case Statement are obviously of great importance to the defendant. An inaccurate or inadequate statement of the defence could have serious repercussions for the defendant, if the trial judge permits 'appropriate' comment;

    (iii) Whilst it will be the natural instinct of most defence counsel to keep the Defence Case Statement short, a short and anodyne statement may be insufficient to trigger any obligation on the prosecution to give secondary disclosure of prosecution material.

3. Normally it will be more appropriate for instructing solicitors to draft the Defence Case Statement, since typically counsel will have had little involvement at this stage.

4. However, there is nothing unprofessional about counsel drafting or settling a Defence Case Statement, although it must be appreciated that there is no provision in the current regulations for graduated fees allowing for counsel to be paid a separate fee for his work. This most unsatisfactory situation (which has arisen, as a result of the 1996 Act, since the graduated fees regulations were negotiated) is being addressed urgently by the Fees and Legal Aid Committee. A barrister has no obligation to accept work for which he will not be paid. The absence of a fee will justify refusal of the instructions of counsel who are not to be retained for the trial and are simply asked to do no more than draft or settle the Defence Case Statement. Where counsel is retained for the trial, Rule 502(b) of the Code of Conduct deems instructions in a legally aided matter to be at a proper fee and counsel would not be justified in refusing to draft or settle a Defence Case Statement on the sole ground that there is no separate fee payable for this work.

5. Many members of the Bar will nevertheless feel that, in the interests of their lay client and or of good relations with instructing solicitors, they cannot refuse work, even where they would otherwise be entitled to do so. Those who do so need to recognise the crucial importance of:

    (i) Obtaining all prosecution statements and documentary exhibits;

---

1   See the Defence Disclosure Time Limit Regulations 1997 made pursuant to the Act: [Paragraph 12–94 of Archbold, 2002 edition].

(ii)   Getting instructions from the lay client, from a properly signed proof and preferably a conference. Those instructions need to explain the general nature of the defence, to indicate the matters on which issue is taken with the prosecution and to give an explanation of the reason for taking issue. They must also give details of any alibi defence, sufficient to give the information required by Section 5(7) of the 1996 Act;

(iii)   Getting statements from other material witnesses;

(iv)   Ensuring that the client realises the importance of the Defence Case Statement and the potential adverse consequences of an inaccurate or inadequate statement;

(v)   Getting proper informed approval for the draft from the client. This is particularly important, given the risks of professional embarrassment if the client seeks to disown the statement during the course of the trial, perhaps when the trial is not going well or when under severe pressure in cross-examination. Counsel ought to insist on getting written acknowledgement from the lay client that:

   (a)   he understands the importance of the accuracy and adequacy of the Defence Case Statement for his case;

   (b)   he has had the opportunity of considering the contents of the statement carefully and approves it.

This may often mean having a conference with the lay client to explain the Defence Case Statement and to get informed approval, although in straightforward cases where counsel has confidence in the instructing solicitor, this could be left to the solicitor. Where the latter course is taken, a short written advice (which can be in a standard form) as to the importance of obtaining the written acknowledgement before service of the statement should accompany the draft Defence Case Statement. A careful record should be kept of work done and advice given.

(vi)   If there is inadequate time, counsel should ask the instructing solicitor to apply for an extension of time. This needs to be considered at a very early stage, since the application must be made before the expiry of the time limit.

6.   It follows that counsel ought not to accept any instructions to draft or settle a Defence Case Statement unless given the opportunity and adequate time to gain proper familiarity with the case and to comply with the fundamental requirements set out above. In short, there is no halfway house. If instructions are accepted, then the professional obligations on counsel are considerable.

SERVICE STANDARDS ON RETURNED BRIEFS AGREED WITH THE CPS

SERVICE STANDARDS ON RETURNED BRIEFS

1   **PRINCIPLE**

1.1   This Standard applies to all advocates instructed to prosecute on behalf of the CPS.

1.2   The fundamental principle upon which the Standard is based is that the advocate initially instructed should conduct the case.

1.3   This applies to all cases irrespective of whether or not they are contested.

1.4   For the purpose of this Standard a return means a brief which is passed to another advocate because the advocate instructed is unable to appear to represent the prosecution at any hearing, subject to the exceptions for interlocutory hearings referred to in paragraphs 1.13–1.15 below.

1.5   There is a need for positive action to be taken by all advocates, acting in conjunction with the CPS, to minimise the level of returns in order to ensure that the best possible service is provided. Such action will include ensuring that the advocate's availability is considered when cases are being fixed and that efforts are made to take this into account.

1.6   Whatever positive action is taken to reduce the level of returns, it is recognised that there will always be some briefs which are returned.

1.7   The impact of a return is dependent upon the nature of the case and the timing of its return.

1.8   There will be some degree of flexibility in uncontested cases in that the acceptability of the return will be influenced by the nature, complexity and seriousness of the case and the degree of involvement of the advocate before committal or transfer.

1.9   Where a return is unavoidable, the advocate will be responsible for ensuring that immediate notice is given to enable the CPS to choose and instruct another advocate and for that advocate fully to prepare the case.

1.10   Special attention must be paid to retrials, sensitive cases or those involving vulnerable witnesses, especially children, and those cases in which the advocate has settled the indictment, provided a substantive advice, attended a conference or been present at an ex parte hearing.

1.11   The advocate prosecuting a case in which the brief has been returned should not, without good reason and prior consultation with the CPS, reverse a decision previously taken by the advocate originally instructed. This is especially important in cases involving child witnesses and video evidence.

1.12   Whenever a brief is returned, the choice of an alternative advocate will always be a matter for the CPS. Where counsel has been instructed, the availability of alternative counsel in the chambers holding the brief will not be the determining factor in selecting a new advocate. Counsel's clerk will be expected to make realistic proposals as to an alternative advocate, whether or not within the same chambers, and consideration will be given to them.

1.13   When the CPS instructs an advocate to appear at an interlocutory hearing, including plea and directions hearings (PDH), bail applications, applications to make or break fixtures and mentions, the advocate instructed in the case will, wherever practicable, be expected to attend. If the advocate instructed is not available, an alternative advocate may be instructed provided that advocate is acceptable to the CPS and following consultation with the CPS.

1.14   If an advocate is unable to attend a PDH as a result of work commitments elsewhere, a returned brief will not be treated as a return for the purpose of monitoring compliance with this Standard, unless the advocate's clerk was consulted about, and had confirmed, the advocate's availability for the PDH before the brief was delivered.

1.15   In the case of other interlocutory hearings, which may be potentially difficult or sensitive, the CPS will, whenever possible, consult the advocate's clerk about the advocate's availability before the date of hearing is arranged. Unless such consultation has taken place, a returned brief will not be counted as a return for the purpose of monitoring compliance with this Standard.

1.16   Following any interlocutory hearing, the brief will revert to the advocate originally instructed, subject to the CPS exercising its discretion to depart from this practice in any particular case.

1.17   In any case in which a brief is returned, and whatever the nature of the hearing, it will be the responsibility of the advocate holding the brief to ensure that the advocate to whom the brief is returned is fully informed of all matters relating to that hearing and, where *practicable*, to endorse the brief accordingly.

1.18   Notwithstanding the responsibility resting with the advocate returning the brief, the advocate accepting the brief also has a duty to be fully prepared to deal with any matter likely to arise at the hearing.

1.19   Subject to any other agreement negotiated with the CPS on the transfer of papers between advocates, whenever a brief is returned it will be the responsibility of the advocate or the advocate's clerk holding the brief to make arrangements to transfer the brief promptly to the agreed alternative advocate.

1.20   Neither the advocate nor the advocate's clerk should permit the number of briefs held by a single advocate to reach a point where returns are inevitable. The CPS must be informed if it appears that this situation might arise.

1.21   The CPS will make arrangements for the distribution of work to individual advocates so as to minimise the possibility of this happening.

2   GUIDANCE

2.1   Recommendations and guidance on counsel's responsibilities in relation to returned briefs have been given in the following reports:

Seabrook Report on the Efficient Disposal of Business in the Crown Court — June 1992.

- Counsel should ensure that the CPS is notified as soon as he or his clerk knows he might have to return a brief due to other professional commitments.
- Counsel should ensure that immediate steps are taken to return a brief to another barrister acceptable to the CPS as soon as he or his clerk becomes aware that he will not be able to conduct the case.

Bar Standards Review Body Report — Blueprint for the Bar — September 1994.

- Counsel should provide written reasons upon request as to why a brief is returned.

- Counsel returning a brief should do so with as little disruption to the conduct of the case as practicable. This involves the provision of information to counsel taking on the case.

2.2   It is against this background that the procedures which follow have been developed.

3   **PROCEDURE**

Categorisation of cases

3.1   For the purpose of setting standards aimed at reducing the level of returns cases will fall within 3 categories.

3.2   **Category A** will comprise the following:

- cases in which the fees will be assessed ex post facto;
- pre-marked cases in which a Grade 4 Advocate or Special List Advocate (London and South Eastern Circuit) is instructed;
- cases in which Leading Counsel (including a Leading Junior) has been instructed by the CPS;
- cases falling within classes 1 and 2 of the Lord Chief Justice's Practice Direction classifying business within the Crown Court.

3.3   In category A cases no return of the brief is acceptable save where the following applies:

- the advocate is unable to attend court because of illness, accident, childbirth or unexpected incapacity;
- attending court would cause the advocate grave personal hardship as, for example, following a bereavement;
- subject to paragraph 3.8 below, circumstances have arisen outside the advocate's, or the advocate's clerk's, control which are such as to make a return inevitable;
- the case has been fixed for trial by the court in the knowledge that the advocate instructed will not be available.

3.4   Where a case has been so fixed, the CPS will decide whether to apply to the court to change the fixed date or to instruct a different advocate.

3.5   **Category B** will comprise cases in which the brief has been pre-marked and which do not fall within category A, and standard fee cases in which a fixed trial date has been allocated.

3.6   If a trial date has been fixed, no return of the trial brief is acceptable except as in 3.3 above.

3.7   If a trial date has been fixed before the brief is delivered, or has been fixed regardless of the advocate's availability, immediate steps will be taken by the CPS in liaison with the advocate or the advocate's clerk, to identify an appropriate advocate who will be available on the fixed date. Once the brief has been delivered or reallocated, no return is acceptable.

3.8   The advocate's involvement in a part-heard trial will not in itself justify a return in a category A or B case, unless the part-heard trial has been prolonged by unforeseeable circumstances. Where the advocate is involved in a part-heard trial, the position must be kept under constant review, and the CPS kept fully informed, so that an early decision can be made by the CPS as to whether to require a brief to be returned.

3.9   If a brief in a category A or B case is returned, the advocate will, upon CPS request, provide a written explanation as to why the return was unavoidable.

3.10 **Category C** will comprise standard fee cases which have not been given fixed trial dates.

3.11 It is recognised that, for cases which attract standard fees, a higher return rate is more difficult to avoid.

3.12 Subject to the requirements of Bar/CPS Standard 2 on pre-trial preparation having been carried out, if the advocate originally instructed in a category C case is not available, the CPS will agree to the brief being returned to another advocate of appropriate experience, who has adequate time to prepare for the hearing.

General procedural matters

3.13 If a case appears in a warned list or firm date list and the advocate instructed will not be available, the advocate or the advocate's clerk must notify the CPS immediately.

3.14 The CPS will then decide whether to make representations to the court to take the case out of the list, or to allow the brief to be returned to another advocate.

3.15 Where a case has appeared in a reserve list, or where a system of overnight listing operates within the warned list, it is accepted that some returns will be inevitable.

3.16 The advocate or the advocate's clerk should give as much notice as possible of returns in these instances and should aim to give the CPS **two working days notice**. This situation could apply, for example, when an advocate becomes committed part way through the week to a case expected to last several days.

3.17 Where a system of firm dates operates within the warned list period, the CPS must be notified if it appears likely that the advocate may be unavailable, so that an early decision can be made on whether to instruct another advocate or whether to defer the decision.

3.18 The timing of the decision whether to instruct another advocate will always be a matter for the CPS and will be influenced by the nature of the case as well as the information provided by the advocate or the advocate's clerk.

August 1996

BarDIRECT TERMS OF ENGAGEMENT

BarDIRECT GUIDANCE HANDBOOKS FOR BARRISTERS AND CHAMBERS AND BarDIRECT CLIENTS

(INFORMATION PACKS INCLUDING HANDBOOKS AND APPENDICES ARE AVAILABLE FROM THE GENERAL COUNCIL OF THE BAR)

INFORMATION PACK FOR BARRISTERS

Introduction

1.1   This handbook comprises the following sections:

(1) A general introduction which sets out what BarDIRECT is and the nature of the work covered by the scheme.

(2) A check list for barristers considering whether to accept instructions under the BarDIRECT scheme.

(3) Guidance for individual barristers and chambers who are considering whether to accept instructions under the BarDIRECT scheme. The notes cover matters such as the qualifications for acceptance of instructions and the obligations arising upon receipt of instructions and thereafter. Where appropriate, the notes contain references to the relevant rules of the Bar Direct Rules.

1.2   There are also attached to this handbook a number of appendices, as follows:

(1) The information pack given to existing and prospective BarDIRECT clients comprising the following:
  (a)   An introduction;
  (b)   Guidance for those seeking recognition as BarDIRECT clients.
  (c)   Guidance notes for BarDIRECT clients.

(2) An application form for those seeking recognition as BarDIRECT clients (Not printed in this Code).

(3) The BarDIRECT terms of work.

(4) The BarDIRECT Rules ('the BDR') (Printed in Annex F in this Code).

(5) The BarDIRECT Recognition Rules ('the BDDR') (Printed in Annex F in this Code).

1.3   Any inquiries about the BarDIRECT scheme should be directed in the first instance to Jan Bye/Mark Makinney, The General Council of the Bar, 3 Bedford Row, London WC1R 4DB Tel: 020 7242 0082.

INTRODUCTION TO BarDIRECT

What is BarDIRECT?

2.1   BarDIRECT seeks to maximise client access to the legal profession whilst at the same time ensuring that the Bar retains its identity as a referral profession. The legal profession is responsible to the public for the provision of competitive and cost effective legal services of the highest professional standards. In meeting these goals the legal profession must ensure that the interests of the client are prioritised. BarDIRECT has been established to provide those organisations and individuals who possess the necessary skills and knowledge to do so, to have the opportunity to refer to the expertise of a Barrister without the intervention of a solicitor.

2.2 BarDIRECT recognises that there are significant areas of work in which the traditional two layered legal system in which the Bar insists that only a solicitor can refer work to it may unnecessarily increase the costs which the client is required to bear. BarDIRECT seeks to highlight the fields of practice in which barristers are positioned to provide specialised advisory and advocacy services on a competitive and cost effective basis without the intervention of a solicitor. It demonstrates the areas of work in which the skills and training of a barrister are compatible with direct access from organisations and individuals whose own training, skills and experience equip them to instruct a barrister directly.

2.3 Building upon the experience of Direct Professional Access (DPA), BarDIRECT will allow direct access to the services of a barrister from a far wider range of organisations and individuals than previously permitted. It will mean that under certain conditions, suitable organisations and individuals (from the business community to the voluntary sector) will have direct access to a barrister.

2.4 The Bar Council will carefully regulate BarDIRECT to ensure that the organisation or individual is properly equipped to instruct the Bar. Through a Licensing Scheme known as BarDIRECT, The Bar Council will identify the particular type and scope of work in respect of which organisations and individuals which it licenses will in future have the opportunity to instruct a barrister directly. BarDIRECT will give those organisations the choice of consulting either a solicitor or a barrister in cases where it is unnecessary and not cost effective to instruct both a solicitor and a barrister.

2.5 In short, BarDIRECT is about ensuring that the Bar is a premier provider of competitive and cost effective legal services and that in offering those services to the public it does not impose unnecessary restrictions.

BarDIRECT Work

2.6 The Courts and Legal Services Act ('CLSA') recognises a distinction between advocacy services and litigation services. The Bar believes that this is an important distinction in the provision of legal services and one which should be maintained in the interests of the public. The Bar is not equipped to and does not have the facilities to conduct litigation or offer litigation services. The principle of a primarily referral based profession remains central to the profession and practice of a barrister. BarDIRECT does not permit barristers to conduct litigation within the definition set out in the CLSA or to perform 'excepted work' as defined in the Code of Conduct.

2.7 The BarDIRECT licensing scheme ensures that the referrer has the skills necessary and the facilities available to instruct the Bar direct. BarDIRECT will not lead to referrals 'off the street'.

Implementation

2.8 Pilot schemes began in the summer of 1999. Client access to the scheme is governed by the BDRR a copy of which is at Appendix 5 (Annex F in this Code). The role of counsel under the scheme is governed by the BarDIRECT Rules ('BDR') which is at Appendix 4 (Annex F in this Code). Any barrister wishing to accept instructions under BarDIRECT must be familiar with the terms of both the Regulations and the Rules.

BarDIRECT CHECKLIST

The Client

- Is the client an approved organisation permitted to instruct under BarDIRECT?

- Does the BarDIRECT client have sufficient authority to instruct you on the type of work that it wishes to — i.e. does the work fall within the authority shown on the BarDIRECT licence forwarded to you at the time of instruction?

- Is the particular type of work actually suitable for instruction under BarDIRECT or will it require the intervention of an intermediary to provide litigation services?

Counsel

- Have you notified BMIF that you will be accepting instructions under BarDIRECT?

- Are you familiar with the terms of the BarDIRECT Recognition Regulations and the Bar-DIRECT Rules?

- Are you satisfied that you and your chambers are sufficiently equipped to facilitate the additional administrative requirements necessary to accept BarDIRECT instructions?

GUIDANCE FOR BARRISTERS AND CHAMBERS

Who can accept Instructions?

3.1   The BDR covers every barrister in independent practice and governs the terms under which they are permitted to accept instructions.

3.2   As set out below, BarDIRECT imposes requirements on Counsel to assess the suitability of instructions under the scheme, obligations to advise clients as to the nature of scheme in each particular case and a duty in respect of the organisation of paperwork etc.

3.3   To be eligible to accept BarDIRECT instructions a barrister must have completed the first six months of pupillage and either be a tenant in chambers or a working pupil/squatter.

3.4   A barrister is only entitled to accept instructions from a BarDIRECT client where s/he has notified the BMIF that s/he intends to accept instructions under BarDIRECT and has paid the appropriate premium (see BDR Rule 3).

The Obligation Upon Counsel Upon Receipt of Instructions

3.5   Accompanying every instruction the client is obliged to send the barrister a copy of its Bar-DIRECT licence and identify exactly who is providing instructions (see BDR Rule 4). A barrister can only accept instructions if satisfied that the type of work offered is appropriate for the scheme. Whilst the licensing scheme should result in a clear definition of what work should be forwarded to counsel, it remains the responsibility of a barrister in each individual case to satisfy her/himself that s/he has sufficient facilities to support the case without the need of a solicitor or other similar intermediary (see BDR Rule 5). Similarly, if at any time during the course of a case, a barrister feels that the client's best interests and the interests of justice are best served by the introduction of a solicitor, or other such intermediary, then s/he must advise in writing the client of the need to instruct them forthwith (see BDR Rule 8(a)). If a solicitor (or other duly authorised person) is not so instructed then the barrister is under an obligation to return instructions and cease to act (see BDR Rule 8(b)).

3.6   Upon receipt of instructions a barrister must write to the client stating that the instructions have been accepted (as the case may be) on the standard terms previously agreed in writing with that BarDIRECT client or on the BarDIRECT Terms of Work or if s/he has accepted instructions otherwise than on such standard terms a copy of the agreement in writing with the BarDIRECT client setting out the terms upon which s/he has agreed to do the work and the basis upon which s/he is to be paid. If requested so to do a barrister should send a copy of the BarDIRECT Terms of Work to the BarDIRECT client. Unless s/he has accepted instructions on the terms of the BarDIRECT Terms of Work or on terms which incorporate the following particulars s/he must advise the BarDIRECT client in writing of the effect of paragraph 210 of the Code of Conduct in the circumstances of the instructions, of the fact that the barrister cannot be expected to perform excepted work and that circumstances may arise in which it will be necessary or appropriate, often at short notice and possibly during the case, to retain the services of a solicitor or authorised litigator (see BDR Rule 7).

Administrative Obligations

3.7   A barrister who is instructed by a BarDIRECT client must keep a case record (either on card or computer). Rule 10 sets out what must be included in the record (such as details as to the date of receipt of and acceptance of instructions, time limits, dates of advices and conferences, the fee (when agreed) etc.).

3.8   Instructions (including a list of enclosures), advices, drafts of documents, notes of all conferences (including on the telephone) and all advice given must either be retained by the barrister or the barrister must take reasonable steps to ensure that the BarDIRECT client will retain these documents for 6 years after the date of the last item of work done (see BDR Rule 11).

3.9   The barrister is under a duty to ensure that the licence covers the client and the scope and type of work the subject matter of the instructions to the barrister. A copy of the Bar-DIRECT Licence must be sent to the barrister with the instructions (see BDR Rule 4). If a barrister believes that a BarDIRECT client has in some significant respect failed to comply with the terms of its licence or with the Terms of Work, then the barrister must report the fact to the BarDIRECT committee (see BDR Rule 9).

APPENDICES

1.   The information pack given to existing and prospective BarDIRECT clients comprising:

   - An introduction;
   - Guidance for those seeking recognition as BarDIRECT clients.
   - Guidance notes for BarDIRECT clients.

2.   An application form for those seeking recognition as BarDIRECT clients. (Not printed in this Code)

3.   The BarDIRECT terms of work.

4.   The BarDIRECT Rules ('the BDR') (Printed in Annex F of this Code).

5.   The BarDIRECT Recognition Rules ('the BDDR') (Printed in Annex F of this Code).

INFORMATION PACK FOR CLIENTS

Introduction

1.1 This handbook, which is provided to existing or potential BarDIRECT clients, comprises the following sections:

(1) Guidance for those seeking recognition under the BarDIRECT scheme. The purpose of this section is to set out, in general terms, the principles which govern the grant of licences to use the BarDIRECT scheme and the nature of such licences.

(2) A check list for BarDIRECT clients who are proposing to instruct a barrister under the terms of their licence.

(3) Guidance notes for BarDIRECT clients. This section is designed to be of assistance to clients who are proposing to instruct a barrister under the terms of their licence. It covers matters such as the type of cases in which it is appropriate to instruct a barrister, choice of barrister, the manner in which a barrister should be instructed, the steps following the initial instruction and billing.

1.2 There are also attached to this handbook a number of appendices, as follows:

(1) An application form for those seeking recognition as BarDIRECT clients (Not printed in this Code).

(2) The BarDIRECT terms of work.

(3) The BarDIRECT Rules (Printed in Annex F of this Code).

(4) The BarDIRECT Recognition Rules (Printed in Annex F of this Code).

1.3 Any inquiries about the BarDIRECT scheme should be directed in the first instance to Jan Bye/Mark Makinney, The General Council of the Bar, 3 Bedford Row, London WC1R 4DB Tel: 020 7242 0082.

GUIDANCE FOR THOSE SEEKING RECOGNITION UNDER THE BarDIRECT SCHEME

2.1 BarDIRECT recognises that solicitors are not alone in having the skills and knowledge to benefit from the legal services offered by the Bar. BarDIRECT provides the opportunity for the widest diversity of organisations and individuals to be licensed to instruct a barrister directly whether in the commercial, profit, non-profit or voluntary sector and irrespective of size or of type of work. These Guidance Notes use the generic term 'organisation' to describe the full range of bodies from large public limited companies to small charities and advice centres.

2.2 A fundamental principle of BarDIRECT is that access under its provisions is *licenced access*. An organisation or individual must be licenced by the Bar Council to use the scheme and the licence will govern who in the organisation may use the scheme and the type and scope of work in respect of which the organisation or individual is licensed to instruct a barrister directly. Within the Bar Council the licensing functions will be carried out by the BarDIRECT Committee (see BDRR Regulation 1). The organisation or individual seeking a licence must apply to the Bar Council and for this purpose must complete an Application Form and provide such further information as may be required.

2.3 Whilst there is no limitation to the type of organisation that can seek authorisation the BarDIRECT Committee will ensure that the body is equipped to provide direct instructions to Counsel. The Committee will examine a wide range of criteria in determining whether a proposed organisation or individual should be granted a licence, including for example the type of work which it wishes to refer directly to a barrister, its expertise or experience, its familiarity with any relevant area of law, its ability to obtain and prepare information and to organise papers and information for the barrister and in a contentious matter for the court, its ability to take charge and have the general conduct of the matter on which it wishes to instruct the barrister directly, the extent to which it has arrangements for holding in separate accounts and maintaining as trust monies any monies received from third parties, the extent to which the affairs and conduct of the person or organisation or its members are subject to professional, disciplinary, regulatory or other organisational rules and have professional indemnity insurance (see BDRR Regulation 6).

2.4 The scope and type of work embraced by the licence will depend on the expertise, skills and knowledge of the organisation or individual applying for the licence. For example, whilst some organisations may be licensed simply to use BarDIRECT to obtain written advices on policy matters, others may be permitted to approach counsel for a wide range of services including advocacy (see BDRR Regulation 3).

2.5 The terms of a licence specifying the name of the person or organisation, the period for which the licence has been granted, the limitations or conditions on which the licence has been granted are within the complete discretion of the BarDIRECT Committee. Such limitations and conditions may for example define the matters upon which they may instruct counsel through BarDIRECT, set out the tribunals or courts in which a barrister may be instructed to exercise a right of audience and/or provide that unless otherwise first agreed in writing all instructions will be deemed to be given and accepted on the terms of the BarDIRECT Terms of Work as approved by the BarDIRECT Committee (see BDRR Regulation 4(b)). A copy of the Licence must be sent to the Barrister at the time of instruction enabling the barrister to ensure that the licence covers the instructions (see BDR Rule 4(c)).

2.6 The status of an organisation can be considered by the BarDIRECT committee. Approval can be given to an organisation or an individual, or to all or some of the members of an organisation or to all or some of the employees of an organisation or its members or of the individual (BDRR Regulation 3(c)). Approval can be on a provisional or full basis and can be limited in time (BDRR Regulation 3(a), (b)).

2.7 The BarDIRECT Committee may from time to time, approve additional persons or organisations, withdraw approval either in whole or in part from any person or organisation who has been licensed, increase reduce or otherwise alter the period for which a licence has been granted, alter or revoke the conditions or limitations which have been imposed under the licence and cancel and demand surrender of any licence which has been issued (see BDRR Regulation 5).

2.8 Instructions under BarDIRECT can only be accepted where the client is properly authorised for the type of work sought to be offered (see BDRR Regulation 3(e) and BDR Rule 1).

2.9 A barrister is not required to accept work from a BarDIRECT client and should not do so if the barrister considers it in the interests of the lay client or the interests of justice that an intermediary be instructed together with or in place of the barrister. Such intermediary may be a solicitor or other authorised litigator or some other appropriate person or organisation (see BDR Rule 5(b)). If a barrister having accepted instructions from a BarDIRECT client considers it in the interests of the lay client or the interests of justice that an intermediary be instructed together with or in place of the barrister the barrister must forthwith advise the BarDIRECT client in writing to instruct such intermediary and unless such intermediary is as soon as reasonably practicable instructed the barrister must cease to act and must return any instructions to the BarDIRECT client (see BDR Rule 8).

CHECKLIST FOR BarDIRECT CLIENTS PROPOSING TO INSTRUCT BARRISTERS

- Is my case an appropriate case for instructing a barrister: see guidance notes in section 3, paragraphs 3.2 to 3.5.

- How do I choose the right barrister for my case: see guidance notes in section 3, paragraphs 3.6 to 3.8.

- How do I go about instructing a barrister: see guidance notes in section 3, paragraphs 3.9 to 3.10.

- How are a barrister's fees calculated and how should they be agreed: see guidance notes in section 3, paragraphs 3.6(4) and 3.10(4).

- What should I send to a barrister: see guidance notes in section 3, paragraphs 3.11 to 3.15.

- What happens after I have instructed a barrister: see guidance notes in section 3, paragraphs 3.16 to 3.20.

- How will I be billed: see guidance notes in section 3, paragraphs 3.21 to 3.22.

- What do I do if I am unhappy about the service which has been provided: see guidance notes in section 3, paragraphs 3.23 to 3.24.

GUIDANCE ON INSTRUCTING BARRISTERS UNDER THE BarDIRECT SCHEME

Introduction

3.1   These guidance notes are intended for use by BarDIRECT clients who are considering instructing a barrister or barristers direct, whether for the purposes of obtaining their advice or for the purposes of obtaining representation in court under the new arrangements for direct licensed access.

In which cases is it appropriate to instruct a barrister?

3.2   The overriding consideration when deciding whether it is appropriate to instruct a barrister alone, or whether to instruct a solicitor (whether that solicitor in turn instructs a barrister or not), is whether to do so would be in the best interests of the client. This means that it is essential to have a proper understanding of what a barrister can and cannot do.

3.3   The following is an outline of those things which a barrister is normally expected and entitled to do:

    (1) Advisory work (e.g., giving advice on the law generally and/or on the merits of any particular matter, whether contentious or non-contentious, and/or on the drafting of documents such as contracts, standard terms and conditions, correspondence, letters before actions, reports etc.,);

    (2) Drafting of claim forms, petitions and other applications;

    (3) Drafting of statements of case;

    (4) Advice on the factual and expert evidence which will be needed in order to establish the case at the hearing, whether oral or written;

    (5) Advice on which witness statements, expert reports and documents must or should be disclosed to the other side;

(6) Assistance in the preparation of affidavits and witness statements for use at a hearing. There is an important distinction between (i) taking a statement from a witness, which involves interviewing the witness in order to elicit his or her evidence, and (ii) assisting in the preparation of a witness statement.[1] The latter task typically includes identifying the matters the statement should cover, reviewing a draft witness statement, advising on questions of admissibility and weight of particular passages of draft statements, and by settling from drafts a final form of witness statement;

(7) Preparation of any documents, such as skeleton arguments, chronologies, etc., used for the purposes of presenting a case in court;

(8) Representation at any court hearing;

(9) Representation at a hearing before a tribunal other than a court, for example a disciplinary tribunal;

(10) Advice on tactics in relation to the litigation generally and its settlement.

3.4 There are some things, on the other hand, which a barrister would not normally be expected or entitled to do. In general barristers do not have the facilities or the office back-up to undertake much of the general preparatory work necessary to get a more complex case to trial. In particular, barristers are not permitted to do the following:

(1) The management, administration and general conduct of litigation including written or oral communication between the parties or their advisors;[2]

(2) Investigating and collecting evidence for use in court;

(3) The receipt or handling of client money.[3]

3.5 In general, accordingly, unless the BarDIRECT client is equipped and prepared to undertake the type of litigation support function normally undertaken by a solicitor, the typical case in which a barrister might be instructed directly to appear in court will be one:

(1) of lesser factual complexity; and

(2) where there is unlikely to be a need for extensive investigation into and gathering of evidence, whether oral or documentary.

Even in the more complex cases, or cases where extensive investigation is required, it may be appropriate to instruct a barrister direct to advise, or to appear in court on a particular application within the litigation.

Choosing a barrister

3.6 The following factors are relevant in determining the appropriate barrister.

(1) *Whether the case merits more then one barrister.* It may be appropriate to instruct two (or more) barristers to work as a team, possibly each from a different field of expertise.

---

1 Save in exceptional circumstances, it is not appropriate for a barrister who has actually taken (as opposed to having assisted in the preparation of) a witness statement to act as an advocate at the trial. Usually, accordingly, it is not appropriate for the barrister, in the event that he or she is intended to appear as the advocate at trial, to take a witness statement. It is open to the BarDIRECT client, however, to instruct a barrister, either a junior in the case where there is to be a more senior barrister presenting the case in court, or a barrister who is not to be instructed at the trial, specifically to take witness statements. The primary requirement is that the witness statement is in the intended witness' own words.

2 Barristers do, however, frequently assist their clients in the drafting of correspondence which is sent to the parties under the client's own name.

3 This may have important consequences, particularly in relation to settlement negotiations.

(2) *Whether the case merits the use of a Queen's Counsel, or a junior barrister, or both.* There is no hard and fast rule as to when it is appropriate to use a Queen's Counsel. In general, it is appropriate where the issues involved in the case are particularly complex, where the result is likely to have significant consequences for the client, and where there is a sufficient amount at stake to warrant the higher cost. Similarly, there is no hard and fast rule as to when it is appropriate to instruct both a junior barrister and a Queen's Counsel. In general, it is appropriate to do so where the criteria for the use of a Queen's Counsel are satisfied *and* there is likely to be a significant amount of preparatory, drafting or research work which could be carried out by a junior barrister at a significantly lower cost than if the Queen's Counsel were to do so.

(3) *The seniority of the barrister.* A barrister's seniority is denoted in the various published directories and guides (see below) by reference to the year in which he was called to the bar. A barrister is normally called to the bar during the year between completing his final year of studying for the bar (i.e., taking the exams at the end of the bar vocational course) and completion of his pupillage. In practice this means that a barrister called in, say, 1990 will by October 1999 have been in practice since about October 1991, i.e., 8 years. This is not, however, a hard and fast rule. Some barristers might have followed another career path (for example an academic career) between being called to the bar and entering practice. The various directories of barristers denote the seniority of a Queen's Counsel by the year in which he took silk. Queen's Counsel are appointed in the April of each year. The factors which will dictate the appropriate level of seniority for a particular case are similar to those which dictate whether it is appropriate to employ the services of a Queen's Counsel or a junior barrister (see above).

(4) *Expense.* Particular regard should be paid to the cost of employing the services of different barristers. In so doing, the following should be taken into consideration:

  (a) There are three basic methods by which barristers charge for their services:
    (i) an hourly rate so that the fee varies upon the amount of time taken to complete the work;
    (ii) a fixed fee agreed in advance for a particular piece of work;
    (iii) a 'brief' fee, which is a fixed fee to cover preparation for a hearing and the first day in court, and a 'refresher' or a daily charge for each subsequent day.

  Additionally, some barristers may in certain types of case be allowed and prepared to accept instructions pursuant to a conditional fee agreement, in which the payment or the amount of the fee will depend upon the outcome in the case.

  Generally, BarDIRECT clients should be prepared to negotiate with the barrister or his clerk in relation to the method of charging for the barrister's services as well as the overall amount to be charged.

  (b) In comparing hourly rates offered in respect of different barristers, it should be borne in mind that a barrister well versed in the relevant field of expertise is likely to spend fewer hours on the matter than one who has a more general experience.

3.7 Each barrister has a professional duty to advise his client whenever he considers either that the client ought to be represented by someone with a different expertise, or by someone at a lower or higher level of seniority. In addition, each barrister owes a duty to consider, and advise, as to whether the case warrants the assistance of (as the case may be) a

Queen's Counsel or junior barrister, or alternatively no longer merits the continued use of either the Queen's Counsel or junior barrister. The barrister also has a duty to advise whether the case merits the involvement of a solicitor.

3.8   There are a number of ways in which to identify a suitable barrister for the relevant case.

(1) Recommendation from others;

(2) The Bar Council publishes a Bar Directory that lists all barristers currently practising and gives details of the expertise of barristers in particular chambers. The Directory is available on the Internet at *www.BarCouncil.org.uk*.

(3) Directories are published by a number of specialist Bar Associations, for example by the Chancery Bar Association and the Commercial Bar Association, which contains lists of barristers (though not all barristers) practising within those fields and details of the expertise of barristers in particular chambers;

(4) There are a number of directories published by private organisations, many of which indicate the views of the editors of the directory of particular barristers operating in particular fields of expertise. These views, being subjective, need to be treated with caution.

(5) Having identified a set or sets of chambers whose members are held out as having expertise in the relevant field, it is worth contacting the chambers to discuss with the clerk the member or members who would be most suitable for your purposes, and to discuss the possible charging structure and charge-out rates of the relevant members.

Instructing a barrister

3.9   Once the BarDIRECT client has decided upon a barrister to instruct, it is always preferable to contact that barrister's clerk in the first instance in order to ensure that the barrister is available.

3.10   In making enquiries of the barrister's clerk, there are four particular points to check:

(1) Is the barrister available to carry out the specific piece of work in relation to which he or she is to be instructed? Barristers are sole practitioners. This has the advantage that when a barrister is instructed it is the barrister himself or herself who carries out the work. In this respect a barrister differs from a solicitor who will regularly delegate work to an assistant or assistants. It has, however, the disadvantage that any particular barrister will already have commitments to other clients, including commitments to complete paper work by a certain date, or to appear in court on a certain date or dates, so that his or her availability may be limited.

(2) If the barrister is to be instructed in a matter that will be ongoing, is he or she likely to be available for any court dates that are to be arranged in the future? Sometimes court hearings are arranged for the convenience of the parties, so that they can ensure that the barrister of their choice represents them. On other occasions, however, court hearings are arranged without regard to the availability of the parties' barristers. Whilst it will not be possible for the barrister to commit to be free for any lengthy period of time within which hearings might occur, it is sensible when initially instructing a barrister to enquire whether he or she has existing commitments such that it is known, or likely, that they will not be free during the period of time when prospective court hearings are likely to occur. It is sometimes sensible to enquire, at the outset, whether there are other members of chambers of a similar level

of experience and with similar expertise who would be able to take over in respect of future court hearings in case the barrister of first choice subsequently became unavailable.

(3) If the barrister is being asked to advise in conference, or to attend a specific court hearing, his or her clerk should be asked at the outset to reserve the date and time in the barrister's diary for that purpose.

(4) Fees. A barrister's fees are normally negotiated with his or her clerk. The way in which barristers charge for their services is referred to in paragraph 3.6(4) above. Negotiations at the outset should include whether a fixed fee should be paid, and if so for how much, whether payment should be on the basis of an hourly rate, in which case an indication of the number of hours which the matter is likely to take should be asked for and given, or whether a brief fee/refresher approach is appropriate, in which case the amounts should be agreed in advance. In addition, in any case where a fixed fee is agreed, you should ensure that there is clear agreement with the barrister's clerk as to the extent of the work to be included in the fee (e.g., whether it is to include advising both in conference and in writing, or only one of these).

Identifying the information and materials to send to the Barrister

3.11   There is no required form or procedure for informing a barrister of the matters in relation to which he is to advise or represent you. The appropriate quantity of material to provide, and the appropriate form in which to provide it, will depend upon the circumstances of each case and, to an extent, the requirements of the particular barrister. Solicitors have developed a particular format and style of expression in instructions to barristers. Whilst there is no reason why BarDIRECT clients should not adopt a similar format and style, there is also no reason why they should. It is the content of the instructions that is important, not the form. In most cases, it is sufficient that the information is provided to the barrister in the form of a letter or a note.

3.12   In an urgent case it is possible to attend a conference with a barrister without any prior written instructions. Similarly, where urgent applications to court are concerned, it is more important that the barrister is provided with the necessary materials to make the application as soon as possible, than that time is spent on drafting written instructions.

3.13   Whenever you are in doubt as to any aspect of the instructions, telephone the barrister direct. A great deal of unnecessary time and expense can be saved by an initial discussion with the barrister as to the materials he will need at the outset to see.

3.14   The following guidelines are to be read in the light of the preceding paragraphs and are intended to be of general assistance only.

3.15   As a general rule, the following is the information and material which a barrister would normally expect to be sent to him upon his initial instruction:

(1) A brief description of the circumstances giving rise to the issue in relation to which he is instructed, including a brief history of the matter and a description of the parties involved.

(2) An outline of the issue or issues in relation to which he is either instructed to appear in court or to advise.

(3) In the case of existing proceedings, copies of any documents already filed with the court, or exchanged between the parties which are relevant to the issue upon which the barrister is instructed;

(4) A clear statement of what it is the barrister is being asked to do. For example:
  (a) where advice is sought, state whether the barrister is asked to advise on a specific issue, or to advise more generally on the issues which he thinks arise out of the circumstances identified to him;
  (b) where the barrister is requested to draft or settle a document, then state the document or documents which he is required to draft (e.g., a statement of case or application), or settle (e.g., an affidavit or a witness statement);
  (c) where the barrister is requested to attend a hearing, identify the hearing and state clearly what result from the hearing the barrister is instructed to try to obtain.

(5) Photocopies of those documents that you think are relevant to the matters upon which his advice is sought. The following should be noted:
  (a) It is in relation to this aspect that communication with the barrister is particularly recommended, whether prior to sending any instructions, or having sent instructions with a few 'core' documents so as to identify what other documents ought to be sent.
  (b) It is important not to send original documents, since these should not be marked and should remain in their original form and should be available for inspection by third parties, whether by reason of disclosure orders which might be made in litigation or otherwise.
  (c) Where correspondence or similar documentation is to be sent, it will save time and expense if it is arranged in chronological order.
  (d) It is also helpful to include an index of the documents, or of the classes of documents, sent.

(6) A clear statement of the time within which a response is sought from the barrister.

(7) Where there is a time limit on commencing proceedings, or taking a step in existing proceedings, or for any other matter, a clear statement of this in the instructions.

Steps following the initial instructions

3.16 Having received the instructions, the barrister should take an initial look through the papers. There are four potential reasons why at this stage the barrister could decline to continue to act:

(1) It is possible that the barrister will identify a conflict of interest (for example because he is acting or has previously acted for another party in the same case) which was not picked up during your discussions with his or her clerk.

(2) The barrister (in cases other than where the BarDIRECT client is able to undertake litigation support such as that normally undertaken by a solicitor) may decide that, because the case requires taking detailed statements from witnesses, or extensive office back-up that he or she does not have, it is not an appropriate case for direct access and needs the expertise of a solicitor. In those circumstances the barrister is required to take no action until an appropriate intermediary is instructed.

(3) The barrister may decide that on closer inspection of the papers the subject matter falls outside his or her area of expertise, or that the case is more complex than he or she is equipped to deal with. He or she is then entitled to decline the instructions.

(4) The barrister may decide, having accepted the instructions on the basis that they were likely to occupy a certain amount of time, which he or she had available, that the instructions will in fact require considerably more of his or her time, which is

not available.

3.17   Alternatively, the barrister may decide that whilst the case is within his or her expertise, it is more suitable for a barrister of different seniority. In that case, the barrister is obliged to advise you of his view, but you may choose whether or not to accept that advice.

3.18   Assuming that the barrister is able to continue to work on the case, the course of conduct thereafter will depend upon the circumstances of the individual case.

3.19   It will often be useful to arrange a face to face meeting with the barrister in order either to discuss the advice that the barrister is to give, or to discuss what work needs to be done in preparing the case for court. Such a meeting may take place either at the barrister's chambers, or at the premises of the BarDIRECT client. It is often easier for the barrister to hold the meeting at his or her chambers, where he or she has ready access to the background material needed in order to advise, unless the volume of material, the need to view equipment or a site or the convenience of the client or witnesses suggests otherwise.

3.20   A face to face meeting is particularly useful in order to discuss and agree upon the division of work as between the barrister and the BarDIRECT client in progressing a case towards a court hearing (bearing in mind those matters which the BarDIRECT client can expect, or should not expect, the barrister to do, as set out earlier in these guidelines).

Billing

3.21   The barrister will send a fee note, either at the end of the case, or after each separate item of work done or, in an ongoing matter, at periodic intervals.

3.22   The BarDIRECT client is contractually liable for the fees of the barrister. Any disputes with the barrister over the fee should be taken up with the barrister's chambers as soon as possible. It will often be the case that any dispute over the fee, or other complaint, can be resolved informally with the barrister's chambers.

3.23   The Bar Council is not usually able to involve itself in disputes over fees, except where there is an allegation of professional misconduct.[4] If the fee dispute cannot be resolved informally, accordingly, there is little alternative but for the matter to go to court.

3.24   If you have any concerns about the services provided by your barrister, you should, in the first instance, refer these to the barrister himself to be resolved through the chambers complaints procedure if possible. If you remain dissatisfied, it is open to you to approach the Bar Council and you should write to the Secretary of the Professional Conduct and Complaints Committee at the Bar Council for further information about this.

Practical matters

3.25   Appended to these guidance notes is guidance on the preparation of witness statements.[5]

APPENDICES

1.   An application form for those seeking recognition as BarDIRECT clients (Not printed in this Code).

2.   The BarDIRECT terms of work.

3.   The BarDIRECT Rules (Printed in Annex F of this Code).

---

4   See the Bar Code of Conduct published by the General Council of the Bar.
5   Taken from section 3 of the Bar Code of Conduct.

4. The BarDIRECT Recognition Rules (Printed in Annex F of this Code).

BarDIRECT

THE BarDIRECT TERMS OF WORK

1. **Application of these terms:** These terms apply to all instructions accepted by barristers where the instructions are given by a BarDIRECT client in accordance with the terms of a licence issued by the Bar Council. They apply save to the extent that they have been varied or excluded by written agreement and subject to the following:

    (1) These Terms will apply to instructions only where the instructions have been accepted by the barrister.

    (2) These terms do not apply to legal aid work.

2. **The Licence:** A copy of the Licence issued to the BarDIRECT client by the BarDIRECT Committee of the Bar Council shall be sent with every set of instructions.

3. **Acceptance of instructions:** Notwithstanding that instructions have been delivered to a barrister, he shall not be deemed to have accepted them until he has satisfied himself that the instructions are given in accordance with the licence granted by the Bar Council by a person entitled by that licence to give those instructions and has expressly accepted them orally or in writing.

4. **Code of Conduct to prevail:** A barrister accepts instructions upon the understanding that in carrying them out he must and will comply with the Code of Conduct and the general law. In this regard:

    (1) Paragraph 210 of the Code of Conduct provides that a barrister must not:

    (i) receive or handle client money securities or other assets other than by receiving payment of remuneration;

    (ii) undertake the management administration or general conduct of a lay client's affairs;

    (iii) conduct litigation or the inter-partes work (for example the conduct of correspondence with an opposite party);

    (iv) investigate or collect evidence for use in any court;

    (v) except as permitted in certain limited circumstances, take any proof of evidence in any criminal case;

    (vi) attend at a police station without the presence of a solicitor to advise a suspect or interviewee as to the handling and conduct of police interviews.

    (2) The BarDIRECT Rules (which form part of the Code of Conduct) provide:

    (a) by rule 5 that a barrister must not accept any instructions from a BarDIRECT client

    (i) unless the barrister and his Chambers are able to provide the services required of them by that BarDIRECT client;

    (ii) if the barrister considers it in the interests of the lay client or the interests of justice that a solicitor or other authorised litigator or some other appropriate intermediary (as the case may be) be instructed either together with or in place of the barrister;

    (b) by rule 8 that if at any stage a barrister who is instructed by a BarDIRECT client considers it in the interests of the lay client or the interests of justice that a solicitor or other authorised litigator or some other appropriate intermediary

(as the case may be) be instructed either together with or in place of the barrister:

(i)   the barrister must forthwith advise the BarDIRECT client in writing to instruct a solicitor or other authorised litigator or other appropriate intermediary (as the case may be); and

(ii) unless a solicitor or other authorised litigator or other appropriate intermediary (as the case may be) is instructed as soon as reasonably practicable thereafter the barrister must cease to act and must return any instructions.

5. **Duty to the lay client:** Where instructions are given to a barrister by a BarDIRECT client in relation to a matter concerning a lay client the BarDIRECT client warrants that he has or will as soon as practicable.

(1) Send the lay client a copy of the BarDIRECT Terms of Work.

(2) Advise the lay client in writing of:

(a)   the effect of paragraph 210 of the Code of Conduct as it relevantly applies in the circumstances;

(b)   the fact that the barrister cannot be expected to perform the functions of a solicitor or other authorised litigator and in particular to fulfil limitation obligations disclosure obligations and other obligations arising out of or related to the conduct of litigation;

(c)   the fact that circumstances may require the lay client to retain a solicitor or other authorised litigator at short notice and possibly during the case.

(3) Send to the lay client a copy of any advice received by the BarDIRECT client from the barrister to the effect that:

(a)   a solicitor or other authorised litigator or some other appropriate intermediary (as the case may be) is capable of providing any services to the lay client which the barrister himself is unable to provide; or

(b)   the barrister considers it in the interests of the lay client or the interests of justice that a solicitor or other authorised litigator or some other appropriate intermediary (as the case may be) be instructed either together with or in place of the barrister; or

(c)   the BarDIRECT client should instruct a solicitor or other authorised litigator or other appropriate intermediary (as the case may be).

6. **Liability for the fees:** The BarDIRECT client is liable for a barrister's fee due in respect of work carried out by the barrister under any instructions. In a case where the matter concerns a lay client, the BarDIRECT client is solely and exclusively liable to the barrister for the fees. In this regard:

(1) The relationship between the barrister and the BarDIRECT client is a contractual one.

(2) Any individual giving or purporting to give the instructions on behalf of any partnership firm, company, individual or other person warrants to the barrister that he is authorised by the latter to do so.

(3) If the BarDIRECT client is a partnership or a firm or unincorporated association, the liability of the partners or members and on death that of their estates for the barrister's fees is joint and several.

(4) Neither the sending by a BarDIRECT client of instructions to a barrister nor the acceptance of those instructions by a barrister nor anything done in connection therewith nor these Terms nor any arrangement or transaction entered into under them shall give rise to any contractual relationship rights duties or consequences whatsoever either (i) between the barrister or the General Council of the Bar and any lay client or (ii) between the General Council of the Bar and the BarDIRECT client.

7. **Time for performance of instructions:** Unless otherwise expressly stipulated by written agreement

   (a) a barrister will carry out the instructions as soon as he reasonably can in the ordinary course of his work, but

   (b) time will not be of the essence.

8. **Duty of care:** A barrister will exercise reasonable care and skill in carrying out instructions. This is however subject to

   (a) any immunity from suit which the barrister may enjoy under the general law in respect of any work done in the course of carrying out instructions and

   (b) paragraph 11(1) below.

9. **Copies of Briefs and Instructions and Records of Advice:** A barrister shall be entitled on completion of any work to take and retain a copy of such instructions and papers and of any written work.

10. **Fees:** other cases. Subject to the Code of Conduct, the following provisions apply:

    (1) **Fees and/or charging rates:** These shall be as agreed between the barrister and the BarDIRECT client before the barrister commences work under the instructions or, in default of such agreement, shall be a reasonable professional rate for the barrister instructed.

    (2) **Submission of fee notes:** The barrister shall (a) as soon as reasonably practicable comply with a written request by the BarDIRECT client for a fee note and (b) in any event submit a fee note not later than 3 months after the work to which the fee note relates has been done.

    (3) **Time for payment:** A barrister's fees in respect of instructions to which these Terms apply are payable and must be paid by the BarDIRECT client 30 days after receipt by the BarDIRECT client of the fee note submitted by him to the BarDIRECT client in respect of such fees.

    (4) **Default in payment:** In the event that a barrister's fees are not paid in full in accordance with sub-paragraph (3) above, the fees and/or the balance thereof outstanding from time to time will carry simple interest at the stipulated rate from the date they became due until payment in full.

11. **Complaints:** In the event that the BarDIRECT client or the lay client (if any) has any Complaint about the services provided by a barrister under any instructions

    (1) The fees shall be paid in accordance with paragraph 10(3) above and no Complaint shall afford a valid ground for non-payment of the fees whether on grounds of set-off or otherwise.

    (2) Sub-paragraph (1) above is without prejudice to any rights of the BarDIRECT client and the lay client to institute any proceedings against the barrister and/or a

complaint against the barrister under the Complaints Rules in Annexe M to the Code of Conduct.

12. **Definitions:** In these Terms:

(1) 'Instructions' includes a brief and any other instructions to a barrister.

(2) 'BarDIRECT Client' means the individual, firm, company or other person instructing or seeking to instruct a barrister, whether on his, their or its own behalf or on behalf of some other person under the terms of a licence issued by the Bar Council.

(3) In a case where the Bar Direct client is instructing or seeking to instruct a barrister not on his, their or its own behalf but on behalf of some other person, 'lay client' means that other person;

(4) 'Written agreement' means an agreement in writing between (a) one or more barristers (including a set of Chambers) and (b) a BarDIRECT Client;

(5) 'Written work' includes any draft pleading or other document and any written opinion or advice prepared by a barrister pursuant to any instructions;

(6) 'Legal aid work' means instructions which are publicly funded under the Legal Aid Act 1988 or Access to Justice Act 1999 as in force from time to time or any legislation which may replace them, and any work carried out pursuant to such instructions;

(7) 'Stipulated rate' means the rate at which interest is payable from time to time on High Court judgment debts;

(8) 'Complaint' includes any complaint whatsoever relating to anything done by a barrister pursuant to any instructions or to the time taken or alleged to have been taken by him in carrying them out and whether the same involves issues of competence, quantum or otherwise.

(9) 'Code of Conduct' means the Code of Conduct of the Bar of England and Wales as promulgated and amended by the General Council of the Bar from time to time.

(10) In these Terms any reference to the masculine shall be deemed to include the feminine.

APPROVED LIST OF DIRECT PROFESSIONAL ACCESS BODIES

Registrar
The Architects Registration Council of the UK   **APPROVED**
73 Hallam Street   **November 1989**
London
W1N 6EE

Chief Executive
The Architects and Surveyors Institute   **APPROVED**
St Mary House   **September 1995**
15 St Mary Street
Chippenham
Wiltshire
SN15 3WD

Executive Secretary
The Association of Authorised Public Accountants   **APPROVED**
10 Cornfield Road   **September 1989**
Eastbourne
East Sussex
BN21 4QE

Joint Secretary
The Association of Average Adjusters   **APPROVED**
H.Q.S. 'Wellington'   **June 1989**
Temple Stairs
Victoria Embankment
London
WC2R 2PN

General Secretary
Association of Consultant Architects   **APPROVED**
7 Park Street   **November 1989**
Bristol
BS1 5NF

Association of Taxation Technicians   **APPROVED**
12 Upper Belgrave Street   **September 1996**
London
SW1X 8BB

Banking Ombudsman   **APPROVED**
70 Gray's Inn Road   **March 1990**
London
WC1X 8NB

Building Society Ombudsman   **APPROVED**
Grosvenor Gardens House   **March 1990**
35–37 Grosvenor Gardens
London SW1

Secretary
The Chartered Association of Certified Accountants   **APPROVED**
29 Lincoln's Inn Fields   **April 1989**
London
WC2A 3EE

The Chartered Institute of Loss Adjusters   **APPROVED**
Mansfield House   **July 1990**
376 Strand
London
WC2R 0LR

Secretary
The Chartered Institute of Management Accountants   **APPROVED**
63 Portland Place   **September 1989**
London
W1N 4AB

Secretary
The Chartered Insurance Institute   **APPROVED**
20 Aldermanbury   **May 1990**
London
EC2V 7HY

Commissioner for Local Administration   **APPROVED**
21 Queen Annes Gate   **March 1990**
London SW1

Commissioner for Local Administration   **APPROVED**
Derwen House   **March 1990**
Bridge End
Mid Glamorgan

Health Service Commissioner   **APPROVED**
Church House   **March 1990**
Great Smith Street
London
SW1P 3BW

Secretary
The Faculty of Actuaries   **APPROVED**
23 St Andrews Square   **November 1989**
Edinburgh
EH2 1AQ

Chief Executive
The Incorporated Society of Valuers & Auctioneers   **APPROVED**
3 Cadogan Gate   **July 1989**
London
SW1X 0AS

President
Insolvency Practitioners Association   APPROVED
Buchlet Phillips & Co.   September 1989
43/44 Albermarie Street
Mayfair
London
W1N 4AB

Secretary General
Institute of Actuaries   APPROVED
Staple Inn Hall   November 1989
High Holborn
London
WC1V 7QJ

Secretary, Management Committee
Institute of Chartered Accountants   APPROVED
PO Box 433   April 1989
Chartered Accountants Hall
London
EC2P 2BY

Director
The Institute of Chartered Accountants in Ireland   APPROVED
Chartered Accountants House   July 1989
87/89 Pembroke Road
Dublin 4
Ireland

Secretary
Institute of Chartered Accountants in Scotland   APPROVED
27 Queen Street   July 1989
Edinburgh
EH2 1LA

Under Secretary
The Institute of Chartered Secretaries and Administrators APPROVED
19 Park Crescent   July 1989
London
W1N 4AH

Secretary
The Chartered Institute of Taxation   APPROVED
12 Upper Belgrave Street   July 1989
London
SW1X 8BB

Administration Manager
The Institution of Chemical Engineers   APPROVED
George E Davis Building   July 1989
165–171 Railway Terrace
Rugby
CV21 3HQ

Executive Director
The Institution of Civil Engineering Surveyors   **APPROVED**
26 Market Street   **November 1997**
Altrincham
Cheshire
WA14 1PF

The Institute of Civil Engineers   **APPROVED**
Great George Street   **November 1989**
Westminster
London
SW1P 3AA

Director, Technical Affairs
The Institute of Electrical Engineers   **APPROVED**
Savoy Place   **November 1991**
London
WC2R 0BL

Chief Executive
The Institute of Financial Accountants   **APPROVED**
Burford House   **January 1995**
44 London Road
Sevenoaks
Kent

Secretary
Institution of Mechanical Engineers   **APPROVED**
1 Birdcage Walk   **July 1989**
London
SW1H 9JJ

Assistant Director, Administration & Finance
The Institution of Structural Engineers   **APPROVED**
11 Upper Belgrave Street   **July 1991**
London
SW1X 8BH

Insurance Ombudsman Bureau   **APPROVED**
City Gate One   **July 1990**
135 Park Street
London
SE1

Parliamentary Commissioner for Administration   **APPROVED**
Church House   **March 1990**
Great Smith Street
London
SW1P 3BW

Senior Legal Officer
The Personal Investment Authority   **APPROVED**
Ombudsman Bureau Ltd   **January 1998**
Hertsmere House
Hertsmere Road
London
E14 4AB

Director General
The Royal Institute of British Architects   **APPROVED**
66 Portland Place   **September 1989**
London
W1N 4AD

President
The Royal Institution of Chartered Surveyors   **APPROVED**
12 Great George Street   **April 1989**
Parliament Square
London
SW1P 3AD

Director, Public Affairs
The Royal Town Planning Institute   **APPROVED**
26 Portland Place   **April 1989**
London
W1N 4BE

The Institute of Indirect Taxation   **APPROVED**
PO Box 96   **May 1999**
Oxted
Surrey
RH8 0FX

JOINT TRIBUNAL STANDING ORDERS FOR FEE DISPUTES WITH SOLICITORS

JOINT TRIBUNAL STANDING ORDERS

Standard Time Scale Proposed

(1)   The Applicant shall within 28 days of submitting written agreement to be bound by the decision of the Joint Tribunal send:

    (a) direct to the OSS;

        (i)   two further copies of the agreement,

        (ii)   two copies of the Statement of Case with any supporting documents which must include relevant fee notes and correspondence (one set for the OSS and one for the Joint Tribunal Law Society member) and,

    (b) (i)   direct to the Bar Council two further copies of the Statement of Case and supporting documents; (one set for the Bar Council and one for the Joint Tribunal Bar Council member), and,

    (c) direct to the Respondent;

        (i)   a Statement of Case, together with all documents relied upon, which must include relevant fee notes and correspondence.

(2)   The Respondent shall, within 28 days of receipt of the Applicant's Statement of Case, supply:

    (a) two copies of their Statement of Response direct to the OSS (as in (1) above) and,

    (b) two copies to the Bar Council (as in (1) above), and,

    (c) supply to the Applicant a Statement of Response, together with all documents relied upon.

(3)   All documents which are submitted shall be indexed and paginated consecutively in the top right hand corner.

(4)   If either party relies upon the evidence of another person a statement of such evidence shall be signed and dated by the witness.

(5)   The Joint Tribunal shall be appointed within 14 days of the receipt by the OSS and the Bar Council of the Statement of Case. The members of the Joint Tribunal shall be supplied with copies of the Statements, by the OSS and the Bar Council respectively. Upon receipt of the Statements by the Joint Tribunal, it shall notify the parties of a date for the determination of the dispute which is not later than 56 days after the date provided above for the supply of the Statement of Response.

(6)   If, in exceptional circumstances, the Applicant wishes to submit a Statement of Reply, or either party wishes to submit additional material to the Joint Tribunal, they shall request permission to do so within 14 days of the receipt by the Applicant of the Statement of Response. Such requests shall be accompanied by a draft Statement of Reply and/or any material sought to be relied upon. The Tribunal shall rule upon the admissibility of such documents and its ruling shall be final.

(7)   Any applications by either party in respect of the conduct of the dispute shall be included within the Statement of Case/Response. The Joint Tribunal shall determine the dispute on the basis of the written submissions of the parties unless in the opinion of the Joint Tribunal an oral hearing is appropriate.

(8)   If an oral hearing has been requested the Joint Tribunal shall, when fixing the date for the determination of the dispute, inform the parties, the OSS and the Bar Council, whether or not a hearing is considered to be appropriate, of the date, time and venue for the hearing.

(9)   The Joint Tribunal shall rule upon any application by either party in respect of the conduct of the dispute, and shall notify the parties, the OSS and the Bar Council, of any consequential directions when giving notice of the date for the determination of the dispute.

(10)   Payment of any sum found to be due shall be made within 14 days of the date of notification of any determination by the Joint Tribunal.

(11)   Non-compliance with these directions shall entitle the Joint Tribunal to dismiss any case or response and to determine the dispute as the Tribunal thinks fit.

(12)   The Joint Tribunal shall have power in its absolute discretion to award interest upon unpaid fees for such period and at such rate as it deems appropriate in the circumstances.

(13)   The Joint Tribunal shall have power to direct payment of undisputed sums forthwith and payment shall be made within 14 days of any interim determination.

(14)   In the event of non-payment within the due time of any determination or interim determination the Joint Tribunal shall refer the matter as professional misconduct to the Office for the Supervision of Solicitors or to The General Council of the Bar.

Implemented 1 May 1998

GUIDANCE ON COUNSEL'S FEE NOTES

COUNSEL'S FEE NOTES AND RECORDS

Guidance from the Professional Standards and Remuneration Committees

1. Lay clients are entitled to know the basis on which fees are charged, not least so that they can protect their interests in respect of opposed assessments of costs, summary or detailed.

2. In order to assist lay and professional clients, Judges, Costs Judges and, in the event of opposed assessments of costs, lay and professional clients justifying Counsel's fees to opposing parties, Counsel should keep careful records of the time taken on each individual item of work done, such as:

   (a) Pleadings, indictments, or other procedural documents;

   (b) Witness statements;

   (c) Experts' reports;

   (d) Schedules;

   (e) Written Advices and Opinions;

   (f) Letters;

   (g) Skeleton arguments;

   (h) Written submissions;

   (i) Preparation of Briefs;

   (j) Conferences and telephone conferences and the preparation for such conferences.

3. The following further steps are also advised as a matter of good practice:

   (i) When Counsel is instructed orally, including by telephone, Counsel should make a note of the nature of the instructions and of the response given.

   (ii) When Counsel asks orally for further information, Counsel should make a note of the nature of the request, and of the answer if the answer is given orally.

   (iii) When any particularly novel or complex issue of fact or law arises in the course of the conduct of a case, Counsel should (unless the subject is dealt with in a written advice or opinion) make a note summarising the relevant issue or issues and the research undertaken in like manner as is required by (i) above.

   (iv) When a Consultation or Conference takes place, unless the professional client makes an attendance note which he sends to Counsel for approval or amendment, Counsel should make a note of the topics covered and the general nature of the advice given.

   (v) When Counsel is involved in negotiations, either between Counsel or by way of leading, assisting or supporting the professional client in the conduct of negotiations, Counsel should make a note of the general nature of the involvement.

   (vi) Notes made pursuant to subparagraphs (i) to (v) above should be kept by Counsel unless they are returned to an instructing solicitor.

   In cases where there is not an instructing solicitor, it may be advisable to keep more detailed records.

4. When a brief fee has not been agreed and is claimed by Counsel in a sum greater than the product of an hourly rate and the number of hours actually worked in preparation of the

brief, this should be recorded in a note to be submitted with the fee note. Details in the supplementary note should include, but are not limited to:

(i) The seniority, reputation and relevant expertise of Counsel;

(ii) The complexity of the case;

(iii) The amount of preparation required in advance of the hearing;

(iv) Counsel's commitment to a fixed hearing date, if any;

(v) The expected length of the case and, therefore, the time reserved for it in Counsel's diary;

(vi) The urgency of the matter when Counsel was briefed;

(vii) The amount of work required out of Court and in the preparation of any kind of written submission during the hearing;

(viii) The importance of the case to the parties or any of them, or to the public interest.

5. When a brief fee has been agreed Counsel or Counsel's Clerk should keep such records as will enable a note containing the details set out at paragraph 4(i)–(viii) above to be produced on request.

6. Clients in cases where Counsel fail to keep proper records to support claimed fees may find the fees reduced. Counsel may then find that a complaint of inadequate professional service may be upheld, in which circumstance Counsel can be ordered to reduce or waive fees and/or to pay compensation up to £5,000. In addition, the Legal Services Ombudsman has power to require Counsel to pay unlimited compensation.

7. In any case in which Counsel appears properly in a privately paid case at a hearing without a brief fee having been agreed (for example on an interim application) Counsel should make and keep a record of the time spent at Court before the start of the hearing, and of the length of the hearing.

GUIDANCE ON HOLDING OUT AS A BARRISTER

CODE OF CONDUCT: 7th EDITION

NON-PRACTISING BARRISTERS OFFERING LEGAL SERVICES

The new 7th edition of the Code of Conduct sets out the conditions which barristers must satisfy in order to be entitled to practise. The Code also contains the rules of conduct which practising barristers, be they in independent practice or employment, must observe. This note provides guidance for barristers who have not satisfied the conditions required to practise as a barrister or who for other reasons wish to supply legal services other than as practising barristers.

The Code does not prohibit non-practising barristers from supplying legal services. It merely prevents them, in connection with the supply of such services, from holding themselves out as barristers and from exercising rights which they have as barristers.

Holding Out as a Barrister

The restriction on holding out prevents non-practising barristers who are supplying or offering to supply legal services from using the title 'barrister' or otherwise conveying the impression that they are practising as barristers. It is not possible to provide a comprehensive list of the circumstances which might amount to 'holding out' but it is hoped that the following examples will give an idea of what is prohibited.

- Describing oneself as a barrister in any printed material used in connection with the provision of legal services: in particular in advertising or publicity, on a card or letterhead, or on premises.

- Describing oneself as a barrister to clients or prospective clients.

- Indicating to opposing parties or their representatives (e.g. in correspondence) that one is a barrister.

- Describing oneself as a barrister or as 'counsel', wearing robes, or sitting in a place reserved for counsel, in court.

- Using other descriptions in such contexts which imply that the individual is a barrister (e.g. membership of an Inn of Court).

These examples are not exhaustive.

Exercising Rights as a Barrister

Non-practising barristers may not exercise any rights that they have by reason of being barristers, the most obvious example being rights of audience. This means that such a barrister may not appear as an advocate in any court or tribunal unless it is one in which lay representatives are permitted to appear or unless the barrister has a right of audience by virtue of some other qualification (e.g. as a solicitor).

There are other rights which a practising barrister may exercise but a non-practising barrister may not. For example, section 22 of the Solicitors Act 1974 prohibits an unqualified person from preparing for reward any instrument relating to real or personal estate, or to any legal proceeding. Section 23 contains a similar prohibition against preparing papers for probate. It would not be permissible for a non-practising barrister to charge for preparing such an instrument or papers.

What Is Not Prohibited

The Code does not prohibit non-practising barristers from describing themselves as barristers when they are not supplying legal services. In particular, the following activities are excluded from the definition of 'legal services' in the Code.

- Lecturing or teaching law.
- Writing or editing law books, articles or reports.
- Reading for libel.
- Acting as an arbitrator or mediator.
- Acting as an honorary legal adviser to a charity.

In connection with those activities (and in other circumstances where the barrister is not supplying legal services at all) it is perfectly permissible to use the title 'barrister'.

There may be occasions on which it is unavoidable for non-practising barristers who are supplying or offering to supply legal services to disclose that they are qualified as barristers. These might include, for example, job applications or enquiries by clients as to the barrister's background. In these cases there is no objection to indicating that you have qualified as a barrister but, particularly if the issue arises in the course of conversation with clients, it should be made clear that you are not practising as a barrister, are not able to exercise any rights as a barrister and are not subject to the rules that practising barristers have to obey.

There is no prohibition on non-practising barristers who are in silk using the title QC.

THE CONSOLIDATED REGULATIONS OF THE HONOURABLE SOCIETIES OF LINCOLN'S INN, INNER TEMPLE, MIDDLE TEMPLE AND GRAY'S INN

INTRODUCTION

1. **Definitions** — In these Regulations and their Schedules unless the context otherwise requires the words and expressions contained in Schedule 1 bear the meanings thereby ascribed to them.

PART I
ADMISSION AND TERM KEEPING

2. **Admission and Educational Qualifications**

   (a) A person applying for admission to an Inn as a student ('an applicant') who is not exempted under any of the Regulations in Part IV must fall within one of the categories specified in Schedule 2.

   (b) The Masters of the Bench may delegate to any committee specified by them any of the functions conferred on them by Schedule 2. Such delegation may be permanent or otherwise and may be revoked at any time.

   (c) A student must first be admitted to one of the Inns before he can be registered on and attend a Vocational Course.

3. **Certificates of Good Character**

   (a) An applicant who is not exempted under any of the Regulations in Part IV must produce two certificates of good character complying to the satisfaction of the Masters of the Bench with the requirements specified in Schedule 3.

   (b) No such certificate shall be from a spouse or close relative.

   (c) A certificate of good character shall be in whichever is appropriate of the forms set out in Schedule 3 with such modifications as may be appropriate.

   (d) The Masters of the Bench may accept in place of any certificate referred to in this Regulation such other evidence of good character as they think fit.

   (e) The Masters of the Bench shall be entitled to make such further enquiries as to the character of an applicant as they may think fit.

4. **Ineligibility for and Refusal of Admission**

   (a) **Other Occupations:** An applicant who is engaged in any occupation which in the opinion of the Masters of the Bench is incompatible with the position of a student seeking Call to the Bar may be refused admission.

   (b) **Convicted Persons:** An applicant who has been convicted of a relevant criminal offence may be refused admission if the circumstances in the opinion of the Masters of the Bench are such as to make his admission undesirable.

   (c) **Insolvency:** An applicant who has had a bankruptcy order or directors disqualification order made against him or has entered into an individual voluntary arrangement with his creditors may be refused admission if in the opinion of the Masters of the Bench the circumstances involved make his admission undesirable.

   (d) **Prohibition on practising:** An applicant who has been prohibited from practising any profession (whether of law or any other profession) may be refused admission if in the opinion of the Masters of the Bench the circumstances are such as to make his admission undesirable.

(e) **Other Cases:** An applicant who is for any other reason in the opinion of the Masters of the Bench unsuitable for admission may be refused admission.

5. **Admission Declaration**

(a) An applicant who is not exempted under any of the Regulations in Part IV must before admission duly complete and sign an Admission Declaration in the form set out in Schedule 4 hereto.

(b) A person who has ceased to be a student otherwise than by call to the Bar and who applies for readmission as a student shall before readmission sign a further Admission Declaration substituting the word 'readmission' for the word 'admission'.

6. **Fees on Admission**

(a) Application for admission as a student must be made upon a form provided for that purpose which may be obtained from the Under Treasurer.

(b) The fees payable by an applicant to the Inn and to the Bar Council under paragraph (c) below will be notified to the applicant upon his application for admission or upon earlier enquiry and are payable upon admission.

(c) A fee is payable in respect of services to be provided by the Bar Council for the benefit of students. This fee is payable to the Inn upon admission but will be transmitted by the Inn to the Bar Council.

(d) No educational fee is payable to the Inn but fees are payable to the Bar Council as prescribed from time to time under Part II of these Regulations.

7. **Conduct of Students**

(a) A student shall observe such regulations (if any) as may be made by his Inn concerning the conduct and discipline of its students.

(b) If a student shall:
   (i)   have a bankruptcy order or directors disqualification order made against him or enter into an individual voluntary arrangement with his creditors; or
   (ii) be convicted of a relevant criminal offence; or
   (iii) be prohibited or suspended from practising any profession (whether of law or any other profession); or
   (iv) engage for a period exceeding three months in any occupation other than an occupation stated in his Admission Declaration or an occupation already notified under this Regulation

he shall give notice in writing thereof to the Masters of the Bench through the Under Treasurer and must abide by and carry out any order of the Masters of the Bench arising out of that notification.

(c) If a student shall:
   (i)   make any false statement in the Admission Declaration made by him pursuant to Regulation 5 or in any such form as is mentioned in Regulation 6(a); or
   (ii) commit any breach of any such regulations as are mentioned in paragraph (a); or
   (iii) fail to carry out any order of the Masters of the Bench made under these Regulations; or
   (iv) be guilty of any other act or omission which in the opinion of the Masters of the Bench demonstrates his unfitness to be called to the Bar or is likely to bring

his Inn or the profession of barrister into disrepute or otherwise to merit punishment as hereafter provided

then the Masters of the Bench may (according to their view of the gravity of the offence)

(1) expel him from student membership of his Inn; or

(2) order that his Call to the Bar shall be postponed for such period as they may specify; or

(3) order that he be admonished as to his future conduct by the Treasurer of his Inn or such other person as the Treasurer may appoint for that purpose.

(d) In this regulation references to 'a student' are references to a student so long as he remains a student.

8. Terms

(a) The four Terms shall be:

Michaelmas Term — from 1 October to 21 December;

Hilary Term — from 11 January to the Wednesday before Easter Sunday;

Easter Term — from the second Tuesday after Easter Sunday to the last Friday in May;

Trinity Term — from the second Tuesday after the end of the Easter Term to 31 July.

(b) During the four Terms an Inn is to offer sufficient qualifying sessions to its students to enable them, over the period of a year, to satisfy the term keeping requirement prescribed by Regulation 9.

(c) It is the responsibility of individual Inns to promulgate to their students the dates in each of the four Terms on which qualifying sessions will take place.

9. Keeping Terms

(a) Subject to the provisions of Regulation 10 and (in the case of a person admitted under Part IV) Regulations 30(h), 31(h), 32(h), 35(j), and 36(i), a student must, before being called to the Bar after 31st May 1998, have kept terms by attending 12 qualifying sessions. The requirement for Call to the Bar before that date shall remain 18 qualifying sessions.

(b) A student who kept any term before 1st September 1997 shall be deemed to have attended 3 qualifying sessions in each term so kept;

(c) A student who, after 1st September 1997, attends more than 6 qualifying sessions in any term shall, for the purposes of paragraph (a), be credited with having attended only 6 qualifying sessions in that term unless, upon a petition in writing showing proper grounds, the Masters of the Bench determine that he is to be credited with having attended a greater number of qualifying sessions (not exceeding 9 or the number actually attended, whichever shall be the less);

(d) Save with the consent of the Masters of the Bench, the qualifying sessions specified in (a) above must be kept during not more than two years;

(e) A student shall not be treated as having attended a qualifying session unless he is present at the formal commencement and remains until the formal conclusion provided that the Treasurer or acting Treasurer of an Inn may during any qualifying session on any day relax this requirement for any student in respect of that qualifying session;

(f) 'Qualifying session' means an event of an educational and collegiate nature arranged by or on behalf of an Inn and may include a residential educational and collegiate activity at Cumberland Lodge, West Dean or elsewhere arranged by or on behalf of an Inn, or a non-residential educational and collegiate activity of similar scope arranged by or on behalf of an Inn;

(g) Students attending any such activities arranged by or on behalf of an Inn may be credited with such numbers of qualifying sessions as the Inn, acting in comity with the other Inns, may consider appropriate;

(h) Each Inn shall be responsible, in comity with the other Inns, for (i) arranging suitable numbers of qualifying sessions to be available for the students who are members of the Inn, and (ii) ensuring that all the activities arranged by or on behalf of the Inn are educational and collegiate activities for the purpose of this Regulation;

(i) Term dinners taken before the coming into force of this Regulation on 31 May 1998 shall be deemed to be qualifying sessions.

10. **Relaxation of and Dispensing with Term Keeping**

(a) On petition showing substantial grounds the Masters of the Bench may permit any student:

(i)   to attend not more than 2 qualifying sessions after Call (provided always that such qualifying sessions are attended within 12 months of the date of Call, and a written undertaking to attend such qualifying sessions is given to the Masters of the Bench by the student on or before Call);

(ii)   to have credit for not more than 2 qualifying sessions in absentia;

provided that the total number of qualifying sessions permitted under this paragraph shall not exceed 2.

(b) In exceptional circumstances the Joint Regulations Committee may relax or dispense with any of the requirements of these Regulations in relation to keeping terms, subject to and in accordance with the procedure identified in Regulation 58.

PART II

THE TRAINING AND ASSESSMENT OF STUDENTS (WHO ARE NOT EXEMPTED UNDER PART IV)

11. **The Academic and Vocational Stages of Training**

(a) There shall be two stages of training: the Academic Stage and the Vocational Stage.

(b) Except with the permission of the Head of Education and Training, which will be given only in exceptional circumstances, a student may not enter the Vocational Stage until he has completed the Academic Stage.

(c) A student must complete both stages before being called to the Bar.

12. **Completion of Academic Stage**

(a) Subject to Regulation 15, a student completes the Academic Stage:

(i)   by obtaining a Qualifying Law Degree as defined in Schedule 1; or

(ii)   having obtained a degree in any discipline of a standard which the Bar Council considers satisfactory or having been accepted by an Inn as a mature student (in accordance with paragraph (d) of Category II of Schedule 2), by subsequently successfully completing a Common Professional Examination Course (or those sections thereof from which he was not granted exemption).

(b) In the case of a Qualifying Law Degree or a degree referred to in paragraph (a)(ii) above the standard which the Bar Council considers satisfactory is a lower second class or above, save that the Head of Education and Training has a discretion, which may only be exercised in exceptional circumstances, to waive this requirement.

13. **Attending a Common Professional Examination Course**

(a) Subject to Regulation 14, only a person whose educational qualifications are within paragraphs (a), (c) or (d) of Category II of Schedule 2 may complete the Academic Stage by attending a Common Professional Examination Course.

(b) In order to be certified as having completed the Academic Stage, a student attending a Common Professional Examination Course or attempting any assessments and examinations in such a course must comply with any rules or regulations in relation thereto approved by the CPE Board and for the time being in force in the institution approved by the CPE Board to provide the course or to conduct the examination.

14. **Certificate of Academic Standing**

(a) (i)   A person who obtains a Qualifying Law Degree following a course of study at two or more institutions or (ii) whose educational qualifications are within paragraphs (c) or (d) of Category II of Schedule 2 and who completes the Academic Stage by completing successfully a Common Professional Examination Course must apply to the Bar Council for and be granted a Certificate of Academic Standing before being admitted to the Vocational Stage.

(b) A Certificate of Academic Standing in respect of paragraph (a)(i) of this Regulation shall remain in force for seven years from 1st October in the year in which it was issued.

(c) Subject to Regulation 15, a student to whom a Certificate of Completion has been issued prior to 1st October 1998 is not required to apply for a Certificate of Academic Standing under this Regulation.

15. **The Academic Stage — Stale Qualifications**

(a) A student may not take the Bar Examination or attend the Vocational Course or attend the Vocational Conversion Course after the expiration of a prescribed period, specified in Schedule 11.

(b) The periods specified in Schedule 11 may be extended by the Head of Education and Training if he certifies that he is satisfied that either

(i)   the student has complied with such requirements as to courses of study, written tests or otherwise as the Head of Education and Training may have imposed as a condition for the granting of a Certificate of Extension of Academic Stage Qualifications; or

(ii)   there are special reasons why the period should be extended without further study or tests.

Any extension granted under this subsection shall be for such a period not exceeding seven years as the Head of Education and Training considers appropriate in the circumstances of each particular case.

(c) Subject to paragraph 5 of Schedule 12 a student who fails to complete the Vocational Stage within the period of extension granted under subsection (b) above may apply for a further extension under that subsection.

16. **Completion of Vocational Stage**

    (a) A student may complete the Vocational Stage either:

        (i) by attending and being certified as having successfully completed a Vocational Course; or

        (ii) by passing the Bar Examination in accordance with Schedule 13 provided he has registered for it on or before 21 July 1997.

17. **Compliance with Regulations relating to a Vocational Course**

In order to be certified as having completed the Vocational Stage, a student attending a vocational course or attempting any assessments and examinations in such a course must comply with any rules or regulations in relation thereto approved by the Bar Council and for the time being in force in the institution approved by the Bar Council to provide the course or to conduct the assessment and examinations.

18. **Exempting Law Degrees and Integrated Courses; Completion of the Academic and Vocational Stages**

A person may complete both the Academic Stage and the Vocational Stage by attending and being certified as completing:

    (i) an exempting law degree; or

    (ii) an integrated course.

19. **Fees**

The Bar Council may charge such fees as it may from time to time prescribe in respect of:

    (i) courses of instruction provided by the Bar Council;

    (ii) examination and other forms of assessment conducted by the Bar Council;

    (iii) applications for certification made in accordance with this part of the Regulations.

Fees currently payable are set out in Schedule 10.

20. **Supplementary**

    (a) The Bar Council may appoint such Boards of Examiners as from time to time it thinks fit to exercise its powers in relation to examinations and assessment, and may from time to time delegate to a Board of Examiners, or to the Head of Education and Training or any other member of the Bar Council's permanent staff, any of the powers in relation to examination and assessment conferred upon it by these Regulations, and may from time to time revoke such delegation.

    (b) Subject to any directions given by the Bar Council, the Head of Education and Training may from time to time delegate to any member of the Bar Council's permanent staff any of the powers conferred upon him by these Regulations, and may from time to time revoke any such delegation.

    (c) A student who is readmitted under Regulation 5(b) shall be treated for the purposes of Part II of these Regulations as having been admitted on the date of his readmission, provided that if under any provision of the said Part II such a student would have been entitled, had he not ceased to be a student, to any exemption, concession or advantage to which by reason of such treatment he is not entitled, the Head of Education and Training may in his discretion apply such provision to him to such extent and with such modifications, if any, as he thinks fit.

PART III

CALL TO THE BAR

21. **Call Days and Procedure**

    (a) Calls to the Bar take place on the following days:
        (i)   Hilary Term: the second Thursday in March;
        (ii)   Trinity Term: the fourth Thursday in July;
        (iii) Michaelmas Term: the fourth Thursday in November;

    (b) A deferred Trinity Call for intending practitioners takes place on the second Thursday in October in each year;

    (c) Other days for Call to the Bar may be authorised from time to time by the Council of the Inns of Court;

    (d) Subject to paragraph (e) below the student whose name is screened for Call in accordance with Regulation 22(d) is obliged to attend in person at the ceremony of Call to the Bar on the Call Day on which his Call is to take place;

    (e) The Masters of the Bench may on petition showing proper grounds permit a student to be called in absentia if they consider it appropriate in all the circumstances.

22. **Eligibility for Call**

    A student is not eligible for Call to the Bar:

    (a) when under the age of 21 years; or

    (b) before he has satisfied such of the requirements of these Regulations relating to the keeping of terms and either the passing of the examination or Call to the Bar or the completion of the Vocational Course or satisfying the conditions of eligibility under Part IV as are applicable to his case; or

    (c) before he has duly completed and signed the Call Declaration and paid the fees payable on Call; or

    (d) until his name and description have been screened in the Hall, Bencher's Rooms and Treasurer's office of his Inn four days in the term in which such Call is to take place.

23. **Screening**

    The name and description of every student who is to be screened for Call shall be sent by the Under Treasurer to each of the other Inns for similar screening.

24. **Declaration and Undertaking before Call or Readmission**

    (a) Every person shall before being called or readmitted to the Bar duly complete and sign a Declaration and Undertaking ('the Call Declaration').

    (b) Subject to the right of the Masters of the Bench to modify the terms of the Call Declaration to meet particular circumstances the following forms of the Call Declaration shall apply:
        (i)   In the case of a person seeking Temporary Membership of the Bar under Part IV(E), Schedule 6 hereto;
        (ii)   In the case of a person seeking to be readmitted to the Bar under Regulation 56, Schedule 7 hereto;
        (iii) In all other cases Schedule 5 hereto.

(c) If the declaration made by a barrister on Call to the Bar is found to have been false in any material respect or if there is a breach of any undertaking embodied in that declaration that shall constitute professional misconduct.

25. **Seniority on Call**

At every Call to the Bar:

(i) Students who hold Certificates of Honour shall rank in seniority over all other students called on the same day and *inter se* in order of seniority as students;

(ii) Students who have been awarded Scarman Scholarships shall rank in seniority over students called on the same day who have not been awarded such Scholarships or Certificates of Honour and, *inter se*, in order of seniority as scholars (earlier Scholarships being deemed to confer seniority over later Scholarships and Scholarships awarded in the same year being deemed to confer seniority in order of merit);

(iii) subject as aforesaid students called on the same day shall rank in order of their seniority as students.

PART IV

CALL TO THE BAR OR REGISTRATION OF CERTAIN QUALIFIED LAWYERS

(A) GENERAL

26. **Permanent or Temporary Call to the Bar; Registration as a Registered European Lawyer**

(a) A qualified lawyer falling within one of the categories mentioned in Sections (B), (C), (D) or (E) of this Part may seek

(i) permanent membership of an Inn and Call to the Bar in accordance with such of sections (B), (C) and (D) of this Part as are applicable to his case: or

(ii) registration with an Inn and with the Bar Council as a Registered European Lawyer in accordance with section (B) of this Part; or

(iii) temporary membership of an Inn and Call to the Bar in accordance with section (E) of this Part.

(b) Nothing contained in this Part shall prevent a qualified lawyer from seeking admission to an Inn as a student and Call to the Bar in accordance with Parts I to III of these Regulations.

(c) Certain expressions defined in the European Communities (Recognition of Professional Qualifications) Regulations 1991 ('the 1991 Regulations') and in the European Communities (Lawyer's Practice) Regulations 2000 (the 2000 Regulations) have, when used in this Part, the meanings thereby ascribed to them. For the sake of convenience the relevant definitions are set out in Schedule 1 hereto.

27. **Delegation to the JRC**

(a) The Bar Council (which is pursuant to the 1991 Regulations the authority designated in relation to the profession of barrister of England and Wales) and the Bar Council and the Inns (which are pursuant to the 2000 Regulations the authorities designated in relation to this profession) have by resolution delegated to the Joint Regulations Committee ('the JRC') the discharge of their functions as designated authorities, and those functions shall be discharged by the JRC in accordance with this Part.

(b) So long as the Bar Council and the Inns remain the designated authorities as aforesaid they may by resolution wholly or partially revoke or vary the delegation of their said functions to the JRC.

(B)   LAWYERS FROM OTHER MEMBER STATES

28.   **Registration as a Registered European Lawyer**

(a) A European lawyer who desires to apply for registration with a view to practising on a permanent basis in England and Wales under his home professional title may apply to the JRC for a direction that he be registered by the Bar Council and by the Inn of his choice as a Registered European Lawyer, and is referred to herein as 'a CR28 applicant'.

(b) The application by a CR28 applicant shall be in such form as may be prescribed by the JRC and shall contain or be accompanied by the following:

(i)   A certificate, not more than three months old at the date of receipt of the application by the JRC, attesting to the registration of the CR28 applicant with the competent authority in his home State as a lawyer qualified to practise in his home State under his home professional title.

(ii)   A declaration that:

(1) he has not on the ground of professional misconduct or the commission of a criminal offence been prohibited from practising in his home State and is not currently suspended from so practising;

(2) no bankruptcy order or directors disqualification order has been made against him and he has not entered into an individual voluntary arrangement with his creditors;

(3) he is not aware of any other circumstances relevant to his fitness to practise under his home professional title in England and Wales; and

(4) he is not registered with the Law Society of England and Wales, of Scotland or of Northern Ireland.

(iii) Payment of the fees prescribed in Schedule 10.

(c) On receipt of a certificate satisfying the requirements of sub-paragraph (b)(i) and a declaration satisfying the requirements of sub-paragraph (b)(ii) above, the JRC shall make a direction that the CR28 applicant be registered by the Bar Council and by one of the Inns as a Registered European Lawyer, and the direction shall be given effect by the Bar Council and by such of the Inns as shall receive his application for membership.

(d) On making such direction the JRC shall inform the competent authority in his home State by whom the certificate referred to in sub-paragraph (b)(i) above has been made.

(e) A Registered European Lawyer shall be subject to the Code of Conduct in the manner provided for in Annex B.

(f) A Registered European Lawyer applying for exemption from the requirement under Annex B of the Code of Conduct to take out professional indemnity insurance shall provide to the JRC evidence to establish that he is covered by insurance taken out or a guarantee provided in accordance with the rules of his home State, and that such insurance or guarantee is equivalent in terms of conditions and extent of cover to the conditions and extent of cover required pursuant to the Code of Conduct. If the JRC is fully satisfied in respect of such matters, the JRC may exempt him wholly from the requirement to take out professional indemnity insurance in accordance with the Code of Conduct. If the JRC is satisfied that the equivalence is only partial, the JRC may require that additional insurance or an additional guarantee be contracted by him to cover the elements which are not already covered by the insurance or guarantee contracted by him in accordance with the rules of his home State.

29. **Applications to become barristers**

A lawyer who is a national of another Member State and who wishes to practise as a barrister and for that purpose to be called to the Bar under Regulation 30, 31 or 32

(a) shall apply in writing to the JRC and shall pay the fees prescribed in Schedule 10;

(b) shall indicate in his application whether he is an applicant under Regulation 30, 31 or 32 of these Regulations.

30. **Applications by reference to the 1991 Regulations**

(a) A lawyer who is a national of and fully qualified in another Member State and desires to apply under this Regulation with a view to establishing himself in England and Wales in order to practise as a barrister and for that purpose to be called to the Bar is referred to herein as 'a CR30 applicant'.

(b) The application by a CR30 applicant shall be in such form as may be prescribed by the JRC and shall contain or be accompanied by the following:

(i) Particulars of the Diploma or other evidence relied on by the CR30 applicant as entitling him to authority to practise pursuant to Regulation 5 of the 1991 Regulations.

(ii) The original or a duly authenticated copy, together with an English translation where necessary, of every certificate or other document relied on by the CR30 applicant as establishing any matter required to be established pursuant to Regulation 5 or 6 of the 1991 Regulations.

(iii) Such evidence as is relied on by the CR30 applicant to establish all the following matters:

(1) that he is of good character and repute;

(2) that he has not on the ground of professional misconduct or the commission of a criminal offence been prohibited from practising in any Member State in which he qualified or practised and is not currently suspended from so practising;

(3) that no bankruptcy order or directors disqualification order has been made against him and he has not entered into an individual voluntary arrangement with his creditors.

(iv) Such representations or evidence as the CR30 applicant may wish to make or rely upon in support of any application that he be wholly or partially exempted from passing an Aptitude Test in accordance with this Regulation.

(v) Any other representations or material (including particulars of the arrangements which he has made or proposes to make as to taking up practice as a barrister if and when he is called to the Bar) as he may wish to rely upon in support of his CR30 application.

(vi) English translations of every certificate and other document on which he relies and which is not in the English language.

(vii) In the case of a second or subsequent CR30 application by the same person, particulars of every previous application made by him.

(c) If a CR30 applicant is unable to establish any of the matters referred to in paragraph (b)(iii), the JRC may nevertheless entertain his application and (if otherwise appropriate) issue a certificate pursuant to paragraph (e)(i) (ii) or (iii) if the JRC is satisfied that the circumstances resulting in his inability to establish those matters are not such as to make it undesirable for him to be authorised to practise as a barrister and for that purpose to be called to the Bar.

The Aptitude Test

(d) The Aptitude Test shall be a test conducted in accordance with Schedule 13A.

   (i)   Subject to the provisions of this Regulation the JRC may require a CR30 applicant to pass the Aptitude Test or

   (ii)   In determining whether a CR30 applicant is to be required to pass the Aptitude Test or a part of it, the JRC

      1   shall observe the requirements of Regulation 7 of the 1991 Regulations;

      2   may exempt a CR30 applicant from passing the whole or any part of the Aptitude Test if, on having regard to the nature or scope or quality of his Diploma or other evidence of formal qualifications or practice, the JRC thinks fit to do so;

      3   shall grant exemption from any part of the Aptitude Test in respect of which the JRC is satisfied that the relevant subject is already covered to a standard not lower than that of the Aptitude Test by his Diploma or other evidence of formal qualifications; and

      4   shall exempt a CR30 applicant who has been a practising member of the Bar of Ireland in independent practice for not less than 3 years immediately before the date of receipt of his CR30 application.

(e) The JRC shall consider a CR30 application as soon as is reasonably practicable and

   (i)   if the JRC considers that the CR30 applicant ought to be authorised to practise as a barrister without being required to pass any part of the Aptitude Test, the JRC shall issue to him a certificate to that effect;

   (ii)   if the JRC considers that he ought to be authorised to practise as a barrister if and when he passes the whole of the Aptitude Test, the JRC shall issue to him a certificate to that effect;

   (iii)   if the JRC considers that he ought to be authorised to practise as a barrister if and when he passes some part of the Aptitude Test the JRC shall issue to him a certificate to that effect specifying the part of the Aptitude Test which he is required to pass;

   (iv)   if the JRC considers that he ought not to be authorised to practise as a barrister in accordance with sub-paragraph (i) (ii) or (iii) the JRC shall inform him in writing of its decision.

Any certificate pursuant to sub-paragraph (ii) or (iii) or notification of a decision pursuant to sub-paragraph (iv) shall be accompanied by a statement of the reasons on which the decision of the JRC is based.

(f) The JRC shall issue to the CR30 applicant the relevant certificate or notification of its decision no later than four months after the receipt of all relevant documents.

Admission to an Inn and Call to the Bar

   (g) (i)   A CR30 applicant to whom a certificate under sub-paragraph (e)(i) is issued may be admitted to an Inn as a student without complying with Regulations 2 and 3 and (subject to paragraph (h)) shall be eligible for Call to the Bar notwithstanding non-compliance with Regulation 22(b).

(ii)   A CR30 applicant to whom a certificate under sub-paragraph (e)(ii) or (iii) is issued may be admitted to an Inn without complying with Regulations 2 and 3 and (subject to paragraph (h)) shall be eligible for Call to the Bar when he has passed the Aptitude Test or such part of it as he is required to pass notwithstanding non-compliance with Regulation 22(b).

Term Keeping and Call Declaration

(h) (i)   In lieu of complying with Regulation 9(a) a CR30 applicant to whom a certificate under sub-paragraph (e)(i) (ii) or (iii) is issued shall keep terms by attending in person not less than six qualifying sessions.

(ii)   A CR30 applicant who has not complied with sub-paragraph (i) before being called to the Bar may be called notwithstanding such non-compliance but must before being called undertake to the Masters of the Bench that he will comply or complete his compliance with sub-paragraph (i) within three years after Call.

(i) Where the JRC is satisfied that a CR30 applicant cannot reasonably comply with paragraph (h) or with any undertaking given by him pursuant to sub-paragraph (h)(ii), it may reduce the number of qualifying sessions which he is required to attend and any undertaking given by him pursuant to sub-paragraph (h)(ii) shall be deemed to be modified accordingly.

Call Declaration

(j) A CR30 applicant shall before being called to the Bar duly complete and sign a Call Declaration in the form set out in Schedule 5.

Exemptions from the Requirements of Part V

(k) In accordance with the provisions of the 1991 Regulations which do not permit a requirement for a CR30 applicant to complete an adaptation period in addition to passing the Aptitude Test, a CR30 applicant who is called to the Bar pursuant to this Part of the Regulations is exempt from the requirements of Part V.

31.   **Applications based on three years practice in England and Wales in English law including Community law**

(a) A Registered European lawyer who desires to apply under this Regulation to be called to the Bar is referred to herein as 'a CR31 applicant'.

(b) A CR31 applicant who practises under his home professional title, and who has effectively and regularly pursued for a period of at least three years since registration as a Registered European Lawyer under these Regulations an activity in England and Wales in English law including Community law, may apply as a CR31 applicant in writing to the JRC, with a view to being called to the Bar in accordance with this Regulation.

(c) 'Effective and regular pursuit' shall mean actual exercise of the activity without any interruption other than that resulting from the events of every day life.

(d) The application by a CR31 applicant shall be accompanied by payment of the fees prescribed in Schedule 10, and shall contain or be accompanied by

(i)   certificates not more than three months old at the date of receipt of the application by the JRC, attesting to his registration (1) with the competent authority in his home State as a lawyer qualified to practise in his home State under his home professional title, and (2) with the Bar Council and an Inn as a Registered European Lawyer under these Regulations;

(ii) evidence of the activity pursued by him in England and Wales in English law including Community law, giving as full information as practicable of such activity with accompanying documentation and of the number of matters he has dealt with and their nature;

(iii) such evidence as is relied on by him to establish

(1) that he is of good character and repute;

(2) that he has not on the ground of professional misconduct or the commission of a criminal offence been prohibited from practising in his home State and is not currently suspended from so practising;

(3) that no bankruptcy order or directors disqualification order has been made against him and he has not entered into an individual voluntary arrangement with his creditors.

(iv) English translations of every certificate and other document on which he relies and which is not in the English language.

(e) The JRC shall verify the effective and regular nature of the activity pursued by the CR31 applicant, and shall be entitled to request him to provide, orally or in writing, clarification of or further details of the information and documentation mentioned in paragraph (d)(ii) above.

(f) The JRC shall consider a CR31 application as soon as is reasonably practicable, and

(i) if the JRC considers that the CR31 applicant ought to be authorised to practise as a barrister, the JRC shall issue to him a certificate to that effect;

(ii) if the JRC considers that he ought not to be authorised to practise as a barrister, the JRC shall give notice to him accordingly, accompanied by a statement of the reasons on which the decision of the JRC is based.

(g) The JRC shall issue to the CR31 applicant the relevant certificate or notification of its decision no later than four months after the receipt by the JRC of all relevant information and documents, including any provided pursuant to paragraph (e) above.

(h) If the JRC issues to the CR31 applicant a certificate under sub-paragraph (f)(i) above, sub-paragraph (g)(i) and paragraphs (h), (i) and (j) of Regulation 30 shall apply, *mutatis mutandis*, to the CR31 applicant.

32. **Applications based on less than three years practice in England and Wales in English law including Community law**

(a) A Registered European lawyer who desires to apply under this Regulation to be called to the Bar is referred to herein as 'a CR32 applicant'.

(b) A CR32 applicant who practises under his home professional title, and who has effectively and regularly pursued for a period of less than three years since registration as a Registered European Lawyer under these Regulations an activity in England and Wales in English law including Community law, may apply as a CR32 applicant in writing to the JRC, with a view to being called to the Bar in accordance with this Regulation.

(c) 'Effective and regular pursuit' shall have the same meaning as provided in paragraph (c) of Regulation 31.

(d) The application by a CR32 applicant shall be accompanied by payment of the fees prescribed in Schedule 10, and shall contain or be accompanied by (i) the certificates and evidence (and English translations) referred to in paragraph (d) of Regulation 31, *mutatis mutandis*; and (ii) such evidence as is relied on by him to show any knowledge and professional experience of English law, and any attendance at lectures or seminars on English law, giving as full information as practicable of such matters with accompanying documentation.

(e) The JRC shall assess (i) his effective and regular pursuit of a professional activity in England and Wales in English law, and (ii) his capacity to continue such activity, by means of an interview, and shall be entitled to request him to provide, orally or in writing, clarification of or further details of the information and documentation mentioned in paragraph (d) above.

(f) The JRC shall consider a CR32 application as soon as is reasonably practicable, and

   (i) if the JRC considers that the CR32 applicant ought to be authorised to practise as a barrister, the JRC shall issue to him a certificate to that effect;

   (ii) if the JRC considers that he ought not to be authorised to practise as a barrister, the JRC shall give notice to him accordingly, accompanied by a statement of the reasons on which the decision of the JRC is based.

(g) The JRC shall issue the relevant certificate or notification of its decision no later than four months after the interview referred to in paragraph (e) above, or after receipt of further information and documents from the CR31 applicant, if later.

(h) If the JRC issues to the CR32 applicant a certificate under sub-paragraph (f)(i) above, sub-paragraph (g)(i) and paragraphs (h), (i) and (j) of Regulation 30 shall apply, *mutatis mutandis*, to the CR32 applicant.

33. **Public Policy**

The JRC may refuse to give a direction in respect of a CR28 applicant or to authorise a CR30 applicant, a CR31 applicant or a CR32 applicant to be called to the Bar or to practise as a barrister if the JRC considers that this would be against public policy, in particular because of disciplinary proceedings, complaints or incidents of any kind, and if the JRC refuses on the ground of public policy, the JRC shall include in its statement of reasons the reasons why it considers that such a direction or authorisation would be against public policy.

34. **Applications under CR31 or CR32 treated as also applications under CR30**

If the JRC decides to refuse to authorise a CR31 applicant or a CR32 applicant, the JRC may with the written consent of the applicant treat the application as being made also as a CR30 application, and in that event Regulation 30 shall be applied, *mutatis mutandis*, to the applicant and his application.

(C) **SOLICITORS**

35. **Applications**

(a) A Solicitor admitted and enrolled in England and Wales or Northern Ireland ('a solicitor') who wishes to practise as a barrister of the Bar of England and Wales and for that purpose to be called to the Bar in accordance with this Part of the Regulations shall apply in writing to the JRC and shall pay the fee prescribed in Schedule 10.

(b) The application shall be in such form as may be prescribed by the JRC and shall contain or be accompanied by the following:

(i)   Particulars of (1) the educational or professional qualifications which entitled the solicitor to be admitted as a solicitor; (2) his admission; and (3) any period of practice as a solicitor.

(ii) A certificate of good standing issued by the Law Society of England and Wales or the Law Society of Northern Ireland.

(iii) A declaration that

(1) he has not on the ground of professional misconduct or the commission of any criminal offence been prohibited from practising in any jurisdiction in which he has been admitted as a solicitor and is not currently suspended from so practising; and

(2) no bankruptcy order or directors disqualification order has been made against him and he has not entered into an individual voluntary arrangement with his creditors; and

(3) he is not aware of any circumstances which might lead to an event falling within (1) or (2) above to taking place; and

(4) he has disclosed to the JRC in writing any circumstances affecting him which might reasonably be considered to be relevant to the question whether he should be permitted to be called to the Bar.

(iv) Evidence (where applicable) that he is or has been entitled to exercise rights of audience as a solicitor, specifying the rights concerned and the manner in which he has or had become entitled to exercise such rights.

(v)   Any other representations or evidence on which he may wish to rely in support of any application to be wholly or partially exempted from any of the requirements of these Regulations.

(c) If a solicitor is unable to provide the certificate referred to in paragraph (b)(ii) or to make the declaration referred to in paragraph (b)(iii), the JRC may nevertheless entertain his application and (if otherwise appropriate) issue a certificate pursuant to paragraph (e), (f) or (g), if the JRC is satisfied that the circumstances (including those resulting in his inability to establish those matters) are not such as to make it undesirable for him to be called to the Bar and to practise as a barrister.

(d) The JRC shall consider the solicitor's application as soon as reasonably practicable.

(e) In the case of a solicitor who has been permitted by the Law Society to exercise the right of audience in all higher courts in relation to all proceedings both civil and criminal,

(i)   the JRC shall so certify;

(ii) if the JRC is satisfied that there are no grounds on which permission to be admitted to an Inn, to be called to the Bar, and to practise as a barrister, ought to be refused, the JRC shall so certify;

(iii) the solicitor shall be exempt from all parts of the aptitude test, and from the requirements in Part V of these Regulations;

(iv) the solicitor may be admitted to an Inn as a student without complying with Regulations 2 and 3 provided that before admission the solicitor shall declare (and if so required by the JRC shall furnish evidence) that he has ceased to practise and to be financially involved in any practice of a solicitor or legal attorney in any part of the world;

(v)   the solicitor shall (subject to paragraph (k) be eligible for Call to the Bar notwithstanding non-compliance with regulation 22(b);

(vi) the solicitor shall before being called to the Bar duly complete and sign a Call Declaration in the form set out in Schedule 5;

(vii) the solicitor shall on Call to the Bar become entitled to practise as a barrister, subject to (1) complying with paragraph (j); and (2) complying with all requirements applicable to him as a barrister to undertake continuing professional development.

(f) In the case of a solicitor who has been permitted by the Law Society to exercise the right of audience in the higher courts in relation to **either** all civil proceedings **or** all criminal proceedings, but not all such proceedings,

    (i) the JRC shall so certify;

    (ii) the solicitor shall be exempt from all parts of the aptitude test;

    (iii) the JRC shall exempt the solicitor from all pupillage requirements under Part V of these Regulations, unless the JRC shall determine (having regard in particular to the experience, previous practice and intended future practice of the solicitor) that there are exceptional circumstances applying to the solicitor, in which case the JRC shall determine and certify what period (if any, not exceeding six months) of non-practising pupillage and practising pupillage the solicitor shall undertake;

    (iv) if the JRC is satisfied that there are no grounds on which permission to be admitted to an Inn and to be called to the Bar ought to be refused, the JRC shall so certify;

    (v) the solicitor may be admitted to an Inn and called to the Bar, and paragraph (e)(iv) (v) and (vi) shall apply, *mutatis mutandis*, subject to complying with paragraph (k);

    (vi) the solicitor, having been called to the Bar and having undertaken any period of pupillage certified by JRC, shall be entitled to practise as a barrister, subject to complying with all requirements applicable to him as a barrister to undertake continuing professional development.

(g) In the case of a solicitor who has not been permitted by the Law Society to exercise any right of audience in the higher court,

    (i) the JRC shall so certify;

    (ii) the JRC shall determine whether the solicitor is to be required to pass either or both of the oral parts of the aptitude test (but not any of the written parts thereof from which the solicitor shall be exempt), and the JRC shall so certify;

    (iii) the JRC shall determine and certify what period (if any) of non-practising pupillage and practising pupillage under Part V of these Regulations the solicitor shall undertake;

    (iv) if the JRC is satisfied that there are no grounds on which permission to be admitted to an Inn should be refused, the JRC shall so certify;

    (v) the solicitor, on successfully completing any oral part of the aptitude test which he is required by the JRC to pass, may be admitted to an Inn and called to the Bar, and paragraph (e)(iv), (v) and (vi) shall apply, *mutatis mutandis*, subject to complying with paragraph (k);

    (vi) the solicitor, on successfully completing any period of pupillage and further training which he is required by the JRC to undertake, shall be entitled to practise as a barrister, and shall comply with all requirements applicable to him as a barrister to undertake continuing professional development.

(h) In the case of any solicitor, if the JRC shall determine that there are grounds on which permission to be admitted to an Inn, to be called to the Bar and to practise as a barrister should be refused, the JRC shall so certify, setting out the grounds on which the determination is based.

(i) Any certificate to be issued by the JRC pursuant to paragraphs (e), (f), (g) and (h) shall be furnished to the solicitor no later than four months after receipt of the application and fee referred to in paragraph (a) above and of all the information and documents referred to in paragraph (b) above.

(j) In lieu of complying with Regulation 9(a), a solicitor falling within paragraph (e), (f) or (g) shall keep terms by attending in person not less than six qualifying sessions.

(k) A solicitor who has not complied with paragraph (j) before being called to the Bar may be called notwithstanding such non-compliance, but must before being called undertake to the Masters of the Bench that he will comply or complete his compliance with paragraph (j) within three years after Call.

(l) A solicitor who is contemplating Call to the Bar may, on providing to the JRC such evidence as would be required in support of an application under this Regulation, but before taking steps to terminate practice as a solicitor, apply to the JRC for information concerning the requirements the JRC would be likely to impose or the exemptions the JRC would be likely to grant if he were to make an application under this Regulation.

(m) A requirement to undergo a pupillage or to undertake an aptitude test imposed upon a solicitor in accordance with the powers contained in sub paragraphs (f)(iii) or g(ii) or (iii) shall not preclude that solicitor from exercising those rights of audience (if any) which he or she is already entitled to exercise pursuant to Section 39 of the Access to Justice Act.

(D)   OTHER QUALIFIED LAWYERS

36.   'Qualified Applicants'

(a) An application under this section of Part IV may be made by a qualified lawyer who falls into one of the following categories:

   (i)   Members of the Bar of Northern Ireland

   (ii)   Members of the Faculty of Advocates in Scotland

   (iii) Legal practitioners in other Common Law jurisdictions who have for a period of not less than 3 years regularly exercised rights of audience in superior courts which administer law which is substantially equivalent to the common law of England and Wales.

(b) In this section any such lawyer is referred to as a 'qualified applicant' or (where it is necessary to distinguish the category into which he falls) as 'a Northern Ireland barrister' 'a Scottish advocate' or 'a common law practitioner' as the case may be.

Applications

(c) A qualified applicant who wishes to practise as a barrister of England and Wales and for that purpose to be called to the Bar in accordance with this Part of these Regulations shall apply in writing to the JRC and shall pay the fee prescribed in Schedule 10.

(d) The application shall be in such form as may be prescribed by the JRC and shall include the following:

(i)   Particulars of the educational or professional qualifications relied upon as constituting him a qualified applicant.

(ii)   The original or a duly authenticated copy of every document relied upon as establishing those educational or professional qualifications.

(iii)   Particulars showing that he has reasonable grounds to expect that, upon Call, he will be able to practise at the Bar of England and Wales or the Channel Islands.

(iv)   Such evidence as is relied upon by the qualified applicant to establish all the following matters:

     (1)   that he is of good character and repute;

     (2)   that he has not on the ground of professional misconduct or the commission of a criminal offence been prohibited from practising in any jurisdiction in relation to which he is a qualified legal practitioner and is not currently suspended from so practising;

     (3)   that no bankruptcy order or directors disqualification order has been made against him and he has not entered into an individual voluntary arrangement with his creditors.

(v)   Such representations or evidence as the qualified applicant may wish to make in support of any application that he be wholly or partially exempted from passing an Aptitude Test in accordance with paragraph (g) of this Regulation and from the requirements in Part V of these Regulations.

(e) Unless in any particular case it considers that further evidence is required the JRC shall accept as sufficient evidence of the matters referred to in paragraph (d) (i) (ii) and (iv) above such certificates as are mentioned in Schedule 9; and without prejudice to its right to require further evidence it may accept as sufficient evidence of the matters referred to in paragraph (d) (iii) above a statement in writing signed by the qualified applicant.

(f) If a qualified applicant is unable to establish any of the matters referred to in paragraph (d)(iv) of this Regulation the JRC may nevertheless entertain his application and (if otherwise appropriate) issue a certificate pursuant to paragraph (h) of this Regulation if it is satisfied that the circumstances resulting in his inability to establish those matters are not such as to make it undesirable for him to be authorised to practise.

The Aptitude Test

(g) The JRC may require a qualified applicant to pass the Aptitude Test referred to in Regulation 30(d) or any part of it provided always that the JRC shall exempt a qualified applicant who has been a practising Northern Ireland barrister in independent practice for not less than three years immediately before the date of his application from passing the whole of the Aptitude Test.

Consideration of the Application by the JRC

(h) Regulation 30(e) and (f) (grant or refusal of a certificate) shall apply (*mutatis mutandis*) in relation to an application by a qualified applicant under this Regulation as it applies to a CR30 applicant.

(i) If the JRC issues to the qualified applicant a certificate under paragraph (h) above, Regulation 30(g) (admission to an Inn and Call to the Bar) Regulation 30(h) and (i) (term keeping) and Regulation 30(j) (Call declaration) shall apply to a qualified applicant under this regulation, *mutatis mutandis*.

Pupillage and Entry into Practice

(j) Part V of these Regulations shall apply to qualified applicants as follows:-

(i) A Northern Ireland barrister who has completed pupillage in Northern Ireland and who is called to the Bar under this Part of the Regulations is exempt from the requirements of Part V.

(ii) A Scottish advocate, or a Common Law practitioner who is called to the Bar under this Part of the Regulations is subject to the requirements of Part V but the JRC may grant him exemptions from those requirements to the extent that it is satisfied that his practical experience is such as to render the satisfaction of those requirements inappropriate in his case.

(E)   TEMPORARY MEMBERSHIP OF THE BAR

37.   Qualified Lawyers

A person who is qualified to apply for permanent membership of the Bar under Section (C) or (D) of this Part of these Regulations ('a qualified lawyer') shall be eligible to be admitted to temporary membership of an Inn and of the Bar for the purpose of conducting a particular case or particular cases before a court or courts of England and Wales.

38.   Certificates and Evidence to be Produced to the JRC

An applicant under this Section must obtain a certificate from the Joint Regulations Committee that the applicant is a qualified lawyer and such certificate shall specify the case or cases in respect of which the applicant seeks temporary membership. Before issuing such a certificate the JRC will normally require to see:

(a) the appropriate certificate of good standing specified in Schedule 9; and

(b) evidence which establishes that a solicitor or solicitors of the Supreme Court in England and Wales wish to brief the applicant to appear in the case or cases in respect of which he seeks temporary membership.

39.   Admission to Temporary Membership of an Inn and Call to the Bar

An applicant under this Section:

(a) who has obtained a certificate of qualification may present the same, together with a petition for temporary admission to an Inn and Call to the Bar, to the Inn of his choice and any Bencher authorised by the Treasurer for this purpose may admit the applicant to temporary membership of the Inn and call him to the Bar;

(b) will be required to pay the fees for temporary membership of an Inn and for temporary membership of the Bar specified in Schedule 10;

(c) shall sign a Call Declaration in the form set out in Schedule 6;

(d) on conclusion of the case or cases for which he was admitted to temporary membership will automatically cease to be a member of the Inn of Court to which he was admitted and of the Bar;

(e) is exempt from complying with any Regulations other than those in this Section.

(F)   REVIEW AND APPEAL

40.   Review by the JRC

(a) A person who has made an application to the JRC under Part IV and who is dissatisfied with the decision of the JRC on that application may request in writing that the

JRC shall review its decision and on making such request shall pay the fee prescribed in Schedule 10.

(b) On receipt of any such request the JRC shall as soon as reasonably practicable review its decision and in doing so shall take into account both such material or information as was provided for its consideration when the application was originally made and also such additional material or information (if any) as may be furnished by the applicant in support of his request for review; and it may either affirm its original decision or substitute for it any other decision which it could have made on the original application.

Appeal to the Visitors to the Inns of Court

(c) A decision by the JRC on a review under the Regulations shall not be subject to further review by the JRC at the instance of the applicant; but the applicant may appeal to the Visitors to the Inns of Court in accordance with the Hearings before the Visitors Rules 1991 or any modification thereof for the time being in force.

Further Review by the JRC

(d) Nothing herein contained shall prevent the JRC from reviewing any of its decisions (including a decision on a review under this regulation) if it thinks fit to do so but except as provided by paragraphs (a) and (b) of this regulation the JRC is not obliged to carry out any such review.

PART V

PUPILLAGE AND ENTRY INTO PRACTICE

41. **Obligation to Undertake Pupillage**

41.1 Unless exempted under Part IV or Part VI of these Regulations, a person who intends to practise as a barrister in accordance with paragraph 202 of the Code of Conduct is required:

(i) to train as a pupil for an aggregate period of not less than 12 months; and

(ii) to complete such further training after completion of the Vocational Stage as may be required from time to time by the Bar Council.

41.2 Pupillage shall be divided into two parts:

(i) the non-practising six months, which, save with the approval in writing of the designated body (which shall, for the purposes of this Part V be the JRC subject to any change hereafter in its designation, and which is referred to in this Part V as 'the JRC'), shall be undertaken in a continuous period of 6 months in England and Wales; and

(ii) the practising six months

(1) which, save with the approval in writing of the JRC, shall be undertaken in a continuous period of six months or with only such intervals (each not exceeding one month) as to ensure that the practising six months is completed within an overall period of nine months;

(2) which, save with the approval in writing of the JRC, shall commence not later than 12 months after the completion of the non-practising six months;

(3) all of which shall be undertaken after Call; and

(4) which may be undertaken in any Member State.

41.3   The approval of the JRC under Regulation 41.2(ii)(1) or (2) may be subject to such conditions as to additional training as the JRC deems appropriate having regard to the particular circumstances of the person seeking the approval.

42.   Registration of Pupils

42.1   On arranging any period of pupillage, which shall include any period of training service under Regulation 46 ('external training'), a pupil shall give notice in writing to the Masters of the Bench and the Bar Council in the form specified in Schedule 14 Part 1.

42.2   It is the duty of each pupil to notify the Masters of the Bench and the Bar Council of all material changes in the arrangements for pupillage of such pupil in writing in the form specified in Schedule 14 Part 2.

43.   Commencement of Pupillage

Subject to Regulation 45, a person who is required by Regulation 41 to train as a pupil may not commence pupillage unless:-

either

    (1) he has completed the Vocational Stage, and in the case of a person who has completed the Vocational Stage by passing the Bar Examination he has also successfully completed a Vocational Conversion Course or such other training as the Bar Council may require; or

    (2) he has been authorised to be called or readmitted to the Bar under Part IV or Part VI of these Regulations and in the case of a person who has been required to take the Aptitude Test or any part of it he has been certified as having passed the Aptitude Test or relevant part thereof:

and

    (3) he has registered his pupillage under Regulation 42.

44.   The Vocational Stage — Stale Qualifications

44.1   A person may not commence pupillage after the expiration of a period of five years (or such other period as the Bar Council may stipulate) from the date when that person was certified as having completed and passed a Vocational Course or a Vocational Conversion Course or any relevant part of the Aptitude Test or as having successfully completed any further training which he was required by the Bar Council to undertake before commencing pupillage.

44.2   Such period may be extended by the Bar Council in an individual case for such period and on such terms as it thinks fit including the requirements as to further courses of study or training to be undertaken by the person seeking the extension.

44.3   This regulation shall not apply to persons who registered for the Vocational Course or Vocational Conversion Course or were required to take the Aptitude Test or any section or sections or part or parts thereof before 1st September 1998.

45.   Exceptions and Dispensations from Pupillage

The JRC may exempt wholly or in part any person from any of the obligations of this Part subject to such conditions, including conditions as to additional training, as it considers appropriate having regard to the qualifications, experience and other particular circumstances of the person concerned.

46.   External Training

46.1   Pupillage must be spent with one or more Pupil Masters save that with the prior approval of the JRC (subject to CR58) all or part of the practising six months of pupillage may be satisfied by any or any combination of the following forms of external training:

(i)   up to six months pupillage may be satisfied by an equivalent period of training spent with a solicitor who is practising in the United Kingdom or in another member State.

(ii)   up to six months pupillage may be satisfied by an equivalent period of training spent with a lawyer qualified and practising in another Member State;

(iii)   six months pupillage may be satisfied by undertaking a 'stage' of five months duration or more, in the legal departments of the European Commission in Brussels or Luxembourg, or a 'placement' at the European Commission in London;

(iv)   up to six weeks pupillage may be satisfied by serving as a marshal with a Judge of the High Court of Justice or with a Circuit judge;

(v)   up to four weeks pupillage may be satisfied by a pupil, with the permission of his Pupil Master, working with a solicitor or other professional person whose work is relevant to his Pupil Master's practice;

(vi)   up to four weeks pupillage may be satisfied by a pupil, with the permission of his Pupil Master, working under supervision for a body, such as a law centre or pro bono or free representation unit which supplies legal services to the public without a fee or for a nominal fee;

(vii)   the JRC may, in an individual case, recognise such other form of training as satisfying part of pupillage as it considers appropriate having regard to the particular circumstances of the person concerned.

46.2   Subject to Regulation 41.2, external training may be undertaken at any time, but in no case shall count towards the non-practising six months of pupillage.

46.3   A solicitor or a lawyer qualified and practising in another member State with whom a period of training is spent pursuant to Regulation 46.1(i) or (ii) shall be a person whose qualifications experience and place of practice are comparable to those which in the case of a barrister would render him eligible to act as a Pupil Master, unless in an individual case the JRC shall permit a person with different qualifications experience and place of practice to conduct the training.

47.   Pupil Masters

47.1   A practising barrister may act as a Pupil Master if:

(i)   he is entered on the register of approved Pupil Masters kept by the Bar Council;

(ii)   his practice is and has been for the previous two years his primary occupation; and

(iii)   his principal place of practice is a chambers or office which is also the principal place of practice of at least one other barrister or member of another authorised body who is of at least three years' standing (as defined in paragraph 203.2 of the Code of Conduct).

47.2   A Pupil Master may not be responsible for more than one pupil at a time save with the approval in writing of the JRC.

48.   **Eligibility for Approval and Registration as a Pupil Master**

48.1   In order to be entered on the register of approved Pupil Masters kept by the Bar Council, a barrister must be approved as a Pupil Master by his Inn.

48.2   Each Inn shall, from time to time, provide the Bar Council with a list of approved Pupil Masters.

48.3   A practising barrister may apply to his Inn to be approved as a Pupil Master. An applicant shall at the date of his application:

(i)   have practised in the United Kingdom or another member State as a barrister (other than as a pupil who has not completed pupillage in accordance with these Regulations) or as a member of another authorised body for a period (which need not have been continuous and need not have been as a member of the same authorised body) of at least six years in the previous eight years; and

(ii)   have made his practice his primary occupation and been entitled to exercise a right of audience as a barrister during the two years immediately preceding the date of the application.

48.4   The Masters of the Bench may approve a person as a Pupil Master even though that person who does not satisfy the conditions set out in Regulation 48.3 above provided they are satisfied that he has the necessary experience to be so approved.

48.5   No Queen's Counsel other than an employed barrister may be registered as a Pupil Master.

48.6   The Bar Council, in consultation with the Inns' Council, shall prescribe what training, if any, shall be undertaken by persons either before or after such persons have been entered on the register of approved Pupil Masters.

48.7   A Pupil Master who fails to undertake the training prescribed under Regulation 48.6 above, within the time prescribed by the Masters of the Bench, shall not be registered or (if already registered) shall have his name removed from the register of approved Pupil Masters held by the Bar Council.

48.8   An appeal against a refusal to register or removal of a person's name from the register under Regulation 48.7 shall lie to the JRC under Regulation 51.

49.   **Application for Approval and Registration as Pupil Master**

The procedure as regards applications for approval and registration as a Pupil Master is as follows:

(i)   An eligible barrister who wishes to act as a Pupil Master must submit to the Masters of the Bench an application in the form specified in Schedule 8.

(ii)   The application must be supported in the following respects:

(a)   In the case of a barrister in independent practice, by the applicant's Head of Chambers, and in the case of an employed barrister by a more senior lawyer employed in the same organisation and having direct knowledge of the work of the applicant; or

(b)   If the applicant is himself the Head of Chambers, or there is no more senior lawyer employed in the same organisation with such direct knowledge, or for any other reason the support referred to in sub-paragraph (a) is not available, by an independent person who is a Master of the Bench of an Inn, a Queen's Counsel, a Leader of a Circuit, a Recorder or Deputy High Court Judge,

Treasury Counsel or a person of comparable standing who is able to comment from personal knowledge on the applicant's suitability to act as a Pupil Master; and

(c) In every case, by a second person falling within the requirements in sub-paragraph (b) above.

(iii) If the Masters of the Bench approve the application, they shall notify the applicant and the Bar Council, which shall cause the applicant to be entered on the register of approved Pupil Masters accordingly.

(iv) Any approval may be provisional and subject to such terms as the Masters of the Bench may at any time in their discretion impose to ensure that the Pupil Master is qualified and able to discharge his responsibilities.

(v) If the Masters of the Bench refuse the application they shall notify the applicant accordingly.

(vi) An appeal shall lie from such a refusal to the JRC in accordance with Regulation 51.

50.   Removal from the Register of Pupil Masters

50.1   Any complaint or other matter which appears to affect the fitness of a barrister to continue as a Pupil Master or the desirability of his continued registration as such, shall be referred to the Masters of the Bench who shall investigate the same, and if thought necessary or desirable, invite the barrister concerned to comment thereon in writing or in person.

50.2   The Masters of the Bench may pending the outcome of such enquiries resolve that a barrister's registration as a Pupil Master be suspended, and shall notify the barrister accordingly.

50.3   Having considered any such case, the Masters of the Bench may:

(i)   dismiss the complaint (if any);

(ii)   take no action;

(iii)   refer the case to the Professional Conduct and Complaints Committee of the Bar Council;

(iv)   if in the opinion of the Masters of the Bench the case is such as to require informal treatment, draw it to the barrister's attention in writing and, if thought necessary, direct him to attend upon the Treasurer or some other person nominated by the Treasurer;

(iv)   in any case where the conduct disclosed is such as, in the opinion of the Masters of the Bench, to render the barrister unfit to continue as a Pupil Master, resolve that the barrister be removed from the register or suspended from the register for such period as they may determine.

50.4   A barrister shall in any event have his name removed from the register of Pupil Masters if:

(a) he requests the Bar Council to remove his name from the register;

(b) not being an employed barrister, he is appointed as Queen's Counsel;

(c) he ceases to practise as a barrister or is suspended from practice as a barrister;

(d) the Masters of the Bench resolve to remove his name from the register because he has not taken a pupil for five years.

50.5   If a resolution is passed for the removal or suspension of a barrister from the register, the Masters of the Bench shall notify the barrister accordingly.

50.6   An appeal shall lie from any resolution for the removal or suspension from the register under Regulation 50 to the JRC in accordance with Regulation 51.

51.   **Appeal to the JRC**

    (a) An appeal under Regulations 48.7, 49 (vi), 50.6 or 52.6 shall be by way of a rehearing.

    (b) Notice of appeal shall be given in writing to the Secretary of the JRC.

    (c) Notice of appeal must be served on the said Secretary within 28 days from the date on which notification of the decision or the resolution of the Inn was given to the appellant, provided always that the JRC may, on such terms as it thinks fit, extend the period for appeal.

    (d) For the purposes of determining an appeal under this Regulation the quorum shall be three members of the JRC.

    (e) The appellant shall be entitled to appear in person or be represented before the JRC and (in addition or as an alternative) to submit a written statement of his case.

    (f) Having considered the appeal the JRC may:

        (i)   dismiss it; or

        (ii)   allow it unconditionally or subject to conditions.

52.   **Qualification Certificates**

52.1   On completion of the non-practising six months of pupillage, a pupil shall obtain from his Pupil Master a certificate for submission both to the Masters of the Bench and to the Bar Council certifying that he has satisfactorily completed this period. Provided that the pupil has completed such further training as is referred to in Regulation 41.1(ii), on receipt of such certificate, the Bar Council shall forthwith register the same and, if the pupil has been called to the Bar, issue the pupil with a Provisional Qualification Certificate.

52.2   On completion of the practising six months of pupillage, a pupil shall obtain from his Pupil Master and from any person with whom the pupil has undertaken external training a certificate for submission both to the Masters of the Bench and to the Bar Council certifying that he has satisfactorily completed this period. Provided that the pupil has completed such further training as is referred to in Regulation 41.1(ii), on receipt of such certificate, the Bar Council shall forthwith register the same and issue the pupil with a Full Qualification Certificate.

52.3   If a pupil is unable to obtain a relevant certificate from his Pupil Master or from any relevant person, the Masters of the Bench and the Bar Council may accept a certificate from the Pupil Master's Head of Chambers, or from the member of those chambers designated by the Head of Chambers as the person in charge of pupillage, or such other person as is acceptable to the Masters of the Bench and the Bar Council, that the pupil has satisfactorily completed the periods specified in Regulation 41.2, provided that the certificate contains an explanation of the reason why the Pupil Master or any relevant person has not provided such a certificate which is satisfactory to the Masters of the Bench and the Bar Council.

52.4   If a Pupil Master or any other person mentioned in Regulations 52.1, 52.2 or 52.3 refuses to sign a relevant certificate for any reason, the pupil may ask the Masters of the Bench, on the grounds that the signature has been wrongfully withheld, to grant a certificate themselves and to request the Bar Council

(i) to register the same; and

(ii) to issue the pupil with a Provisional Qualification Certificate or a Full Qualification Certificate as the case may be.

52.5   On receipt of a certificate under Regulation 52.3 above, or on the grant of a certificate by the Masters of the Bench under Regulation 52.4 above, the Masters of the Bench will request the Bar Council to issue the pupil forthwith with a Provisional Qualification Certificate or a Full Qualification Certificate as the case may be.

52.6   A pupil may appeal to the JRC against any refusal by the Masters of the Bench to take any of the steps set out in Regulations 52.3, 52.4 or 52.5.

53. Duties of a Pupil

53.1   During each pupillage including any external training it is the duty of the pupil to be conscientious in receiving the instruction given, to apply himself full time thereto, to preserve the confidentiality of every client's affairs, and to comply with the Code of Conduct and with such other rules or guidelines relating to pupillage as may be approved from time to time by the Bar Council in consultation with the Inns' Council.

53.2   Where on the conclusion of a period of pupillage including any external training a pupil does not intend to serve another pupillage or period of external training he shall notify the Records Office of the Bar Council and the Under Treasurer in writing:

(i) of any tenancy or employment he has secured, giving details of the chambers or employer; or

(ii) if he has not secured a tenancy or employment, whether he is seeking a tenancy or employment in England and Wales, whether he intends to practise abroad, or whether he is seeking employment abroad, and in each case shall give all relevant details.

54. Duties of a Pupil Master

The duties of a Pupil Master are set out in paragraph 804 of the Code of Conduct.

PART VI

MISCELLANEOUS REGULATIONS

55. Teachers of the Law of England and Wales of Experience and Distinction

(a) A person who is a teacher of the law of England and Wales and who desires to be called to the Bar without complying in full with the requirements and provisions of Parts I to V of these Regulations may make an application to the Joint Regulations Committee for the relaxation of those requirements and provisions in respect of his case and the JRC shall have power to grant such application (whether in whole or in part) in accordance with the provisions of this Regulation.

(b) Any such application shall be made to the JRC in such manner as the JRC shall prescribe and shall be accompanied by payment of such fee as the JRC shall from time to time determine, having due regard to cost.

(c) The application shall be considered in the first instance by a subcommittee of the JRC known as the Legal Academics Committee which shall make such recommendations as it thinks fit as to the relaxation (if any) which in its opinion ought to be granted, but the JRC shall not be bound to accept any such recommendation.

(d) In considering whether to recommend or to grant any such relaxation the Legal Academics Committee or the JRC (as the case may be) shall have regard to all the circumstances of the case including, but not limited to, the matters specified in the next paragraph; and shall act in accordance with the principle stated in paragraph (f).

(e) The circumstances referred to in the preceding paragraph are the following:

    (i)   The academic achievements of the applicant;

    (ii)   The seniority standing and distinction of the applicant as a teacher of law;

    (iii) The nature and extent of the applicant's contacts with barristers in independent practice;

    (iv) The intentions of the applicant in relation to practice at the Bar and any arrangements made for the purpose of fulfilling those intentions;

    (v)   The benefits to the Bar which may be expected to flow from the applicant's Call to Bar.

(f) The principle referred to in paragraph (d) is that this regulation makes available a wholly exceptional route by which a person may be called to the Bar and that a relaxation should be granted only in cases where the Legal Academics Committee and the JRC are satisfied:

    (i)   that the applicant is of such academic distinction or likely to be of such value to the profession that his admission by such an exceptional route is justified; and

    (ii)   that no useful purpose would be satisfied by requiring the applicant to comply with the requirements or provisions which are proposed to be relaxed.

(g) In this regulation references to 'relaxation' include, but are not limited to:

    (i)   the relaxation or modification of

    (ii)   the complete or partial exemption from

    (iii) the complete or partial dispensation from compliance with, and

    (iv) the conditional or unconditional waiver or excusing of

        any breach of or non-compliance with any requirement or provision contained in Parts I to V of these Regulations; and the word 'relax' shall be construed accordingly.

(h) In relation to the requirements and provisions or Part II of these Regulations the power of relaxation conferred by this Regulation shall be exercised by the JRC and not by the Bar Council; and the JRC may as a condition of any relaxation of such requirements or provisions require the applicant to pass the Aptitude Test referred to in Regulation 30(d) or one or more parts of the Aptitude Test.

(i) The powers of relaxation conferred by this rule are in addition to and not in substitution for the power referred to in Regulation 58 and every other power of relaxation conferred by these Regulations.

(j) No appeal shall lie from any decision of the JRC under this Regulation but the JRC may at its discretion review any such decision insofar as it is not in favour of the applicant and (whether in connection with such a review or otherwise) may refer any application back to the Legal Academics Committee for further consideration by it.

(k) An applicant whose application for a relaxation pursuant to this Regulation is wholly rejected may not, without the prior consent of the JRC, make a further application under this Regulation before the expiration of three years from such rejection; but an applicant whose application is wholly or partially successful may at any time make an application for a further relaxation (including the removal or modification of any condition imposed in relation to a previous relaxation).

56. **Readmission of Barristers Disbarred at own Request**

(a) A former barrister who has been disbarred at his own request and who seeks readmission to the Bar shall apply to the Masters of the Bench and shall pay the fees specified in Schedule 10 to reflect the administrative costs involved in processing the application.

(b) If the Masters of the Bench decide to entertain the application they shall cause notice thereof to be screened in the Hall, Benchers' Rooms, and Treasurer's Office of the Inn for not less than 8 days and shall cause a copy of the notice so screened to be sent to each of the other Inns for screening.

(c) The notice of application shall contain the name and description of the applicant and the dates of his original call and disbarment and any information deemed relevant by the Inn.

(d) Subject to payment by the applicant of the further admission fee specified in Schedule 10 and to his making a further Call Declaration in the form specified in Schedule 7, the Masters of the Bench may at any time within 3 months after such screening readmit him.

57. **Readmission of Barristers Disbarred for Disciplinary Offences**

(a) A former barrister who has been disbarred for a disciplinary offence and who seeks readmission to the Bar shall apply to the Masters of the Bench and shall pay the fee specified in Schedule 10 to reflect the administrative costs involved in processing the application.

(b) The application must be supported in writing:
  (i)   by at least one practising or employed barrister of not less than 10 years standing or by a Master of the Bench;
  (ii) by the applicant's employer or last employer if applicable;
  (iii) by two other references as to general character in the form adapted from Certificate A in Schedule 3; and must be accompanied by a statement signed by the applicant setting out all relevant matters affecting him since disbarment, including his record of employment and any relevant medical certificate.

(c) The Masters of the Bench shall refer the application to the Professional Conduct and Complaints Committee of the Bar Council ('the PCC') together with all relevant documents in its possession relating to the original complaint and any other matters concerning the applicant.

(d) The PCC shall consider the matter in accordance with the provisions of the Code of Conduct and shall in writing inform the Masters of the Bench of its recommendation or of the fact that it makes no recommendation.

(e) Upon receipt of the views of the PCC the Masters of the Bench shall decide whether or not to entertain the application and if they decide so to do may impose such conditions on the applicant as to further training, assessment or pupillage as they think fit.

(f) Subject to satisfaction of any further conditions imposed under paragraph (e) above, the procedure for readmission of a successful applicant shall follow that set out in paragraphs (b), (c) and (d) of Regulation 56.

58. **Relaxation of Regulations**

(a) In addition to any powers exercisable by the Masters of the Bench under these Regulations, the Bar Council in relation to Part II and the JRC in relation to all other parts of the Regulations, may in any particular case either unconditionally or subject to conditions:

(i) modify or dispense with any requirement or provision of these Regulations (including any term of any undertaking given thereunder); or

(ii) excuse any breach of or non-compliance with any such requirement or provision (including any such terms as aforesaid).

(b) Any petition for the exercise of the power of the JRC referred to in this Regulation shall be addressed to the Masters of the Bench through the Under Treasurer who shall forward the same to the JRC for adjudication together with such observations thereon as the Masters of the Bench may think fit to make.

59. **Amendment of Regulations**

(a) In relation to Part II, Regulation 30(d) and Part V of these Regulations and the associated Schedules, the Bar Council acting in consultation with the Inns' Council; and

(b) in relation to the remainder of these Regulations, the Inns' Council acting in consultation with the Bar Council

have power to amend these Regulations from time to time in any manner they think fit and any such amendment shall forthwith be binding on all members of all the Inns.

60. **Breach of Regulations or Undertakings**

Any breach of any requirement or provision of these Regulations or of any term of any undertaking given thereunder or any misstatement of fact in any declaration made thereunder may involve disciplinary action.

SCHEDULE 1

Definitions

'The 1991 Regulations' and 'the 1999 Order' bear the meanings set out in Regulation 26(c).

'Admission Declaration' means the Declaration and Undertaking referred to in Regulation 5.

'Applicant' means a person applying for admission to an Inn as a student.

'Authorised body' means any body other than the Bar Council authorised to grant rights of audience or rights to conduct litigation under the Courts and Legal Services Act 1990.

'Bankruptcy order' includes a bankruptcy order made pursuant to the Insolvency Act 1986 and any similar order made in any jurisdiction in the world.

' The Bar' means the Bar of England and Wales.

'Bar Council' means the General Council of the Bar.

'The Bar Examination' means the examination for Call to the Bar as constituted by paragraph 1 of Schedule 12.

'Barrister in independent practice' has the meaning assigned to it in the Code of Conduct.

'The Board of Examiners' means any Board of Examiners appointed from time to time by the Bar Council.

'Call Declaration' means the Declaration and Undertaking referred to in Regulation 24.

'The Code of Conduct' means the Code of Conduct of the Bar of England and Wales adopted by the Bar Council, and as amended, from time to time.

'Common Professional Examination Course' means a course in preparation for a Common Professional Examination approved by the CPE Board or a course in preparation for a Law Society recognised Diploma in Law approved by the CPE Board which:

(a) in respect of a course begun by a student before 1st September 1996, includes the six Core Subjects; and

(b) in respect of a course begun by a student on or after 1st September 1996, includes a study of the foundations of legal knowledge and one other area of legal study, and assessments and examinations in those subjects.

'The Core Subjects' means the following six subjects:

(i)   The Law of Contract.

(ii)   The Law of Tort.

(iii)   Criminal Law.

(iv)   Land Law.

(v)   Constitutional and Administrative Law.

(vi)   Equity and Trusts.

'The CPE Board' means

(a) the Common Professional Examination Board set up pursuant to resolutions passed by the Council of the Inns of Court and the Law Society, and which administers any Common Professional Examination Course specified in Regulations 12, 13 and 14; or

(b) any successor to that Board which is established for the purposes of administering any such Common Professional Examination Course.

'A CR28 applicant', 'a CR30 applicant', 'a CR31 applicant' and 'a CR32 applicant' bear the meanings set out in Regulations 28, 30, 31 and 32 respectively.

'Designated Body' means a person, committee or other body to whom the Bar Council, in consultation with the Inns' Council, has delegated the exercise of a function or power under these Regulations.

'Diploma' means any diploma, certificate or other evidence of formal qualifications awarded by a competent authority in an European Union Member State which

(a) shows that the holder:

(i)   has successfully completed a post-secondary course of at least three year's duration (or equivalent duration part-time) at a university or establishment of higher education or establishment of similar level;

(ii)   has successfully completed any additional professional training required; and

(iii)   has the qualifications required for the practice of a regulated profession in that State; provided that either:

(A) the education and training so attested were received mainly within the European Union; or

(B) the holder has had at least three years professional experience certified by a competent authority in that State (being a State which recognised a qualification obtained in a non-member State); or which

(b) was awarded by a competent authority in an European Union Member State on the successful completion of education and training received within the European Union, and which

(i) has been recognised by a competent authority in that State as equivalent in level to a diploma to which sub-paragraph (a) applies; and

(ii) confers the same rights in respect of the practice of a regulated profession in that State.

'Employed Barrister' has the meaning assigned to it in the Code of Conduct service or for services.

'European lawyer' means a person who is a national of a State listed in article 2(2) of the 1999 Order and who is authorised in any of those States to pursue professional activities under any of the professional titles appearing in article 2(2) of the 1999 Order, but who is not any of the following:

(a) a solicitor or barrister of England and Wales or Northern Ireland; or

(b) a solicitor or advocate under the law of Scotland.

'Exempting Law Degree' means a degree which is recognised by the Bar Council as satisfying both the Academic Stage and the Vocational Stage of training.

'EU' means the European Union.

'Foundations of Legal Knowledge' means those subjects the study of which is prescribed by the Bar Council for the purpose of obtaining a Qualifying Law Degree by a course of study begun on or after 1st September 1995 and by the CPE Board for inclusion in any Common Professional Examination Course beginning on or after 1st September 1996:

(i)   Obligations I (Contract)

(ii)   Obligations II (Tort)

(iii) Criminal Law

(iv)   Public Law

(v)   Property Law

(vi)   Equity & The Law of Trusts

(vii) Foundations of EU Law.

'The Head of Education' or 'The Head of Education and Training' means the Head of the Education and Training Department of the General Council of the Bar.

'Home professional title' means, in relation to a European lawyer, the professional title or any of the professional titles specified in relation to his home State in article 2(2) of the 1999 Order under which he is authorised in his home State to pursue professional activities.

'Home State' means the State listed in article 2(2) of the 1999 Order in which a European lawyer acquired the authorisation to pursue professional activities under any of the professional titles appearing in article 2(2) of the 1999 Order and, if he is authorised in more than one of those States, it shall mean any of those States.

'Inn' means one of the four Inns of Court namely the Honourable Societies of Lincoln's Inn, Inner Temple, Middle Temple and Gray's Inn.

'Inns' Council' means the Council of the Inns of Court.

'Integrated Course' means a course (for those whose educational qualifications are within paragraphs (a), (c) or (d) of Category II of Schedule 2) which is recognised by the Bar Council as satisfying both the Academic Stage and the Vocational Stage of training.

'Joint Regulations Committee' or 'JRC' means the Joint Consolidated Regulations and Transfer Committee of the Inns' Council and the Bar Council.

'The Masters of the Bench' means the Masters of the Bench of the Inn to which the applicant seeks admission or of which the student or barrister concerned is a member.

'Member State' means a Member State of the European Communities, and 'another Member State' means a Member State other than the United Kingdom;

'Month' means a calendar month.

'Overseas Applicant' means an applicant whose permanent residence is not in the United Kingdom and 'overseas student' has a corresponding meaning.

'Practical Exercises' means the Forensic Exercises in Advocacy, the Chambers Exercises in Drafting, the Professional Ethics Course and the Film Work arranged or conducted by the Bar Council.

'Practice' in relation to any regulated profession, includes—

- (a) the taking up or pursuit of the profession in a Member State, whether in a self-employed capacity or as an employed person; and
- (b) the right to use, in the course of such pursuit, a professional title or abbreviator letters, or the enjoyment of any special status, granted by a designated authority for that profession;

'Practising as a barrister' has the meaning set out in paragraph 201 of the Code of Conduct.

'Pupil Master' has the meaning assigned to it by Regulation 47.1.

'Qualifying Law Degree' (whether a single honours degree in law, a joint honour's degree, or a mixed honours degree) means a degree passed at such a standard as the Bar Council considers satisfactory, and which:

- (a) in the case of a degree conferred upon the successful completion of a course of study begun before 1st September 1995, includes subjects which the Bar Council considers to be sufficiently equivalent to the six core subjects, being
  - (i) a degree conferred by a university in the United Kingdom or Republic of Ireland;
  - (ii) a degree conferred by the Council for National Academic Awards before its dissolution on 31st March 1993; or
  - (iii) a License in Law conferred by the former University College of Buckingham before that college was granted university status; and

(b) in the case of a degree conferred upon the successful completion of a course of study, acceptable to the Bar Council, begun on or after 1st September 1995, a degree conferred by a university in the United Kingdom or the Republic of Ireland which includes the study of the foundations of legal knowledge and such other optional law subjects as may from time to time be required by the Bar Council and the passing of appropriate assessments and examinations therein. In deciding whether such a course of study is acceptable to the Bar Council, the Bar Council shall have regard to the provision of adequate learning resources.

'Registered European lawyer' means a person registered as such by the Bar Council and by an Inn pursuant to a direction by the JRC under Regulation 28.

'Relevant Criminal Offence' means any criminal offence committed in any part of the world (including an offence the conviction for which is a spent conviction within the meaning of the Rehabilitation of Offenders Act 1974) except:

(i) an offence committed in the United Kingdom which is a fixed penalty offence for the purposes of the Road Traffic Offenders Act 1988 or any statutory modification or replacement thereof for the time being in force;

(ii) an offence committed in the United Kingdom or abroad which is dealt with by a procedure substantially similar to that applicable to such a fixed penalty offence; and

(iii) an offence whose main ingredient is the unlawful parking of a motor vehicle.

'Solicitor' means a solicitor of the Supreme Court of England and Wales.

'Student' means a person who is a member of an Inn but who has not yet been called to the English Bar.

'The Under Treasurer' means the Under Treasurer or Sub-Treasurer of the Inn to which the applicant seeks admission or of which the student or barrister concerned is a member.

'United Kingdom' means England, Scotland, Wales and Northern Ireland.

'Vocational Course' is a course designed to provide instruction in the skills, knowledge and attitudes required by those who intend to become practising barristers in the territory of any Member State and recognised by the Bar Council as satisfying the requirements of the Vocational Stage.

Any reference to the masculine shall be deemed to include the feminine and any use of the singular shall be deemed to include the plural.

SCHEDULE 2

Educational Qualifications for Admission to an Inn of Court

Category I — Persons who have completed the Academic Stage in accordance with Regulation 12, and are thus qualified for admission to the Vocational Stage.

Category II — Persons who have not yet completed the Academic Stage and therefore have not yet qualified for admission to the Vocational Stage:

(a) Persons holding a degree (other than an honorary degree) passed at a standard which the Bar Council considers satisfactory in any subject or subjects conferred by a university in the United Kingdom or the Republic of Ireland or by the Council for National Academic Awards before its dissolution on 31st March 1993 or a license conferred by the former University College of Buckingham before that college was granted university status. For this purpose a degree means a degree obtained by examination after a minimum of 3 years study, although a research degree obtained by thesis, or a degree obtained by examination in less than 3 years, may be considered on its merits, including (if necessary) the qualifications on which registration for the degree was based.

(b) Persons reading as students for such degree as is mentioned in paragraph (a) and who have passed the English Language Examination for the General Certificate of Education at Ordinary Level or have obtained the General Certificate of Secondary Education in English Language, or, exceptionally, have satisfied the Head of Education that they hold an equivalent qualification or have otherwise demonstrated their competence in the English language to the satisfaction of the Head of Education.

(c) Persons holding a degree (other than an honorary degree) in any subject or subjects passed at a standard which the Bar Council considers satisfactory and conferred by a university outside the United Kingdom and the Republic of Ireland, and who have obtained a Certificate of Academic Standing from the Bar Council.

(d) Persons who have been accepted by the Masters of the Bench as mature students. Such an applicant must:

(i)   have had considerable experience or shown exceptional ability in an academic, professional, business or administrative field;

(ii)   ordinarily have reached the age of 25;

(iii) have obtained such academic and vocational qualifications as the Masters of the Bench may consider equivalent to a degree under paragraph (a) of Category II of this schedule or have attained such standard of general education as the Masters of the Bench may consider sufficient;

(iv)   be able to satisfy the Masters of the Bench that there is a good reason why he should not be required to obtain a Qualifying Law Degree; and

(v)   be considered by the Masters of the Bench to be suitable for admission as a mature student.

SCHEDULE 3

(Persons from whom the certificates specified in Regulation 3 are to be provided, and the form of such certificates. Such certificates may not be supplied by a spouse or a close relative).

Applicant	Certificates required
1. United Kingdom.	Certificates from two responsible people resident in the United Kingdom who have known the applicant for one year or more, in the form specified in Certificate A overleaf.
2. Overseas applicant who has received (or is receiving) the whole or part of such applicants general education in the United Kingdom.	A certificate from the past or present Head of the School or College (or a tutor at such School or College) in general education in the United Kingdom in the form specified in Certificate B [below], and a certificate from a responsible person resident in the United Kingdom who has known the applicant for one year or more, in the form specified in Certificate A [below].

Applicant	Certificates required
3. Other overseas applicants.	One certificate from the past or present Head of the School or College (or a tutor at such School or College) last attended by the applicant in the form specified in Certificate B [below], and a certificate from a Judge or Magistrate or any other responsible person in the country in which the applicant is permanently resident, in the form specified in Certificate A [below].

CERTIFICATE A

I, (name) .... (job title) ....

of address) ....

....

certify that I have known (name of applicant) ....

of (address of applicant) ....

....

for .... year(s). I have had the following opportunities of judging his/her character:

....

....

I believe the applicant to be of good character and a proper person to be admitted as a

student of the Honourable Society of ....

[*insert name of Inn if known; otherwise substitute from the beginning of the line 'as a student of any of the Honourable Societies'*] with a view to being called to the Bar.

Dated ....   (Signature) ....

CERTIFICATE B

I, (name) .... (job title) ....

of address) ....

....

certify that I have known (name of applicant) ....

of (address of applicant) ....

....

....

has been known to me in my capacity as ....

I further certify that the applicant pursued the following course(s) of study for which I was

responsible, namely ....

between .... and ....

I believe the applicant to be of good character and a proper person to be admitted as a

student of the Honourable Society of ....

[*insert name of Inn if known; otherwise substitute from the beginning of the line 'as a student of any of the Honourable Societies'*] with a view to being called to the Bar.

Dated ....   (Signature) ....

SCHEDULE 4

Admission Declaration (Regulation 5)

[Amended 23 October 2000]

To the Masters of the Bench of the Honourable Society of ....

I, (full names) ....

of (home address) ....

....   Tel: ....

for the purpose of obtaining admission as a student member of the Inn hereby DECLARE
AND UNDERTAKE as follows:—

1. I was born on .... 19 .... at ....

2. I declare that:—

    (a) I am engaged in the following occupations (to be specified)

        (i)   ....

        (ii)   ....

    (b) I do not intend to practise as a solicitor in any part of the United Kingdom save in the
exercise of my existing rights of audience (if any) as a solicitor.

3.[1] (a) Have you ever been convicted of any relevant criminal offence[2] in any part of the
world or are any criminal proceedings pending against you anywhere in respect of
any relevant criminal offence?

YES		NO	

    (b) Has any bankruptcy order ever been made against you in any part of the world?[3]

YES		NO	

    (c) Has any order been made against you in civil proceedings in any jurisdiction restricting your conduct in any manner?[4]

YES		NO	

---

1 Answer the questions in (a), (b), (c) and (d) by ticking the relevant YES or NO box.
2 'Relevant criminal offence' means any criminal offence committed in any part of the world (including
an offence the conviction for which is a spent conviction within the meaning of the Rehabilitation of
Offenders Act 1974) except (i) an offence committed in the United Kingdom which is a fixed penalty
offence for the purposes of the Road Traffic Offenders Act 1988 or any statutory modification or replacement thereof for the time being in force; (ii) an offence committed in the United Kingdom or
abroad which is dealt with by a procedure substantially similar to that applicable to such a fixed penalty
offence; and (iii) an offence whose main ingredient is the unlawful parking of a motor vehicle.
3 'Bankruptcy Order' includes a bankruptcy order made pursuant to the Insolvency Act 1986 and any
similar order made in any jurisdiction in the world.
4 Order includes any order in which an undertaking is given restricting your conduct in any manner. The
following list is not exhaustive but gives an idea of the type of matters which should be disclosed:
    a. Order pursuant to section 42 of the Supreme Court Act 1981 (Restriction of vesatious legal proceed-
ings)
    b. Civil or other injunction restricting your conduct in any manner.
    c. The imposition of a *Grepe v Loam Order*.
    d. Disqualification order as a Director of Companies.

(d)   Do you know of any other matter which might reasonably be expected to affect the mind of a Bencher of the Inn considering your application?[5]

YES		NO	

(e)

SUPPLEMENTARY INFORMATION   *(If the answer to any of the above questions is YES please give details and attach supporting documents — use a continuation sheet if necessary. Please ensure you give details of any sentence awarded)*

---

5   Include any incident of behaviour which if known by a Bencher might cause him/her to consider your application more carefully. If in doubt disclose the incident/behaviour. Two examples are given by way of illustration but not as limitations on disclosure.
    a.   The receipt of a police caution.
    b.   Breach of the rules of any professional body leading to a restriction of the right to practice or membership.

4. I undertake that while I am a student:—

(a) I will observe such regulations (if any) as may from time to time be made by the Inn concerning the conduct and discipline of its students;[6]

(b) If:

(i) I am convicted of a relevant criminal offence; or

(ii) I have a bankruptcy or Section 42 order made against me;

(iii) I have been disqualified under the Company Directors Disqualification Act

(iv) I engage for a period exceeding three months in an occupation other than that stated above or an occupation not previously notified to you.

I will give notice in writing thereof to you through the Under Treasurer and I will abide by and carry out any order you may make arising out of such notification.

5. I declare that I have read and understood the terms of the further declaration, which I shall be called upon to sign before I can be Called to the Bar.

6. I will keep the Inn informed of any changes to my address.

Dated ....   Signature ....

SCHEDULE 5

Standard Call Declaration (Regulation 25)

[Amended 23 October 2000]

To the Masters of the Bench of the Honourable Society of ....

I, (full names) ....

of (address) ....

....   Tel: ....

for the purpose of being Called to the Bar do hereby DECLARE AND UNDERTAKE as follows:

1. (a) Do you confirm that the declaration which you made for the purpose of obtaining admission as a student member of this Honourable Society was true and accurate in every respect when you made it?[1]

YES		NO	

(b) Does the declaration, which you made for the purpose of obtaining admission as a student member of this Honourable Society, remain true and accurate in every respect?[2]

YES		NO	

2. While you have been a student of the Honourable Society

(a) Have you been engaged, for a period exceeding three months, in any occupation which you did not either state in your Admission Declaration or notify in writing to the Under Treasurer?

YES		NO	

---

6 Copies of the Disciplinary Rules of the Inn, Equal Opportunities Codes etc. are available for inspection in the Treasury Office.

1 If the answer to any of the questions listed below is YES give details in the box at paragraph 6.

2 You are entitled to practice as a solicitor post Call but if you intend or might do so please declare it in the box at paragraph 5

(b) Have you been convicted of any relevant criminal offence[3] in any part of the world or are criminal proceedings pending against you anywhere in respect of any relevant criminal offence?

YES		NO	

(c) Has any bankruptcy order[4] been made against you in any part of the world?

YES		NO	

(d) Has an order been made against you or undertaking/promise given by you restricting you from instituting any form of legal proceedings?[5]

YES		NO	

(e) Do you know of any other matter which might reasonably be expected to affect the mind of a Bencher of the Inn considering your application?[6]

3. So long as I remain a barrister I will observe the Code of Conduct.

4.[7] If Called to the Bar I will, unless otherwise authorised, keep not less than .... terms, which shall be the terms immediately following my Call unless you authorise me to keep other terms.

5.

SUPPLEMENTARY INFORMATION   *(If the answer to any of the above questions is YES please give details and attach supporting documents — use a continuation sheet if necessary. Please ensure you give details of any sentence awarded)*

---

3 'Relevant criminal offence' means any criminal offence committed in any part of the world (including an offence the conviction for which is a spent conviction within the meaning of the Rehabilitation of Offenders Act 1974) except (i) an offence committed in the United Kingdom which is a fixed penalty offence for the purposes of the Road Traffic Offenders Act 1988 or any statutory modification or re-placement thereof for the time being in force; (ii) an offence committed in the United Kingdom or abroad which is dealt with by a procedure substantially similar to that applicable to such a fixed penalty offence; and (iii) an offence whose main ingredient is the unlawful parking of a motor vehicle.

4 'Bankruptcy Order' includes a bankruptcy order made pursuant to the Insolvency Act 1986 and any similar order made in any jurisdiction in the world.

5 The following list is not exhaustive but gives an idea of the type of matters which should be disclosed:
   a. Order pursuant to section 42 of the Supreme Court Act 1981 (restriction of vexatious legal proceedings).
   b. Civil or other injunction restricting your conduct in any manner.
   c. The imposition of a *Grepe v Loam* Order.

6 Include any incident of behaviour, which if known by a Bencher might cause him/her to consider your application more carefully. If in doubt disclose the incident/behaviour. Three examples are given by way of illustration but not as limitations on disclosure.
   a. The receipt of a police caution.
   b. Breach of the rules of any professional body leading to a restriction of the right to practise or membership.
   c. Disqualification order as a Director of Companies.

7 This paragraph is to be deleted except where the declarant has not completed his term keeping obligations at the time of Call and is permitted to keep the outstanding terms after Call.

6. I understand that if this declaration is found to have been false in any material respect or if there is a breach of any undertaking embodied in it that falsity or breach shall constitute professional misconduct.

Dated .... Signature ....

SCHEDULE 6

Call Declaration for Applicants for Temporary Membership of the Bar (Part IV(E))

[Amended 23 October 2000]

To the Masters of the Bench of the Honourable Society of

I, (full names) ....

of (address) ....

.... Tel: ....

for the purpose of obtaining temporary membership of the Honourable Society and of the Bar pursuant to Regulations 38 to 40 do hereby DECLARE AND UNDERTAKE as follows:

1. I will not while in England and Wales do anything in relation to the provision of legal services in England and Wales which may not properly be done by a barrister in independent practice in England and Wales.

2. I will not while in England and Wales provide any legal services to any person except legal services in connection with the conduct of

    (a) the case or cases in respect of which I sought temporary membership of the Bar; and

    (b) any other case or cases which I may be specifically authorised in writing by the Joint Regulations Committee to conduct.

3.[1] (a) Have you ever been convicted of any relevant criminal offence[2] in any part of the world or are any criminal proceedings pending against you anywhere in respect of any relevant criminal offence?

YES		NO	

(b) Has any bankruptcy order or directors disqualification order ever been made against you in any part of the world?[3]

YES		NO	

(c) Have you entered into any individual voluntary arrangement with your creditors?

YES		NO	

4. Have you been prohibited or suspended from practising as a member of any professional body in any part of the world?

YES		NO	

---

1 Answer the questions by ticking the relevant YES or NO box. Any answer to a question of YES should be expanded in the box provided. Use a supplementary sheet if necessary.
2 'Relevant criminal offence' means any criminal offence committed in any part of the world (including an offence the conviction for which is a spent conviction within the meaning of the Rehabilitation of Offenders Act 1974) except (i) an offence committed in the United Kingdom which is a fixed penalty offence for the purposes of the Road Traffic Offenders Act 1988 or any statutory modification or replacement thereof for the time being in force; (ii) an offence committed in the United Kingdom or abroad which is dealt with by a procedure substantially similar to that applicable to such a fixed penalty offence; and (iii) an offence whose main ingredient is the unlawful parking of a motor vehicle.
3 'Bankruptcy Order' includes a bankruptcy order made pursuant to the Insolvency Act 1986 and any similar order made in any jurisdiction in the world.

5. Have you set out on a separate sheet attached to this Declaration a statement signed and dated by you containing such further information about yourself as may reasonably be regarded as relevant to be considered by the Masters of the Bench in connection with your proposed Call to the Bar?

YES		NO	

6. I will not, whether in England or Wales or elsewhere, rely on the fact that I am or have been a member of the Bar for any purpose whatsoever other than for the purpose of conducting the case or cases referred to in paragraph 2.

7. So long as I remain a member of the Bar of England and Wales I will observe the Code of Conduct.

8. I understand that if this declaration is found to have been false in any material respect or if there is a breach of any undertaking embodied in it that falsity or breach shall constitute professional misconduct.

Dated .... Signature ....

SUPPLEMENTARY INFORMATION *(If the answer to any of the above questions is YES please give details and attach supporting documents — use a continuation sheet if necessary. Please ensure you give details of any sentence awarded)*

SCHEDULE 7

Call Declaration on Readmission (Regulations 57(d) and 58(f))

[Amended 23 October 2000]

To the Masters of the Bench of the Honourable Society of

I, (full names) ....

of (address) ....

.... Tel: ....

for the purpose of obtaining readmission to the Bar by the Honourable Society do hereby
DECLARE AND UNDERTAKE as follows:

1. Have you during the twelve months immediately before the date hereof engaged for any
    period in any occupation which you have not disclosed to the Under Treasurer?

2.[1] (a) Have you ever been convicted of any relevant criminal offence[2] in any part of the
            world or are any criminal proceedings pending against you anywhere in respect of
            any relevant criminal offence?

YES		NO	

   (b) Has any bankruptcy order or directors disqualification order ever been made against
        you in any part of the world?[3]

YES		NO	

   (c) Have you entered into any individual voluntary arrangement with your creditors?

YES		NO	

3. Have you been prohibited or suspended from practising as a member of any professional
    body in any part of the world?

YES		NO	

4. Have you set out in a statement annexed to this Declaration and signed and dated by you
    such further information about yourself as may reasonably be regarded as relevant to be
    considered by the Masters of the Bench in connection with your proposed readmission to
    the Bar.

YES		NO	

5. So long as I remain a barrister I will observe the Code of Conduct.

6. I understand that if this declaration is found to have been false in any material respect or
    if there is a breach of any undertaking embodied in it that falsity or breach shall constitute
    professional misconduct.

   Dated ....   Signature ....

1 Answer the questions by ticking the relevant YES or NO box. Any answer to a question of YES should be
   expanded in the box provided. Use a supplementary sheet if necessary.
2 'Relevant criminal offence' means any criminal offence committed in any part of the world (including
   an offence the conviction for which is a spent conviction within the meaning of the Rehabilitation of
   Offenders Act 1974) except (i) an offence committed in the United Kingdom which is a fixed penalty
   offence for the purposes of the Road Traffic Offenders Act 1988 or any statutory modification or replacement thereof for the time being in force; (ii) an offence committed in the United Kingdom or
   abroad which is dealt with by a procedure substantially similar to that applicable to such a fixed penalty
   offence; and (iii) an offence whose main ingredient is the unlawful parking of a motor vehicle.
3 'Bankruptcy Order' includes a bankruptcy order made pursuant tot he Insolvency Act 1986 and any
   similar order made in any jurisdiction in the world.

SUPPLEMENTARY INFORMATION   *(If the answer to any of the above questions is YES please give details and attach supporting documents — use a continuation sheet if necessary. <u>Please ensure you give details of any sentence awarded</u>)*

SCHEDULE 8

Application for approval and registration as a Pupil Master (Regulation 50)

To the Masters of the Bench of the Honourable Society of ....

I, (full names) ....

of (home address) ....

....

Telephone/fax/email ....

Apply to be registered as a Pupil Master in the chambers/employment of:

Name: ....

of (Address) ....

....

Telephone/fax/email ....

I can confirm that:

(i)   I have practised in the United Kingdom or another Member State as a barrister (other than as a pupil who has not completed pupillage in accordance with these Regulations) or as a member of another authorised body for a period (which need not have been continuous and need not have been as a member of the same authorised body) of at least six years in the previous eight years.

YES		NO	

(ii)   I have made my practice my primary occupation and been entitled to exercise a right of audience as a barrister in the two years immediately preceding the date of this application.

YES		NO	

(iii)   I am not a QC in independent practice.

YES		NO	

If the answer to all of the above questions is YES, please supply the following information:

(iv)   I was called to the Bar on

(v)   I completed my 12 months pupillage on

(vi)   I have practised as a barrister or a member of another authorised body at

....

....

....

(vii)   Save for the breaks in practice noted below

....

....

....

(viii) I agree to undertake the training prescribed for new Pupil Masters before or after entry on the register of Pupil Masters, but before I can take a pupil.

Date ....   Signature ....

Notes:

(1)   The duties of Pupil Masters are set out in paragraph ** of the Code of Conduct.

(2)   The eligibility requirements for Pupil Masters are set out in Regulation 49.

(3)   Applicants for Pupil Master status are required to complete this form and a supplementary application form.

(4)   On completion by the applicant, both forms should be sent to the applicant's referees for comment before being sent to the applicant's Inn of Court.

(5)   Two supporting references are required:

(a) In the case of a barrister in independent practice, by the applicant's Head of Chambers and in the case of an employed barrister by a more senior lawyer employed in the same department/organisation and having direct knowledge of the work of the applicant: or

(b) If the applicant is himself the Head of Chambers, or there is no more senior lawyer employed in the same department/organisation with such direct knowledge of the work of the applicant or for any other reason the support referred to in sub paragraph (a) is not available, by an independent person who is Master of the Bench of an Inn, a Queen's Counsel, a Leader of a Circuit, a Recorder or Deputy High Court Judge, Treasury Counsel or a person of comparable standing who is able to comment from personal knowledge on the applicant's suitability to act as a Pupil Master; and

(c) In every case, by a second person falling within the requirements in sub paragraph (b) above.

(SCHEDULE 8)

Application to be approved as a Pupil Master

Supplementary Information Form

Name

....

(6)   Please give details of the nature, scope and principal areas of your practice (independent barrister)/work (employed barrister) [details of the number and type of cases handled annually should be provided].

....

....

....

....

(7)   Describe the sort of training and experience that you could offer a pupil (e.g.: in terms of paper work, court work, advocacy, instruction in conduct and etiquette and opportunities for feedback).

....

....

....

....

(8)   Do you practise mainly on Circuit? If so, which Circuit?

....

(9)Are you covered by indemnity insurance?

YES		NO	

(10) a)   Please provide details of any complaints about you to the Bar Council/other authorised body? [Delete if inapplicable]

....

b)   Do we have your permission to ask the Bar Council/other authorised body to release any information that it might hold on you relating to complaints that is considered material to this application?

YES		NO	

(11) Is there any urgency about this application?

YES		NO	

If yes, why?

Date ....   Signature ....

(SCHEDULE 8)

Application to be approved as a Pupil Master

Referee Form

Applicants for Pupil Master status are required to send their referees completed copies of Schedule 8 and the Supplementary Information form for comment prior to them being forwarded to the applicant's Inn of Court.

Two supporting referees are required:

(a)   In the case of a barrister in independent practice, by the applicant's Head of Chambers and in the case of an employed barrister by a more senior lawyer employed in the same organisation and having direct knowledge of the work of the applicant: or
(b)   If the applicant is himself the Head of Chambers, or there is no more senior lawyer employed in the same organisation with such direct knowledge of the work of the applicant or for any other reason the support referred to in sub paragraph (a) is not available, by an independent person who is Master of the Bench of an Inn, a Queen's Counsel, a Leader of a Circuit, a Recorder or Deputy High Court Judge, Treasury Counsel or a person of comparable standing who is able to comment from personal knowledge on the applicant's suitability to act as a Pupil Master; and
(c)   In every case, by a second person falling within the requirements in sub paragraph (b) above.

* * *

Name of Referee

....

Status (please indicate)

Head of Chambers	
Master of the Bench of an Inn	
Queen's Counsel	
Leader of a Circuit	
Recorder	
Deputy High Court Judge	
Treasury Counsel	

Other person of comparable standing

....

Is the information contained in the application form accurate?

YES		NO	

Please comment on the nature, scope and content of the applicant's practice.

....

....

....

....

Please comment on the applicant's suitability to be a Pupil Master

....

....

....

Date ....   Signature ....

SCHEDULE 9

Certificates of Qualification and Good Standing
(Regulations 37(d) and 39(a))

APPLICANTS	CERTIFICATES REQUIRED	
	As to Qualification	As to Good Standing
1. Northern Ireland Barrister Irish Barrister	Certificate of Call to the relevant Bar, and stating the date from which he has been practising as such.	Certificate of the respective Attorney General that the applicant is a fit and proper person to be Called to the Bar.
2. Scottish Advocate	Certificate from the Dean of the Faculty of Advocates, stating that the applicant is a member of the Faculty and date from which he has been practising as such.	Certificate from the Dean of the Faculty of Advocates that the applicant is a fit and proper person to be Called to the Bar.
3. Common Law Practitioner	Certificate of the Senior Judge, Attorney General or Senior Law Officer of the Superior Court in which the applicant has practised showing that for a period of not less than 3 years within the period of 5 years immediately preceding the date of his application the applicant has regularly exercised rights of audience in such courts (identifying the period or periods in question) and is a fit and proper person to be Called to the Bar; and degrees admission certificate or certificates.	

[**Note:** The Committee may be prepared to accept certificates from other persons of comparable status if the reason for non-compliance is explained]

SCHEDULE 10

Fees

1. For a Certificate of Academic Standing under Regulation 14(a): £60.

2. (a) For a certificate entitling a student to proceed to the Vocational Stage under Regulation 15(b): £120.

    (b) For a written or oral test required to be taken under Regulation 15(b)(i) if conducted by the Bar Council: £150 per Core Subject.

    Provided that the Head of Education *and* Training may in his discretion reduce or waive either of the fees prescribed by this paragraph if the student is at the same time applying for a certificate under Regulation *14*(a), or if he is satisfied that there are other special reasons for such reduction or waiver.

3. For an application for a waiver under Regulation 12 by a student who fails to achieve the standard of degree which the Bar Council considers satisfactory: £120. (A further fee of £120 is required for students seeking reconsideration of such an application.)

4. For an application to the Masters of the Bench as a mature student under Schedule 2, Category II, paragraph (d): £120.

5. For the Bar Examination under Regulation 16(a)(ii) and Schedule 12:

    (a) Examinations in London: On the occasion of each entry:-

    For a single section (where permitted): £80

    For the whole examination: £470

    (b) Examinations at Overseas Centres: On the occasion of each entry (where permitted):

    For a single section: £122

    For the whole examination: £732

    Note: There is also an overseas local centre fee which varies according to the overseas centre, and which is paid direct to the body making the local arrangements for holding the examinations.

    (c) Late Entries: A student who is permitted, either by virtue of a general direction or personally, to enter for any examination after the last date fixed for receipt of applications shall, in addition to the above fees, pay a late entry fee equal to the amount of the examination entry fee for the Section or Examination for which he is permitted to enter.

6. For applications under Part IV (other than a request for a review of a decision): £300.

7. For a request for a review of a decision under Part IV: £150.

8. For the whole Aptitude Test under Regulation 32(d) and Schedule 13 or for any individual written paper, part of a written paper or oral assessment taken otherwise than as part of the whole Test, such fee or fees as may be determined from time to time by the Council which, in doing so, shall have due regard to the cost of conducting the Test.

9. For temporary membership of an Inn (Regulation 40): Such sum as may be required by the Inn, being not less than £100. For temporary membership of the Bar (Regulation 40): £200.

10. For readmission to the Bar (Regulations 57 and 58): Such sum as may be required by the Inn, being not less than £30, to reflect the administrative costs involved in processing the application; and not less than £50 for readmission.

SCHEDULE 11

Periods of time after which a student may not take the Bar Examination or attend the Vocational Course (Regulation 15)

Method of completing Academic Stage	Period within which Vocational Stage Must be completed
By obtaining a Qualifying Law Degree [Regulation 12(a)]	7 years from 1st October in the year in which the student completed the Academic Stage of Training.
By passing any assessments and examinations contained in a Common Professional Examination course or a Diploma in Law Course [Regulation 12(b)]	7 years from 1st October in the year in which the student completed the Academic Stage of Training.
By being granted exemption from certain sections of the Common Professional Examination or Diploma in Law Examinations, and then passing examinations in the outstanding sections [Regulation 12(b)]	7 years from 1st October in the year in which the student completed the degree by virtue of which he was granted exemption from sections of the Common Professional Examination or Diploma in Law Examinations.

SCHEDULE 12

Completion of the Vocational Stage by Examination (Regulation 16(a)(ii))

1. **The Vocational Stage — The Examination for Call to the Bar**

    (a) The Bar Examination consists of six sections, as follows:

    I   General Paper 1 — Law of Tort and Criminal Law

    II   General Paper 2 — Equity and Trusts, and Remedies for Breach of Contract

    III   Civil and Criminal Procedure

    IV   Evidence

          and two of the following:

    V   Revenue Law

    VI   Family Law (and Procedure)

    VII   The Sale of Goods and Credit

    VIII Practical Conveyancing

    IX   Conflict of Laws

    X   The Law of International Trade

    XI   European Community Law and Human Rights

    (b) In order to pass the Bar Examination a student must pass each of the six sections for which he enters, except in so far as he may be exempted from so doing under paragraph 3 of this Schedule.

    (c) A student is not permitted to take any of Sections V to XI inclusive if his completion of the Academic Stage is based on an examination which includes a subject or subjects which the Bar Council considers to be equivalent to such section.

2. **Examinations**

(a) The Bar Examination is conducted under the supervision and direction of the Bar Council and is held at such times and at such places as the Bar Council appoints. A student may not take the Bar Examination or any section of the Bar Examination at any place overseas except with the permission of the Bar Council.

(b) The Bar Examination is by written papers and such viva voce questions (if any) as the Bar Council may consider desirable.

(c) Except with the permission of the Bar Council (which will be granted only in exceptional circumstances), a student may not enter for the Bar Examination until:

(i)   he has completed the Academic Stage, and

(ii) attended 9 qualifying sessions in accordance with Regulation 8.

(d) Except with the permission of the Bar Council, a student shall not be allowed to enter for any examination so long as any sums due from him to the Bar Council or an Inn in respect of any fees remain unpaid.

(e) Subject to paragraphs 3 and 4 of this Schedule, a student must take all sections of the Bar Examination at the same examination.

(f) In the case of a third or subsequent attempt at the Bar Examination, or any section thereof, a double-marking system will apply.

3. **Illness**

If on account of his illness or other sufficient cause beyond his control a student fails to sit for any section for which he has entered, or having sat fails to pass such section, the Bar Council may, if it is in its opinion appropriate to do so, direct

(i)   that the student shall be deemed to have passed such section;

(ii) that in an ensuing examination he be not required to satisfy the examiners again in any section in which he has already satisfied them;

(iii) that the examination fees paid by the student in respect of that section be refunded to him, less a deduction for administrative expenses at such rate as the Bar Council may from time to time direct;

(iv) that his appearance at the examination during which the illness occurred shall be wholly disregarded, and in particular shall not be counted for the purposes of paragraph 5 of this Schedule.

4. **Conditional Passes**

(a) Subject as hereinafter provided, if at any examination a student would have passed the whole of the Bar Examination, but for his failure in any one section thereof, the Bar Council may, having regard to the standard which he has attained in the section which he has failed, allow him to be treated as having passed the Bar Examination conditionally on his subsequently passing the section in which he has failed. If a student fails in one half only of each of Sections I and II (General Papers 1 and 2) but satisfies the Examiners in the remaining sections, the Bar Council may treat him as having failed in one section and may, having regard to the standard which he has attained in the General Papers, allow him to be treated as having passed the Bar Examination conditionally on his subsequently passing a special paper ('Section SP') comprising two halves corresponding to those in which he has failed.

(b) Where a student does not qualify for a Conditional Pass under paragraph (a) above, the Bar Council may order that he shall not be required to pass again any one or more sections in which his performance was in the opinion of the Bar Council sufficiently meritorious to justify the making of such an order.

5. **Number of Permitted Attempts and Exclusion of Candidates**

(a) A student may not attempt the whole of the Bar Examination more than 4 times except with the permission of the Bar Council.

(b) A student must pass the whole of the Bar Examination within 3 years of his first registering for it.

(c) Permission to make a fifth attempt at the whole of the Bar Examination shall be given only in exceptional circumstances, and permission shall not be given for more than a fifth attempt at the whole examination.

(d) Where a student obtains a Conditional Pass at any attempt at the Bar Examination which he is permitted to make, he may make further attempts at the outstanding subject, provided that, subject to sub-paragraphs (a), (b) and (c) above, he does not make more than six attempts in all at the whole examination and the outstanding subject.

(e) For the purpose of paragraphs 4 and 5 of this Schedule:

   (i)   where a student obtains relief under paragraph 4(d) of this Schedule then, in ascertaining the number of attempts made by him to pass the Bar Examination, any attempt to pass the outstanding sections shall be treated as attempting the whole examination;

   (ii) in ascertaining the number of times a student has attempted a particular section, there shall be aggregated all occasions on which he has attempted that section either alone or with any others and whether before, when or after obtaining a Conditional Pass;

   (iii) in ascertaining the number of times a student has attempted Section SP there shall be aggregated all occasions on which he has attempted the General Papers and that section.

(f) The Bar Council may direct that any student whose performance in the Examination is of insufficient merit shall not enter for the Examination again for such period not exceeding one year as they may decide, and may at any time on the application of the student concerned forthwith terminate or abridge the period.

(g) Applications by students for relief under any of the provisions of this paragraph shall be made in writing to the Bar Council.

(h) In the performance of any of their functions under this Regulation, the Bar Council may take into account any matter they consider relevant, but before reaching a decision it will afford the student an opportunity to appear and make oral representations.

6. **Entry for Additional Subjects**

Subject to paragraph 5 of this Schedule:

(a) A person who has passed the Bar Examination may at any subsequent examination enter for any section of the Bar Examination which he has not already passed;

(b) A person who has obtained a Conditional Pass in the Bar Examination may with the permission of the Bar Council at any subsequent examination, in addition to the outstanding section, enter for any section which he has not already passed.

7. **Class Lists**

   (a) At each examination successful candidates will be classified as Class I, Class II Division I, Class II Division II, or Class III, and candidates who are awarded a Conditional Pass will be so published.

   (b) Candidates successfully completing the Bar Examination after having obtained a Conditional Pass or an exemption under paragraph 4(c) of this Schedule will be placed in Class III.

   (c) In Class I and Class II Division I names will be published in order of merit; otherwise names will be published in the order of examination numbers allotted to candidates.

8. **Certificates of Honour and Prizes**

   (a) A student who is placed in Class I in the Bar Examination shall be entitled to receive from the Bar Council a Certificate of Honour.

   (b) Upon the result of each Bar Examination the Bar Council may make the following awards provided that in each case the candidate has achieved not less than Upper Second Class Honours in the Examination:

   (i)   to the candidate who obtains the highest aggregate mark, a prize of £1,000;

   (ii) to the candidate who obtains the second highest aggregate mark, a prize of £600;

   (iii) to the candidate who obtains the third highest aggregate mark, a prize of £400.

   (c) If at any examination two or more candidates satisfy the conditions for any of the prizes referred to in paragraph (b), the Bar Council may:

   (i)   divide the prize between such candidates in equal shares; or

   (ii) vary the amounts of the prizes in such manner as the Bar Council considers appropriate.

   (d) Certificates of Honour and Prizes may only be awarded by the Bar Council under this paragraph to candidates who pass the whole Bar Examination and, save in exceptional circumstances, at the first attempt.

   (e) The Bar Council may in its discretion accept offers from other persons or bodies to provide prizes in connection with the whole Bar Examination, or any section of it upon such terms as the Bar Council thinks fit.

SCHEDULE 13

The Aptitude Test (Regulation 32(d))

1. The Bar Council shall provide an Aptitude Test for candidates for admission to the Bar of England and Wales who are required by the JRC pursuant to Part IV of these Regulations to pass all or any part of the Aptitude Test.

2. The Aptitude Test shall consist of such written and oral papers and tests as the Bar Council or the Board of Studies may from time to time prescribe under Examination Regulations.

3. The Aptitude Test shall be conducted under the supervision and direction of the Bar Council and shall be held at such times and at such place or places as the Bar Council

appoints but so that the Aptitude Test shall be held not less than twice in every year and not more than eight months shall elapse between one Aptitude Test and the next.

4. Unless the JRC with the concurrence of the Bar Council decides otherwise, the Aptitude Test shall be held in London.

5. In the conduct of the Aptitude Test the Bar Council will act through the Education and Training Committee. The detailed planning of the conduct of the Aptitude Test will be controlled by the Aptitude Test Sub-Committee of the Education and Training Committee and the Board of Examiners for the Aptitude Test, which shall be constituted by the Education and Training Committee exercising equivalent powers to those conferred upon the Education and Training Committee by Regulation 21.

6. The examination of candidates shall be carried out in accordance with the Examination Regulations in force at the time that candidates take the Aptitude Test. The Examination Regulations shall be made by the Bar Council and may be amended from time to time by the Bar Council acting on the advice of the Education and Training Committee.

7. Subject to the provisions of paragraphs 9 and 10 below and of Examination Regulations made under paragraph 6 above, a candidate who is required to pass the Aptitude Test must pass all parts of the Aptitude Test (or all parts which he is required to pass) at the same occasion on which the Aptitude Test is held.

8. A candidate must pass the Aptitude Test or such part or parts thereof as he is required by the JRC to take within two years after the date of the certificate issued to him by the JRC under Regulation 32. The JRC may on application to it extend the period of two years in any particular case when it appears to be appropriate to do so.

9. Where a candidate has not satisfied the requirements of the Examination Regulations to be certified as having passed the Aptitude Test or the part or parts thereof required to be passed he may (where his overall performance merits such certification) be certified as having passed the Aptitude Test conditionally on his subsequently (but not more than three years after the date of the certification issued to him by the JRC under Regulation 32) passing the part or parts which he has failed.

10. If on account of mitigating circumstances a candidate fails to sit for or take any part of the Aptitude Test for which he has entered, or having taken such part fails to pass it,

   (a) the Head of Education and Training may direct that the fees paid by the candidate in respect of that part be refunded to him, less a deduction for administrative expense at such rate as he may from time to time direct; and/or

   (b) the Board of Examiners may direct that the periods of two years and three years mentioned in paragraphs 8 and 9 of this Schedule be extended in the case of the candidate in question by not more than two further years.

SCHEDULE 14

PART 1(a)

Application to be registered as a pupil (Regulation 42)

I (name) ....

Of (address) ....

....

Date of Birth ....

Telephone/Fax/Email ....

Being a member of the Honourable Society of .... (1)

and Called to the Bar on .... (2)

apply to be registered as a pupil in the chambers/employment of:

(Name) ....

Of (address) ....

....

Telephone/Fax/email ....

To undertake the non-practising six months/the practising six months/the full twelve months/non-practising ...... (number) months/practising ...... (number) months (delete as appropriate) (3)

The proposed date of the commencement of my pupillage is .... (4)

My pupil master will be (name) .... (5)

I agree to comply with the Code of Conduct and relevant provisions of the Consolidated Regulations (6) and to notify the Bar Council of any material change in my pupillage arrangements (7).

Signed .... Date ....

I confirm that the above person has been offered and has accepted a pupillage in my chambers/with my employer (delete as appropriate) for the period stated. (8)

Signed .... Status .... Date ....

Notes:

1. A pupil may not commence pupillage until his or her pupillage is registered with the Bar Council and the Masters of the Bench (Regulation 42). This form should be submitted to the Bar Council which undertakes to provide a copy to the relevant Masters of the Bench. A supplementary information sheet must also be completed and submitted with this form. A copy can be obtained from the Bar Council.

2. Provide the date or prospective date of Call.

3. Insert the appropriate number of months if permission has been received from the Joint Regulations Committee to undertake a reduced pupillage or if only part of the practising or non-practising six months is being undertaken with this chambers or employer.

4. If the date of registration is later than the date of commencement set out on the form, the pupillage will be deemed to commence on the date of registration.

5. The name of the pupil master/mistress must be included if known. If not yet known, the form may be submitted to the Bar Council, but the pupillage will not be registered until the name of the pupil master/mistress is notified to the Bar Council. It is the pupil's responsibility to notify the Bar Council.

6. Attention is drawn in particular to paragraph 801–803 of the Code, the Pupillage Guidelines and Part 5 of the Consolidated Regulations. In addition regard should be had to information contained in the Pupillage File.

7. Any material changes to pupillage arrangements must be notified to the Bar Council and the Masters of the Bench using Schedule 14 Part 2. These include a change of home or pupillage address, a change in the date of commencement of pupillage, a

change of pupil master/mistress or a change in the proposed end date of pupillage (e.g. resulting from illness). Advice should be sought from the Bar Council's Education and Training Department if there is uncertainty as to whether other changes are material.

8.   The form must be signed by the Head of Chambers or other person authorised by him or her. In the case of a pupillage in employment, the form must signed by a person authorised by the employer.

SCHEDULE 14

PART 1(b)

Application to register external training (Regulation 42)

I (name) ....

Of (address) ....

Telephone/Fax/email ....

Date of Birth ....

Being a member of the Honourable Society of .... (1)

and Called to the Bar on .... (2)

apply to register the following period of external training:

Type .... (3)

(Name) ....

Of (address) ....

Telephone/Fax/email ....

From (date) ....   To (date) .... (4)

My supervisor will be (name) .... (5)

I agree to comply with the Code of Conduct and relevant provisions of the Consolidated Regulations (6) and to notify the Bar Council of any material change in my pupillage arrangements (7).

Signed .... Date ....

I confirm that the above person has been offered and has accepted a period of external training in my organisation for the period stated/I confirm that I have given permission for the above person to undertake a period of external training in the above organisation (Please delete as appropriate) (8)

Signed .... Status .... Date ....

Notes:

1.   A pupil may not commence external training until the training has been registered with the Bar Council and the Masters of the Bench (Regulation 42). This form should be submitted to the Bar Council which undertakes to provide a copy to the relevant Masters of the Bench.

2.   Provide the date or prospective date of Call. You may not undertake external training before Call.

3.   (i) Training spent with a solicitor practising in the UK or another member state, (ii) training spent with a lawyer qualified and practising in another member state, (iii) a 'stage' at the European Commission, (iv) marshalling with a High Court or Circuit judge, (v) working with a solicitor or other professional person whose work is relevant

to the pupil master's/mistress' practice, (vi) working under supervision for a body supplying legal services to the public for a nominal fee, (vii) other form of training for which the Joint Regulations Committee has granted permission in an individual case.

4.   If the date of registration is later than the date of commencement set out on the form, the pupillage will be deemed to commence on the date of registration.

5.   The name should be given of the supervising solicitor, lawyer, judge or person with whom the external training will be undertaken. If external training is undertaken with a solicitor or a lawyer qualified and practising in another member state under (i) or (ii) in note 3 above, the person must have qualifications, experience and place of practice comparable to those, which in the case of a barrister, would render him or her eligible to take pupils, unless the JRC has waived these requirements in an individual case. If the name of the supervising person is not yet known, the form may be submitted to the Bar Council, but the pupillage will not be registered until the name of the person is notified to the Bar Council.

6.   Attention is drawn in particular to paragraph 801–803 of the Code, the Pupillage Guidelines and Part 5 of the Consolidated Regulations. In addition regard should be had to information contained in the Pupillage File.

7.   Any material changes to these arrangements must be notified to the Bar Council and the Masters of the Bench using the form specified by Schedule 14 Part 2. These include a change of home or training address, a change in the date of commencement of external training, a change of supervisor or a change in the proposed end date of training (e.g. resulting from illness). Advice should be sought from the Bar Council's Education and Training Department if there is uncertainty as to whether other changes are material.

8.   The form must be signed by supervisor or other person or other person authorised by the organisation where the training is being undertaken, except in the cases of (v) and (vi) above, where the form should be signed by the pupil master or mistress.

SCHEDULE 14

PART 2

Notification of a material change in pupillage or external training arrangements (Regulation 42)

I (name) ....

Of (address) ....

Telephone/Fax/email ....

Date of Birth ....

Being a member of the Honourable Society of .... (1)

and Called to the Bar on .... (2)

and currently/formerly (delete as appropriate) a pupil in the chambers/employment of or currently/formerly (delete as appropriate) undertaking external training at:

(Name) ....

Of (address) ....

Telephone/Fax/email ....

Give notice of the following material change in these arrangements (3):

The proposed date of the commencement of the new arrangements is .... (4)

My pupil master/supervisor will be (name) ....

Signed (pupil) .... Date ....

I confirm that the arrangements set out above have been agreed through the appropriate procedures in my chambers/with my employer/with my external training organisation (5)

Signed .... Status .... Date ....

Notes:

1.   This form should be submitted to the Bar Council, which undertakes to provide a copy to the relevant Masters of the Bench.

2.   Provide date or prospective date of Call.

3.   A material change includes a change of home or pupillage or training address, a change to the date of the commencement of pupillage or external training, a change in pupil master/mistress or supervisor or a change in the proposed end date of pupillage or external training (e.g. resulting from illness). Advice should be sought from the Education and Training Department at the Bar Council if there is uncertainty as to whether other changes are material.

4.   Under the Regulations, the 'non-practising' period of pupillage must be a continuous period of six months. The second or practising period of pupillage must be commenced not later than twelve months after the completion of the 'non practising' six months. The practising period of pupillage must be a continuous period of six months or with only such interval (each not exceeding one month) as to ensure that it is completed within the overall period of nine months. Permission must be obtained from the Joint Regulations to waive any or these requirements.

5.   The form must be signed by the Head of Chambers or other person authorised by him or her. In the case of a pupillage in employment, the form must signed by a person authorised by the employer. In the case of external training, the form must be signed by a person authorised by the training organisation.

APPENDIX 2
ANSWERS TO PROBLEMS

The following are the answers to the problems set in the course of **Chapter 2** and **Chapter 5**. The problems in **Chapter 8** will be dealt with during the practitioner large group sessions.

2.1 Relationship with the court

2.1.1 Duties and responsibilities owed to the court

(1) Para. 708(c) makes it clear that you have no choice (in civil or criminal proceedings) but to bring the authority to the attention of the court, whether or not you believe that you can distinguish it by argument (see *Copeland v Smith and Another* [2000] 1 All ER 457).

(2) It would be impolite and embarrassing to interrupt counsel for the claimant or stand up and address the court on the point. Inform counsel for the claimant of his error as soon as practicable, either by passing a note or speaking to him or her as he or she is leaving or just outside the court. It is then for him or her, knowing his or her duty, to return to the court, apologise and put the matter right.

(3) Accept his or her ruling with good grace, carry on as best you can and, if your client is convicted, appeal. Once the judge has ruled you must accept it. Do not argue with the tribunal, whatever your feelings; remember your duty to be courteous to the court. Contrast this position with one where there has been a procedural irregularity in the proceedings (see para 708(d)).

2.1.3 Further duties

(1) Your views on the reason for the jump are largely irrelevant! The defence are entitled to see the note. You remain under a continuing duty to review questions of disclosure (s 9 of the Criminal Procedure and Investigations Act 1996). If you, at any time before the accused is acquitted or convicted, form the opinion that there is material that might undermine the prosecution case, or be reasonably expected to assist the accused's defence, then it must be disclosed to the accused as soon as reasonably practicable (subject to the court's ruling to the contrary). In these circumstances your duty would probably be to get the witness back to court if requested. If the note were very much older then it would be better for defence counsel to apply to reopen cross-examination and satisfy the judge that the

information was relevant (see also para 11.2, Standards Applicable to Criminal Cases in the Written Standards for the Conduct of Professional Work in Section 3, Miscellaneous Guidance).

(2) The principle is the same as that involved where the judge makes an error in summing-up (para 11.7, Standards Applicable to Criminal Cases in the Written Standards for the Conduct of Professional Work in Section 3, Miscellaneous Guidance). You are bound to draw the error to his or her attention. If he or she does not correct it, consider carefully whether you still want to adduce the evidence or otherwise take advantage of the ruling. What is the point of securing a conviction which will be overturned on appeal? See, further, *R v Langford* The Times, 12 January 2001.

(3) It would be quite wrong for you not to tell your opponent. You could be professionally embarrassed under para 603(f) and if so, must withdraw from the case under para 608(a). Even if, having taken instructions from the defendant, no objection is raised you should think very carefully before continuing to act. You might well feel inhibited in the conduct of your case. More importantly, you risk a possible complaint if the defendant is convicted.

2.1.4 Specific responsibilities of defence counsel

(1) From a practical point of view, it is to be hoped that you kept a careful note of what your client told you. Ideally that should have been copied to your instructing solicitor, or the account at least communicated to him or her at the time. In that way, the account should be in the defendant's proof of evidence in any event. If it was not in the proof when the brief was delivered you should have spotted and rectified the omission prior to the trial. Prior to the Criminal Justice and Public Order Act 1994, guidance was given in the case of *R v Jaquith*; *R v Emode* [1989] Crim LR 508 and 563, CA. The basic rule is still the same: you should not give evidence unless it is absolutely necessary. It is necessary if your client will suffer if you do not and there is no other way. In this case your client may not be able to avoid the statutory inferences deriving from his silence *in interview*, but the suggestion of recent fabrication is obviously unfair. Your first move is to tell your opponent of the position (by interrupting him or her, if necessary), as discreetly as you can. If you have conducted yourself properly thus far, he or she will probably accept your word and withdraw the specific suggestion after you have agreed a formula about the date. Showing him or her your client's proof should be avoided if possible. If no agreement can be reached you must explain the situation to your clients (lay and professional) and may withdraw provided that your client's interests are not jeopardised (para 3.6, General Standards in Written Standards for the Conduct of Professional Work in Section 3, Miscellaneous Guidance). The trial will have to restart with fresh counsel so that you can give evidence. If you have a leader the trial can continue without you. If you are sure that withdrawal is the only proper course, do not be put off by any unsatisfactory compromise whether suggested by your opponent or the judge, merely to avoid a threat of wasted costs orders.

(2) Obviously if you have simply not put your case properly, you should immediately make that clear in front of the jury. Your client must not be prejudiced by your mistake and cannot be prejudiced by its correction. However, in the circumstances described here much will depend on what the judge has said. Most judges would realize what has happened and simply smile to themselves or at prosecution counsel. If, however, the judge asks you: 'That is not how it was put, was it Mr or Ms

Smith?' or 'You did not challenge the evidence of your client's presence, did you Mr or Ms Smith?', you can simply agree. If the judge asks, 'Mr or Ms Smith, what on earth is going on?', you can simply state that you have put the case according to your instructions. Do not engage in or rise to comments about whose 'fault' it is. If there is some explicit demand to know your client's instructions, you should politely but firmly refuse to answer such a question: 'Your Honour, should not ask me such a question …' or 'Your Honour, it is not appropriate for me to answer that question …' If the judge presses the matter then ask him or her to send the jury out. In the absence of the jury you should point out that you cannot under any circumstances reveal your client's instructions and waive privilege without your client's consent (para 702). For the same reason you should not show your instructions to the judge.

(3) Paragraph 702 applies here. With regard to the first part of the problem, you are under no obligation to volunteer the information, but *you must not* refer to the defendant's character in any way which suggests that he or she has no previous convictions. In other words, you must never mislead the court (para 302). This is bound severely to restrict what may be said in mitigation and may have the effect of preventing any reference at all to character. You may then be faced by a penetrating question from the court, in which case (subject to your client's instructions, as to which see below) you would use a formula such as 'There is nothing further I can add.'. If you have not got clear instructions from your client, then ask for time to take some. From a practical point of view, as soon as you realize the police antecedents are incomplete (which ought to be before you go into court) you should explain the position to your client and obtain from him or her clear instructions as to whether he or she wishes you to disclose straight away, or only if asked, or not at all. Tactics will play a part in any advice you give. If the court puts the case over for reports then the information is likely to come out anyway. A virtue can be made in mitigation of the fact that disclosure has been made.

The answer to the second part of the question is the same, although your advice will almost inevitably be to make disclosure. The original sentencing court is likely to find out about the breach and may take the view, if the defendant is called back to that court, that the instant court imposed too lenient a sentence because it was not in possession of all the pertinent information.

2.2 Relationship with the lay client

(1) Distinguish between your duty and his or her rights. You must put in cross-examination all those instructions which are relevant and material to the defence. You are the arbiter of that (see para 708(a)). He or she is entitled to give evidence himself or herself and call witnesses who can give material evidence. You can only advise him or her. If he or she rejects your advice you must still pursue his or her case with vigour, but you must not make submissions you consider not to be properly arguable (see para 708(f)). (See paras 708(g) and (j) and 508, General Standards and 12.4, Standards Applicable to Criminal Cases in Written Standards for the Conduct of Professional Work in Section 3, Miscellaneous Guidance.)

(2) The first step is to obtain instructions from the client as to what really happened. Write this down and invite him or her to sign your note. This is to guard against him or her subsequently alleging that you acted improperly or contrary to his or her

instructions. Explain to the client the consequences, if any, of this new information upon the conduct or likely outcome of his or her case. It may be you are now unable to pursue part of his or her claim/defence. You may be professionally embarrassed (see para 603). If this is so, inform your opponent and the court as soon as possible. You do not need to say why (para 702). Alternatively, it may be necessary to apply to amend your statement of case. Inform your opponent of your intention to do so and the extent of the amendment you will seek. Explain to the client the likely implications upon the question of costs. Ensure he or she understands the nature of the oath he or she will take in court and the necessity to give evidence in accordance with the truth of what he or she says actually happened. After the case, telephone your instructing solicitor and inform him or her of what took place. This may affect the future relationship between him or her and the lay client. Also consider whether any conflicts of interest exist (see para 703).

(3) Clients frequently react in emotional terms to losing in court, both in civil and criminal proceedings. They may threaten harm to others or even to themselves. Do not 'disappear' without speaking to your client after the case. Poor communication is often the cause of dissatisfied clients lodging a complaint with the Professional Conduct and Complaints Committee. It is important to spend some time with the client after the hearing of the case, explaining precisely what has happened, why it has happened and whether there are any grounds of appeal. Warn the client of the consequences both to him and others (in this example, his children and the nature of his future relationship with them) of either making or carrying out such threats. Do not repeat to any third party what the client has said unless your duty of confidentiality is being used to conceal a crime (see para 702).

2.3 Relationship with the professional client

2.3.1 Duties and responsibilities owed to the professional client

(1) You should not agree to supply such an opinion. It is a breach of the Code (para 307) if you compromise your professional standards in order to please your client or permit your absolute independence to be compromised.

It is a clear abuse of your position, and it is tantamount to fraud, to supply an opinion for publication to others which is at odds with your true opinion. In various individual situations it may be proper for you to write an opinion for your client which will be shown to a third party, in which you deal with the matter differently from an opinion given to the client for the client's consumption only, eg by omission of reference to privileged matters or to considerations or qualifications which do not ultimately alter the effect or emphasis of your conclusions, but it is an area fraught with technical difficulty and one in which you will always be wise to discuss the points of concern with your colleagues in chambers.

Note: In any case where a solicitor asks for your advice in general terms, or on a particular basis without sufficient details for the giving of definitive advice governing an individual case, if you have any reason to suspect that the opinion is for circulation to others than an individual client, you should carefully state the assumed facts or other basis on which you advise in the body of the opinion itself.

(2) Remember your duty to act fearlessly on behalf of your lay client without regard to any consequences to yourself (para 303(a)). You should make an application for the 'costs thrown away' to be paid by the defendant's solicitors irrespective of the extent of your personal or professional relationship with them. Otherwise your client will suffer loss through no fault of his or her own. It is for the court to determine the merits of your application.

2.3.3 Prosecuting counsel and the Crown Prosecution Service

Whilst para 11.6, Standards Applicable to Criminal Cases in Written Standards for the Conduct of Professional Work in Section 3, Miscellaneous Guidance gives some guidance, the problem is one of communication. You have given weight to factors which you consider important. The solicitor may have others, including the need to adopt a consistent approach to all cases. You should listen to his or her arguments and explain yours clearly to him or her. If you are unable to persuade him or her and you maintain your original opinion, you should consider withdrawing.

2.4 Relationship with other members of the profession

(1) Almost certainly no, particularly if there is an issue on liability. Your knowledge of the view taken by your colleague of the strength of the claimant's case gives you an unfair advantage, particularly if, on the papers before you, the claimant's case does not strike you as being so weak (see para 603(g)). It is only if liability is not in dispute that you could consider continuing. Even if you do not feel embarrassed you should disclose to your colleague what has happened and ensure that he or she feels that his or her case is not unfairly disadvantaged by your earlier discussion.

(2) The first step is to speak to your senior clerk. It is courteous to ask for a word with him or her in private, as it is likely to embarrass him or her if you question him or her in front of the junior clerks. Ask him or her for an explanation as to why this particular brief was given to the pupil when you have advised on the case previously. There may be a good reason, for example, the solicitor may have asked for a pupil to do the case for reasons of cost or he or she may have indicated to the clerk that the client was not happy with your previous advice and did not feel confident about you conducting his or her case. If no satisfactory explanation is forthcoming, ask your clerk what reason the solicitor was given for your unavailability. If you are satisfied that the clerk has deliberately lied to the professional client in order to stop your work, speak to the head of chambers about the matter. You should not 're-trieve' the brief from the pupil for the next day when the solicitor has already been informed that he or she is doing the case. At the very least, however, you should ensure that the situation does not recur.

5.7 Court etiquette: problems

(1) Don't panic. The first step is to telephone your clerk. Instruct him or her to contact the court and your solicitors to inform them of your delay and your expected time of arrival at court. On arrival at court, you must apologise to your client, instructing

solicitor and opponent. If you have kept the judge (and jury) waiting, it will be necessary to apologise in open court. Do not make excuses which are untrue such as 'my car broke down'. You have a duty to be candid no matter how embarrassed or concerned you are about the consequences (para 302). Punctuality is vital so do not make a habit of being late (para 701(a)). Having said that, most members of the Bar have had one experience of this!

(2) Unfortunately, this situation is a not uncommon one to face members of the Criminal Bar, known as 'double-courting'. Once the first case has finished you have no option but to hasten to the second court and make your apologies to the judge. Expect a reprimand from the judge, and possibly the consideration of a wasted costs order. This is a situation that ought not to have arisen: Written Standards for the Conduct of Professional Work in Section 3, Miscellaneous Guidance of the Code of Conduct provides at para 4.1 that 'When a barrister has accepted a brief for the defence of a person charged with a serious criminal offence, he should so far as reasonably practicable ensure that the risk of a conflicting professional engagement does not arise'. Both cases ought not to have been accepted. You should have discussed the matter with your clerk before going to court. It is sometimes difficult to have a discussion in which you are asking the clerk to alter something he or she has put into the diary. Remember, however, that you are responsible for the proper administration of your practice, and you will get the flak from the judge, not your clerk (para 306, and see *Wasted Costs Order (No 4 of 1993)* The Times, 21 April 1995).

Speak to your clerk on your return to chambers. Tell him or her what has occurred and try to ensure that it never happens again. In the event of a dispute with your clerk which cannot be resolved between you, consult your head of chambers.

INDEX